Outlooks
and Insights

A READER FOR COLLEGE WRITERS

Second Edition

Edited by PAUL ESCHHOLZ
and ALFRED ROSA
University of Vermont

Outlooks
and Insights

A READER FOR COLLEGE WRITERS

Second Edition

St. Martin's Press / New York

For information, write St. Martin's Press, Inc.
175 Fifth Avenue, New York, N.Y. 10010

ISBN: 0-312-59166-7

Interior design: BETTY BINNS GRAPHICS
Photo research: JUNE LUNDBORG WHITWORTH
Cover design: DARBY DOWNEY
Cover photograph: VICTOR SCHRAGER

Part Opening Photographs

Private Lives: © Jean-Claude Lejeune
Family and Friends: © Joel Gordon 1984
Men and Women: © Joel Gordon 1981
The Aims of Education: © Jean-Claude Lejeune
Work: Martin J. Dain/Photo Researchers, Inc.
Language in America: Harvey Stein © 1974
The Politics of Technology and Science: © Jean-Claude Lejeune
The Individual and Society: M. E. Warren/Photo Researchers. Inc.

Acknowledgments

Gordon W. Allport, "Prejudice," from THE NATURE OF PREJUDICE. Copyright © 1979 by Addison-Wesley, Reading, Massachusetts. Excerpted material. Reprinted by permission.

W. H. Auden, "The Unknown Citizen," from W. H. AUDEN: COLLECTED POEMS. Copyright © 1940 and renewed 1968 by W. H. Auden. Reprinted from W. H. AUDEN: COLLECTED POEMS, edited by Edward Mendelson, by permission of Random House, Inc.

Acknowledgments and copyrights continue at the back of the book on pages 790–795, which constitute an extension of the copyright page.

Preface

The second edition of *Outlooks and Insights*, like the first, is an exciting yet practical and classroom-tested solution to an old problem: how best to use readings to help students improve their writing. Most teachers of writing, and indeed most writers, would agree that reading supports writing in many ways. A fine essay can serve as an example of masterful writing, and also of mature thought and insight; such examples can give inexperienced writers a sense of what is possible and inspire them to aim high. An essay can also provide students with information and ideas for use in their writing, or it may stimulate them to pursue new lines of inquiry and to write on new topics of their own. And of course an essay can illustrate the effective use of rhetorical strategies and techniques. The readings collected here will serve all of these familiar purposes. But *Outlooks and Insights* has an additional dimension: It provides students with explicit guidance—through discussion, examples, and exercises—in reading well and in using their reading in their writing.

This guidance is provided, first of all, in an introductory chapter, "On Reading and Writing." Here we offer well-grounded, sympathetic, and practical instruction to students on how to become more active and accurate readers and how to turn what they read to effective use in their compositions. We acknowledge that different people respond differently to the same text, and also that one reader may use different reading strategies at different times according to the particular purpose. But we also insist that any interpretation of a text should be supported by evidence drawn from the words on the page, so that diverse readers can find common ground for discussion and agreement. To this end we offer criteria and a set of questions designed to help students respond fully to what they read and to help them distinguish between a purely personal response and reasoned understanding.

Many students are unaware of the choices they have available to them when they are required to write about something they have read. To help them better understand these options, "On Reading and Writing" offers not only advice but full-length examples of three different kinds of papers that composition students are frequently required to write: the paper that analyzes a reading, the expository or argumentative essay on a topic derived from the reading, and the personal experience essay.

All three essays were written in response to the same selection, George Orwell's "A Hanging." The first analyzes some aspects of Orwell's rhetoric, showing how he uses certain details to support his thesis. The second argues in support of capital punishment, engaging Orwell's topic but taking an independent position on it. The third recounts a personal experience in which the student writer discovered her own aptitude for thoughtless cruelty. Taken together, these compositions suggest the wide range of original responses that are possible in college writing assignments.

The heart of any anthology is, of course, the selections it contains. The readings in this new edition of *Outlooks and Insights* are both numerous and fresh. We have chosen 85 essays, 6 short stories, and 11 poems, offering instructors a large variety of options for making individual assignments and for organizing the course. The readings are grouped in eight large thematic units, beginning with themes of personal experiences and relationships, continuing with such aspects of our lives as education, work, language, and technology, and finally arriving at considerations of contemporary social issues and ethical questions. New to this edition are the focused subsections within each large thematic unit. These subsections are designed to concentrate classroom discussion and student writing on well-defined issues, concerns, and questions. For example, in the thematic unit "Men and Women" we have the subsections "Gender Roles" and "Marriage and Its Alternatives," and in "Language in America" we have "Is There a Language Crisis?" "Prejudice," and "Language That Manipulates." The selections in each subsection play off one another and encourage stimulating debate and controversy in the classroom and help to both focus and direct student writing. Because we've used these selections in our own classrooms, we know that each subsection provides a manageable and balanced assignment for a college composition class.

Each reading in this new edition has been chosen to be challenging but not baffling, and we have sought not only to appeal to students' interests and concerns but to broaden them. The selections are a mixture of the new and the familiar—familiar to composition instructors, that is, for few freshmen will have read even such durable pieces as E. B. White's "Once More to the Lake," Rachel Carson's "The Obligation to Endure," and George Orwell's "Politics and the English Language," essays that have earned their places in the small canon of essential readings for compositions classes. We have been particularly careful to choose readings that are provocative or have an argumentative bent and that contain information that students can use to effect in their own writing.

Most of the essays in *Outlooks and Insights* were written in the last decade or two, but we have seasoned them with a few selections from classic authors—Jefferson, Thoreau, the apostle Matthew. In most sections we have also included a poem and a story which we think can be used effectively in a composition course; any writer can learn from the meticulously sustained irony of Auden's "The Unknown Citizen" as well as from Gregory's "Shame," from the controlled and modulated prose style of a Welty or Oates story as well as from that of a White or Didion essay. The questions and writing suggestions for the stories and poems are much like those supplied for the essays, with minimal attention to questions of literary form, but at the end of "On Reading and Writing" we do alert students to some important generic differences, so that they will not read stories and poems in exactly the same way they read essays.

The questions and writing topics supplied for each selection further develop and exploit the advice and instruction given in "On Reading and Writing." The study questions about each essay, story, and poem, like the general questions in the introduction, help students to test and increase their understanding of what they have read, and may also help them gather material for analytical papers. The assignments, which are called "Writing Topics," focus the students' attention on the central issues and questions of the thematic units. Often we use these topics to generate classroom discussion and debate before we ask our students to write. We find that such discussions coax students to develop their own lines of thinking and to articulate clearly their views on a specific issue. The writing topics suggest ways that students may use a reading in their writing, and they are designed to elicit results ranging from autobiographical essays to research papers.

Each thematic section begins with a picture and several epigraphs which highlight the issues of that section. These materials, particularly the epigraphs, may find use in their own right as objects of discussion and as sources of writing assignments. Each selection is provided with a biographical headnote which sets the piece in the context of the author's work and where necessary supplies information about the author's original audience and purpose. To make *Outlooks and Insights* still more flexible and useful, there is a rhetorical table of contents that classifies the selections by type and by principle of organization, as well as a glossary that will help students understand rhetorical and literary terms in the questions without having to refer to other sources.

In working on the second edition of *Outlooks and Insights* we have benefitted inestimably from the observations and suggestions of our fellow teachers from across the country: Dorothea L. Alex, North Central College; Mia Anderson, Bergen Community College; Ronnie Apter, Fairleigh Dickinson University; Helen Aron, Union County College; Kathleen Ashley, University of Southern Maine; Bruce Bashford, SUNY at Stony Brook; Patricia Bennett, University of Connecticut; Kimberly M. Blaeser, University of Notre Dame; Deborah Bosley, Millikin University; Joe S. Britton, Kentucky Wesleyan College; Ada Brotman, American River College; Carol Burns, Southern Illinois University; Richard Cloyed, Kearney State College; Peter Cortland, Santa Rosa Junior College; Faye Curran, Wilmington College; Mary Depriest, University of Orgeon; Wayne G. Deahl, University of Wyoming; Wilma Delaney, North Central College; Eloise Dielman, University of Oregon; Carol Domblewski, Suffolk University; Leonard Engel, Quinnipiac College; Charles Fishman, SUNY at Farmingdale; Grace Flisser, Community College of Philadelphia; Barbara Friedman, St. John's University; Susan Frisbie, University of Santa Clara; Genie Goicoechea, Northern Nevada Community College; Bruce Gold, Pennsylvania State University; Gloria Gross, California State University at Los Angeles; Elizabeth Gruen, Union County College; Sheila Gullickson, Moorhead State University; Karen M. Henry, North Central College; Jean Hodgin, North Shore Community College; Dorothea Hoffner, Union County College; Joan Hunter, New Mexico State University; Madelyn Jablon, Clarion University of Pennsylvania; Johanna Jung, Southampton College; Daniel Kaderli, University of Texas at San Antonio; Thomas M. Kitts, St. John's University; Ali Lang, Southeastern Massachusetts University; Anne Laskaya, University of Oregon; Mary Lauberg, St. Louis Community College at Florissant Valley; Milton Levin, Trenton State College; Emily M. Liebman, St. Louis Community College at Florissant Valley; Marcus C. Lopez, Solano Community College; Joanne L. Lynn, California State University at Fullerton; Sharon Malone, Wilmington College; Bonnie Martin, George Mason University; Wolfgang McAninch-Rünzi, University of Oregon; Margaret McBride, University of Oregon; Alfred McDowell, Bergen Community College; Barbara G. Merkel, Barber-Scotia College; Jeanne Millhuff, Mid America Nazarene College; Lynne Moncus, New Mexico State University; Claudia Mon Pere, University of Santa Clara; Margo J. Moore, Southeastern Massachusetts University; Thomas Mullen, Slippery Rock University; John S. Nelson, Rocky Mountain College; Eric W. Nye, University of Wyoming; Patrick O'Brien, Cypress College; Kevin Oderman, Iowa State University; Twila Yates Papay, Hofstra University; William Powell, Lane Community College; Robert Reilly, Rider College; Gerald Richman, Suffolk University; Gertrude Robertson, University of Toledo; Lyn Robertson, Denison University; Pamela S. Rosenbaum, Roosevelt University; Steven Serafin, C. W. Post Center, Long Island University; Marvin W.

Sherak, Santa Rosa Junior College; Joan G. Silberman, Rockland Community College; Henry Silverman, Michigan State University; Lawrence Skinner, St. Louis Community College at Florissant Valley; Marcy Golant Solomon, Mount Ida College; Patricia Spano, Columbus College; Ada-Marie Steven, Metropolitan State College; Paul Strong, Alfred University, Christi Sutphin, University of Oregon; Betty L. Taylor, University of Oregon; Mary Ann Trevathon, University of Wyoming; Barnard Turner, University of Oregon; Connie Van Zelm, SUNY at Buffalo; Kathryn Young, University of Oregon; and Rafia Zafar, Harvard University. In particular we would like to thank Nancy Barry, University of Iowa; Gwendolyn Gong, Texas A & M University; Irene Isley, University of Oregon; Carol Schrieber, California State Polytechnic University; and Randal Woodland, University of North Carolina. Our colleagues at the University of Vermont helped us by assigning George Orwell's "A Hanging" to their composition classes and providing us with student papers for the introduction "On Reading and Writing." Finally, we want particularly to acknowledge the contribution of our students, who teach us something new every day.

Contents

8.   The Individual and Society   641

xvi   *Contents*

Rhetorical Table of Contents

The selections in *Outlooks and Insights* are arranged in eight sections according to their themes. The following contents, which is certainly not exhaustive, first classifies many of the essays according to the rhetorical strategies they exemplify. It then classifies selections by genre—poems, short stories, autobiographical and biographical writings, speeches, and so forth.

Analogy

Argument and Persuasion

Cause and Effect

Illustration

Narration

Poems

Comparison and Contrast

Definition

Description

Short Stories

Outlooks
and Insights

A READER FOR COLLEGE WRITERS

Second Edition

Introduction: On Reading and Writing

PEOPLE read for many different reasons, and they read in different
ways as well. They may read for enjoyment, or to improve themselves, or to gather information, or to obtain an education or do a job;
sometimes their reading benefits them in several ways at once, and in
ways they did not expect. Sometimes they read with painstaking care,
while at other times they may skip and skim, or even begin reading in the
middle or at the end, all depending on what they are reading and what
they want from it. But whatever the reason and whatever the method,
reading is most rewarding when it is done actively, in a thoughtful spirit
and with an inquiring mind.

Many people believe that the right way to read is passively, taking
in what they read and storing it away for later use. But this kind of reading
is seldom either fulfilling or useful. Unless you bring to bear on your reading what you know and believe, testing what you read and allowing it to
test you, you will seldom find the experience particularly rewarding, and
you may have some trouble even remembering much of what you have
read. Active reading is like conversation: You give as well as take. You
examine and question the author's claims, you remember and ponder ideas

and information that relate to your reading, you even laugh at the jokes—at least the good ones. By responding so fully, you are taking possession of what you read, making it your own and getting it ready for use—in discussions with your friends, classmates, and teachers, for example, or in writing of your own.

Unquestionably, one of the benefits of active reading is that it can help you become a better writer. Reading can provide you with information and ideas for use in your writing, and often with subjects to write about. Moreover, it can provide you with examples to learn from. Writing is a skill that can be learned, like playing tennis or playing the piano, and one of the best ways to improve your writing is by observing how accomplished writers get their results. As you read you can see for yourself what a writer's strategies are, analyze how they work, and then adapt them to your own writing purposes. By picking up ideas and techniques from many different writers and incorporating them into your writing, you can increase your mastery and develop your own personal style.

In using *Outlooks and Insights,* you will learn to read as a writer. To read as a writer, you must be able to discover what is going on in an essay, to figure out the writer's reasons for shaping the essay in a particular way, to decide whether the result works well or poorly—and why. Like writing itself, analytical reading is a skill that takes time to acquire. But the skill is necessary if you are to understand the craft of a piece of writing. Perhaps the most important reason to master the skills of analytical reading is that, for everything you write, you will be your own first reader and critic. How well you are able to analyze your own drafts will powerfully affect how well you revise them; and revising well is crucial to writing well. So reading others' writings analytically is useful and important practice.

Outlooks and Insights is a reader for writers, as the subtitle says. The selections in this book can entertain you, inform you, and even contribute to your self-awareness and understanding of the world around you. The writers included here are among the most skillful of their time, many of them well known and widely published. From their work you can learn important and useful writing strategies and skills. Most are contemporary, writing on issues of our own day for readers like us, but some great writers of the past are here as well. The idealism of a Henry David Thoreau, the moral indignation of an Elizabeth Cady Stanton, the noble vision of a Martin Luther King continue to move readers despite the intervening years.

Outlooks and Insights is an anthology of writings arranged according to their subjects and themes. The first of its eight sections includes narratives and discussions of personal experiences and relationships, while the following sections broaden to increasingly wide frames of reference, finally arriving at themes concerning our society and, ultimately, all humanity. Each section begins with several aphorisms that highlight the issues addressed and serve as topics for thought, discussion, and writing. Within each section, every piece has its own brief introduction providing information about the author and often about the selection's original purpose and audience. After each piece comes "Questions for Study and Discussion," an aid to active reading. These questions ask you to analyze what you have just read in order to discover, or rediscover, important points about its content and its writing. In addition, each selection has two or more "Writing Topics."

Although intended primarily to stimulate writing, these suggested writing topics may be used as a starting point for your own thoughts, or for class discussion.

Getting the Most Out of What You Read

What does it mean, to understand a piece of writing—an essay, for example? It means, of course, that you comprehend all the words in it. It also means that you have enough background knowledge to grasp its subject matter; a discussion of Brownian motion would mean little to someone who knew no physics, nor would un analysis of Elizabethan metrics enlighten someone unfamiliar with sixteenth-century English poetry. You have only understood the essay if you have grasped it as a whole, so that you can summarize and explain its chief points in your own words and show what each part contributes to the whole.

As you read, you absorb the essay part by part. You cannot "read" the whole all at once, as you can take in a building or a face, but must hold most of the essay in your memory and form your impression of it bit by bit as you read. How this works—what the mind does—is not fully understood, and different readers may well have different ways of doing it. That could be yet another reason why a single piece can evoke so many diverse responses. But there are some guidelines that can help you achieve an understanding of what you read.

UNDERSTANDING THE PARTS OF AN ESSAY

As you progress through an essay, word by word and sentence by sentence, keep the following guidelines in mind:

• Make sure you understand what each word means. If a word is new to you and the context does not make its meaning clear, don't guess—look it up.

• Stay sensitive to connotations, the associations words carry with them.

The words *falsehood* and *fib* mean about the same thing, but they convey quite different attitudes and feelings.

• Watch for allusions and try to interpret them. If the author refers to "the patience of Job," you don't really understand the passage unless you know how patient Job was. If you don't understand the allusion, check standard reference works such as dictionaries, encyclopedias, and books of quotations, or ask someone you think might know the answer.

• Be on the alert for key words and ideas. The two often go together. Key words in this introduction, for example, are *reading* and *writing*; their repetition points up the key idea that these activities are really inseparable and mutually beneficial. A key idea within an essay is normally developed at some length in one or more paragraphs, and it may be stated directly at the beginning or end of a paragraph.

• Use your knowledge and your critical sense to test what you read. Is each "fact" true, as far as you know (or can find out)? Is the author's reasoning logical?

• Interpret figures of speech. When George Orwell speaks of a writer who "turns as it were instinctively to long words and exhausted idioms, like a cuttlefish squirting out ink," you must not only know or find out what a cuttlefish is but also find out how and why it squirts ink and consider how the image expresses the author's idea.

• Pay attention to where you are in the essay. Note where the introduction ends and the body of the essay begins, and where the body gives way to the conclusion. Note where the author turns, let us say, from personal narrative to a series of arguments, or where those arguments are succeeded by refutation of other people's views. And be on the alert for the point at which you discover what the essay is really about—the point where it "makes its move," like a chess player going on the attack or a basketball forward streaking toward the basket. Often the essay's purpose and main idea are clear from the beginning, but sometimes the author withholds or even conceals them until much later.

UNDERSTANDING THE WHOLE ESSAY

As you read, you are constantly creating and recreating your idea of the essay as a whole. At the end you will have reached some conclusions about it. Here, again, are some points to keep in mind while reading:

• Look for the main idea of the essay—what is often called the *thesis*. Sometimes the main idea is directly stated, either in the introduction or later on; sometimes it is not stated but can be inferred from the essay as a whole. Define the thesis of an essay as narrowly and specifically as you can while still taking the whole of the essay into account.

• Determine the author's purpose. Is it to persuade you to a point of view?

to explain a subject to you? The author may directly state his or her purpose, or it may be clearly implied by the thesis.

• Consider the relation between the whole and its parts. How does the main idea of each paragraph relate to the thesis? Does the information supplied in the body of the essay support the thesis—make it more persuasive or easier to understand? Does the author ever seem to get away from the main point, and if so why?

• Look for omissions. Has the author left out any information that you think might be relevant to the thesis? Does he or she fail to consider any important views—including perhaps your own view? Does the author assume anything without supporting the assumption or even stating it? How important are these omissions—do they lessen the clarity or the persuasiveness of the essay?

• Evaluate the essay. Whether or not you like the essay or agree with it is important, but don't stop there; ask yourself why. Test its reasoning for errors and omissions. Test its explanations for clarity and completeness. Consider the author's style, whether it is suitable to the subject, agreeable or powerful in itself, and consistently maintained. In short, assess all the strengths and weaknesses.

Some Tips and Techniques for Reading an Essay

Each essay offers its own distinctive challenges and rewards, but there are some reading techniques that you can use successfully with all of them in your quest for understanding. Here are some tips on reading.

Prepare Yourself. Before you plunge into reading the essay itself, form some expectations of it. Ponder the title: What does it tell you about the essay's subject matter? About its tone? Think about the author: Have you read anything else by him or her? If so, what do you know about the author's attitudes and style that may help prepare you now? If any materials accompany the essay, like the introductions in *Outlooks and Insights,* read them. These preparations will help you put yourself into an alert, ready frame of mind.

Read and Reread. You should read the selection at least twice, no matter how long or short it is. Very few essays yield their full meaning on first reading, and their full meaning is what you should be aiming to extract.

The first reading is for getting acquainted with the essay and forming your first impressions of it. The essay will offer you information, ideas, and arguments you did not expect, and as you read you will find yourself continually modifying your sense of its purpose, its strategy, and sometimes even what it is about or what point it is intended to make. (This is especially true when the author delays stating the thesis—or makes no thesis statement at all.) Only when you have finished your first reading can you be confident that you have then really begun to understand the piece as a whole.

The second reading is quite different from the first one. You will know what the essay is about, where it is going and how it gets there; now you can relate the parts more accurately to the whole. You can work at the difficult passages to make sure you fully understand what they mean. You can test your first impressions against the words on the page, developing and deepening your sense of the essay's core meaning—or possibly changing your mind about it. And as a writer, you can now pay special attention to the author's purpose and means of achieving that purpose, looking for features of organization and style that you can learn from and adapt to your own work.

Ask Yourself Questions. As you probe the essay, focus your attention by asking yourself some basic questions about it. Here are some you may find useful:

1. Do I like the essay or not? What, for me, are the most interesting parts of it? What parts do I find least interesting or hardest to understand?

2. What is the essay's main idea? What are the chief supporting ideas, and how do they relate to the main idea?

3. What is the author's attitude toward the essay's subject? What is the author's purpose? What readers was the author apparently writing for, and what is his or her attitude toward them? How am I part of the intended audience—if I am?

4. How is the essay structured? How does its organization relate to its main idea, and to the author's purpose?

5. Can I follow the essay's line of reasoning? Is its logic valid, however complex, or are there mistakes and fallacies? If the reasoning is flawed, how much damage does this do to the essay's effect?

6. Does the author supply enough information to support the essay's ideas, and enough details to make its descriptions precise? Is all of the information relevant and, as far as I know, accurate? Are all of the details convincing? What does the author leave out, and how do these omissions affect my response to the essay?

7. What are the essay's basic, underlying assumptions? Which are stated and which are left unspoken? Are they acceptable, or do I challenge them? If I do, and I am right, how does this affect the essay's main idea?

8. Do all the elements of the essay relate, directly or indirectly, to its

main idea? Can I explain how they relate? If any do not, what other purposes do they serve, if any?

9. Where do I place this essay in the context of my other reading? In the context of my life and thought? What further thoughts, and further reading, does it incite me to? Would I recommend it to anyone else to read? To whom, and why?

Each selection in *Outlooks and Insights* is followed by a set of questions, similar to the ones just suggested but usually more specific, which should help you in your effort to understand the piece. All of these questions work best when you try to answer them as fully as you can, remembering and considering many details from the selection to support your answers. Most of the questions are variations on these three basic ones: "What's going on here?" and "Why?" and "How do I feel about it?"

Make Notes. Keep a pencil in hand and use it. Some readers like to write in their books, putting notes and signals to themselves in the margins and underlining key passages; others keep notebooks and jot their responses down there.

There is no all-purpose, universal method for annotating a text; what you write will depend on the details of the work at hand and how you respond. But you may find these tips useful:

• Keep track of your responses. Jot down ideas that come to mind whether or not they seem directly relevant to what you are reading. If you think of a fact or example that supports the author's ideas, or disproves them, make a note. If a passage impresses or amuses you, set it off with an exclamation point in the margin. Converse with the text. Write *yes* or *no* or *why?* or *so what?* in response to the author's ideas and arguments.

• Mark words or passages you don't understand at first reading. A question mark in the margin may do the job, or you may want to circle words or phrases in the text. During the second reading you can look up the words and allusions and puzzle out the more difficult passages.

• Mark key points. Underline or star the main idea, or write it down in your notebook. Mark off the selection into its main sections, such as the introduction, body, and conclusion.

When annotating your text, don't be timid. Mark up your book as much as you please. Above all, don't let annotating become burdensome; it's an aid, not a chore. A word or phrase will often serve as well as a sentence. You may want to delay much of your annotating until your second reading, so that the first reading can be fast and free.

Using Your Reading in the Writing Process

What does analytical reading have to do with your own writing? Reading is not simply an end in itself; it is also a means to help you become a better writer. In *Outlooks and Insights* we are concerned with both the content and the form of an essay—that is, with what an essay has to say and with the strategies used to say it. All readers pay attention to content, to the substance of what an author is saying. Far fewer, however, notice the strategies that authors use to organize their writing, to make it understandable and effective. Yet using these strategies is an essential element of the writer's craft, an element that must be mastered if one is to write well.

There is nothing mysterious or highly sophisticated about the strategies themselves. When you want to tell a story about being unemployed, for example, you naturally use the strategy called *narration*. When you want to show the differences between families in the 1940s and families today, you naturally *compare and contrast* representative families of the two eras. When you want to explain how toxins enter the food chain, you fall automatically into the strategy called *process analysis*. And when you want to determine the reasons for the disaster at the Chernobyl nuclear plant, you use *cause and effect analysis*. These and other strategies are ways we think about the world and our experiences in it. What makes them seem mysterious, especially in writing, is that most people use them more or less unconsciously, with little awareness that they're doing so. Sophistication, whether in thought or in writing, does not come from simply using these structures—everyone does that—but from using them consciously, purposefully, and well.

At the simplest level, reading can provide you with information and ideas both to give authority to your writing and to enliven it. Moreover, your reading often provides you with subjects to write about. For example, one of our students, after reading James Rachels's "Active and Passive Euthanasia" (p. 765), wrote an essay analyzing the strengths and weaknesses of the author's argument. Another student read "What Is Job Burnout?" by Robert L. Veninga and James P. Spradley (p. 388), and used it as a springboard to her own essay defining "student burnout." In a more subtle way, analytical reading can increase your awareness of how the writing of others affects you, and thus make you more sensitive to how your own writing will affect your readers. If you've ever been irritated by an article that makes an outrageous claim without a shred of supporting evidence, you might be more likely to back up your own claims more carefully. If you've been delighted by a happy turn of phrase or absorbed by a new idea, you might be less inclined to feed your own readers on clichés and platitudes. You will begin to consider in more detail how your own readers are likely to respond.

More to the point, however, analytical reading of the kind you'll be encouraged to do in this text will help you master important strategies of thinking and writing that you can use very specifically throughout the writing process. During the early stages of your writing you will need to focus on the large issues of choosing a subject, gathering information, planning the strategies suited to your purpose, and organizing your ideas. As you move from a first draft through further revisions, your concerns will begin to narrow. In conference with your instructor you may discover a faulty beginning or ending, or realize that your tone is inappropriate, or see that the various parts of your essay are not quite connected, or notice awkward repetitions in your choice of words and phrases. Analytical reading can lead you to solutions for such problems at every stage of your writing, from selecting a subject to revising and editing your final draft.

Reading George Orwell's "A Hanging": A Case Study

Some writers, and some essays, become classics—people continue to read them for decades or centuries. Such a writer is George Orwell, the English author best known for his novel, *1984*, a vivid and terrifying evocation of life in a totalitarian state. But that was his last major work. One of his first works was an essay, "A Hanging," which he wrote in 1931 (he was then twenty-eight) about one of his experiences as a police official in Burma, where he had served from 1922 to 1927. "A Hanging" was published in *The Adelphi*, a socialist literary magazine whose readers would have been sympathetic to Orwell's attitudes.

As you read "A Hanging," note your own questions and responses in the margins or in your notebook. At the end of the essay you will find one reader's notes to which you can compare your responses.

A Hanging

GEORGE ORWELL

It was in Burma, a sodden morning of the rains. A sickly light, like yellow tinfoil, was slanting over the high walls into the jail yard. We were waiting outside the condemned cells, a row of sheds fronted with double bars, like small animal cages. Each cell measured about ten feet by ten and was quite bare within except for a plank bed and

1

a pot for drinking water. In some of them brown silent men were squatting at the inner bars, with their blankets draped around them. These were the condemned men, due to be hanged within the next week or two.

One prisoner had been brought out of his cell. He was a Hindu,   2
a puny wisp of a man, with a shaven head and vague liquid eyes. He had a thick, sprouting moustache, absurdly too big for his body, rather like the moustache of a comic man on the films. Six tall Indian warders were guarding him and getting him ready for the gallows. Two of them stood by with rifles and fixed bayonets, while the others handcuffed him, passed a chain through his handcuffs and fixed it to their belts, and lashed his arms tight to his sides. They crowded very close about him, with their hands always on him in a careful, caressing grip as though all the while feeling him to make sure he was there. It was like men handling a fish which is still alive and may jump back into the water. But he stood quite unresisting, yielding his arms limply to the ropes, as though he hardly noticed what was happening.

Eight o'clock struck and a bugle call, desolately thin in the wet   3
air, floated from the distant barracks. The superintendent of the jail, who was standing apart from the rest of us, moodily prodding the gravel with his stick, raised his head at the sound. He was an army doctor, with a gray toothbrush moustache and a gruff voice. "For God's sake hurry up, Francis," he said irritably. "The man ought to have been dead by this time. Aren't you ready yet?"

Francis, the head jailer, a fat Dravidian in a white drill suit and   4
gold spectacles, waved his black hand. "Yes sir, yes sir," he bubbled. "All iss satisfactorily ₁ repared. The hangman iss waiting. We shall proceed."

"Well, quick march, then. The prisoners can't get their breakfast   5
till this job's over."

We set out for the gallows. Two warders marched on either side   6
of the prisoner, with their rifles at the slope; two others marched close against him, gripping him by arm and shoulder, as though at once pushing and supporting him. The rest of us, magistrates and the like, followed behind. Suddenly, when we had gone ten yards, the procession stopped short without any order or warning. A dreadful thing had happened—a dog, come goodness knows whence, had appeared in the yard. It came bounding among us with a loud volley of barks, and leapt round us wagging its whole body, wild with glee at finding so many human beings together. It was a large woolly dog, half Airedale, half pariah. For a moment it pranced round us, and then, before anyone could stop it, it had made a dash for the prisoner and, jumping up, tried to lick his face. Everyone stood aghast, too taken aback even to grab at the dog.

"Who let that bloody brute in here?" said the superintendent   7
angrily. "Catch it, someone!"

A warder, detached from the escort, charged clumsily after the   8 dog, but it danced and gamboled just out of his reach, taking every-thing as part of the game. A young Eurasian jailer picked up a handful of gravel and tried to stone the dog away, but it dodged the stones and came after us again. Its yaps echoed from the jail walls. The prisoner, in the grasp of the two warders, looked on incuriously, as though this was another formality of the hanging. It was several minutes before someone managed to catch the dog. Then we put my handkerchief through its collar and moved off once more, with the dog still straining and whimpering.

It was about forty yards to the gallows. I watched the bare brown 9 back of the prisoner marching in front of me. He walked clumsily with his bound arms, but quite steadily, with that bobbing gait of the Indian who never straightens his knees. At each step his muscles slid neatly into place, the lock of hair on his scalp danced up and down, his feet printed themselves on the wet gravel. And once, in spite of the men who gripped him by each shoulder, he stepped slightly aside to avoid a puddle on the path.

It is curious, but till that moment I had never realized what it 10 means to destroy a healthy, conscious man. When I saw the prisoner step aside to avoid the puddle I saw the mystery, the unspeakable wrongness, of cutting a life short when it is in full tide. This man was not dying, he was alive just as we are alive. All the organs of his body were working—bowels digesting food, skin renewing itself, nails grow-ing, tissues forming—all toiling away in solemn foolery. His nails would still be growing when he stood on the drop, when he was falling through the air with a tenth of a second to live. His eyes saw the yellow gravel and the gray walls, and his brain still remembered, fore-saw, reasoned—reasoned even about puddles. He and we were a party of men walking together, seeing, hearing, feeling, understanding the same world; and in two minutes, with a sudden snap, one of us would be gone— one mind less, one world less.

The gallows stood in a small yard, separate from the main grounds 11 of the prison, and overgrown with tall prickly weeds. It was a brick erection like three sides of a shed, with planking on top, and above that two beams and a crossbar with the rope dangling. The hangman, a gray-haired convict in the white uniform of the prison, was waiting beside his machine. He greeted us with a servile crouch as we entered. At a word from Francis the two warders, gripping the prisoner more closely than ever, half led half pushed him to the gallows and helped him clumsily up the ladder. Then the hangman climbed up and fixed the rope round the prisoner's neck.

We stood waiting, five yards away. The warders had formed in 12 a rough circle round the gallows. And then, when the noose was fixed, the prisoner began crying out to his god. It was a high, reiterated cry of "Ram! Ram! Ram! Ram!"[1] not urgent and fearful like a prayer or

---

[1] In the Hindu religion, Rama is the incarnation of the god Vishnu.

cry for help, but steady, rhythmical, almost like the tolling of a bell. The dog answered the sound with a whine. The hangman, still standing on the gallows, produced a small cotton bag like a flour bag and drew it down over the prisoner's face. But the sound, muffled by the cloth, still persisted, over and over again: "Ram! Ram! Ram! Ram! Ram!"

The hangman climbed down and stood ready, holding the lever.   13 Minutes seemed to pass. The steady, muffled crying from the prisoner went on and on, "Ram! Ram! Ram!" never faltering for an instant. The superintendent, his head on his chest, was slowly poking the ground with his stick; perhaps he was counting the cries, allowing the prisoner a fixed number—fifty, perhaps, or a hundred. Everyone had changed color. The Indians had gone gray like bad coffee, and one or two of the bayonets were wavering. We looked at the lashed, hooded man on the drop, and listened to his cries—each cry another second of life; the same thought was in all our minds: oh, kill him quickly, get it over, stop that abominable noise!

Suddenly the superintendent made up his mind. Throwing up   14 his head he made a swift motion with his stick. "Chalo!"[2] he shouted almost fiercely.

There was a clanking noise, and then dead silence. The prisoner   15 had vanished, and the rope was twisting on itself. I let go of the dog, and it galloped immediately to the back of the gallows; but when it got there it stopped short, barked, and then retreated into a corner of the yard, where it stood among the weeds, looking timorously out at us. We went round the gallows to inspect the prisoner's body. He was dangling with his toes pointed straight downward, very slowly revolving, as dead as a stone.

The superintendent reached out with his stick and poked the   16 bare brown body: it oscillated slightly. "*He's* all right," said the superintendent. He backed out from under the gallows, and blew out a deep breath. The moody look had gone out of his face quite suddenly. He glanced at his wrist watch. "Eight minutes past eight. Well, that's all for this morning, thank God."

The warders unfixed bayonets and marched away. The dog, so-   17 bered and conscious of having misbehaved itself, slipped after them. We walked out of the gallows yard, past the condemned cells with their waiting prisoners, into the big central yard of the prison. The convicts, under the command of warders armed with lathis,[3] were already receiving their breakfast. They squatted in long rows, each man holding a tin pannikin, while two warders with buckets marched round ladling out rice; it seemed quite a homely, jolly scene, after the hanging. An enormous relief had come upon us now that the job was

---

[2]"*Let go*," in Hindi.
[3]Wooden batons.

done. One felt an impulse to sing, to break into a run, to snigger. All at once everyone began chattering gaily.

The Eurasian boy walking beside me nodded toward the way we had come, with a knowing smile: "Do you know, sir, our friend [he meant the dead man] when he heard his appeal had been dismissed, he pissed on the floor of his cell. From fright. Kindly take one of my cigarettes, sir. Do you not admire my new silver case, sir? From the boxwalah, two rupees eight annas.[4] Classy European style."   18

Several people laughed—at what, nobody seemed certain.   19

Francis was walking by the superintendent, talking garrulously: "Well, sir, all hass passed off with the utmost satisfactoriness. It was all finished—flick! like that. It iss not always so—oah, no! I have known cases where the doctor wass obliged to go beneath the gallows and pull the prissoner's legs to ensure decease. Most disagreeable!"   20

"Wriggling about, eh? That's bad," said the superintendent.   21

"Ach, sir, it iss worse when they become refractory! One man, I recall, clung to the bars of hiss cage when we went to take him out. You will scarcely credit, sir, that it took six warders to dislodge him, three pulling at each leg. We reasoned with him. 'My dear fellow,' we said, 'think of all the pain and trouble you are causing to us!' But no, he would not listen! Ach, he wass very troublesome!"   22

I found that I was laughing quite loudly. Everyone was laughing. Even the superintendent grinned in a tolerant way. "You'd better all come out and have a drink," he said quite genially. "I've got a bottle of whisky in the car. We could do with it."   23

We went through the big double gates of the prison into the road. "Pulling at his legs!" exclaimed a Burmese magistrate suddenly, and burst into a loud chuckling. We all began laughing again. At that moment Francis' anecdote seemed extraordinarily funny. We all had a drink together, native and European alike, quite amicably. The dead man was a hundred yards away.   24

One Reader's Notes

Here are the notes one reader made in his notebook during and after his first reading of "A Hanging." They include personal comments, queries concerning the meaning of words and details, and some reflections on the piece and its subject. The numbers in parentheses indicate which paragraphs the notes refer to.

NOTES MADE DURING THE READING

(2) puny prisoner, 6 tall guards, handcuffs, rope, chains. handled "like a fish"—cells like animal cages. suggests prisoner thought less than human.

---

[4]Indian currency worth less than 50 cents. *Boxwalah:* in Hindi, a seller of boxes.

(4)   natives do dirty work, Brits stand around supervising. what's a Dravidian?

(6)   dog—half Airedale, half pariah, like prison staff a mixture of Brits and natives. prisoner its favorite person. why? pet?

(10) main idea (?): "I saw the mystery, the unspeakable wrongness, of cutting a life short when it is in full tide."

But what was the man's crime? might have been a murderer or terrorist. Does O. mean that *all* cap. pun. is wrong?

Dog incident—dog recog. prisoner's humanity, behaves naturally, O. claims the execution is unnatural.

(11) hangman a convict, not an official. yard overgrown—significance?

(12) what god is Ram? prisoner a Hindu.

(13) why everyone transfixed? more than surprise? "kill him quickly"—selfish.

(15) the dog again. what was O. doing there anyway? all he does is hold dog. observer from P.D.?

(17) what's a lathi? or lathis? dog "conscious of having misbehaved"—how does O. know?

(18) prisoner afraid before, found courage to face death—humanizes him. what's a boxwalah?

Anticlimax from here on. prisoners impassive, officials near hysteria. again, why such a big deal, if they do executions often (other condemned men there). take O's word that this time was different. laughing it off, life goes on, etc.

(24) Euros and natives on same side, against prisoners. still nothing about dead man's crime, but can't have been so bad given everyone's reactions—? nobody says it's what he deserved.

NOTES MADE AFTER FINISHING THE READING

did this really happen? seems too pat, with dog and all, and O. hanging around doing nothing instead of whatever he usually did. Could have happened, maybe that's enough.

no argument against cap. pun., just personal insight from personal experience. can't make laws that way. no reasons pro or con except O. thinks it unnatural, with dog's behavior as the proof.

form—chron. narration, no gaps or flashbacks. intro para 1, sets scene. climax: the hanging. conclusion starts para 17 (?), winds story down. style clear, direct, not fancy, strong words, lots of detail and color, etc. good writing obviously, but he doesn't persuade me about cap. pun.

Looking over this reader's shoulder, you can see that he gets increasingly skeptical about Orwell's thesis statement, and you may guess that he himself supports capital punishment—or at least sees some point in it. The reader has noted a good deal of what Orwell put into the essay, such as who does what at the prison; perhaps on the second reading he will get more out of the essay's concluding paragraphs, which are skimmed over in his notes. And the reader has also noticed some of the things Orwell left out, such as the nature of the prisoner's offense. He has begun to find relations between the details and the whole, notably by thinking about the significance of the dog's behavior. All in all, he has made a good beginning at understanding "A Hanging."

From Reading to Writing

In many college courses you will be required to discuss your reading in some writing of your own. In composition courses, such writing assignments often take these forms:

1. An analysis of the reading's content, form, or both.
2. An original composition on the topic of the reading, or on a related topic.
3. An original composition on a topic of your choice, inspired in some way by the reading but not bound by its subject matter.

Which kind of paper you write may be specified by your instructor, or the choice may be left to you.

Three Student Essays in Response to George Orwell's "A Hanging"

In the following pages you will find papers of all three types, each a response to Orwell's "A Hanging" and each typical of how students write for their composition courses.

An Analytical Essay

When you write an analysis of something you have read, your purpose is to show that you have understood the work and to help your readers increase their understanding of it too. You do this by drawing attention to aspects of its meaning, structure, and style that are important but not obvious. Such an analysis grows directly out of your reading, and more specifically out of the notes you made during your first and subsequent readings of the text.

When planning your analytical paper, start by considering what point you most want to make—what your thesis will be. If you can think of several possible theses for your paper, and you often will be able to, select the one that seems to you the most important—and that you think you can support and defend most strongly and effectively using evidence from the piece you are writing about. Many different theses would be possible for an analytical paper about Orwell's "A Hanging." Here are a few:

In "A Hanging," George Orwell carefully selects details in order to persuade us that capital punishment is wrong.

"A Hanging" reveals how thoroughly the British had imposed their laws, customs, and values on colonial Burma.

Though "A Hanging" appeals powerfully to the emotions, it does not make a reasoned argument against capital punishment.

In "A Hanging," George Orwell employs metaphor, personification, and dialogue to express man's inhumanity to other men.

This last is the thesis of the student paper that follows, "The Disgrace of Man."

Think, too, about your audience. Who will read your paper? Will they know the work you are analyzing? If not, then you need to supply enough information about the work so that your readers can understand you. But if you expect your essay to be read by your instructor and classmates, and if it is about an assigned reading, you can usually assume that they know the work and need no summary of it, though they may need clear reminders of specific details and passages that you analyze closely and that may have escaped their attention.

Students writing papers for their courses have a special problem: What can they say that their readers, especially their instructors, do not already know? This is a problem all writers face, including instructors themselves when writing professional articles, and the answer is always the same: Write honestly about what you see in the work and what you think about it. Since all readers respond differently to the same text, any one of them—including you—may notice details or draw conclusions that others miss. Teachers may be experienced, knowledgeable readers, but they do not know everything. Some might not have noticed that Orwell excludes from "A Hanging" any hint of the prisoner's crime, yet this omission is important because it reinforces Orwell's main point: Capital punishment is always wrong, no matter what the circumstances. And even if you think you have no such discoveries to offer, your individual point of view and response to the text will lend your writing originality and interest. As the poet James Stephens once wrote, "Originality does not consist in saying what no one has ever said before, but in saying exactly what you think yourself."

The following student essay, "The Disgrace of Man," is original in Stephens's sense, and the student has also discovered something in "A Hanging" that other readers might well have missed, something about Orwell's way of telling his story that contributes, subtly but significantly, to its effect.

The Disgrace of Man

George Orwell's "A Hanging" graphically depicts the execution of a prisoner in a way that expresses a universal tragedy. He artfully employs metaphor, personification, and dialogue to indicate man's inhumanity toward other men, and to prompt the reader's sympathy and self-examination.

Orwell uses simile and metaphor to show that the prisoner is treated more like an animal than like a human being. The cells of the condemned men, "a row of sheds . . . quite bare within," are "like small animal cages." The warders grip the prisoner "like men handling a fish." Though they refer to the prisoner as "the man" or "our friend," the other characters view him as less than human. Even his cry resounds like the "tolling of a bell" rather than a human "prayer or cry for help," and after he is dead the superintendent pokes at the body with a stick. These details direct the reader's attention to the lack of human concern for the condemned prisoner.

In contrast, Orwell emphasizes the "wrongness of cutting a life short" by representing the parts of the prisoner's body as taking on human behavior. He describes the lock of hair "dancing" on the man's scalp, his feet "printing themselves" on the gravel, all his organs "toiling away" like a team of laborers at some collective project. In personifying these bodily features, Orwell forces the reader to see the prisoner's vitality, his humanity. The reader, in turn, associates each bodily part with himself; he becomes highly aware of the frailty of life. As the author focuses on how easily these actions can be stopped, in any human being, "with a sudden snap," the reader feels the "wrongness" of the hanging as if his own life were threatened.

In addition to creating this sense of unmistakable life, Orwell uses the dog as a standard for evaluating the characters' appreciation of human life. The dog loves people—he is "wild with glee to find so many human beings together"—and the person he loves the most is the prisoner, who has been treated as less than human by the jail attendants. When the prisoner starts to pray, the other people are silent, but the dog answers "with a whine." Even after the hanging, the dog runs directly to the gallows to see the prisoner again. The reader is forced to reflect on his own reaction: Which is more shocking, the dog's actions or the observers' cold response?

Finally, Orwell refers to the characters' nationalities to stress that this insensitivity extends to all nationalities and races. The hanging takes place in Burma, in a jail run by a European army doctor and a native of southern India. The warders are also Indians, and the hangman is actually a fellow prisoner. The author calls attention to each of these participants, and implies that each one of them might have halted the brutal proceedings. He was there too and could have intervened when he suddenly realized that killing the prisoner would be wrong. Yet the "formality of the hanging" goes on.

As he reflects on the meaning of suddenly destroying human life, Orwell emphasizes the similarities among all men, regardless of nationality. Before the hanging, they are "seeing, hearing, feeling, understanding the same world," and afterward there would be "one mind less, one world less." Such feelings do not affect the other characters, who think of the hanging not as killing but as a job to be done, a job made unpleasant by those reminders (the incident of the dog, the prisoner's praying) that they are dealing with a human being. Orwell uses dialogue to show how selfish and callous the observers are. Though they have different accents—the superintendent's "for God's sake hurry up," the Dravidian's "It wass all finished"—they think and feel the same. Their words, such as "*He's* all right," show that they are more concerned about their own lives than the one they are destroying.

Although George Orwell sets his story in Burma, his point is universal; although he deals with capital punishment, he implies other questions of life and death. We are all faced with issues such as capital punishment, abortion, and euthanasia, and sometimes we find ourselves directly involved, as Orwell did. "A Hanging" urges us to examine ourselves and to take very seriously the value of a human life.

Most teachers would consider "The Disgrace of Man" a fine student essay. It is well organized, stating its thesis early, supporting it effectively, and sticking to the point. The discussion is clear and coherent, and it is firmly based on Orwell's text—the student author has understood the core meaning of "A Hanging." She has also noticed many details that express Orwell's attitude toward the hanging and toward his imperial colleagues, and she has interpreted them so that her readers can plainly see how those details contribute to the total effect of "A Hanging." How many would have observed that Orwell actually personifies the parts of the prisoner's body? How many, having noticed it, would have grasped the relation of this detail to Orwell's point? That's accurate, active reading.

An Argumentative Essay

Perhaps you recall the annotations of "A Hanging" on pages 13–14. The writer of those notes was attentive to the meaning of the text, but as he read he found himself disagreeing with Orwell's view that taking human life is always unspeakably wrong. He might have gone on to analyze "A Hanging," as he was obviously capable of doing, but he did not. Instead, given the opportunity to choose his own topic, he decided to present his own views on Orwell's subject: capital punishment.

The writer began by exploring the topic, jotting down notes on what he knew and believed. He also went to the library to look up recent research into the effects of capital punishment, but found that authorities still cannot agree on whether the death penalty deters crime or protects society, so his efforts led only to a few sentences in his first paragraph. Why go to so much trouble for a short writing assignment? Evidently the writer cared enough about his topic to want to do it justice, not just for the assignment's sake but for his own. As the English philosopher John Stuart Mill wrote, "If the cultivation of the understanding consists in one thing more than in another, it is surely in learning the grounds of one's own opinions." The author of "For Capital Punishment" knew what he believed, and he used the occasion of a writing assignment to work out a rationale for that belief.

For Capital Punishment

The debate on capital punishment goes on and on. Does the death penalty deter people from committing murder? Does it protect us from criminals who would murder again if they were returned to society? These questions have not yet been answered beyond any doubt, and maybe they never will be. But is the death penalty cruel and unnatural? This is a different kind of question, having to do with the nature of the punishment itself, and it can be answered. I think the answer is no, and that capital punishment has a place in a civilized society. I also feel that it should be imposed as the penalty for the worst crimes.

In the United States this is a constitutional issue, because the Bill of Rights does not allow cruel and unusual punishment. The Supreme Court has interpreted these words not to include capital punishment, and there is a basis in the Constitution for their decision: The fifth amendment says that "no person shall . . . be deprived of life, liberty, or property, without due process of law," which means that a person can be deprived of life if due process has been observed. The Court did find some years ago that the death penalty was being imposed much more often on poor black people than on any others, and suspended capital punishment throughout the nation because due process was obviously *not* being observed, but when the Court considered that that situation had been corrected it permitted executions to resume in 1977 with the death of Gary Gilmore.

But beyond the constitutionality of capital punishment there is the deeper question of whether it is morally wrong. We accept some punishments as just, while others seem barbaric. The difference, I think, has to do with what the condemned man is made to suffer. The lightest punishments take away some of his money or restrict his freedom of movement in society; some examples are fines, probation, and work-release programs. Then there are punishments that remove the criminal from society, such as imprisonment and deportation. The kind of punishment we do not accept, though it is still used in some countries, is the kind that is meant to do physical harm: beating, maiming, torture. The death penalty is a special case. It removes criminals from society permanently and economically, but it also involves physical harm. It is in the balance between these two effects, I think, that we can find out whether capital punishment is morally acceptable.

If we condemned people to death because we wanted them to suffer, you would expect that methods of execution would have been made more painful and frightening over the years. Instead, the opposite has happened. Traitors used to be tortured to death before screaming mobs, but now the condemned man dies in private as painlessly as possible; Texas now uses chemical injections that are apparently almost painless. It must be, then, that the reason for execution is not physical harm but removal from society, which is a widely accepted purpose for judicial punishment.

But why, then, would not life imprisonment serve the same purpose just as well? There are two main reasons why it does not. First, "life imprisonment" does not mean what it says; most lifers are considered for parole after fifteen years or less, even monsters like Charles Manson and Sirhan Sirhan. It's true that these two have not been released, but they might be at any time their California parole board changes its mind. So life imprisonment does not insure that the worst criminals will be removed from society permanently. Second, as long as a criminal stays in prison he is a burden on the very society he has offended against, costing society tens of thousands of dollars each year to keep him secure and healthy. There is also a real question in my mind whether caging a prisoner for life, if it actually *is* for life, is any more merciful than putting him to death. The conditions in American prisons, where the inmates are often brutalized and degraded by each other and even by their guards, must often seem a "fate worse than death."

Most nations of the world, and most states in the United States, have legalized capital punishment and used it for many years. They—we—are not bloodthirsty monsters, but ordinary people seeking safety and justice under the law. Maybe the time will come when the death penalty is no longer needed or wanted, and then it will be abolished. But that time is not yet here.

The writer of "For Capital Punishment" has taken on a large subject, on which many books have been and many more will be written. When discussing a controversial topic of wide interest, many people tend to parrot back uncritically the opinions they have read and heard, which is easy to do but does not add much to what everyone knows. This writer has escaped that temptation and thought his subject through, in the process working out reasoned and partly original arguments of his own to support his view. His discussion is clear and well-organized; he states his thesis at the end of the first paragraph and supports it with evidence and reasoning throughout the paper. Of course many reasonable people will disagree with his support of capital punishment, just as he disagrees with Orwell's opposition to it. But most composition teachers, even those who do not share this writer's views, would consider "For Capital Punishment" a good student paper.

A Narrative Essay

In "A Hanging," George Orwell writes about an incident that brought him to an important insight. The author of the following essay did the same. Reading Orwell brought back to mind a childhood experience which had made her aware of the potential for thoughtless violence that lies within us all. Part of Orwell's influence on her is revealed by her choice of subject—the heedless killing of three helpless nestlings. But she also follows Orwell in her choice of a writing strategy; like him she narrates a personal experience that illustrates a general moral principle.

Killing for Fun

Every summer my family returns to our ancestral home, which is in a community where the same families have lived generation after generation. There are tennis courts, a golf course, boats, and other occupations to help pass the long, hot days. This all sounds very enjoyable, and it usually was, but sometimes it got very boring. Spending every summer with the same gang and doing the same things, under the same grown-ups' noses, began to seem dull, and by the time I was thirteen I was ready to experience the thrill of the forbidden.

One afternoon in July, I was supposed to sail in some races with my best friend Mitchell, but the air was so thick and heavy that we decided not to go. We sat around his house all day, waiting for his brother to bring back the family power boat so that we could water ski. Thinking back to that summer, I remember how frustrated and irritable we were, our pent-up energy ready to explode. We roamed his house searching for something—anything—to do, but we only succeeded in making one mess after another and angering his mother. Finally we hit on something. We were eating lunch on Mitchell's back porch when we both noticed his father's rifle propped in a corner.

Now Mitchell's father had often warned all of us that his rifle was strictly off limits. The rifle itself was not very dangerous, as it was only an air gun that shot small pellets, but he was afraid of its being misused and hurting someone. He himself used it to scare off stray dogs and was usually very careful to put it away, but for some reason on that particular day he had forgotten. We decided that it would be fun to take the rifle out in the nearby woods and shoot at whatever we found there.

We had to be very careful not to be seen by the borough residents as they all knew us. For most parents, kids heading for the woods meant trouble. So Mitchell and I sneaked out of his house with the gun and went slinking through some old horse stables on our way to the woods. By the time we arrived at the edge of the woods we felt like spies. There was a caretaker's cottage there, and the caretaker was forever on the lookout for what he thought were troublesome kids. When we successfully passed the cottage our spirits were high, as we had gotten safely through the danger zone on the way to our forbidden project.

As we went into the woods we began to find some animals and birds to use as targets, but try as we might, we could not hit anything. Our pellets seemed to disappear in flight, not even giving us the satisfaction of hitting a tree and making a noise. Our mission was not succeeding, and we decided to look for an easier target.

Finally we startled a mother bird, who flew away leaving her nest behind. We thought the nest would make a fine target, stationary as it was and with live creatures inside. We took turns shooting at it in an attempt to knock it out of the tree, intoxicated with our power and carried away by the thrill of it all. Mitchell was the one to knock it down. It tottered, and after a little rustling a small object fell out, and the nest followed, landing upside down.

Mitchell ran up and excitedly turned it over. The sight was horribly repulsive. Underneath lay three naked pink corpses, staring up at us silently with wide dark eyes and wide, underdeveloped, faintly yellow beaks. They looked as if they had been savagely strangled one by one, except for the small pellet holes in each tiny body. A few feet away a slight movement caught my eye. The object that had fallen first was a fourth baby bird. It had survived the shooting and the fall and was flopping around, mutilated as it was. I poked Mitchell, who was staring at the massacre underneath the nest, and directed his attention to the desperately flapping pink lump a few feet away.

I could see that Mitchell was repulsed by the sight, but being a thirteen-year-old boy he refused to show it. He made an attempt to maintain a hunter's attitude, and fiercely drove pellet after pellet into the injured bird. We tried to joke about it, and as soon as we were out of sight of the nest we broke into hysterically uncontrollable laughter, trying to avoid thinking about what we had done. On the way home we avoided talking about it, and I felt relieved to part company with Mitchell when we got home.

That incident shocked me into thinking about the results of my actions. Mitchell and I were not inhuman monsters, determined to massacre baby birds; we were just bored kids looking for an adventure and not thinking about the consequences. I wonder how much unhappiness and even crime comes from young people acting selfishly and thoughtlessly, out for a thrill. If they had to see the suffering they cause, they would surely think harder before they act.

The author of "Killing for Fun" tells her story well. She describes her experience vividly, with much closely observed detail, and builds suspense to hold her readers' attention. What makes "Killing for Fun" not just a story but a personal essay is the last paragraph, where she turns her experience to an observation about life. The observation may not be brand new, but then it needn't be—few important truths are. George Orwell was certainly not the first to oppose capital punishment. In both narrative essays it is the authors' personal experience, honestly and precisely recounted, that gives their general observations force.

These three essays, each different from the other two and from Orwell's, illustrate but a few of the many ways different people can respond to their reading and use their responses in their writing. Each paper also shows how a student, working under the limitations of an assigned reading and a specific writing assignment, can create an interesting and original piece of writing by analyzing the reading carefully, or exploring his or her own beliefs, or drawing upon personal experience. Each of the selections in *Outlooks and Insights* provides you with opportunities to do the same.

Some Notes on Fiction and Poetry

The poems and short stories in *Outlooks and Insights* explore many of the same themes the essays do, and can serve your writing purposes in similar ways. A story or a poem may give you ideas for your writing or topics to write about, and even though you may never write poetry or fiction you can still learn much about structure and style from reading literature. These selections will be most useful to you, however, if you know something about the basic elements of fiction and poetry, and so the following pages provide a brief, highly selective introduction to some of their most important qualities and forms.

READING SHORT STORIES

Short stories look much like essays, and the two forms are similar in other ways as well. Both are written in prose; some essays, like nearly all stories, are narratives; both may contain dialogue. And certainly a reader can learn from fiction as well as from nonfiction about the ways other people think, feel, and behave, and how they deal with ethical problems. But stories also differ from essays in fundamental respects, and call for different expectations and responses from their readers.

Though a short story may incorporate materials from real life, including places and even characters and incidents, it is essentially the product of the author's imagination. Eudora Welty says that she got the idea for her short story "A Worn Path" (page 136) from watching an old woman walking slowly across a winter country landscape, but that the rest of the story was pure invention. In an essay, on the other hand, we expect the events and characters to be rendered accurately from real life. Part of the force of George Orwell's "A Hanging" comes from our belief that he is reporting a personal experience—that he did indeed attend a hanging at which the events he narrates actually took place.

Both essays and stories can make points about life, but each type does so differently. An essay normally states its main idea or *thesis* openly and explains or argues that idea at length in a direct and orderly way. A story, however, does not tell—it shows. Its main idea, called its *theme*, is not so much discussed as embodied in the characters and action, and is seldom presented openly—each reader has to discover a story's theme for himself or herself. As Eudora Welty puts it, "A narrative line is in its deeper sense . . . the tracing out of a meaning"—which is the story's theme. Theme is not the same as subject. The subject of "A Worn Path" is an old woman's long, wearying trip to town to get medicine for her ill grandson—a trip which she has made many times before and will make again. The story's theme, however, is the general observation it illustrates and embodies. Different readers may put the theme of "A Worn Path" into different words. Welty says it this way: "The habit of love cuts through confusion and stumbles or contrives its way out of difficulty, it remembers the way even when it forgets, for a dumbfounded moment, its reason for being." This is the story's true meaning and encompasses all of its details, right down to the path itself, worn by the old woman's often-repeated errand of love. As this suggests, a story's theme reveals the unity of the whole work—or can even be said to give the work its unity.

Most short stories have other elements in common which are seldom found in nonfiction writing. The action in a short story, called its *plot,* typically unfolds in a pattern consisting of a series of stages that can be diagrammed in this way:

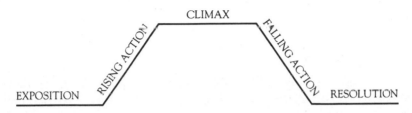

The *exposition* sets the scene, describes the situation, and begins to introduce some of the characters. The *rising action* (sometimes called the *complication*) sets the characters into conflict—with each other or within themselves—and the conflict rises in tension and complexity. At the *climax* the tension and complexity reach their peak, and the central character takes an action or undergoes an experience that is the turning point of the story. After the climax comes the *falling action,* in which the tension slackens and the story moves toward its conclusion. The end of the story is the *resolution,* in which the conflict of the plot gives way to a new stability. "A Worn Path" follows this pattern. Its exposition consists of the first two paragraphs. The rising action, beginning in paragraph 3, builds to a climax when Phoenix meets the hunter. After the falling action, in which she makes her way into town, the resolution begins in paragraph 70 when she arrives at the doctor's office. These conventions of plot have served countless writers for more than two thousand years with no loss in effectiveness and vitality, and still provide the structure for novels, short stories, plays—even movies and television dramas.

How we take in the events of the plot is determined by the author's use of a narrative *point of view.* Sometimes the story is told by one of the characters, as in Isaac Bashevis Singer's "Gimpel the Fool" (page 57). This is called *first person point of view* because the narrator often uses the first person pronoun *I.* When the story is told by a narrator standing somewhere outside the events of the story, this is called *third person point of view* because the narrator uses the third person pronouns *he, she,* and *they.* "A Worn Path" is told from the third person point of view; the narrator, like a movie camera's eye, tracks old Phoenix Jackson all the way to town, reporting on her doings from outside the story.

The third person point of view has two main forms: *omniscient* and *limited*. If the narrator tells us what all the characters are doing, wherever they are, and even what they are thinking and feeling, the author is using the third person omniscient point of view. An example is James Joyce's "Counterparts" (p. 400). In "A Worn Path," on the other hand, the narrator tells us only what Phoenix Jackson does, says, hears, and sees; we can only infer what the characters are thinking from what they say and do.

READING POEMS

Almost anything can be subject matter for poetry, and the range of poetic styles and forms is enormous: John Updike's "Ex-Basketball Player" (p. 361), for example, uses special poetic devices such as simile and metaphor, while Donald Hall's "Ox Cart Man" (p. 398) seems as plain as prose. But even the plainest poetry should never be read merely to understand its message, for that would be to ignore the special delights and the special kinds of meaning which only poetry can convey.

Let's look at one poem as an active reader would, trying to respond not only to its literal meaning but also to its special qualities as a poem. The poem is by William Shakespeare:

That time of year thou may'st in me behold
When yellow leaves, or none, or few, do hang
Upon those boughs which shake against the cold,
Bare ruined choirs where late the sweet birds sang.
In me thou seest the twilight of such day   5
As after sunset fadeth in the west,
Which by and by black night doth take away,
Death's second self that seals up all in rest.
In me thou seest the glowing of such fire
That on the ashes of his youth doth lie,   10
As the deathbed whereon it must expire,
Consumed with that which it was nourished by.
  This thou perceiv'st, which makes thy love more strong,
  To love that well which thou must leave ere long.

One of the first things a reader would notice about this poem is that it conveys its meaning in a special way. The speaker of the poem says, in effect, that he is old, but he only tells us so indirectly. He compares his time of life with a season, a time of day, and a stage in the life of a fire, and these three images evoke our own experience so that we understand what he means. In autumn the days grow shorter and colder, at twilight the day's heat and light are going fast, and the embers of a dying fire grow dimmer and cooler with every minute; so too with advancing age, when the vigor and passions of earlier years have faded and death is soon to come. The images also reinforce each other, each describing a natural process that cannot be avoided or stopped and evoking the same progression from warmth to cold, from light to dark. And there is a progression from one image to the next: Autumn, a span of months and days, is succeeded by twilight, a matter of an hour or less, and last comes fire, which can rise and go out in a few minutes. This speeding up of time prepares for the last line's suggestion that death will come "ere long." Images such as these, which occur only occasionally in prose, can often be a poem's chief means of conveying its meaning.

Another resource which prose writers use sparingly but which is vital to poetry is the *sound* of the language—its vowels and consonants, and the rhythms of words and phrases. Tradition has it that poetry began as song, and poets often choose their words not only to convey meaning but to make a kind of music through planned patterns of verbal sounds. To hear and appreciate that music to the fullest, it's a good idea to read a poem aloud, listening for those patterns. And even if you can't read aloud (for example, if you are in a library reading room or on the bus), try to "hear" the poem in your imagination.

Even on first reading "That Time of Year" you probably noticed that Shakespeare has written his poem with not only its sense but its sound in mind. The rhythm is regular, as each of the fourteen lines has exactly ten syllables, and those syllables alternate regularly between weak and strong stress: "That *time* of *year* thou *may'st* in *me* be*hold.*" Shakespeare's skill is such that to achieve this musical effect he never needs to sacrifice clarity, and indeed he rarely departs from natural phrasing. There is evidence, too, that Shakespeare has coordinated the vowel and consonant sounds of his poem. For one thing, he rhymes his lines in a complex but regular pattern. For another, two particular consonants, *l* and *s*, recur throughout the poem. They are most conspicuous in phrases like "second *self* that *seals*" (line 8) and "*leave* ere *long*" (line 14), which are examples of alliteration, but on closer examination you will find that one or both sounds appear, usually more than once, in each line of the poem, and help to give it its special music.

Shakespeare's use of rhyme deserves special attention, because it fits perfectly the meaning and even the grammar of his poem. Each of the three images is expressed in a single sentence that takes up four lines, and those lines are rhymed in an interlocking pattern that makes the image, and the sentence, seem all the more self-contained. The arrival of a new image brings the beginning not only of a new sentence but also of a new and different set of rhymes. The last two lines of the poem are not an image but a direct statement, and they have a rhyme pattern of their own using *strong* and *long*. Some readers may even notice in this last rhyme a distant echo of *hang* and *sang* from the beginning of the poem.

Shakespeare's rhyme scheme fits the meaning of his poem so closely that you might think he had invented both as part of the same creative act. In fact this is not so. He wrote 153 other poems in exactly the same form, which is sometimes called the Shakespearean sonnet in his honor. Moreover, Shakespeare did not invent the form, which had existed for forty years and been used by many poets before he took it up. Here we have a strange thing: Maybe the form itself gave Shakespeare ideas for poems, or at least set him challenges that heated rather than cooled his imagination. How versatile the sonnet form was in Shakespeare's hands you can see from the following, which has exactly the same structure as "That Time of Year" but a very different theme:

My mistress' eyes are nothing like the sun;
Coral is far more red than her lips' red;
If snow be white, why then her breasts are dun;
If hairs be wires, black wires grow on her head.
I have seen roses damasked, red and white,   5
But no such roses see I in her cheeks;
And in some perfumes is there more delight
Than in the breath that from my mistress reeks.
I love to hear her speak; yet well I know
That music hath a far more pleasing sound: 10
I grant I never saw a goddess go;
My mistress, when she walks, treads on the ground.
    And yet, by heaven, I think my love as rare
    As any she belied with false compare.

1 *Private Lives*

Our entire life, with our fine moral code and our precious freedom, consists ultimately in accepting ourselves as we are.
JEAN ANOUILH

Is happiness measured by the size of our home, the quality of our clothes, and the vacations we take?
THE PEOPLE'S BICENTENNIAL COMMISSION, COMMON SENSE II

The road to psychological maturity is twisting, hilly, and poorly surfaced.
ROBERT E. NIXON

A Sense of Self

DICK GREGORY

Dick Gregory was one of the angry black comics who emerged at the beginning of the 1960s who, as entertainers, could speak of racial injustice to audiences that would not listen to other black leaders. A contemporary of Martin Luther King, Jr., and Malcolm X, Gregory played a significant part in the civil rights movement of the sixties with his comedy, his political advocacy, and his writing. His books include *From the Back of the Bus* (1962) and *nigger* (1964).

Gregory's childhood was hard. He was born in the Depression year of 1932 in the segregated state of Missouri, and grew up burdened by deprivations of all kinds. The following excerpt from his autobiography, *nigger*, gives a hint of what his early years were like, describing a childhood experience that made him aware of how others saw him—and of the meaning of shame.

Shame

I never learned hate at home, or shame. I had to go to school for 1 that. I was about seven years old when I got my first big lesson. I was in love with a little girl named Helene Tucker, a light-complected little girl with pigtails and nice manners. She was always clean and she was smart in school. I think I went to school then mostly to look at her. I brushed my hair and even got me a little old handkerchief. It was a lady's handkerchief, but I didn't want Helene to see me wipe my nose on my hand. The pipes were frozen again, there was no water in the house, but I washed my socks and shirt every night. I'd get a pot, and go over to Mister Ben's grocery store, and stick my pot down into his soda machine. Scoop out some chopped ice. By evening the ice melted to water for washing. I got sick a lot that winter because the fire would go out at night before the clothes were dry. In the morning I'd put them on, wet or dry, because they were the only clothes I had.

Everybody's got a Helene Tucker, a symbol of everything you want.   2
I loved her for her goodness, her cleanness, her popularity. She'd walk
down my street and my brothers and sisters would yell, "Here comes
Helene," and I'd rub my tennis sneakers on the back of my pants and
wish my hair wasn't so nappy and the white folks' shirt fit me better. I'd
run out on the street. If I knew my place and didn't come too close,
she'd wink at me and say hello. That was a good feeling. Sometimes I'd
follow her all the way home, and shovel the snow off her walk and try
to make friends with her Momma and her aunts. I'd drop money on her
stoop late at night on my way back from shining shoes in the taverns.
And she had a Daddy, and he had a good job. He was a paper hanger.

I guess I would have gotten over Helene by summertime, but some-   3
thing happened in that classroom that made her face hang in front of
me for the next twenty-two years. When I played the drums in high ·
school it was for Helene and when I broke track records in college it was
for Helene and when I started standing behind microphones and heard
applause I wished Helene could hear it, too. It wasn't until I was twenty-
nine years old and married and making money that I finally got her out
of my system. Helene was sitting in that classroom when I learned to be
ashamed of myself.

It was on a Thursday. I was sitting in the back of the room, in a   4
seat with a chalk circle drawn around it. The idiot's seat, the troublemaker's seat.

The teacher thought I was stupid. Couldn't spell, couldn't read,   5
couldn't do arithmetic. Just stupid. Teachers were never interested in
finding out that you couldn't concentrate because you were so hungry,
because you hadn't had any breakfast. All you could think about was
noontime, would it ever come? Maybe you could sneak into the cloak-
room and steal a bite of some kid's lunch out of a coat pocket. A bite
of something. Paste. You can't really make a meal of paste, or put it on
bread for a sandwich, but sometimes I'd scoop a few spoonfuls out of the
big paste jar in the back of the room. Pregnant people get strange tastes.
I was pregnant with poverty. Pregnant with dirt and pregnant with smells
that made people turn away, pregnant with cold and pregnant with shoes
that were never bought for me, pregnant with five other people in my
bed and no Daddy in the next room, and pregnant with hunger. Paste
doesn't taste too bad when you're hungry.

The teacher thought I was a troublemaker. All she saw from the   6
front of the room was a little black boy who squirmed in his idiot's seat
and made noises and poked the kids around him. I guess she couldn't see
a kid who made noises because he wanted someone to know he was
there.

It was on a Thursday, the day before the Negro payday. The eagle   7
always flew on Friday. The teacher was asking each student how much
his father would give to the Community Chest. On Friday night, each
kid would get the money from his father, and on Monday he would bring
it to the school. I decided I was going to buy a Daddy right then. I had
money in my pocket from shining shoes and selling papers, and whatever
Helene Tucker pledged for her Daddy I was going to top it. And I'd hand
the money right in. I wasn't going to wait until Monday to buy me a
Daddy.

I was shaking, scared to death. The teacher opened her book and   8
started calling out names alphabetically.

"Helene Tucker?"   9

"My Daddy said he'd give two dollars and fifty cents."   10

"That's very nice, Helene. Very, very nice indeed."   11

That made me feel pretty good. It wouldn't take too much to top   12
that. I had almost three dollars in dimes and quarters in my pocket. I
stuck my hand in my pocket and held onto the money, waiting for her
to call my name. But the teacher closed her book after she called everybody else in the class.

I stood up and raised my hand.   13

"What is it now?"   14

"You forgot me?"   15

She turned toward the blackboard. "I don't have time to be playing   16
with you, Richard."

"My Daddy said he'd . . ."   17

"Sit down, Richard, you're disturbing the class."   18

"My Daddy said he'd give . . . fifteen dollars."   19

She turned around and looked mad. "We are collecting this money   20
for you and your kind, Richard Gregory. If your Daddy can give fifteen
dollars you have no business being on relief."

"I got it right now, I got it right now, my Daddy gave it to me to   21
turn in today, my Daddy said . . ."

"And furthermore," she said, looking right at me, her nostrils get-   22
ting big and her lips getting thin and her eyes opening wide. "We know
you don't have a Daddy."

Helene Tucker turned around, her eyes full of tears. She felt sorry   23
for me. Then I couldn't see her too well because I was crying, too.

"Sit down, Richard."   24

And I always thought the teacher kind of liked me. She always   25
picked me to wash the blackboard on Friday, after school. That was a
big thrill, it made me feel important. If I didn't wash it, come Monday
the school might not function right.

"Where are you going, Richard?"   26

I walked out of school that day, and for a long time I didn't go   27
back very often. There was shame there.

Now there was shame everywhere. It seemed like the whole world   28
had been inside that classroom, everyone had heard what the teacher
had said, everyone had turned around and felt sorry for me. There was
shame in going to the Worthy Boys Annual Christmas Dinner for you
and your kind, because everybody knew what a worthy boy was. Why
couldn't they just call it the Boys Annual Dinner, why'd they have to
give it a name? There was shame in wearing the brown and orange and
white plaid mackinaw the welfare gave to 3,000 boys. Why'd it have to
be the same for everybody so when you walked down the street the people
could see you were on relief? It was a nice warm mackinaw and it had a
hood, and my Momma beat me and called me a little rat when she found
out I stuffed it in the bottom of a pail full of garbage way over on Cottage
Street. There was shame in running over to Mister Ben's at the end of
the day and asking for his rotten peaches, there was shame in asking
Mrs. Simmons for a spoonful of sugar, there was shame in running out
to meet the relief truck. I hated that truck, full of food for you and your
kind. I ran into the house and hid when it came. And then I started to
sneak through alleys, to take the long way home so the people going
into White's Eat Shop wouldn't see me. Yeah, the whole world heard
the teacher that day, we all know you don't have a Daddy.

It lasted for a while, this kind of numbness. I spent a lot of time   29
feeling sorry for myself. And then one day I met this wino in a restaurant.
I'd been out hustling all day, shining shoes, selling newspapers, and I
had googobs of money in my pocket. Bought me a bowl of chili for fifteen
cents, and a cheeseburger for fifteen cents, and a Pepsi for five cents,
and a piece of chocolate cake for ten cents. That was a good meal. I was
eating when this old wino came in. I love winos because they never hurt
anyone but themselves.

The old wino sat down at the counter and ordered twenty-six cents   30
worth of food. He ate it like he really enjoyed it. When the owner,
Mister Williams, asked him to pay the check, the old wino didn't lie or
go through his pocket like he suddenly found a hole.

He just said: "Don't have no money."   31

The owner yelled: "Why in hell you come in here and eat my food   32
if you don't have no money? That food cost me money."

Mister Williams jumped over the counter and knocked the wino   33
off his stool and beat him over the head with a pop bottle. Then he
stepped back and watched the wino bleed. Then he kicked him. And
he kicked him again.

I looked at the wino with blood all over his face and I went over. 34
"Leave him alone, Mister Williams. I'll pay the twenty-six cents."

The wino got up, slowly, pulling himself up to the stool, then up 35
to the counter, holding on for a minute until his legs stopped shaking so
bad. He looked at me with pure hate. "Keep your twenty-six cents. You
don't have to pay, not now. I just finished paying for it."

He started to walk out, and as he passed me, he reached down and 36
touched my shoulder. "Thanks, sonny, but it's too late now. Why didn't
you pay it before?"

I was pretty sick about that. I waited too long to help another man. 37

Questions for Study and Discussion

1. What does Gregory mean by shame? What precisely was he ashamed of,
and what in particular did he learn from the incident at school?

2. What is the teacher's attitude toward Gregory? Consider her own words
and actions as well as Gregory's opinion in arriving at your answer.

3. What role does money play in Gregory's narrative? How does it relate to
his sense of shame?

4. Gregory's use of details—his description of Helene Tucker's manners or
his plaid mackinaw, for example—does more than merely make his narrative
vivid and interesting. Cite several other specific details he gives, and consider
the effect each has on your response to the story.

5. What effect does Gregory's repetition of the word *shame* have on you?
Does Gregory repeat any other words or phrases? If so, with what effect?

Writing Topics

1. Write an essay in which you describe an event in your life that made you
sharply aware of how other people see you. How did you feel—surprised,
ashamed, angry, proud, or something else? Why? Do you still feel the same
way?

2. Social institutions and organizations help to shape our self-esteem, as they
did with Dick Gregory. In an essay, discuss the effect one such institution or
organization has had on you. How did it influence you? Did it help or hinder
you in developing a positive image of yourself?

Nora Ephron was born in New York City in 1941 but was raised in Beverly Hills, California. The daughter of Hollywood screenwriters, she grew up amidst entertainment types and celebrities. After graduating from Wellesley College Ephron began her writing career working as a reporter, editor, and columnist for *Newsweek, Esquire, The New York Post, McCall's,* and *Cosmopolitan.* Women's issues and popular culture are her favorite essay topics and her work has been collected in *Wallflower at the Orgy* (1970), *Crazy Salad: Some Things about Women* (1975), and *Scribble Scribble: Notes on the Media* (1979). In 1983 she published her only novel, *Heartburn.*

In "A Few Words about Breasts," Ephron addresses the topic of sex-role stereotyping and is especially candid as she recounts the trauma of what happened, and what did not happen, to her physically during her preadolescent and adolescent development as a young woman.

A Few Words about Breasts

I have to begin with a few words about androgyny. In grammar school, in the fifth and sixth grades, we were all tyrannized by a rigid set of rules that supposedly determined whether we were boys or girls. The episode in *Huckleberry Finn* where Huck is disguised as a girl and gives himself away by the way he threads a needle and catches a ball—that kind of thing. We learned that the way you sat, crossed your legs, held a cigarette, and looked at your nails—the way you did these things in- stinctively was absolute proof of your sex. Now obviously most children did not take this literally, but I did. I thought that just one slip, just one incorrect cross of my legs or flick of an imaginary cigarette ash would turn me from whatever I was into the other thing; that would be all it took, really. Even though I was outwardly a girl and had many of the trappings generally associated with girldom—a girl's name, for example, and dresses, my own telephone, an autograph book—I spent the early years of my adolescence absolutely certain that I might at any point gum it up. I did not feel at all like a girl. I was boyish. I was athletic, ambi- tious, outspoken, competitive, noisy, rambunctious. I had scabs on my knees and my socks slid into my loafers and I could throw a football. I wanted desperately not to be that way, not to be a mixture of both things, but instead just one, a girl, a definite indisputable girl. As soft and as pink as a nursery. And nothing would do that for me, I felt, but breasts.

I was about six months younger than everyone else in my class, and so for about six months after it began, for six months after my friends

1

2

had begun to develop (that was the word we used, develop), I was not particularly worried. I would sit in the bathtub and look down at my breasts and know that any day now, any second now, they would start growing like everyone else's. They didn't. "I want to buy a bra," I said to my mother one night. "What for?" she said. My mother was really hateful about bras, and by the time my third sister had gotten to the point where she was ready to want one, my mother had worked the whole business into a comedy routine. "Why not use a Band-Aid instead?" she would say. It was a source of great pride to my mother that she had never even had to wear a brassiere until she had her fourth child, and then only because her gynecologist made her. It was incomprehensible to me that anyone could ever be proud of something like that. It was the 1950s, for God's sake. Jane Russell. Cashmere sweaters. Couldn't my mother see that? *"I am too old to wear an undershirt."* Screaming. Weeping. Shouting. "Then don't wear an undershirt," said my mother. "But I want to buy a bra." "What for?"

I suppose that for most girls, breasts, brassieres, that entire thing, has more trauma, more to do with the coming of adolescence, with becoming a woman, than anything else. Certainly more than getting your period, although that, too, was traumatic, symbolic. But you could see breasts; they were there; they were visible. Whereas a girl could claim to have her period for months before she actually got it and nobody would ever know the difference. Which is exactly what I did. All you had to do was make a great fuss over having enough nickels for the Kotex machine and walk around clutching your stomach and moaning for three to five days a month about The Curse and you could convince anybody. There is a school of thought somewhere in the women's lib/women's mag/gynecology establishment that claims that menstrual cramps are purely psychological, and I lean towards it. Not that I didn't have them finally. Agonizing cramps, heating-pad cramps, go-down-to-the-school-nurse-and-lie-on-the-cot cramps. But, unlike any pain I had ever suffered, I adored the pain of cramps, welcomed it, wallowed in it, bragged about it. "I can't go. I have cramps." "I can't do that. I have cramps." And most of all, gigglingly, blushingly: "I can't swim. I have cramps." Nobody ever used the hard-core word. Menstruation. God, what an awful word. Never that. "I have cramps." 3

The morning I first got my period, I went into my mother's bedroom to tell her. And my mother, my utterly-hateful-about-bras mother, burst into tears. It was really a lovely moment, and I remember it so clearly not just because it was one of the two times I ever saw my mother cry on my account (the other was when I was caught being a six-year-old kleptomaniac), but also because the incident did not mean to me what 4 it meant to her. Her little girl, her firstborn, had finally become a woman. That was what she was crying about. My reaction to the event, however, was that I might well be a woman in some scientific, textbook sense (and could at least stop faking every month and stop wasting all those nickels). But in another sense—in a visible sense—I was as androgynous and as liable to tip over into boyhood as ever.

I started with a 28AA bra. I don't think they made them any   5
smaller in those days, although I gather that now you can buy bras for five-year-olds that don't have any cups whatsoever in them; trainer bras they are called. My first brassiere came from Robinson's Department Store in Beverly Hills. I went there alone, shaking, positive they would look me over and smile and tell me to come back next year. An actual fitter took me into the dressing room and stood over me while I took off my blouse and tried the first one on. The little puffs stood out on my chest. "Lean over," said the fitter. (To this day, I am not sure what fitters in bra departments do except to tell you to lean over.) I leaned over, with the fleeting hope that my breasts would miraculously fall out of my body and into the puffs. Nothing.

"Don't worry about it," said my friend Libby some months later,   6
when things had not improved. "You'll get them after you're married."

"What are you talking about?" I said.   7

"When you get married," Libby explained, "your husband will touch   8
your breasts and rub them and kiss them and they'll grow."

That was the killer. Necking I could deal with. Intercourse I could   9
deal with. But it had never crossed my mind that a man was going to touch my breasts, that breasts had something to do with all that, petting, my God, they never mentioned petting in my little sex manual about the fertilization of the ovum. I became dizzy. For I knew instantly—as naive as I had been only a moment before—that only part of what she was saying was true: the touching, rubbing, kissing part, not the growing part. And I knew that no one would ever want to marry me. I had no breasts. I would never have breasts.

My best friend in school was Diana Raskob. She lived a block from   10
me in a house full of wonders. English muffins, for instance. The Raskobs were the first people in Beverly Hills to have English muffins for breakfast. They also had an apricot tree in the back, and a badminton court, and a subscription to *Seventeen* magazine, and hundreds of games, like Sorry and Parcheesi and Treasure Hunt and Anagrams. Diana and I spent three or four afternoons a week in their den reading and playing and eating. Diana's mother's kitchen was full of the most colossal assortment of junk food I have ever been exposed to. My house was full of apples and peaches and milk and homemade chocolate-chip cookies—which were nice, and

good for you, but-not-right-before-dinner-or-you'll-spoil-your-appetite. Diana's house had nothing in it that was good for you, and what's more, you could stuff it in right up until dinner and nobody cared. Bar-B-Q potato chips (they were the first in them, too), giant bottles of ginger ale, fresh popcorn with melted butter, hot fudge sauce on Baskin-Robbins jamoca ice cream, powdered-sugar doughnuts from Van de Kamp's. Diana and I had been best friends since we were seven; we were about equally popular in school (which is to say, not particularly), we had about the same success with boys (extremely intermittent), and we looked much the same. Dark. Tall. Gangly.

It is September, just before school begins. I am eleven years old, about to enter the seventh grade, and Diana and I have not seen each other all summer. I have been to camp and she has been somewhere like Banff with her parents. We are meeting, as we often do, on the street midway between our two houses, and we will walk back to Diana's and eat junk and talk about what has happened to each of us that summer. I am walking down Walden Drive in my jeans and my father's shirt hanging out and my old red loafers with the socks falling into them and coming toward me is . . . I take a deep breath . . . a young woman. Diana. Her hair is curled and she has a waist and hips and a bust and she is wearing a straight skirt, an article of clothing I have been repeatedly told I will be unable to wear until I have the hips to hold it up. My jaw drops, and suddenly I am crying, crying hysterically, can't catch my breath sobbing. My best friend has betrayed me. She has gone ahead without me and done it. She has shaped up.

Here are some things I did to help:

Bought a Mark Eden Bust Developer.

Slept on my back for four years.

Splashed cold water on them every night because some French actress said in *Life* magazine that that was what *she* did for her perfect bustline.

Ultimately, I resigned myself to a bad toss and began to wear padded bras. I think about them now, think about all those years in high school I went around in them, my three padded bras, every single one of them with different-sized breasts. Each time I changed bras I changed sizes: one week nice perky but not too obstrusive breasts, the next medium-sized slightly pointy ones, the next week knockers, true knockers; all the time, whatever size I was, carrying around this rubberized appendage on my chest that occasionally crashed into a wall and was poked inward and had to be poked outward—I think about all that and wonder how anyone kept a straight face through it. My parents, who normally had no restraints about needling me—why did they say nothing as they watched

11

12

13

my chest go up and down? My friends, who would periodically inspect my breasts for signs of growth and reassure me—why didn't they at least counsel consistency?

And the bathing suits. I die when I think about the bathing suits.   14
That was the era when you could lay an uninhabited bathing suit on the beach and someone would make a pass at it. I would put one on, an absurd swimsuit with its enormous bust built into it, the bones from the suit stabbing me in the rib cage and leaving little red welts on my body, and there I would be, my chest plunging straight downward absolutely vertically from my collarbone to the top of my suit and then suddenly, wham, out came all that padding and material and wiring absolutely horizontally.

Buster Klepper was the first boy who ever touched them. He was   15
my boyfriend my senior year of high school. There is a picture of him in my high-school yearbook that makes him look quite attractive in a Jewish, horn-rimmed-glasses sort of way, but the picture does not show the pimples, which were air-brushed out, or the dumbness. Well, that isn't really fair. He wasn't dumb. He just wasn't terribly bright. His mother refused to accept it, refused to accept the relentlessly average report cards, refused to deal with her son's inevitable destiny in some junior college or other. "He was tested," she would say to me, apropos of nothing, "and it came out a hundred and forty-five. That's near-genius." Had the word "underachiever" been coined, she probably would have lobbed that one at me, too. Anyway, Buster was really very sweet—which is, I know, damning with faint praise, but there it is. I was the editor of the front page of the high-school newspaper and he was editor of the back page; we had to work together, side by side, in the print shop, and that was how it started. On our first date, we went to see *April Love*, starring Pat Boone. Then we started going together. Buster had a green coupe, a 1950 Ford with an engine he had hand-chromed until it shone, dazzled, reflected the image of anyone who looked into it, anyone usually being Buster polishing it or the gas-station attendants he constantly asked to check the oil in order for them to be overwhelmed by the sparkle on the valves. The car also had a boot stretched over the back seat for reasons I never understood; hanging from the rearview mirror, as was the custom, was a pair of angora dice. A previous girl friend named Solange, who was famous throughout Beverly Hills High School for having no pigment in her right eyebrow, had knitted them for him. Buster and I would ride around town, the two of us seated to the left of the steering wheel. I would shift gears. It was nice.

There was necking. Terrific necking. First in the car, overlooking   16
Los Angeles from what is now the Trousdale Estates. Then on the bed

of his parents' cabana at Ocean House. Incredibly wonderful, frustrating necking, I loved it, really, but no further than necking, please don't, please, because there I was absolutely terrified of the general implications of going-a-step-further with a near-dummy and also terrified of his finding out there was next to nothing there (which he knew, of course; he wasn't that dumb).

I broke up with him at one point. I think we were apart for about two weeks. At the end of that time, I drove down to see a friend at a boarding school in Palos Verdes Estates and a disc jockey played "April Love" on the radio four times during the trip. I took it as a sign. I drove straight back to Griffith Park to a golf tournament Buster was playing in (he was the sixth-seeded teen-age golf player in southern California) and presented myself back to him on the green of the 18th hole. It was all very dramatic. That night we went to a drive-in and I let him get his hand under my protuberances and onto my breasts. He really didn't seem to mind at all.   17

"Do you want to marry my son?" the woman asked me.   18
"Yes," I said.   19
I was nineteen years old, a virgin, going with this woman's son, this big   20
strange woman who was married to a Lutheran minister in New Hampshire
and pretended she was gentile and had this son, by her first husband, this total
fool of a son who ran the hero-sandwich concession at Harvard Business School
and whom for one moment one December in New Hampshire I said—as much
out of politeness as anything else—that I wanted to marry.

"Fine," she said. "Now, here's what you do. Always make sure you're   21
on top of him so you won't seem so small. My bust is very large, you see, so
I always lie on my back to make it look smaller, but you'll have to be on top
most of the time."

I nodded. "Thank you," I said.   22
"I have a book for you to read," she went on. "Take it with you when   23
you leave. Keep it." She went to the bookshelf, found it, and gave it to me.
It was a book on frigidity.

"Thank you," I said.   24

That is a true story. Everything in this article is a true story, but I   25
feel I have to point out that that story in particular is true. It happened on December 30, 1960. I think about it often. When it first happened, I naturally assumed that the woman's son, my boyfriend, was responsible. I invented a scenario where he had had a little heart-to-heart with his mother and had confessed that his only objection to me was that my breasts were small; his mother then took it upon herself to help out. Now I think I was wrong about the incident. The mother was acting on her own, I think: that was her way of being cruel and competitive under

the guise of being helpful and maternal. You have small breasts, she was saying; therefore you will never make him as happy as I have. Or you have small breasts; therefore you will doubtless have sexual problems. Or you have small breasts; therefore you are less woman than I am. She was, as it happens, only the first of what seems to me to be a never-ending string of women who have made competitive remarks to me about breast size. "I would love to wear a dress like that," my friend Emily says to me, "but my bust is too big." Like that. Why do women say these things to me? Do I attract these remarks the way other women attract married men or alcoholics or homosexuals? This summer, for example. I am at a party in East Hampton and I am introduced to a woman from Washington. She is a minor celebrity, very pretty and Southern and blonde and outspoken, and I am flattered because she has read something I have written. We are talking animatedly, we have been talking no more than five minutes, when a man comes up to join us. "Look at the two of us," the woman says to the man, indicating me and her. "The two of us together couldn't fill an A cup." Why does she say that? It isn't even true, dammit, so why? Is she even more addled than I am on this subject? Does she honestly believe there is something wrong with her size breasts, which, it seems to me, now that I look hard at them, are just right? Do I unconsciously bring out competitiveness in women? In that form? What did I do to deserve it?

As for men.

There were men who minded and let me know that they minded. There were men who did not mind. In any case, *I* always minded.

And even now, now that I have been countlessly reassured that my figure is a good one, now that I am grown-up enough to understand that most of my feelings have very little to do with the reality of my shape, I am nonetheless obsessed by breasts. I cannot help it. I grew up in the terrible fifties—with rigid stereotypical sex roles, the insistence that men be men and dress like men and women be women and dress like women, the intolerance of androgyny—and I cannot shake it, cannot shake my feelings of inadequacy. Well, that time is gone, right? All those exaggerated examples of breast worship are gone, right? Those women were freaks, right? I know all that. And yet here I am, stuck with the psychological remains of it all, stuck with my own peculiar version of breast worship. You probably think I am crazy to go on like this: here I have set out to write a confession that is meant to hit you with the shock of recognition, and instead you are sitting there thinking I am thoroughly warped. Well, what can I tell you? If I had had them, I would have been a completely different person. I honestly believe that.

After I went into therapy, a process that made it possible for me   29
to tell total strangers at cocktail parties that breasts were the hang-up of
my life, I was often told that I was insane to have been bothered by my
condition. I was also frequently told, by close friends, that I was extremely boring on the subject. And my girl friends, the ones with nice
big breasts, would go on endlessly about how their lives had been far
more miserable than mine. Their bra straps were snapped in class. They
couldn't sleep on their stomachs. They were stared at whenever the word
"mountain" cropped up in geography. And *Evangeline*, good God what
they went through every time someone had to stand up and recite the
Prologue to Longfellow's *Evangeline*: ". . . stand like druids of eld . . . /
With beards that rest on their bosoms." It was much worse for them,
they tell me. They had a terrible time of it, they assure me. I don't know
how lucky I was, they say.

I have thought about their remarks, tried to put myself in their   30
place, considered their point of view. I think they are full of shit.

Questions for Study and Discussion

1. What exactly is Nora Ephron's problem? How does this problem affect her
self-image?

2. What are the sex-role stereotypes of the 1950s as Ephron describes them?
How was Ephron affected psychologically by these stereotypes? Why does she
feel the need to talk about her adolescent obsession?

3. Ephron refers to a passage in Mark Twain's *The Adventures of Huckleberry
Finn* in which Huck, who is disguised as a girl, betrays himself by his actions.
What types of activities does Ephron mention and how do boys supposedly
perform them differently than girls? What do you think is Ephron's point in
starting her essay in this manner?

4. How does Ephron's mother react to her problem? How would you characterize Ephron's attitude toward her mother?

5. What is Ephron's purpose in discussing her friend Diana and in telling of
her experiences with Buster Klepper? What are the connotations of each
name, and how do these connotations work in the context of Ephron's overall meaning?

6. Having read the essay, how would you characterize Nora Ephron? Cite
specific words and/or ideas to support your conclusions.

7. What is the author's tone in this essay? Did you feel comfortable reading
it? Why, or why not?

8. Would you characterize Ephron's narrative as a feminist or antifeminist
statement?

Writing Topics

1. For Ephron breasts became an obsession. She writes, "If I had had them, I would have been a completely different person. I honestly believe that." Like Ephron, each of us can remember a time when some particular trait became so important that it dominated our life. Write an essay in which you reflect upon the experience and how you came to terms with your self-image.

2. To what extent did sex roles have an influence on your adolescent development? Do you consider the influence of sex roles beneficial or detrimental to the formation of your personality? Using examples from your own experiences (or those of your friends), write an essay in which you discuss the positive and negative effects of sex roles on the development of a healthy self-image.

GEORGE ORWELL

George Orwell (1903–1950) was one of the most brilliant social critics of our times. He was born in Bengal, India, but he grew up in England and received a traditional education at the prestigious school of Eton. Instead of going on to a university, he joined the civil service himself and was sent to Burma at nineteen as an assistant superintendent of police. Disillusioned with British imperialism, Orwell resigned in 1929 and began a decade of studying social and political issues first-hand and then writing about them in such works as *Down and Out in Paris and London* (1933) and *The Road to Wigan Pier* (1937). His most famous books are *Animal Farm* (1945), a satire on the Russian Revolution, and *1984* (1949), a chilling novel set in an imagined totalitarian state of the future.

"Shooting an Elephant" was published in the British magazine *New Writing* in 1936. Hitler, Mussolini, and Stalin were in power, building the "younger empires" Orwell refers to in his second paragraph, and the old British Empire was soon to decline, as Orwell predicted. In this essay, Orwell tells of a man in authority who finds himself compelled to act against his convictions.

Shooting an Elephant

In Moulmein, in lower Burma, I was hated by large numbers of   1
people—the only time in my life that I have been important enough for this to happen to me. I was sub-divisional police officer of the town, and in an aimless, petty kind of way anti-European feeling was very bitter. No one had the guts to raise a riot, but if a European woman went through the bazaars alone somebody would probably spit betel juice over her dress. As a police officer I was an obvious target and was baited whenever it seemed safe to do so. When a nimble Burman tripped me up on the football field and the referee (another Burman) looked the other way, the crowd yelled with hideous laughter. This happened more than once. In the end the sneering yellow faces of young men that met me everywhere, the insults hooted after me when I was at a safe distance, got badly on my nerves. The young Buddhist priests were the worst of all. There were several thousands of them in the town and none of them seemed to have anything to do except stand on street corners and jeer at Europeans.

All this was perplexing and upsetting. For at that time I had already   2
made up my mind that imperialism was an evil thing and the sooner I chucked up my job and got out of it the better. Theoretically—and

secretly, of course—I was all for the Burmese and all against their op-
pressors, the British. As for the job I was doing, I hated it more bitterly
than I can perhaps make clear. In a job like that you see the dirty work
of Empire at close quarters. The wretched prisoners huddling in the
stinking cages of the lock-ups, the gray, cowed faces of the long-term
convicts, the scarred buttocks of the men who had been flogged with
bamboos—all these oppressed me with an intolerable sense of guilt. But
I could get nothing into perspective. I was young and ill educated and I
had had to think out my problems in the utter silence that is imposed
on every Englishman in the East. I did not even know that the British
Empire is dying, still less did I know that it is a great deal better than
the younger empires that are going to supplant it. All I knew was that I
was stuck between my hatred of the empire I served and my rage against
the evil-spirited little beasts who tried to make my job impossible. With
one part of my mind I thought of the British Raj as an unbreakable
tyranny, as something clamped down, in *saecula saeculorum,* upon the
will of prostrate peoples; with another part I thought that the greatest
joy in the world would be to drive a bayonet into a Buddhist priest's
guts.[1] Feelings like these are the normal by-products of imperialism; ask
any Anglo-Indian official, if you can catch him off duty.

One day something happened which in a roundabout way was en-   3
lightening. It was a tiny incident in itself, but it gave me a better glimpse
than I had had before of the real nature of imperialism—the real motives
for which despotic governments act. Early one morning the sub-inspector
at a police station the other end of the town rang me up on the 'phone
and said that an elephant was ravaging the bazaar. Would I please come
and do something about it? I did not know what I could do, but I wanted
to see what was happening and I got on a pony and started out. I took
my rifle, an old .44 Winchester and much too small to kill an elephant,
but I thought the noise might be useful *in terrorem.* Various Burmans
stopped me on the way and told me about the elephant's doings. It was
not, of course, a wild elephant, but a tame one which had gone "must."[2]
It had been chained up, as tame elephants always are when their attack
of "must" is due, but on the previous night it had broken its chain and
escaped. Its mahout, the only person who could manage it when it was
in that state, had set out in pursuit, but had taken the wrong direction
and was now twelve hours' journey away, and in the morning the elephant had suddenly reappeared in the town. The Burmese population
had no weapons and were quite helpless against it. It had already de-

---

[1]Raj: rule, especially in India. *Saecula saeculorum:* from time immemorial.
[2]That is, gone into an uncontrollable frenzy.

stroyed somebody's bamboo hut, killed a cow and raided some fruit-stalls and devoured the stock; also it had met the municipal rubbish van and, when the driver jumped out and took to his heels, had turned the van over and inflicted violences upon it.

The Burmese sub-inspector and some Indian constables were wait-   4
ing for me in the quarter where the elephant had been seen. It was a very poor quarter, a labyrinth of squalid bamboo huts, thatched with palm-leaf, winding all over a steep hillside. I remember that it was a cloudy, stuffy morning at the beginning of the rains. We began questioning the people as to where the elephant had gone and, as usual, failed to get any definite information. That is invariably the case in the East; a story always sounds clear enough at a distance, but the nearer you get to the scene of events the vaguer it becomes. Some of the people said that the elephant had gone in one direction, some said that he had gone in another, some professed not even to have heard of any elephant. I had almost made up my mind that the whole story was a pack of lies, when we heard yells a little distance away. There was a loud, scandalized cry of "Go away, child! Go away this instant!" and an old woman with a switch in her hand came round the corner of a hut, violently shooing away a crowd of naked children. Some more women followed, clicking their tongues and exclaiming; evidently there was something that the children ought not to have seen. I rounded the hut and saw a man's dead body sprawling in the mud. He was an Indian, a black Dravidian coolie, almost naked, and he could not have been dead many minutes. The people said that the elephant had come suddenly upon him round the corner of the hut, caught him with its trunk, put its foot on his back and ground him into the earth. This was the rainy season and the ground was soft, and his face had scored a trench a foot deep and a couple of yards long. He was lying on his belly with arms crucified and head sharply twisted to one side. His face was coated with mud, the eyes wide open, the teeth bared and grinning with an expression of unendurable agony. (Never tell me, by the way, that the dead look peaceful. Most of the corpses I have seen looked devilish.) The friction of the great beast's foot had stripped the skin from his back as neatly as one skins a rabbit. As soon as I saw the dead man I sent an orderly to a friend's house nearby to borrow an elephant rifle. I had already sent back the pony, not wanting it to go mad with fright and throw me if it smelt the elephant.

The orderly came back in a few minutes with a rifle and five car-   5
tridges, and meanwhile some Burmans had arrived and told us that the elephant was in the paddy fields below, only a few hundred yards away. As I started forward practically the whole population of the quarter flocked out of the houses and followed me. They had seen the rifle and were all

shouting excitedly that I was going to shoot the elephant. They had not shown much interest in the elephant when he was merely ravaging their homes, but it was different now that he was going to be shot. It was a bit of fun to them, as it would be to an English crowd; besides they wanted the meat. It made me vaguely uneasy. I had no intention of shooting the elephant—I had merely sent for the rifle to defend myself if necessary—and it is always unnerving to have a crowd following you. I marched down the hill, looking and feeling a fool, with the rifle over my shoulder and an ever-growing army of people jostling at my heels. At the bottom, when you got away from the huts, there was a metalled road and beyond that a miry waste of paddy fields a thousand yards across, not yet ploughed but soggy from the first rains and dotted with coarse grass. The elephant was standing eight yards from the road, his left side toward us. He took not the slightest notice of the crowd's approach. He was tearing up bunches of grass, beating them against his knees to clean them, and stuffing them into his mouth.

I had halted on the road. As soon as I saw the elephant I knew   6 with perfect certainty that I ought not to shoot him. It is a serious matter to shoot a working elephant—it is comparable to destroying a huge and costly piece of machinery—and obviously one ought not to do it if it can possibly be avoided. And at that distance, peacefully eating, the elephant looked no more dangerous than a cow. I thought then and I think now that his attack of "must" was already passing off; in which case he would merely wander harmlessly about until the mahout came back and caught him. Moreover, I did not in the least want to shoot him. I decided that I would watch him for a little while to make sure that he did not turn savage again, and then go home.

But at that moment I glanced round at the crowd that had followed   7 me. It was an immense crowd, two thousand at the least and growing every minute. It blocked the road for a long distance on either side. I looked at the sea of yellow faces above the garish clothes—faces all happy and excited over this bit of fun, all certain that the elephant was going to be shot. They were watching me as they would watch a conjurer about to perform a trick. They did not like me, but with the magical rifle in my hands I was momentarily worth watching. And suddenly I realized that I should have to shoot the elephant after all. The people expected it of me and I had got to do it; I could feel their two thousand wills pressing me forward, irresistibly. And it was at this moment, as I stood there with the rifle in my hands, that I first grasped the hollowness, the futility of the white man's dominion in the East. Here was I, the white man with his gun, standing in front of the unarmed native crowd— seemingly the leading actor of the piece; but in reality I was only an

absurd puppet pushed to and fro by the will of those yellow faces behind.
I perceived in this moment that when the white man turns tyrant it is
his own freedom that he destroys. He becomes a sort of hollow, posing
dummy, the conventionalized figure of a sahib. For it is the condition of
his rule that he shall spend his life in trying to impress the "natives,"
and so in every crisis he has got to do what the "natives" expect of him.
He wears a mask, and his face grows to fit it. I had got to shoot the
elephant. I had committed myself to doing it when I sent for the rifle.
A sahib has got to act like a sahib; he has got to appear resolute, to
know his own mind and do definite things. To come all that way, rifle
in hand, with two thousand people marching at my heels, and then to
trail feebly away, having done nothing—no, that was impossible. The
crowd would laugh at me. And my whole life, every white man's life in
the East, was one long struggle not to be laughed at.

But I did not want to shoot the elephant. I watched him beating   8
his bunch of grass against his knees with that preoccupied grandmotherly
air that elephants have. It seemed to me that it would be murder to shoot
him. At that age I was not squeamish about killing animals, but I had
never shot an elephant and never wanted to. (Somehow it always seems
worse to kill a *large* animal.) Besides, there was the beast's owner to be
considered. Alive, the elephant was worth at least a hundred pounds;
dead, he would only be worth the value of his tusks, five pounds, possibly.[3] But I had got to act quickly. I turned to some experienced-looking
Burmans who had been there when we arrived, and asked them how the
elephant had been behaving. They all said the same thing: he took no
notice of you if you left him alone, but he might charge if you went too
close to him.

It was perfectly clear to me what I ought to do. I ought to walk up   9
to within, say, twenty-five yards of the elephant and test his behavior.
If he charged, I could shoot; if he took no notice of me, it would be safe
to leave him until the mahout came back. But also I knew that I was
going to do no such thing. I was a poor shot with a rifle and the ground
was soft mud into which one would sink at every step. If the elephant
charged and I missed him, I should have about as much chance as a toad
under a steam-roller. But even then I was not thinking particularly of
my own skin, only of the watchful yellow faces behind. For at that
moment, with the crowd watching me, I was not afraid in the ordinary
sense, as I would have been if I had been alone. A white man mustn't
be frightened in front of "natives"; and so, in general, he isn't frightened.
The sole thought in my mind was that if anything went wrong those two

---

[3]The British pound would have been worth $5.00 at the time.

thousand Burmans would see me pursued, caught, trampled on, and reduced to a grinning corpse like that Indian up the hill. And if that happened it was quite probable that some of them would laugh. That would never do. There was only one alternative. I shoved the cartridges into the magazine and lay down on the road to get a better aim.

The crowd grew very still, and a deep, low, happy sigh, as of people   10
who see the theater curtain go up at last, breathed from innumerable throats. They were going to have their bit of fun after all. The rifle was a beautiful German thing with cross-hair sights. I did not then know that in shooting an elephant one would shoot to cut an imaginary bar running from ear-hole to ear-hole. I ought, therefore, as the elephant was sideways on, to have aimed straight at his ear-hole; actually I aimed several inches in front of this, thinking the brain would be further forward.

When I pulled the trigger I did not hear the bang or feel the kick—   11
one never does when a shot goes home—but I heard the devilish roar of glee that went up from the crowd. In that instant, in too short a time, one would have thought, even for the bullet to get there, a mysterious, terrible change had come over the elephant. He neither stirred nor fell, but every line of his body had altered. He looked suddenly stricken, shrunken, immensely old, as though the frightful impact of the bullet had paralyzed him without knocking him down. At last, after what seemed a long time—it might have been five seconds, I dare say—he sagged flabbily to his knees. His mouth slobbered. An enormous senility seemed to have settled upon him. One could have imagined him thousands of years old. I fired again into the same spot. At the second shot he did not collapse but climbed with desperate slowness to his feet and stood weakly upright, with legs sagging and head drooping. I fired a third time. That was the shot that did for him. You could see the agony of it jolt his whole body and knock the last remnant of strength from his legs. But in falling he seemed for a moment to rise, for as his hind legs collapsed beneath him he seemed to tower upward like a huge rock toppling, his trunk reaching skyward like a tree. He trumpeted, for the first and only time. And then down he came, his belly toward me, with a crash that seemed to shake the ground even where I lay.

I got up. The Burmans were already racing past me across the mud.   12
It was obvious that the elephant would never rise again, but he was not dead. He was breathing very rhythmically with long rattling gasps, his great mound of a side painfully rising and falling. His mouth was wide open—I could see far down into caverns of pale pink throat. I waited a long time for him to die, but his breathing did not weaken. Finally I fired my two remaining shots into the spot where I thought his heart must be. The thick blood welled out of him like red velvet, but still he

did not die. His body did not even jerk when the shots hit him, the tortured breathing continued without a pause. He was dying, very slowly and in great agony, but in some world remote from me where not even a bullet could damage him further. I felt that I had got to put an end to that dreadful noise. It seemed dreadful to see the great beast lying there, powerless to move and yet powerless to die, and not even to be able to finish him. I sent back for my small rifle and poured shot after shot into his heart and down his throat. They seemed to make no impression. The tortured gasps continued as steadily as the ticking of a clock.

In the end I could not stand it any longer and went away. I heard later that it took him half an hour to die. Burmans were bringing dahs[4] and baskets even before I left, and I was told they had stripped his body almost to the bones by the afternoon.

Afterward, of course, there were endless discussions about the shooting of the elephant. The owner was furious, but he was only an Indian and could do nothing. Besides, legally I had done the right thing, for a mad elephant has to be killed, like a mad dog, if its owner fails to control it. Among the Europeans opinion was divided. The older men said I was right, the younger men said it was a damn shame to shoot an elephant for killing a coolie, because an elephant was worth more than any damn Coringhee coolie. And afterwards I was very glad that the coolie had been killed; it put me legally in the right and it gave me a sufficient pretext for shooting the elephant. I often wondered whether any of the others grasped that I had done it solely to avoid looking a fool.

13

14

Questions for Study and Discussion

1. Why is the setting of this narrative significant? What is imperialism, and what does Orwell's essay say about it?

2. Why, according to Orwell, did he shoot the elephant? Do you find his interpretation convincing? Why, or why not?

3. What do you think was Orwell's purpose in telling this story? Cite evidence from the essay that indicates to you that purpose. Does he accomplish his purpose?

4. What part of the essay struck you most strongly? The shooting itself? Orwell's feelings? The descriptions of the Burmans and their behavior? Or something else? Can you identify anything about Orwell's prose that enhances the impact of that passage? Explain.

5. What is Orwell doing in the final paragraph? How does that paragraph affect your response to the whole essay?

---

[4]Heavy knives.

Writing Topics

1. Consider situations in which you have been a leader, like Orwell, or part of a crowd, like the Burmans. As a leader, what was your attitude toward your followers? As a follower, what did you feel toward your leader? From these experiences, what conclusions can you draw? Write an essay about the relationship between leaders and followers.

2. Tell of a situation in which you felt compelled to act against your convictions. What arguments can justify your action? How much freedom of choice did you actually have, and what were the limits on your freedom? On what basis can you refuse to subordinate your convictions to others', or to society's?

3. Orwell has shown one of the ironies of imperialism, that colonial officers are ruled by those they govern, or, to put it another way, that the rulers are ruled by the ruled. What are some other criticisms of imperialism? Using library sources, write an essay on the differing views of imperialism, from the perspective of the imperial power and from that of the people subject to the power.

WILLARD GAYLIN

What is the true measure of character—our inward feelings and motives, or what we actually do? According to Willard Gaylin, a distinguished psychiatrist and teacher, our actions are what count. Born in Cleveland in 1925, Gaylin is professor of clinical psychiatry at Columbia University and president of the Institute of Society, Ethics, and Life Sciences. As this latter position suggests, he is deeply concerned with moral issues in human behavior, a concern reflected in his books *In Service of Their Country: War Resistors in Prison* (1970), *Partial Justice: A Study of Bias in Sentencing* (1974), and *Feelings: Our Vital Signs* (1979). Gaylin's views on the inner and outer person affect not only his social attitudes but also his conception of the self. His notion of what might be called the "integrated self" has a bearing on important questions of social policy.

What You See Is the Real You

It was, I believe, the distinguished Nebraska financier Father Edward J. Flanagan who professed to having "never met a bad boy."[1] Having, myself, met a remarkable number of bad boys, it might seem that either our experiences were drastically different or we were using the word "bad" differently. I suspect neither is true, but rather that the Father was appraising the "inner man," while I, in fact, do not acknowledge the existence of inner people.

Since we psychoanalysts have unwittingly contributed to this confusion, let one, at least, attempt a small rectifying effort. Psychoanalytic data—which should be viewed as supplementary information—is, unfortunately, often viewed as alternative (and superior) explanation. This has led to the prevalent tendency to think of the "inner" man as the real man and the outer man as an illusion or pretender.

While psychoanalysis supplies us with an incredibly useful tool for explaining the motives and purposes underlying human behavior, most of this has little bearing on the moral nature of that behavior.

Like roentgenology, psychoanalysis is a fascinating, but relatively new, means of illuminating the person. But few of us are prepared to substitute an X-ray of Grandfather's head for the portrait that hangs in the parlor. The inside of the man represents another view, not a truer one. A man may not always be what he appears to be, but what he

---

[1]Father Flanagan founded Boys Town, a village for homeless boys. He also created an enormous and highly successful fund-raising system to support the town.

53

appears to be is always a significant part of what he is. A man is the sum total of *all* his behavior. To probe for unconscious determinants of behavior and then define *him* in their terms exclusively, ignoring his overt behavior altogether, is a greater distortion than ignoring the unconscious completely.

Kurt Vonnegut has said, "You are what you pretend to be," which   5
is simply another way of saying, you are what we (all of us) perceive you to be, not what you think you are.

Consider for a moment the case of the ninety-year-old man on his   6
deathbed (surely the Talmud[2] must deal with this?) joyous and relieved over the success of his deception. For ninety years he has shielded his evil nature from public observation. For ninety years he has affected courtesy, kindness, and generosity—suppressing all the malice he knew was within him while he calculatedly and artificially substituted grace and charity. All his life he had been fooling the world into believing he was a good man. This "evil" man will, I predict, be welcomed into the Kingdom of Heaven.

Similarly, I will not be told that the young man who earns his   7
pocket money by mugging old ladies is "really" a good boy. Even my generous and expansive definition of goodness will not accommodate that particular form of self-advancement.

It does not count that beneath the rough exterior he has a heart—   8
or, for that matter, an entire innards—of purest gold, locked away from human perception. You are for the most part what you seem to be, not what you would wish to be, nor, indeed, what you believe yourself to be.

Spare me, therefore, your good intentions, your inner sensitivities,   9
your unarticulated and unexpressed love. And spare me also those tedious psychohistories which—by exposing the goodness inside the bad man, and the evil in the good—invariably establish a vulgar and perverse egalitarianism, as if the arrangement of what is outside and what inside makes no moral difference.

Saint Francis may, in his unconscious, indeed have been compen-   10
sating for, and denying, destructive, unconscious Oedipal impulses identical to those which Attila projected and acted on.[3] But the similarity

---

[2]An ancient collection of Jewish law and commentaries by sages on the written and oral traditions of the Jews.

[3]Saint Francis, founder of the Franciscan order of begging friars, was born into a wealthy family but took vows of poverty. Oedipal impulses, in psychoanalysis, refer to complex emotions resulting from a child's sexual attraction to a parent of the opposite sex and a view of the same-sex parent as a rival to be destroyed. Attila led the Huns, an Asian tribe, in a brutal invasion of ancient Italy.

of the unconscious constellations in the two men matters precious little, if it does not distinguish between them.

I do not care to learn that Hitler's heart was in the right place. A   11
knowledge of the unconscious life of the man may be an adjunct to understanding his behavior. It is *not* a substitute for his behavior in describing him.

The inner man is a fantasy. If it helps you to identify with one, by   12
all means, do so; preserve it, cherish it, embrace it, but do not present it to others for evaluation or consideration, for excuse or exculpation, or, for that matter, for punishment or disapproval.

Like any fantasy, it serves your purposes alone. It has no standing   13
in the real world which we share with each other. Those character traits, those attitudes, that behavior—that strange and alien stuff sticking out all over you—*that's the real you!*

Questions for Study and Discussion

1. What is Gaylin's fullest statement of his thesis? How does he defend it? What counterarguments does he answer? From your point of view, are his answers adequate? Why, or why not?

2. Why does Gaylin believe that we need to think more carefully than we have about two important components of self—the inner and outer person? What is mistaken in the prevailing view, according to him?

3. Toward the end of his essay Gaylin says that "The inner man is a fantasy." Why does he say that? Are there statements or concerns in the essay that imply a contradiction? Explain your answer.

4. In paragraphs 10 and 11 Gaylin refers to famous historical figures as examples. For the purpose of his argument, what are the advantages of doing this? What are the disadvantages?

5. What analogy does Gaylin use to support his statement that "the inside of the man represents another view, not a truer one"? Why do you think he chose that analogy? What are its strong and weak points?

6. Gaylin opens his essay by quoting Father Flanagan. What purpose do Flanagan's thoughts serve in the essay? Why do you think Gaylin chooses to place them at the very beginning of the essay?

Writing Topics

1. Everyone makes mistakes, and probably all of us have at one time or another tried to excuse ourselves by saying we didn't *mean* to do wrong. Gaylin seems to say that intentions do not matter, that they have no standing in the real world which we share with each other. Write an essay in which

you agree or disagree with Gaylin's view. Use examples from your own experiences or reading.

2. Choose an area of society in which you are particularly interested—for example, business, politics, community activities, or criminal justice, and write an essay in which you discuss the implications of the inner/outer man dichotomy for the area you have selected.

ISAAC BASHEVIS SINGER

Born in the small Polish town of Bilgoray in 1904, Isaac Bashevis Singer grew up in the Jewish ghetto in Warsaw. His father was a rabbi of the mystical Hasidic sect, and Singer himself studied to become a rabbi. Instead he began a career as a writer with Warsaw's Yiddish newspaper, meanwhile writing short stories, novellas, and his first novel, *Satan in Goray* (1935). In 1935 he emigrated to New York, four years before Hitler invaded Poland. Though fluent in English, he has continued to write his fiction in Yiddish, saying: "In a figurative way, Yiddish is the wise and humble language of us all, the idiom of frightened and hopeful humanity."

In "Gimpel the Fool," first published in 1953 in Saul Bellow's translation from the Yiddish, Isaac Bashevis Singer explores the tension between faith and doubt. Gimpel is so willing to believe what others tell him that his neighbors think him a fool. Yet trust, the willingness to accept things on faith, is no less important to our public and private lives than our inclination to question and suspect. In the surprising conclusion, Gimpel completely changes his way of life, yet manages to maintain his trust of humankind.

Gimpel the Fool

I am Gimpel the fool. I don't think myself a fool. On the contrary. But that's what folks call me. They gave me the name while I was still in school. I had seven names in all: imbecile, donkey, flax-head, dope, glump, ninny, and fool. The last name stuck. What did my foolishness consist of? I was easy to take in. They said, "Gimpel, you know the rabbi's wife has been brought to childbed?" So I skipped school. Well, it turned out to be a lie. How was I supposed to know? She hadn't had a big belly. But I never looked at her belly. Was that really so foolish? The gang laughed and hee-hawed, stomped and danced and chanted a good-night prayer. And instead of the raisins they give when a woman's lying in, they stuffed my hand full of goat turds. I was no weakling. If I slapped someone he'd see all the way to Cracow. But I'm really not a slugger by nature. I think to myself: Let it pass. So they take advantage of me.

I was coming home from school and heard a dog barking. I'm not afraid of dogs, but of course I never want to start up with them. One of them may be mad, and if he bites there's not a Tartar in the world who can help you. So I made tracks. Then I looked around and saw the whole market place wild with laughter. It was no dog at all but Wolf-Leib the

Thief. How was I supposed to know it was he? It sounded like a howling
bitch.

When the pranksters and leg-pullers found that I was easy to fool,   3
every one of them tried his luck with me. "Gimpel, the Czar is coming
to Frampol: Gimpel, the moon fell down in Turbeen;[1] Gimpel, little
Hodel Furpiece found a treasure behind the bathhouse." And I like a
golem[2] believed everyone. In the first place, everything is possible, as it
is written in the Wisdom of the Fathers. I've forgotten just how: Second,
I had to believe when the whole town came down on me! If I ever dared
to say, "Ah, you're kidding!" there was trouble. People got angry. "What
do you mean! You want to call everyone a liar?" What was I to do? I
believed them, and I hope at least that did them some good.

I was an orphan. My grandfather who brought me up was already   4
bent toward the grave. So they turned me over to a baker, and what a
time they gave me there! Every woman or girl who came to bake a batch
of noodles had to fool me at least once. "Gimpel, there's a fair in heaven;
Gimpel, the rabbi gave birth to a calf in the seventh month; Gimpel, a
cow flew over the roof and laid brass eggs." A student from the yeshiva[3]
came once to buy a roll, and he said, "You, Gimpel, while you stand
here scraping with your baker's shovel the Messiah has come. The dead
have arisen." "What do you mean?" I said. "I heard no one blowing the
ram's horn!" He said, "Are you deaf?" And all began to cry, "We heard
it, we heard!" Then in came Rietze the Candle-dipper and called out in
her hoarse voice, "Gimpel, your father and mother have stood up from
the grave. They're looking for you."

To tell the truth, I knew very well that nothing of the sort had   5
happened, but all the same, as folks were talking, I threw on my wool
vest and went out. Maybe something had happened. What did I stand
to lose by looking? Well, what a cat music went up! And then I took a
vow to believe nothing more. But that was no go either. They confused
me so that I didn't know the big end from the small.

I went to the rabbi to get some advice. He said, "It is written,   6
better to be a fool all your days than for one hour to be evil. You are
not a fool. They are the fools. For he who causes his neighbor to feel
shame loses Paradise himself." Nevertheless the rabbi's daughter took me
in. As I left the rabbinical court she said, "Have you kissed the wall
yet?" I said, "No; what for?" She answered, "It's the law; you've got to
do it after every visit." Well, there didn't seem to be any harm in it.

---

[1]Frampol and Turbeen are mythical towns in Singer's fiction.
[2]A slow-witted simpleton.
[3]In Europe, a rabbinical seminary.

And she burst out laughing. It was a fine trick. She put one over on me, all right.

I wanted to go off to another town, but then everyone got busy matchmaking, and they were after me so they nearly tore my coat tails off. They talked at me and talked until I got water on the ear. She was no chaste maiden, but they told me she was virgin pure. She had a limp, and they said it was deliberate, from coyness. She had a bastard, and they told me the child was her little brother. I cried, "You're wasting your time. I'll never marry that whore." But they said indignantly, "What a way to talk! Aren't you ashamed of yourself? We can take you to the rabbi and have you fined for giving her a bad name." I saw then that I wouldn't escape them so easily and I thought: They're set on making me their butt. But when you're married the husband's the master, and if that's all right with her it's agreeable to me too. Besides, you can't pass through life unscathed, nor expect to.

I went to her clay house, which was built on the sand, and the whole gang, hollering and chorusing, came after me. They acted like bear-baiters. When we came to the well they stopped all the same. They were afraid to start anything with Elka. Her mouth would open as if it were on a hinge, and she had a fierce tongue. I entered the house. Lines were strung from wall to wall and clothes were drying. Barefoot she stood by the tub, doing the wash. She was dressed in a worn hand-me-down gown of plush. She had her hair put up in braids and pinned across her head. It took my breath away, almost, the reek of it all.

Evidently she knew who I was. She took a look at me and said, "Look who's here! He's come, the drip. Grab a seat."

I told her all; I denied nothing. "Tell me the truth," I said, "are you really a virgin, and is that mischievous Yechiel actually your little brother? Don't be deceitful with me, for I'm an orphan."

"I'm an orphan myself," she answered, "and whoever tries to twist you up, may the end of his nose take a twist. But don't let them think they can take advantage of me. I want a dowry of fifty guilders, and let them take up a collection besides. Otherwise they can kiss my you-know-what." She was very plainspoken. I said, "It's the bride and not the groom who gives a dowry." Then she said, "Don't bargain with me. Either a flat 'yes' or a flat 'no'—Go back where you came from."

I thought: No bread will ever be baked from *this* dough. But ours is not a poor town. They consented to everything and proceeded with the wedding. It so happened that there was a dysentery epidemic at the time. The ceremony was held at the cemetery gates, near the little corpse-washing hut. The fellows got drunk. While the marriage contract was being drawn up I heard the most pious high rabbi ask, "Is the bride a widow or a divorced woman?" And the sexton's wife answered for her, "Both a widow and divorced." It was a black moment for me. But what was I to do, run away from under the marriage canopy?

There was singing and dancing. An old granny danced opposite   13
me, hugging a braided white *chalah*.[4] The master of revels made a "God'a mercy" in memory of the bride's parents. The schoolboys threw burrs, as on Tishe b'Av fast day.[5] There were a lot of gifts after the sermon: a noodle board, a kneading trough, a bucket, brooms, ladles, household articles galore. Then I took a look and saw two strapping young men carrying a crib. "What do we need this for?" I asked. So they said, "Don't rack your brains about it. It's all right, it'll come in handy." I realized I was going to be rooked. Take it another way though, what did I stand to lose? I reflected: I'll see what comes of it. A whole town can't go altogether crazy.

At night I came where my wife lay, but she wouldn't let me in.   14
"Say, look here, is this what they married us for?" I said. And she said, "My monthly has come." "But yesterday they took you to the ritual bath, and that's afterward, isn't it supposed to be?" "Today isn't yesterday," said she, "and yesterday's not today. You can beat it if you don't like it." In short, I waited.

Not four months later she was in childbed. The townsfolk hid their   15
laughter with their knuckles. But what could I do? She suffered intolerable pains and clawed at the walls. "Gimpel," she cried, "I'm going. Forgive me." The house filled with women. They were boiling pans of water. The screams rose to the welkin.

The thing to do was to go to the House of Prayer to repeat Psalms,   16
and that was what I did.

The townsfolk liked that, all right. I stood in a corner saying Psalms   17
and prayers, and they shook their heads at me. "Pray, pray!" they told me, "Prayer never made any woman pregnant." One of the congregation put a straw to my mouth and said, "Hay for the cows." There was something to that too, by God!

She gave birth to a boy, Friday at the synagogue the sexton stood   18
up before the Ark, pounded on the reading table, and announced, "The wealthy Reb Gimpel invites the congregation to a feast in honor of the birth of a son." The whole House of Prayer rang with laughter. My face was flaming. But there was nothing I could do. After all, I *was* the one responsible for the circumcision honors and rituals.

---

[4]Bread.

[5]A day of fasting and mourning commemorating the destruction of the Temple in Jerusalem.

Half the town came running. You couldn't wedge another soul in.   19
Women brought peppered chick-peas, and there was a keg of beer from
the tavern. I ate and drank as much as anyone, and they all congratulated
me. Then there was a circumcision, and I named the boy after my father,
may he rest in peace. When all were gone and I was left with my wife
alone, she thrust her head through the bed-curtain and called me to her.

"Gimpel," said she, "why are you silent? Has your ship gone and   20
sunk?"

"What shall I say?" I answered. "A fine thing you've done to me!   21
If my mother had known of it she'd have died a second time."

She said, "Are you crazy, or what?"   22

"How can you make such a fool," I said, "of one who should be   23
the lord and master?"

"What's the matter with you?" she said. "What have you taken it   24
into your head to imagine?"

I saw that I must speak bluntly and openly. "Do you think this is   25
the way to use an orphan?" I said. "You have borne a bastard."

She answered, "Drive this foolishness out of your head. The child   26
is yours."

"How can he be mine?" I argued. "He was born seventeen weeks   27
after the wedding."

She told me then that he was premature. I said, "Isn't he a little   28
too premature?" She said, she had had a grandmother who carried just
as short a time and she resembled this grandmother of hers as one drop
of water does another. She swore to it with such oaths that you would
have believed a peasant at the fair if he had used them. To tell the plain
truth, I didn't believe her; but when I talked it over next day with the
schoolmaster he told me that the very same thing had happened to Adam
and Eve. Two they went up to bed and four they descended.

"There isn't a woman in the world who is not the granddaughter   29
of Eve," he said.

That was how it was; they argued me dumb. But then, who really   30
knows how such things are?

I began to forget my sorrow. I loved the child madly, and he loved   31
me too. As soon as he saw me he'd wave his little hands and want me
to pick him up, and when he was colicky I was the only one who could
pacify him. I bought him a little bone teething ring and a little gilded
cap. He was forever catching the evil eye from someone, and then I had
to run to get one of those abracadabras for him that would get him out
of it. I worked like an ox. You know how expenses go up when there's
an infant in the house. I don't want to lie about it; I didn't dislike Elka
either, for that matter. She swore at me and cursed, and I couldn't get

enough of her. What strength she had! One of her looks could rob you of the power of speech. And her orations! Pitch and sulphur, that's what they were full of, and yet somehow also full of charm. I adored her every word. She gave me bloody wounds though.

In the evening I brought her a white loaf as well as a dark one, and also poppyseed rolls I baked myself. I thieved because of her and swiped everything I could lay hands on: macaroons, raisins, almonds, cakes. I hope I may be forgiven for stealing from the Saturday pots the women left to warm in the baker's oven. I would take out scraps of meat, a chunk of pudding, a chicken leg or head, a piece of tripe, whatever I could nip quickly. She ate and became fat and handsome.   32

I had to sleep away from home all during the week, at the bakery. On Friday nights when I got home she always made an excuse of some sort. Either she had heartburn, or a stitch in the side, or hiccups, or headaches. You know what women's excuses are. I had a bitter time of it. It was rough. To add to it, this little brother of hers, the bastard, was growing bigger. He'd put lumps on me, and when I wanted to hit back she'd open her mouth and curse so powerfully I saw a green haze floating before my eyes. Ten times a day she threatened to divorce me. Another man in my place would have taken French leave and disappeared. But I'm the type that bears it and says nothing. What's one to do? Shoulders are from God, and burdens too.   33

One night there was a calamity in the bakery; the oven burst, and we almost had a fire. There was nothing to do but go home, so I went home. Let me, I thought, also taste the joy of sleeping in bed in mid-week. I didn't want to wake the sleeping mite and tiptoed into the house. Coming in, it seemed to me that I heard not the snoring of one but, as it were, a double snore, one a thin enough snore and the other like the snoring of a slaughtered ox. Oh, I didn't like that! I didn't like it at all. I went up to the bed, and things suddenly turned black. Next to Elka lay a man's form. Another in my place would have made an uproar, and enough noise to rouse the whole town, but the thought occurred to me that I might wake the child. A little thing like that—why frighten a little swallow, I thought. All right then, I went back to the bakery and stretched out on a sack of flour and till morning I never shut an eye. I shivered as if I had had malaria. "Enough of being a donkey," I said to myself. "Gimpel isn't going to be a sucker all his life. There's a limit even to the foolishness of a fool like Gimpel."   34

In the morning I went to the rabbi to get advice, and it made a great commotion in the town. They sent the beadle for Elka right away. She came, carrying the child. And what do you think she did? She denied it, denied everything, bone and stone! "He's out of his head," she said.   35

"I know nothing of dreams or divinations." They yelled at her, warned her, hammered on the table, but she stuck to her guns: it was a false accusation, she said.

The butchers and the horse-traders took her part. One of the lads from the slaughterhouse came by and said to me, "We've got our eye on you, you're a marked man." Meanwhile the child started to bear down and soiled itself. In the rabbinical court there was an Ark of the Covenant, and they couldn't allow that, so they sent Elka away.   36

I said to the rabbi, "What shall I do?"   37

"You must divorce her at once," said he.   38

"And what if she refuses?" I asked.   39

He said, "You must serve the divorce. That's all you'll have to do."   40

I said, "Well, all right, Rabbi. Let me think about it."   41

"There's nothing to think about," said he. "You mustn't remain under the same roof with her."   42

"And what if she refuses?" I asked.   43

"Let her go, the harlot," said he, "and her brood of bastards with her."   44

The verdict he gave was that I mustn't even cross her threshold— never again, as long as I should live.   45

During the day it didn't bother me so much. I thought. It was bound to happen, the abscess had to burst. But at night when I stretched out upon the sacks I felt it all very bitterly. A longing took me, for her and for the child. I wanted to be angry, but that's my misfortune exactly, I don't have it in me to be really angry. In the first place—this was how my thoughts went—there's bound to be a slip sometimes. You can't live without errors. Probably that lad who was with her led her on and gave her presents and what not, and women are often long on hair and short on sense, and so he got around her. And then since she denies it so, maybe I was only seeing things? Hallucinations do happen. You see a figure or a mannikin or something, but when you come up closer it's nothing, there's not a thing there. And if that's so, I'm doing her an injustice. And when I got so far in my thoughts I started to weep. I sobbed so that I wet the flour where I lay. In the morning I went to the rabbi and told him that I had made a mistake. The rabbi wrote on with his quill, and he said that if that were so he would have to reconsider the whole case. Until he had finished I wasn't to go near my wife, but I might send her bread and money by messenger.   46

Nine months passed before all the rabbis could come to an agreement. Letters went back and forth. I hadn't realized that there could be so much erudition about a matter like this.   47

Meanwhile Elka gave birth to still another child, a girl this time.   48
On the Sabbath I went to the synagogue and invoked a blessing on her.
They called me up to the Torah,[6] and I named the child for my mother-
in-law—may she rest in peace. The louts and loudmouths of the town
who came into the bakery gave me a going over. All Frampol refreshed
its spirits because of my trouble and grief. However, I resolved that I
would always believe what I was told. What's the good of *not* believing?
Today it's your wife you don't believe; tomorrow it's God Himself you
won't take stock in.

By an apprentice who was her neighbor I sent her daily a corn or   49
a wheat loaf, or a piece of pastry, rolls or bagels, or, when I got the
chance, a slab of pudding, a slice of honeycake, or wedding strudel—
whatever came my way. The apprentice was a goodhearted lad, and more
than once he added something on his own. He had formerly annoyed
me a lot, plucking my nose and digging me in the ribs, but when he
started to be a visitor to my house he became kind and friendly, "Hey,
you, Gimpel," he said to me, "you have a very decent little wife and
two fine kids. You don't deserve them."

"But the things people say about her," I said.   50

"Well, they have long tongues," he said, "and nothing to do with   51
them but babble. Ignore it as you ignore the cold of last winter."

One day the rabbi sent for me and said, "Are you certain, Gimpel,   52
that you were wrong about your wife?"

I said, "I'm certain."   53

"Why, but look here! You yourself saw it."   54

"It must have been a shadow," I said.   55

"The shadow of what?"   56

"Just of one of the beams, I think."   57

"You can go home then. You owe thanks to the Yanover rabbi. He   58
found an obscure reference in Maimonides[7] that favored you."

I seized the rabbi's hand and kissed it.   59

I wanted to run home immediately. It's no small thing to be sep-   60
arated for so long a time from wife and child. Then I reflected: I'd better
go back to work now, and go home in the evening. I said nothing to
anyone, although as far as my heart was concerned it was like one of the
Holy Days. The women teased and twitted me as they did every day, but

---

[6]The holy scriptures of the Jews, usually in a scroll. On special occasions a member
of the congregation is called upon to read from the scroll. It is considered a great
honor.

[7]Moses ben Maimon (1135–1204), Jewish philosopher and commentator on religious
law.

my thought was: Go on, with your loose talk. The truth is out, like the oil upon the water. Maimonides says it's right, and therefore it is right!

At night, when I had covered the dough to let it rise, I took my share of bread and a little sack of flour and started homeward. The moon was full and the stars were glistening, something to terrify the soul. I hurried onward, and before me darted a long shadow. It was winter, and a fresh snow had fallen. I had a mind to sing, but it was growing late and I didn't want to wake the householders. Then I felt like whistling, but I remembered that you don't whistle at night because it brings the demons out. So I was silent and walked as fast as I could. 61

Dogs in the Christian yards barked at me when I passed, but I thought: Bark your teeth out! What are you but mere dogs? Whereas I am a man, the husband of a fine wife, the father of promising children. 62

As I approached the house my heart started to pound as though it were the heart of a criminal. I felt no fear, but my heart went thump! thump! Well, no drawing back. I quietly lifted the latch and went in. Elka was asleep. I looked at the infant's cradle. The shutter was closed, but the moon forced its way through the cracks. I saw the newborn child's face and loved it as soon as I saw it—immediately—each tiny bone. 63

Then I came nearer to the bed. And what did I see but the apprentice lying there beside Elka. The moon went out all at once. It was utterly black, and I trembled. My teeth chattered. The bread fell from my hands, and my wife waked and said, "Who is that, ah?" 64

I muttered, "It's me." 65

"Gimpel?" she asked. "How come you're here? I thought it was forbidden." 66

"The rabbi said," I answered and shook as with a fever. 67

"Listen to me, Gimpel," she said, "go out to the shed and see if the goat's all right. It seems she's been sick." I have forgotten to say that we had a goat. When I heard she was unwell I went into the yard. The nannygoat was a good little creature. I had a nearly human feeling for her. 68

With hesitant steps I went up to the shed and opened the door. The goat stood there on her four feet. I felt her everywhere, drew her by the horns, examined her udders, and found nothing wrong. She had probably eaten too much bark. "Good night, little goat," I said. "Keep well." And the little beast answered with a "Maa" as though to thank me for the good will. 69

I went back. The apprentice had vanished. 70

"Where," I asked, "is the lad?" 71

"What lad?" my wife answered. 72

"What do you mean?" I said. "The apprentice. You were sleeping   73
with him."

"The things I have dreamed this night and the night before," she   74
said, "may they come true and lay you low, body and soul! An evil spirit
has taken root in you and dazzles your sight." She screamed out, "You
hateful creature! You moon calf! You spook! You uncouth man! Get out,
or I'll scream all Frampol out of bed!"

Before I could move, her brother sprang out from behind the oven   75
and struck me a blow on the back of the head. I thought he had broken
my neck. I felt that something about me was deeply wrong, and I said,
"Don't make a scandal. All that's needed now is that people should
accuse me of raising spooks and *dybbuks*."[8] For that was what she had
meant. "No one will touch bread of my baking."

In short, I somehow calmed her.   76

"Well," she said, "that's enough. Lie down, and be shattered by   77
wheels."

Next morning I called the apprentice aside. "Listen here, brother!"   78
I said. And so on and so forth. "What do you say?" He stared at me as
though I had dropped from the roof or something.

"I swear," he said, "you'd better go to an herb doctor or some   79
healer. I'm afraid you have a screw loose, but I'll hush it up for you."
And that's how the thing stood.

To make a long story short, I lived twenty years with my wife. She   80
bore me six children, four daughters and two sons. All kinds of things
happened, but I neither saw nor heard. I believed, and that's all. The
rabbi recently said to me, "Belief in itself is beneficial. It is written that
a good man lives by his faith."

Suddenly my wife took sick. It began with a trifle, a little growth   81
upon the breast. But she evidently was not destined to live long; she had
no years. I spent a fortune on her. I have forgotten to say that by this
time I had a bakery of my own and in Frampol was considered to be
something of a rich man. Daily the healer came, and every witch doctor
in the neighborhood was brought. They decided to use leeches, and after
that to try cupping. They even called a doctor from Lublin,[9] but it was
too late. Before she died she called me to her bed and said, "Forgive me,
Gimpel."

I said, "What is there to forgive? You have been a good and faithful   82
wife."

----

[8] A demon.
[9] A town in Poland.

"Woe, Gimpel!" she said. "It was ugly how I deceived you all these years. I want to go clean to my Maker, and so I have to tell you that the children are not yours." 83

If I had been clouted on the head with a piece of wood it couldn't have bewildered me more. 84

"Whose are they?" I asked. 85

"I don't know," she said. "There were a lot . . . but they're not yours." And as she spoke she tossed her head to the side, her eyes turned glassy, and it was all up with Elka. On her whitened lips there remained a smile. 86

I imagined that, dead as she was, she was saying, "I deceived Gimpel. That was the meaning of my brief life." 87

One night, when the period of mourning was done, as I lay dreaming on the flour sacks, there came the Spirit of Evil himself and said to me, "Gimpel, why do you sleep?" 88

I said, "What should I be doing? Eating *kreplach*?"[10] 89

"The whole world deceives you," he said, "and you ought to deceive the world in your turn." 90

"How can I deceive all the world?" I asked him. 91

He answered, "You might accumulate a bucket of urine every day and at night pour it into the dough. Let the sages of Frampol eat filth." 92

"What about the judgment in the world to come?" I said. 93

"There is no world to come," he said. "They've sold you a bill of goods and talked you into believing you carried a cat in your belly. What nonsense!" 94

"Well then," I said, "and is there a God?" 95

He answered, "There is no God, either." 96

"What," I said, "*is* there, then?" 97

"A thick mire." 98

He stood before my eyes with a goatish beard and horn, long-toothed, and with a tail. Hearing such words, I wanted to snatch him by the tail, but I tumbled from the flour sacks and nearly broke a rib. Then it happened that I had to answer the call of nature, and, passing, I saw the risen dough, which seemed to say to me, "Do it!" In brief, I let myself be persuaded. 99

At dawn the apprentice came. We kneaded the bread, scattered caraway seeds on it, and set it to bake. Then the apprentice went away, and I was left sitting in the little trench of the oven, on a pile of rags. Well, Gimpel, I thought, you've revenged yourself on them for all the 100

---

[10]A dumpling.

shame they've put on you. Outside the frost glittered, but it was warm beside the oven. The flames heated my face. I bent my head and fell into a doze.

I saw in a dream, at once, Elka in her shroud. She called to me, "What have you done, Gimpel?"   101

I said to her, "It's all your fault," and started to cry.   102

"You fool!" she said. "You fool! Because I was false is everything   103 false too? I never deceived anyone but myself. I'm paying for it all, Gimpel. They spare you nothing here."

I looked at her face. It was black; I was startled and waked, and   104 remained sitting dumb. I sensed that everything hung in the balance. A false step now and I'd lose Eternal Life. But God gave me His help. I seized the long shovel and took out the loaves, carried them into the yard, and started to dig a hole in the frozen earth.

My apprentice came back as I was doing it. "What are you doing   105 boss?" he said, and grew pale as a corpse.

"I know what I'm doing," I said, and I buried it all before his very   106 eyes.

Then I went home, took my hoard from its hiding place, and di-   107 vided it among the children. "I saw your mother tonight," I said. "She's turning black, poor thing."

They were so astounded they couldn't speak a word.   108

"Be well," I said, "and forget that such a one as Gimpel ever ex-   109 isted." I put on my short coat, a pair of boots, took the bag that held my prayer shawl in one hand, my stock in the other, and kissed the *mezzuzah*.[11] When people saw me in the street they were greatly surprised.

"Where are you going?" they said.   110

I answered, "Into the world." And so I departed from Frampol.   111

I wandered over the land, and good people did not neglect me.   112 After many years I became old and white; I heard a great deal, many lies and falsehoods, but the longer I lived the more I understood that there were really no lies. Whatever doesn't really happen is dreamed at night. It happens to one if it doesn't happen to another, tomorrow if not today, or a century hence if not next year. What difference can it make? Often I heard tales of which I said, "Now this is a thing that cannot happen." But before a year had elapsed I heard that it actually had come to pass somewhere.

Going from place to place, eating at strange tables, it often happens   113 that I spin yarns—improbable things that could never have happened—

---

[11]A small oblong container affixed to the door jamb of devout Jews. It contains verses from the Torah and is kissed each time a Jew passes through the door.

about devils, magicians, windmills, and the like. The children run after me, calling, "Grandfather, tell us a story." Sometimes they ask for particular stories, and I try to please them. A fat young boy once said to me, "Grandfather, it's the same story you told us before." The little rogue, he was right.

So it is with dreams too. It is many years since I left Frampol, but as soon as I shut my eyes I am there again. And whom do you think I see? Elka. She is standing by the washtub, as at our first encounter, but her face is shining and her eyes are as radiant as the eyes of a saint, and she speaks outlandish words to me, strange things. When I wake I have forgotten it all. But while the dream lasts I am comforted. She answers all my queries, and what comes out is that all is right. I weep and implore, "Let me be with you." And she consoles me and tells me to be patient. The time is nearer than it is far. Sometimes she strokes and kisses me and weeps upon my face. When I awaken I feel her lips and taste the salt of her tears.

No doubt the world is entirely an imaginary world, but it is only once removed from the true world. At the door of the hotel where I lie, there stands the plank on which the dead are taken away. The gravedigger Jew has his spade ready. The grave waits and the worms are hungry; the shrouds are prepared—I carry them in my beggar's sack. Another *schnorrer*[12] is waiting to inherit my bed of straw. When the time comes I will go joyfully. Whatever may be there, it will be real, without complication, without ridicule, without deception. God be praised: there even Gimpel cannot be deceived.

Questions for Study and Discussion

1. Is Gimpel really a fool? What evidence do you find in the story that he is, or is not? If he is not, why does he let himself be made to seem foolish?

2. Are the lies people tell Gimpel all of the same kind, or are there differences?

3. What does Gimpel's confession of thievery reveal about his character? What of his decision to defile the villagers' bread, and his later decision not to do so?

4. Gimpel speaks of visions—of the devil, of his dead wife. How do you interpret these visions?

5. What is the turning point of the story? What does Gimpel give up, and why? What is his new purpose? How does his later life relate to his earlier life? What has Gimpel discovered about himself in the course of the story?

---

[12]A beggar.

6. What is Singer's theme in this story? What does Gimpel mean in the last paragraph of the story when he talks about the imaginary world and the true world?

Writing Topics

1. Gimpel is often troubled by the relation between appearance and reality. Are things as they seem or is there an explanation which, though perhaps far from obvious, offers more of the truth? This question lies at the root of many personal, professional, and social dilemmas. Choose a topic that you think embodies the problem of appearance and reality and develop it in an essay, drawing on your experience and your reading for examples.

2. "Gimpel the Fool" is, at least in part, a story about how one should live. In this respect it is similar to "The Sermon on the Mount" in the Gospel according to Saint Matthew. In preparation for writing an essay on the philosophy of life presented in each work, read "The Sermon on the Mount." What do the two have in common? Where do they differ?

In Pursuit of Happiness

JOHN CIARDI

Poet, educator, editor, and critic, the late John Ciardi was born in Boston in 1916. After graduating from Tufts University and the University of Michigan, he taught for a number of years at Harvard and Rutgers universities and directed the summer Bread Loaf Writers' Conference. Ciardi has written several volumes of poetry, including *Homeward to America* and *From Time to Time*. The three volumes of his translation of Dante's *Divine Comedy—Inferno* (1954), *Purgatorio* (1961), and *Paradiso* (1970)—are among his finest achievements. Ciardi was for many years poetry editor for the *Saturday Review*. He died in 1986.

In this essay, first published in the *Saturday Review* in 1964, Ciardi, popularly known as a writer of the short essay, attempts to define *happiness*, a term he feels "will not sit still for easy definition."

Is Everybody Happy?

The right to pursue happiness is issued to Americans with their birth certificates, but no one seems quite sure which way it ran. It may be we are issued a hunting license but offered no game. Jonathan Swift seemed to think so when he attacked the idea of happiness as "the possession of being well-deceived," the felicity of being "a fool among knaves." For Swift saw society as Vanity Fair, the land of false goals.

It is, of course, un-American to think in terms of fools and knaves. We do, however, seem to be dedicated to the idea of buying our way to happiness. We shall all have made it to Heaven when we possess enough.

And at the same time the forces of American commercialism are hugely dedicated to making us deliberately unhappy. Advertising is one of our major industries, and advertising exists not to satisfy desires but to create them—and to create them faster than any man's budget can satisfy them. For that matter, our whole economy is based on a dedicated insatiability. We are taught that to possess is to be happy, and then we are made to want. We are even told it is our duty to want. It was only a few years ago, to cite a single example, that car dealers across the country were flying banners that read "You Auto Buy Now." They were calling upon Americans, as an act approaching patriotism, to buy at once, with money they did not have, automobiles they did not really need, and which they would be required to grow tired of by the time next year's models were released.

Or look at any of the women's magazines. There, as Bernard DeVoto   4
once pointed out, advertising begins as poetry in the front pages and ends as pharmacopoeia and therapy in the back pages. The poetry of the front matter is the dream of perfect beauty. This is the baby skin that must be hers. These, the flawless teeth. This, the perfumed breath she must exhale. This, the sixteen-year-old figure she must display at forty, at fifty, at sixty, and forever.

Once past the vaguely uplifting fiction and feature articles, the   5
reader finds the other face of the dream in the back matter. This is the harness into which Mother must strap herself in order to display that perfect figure. These, the chin straps she must sleep in. This is the salve that restores all, this is her laxative, these are the tablets that melt away fat, these are the hormones of perpetual youth, these are the stockings that hide varicose veins.

Obviously no half-sane person can be completely persuaded either   6
by such poetry or by such pharmacopoeia and orthopedics. Yet someone is obviously trying to buy the dream as offered and spending billions every year in the attempt. Clearly the happiness-market is not running out of customers, but what is it trying to buy?

The idea "happiness," to be sure, will not sit still for easy definition: 7
the best one can do is to try to set some extremes to the idea and then work in toward the middle. To think of happiness as acquisitive and competitive will do to set the materialistic extreme. To think of it as the idea one senses in, say, a holy man of India will do to set the spiritual extreme. That holy man's idea of happiness is in needing nothing from outside himself. In wanting nothing, he lacks nothing. He sits immobile, rapt in contemplation, free even of his own body. Or nearly free of it. If devout admirers bring him food he eats it; if not, he starves indifferently. Why be concerned? What is physical is an illusion to him. Contemplation is his joy and he achieves it through a fantastically demanding discipline, the accomplishment of which is itself a joy within him.

Is he a happy man? Perhaps his happiness is only another sort of   8
illusion. But who can take it from him? And who will dare say it is more illusory than happiness on the installment plan?

But, perhaps because I am Western, I doubt such catatonic happiness, as I doubt the dreams of the happiness-market. What is certain is that his way of happiness would be torture to almost any Western man. Yet these extremes will still serve to frame the area within which all of us must find some sort of balance. Thoreau—a creature of both Eastern and Western thought—had his own firm sense of that balance. His aim was to save on the low levels in order to spend on the high.

Possession for its own sake or in competition with the rest of the neighborhood would have been Thoreau's idea of the low levels. The active discipline of heightening one's perception of what is enduring in nature would have been his idea of the high. What he saved from the low was time and effort he could spend on the high. Thoreau certainly disapproved of starvation, but he would put into feeding himself only as much effort as would keep him functioning for more important efforts.

Effort is the gist of it. There is no happiness except as we take on life-engaging difficulties. Short of the impossible, as Yeats put it, the satisfactions we get from a lifetime depend on how high we choose our difficulties. Robert Frost was thinking in something like the same terms when he spoke of "The pleasure of taking pains." The mortal flaw in the advertised version of happiness is in the fact that it purports to be effortless.

We demand difficulty even in our games. We demand it because without difficulty there can be no game. A game is a way of making something hard for the fun of it. The rules of the game are an arbitrary imposition of difficulty. When the spoilsport ruins the fun, he always does so by refusing to play by the rules. It is easier to win at chess if you are free, at your pleasure, to change the wholly arbitrary rules, but the fun is in winning within the rules. No difficulty, no fun.

The buyers and sellers at the happiness-market seem too often to have lost their sense of pleasure of difficulty. Heaven knows what they are playing, but it seems a dull game. And the Indian holy man seems dull to us, I suppose, because he seems to be refusing to play anything at all. The Western weakness may be in the illusion that happiness can be bought. Perhaps the Eastern weakness is in the idea that there is such a thing as perfect (and therefore static) happiness.

Happiness is never more than partial. There are no pure states of mankind. Whatever else happiness may be, it is neither in having nor in being, but in becoming. What the Founding Fathers declared for us as an inherent right, we should do well to remember, was not happiness but the *pursuit* of happiness. What they might have underlined, could they have foreseen the happiness-market, is the cardinal fact that happiness is in the pursuit itself, in the meaningful pursuit of what is life-

9

10

11

12

13

14

engaging and life-revealing, which is to say, in the idea of *becoming*. A nation is not measured by what it possesses or wants to possess, but by what it wants to become.

By all means let the happiness-market sell us minor satisfactions   15
and even minor follies so long as we keep them in scale and buy them out of spiritual change. I am no customer for either puritanism or asceticism. But drop any real spiritual capital at those bazaars, and what you come home to will be your own poorhouse.

Questions for Study and Discussion

1. How does Ciardi define *happiness*? Do you agree with his definition?

2. What does Ciardi mean when he says that "the forces of American commercialism are hugely dedicated to making us deliberately unhappy"? What evidence does he offer in support of his claim?

3. Ciardi feels that *happiness* is a difficult term to define. Do you agree? Why, or why not?

4. What is Ciardi's attitude toward materialistic happiness and spiritual happiness?

5. Ciardi coins the term "happiness-market" in this essay. Define the term. What are its connotations as Ciardi uses it?

6. Why does Ciardi use the quotation from Swift in paragraph 1 and the ones from Yeats and Frost in paragraph 11?

Writing Topics

1. What for you is happiness? Write an essay in which you define happiness, using examples from your own experience.

2. Ciardi believes that "there is no happiness except as we take on life-engaging difficulties." Write an essay in which you agree or disagree with Ciardi's position. Use specific examples to document your essay.

3. Write an essay in which you discuss your understanding of the American Dream and its relationship to happiness. Is it unrealistic to think that money can't buy at least a certain degree of happiness? Does material success preclude happiness?

ERICH FROMM

Erich Fromm (1900–1980) was born in Frankfurt, Germany, and received his Ph.D. from the University of Heidelberg. Fromm emigrated to the United States in 1934 and became a naturalized citizen in 1940. Through his lectures and writing, Fromm established himself as a leading psychoanalyst, social critic, and philosopher. He taught at several universities, including Yale and Columbia, and his most significant books include *Escape from Freedom* (1941), *The Sane Society* (1955), *Life without Illusions* (1962), and *Anatomy of Human Destructiveness* (1973). His most famous book is *The Art of Loving* (1956), in which he maintains that love is the answer to the human predicament.

In the following essay, which first appeared in the *Saturday Evening Post* in 1964, we see Erich Fromm the social critic. Recognizing the growing unhappiness of many Americans amidst great material wealth, Fromm tries to explain what is missing in their lives.

Our Way of Life Makes Us Miserable

Most Americans believe that our society of consumption-happy, fun-loving, jet-traveling people creates the greatest happiness for the greatest number. Contrary to this view, I believe that our present way of life leads to increasing anxiety, helplessness and, eventually, to the disintegration of our culture. I refuse to identify fun with pleasure, excitement with joy, business with happiness, or the faceless, buck-passing "organization man" with an independent individual.

From this critical view our rates of alcoholism, suicide and divorce, as well as juvenile delinquency, gang rule, acts of violence and indifference to life, are characteristic symptoms of our "pathology of normalcy." It may be argued that all these pathological phenomena exist because we have not yet reached our aim, that of an affluent society. It is true, we are still far from being an affluent society. But the material progress made in the last decades allows us to hope that our system might eventually produce a materially affluent society. Yet will we be happier then? The example of Sweden, one of the most prosperous, democratic and peaceful European countries, is not very encouraging: Sweden, as is often pointed out, in spite of all its material security has among the highest alcoholism and suicide rates in Europe, while a much poorer country like Ireland ranks among the lowest in these respects. Could it be that our dream that material welfare per se leads to happiness is just a pipe dream? . . .

75

Certainly the humanist thinkers of the eighteenth and nineteenth   3
centuries, who are our ideological ancestors, thought that the goal of life
was the full unfolding of a person's potentialities; what mattered to them
was the person who *is* much, not the one who *has* much or *uses* much.
For them economic production was a means to the unfolding of man,
not an end. It seems that today the means have become ends, that not
only "God is dead," as Nietzsche said in the nineteenth century, but also
man is dead; that what is alive are the organizations, the machines; and
that man has become their slave rather than being their master.

Each society creates its own type of personality by its way of bringing   4
up children in the family, by its system of education, by its effective
values (that is, those values that are rewarded rather than only preached).
Every society creates the type of "social character" which is needed for
its proper functioning. It forms men who *want* to do what they *have* to
do. What kind of men does our large-scale, bureaucratized industrialism
need?

It needs men who cooperate smoothly in large groups, who want   5
to consume more and more, and whose tastes are standardized and can
be easily influenced and anticipated. It needs men who feel free and
independent, yet who are willing to be commanded, to do what is expected, to fit into the social machine without friction; men who can be
guided without force, led without leaders, prompted without an aim except the aim to be on the move, to function, to go ahead.

Modern industrialism has succeeded in producing this kind of man.   6
He is the "alienated" man. He is alienated in the sense that his actions
and his own forces have become estranged from him; they stand above
him and against him, and rule him rather than being ruled by him. His
life forces have been transformed into things and institutions, and these
things and institutions have become idols. They are something apart from
him, which he worships and to which he submits. Alienated man bows
down before the works of his own hands. He experiences himself not as
the active bearer of his own forces and riches but as an impoverished
"thing," dependent on other things outside of himself. He is the prisoner
of the very economic and political circumstances which he has created.

Since our economic organization is based on continuous and ever-   7
increasing consumption (think of the threat to our economy if people
did not buy a new car until their old one was really obsolete), contemporary industrial man is encouraged to be consumption-crazy. Without
any real enjoyment, he "takes in" drink, food, cigarettes, sights, lectures,
books, movies, television, any new kind of gadget. The world has become
one great maternal breast, and man has become the eternal suckling,
forever expectant, forever disappointed.

Sex, in fact, has become one of the main objects of consumption.   8
Our newsstands are full of "girlie" magazines; the percentages of girls
having premarital sexual relations and of unwed mothers are on a steep
incline. It can be argued that all this represents a welcome emancipation
from Victorian morality, that it is a wholesome affirmation of independence, that it reflects the Freudian principle that repression may produce
neurosis. But while all these arguments are true to some extent, they
omit the main point. Neither independence nor Freudian principle is the
main cause of our present-day sexual freedom. Our sexual mores are part
and parcel of our *cult of consumption,* whose main principle was so succinctly expressed by Aldous Huxley in *Brave New World:* "Never put off
till tomorrow the fun you can have today." Nature has provided men
and women with the capacity for sexual excitement; but excitement in
consumption, whether it is of sex or any other commodity, is not the
same as aliveness and richness of experience.

In general, our society is becoming one of giant enterprises directed   9
by a bureaucracy in which man becomes a small, well-oiled cog in the
machinery. The oiling is done with higher wages, fringe benefits, well-
ventilated factories and piped music, and by psychologists and "human-
relations" experts; yet all this oiling does not alter the fact that man has
become powerless, that he does not wholeheartedly participate in his
work and that he is bored with it. In fact, the blue- and the white-collar
workers have become economic puppets who dance to the tune of au-
tomated machines and bureaucratic management.

The worker and employee are anxious, not only because they might   10
find themselves out of a job (and with installment payments due); they
are anxious also because they are unable to acquire any real satisfaction
or interest in life. They live and die without ever having confronted the
fundamental realities of human existence as emotionally and intellectually productive, authentic and independent human beings.

Those higher up on the social ladder are no less anxious. Their   11
lives are no less empty than those of their subordinates. They are even
more insecure in some respects. They are in a highly competitive race.
To be promoted or to fall behind is not only a matter of salary but even
more a matter of self-esteem. When they apply for their first job, they
are tested for intelligence as well as for the right mixture of submissiveness
and independence. From that moment on they are tested again and
again—by the psychologists, for whom testing is a big business, and by
their superiors, who judge their behavior, sociability, capacity to get
along, etc., their own and that of their wives. This constant need to
prove that one is as good as or better than one's fellow-competitor creates

constant anxiety and stress, the very causes of unhappiness and psycho-somatic illness.

The "organization man" may be well fed, well amused and well   12
oiled, yet he lacks a sense of identity because none of his feelings or his thoughts originates within himself; none is authentic. He has no con-victions, either in politics, religion, philosophy or in love. He is attracted by the "latest model" in thought, art and style, and lives under the illusion that the thoughts and feelings which he has acquired by listening to the media of mass communication are his own.

He has a nostalgic longing for a life of individualism, initiative and   13
justice, a longing that he satisfies by looking at Westerns. But these values have disappeared from real life in the world of giant corporations, giant state and military bureaucracies and giant labor unions. He, the individ-ual, feels so small before these giants that he sees only one way to escape the sense of utter insignificance: He identifies himself with the giants and idolizes them as the true representatives of his own human powers, those of which he has dispossessed himself. His effort to escape his anxiety takes other forms as well. His pleasure in a well-filled freezer may be one unconscious way of reassuring himself. His passion for consumption—from television to sex—is still another symptom, a mechanism which psychiatrists often find in anxious patients who go on an eating or buying spree to evade their problems.

The man whose life is centered around producing, selling and con-   14
suming commodities transforms himself into a commodity. He becomes increasingly attracted to that which is man-made and mechanical, rather than to that which is natural and organic. Many men today are more interested in sports cars than in women; or they experience women as a car which one can cause to race by pushing the right button. Altogether they expect happiness is a matter of finding the right button, not the result of a productive, rich life, a life which requires making an effort and taking risks. In their search for the button, some go to the psychoan-alyst, some go to church and some read "self-help" books. But while it is impossible to find the button for happiness, the majority are satisfied with pushing the buttons of cameras, radios, television sets, and watching science fiction becoming reality.

One of the strangest aspects of this mechanical approach to life is   15
the widespread lack of concern about the danger of total destruction by nuclear weapons; a possibility people are consciously aware of. The ex-planation, I believe, is that they are more proud of than frightened by the gadgets of mass destruction. Also, they are so frightened of the pos-sibility of their personal failure and humiliation that their anxiety about personal matters prevents them from feeling anxiety about the possibility

that everybody and everything may be destroyed. Perhaps total destruction is even more attractive than total insecurity and never-ending personal anxiety.

Am I suggesting that modern man is doomed and that we should return to the preindustrial mode of production or to nineteenth-century "free enterprise" capitalism? Certainly not. Problems are never solved by returning to a stage which one has already outgrown. I suggest transforming our social system from a bureaucratically managed industrialism in which maximal production and consumption are ends in themselves (in the Soviet Union as well as in the capitalist countries) into a humanist industrialism in which man and the full development of his potentialities—those of love and of reason—are the aims of all social arrangements. Production and consumption should serve only as means to this end, and should be prevented from ruling man. 16

To attain this goal we need to create a Renaissance of Enlightenment and of Humanism. It must be an Enlightenment, however, more radically realistic and critical than that of the seventeenth and eighteenth centuries. It must be a Humanism that aims at the full development of the total man, not the gadget man, not the consumer man, not the organization man. The aim of a humanist society is the man who loves life, who has faith in life, who is productive and independent. Such a transformation is possible if we recognize that our present way of life makes us sterile and eventually destroys the vitality necessary for survival. 17

Whether such transformation is likely is another matter. But we will not be able to succeed unless we see the alternatives clearly and realize that the choice is still ours. Dissatisfaction with our way of life is the first step toward changing it. As to these changes, one thing is certain: They must take place in all spheres simultaneously—in the economic, the social, the political and the spiritual. Change in only one sphere will lead into blind alleys, as did the purely political French Revolution and the purely economic Russian Revolution. Man is a product of circumstances—but the circumstances are also his product. He has a unique capacity that differentiates him from all other living beings: the capacity to be aware of himself and of his circumstances, and hence to plan and to act according to his awareness. 18

Questions for Study and Discussion

1. What is Fromm's thesis? Summarize the main points of his argument in your own words.

2. In what ways are people of the twentieth century different from their ideological ancestors of the eighteenth or nineteenth century?

3. What does Fromm mean when he says, "The man whose life is centered around producing, selling and consuming commodities transforms himself into a commodity"?

4. Why is modern man "alienated"?

5. What, in Fromm's view, should be the aims of all social arrangments? What roles do production and consumption play in his scheme of things? Does Fromm argue against production and consumption?

6. Fromm has made a number of generalizations in his essay. Identify several of these generalizations. In your view, has he adequately supported them? Explain.

Writing Topics

1. Fromm asks the question: Could it be that our dream that material welfare per se leads to happiness is just a pipe dream? What do you think? Write an essay in which you argue your position.

2. Fromm believes that competition "creates constant anxiety and stress, the very causes of unhappiness and psychosomatic illness." Write an essay in which you argue for or against the need to have competition in our lives.

ANNIE DILLARD

Annie Dillard was born in Pittsburgh and attended Hollins College. She now makes her home in Middletown, Connecticut, where she is writer in residence at Wesleyan University. A poet, journalist, and contributing editor to *Harper's* magazine, Dillard has written *Tickets for a Prayer Wheel* (1973), *Holy the Firm* (1977), and *Teaching a Stone to Talk* (1982). In 1974 she published *Pilgrim at Tinker Creek*, a fascinating collection of natural observations for which she was awarded the Pulitzer Prize for nonfiction.

In the following selection from *Pilgrim at Tinker Creek*, Dillard uses a childhood activity or game to help her explain the happiness that can be derived from an active perception of the world around us.

Sight into Insight

When I was six or seven years old, growing up in Pittsburgh, I used to take a penny of my own and hide it for someone else to find. It was a curious compulsion; sadly, I've never been seized by it since. For some reason I always "hid" the penny along the same stretch of sidewalk up the street. I'd cradle it at the roots of a maple, say, or in a hole left by a chipped-off piece of sidewalk. Then I'd take a piece of chalk and, starting at either end of the block, draw huge arrows leading up to the penny from both directions. After I learned to write I labeled the arrows "SURPRISE AHEAD" or "MONEY THIS WAY." I was greatly excited, during all this arrowdrawing, at the thought of the first lucky passerby who would receive in this way, regardless of merit, a free gift from the universe. But I never lurked about. I'd go straight home and not give the matter another thought, until, some months later, I would be gripped by the impulse to hide another penny.

There are lots of things to see, unwrapped gifts and free surprises. The world is fairly studded and strewn with pennies cast broadside from a generous hand. But—and this is the point—who gets excited by a mere penny? If you follow one arrow, if you crouch motionless on a bank to watch a tremulous ripple thrill on the water, and are rewarded by the sight of a muskrat kit paddling from its den, will you count that sight a chip of copper only, and go your rueful way? It is very dire poverty indeed for a man to be so malnourished and fatigued that he won't stoop to pick up a penny. But if you cultivate a healthy poverty and simplicity, so that finding a penny will make your day, then, since the world is in fact planted in pennies, you have with your poverty bought a lifetime of days. What you see is what you get.

1

2

Unfortunately, nature is very much a now-you-see-it, now-you-don't   3
affair. A fish flashes, then dissolves in the water before my eyes like so
much salt. Deer apparently ascend bodily into heaven: the brightest ori-
ole fades into leaves. These disappearances stun me into stillness and
concentration; they say of nature that it conceals with a grand noncha-
lance, and they say of vision that it is a deliberate gift, the revelation of
a dancer who for my eyes only flings away her seven veils.

For nature does reveal as well as conceal; now-you-don't-see-it,   4
now-you-do. For a week this September migrating red-winged blackbirds
were feeding heavily down by Tinker Creek at the back of the house.
One day I went out to investigate the racket; I walked up to a tree, an
Osage orange, and a hundred birds flew away. They simply materialized
out of the tree. I saw a tree, then a whisk of color, then a tree again. I
walked closer and another hundred blackbirds took flight. Not a branch,
not a twig budged: the birds were apparently weightless as well as invisible. Or, it was as if the leaves of the Osage orange had been freed from
a spell in the form of red-winged blackbirds; they flew from the tree,
caught my eye in the sky, and vanished. When I looked again at the
tree, the leaves had reassembled as if nothing had happened. Finally I
walked directly to the trunk of the tree and a final hundred, the real
diehards, appeared, spread, and vanished. How could so many hide in
the tree without my seeing them? The Osage orange, unruffled, looked
just as it had looked from the house, when three hundred red-winged
blackbirds cried from its crown. I looked upstream where they flew, and
they were gone. Searching, I couldn't spot one. I wandered upstream to
force them to play their hand, but they'd crossed the creek and scattered.
One show to a customer. These appearances catch at my throat; they
are the free gifts, the bright coppers at the roots of trees.

It's all a matter of keeping my eyes open. Nature is like one of   5
those line drawings that are puzzles for children: Can you find hidden in
the tree a duck, a house, a boy, a bucket, a giraffe, and a boot? Specialists
can find the most incredibly hidden things. A book I read when I was
young recommended an easy way to find caterpillars: you simply find
some fresh caterpillar droppings, look up, and there's your caterpillar.
More recently an author advised me to set my mind at ease about those
piles of cut stems on the ground in grassy fields. Field mice make them;
they cut the grass down by degrees to reach the seeds at the head. It
seems that when the grass is tightly packed, as in a field of ripe grain,
the blade won't topple at a single cut through the stem; instead, the cut
stem simply drops vertically, held in the crush of grain. The mouse severs
the bottom again and again, the stem keeps dropping an inch at a time,
and finally the head is low enough for the mouse to reach the seeds.

Meanwhile the mouse is positively littering the field with its little piles of cut stems into which, presumably, the author is constantly stumbling.

If I can't see these minutiae, I still try to keep my eyes open. I'm always on the lookout for ant lion traps in sandy soil, monarch pupae near milkweed, skipper larvae in locust leaves. These things are utterly common, and I've not seen one. I bang on hollow trees near water, but so far no flying squirrels have appeared. In flat country I watch every sunset in hopes of seeing the green ray. The green ray is a seldom-seen streak of light that rises from the sun like a spurting fountain at the moment of sunset; it throbs into the sky for two seconds and disappears. One more reason to keep my eyes open. A photography professor at the University of Florida just happened to see a bird die in midflight; it jerked, died, dropped, and smashed on the ground.

I squint at the wind because I read Stewart Edward White: "I have always maintained that if you looked closely enough you could *see* the wind—the dim, hardly-made-out, fine débris fleeing high in the air." White was an excellent observer, and devoted an entire chapter of *The Mountains* to the subject of seeing deer: "As soon as you can forget the naturally obvious and construct an artificial obvious, then you too will see deer."

But the artificial obvious is hard to see. My eyes account for less than 1 percent of the weight of my head; I'm bony and dense; I see what I expect. I just don't know what the lover knows; I can't see the artificial obvious that those in the know construct. The herpetologist asks the native, "Are there snakes in that ravine?" "No, sir." And the herpetologist comes home with, yessir, three bags full. Are there butterflies on that mountain? Are the bluets in bloom? Are there arrowheads here, or fossil ferns in the shale?

Peeping through my keyhole I see within the range of only about 30 percent of the light that comes from the sun; the rest is infrared and some little ultraviolet, perfectly apparent to many animals, but invisible to me. A nightmare network of ganglia, charged and firing without my knowledge, cuts and splices what I do see, editing it for my brain. Donald E. Carr points out that the sense impressions of one-celled animals are *not* edited for the brain: "This is philosophically interesting in a rather mournful way, since it means that only the simplest animals perceive the universe as it is."

A fog that won't burn away drifts and flows across my field of vision. When you see fog move against a backdrop of deep pines, you don't see the fog itself, but streaks of clearness floating across the air in dark shreds. So I see only tatters of clearness through a pervading obscurity. I can't distinguish the fog from the overcast sky; I can't be sure if the light is direct or reflected. Everywhere darkness and the presence of the unseen appalls. We estimate now that only one atom dances alone in every cubic meter of intergalactic space. I blink and squint. What planet or power yanks Halley's Comet out of orbit? We haven't seen it yet; it's a question of distance, density, and the pallor of reflected light. We rock, cradled in the swaddling band of darkness. Even the simple darkness of night whispers suggestions to the mind. This summer, in August, I stayed at the creek too late.

Questions for Study and Discussion

1. Dillard seems to be teaching us something she has learned from her experiences as a naturalist. What exactly is her lesson?

2. Dillard uses the analogy of hidden pennies to make her point. Explain how her analogy works. How effective did you find the analogy? Does the analogy seem at all contrived?

3. Dillard uses two clichés: "What you see is what you get" and "now-you-see-it, now-you-don't." Are these clichés used thoughtlessly? What do you suppose her purpose is in using them?

4. What does Dillard mean when she asks us to "cultivate a healthy poverty and simplicity"?

5. Dillard uses a number of examples from the natural world to illustrate her point. How would you characterize these examples? And, why does she develop one more than the others?

Writing Topics

1. Write an essay in which you describe several of the "free gifts" that nature has given you and try to explain the meaning that each had for you. How have they added to your satisfaction and personal happiness?

2. Dillard's essay addresses a theme that has been a concern of writers and naturalists throughout the ages. Consider, for example, the following poem by William Wordsworth.

The World Is Too Much with Us

The world is too much with us; late and soon,
Getting and spending, we lay waste our powers:
Little we see in Nature that is ours;
We have given our hearts away, a sordid boon!

This Sea that bares her bosom to the moon;   5
The winds that will be howling at all hours,
And are up-gathered now like sleeping flowers;
For this, for everything, we are out of tune;
It moves us not.—Great God! I'd rather be
A Pagan suckled in a creed outworn;   10
So might I, standing on this pleasant lea,
Have glimpses that would make me less forlorn;
Have sight of Proteus rising from the sea;
Or hear old Triton blow his wreathèd horn.

Write an essay in which you talk about our relationship to nature. What are the obstacles in contemporary life that prevent us from truly seeing nature and receiving the benefits of the natural world?

EDWIN ARLINGTON ROBINSON

Three-time Pulitzer Prize-winning poet Edwin Arlington Robinson (1869–1935) was born near Gardiner, Maine, the prototype of Tilbury Town where many of his poems are set. He attended Harvard for only two years before moving to New York City, where he earned a precarious living and wrote poetry. President Theodore Roosevelt became such a fan of his poetry that he rescued Robinson from his job as Inspector of Subway Construction by arranging a clerkship for him in the New York Custom House.

"Richard Cory" is one of those dark psychological portraits that Robinson, and indeed modern literature, became famous for in the early decades of this century.

Richard Cory

Whenever Richard Cory went down town,
We people on the pavement looked at him:
He was a gentleman from sole to crown,
Clean favored, and imperially slim.

And he was always quietly arrayed,   5
And he was always human when he talked;
But still he fluttered pulses when he said,
"Good-morning," and he glittered when he walked.

And he was rich—yes, richer than a king—
And admirably schooled in every grace: 10
In fine, we thought that he was everything
To make us wish that we were in his place.

So on we worked, and waited for the light,
And went without the meat, and cursed the bread;
And Richard Cory, one calm summer night,   15
Went home and put a bullet through his head.

Questions for Study and Discussion

1. What does "Richard Cory" suggest about the relationship between happiness and material success? Is Robinson totally pessimistic about the possibility of happiness?

2. What is irony? Where has Robinson used irony in his poem? How effective do you find his use of irony? Explain.

3. How does Robinson's choice of words help to create the character of Richard Cory? Cite specific examples from the poem to illustrate your assessment.

Writing Topics

1. Robinson's "Richard Cory" shows us dramatically that there is often a big difference between appearance and reality. Willard Gaylin takes the opposite position in his essay "What You See Is the Real You" (pp. 53-55). Write an essay in which you interpret Robinson's poem in light of what Gaylin has to say.

2. Argue the proposition that no one can tell what happiness is because happiness is something that each of us must determine for himself or herself.

3. Americans have tended to link monetary success with happiness. Richard Cory is a tragic reminder that material success does not always lead to inner peace. Write an essay in which you propose another measure of success, one that would ensure greater happiness for the individual.

Turning Points

LANGSTON HUGHES

Langston Hughes was born in 1902 in Joplin, Missouri, and though he began writing poetry at an early age, he was at first unable to get his work published and supported himself by traveling about the country, doing whatever work he could find. He was working as a busboy when his poetry was discovered in 1925 by Vachel Lindsay, a famous poet of the time. A year later Hughes published his first book of poems, *The Weary Blues*, and entered Lincoln University in Pennsylvania. He graduated in 1929 and set about making his way as a writer. Hughes's work focuses on American Negro life, often incorporating dialect and jazz rhythms. His writings include novels, plays, and a popular series of newspaper sketches, but his reputation rests most solidly on his poems. Much of his finest poetry has been collected as *Selected Poems* (1959). He died in 1967.

In this selection taken from his autobiography, *The Big Sea*, Hughes narrates his experiences at a church revival meeting he attended when he was twelve years old.

Salvation

I was saved from sin when I was going on thirteen. But not really   1
saved. It happened like this. There was a big revival at my Auntie Reed's church. Every night for weeks there had been much preaching, singing, praying, and shouting, and some very hardened sinners had been brought to Christ, and the membership of the church had grown by leaps and bounds. Then just before the revival ended, they held a special meeting for children, "to bring the young lambs to the fold." My aunt spoke of it for days ahead. That night I was escorted to the front row and placed on the mourners' bench with all the other young sinners, who had not yet been brought to Jesus.

My aunt told me that when you were saved you saw a light, and   2
something happened to you inside! And Jesus came into your life! And

God was with you from then on! She said you could see and hear and feel Jesus in your soul. I believed her. I have heard a great many old people say the same thing and it seemed to me they ought to know. So I sat there calmly in the hot, crowded church, waiting for Jesus to come to me.

The preacher preached a wonderful rhythmical sermon, all moans   3
and shouts and lonely cries and dire pictures of hell, and then he sang a song about the ninety and nine safe in the fold, but one little lamb was left out in the cold. Then he said: "Won't you come? Won't you come to Jesus? Young lambs, won't you come?" And he held out his arms to all us young sinners there on the mourners' bench. And the little girls cried. And some of them jumped up and went to Jesus right away. But most of us just sat there.

A great many old people came and knelt around us and prayed, old   4
women with jet-black faces and braided hair, old men with work-gnarled hands. And the church sang a song about the lower lights are burning, some poor sinners to be saved. And the whole building rocked with prayer and song.

Still I kept waiting to *see* Jesus.   5

Finally all the young people had gone to the altar and were saved,   6
but one boy and me. He was a rounder's son named Westley. Westley and I were surrounded by sisters and deacons praying. It was very hot in the church, and getting late now. Finally Westley said to me in a whisper: "God damn! I'm tired o' sitting here. Let's get up and be saved." So he got up and was saved.

Then I was left all alone on the mourners' bench. My aunt came   7
and knelt at my knees and cried, while prayers and songs swirled all around me in the little church. The whole congregation prayed for me alone, in a mighty wail of moans and voices. And I kept waiting serenely for Jesus, waiting, waiting—but he didn't come. I wanted to see him, but nothing happened to me. Nothing! I wanted something to happen to me, but nothing happened.

I heard the songs and the minister saying: "Why don't you come?   8
My dear child, why don't you come to Jesus? Jesus is waiting for you. He wants you. Why don't you come? Sister Reed, what is this child's name?"

"Langston," my aunt sobbed.   9

"Langston, why don't you come? Why don't you come and be saved?   10
Oh, Lamb of God! Why don't you come?"

Now it was really getting late. I began to be ashamed of myself,   11
holding everything up so long. I began to wonder what God thought about Westley, who certainly hadn't seen Jesus either, but who was now sitting proudly on the platform, swinging his knickerbockered legs and

grinning down at me, surrounded by deacons and old women on their knees praying. God had not struck Westley dead for taking his name in vain or for lying in the temple. So I decided that maybe to save further trouble, I'd better lie, too, and say that Jesus had come, and get up and be saved.

So I got up.   12

Suddenly the whole room broke into a sea of shouting, as they saw   13
me rise. Waves of rejoicing swept the place. Women leaped in the air. My aunt threw her arms around me. The minister took me by the hand and led me to the platform.

When things quieted down, in a hushed silence, punctuated by a   14
few ecstatic "Amens," all the new young lambs were blessed in the name of God. Then joyous singing filled the room.

That night, for the last time in my life but one—for I was a big   15
boy twelve years old—I cried. I cried, in bed alone, and couldn't stop. I buried my head under the quilts, but my aunt heard me. She woke up and told my uncle I was crying because the Holy Ghost had come into my life, and because I had seen Jesus. But I was really crying because I couldn't bear to tell her that I had lied, that I had deceived everybody in the church, that I hadn't seen Jesus, and that now I didn't believe there was a Jesus any more, since he didn't come to help me.

Questions for Study and Discussion

1. Why does the young Langston expect to be saved at the revival meeting? Once the children are in church, what appeals are made to them to encourage them to seek salvation?

2. Trace the various pressures working on Hughes that lead to his decision to "get up and be saved". What important realization finally convinces him to lie about being saved?

3. Even though Hughes's account of the events at the revival is at points humorous, the experience was nonetheless painful for him. Why does he cry on the night of his "salvation"? Why does his aunt think he is crying? What significance is there in the disparity between their views?

4. What paradox or apparent contradiction does Hughes present in the first two sentences of the narrative? Why do you suppose he uses this device?

5. What is the function of the third sentence, "It happened like this"?

6. Hughes consciously varies the structure and length of his sentences to create different effects. What effect does he create through the short sentences in paragraphs 2 and 3 and the long sentence which concludes the final paragraph? How do the short, one-sentence paragraphs aid him in telling his story?

7. Although Hughes tells most of his story himself, he allows Auntie Reed, the minister, and Westley to speak for themselves. What does Hughes gain by having his characters speak for themselves?

8. How does Hughes's choice of words help to establish a realistic atmosphere for a religious revival meeting? Does he use any traditional religious figures of speech?

9. Why does Hughes italicize the word *see* in paragraph 5? What do you think he means by *see*? What do you think his aunt means by *see*? Explain.

Writing Topics

1. Like the young Langston Hughes, we sometimes find ourselves in situations in which, for the sake of conformity, we do things we do not believe in. Consider one such experience you have had. What is it about human nature that makes us occasionally act in ways that contradict our inner feelings?

2. In the end of his essay Langston Hughes suffers alone. He cannot bring himself to talk about his dilemma with other people. Why can it be so difficult to seek the help of others? Consider examples from your experience and what you have seen and read about other people.

3. Sometimes the little, insignificant, seemingly trivial experiences in our daily lives can provide the material for narratives that reveal something about ourselves and the world we live in. Select one seemingly trivial event in your life, and write an essay in which you narrate that experience and explain its significance.

JOAN DIDION

Essayist, novelist, and journalist, Joan Didion was born in Sacramento in 1934 and educated at the University of California at Berkeley. She often writes on aspects of life in California and in the West. She has written for a wide spectrum of magazines, from *Mademoiselle* to the *National Review*, and her essays have been collected in *Slouching Towards Bethlehem* (1969) and *The White Album* (1979). Her novels include *Run River* (1963), *Play It As It Lays* (1971), and *A Book of Common Prayer* (1977).

This selection, taken from her highly acclaimed collection of essays *Slouching Towards Bethlehem*, first appeared in *The Saturday Evening Post*. Didion recalls the experience of going home to her parents' house with her adopted daughter, Quintana, for the child's first birthday.

On Going Home

I am home for my daughter's first birthday. By "home" I do not   1
mean the house in Los Angeles where my husband and I and the baby
live, but the place where my family is, in the Central Valley of California.
It is a vital although troublesome distinction. My husband likes my family
but is uneasy in their house, because once there I fall into their ways,
which are difficult, oblique, deliberately inarticulate, not my husband's
ways. We live in dusty houses ("D-U-S-T," he once wrote with his finger
on surfaces all over the house, but no one noticed it) filled with mementos quite without value to him (what could the Canton dessert plates
mean to him? how could he have known about the assay scales, why
should he care if he did know?), and we appear to talk exclusively about
people we know who have been committed to mental hospitals, about
people we know who have been booked on drunk-driving charges, and
about property, particularly about property, land, price per acre and
C-2 zoning and assessments and freeway access. My brother does not
understand my husband's inability to perceive the advantage in the rather
common real-estate transaction known as "sale-leaseback," and my husband in turn does not understand why so many of the people he hears
about in my father's house have recently been committed to mental
hospitals or booked on drunk-driving charges. Nor does he understand
that when we talk about sale-leasebacks and right-of-way condemnations
we are talking in code about the things we like best, the yellow fields
and the cottonwoods and the rivers rising and falling and the mountain
roads closing when the heavy snow comes in. We miss each other's
points, have another drink and regard the fire. My brother refers to my

93

husband, in his presence, as "Joan's husband." Marriage is the classic betrayal.

Or perhaps it is not any more. Sometimes I think that those of us who are now in our thirties were born into the last generation to carry the burden of "home," to find in family life the source of all tension and drama. I had by all objective accounts a "normal" and a "happy" family situation, and yet I was almost thirty years old before I could talk to my family on the telephone without crying after I had hung up. We did not fight. Nothing was wrong. And yet some nameless anxiety colored the emotional charges between me and the place that I came from. The question of whether or not you could go home again was a very real part of the sentimental and largely literary baggage with which we left home in the fifties; I suspect that it is irrelevant to the children born of the fragmentation after World War II. A few weeks ago in a San Francisco bar I saw a pretty young girl on crystal take off her clothes and dance for the cash prize in an "amateur-topless" contest. There was no particular sense of moment about this, none of the effect of romantic degradation, of "dark journey," for which my generation strived so assiduously. What sense could that girl possibly make of, say, *Long Day's Journey into Night?* Who is beside the point?

That I am trapped in this particular irrelevancy is never more apparent to me than when I am home. Paralyzed by the neurotic lassitude engendered by meeting one's past at every turn, around every corner, inside every cupboard, I go aimlessly from room to room. I decide to meet it head-on and clean out a drawer, and I spread the contents on the bed. A bathing suit I wore the summer I was seventeen. A letter of rejection from *The Nation*, an aerial photograph of the site for a shopping center my father did not build in 1954. Three teacups hand-painted with cabbage roses and signed "E.M.," my grandmother's initials. There is no final solution for letters of rejection from *The Nation* and teacups hand-painted in 1900. Nor is there any answer to snapshots of one's grandfather as a young man on skis, surveying around Donner Pass in the year 1910. I smooth out the snapshot and look into his face, and do and do not see my own. I close the drawer, and have another cup of coffee with my mother. We get along very well, veterans of a guerrilla war we never understood.

Days pass. I see no one. I come to dread my husband's evening call, not only because he is full of news of what by now seems to me our remote life in Los Angeles, people he has seen, letters which require attention, but because he asks what I have been doing, suggests uneasily that I get out, drive to San Francisco or Berkeley. Instead I drive across the river to a family graveyard. It has been vandalized since my last visit and the monuments are broken, overturned in the dry grass. Because I once saw a rattlesnake in the grass I stay in the car and listen to a country-and-Western station. Later I drive with my father to a ranch he has in the foothills. The man who runs his cattle on it asks us to the roundup, a week from Sunday, and although I know that I will be in Los Angeles I say, in the oblique way my family talks, that I will come. Once home I mention the broken monuments in the graveyard. My mother shrugs.

I go to visit my great-aunts. A few of them think now that I am   5
my cousin, or their daughter who died young. We recall an anecdote about a relative last seen in 1948, and they ask if I still like living in New York City. I have lived in Los Angeles for three years, but I say that I do. The baby is offered a horehound drop, and I am slipped a dollar bill "to buy a treat." Questions trail off, answers are abandoned, the baby plays with the dust motes in a shaft of afternoon sun.

It is time for the baby's birthday party: a white cake, strawberry-   6
marshmallow ice cream, a bottle of champagne saved from another party. In the evening, after she has gone to sleep, I kneel beside the crib and touch her face, where it is pressed against the slats, with mine. She is an open and trusting child, unprepared for and unaccustomed to the ambushes of family life, and perhaps it is just as well that I can offer her little of that life. I would like to give her more. I would like to promise her that she will grow up with a sense of her cousins and of rivers and of her great-grandmother's teacups, would like to pledge her a picnic on a river with fried chicken and her hair uncombed, would like to give her *home* for her birthday, but we live differently now and I can promise her nothing like that. I give her a xylophone and a sundress from Madeira, and promise to tell her a funny story.

Questions for Study and Discussion

1. What does Didion mean by "home"? Why does she say that the distinction between her house in Los Angeles and her family's place in the Central Valley of California is "vital although troublesome"?

2. What are Didion's attitudes toward home? Are they in any way contradictory? Explain.

3. What does Didion mean when she says, "Marriage is the classic betrayal"? Explain.

4. Eugene O'Neill's *Long Day's Journey into Night* is an autobiographical domestic tragedy which, as Didion correctly implies, finds "in family life the source of all tension and drama". Why does Didion feel that the pretty young girl who dances in the "amateur-topless" contest would have difficulty making any sense of this play?

5. What details does the author use to support her feelings of being "Paralyzed by the neurotic lassitude engendered by meeting one's past at every turn"? What does she mean when she says of her relationship with her mother, "We get along very well, veterans of a guerrilla war we never understood"?

6. Why do you think Didion gives her daughter a xylophone and a sundress from Madeira for her birthday? What else would she have liked to give her? Why does she feel that she could not make a promise "like that"?

7. Good narrative tells when an action happened, where it happened, and to whom it happened. Where does Didion give us this information?

8. In the context of this essay, comment on the appropriateness of each of the following substitutions for Didion's diction. Which word is better in each case? Why?
a. *important* for *vital* (1)
b. *bothersome* for *troublesome* (1)
c. *dirty* for *dusty* (1)
d. *heirlooms* for *mementos* (1)
e. *argue* for *fight* (2)
f. *uncertainty* for *fragmentation* (2)
g. *immobilized* for *paralyzed* (3)
h. *fear* for *dread* (4)
i. *obscure* for *oblique* (1, 4)
j. *outing* for *picnic* (6)

Writing Topics

1. Drawing on your own experience of home life, do you think that Didion is correct when she says that "those of us who are now in our thirties were born into the last generation to carry the burden of 'home,' to find in family life the source of all tension and drama"? Write a brief narrative which conveys what home is like for you.

2. In "On Going Home" Didion honestly confronts her feelings about her parents, her husband, her child, and the passage of time. In attempting not to deceive herself she gains a measure of what might be called self-respect, or self-understanding. How and why do people deceive themselves? Why is self-deception so difficult to overcome? Finally, what does it mean to have self-respect? Write an essay in which you develop your answers to these questions.

3. In another essay from *Slouching Towards Bethlehem*, Didion defines character as "the willingness to accept responsibility for one's own life." Is that what character means to you? If so, develop the definition into an essay of your own. If not, write an essay explaining what you think character really is.

E. B. WHITE

Master essayist, storyteller, and poet, Elwyn Brooks White (1899–1985) was born in Mount Vernon, New York, lived some years in New York City, and for many years made his home on a salt-water farm in Maine. After studying at Cornell University, he joined the staff of *The New Yorker* in 1926, where he wrote essays, editorials, anonymous fillers, and even cartoon captions that helped to establish the magazine's and his own reputation for witty and graceful prose. A selection of his essays is available in *The Essays of E. B. White* (1977). He is the author of the classic children's stories *Stuart Little* (1945) and *Charlotte's Web* (1952) and he revised William Strunk's celebrated work, *The Elements of Style*, several times beginning in 1959. "Once More to the Lake," first published in *Harper's* in 1941, is a loving account of a trip White took with his son to the site of his own childhood vacations.

Once More to the Lake

One summer, along about 1904, my father rented a camp on a lake in Maine and took us all there for the month of August. We all got ringworm from some kittens and had to rub Pond's Extract on our arms and legs night and morning, and my father rolled over in a canoe with all his clothes on; but outside of that the vacation was a success and from then on none of us ever thought there was any place in the world like that lake in Maine. We returned summer after summer—always on August 1st for one month. I have since become a salt-water man, but sometimes in summer there are days when the restlessness of the tides and the fearful cold of the sea water and the incessant wind which blows across the afternoon and into the evening make me wish for the placidity of a lake in the woods. A few weeks ago this feeling got so strong I bought myself a couple of bass hooks and a spinner and returned to the lake where we used to go, for a week's fishing and to revisit old haunts.

I took along my son, who had never had any fresh water up his nose and who had seen lily pads only from train windows. On the journey over to the lake I began to wonder what it would be like. I wondered how time would have marred this unique, this holy spot—the coves and streams, the hills that the sun set behind, the camps and the paths behind the camps. I was sure that the tarred road would have found it out and I wondered in what other ways it would be desolated. It is strange how much you can remember about places like that once you allow your mind to return into the grooves which lead back. You remember one thing, and that suddenly reminds you of another thing. I guess I remembered

97

clearest of all the early mornings, when the lake was cool and motionless, remembered how the bedroom smelled of the lumber it was made of and of the wet woods whose scent entered through the screen. The partitions in the camp were thin and did not extend clear to the top of the rooms, and as I was always the first up I would dress softly so as not to wake the others, and sneak out into the sweet outdoors and start out in the canoe, keeping close along the shore in the long shadows of the pines. I remembered being very careful never to rub my paddle against the gunwale for fear of disturbing the stillness of the cathedral.

The lake had never been what you would call a wild lake. There   3
were cottages sprinkled around the shores, and it was in farming country although the shores of the lake were quite heavily wooded. Some of the cottages were owned by nearby farmers, and you would live at the shore and eat your meals at the farmhouse. That's what our family did. But although it wasn't wild, it was a fairly large and undisturbed lake and there were places in it which, to a child at least, seemed infinitely remote and primeval.

I was right about the tar: it led to within half a mile of the shore.   4
But when I got back there, with my boy, and we settled into a camp near a farmhouse and into the kind of summertime I had known, I could tell that it was going to be pretty much the same as it had been before— I knew it, lying in bed the first morning, smelling the bedroom, and hearing the boy sneak quietly out and go off along the shore in a boat. I began to sustain the illusion that he was I, and therefore, by simple transposition, that I was my father. This sensation persisted, kept cropping up all the time we were there. It was not an entirely new feeling, but in this setting it grew much stronger. I seemed to be living a dual existence. I would be in the middle of some simple act, I would be picking up a bait box or laying down a table fork, or I would be saying something, and suddenly it would be not I but my father who was saying the words or making the gesture. It gave me a creepy sensation.

We went fishing the first morning. I felt the same damp moss cov-   5
ering the worms in the bait can, and saw the dragonfly alight on the tip of my rod as it hovered a few inches from the surface of the water. It was the arrival of this fly that convinced me beyond any doubt that everything was as it always had been, that the years were a mirage and there had been no years. The small waves were the same, chucking the rowboat under the chin as we fished at anchor, and the boat was the same boat, the same color green and the ribs broken in the same places, and under the floor-boards the same freshwater leavings and débris—the dead helgramite, the wisps of moss, the rusty discarded fishhook, the dried blood from yesterday's catch. We stared silently at the tips of our

rods, at the dragonflies that came and went. I lowered the tip of mine into the water, tentatively, pensively dislodging the fly, which darted two feet away, poised, darted two feet back, and came to rest again a little farther up the rod. There had been no years between the ducking of this dragonfly and the other one—the one that was part of memory. I looked at the boy, who was silently watching his fly, and it was my hands that held his rod, my eyes watching. I felt dizzy and didn't know which rod I was at the end of.

We caught two bass, hauling them in briskly as though they were mackerel, pulling them over the side of the boat in a businesslike manner without any landing net, and stunning them with a blow on the back of the head. When we got back for a swim before lunch, the lake was exactly where we had left it, the same number of inches from the dock, and there was only the merest suggestion of a breeze. This seemed an utterly enchanted sea, this lake you could leave to its own devices for a few hours and come back to, and find that it had not stirred, this constant and trustworthy body of water. In the shallows, the dark, water-soaked sticks and twigs, smooth and old, were undulating in clusters on the bottom against the clean ribbed sand, and the track of the mussel was plain. A school of minnows swam by, each minnow with its small individual shadow, doubling the attendance, so clear and sharp in the sunlight. Some of the other campers were in swimming, along the shore, one of them with a cake of soap, and the water felt thin and clear and unsubstantial. Over the years there had been this person with the cake of soap, this cultist, and here he was. There had been no years.

Up to the farmhouse to dinner through the teeming, dusty field, the road under our sneakers was only a two-track road. The middle track was missing, the one with the marks of the hooves and the splotches of dried, flaky manure. There had always been three tracks to choose from in choosing which track to walk in; now the choice was narrowed down to two. For a moment I missed terribly the middle alternative. But the way led past the tennis court, and something about the way it lay there in the sun reassured me; the tape had loosened along the backline, the alleys were green with plantains and other weeds, and the net (installed in June and removed in September) sagged in the dry noon, and the whole place steamed with midday heat and hunger and emptiness. There was a choice of pie for dessert, and one was blueberry and one was apple, and the waitresses were the same country girls, there having been no passage of time, only the illusion of it as in a dropped curtain—the waitresses were still fifteen; their hair had been washed, that was the only difference—they had been to the movies and seen the pretty girls with the clean hair.

Summertime, oh summertime, pattern of life indelible, the fade-   8
proof lake, the woods unshatterable, the pasture with the sweetfern and
the juniper forever and ever, summer without end; this was the background, and the life along the shore was the design, the cottages with
their innocent and tranquil design, their tiny docks with the flagpole and
the American flag floating against the white clouds in the blue sky, the
little paths over the roots of the trees leading from camp to camp and
the paths leading back to the outhouses and the can of lime for sprinkling,
and at the souvenir counters at the store the miniature birch-bark canoes
and the post cards that showed things looking a little better than they
looked. This was the American family at play, escaping the city heat,
wondering whether the newcomers in the camp at the head of the cove
were "common" or "nice," wondering whether it was true that the people
who drove up for Sunday dinner at the farmhouse were turned away
because there wasn't enough chicken.

It seemed to me, as I kept remembering all this, that those times   9
and those summers had been infinitely precious and worth saving. There
had been jollity and peace and goodness. The arriving (at the beginning
of August) had been so big a business in itself, at the railway station the
farm wagon drawn up, the first smell of the pine-laden air, the first
glimpse of the smiling farmer, and the great importance of the trunks
and your father's enormous authority in such matters, and the feel of the
wagon under you for the long ten-mile haul, and at the top of the last
long hill catching the first view of the lake after eleven months of not
seeing this cherished body of water. The shouts and cries of the other
campers when they saw you, and the trunks to be unpacked, to give up
their rich burden. (Arriving was less exciting nowadays, when you sneaked
up in your car and parked it under a tree near the camp and took out
the bags and in five minutes it was all over, no fuss, no loud wonderful
fuss about trunks.)

Peace and goodness and jollity. The only thing that was wrong   10
now, really, was the sound of the place, an unfamiliar nervous sound of
the outboard motors. This was the note that jarred, the one thing that
would sometimes break the illusion and set the years moving. In those
other summertimes all motors were inboard; and when they were at a
little distance, the noise they made was a sedative, an ingredient of
summer sleep. They were one-cylinder and two-cylinder engines, and
some were make-and-break and some were jump-spark, but they all made
a sleepy sound across the lake. The one-lungers throbbed and fluttered,
and the twin-cylinder ones purred and purred, and that was a quiet sound
too. But now the campers all had outboards. In the daytime, in the hot
mornings, these motors made a petulant, irritable sound; at night, in the

still evening when the afterglow lit the water, they whined about one's ears like mosquitoes. My boy loved our rented outboard, and his great desire was to achieve singlehanded mastery over it, and authority, and he soon learned the trick of choking it a little (but not too much), and the adjustment of the needle valve. Watching him I would remember the things you could do with the old one-cylinder engine with the heavy flywheel, how you could have it eating out of your hand if you got really close to it spiritually. Motor boats in those days didn't have clutches, and you would make a landing by shutting off the motor at the proper time and coasting in with a dead rudder. But there was a way of reversing them, if you learned the trick, by cutting the switch and putting it on again exactly on the final dying revolution of the flywheel, so that it would kick back against compression and begin reversing. Approaching a dock in a strong following breeze, it was difficult to slow up sufficiently by the ordinary coasting method, and if a boy felt he had complete mastery over his motor, he was tempted to keep it running beyond its time and then reverse it a few feet from the dock. It took a cool nerve, because if you threw the switch a twentieth of a second too soon you could catch the flywheel when it still had speed enough to go up past center, and the boat would leap ahead, charging bull-fashion at the dock.

We had a good week at the camp. The bass were biting well and the sun shone endlessly, day after day. We would be tired at night and lie down in the accumulated heat of the little bedrooms after the long hot day and the breeze would stir almost imperceptibly outside and the smell of the swamp drift in through the rusty screens. Sleep would come easily and in the morning the red squirrel would be on the roof tapping out his gay routine. I kept remembering everything, lying in bed in the mornings—the small steamboat that had a long rounded stern like the lip of a Ubangi,[1] and how quietly she ran on the moonlight sails, when the older boys played their mandolins and the girls sang and we ate doughnuts dipped in sugar, and how sweet the music was on the water in the shining night, and what it had felt like to think about girls then. After breakfast we would go up to the store and the things were in the same place—the minnows in a bottle, the plugs and spinners disarranged and pawed over by the youngsters from the boys' camp, the fig newtons and the Beeman's gum. Outside, the road was tarred and cars stood in front of the store. Inside, all was just as it had always been, except there was more Coca-Cola and not so much Moxie and root beer and birch beer and sarsaparilla. We would walk out with a bottle

---

[1] A member of an African tribe whose lower lip is stretched around a wooden, plate-like disk.

of pop apiece and sometimes the pop would backfire up our noses and hurt. We explored the streams, quietly, where the turtles slid off the sunny logs and dug their way into the soft bottom; and we lay on the town wharf and fed worms to the tame bass. Everywhere we went I had trouble making out which was I, the one walking at my side, the one walking in my pants.

One afternoon while we were there at that lake a thunderstorm   12
came up. It was like the revival of an old melodrama that I had seen long ago with childish awe. The second-act climax of the drama of the electrical disturbance over a lake in America had not changed in any important respect. This was the big scene, still the big scene. The whole thing was so familiar, the first feeling of oppression and heat and a general air around camp of not wanting to go very far away. In midafternoon (it was all the same) a curious darkening of the sky, and a lull in everything that had made life tick; and then the way the boats suddenly swung the other way at their moorings with the coming of a breeze out of the new quarter, and the premonitory rumble. Then the kettle drum, then the snare, then the bass drum and cymbals, then crackling light against the dark, and the gods grinning and licking their chops in the hills. Afterward the calm, the rain steadily rustling in the calm lake, the return of light and hope and spirits, and the campers running out in joy and relief to go swimming in the rain, their bright cries perpetuating the deathless joke about how they were getting simply drenched, and the children screaming with delight at the new sensation of bathing in the rain, and the joke about getting drenched linking the generations in a strong in-destructible chain. And the comedian who waded in carrying an um-brella.

When the others went swimming my son said he was going in too.   13
He pulled his dripping trunks from the line where they had hung all through the shower, and wrung them out. Languidly, and with no thought of going in, I watched him, his hard little body, skinny and bare, saw him wince slightly as he pulled up around his vitals the small, soggy, icy garment. As he buckled the swollen belt suddenly my groin felt the chill of death.

Questions for Study and Discussion

1. The first three paragraphs serve as an introduction to White's essay. Taken together, how do they prepare for what follows? What does each paragraph contribute?

2. White returns to the lake wondering whether it will be as he remembers it from his childhood vacations. What remains the same? What significance

does White attach to the changes in the road, the waitresses, and the out-board-motor boats?

3. In paragraph 4 White tells us, "I began to sustain the illusion that [my son] was I, and therefore, by simple transposition, that I was my father." What first prompts this "illusion"? Where else does White refer to it? How does it affect your understanding of what the week at the lake means to White?

4. In paragraph 12 White describes a late afternoon thunderstorm at the lake. How does White organize his description? What does the metaphor of the old melodrama contribute to that description?

5. What is the tone of this essay, and what does it reveal about White's attitude toward his experience? Has he undergone a process of self-discovery? Give examples to support your answer.

6. The closing sentence takes many readers by surprise. Why did White feel the "chill of death"? Has he prepared for this surprise earlier in the essay? If so, where?

Writing Topics

1. Have you ever returned to a place you once knew well but have not seen in years—a house or a city where you once lived, a school you once attended, a favorite vacation spot? What memories did the visit bring back? Did you, like White, find that little had changed and feel that time had stood still, or were there many changes? If possible, you might make such a visit, to reflect on what has happened to the place—and to you—since you were last there.

2. What, for you, is the ideal vacation? Where would you go and what would you do? What do you hope and expect that a good vacation will do for you?

3. Write an essay in which you discuss death and when you first became aware of your own mortality.

JEAN SHEPHERD

Actor, radio announcer, humorist, and writer, Jean Shepherd was born in 1929 in Chicago. As an actor he has had four one-man shows and has appeared in off-Broadway plays, and as an announcer he has worked for radio stations in Cincinnati, Philadelphia, and New York. Shepherd has also contributed columns to the *Village Voice* (1960–1967) and to *Car and Driver* (1968–1977), as well as prize-winning fiction to *Playboy*. His published works include *The America of George Ade* (1961); *In God We Trust: All Others Pay Cash* (1967); *Wanda Hickey's Night of Golden Memories and Other Disasters* (1972); *The Ferrari in the Bedroom* (1973); *The Phantom of the Open Hearth* (1977); and *A Fistful of Fig Newtons* (1981).

In the following essay, Shepherd takes us along as he relives a not-so-easily forgotten blind date. In telling his story he displays his considerable talent for evoking a sense of drama, pathos, and humor.

The Endless Streetcar Ride into the Night, and the Tinfoil Noose

Mewling, puking babes. That's the way we all start. Damply cling- 1
ing to someone's shoulder, burping weakly, clawing our way into life. *All* of us. Then gradually, surely, we begin to divide into two streams, all marching together up that long yellow brick road of life, but on opposite sides of the street. One crowd goes on to become the Official people, peering out at us from television screens; magazine covers. They are forever appearing in newsreels, carrying attaché cases, surrounded by banks of microphones while the world waits for their decisions and state-ments. And the rest of us go on to become . . . just us.

They are the Prime Ministers, the Presidents, Cabinet members, 2
Stars, dynamic molders of the Universe, while we remain forever the onlookers, the applauders of their real lives.

Forever down in the dark dungeons of our souls we ask ourselves: 3

"How did they get away from me? When did I make that first 4
misstep that took me forever to the wrong side of the street, to become eternally part of the accursed, anonymous Audience?"

It seems like one minute we're all playing around back of the garage, 5
kicking tin cans and yelling at girls, and the next instant you find yourself doomed to exist as an office boy in the Mail Room of Life, while another ex-mewling, puking babe sends down Dicta, says "No comment" to the Press, and lives a real, genuine *Life* on the screen of the world.

104

Countless sufferers at this hour are spending billions of dollars and   6
endless man hours lying on analysts' couches, trying to pinpoint the exact
moment that they stepped off the track and into the bushes forever.

It all hinges on one sinister reality that is rarely mentioned, no   7
doubt due to its implacable, irreversible inevitability. These decisions
cannot be changed, no matter how many brightly cheerful, buoyantly
optimistic books on HOW TO ACHIEVE A RICHER, FULLER, MORE
BOUNTIFUL LIFE or SEVEN MAGIC GOLDEN KEYS TO INSTANT DYNAMIC
SUCCESS or THE SECRET OF HOW TO BECOME A BILLIONAIRE we read,
or how many classes are attended for instruction in handshaking, back-
slapping, grinning, and making After-Dinner speeches. Joseph Stalin was
not a Dale Carnegie graduate. He went all the way. It is an unpleasant
truth that is swallowed, if at all, like a rancid, bitter pill. A star is a star;
a numberless cipher is a numberless cipher.

Even more eerie a fact is that the Great Divide is rarely a matter   8
of talent or personality. Or even luck. Adolf Hitler had a notoriously
weak handshake. His smile was, if anything, a vapid mockery. But inevitably his star zoomed higher and higher. Cinema luminaries of the first
order are rarely blessed with even the modicum of Talent, and often their
physical beauty leaves much to be desired. What is the difference between
Us and Them, We and They, the Big Ones and the great, teeming
rabble?

There are about four times in a man's life, or a woman's, too, for   9
that matter, when unexpectedly, from out of the darkness, the blazing
carbon lamp, the cosmic searchlight of Truth shines full upon them. It
is how we react to those moments that forever seals our fate. One crowd
simply puts on its sunglasses, lights another cigar, and heads for the
nearest plush French restaurant in the jazziest section of town, sits down
and orders a drink, and ignores the whole thing. While we, the Doomed,
caught in the brilliant glare of illumination, see ourselves inescapably for
what we are, and from that day on skulk in the weeds, hoping no one
else will spot us.

Those moments happen when we are least able to fend them off. I   10
caught the first one full in the face when I was fourteen. The fourteenth
summer is a magic one for all kids. You have just slid out of the pupa
stage, leaving your old baby skin behind, and have not yet become a
grizzled, hardened, tax-paying beetle. At fourteen you are made of cel-
lophane. You curl easily and everyone can see through you.

When I was fourteen, Life was flowing through me in a deep, rich   11
torrent of Castoria. How did I know that the first rocks were just ahead,
and I was about to have my keel ripped out on the reef? Sometimes you
feel as though you are alone in a rented rowboat, bailing like mad in the

darkness with a leaky bailing can. It is important to know that there are
at least two billion other ciphers in the same boat, bailing with the same
leaky can. They all think they are alone and are crossed with an evil
star. They are right.

I'm fourteen years old, in my sophomore year at high school. One
day Schwartz, my purported best friend, sidled up to me edgily outside
of school while we were waiting on the steps to come in after lunch. He
proceeded to outline his plan:

"Helen's old man won't let me take her out on a date on Saturday
night unless I get a date for her girlfriend. A double date. The old coot
figures, I guess, that if there are four of us there won't be no monkey
business. Well, how about it? Do you want to go on a blind date with
this chick? I never seen her."

Well. For years I had this principle—absolutely *no* blind dates. I
was a man of perception and taste, and life was short. But there is a time
in your life when you have to stop taking and begin to give just a little.
For the first time the warmth of sweet Human Charity brought the roses
to my cheeks. After all, Schwartz was my friend. It was little enough to
do, have a blind date with some no doubt skinny, pimply girl for your
best friend. I would do it for Schwartz. He would do as much for me.

"Okay. Okay, Schwartz."

Then followed the usual ribald remarks, feckless boasting, and dirty
jokes about dates in general and girls in particular. It was decided that
next Saturday we would go all the way. I had a morning paper route at
the time, and my life savings stood at about $1.80. I was all set to blow
it on one big night.

I will never forget that particular Saturday as long as I live. The
air was as soft as the finest of spun silk. The scent of lilacs hung heavy.
The catalpa trees rustled in the early evening breeze from off the Lake.
The inner Me itched in that nameless way, that indescribable way that
only the fourteen-year-old Male fully knows.

All that afternoon I had carefully gone over my wardrobe to select
the proper symphony of sartorial brilliance. That night I set out wearing
my magnificent electric blue sport coat, whose shoulders were so wide
that they hung out over my frame like vast, drooping eaves, so wide I
had difficulty going through an ordinary door head-on. The electric blue
sport coat that draped voluminously almost to my knees, its wide lapels
flapping soundlessly in the slightest breeze. My pleated gray flannel slacks
began just below my breastbone and indeed chafed my armpits. High-
belted, cascading down finally to grasp my ankles in a vise-like grip. My
tie, indeed one of my most prized possessions, had been a gift from my
Aunt Glenn upon the state occasion of graduation from eighth grade. It

was of a beautiful silky fabric, silvery pearly colored, four inches wide at the fulcrum, and of such a length to endanger occasionally my zipper in moments of haste. Hand-painted upon it was a magnificent blood-red snail.

I had spent fully two hours carefully arranging and rearranging my great mop of wavy hair, into which I had rubbed fully a pound and a half of Greasy Kid Stuff.   19

Helen and Schwartz waited on the corner under the streetlight at the streetcar stop near Junie Jo's home. Her name was Junie Jo Prewitt. I won't forget it quickly, although she has, no doubt, forgotten mine. I walked down the dark street alone, past houses set back off the street, through the darkness, past privet hedges, under elm trees, through air rich and ripe with promise. Her house stood back from the street even farther than the others. It sort of crouched in the darkness, looking out at me, kneeling. Pregnant with Girldom. A real Girlfriend house.   20

The first faint touch of nervousness filtered through the marrow of my skullbone as I knocked on the door of the screen-enclosed porch. No answer. I knocked again, louder. Through the murky screens I could see faint lights in the house itself. Still no answer. Then I found a small doorbell button buried in the sash. I pressed. From far off in the bowels of the house I heard two chimes "Bong" politely. It sure didn't sound like our doorbell. We had a real ripper that went off like a broken buzz saw, more of a BRRRAAAAKKK than a muffled Bong. This was a rich people's doorbell.   21

The door opened and there stood a real, genuine, gold-plated Father: potbelly, underwear shirt, suspenders, and all.   22

"Well?" he asked.   23

For one blinding moment of embarrassment I couldn't remember her name. After all, she was a blind date. I couldn't just say: 24

"I'm here to pick up some girl."   25

He turned back into the house and hollered: 26

"JUNIE JO! SOME KID'S HERE!"   27

"Heh, heh. . . ." I countered.   28

He led me into the living room. It was an itchy house, sticky stucco walls of a dull orange color, and all over the floor this Oriental rug with the design crawling around, making loops and sworls. I sat on an overstuffed chair covered in stiff green mohair that scratched even through my slacks. Little twisty bridge lamps stood everywhere. I instantly began to sweat down the back of my clean white shirt. Like I said, it was a very itchy house. It had little lamps sticking out of the walls that looked like phony candles, with phony glass orange flames. The rug started moaning to itself.   29

I sat on the edge of the chair and tried to talk to this Father. He   30
was a Cub fan. We struggled under water for what seemed like an hour
and a half, when suddenly I heard someone coming down the stairs. First
the feet; then those legs, and there she was. She was magnificent! The
greatest-looking girl I ever saw in my life! I have hit the double jackpot!
And on a blind date! Great Scot!

My senses actually reeled as I clutched the arm of that bilge-green   31
chair for support. Junie Jo Prewitt made Cleopatra look like a Girl Scout!

Five minutes later we are sitting in the streetcar, heading toward   32
the bowling alley. I am sitting next to the most fantastic creation in the
Feminine department known to Western man. There are the four of us
in that long, yellow-lit streetcar. No one else was aboard; just us four.
I, naturally, being a trained gentleman, sat on the aisle to protect her
from candy wrappers and cigar butts and such. Directly ahead of me, also
on the aisle, sat Schwartz, his arm already flung affectionately in a death
grip around Helen's neck as we boomed and rattled through the night.

I casually flung my right foot up onto my left knee so that she could   33
see my crepe-soled, perforated, wind-toed, Scotch bluchers with the two-
toned laces. I started to work my famous charm on her. Casually, with
my practiced offhand, cynical, cutting, sardonic humor I told her about
how my Old Man had cracked the block in the Oldsmobile, how the
White Sox were going to have a good year this year, how my kid brother
wet his pants when he saw a snake, how I figured it was going to rain,
what a great guy Schwartz was, what a good second baseman I was, how
I figured I might go out for football. On and on I rolled, like Old Man
River, pausing significantly for her to pick up the conversation. Nothing.

Ahead of us Schwartz and Helen were almost indistinguishable one   34
from the other. They giggled, bit each other's ears, whispered, clasped
hands, and in general made me itch even more.

From time to time Junie Jo would bend forward stiffly from the waist   35
and say something I could never quite catch into Helen's right ear.

I told her my great story of the time that Uncle Carl lost his false   36
teeth down the airshaft. Still nothing. Out of the corner of my eye I
could see that she had her coat collar turned up, hiding most of her face
as she sat silently, looking forward past Helen Weathers into nothingness.

I told her about this old lady on my paper route who chews tobacco,   37
and roller skates in the backyard every morning. I still couldn't get through
to her. Casually I inched my right arm up over the back of the seat
behind her shoulders. The acid test. She leaned forward, avoiding my
arm, and stayed that way.

"Heh, heh, heh. . . ."   38

As nonchalantly as I could, I retrieved it, battling a giant cramp   39
in my right shoulder blade. I sat in silence for a few seconds, sweating
heavily as ahead Schwartz and Helen are going at it hot and heavy.

It was then that I became aware of someone saying something to   40
me. It was an empty car. There was no one else but us. I glanced around,
and there it was. Above us a line of car cards looked down on the empty
streetcar. One was speaking directly to me, to me alone.

DO YOU OFFEND?

Do I *offend*?!   41

With no warning, from up near the front of the car where the   42
motorman is steering I see this thing coming down the aisle directly
toward *me*. It's coming closer and closer. I can't escape it. It's this blinding, fantastic, brilliant, screaming blue light. I am spread-eagled in it.
There's a pin sticking through my thorax. I see it all now.

I AM THE BLIND DATE!   43

ME!!   44

I'M the one they're being nice to!   45

I'm suddenly getting fatter, more itchy. My new shoes are like   46
bowling balls with laces; thick, rubber-crepe bowling balls. My great tie
that Aunt Glenn gave me is two feet wide, hanging down to the floor
like some crinkly tinfoil noose. My beautiful hand-painted snail is seven
feet high, sitting up on my shoulder, burping. Great Scot! It is all clear
to me in the searing white light of Truth. My friend Schwartz, I can see
him saying to Junie Jo:

"I got this crummy fat friend who never has a date. Let's give him   47
a break and. . . ."

I AM THE BLIND DATE!   48

They are being nice to *me*! She is the one who is out on a Blind   49
Date. A Blind Date that didn't make it.

In the seat ahead, the merriment rose to a crescendo. Helen tit-   50
tered; Schwartz cackled. The marble statue next to me stared gloomily
out into the darkness as our streetcar rattled on. The ride went on and
on.

I AM *THE* BLIND DATE!   51

I didn't say much the rest of the night. There wasn't much to be   52
said.

Questions for Study and Discussion

1. Shepherd develops his long narrative to illustrate his point about turning
points in life. What exactly is his point, and where is it stated? In what way
is the blind date episode a moment of truth?

2. Where does Shepherd's narrative begin?

3. What distinction does Shepherd draw between "Official people" and "just us"? Do you agree with his assessment? Explain.

4. For whom has Shepherd written this essay? How do you know?

5. What event triggers the narrator's moment of insight?

6. Explain Shepherd's title. What is the "tinfoil noose"?

7. What do you know of the narrator from the story he tells? What do you learn of his appearance? His personality?

8. To what extent does Shepherd use figurative language in his essay? Cite several examples of metaphors and similes. What do these figures add to his style?

Writing Topics

1. Shepherd believes that people on average experience four moments of truth in a lifetime. Moreover, he states that "it is how we react to those moments that forever seals our fate." From your own experiences, recount one such moment in your life and how you dealt with it. In retrospect, how do you think you handled the situation?

2. Write an essay in which you argue for or against Shepherd's assertion that Official people are insensitive to or can simply ignore moments of truth.

ROBERT FROST

Robert Frost (1874–1963) was born in San Francisco but moved with his family to Massachusetts when he was eleven, and he became a New Englander through and through. He attended Dartmouth and Harvard briefly, spent some time as a millworker and schoolteacher, and then in 1900 moved to a farm in New Hampshire, where he lived most of the rest of his life. From 1912 to 1915 he lived in England, where he published two books of poems that brought him his first critical recognition. He returned to the United States a popular poet and soon became a highly influential one, to teach at Amherst, Dartmouth, Harvard, and the University of Michigan and to be awarded numerous prizes and honors. Among his most celebrated poems are "The Tuft of Flowers" (1913), "Birches" (1916), and "Fire and Ice" (1923); they can be found in *Complete Poems* (1949).

Completed in 1916, "The Road Not Taken" has become a cultural symbol of the difficulty and consequences of making a choice in life. Ostensibly about the choice between two roads that diverge in the woods, the poem, of course, implies much more. As Frost himself said, "I'm always saying something that's just the edge of something more."

The Road Not Taken

Two roads diverged in a yellow wood,
And sorry I could not travel both
And be one traveler, long I stood
And looked down one as far as I could
To where it bent in the undergrowth;   5

Then took the other, as just as fair,
And having perhaps the better claim,
Because it was grassy and wanted wear;
Though as for that the passing there
Had worn them really about the same,   10

And both that morning equally lay
In leaves no step had trodden black.
Oh, I kept the first for another day!
Yet knowing how way leads on to way,
I doubted if I should ever come back.   15

I shall be telling this with a sigh
Somewhere ages and ages hence:
Two roads diverged in a wood, and I—
I took the one less traveled by,
And that has made all the difference.   20

Questions for Study and Discussion

1. Why did the speaker in the poem make the decision that he did? Was it a difficult choice to make? What things did the speaker consider when making his decision?

2. Can the speaker in the poem really tell that he made the right decision? Explain.

3. Metaphorically, what do the roads and the yellow wood signify?

4. What, if anything, does Frost's poem reveal about turning points, those significant decisions that alter the course of our lives?

Writing Topics

1. Compare the sentiments expressed in Frost's twenty-line poem to those expressed in Langston Hughes's autobiographical essay "Salvation" (pp. 89–91). In what ways are they similar; in what ways different?

2. By the time you enter college you have been exposed to poetry and have formed an opinion about it—you either like it, dislike it, or are merely indifferent to it. What is it in poetry, or your own attitudes, that causes you to respond to it as you do?

3. Write an essay in which you examine a choice or decision you made some time ago. Would you make the same choice again? What do you know now that you didn't know then?

2 Family and Friends

Without a family, man, alone in the world, trembles with the cold.
ANDRÉ MAUROIS

If we judge love by its results, it resembles hatred more than friendship.
FRANÇOIS DE LA ROCHEFOUCAULD

Wishing to be friends is quick work, but friendship is a slow-ripening fruit.
ARISTOTLE

Family Ties

S. I. HAYAKAWA

He has been president of San Francisco State College and a United States Senator, but Samuel Ichiyé Hayakawa has been most influential as a scholar and teacher of general semantics, the study of the meanings of words and how they influence our lives. Born in Vancouver, Canada, in 1906, Hayakawa attended the University of Manitoba, McGill University, and the University of Wisconsin before beginning a career as a professor of English. Since then he has written several books, including *Language in Thought and Action* (1941), which has been widely used as a textbook. Hayakawa has also written many articles on a wide range of social and personal issues, making frequent reference to the use of general semantics in everyday life.

This is one of those articles. It was written for *McCall's* magazine, which is read mainly by women, many of them mothers—some of them no doubt faced with the same dilemma as the Hayakawas, whose son Mark was born with Down's syndrome, a form of retardation. What happened next, and why, is the subject of "Our Son Mark."

Our Son Mark

It was a terrible blow for us to discover that we had brought a retarded child into the world. My wife and I had had no previous acquaintance with the problems of retardation—not even with the words to discuss it. Only such words as imbecile, idiot, and moron came to mind. And the prevailing opinion was that such a child must be "put away," to live out his life in an institution.

Mark was born with Down's syndrome, popularly known as mongolism. The prognosis for his ever reaching anything approaching normality was hopeless. Medical authorities advised us that he would show some mental development, but the progress would be painfully slow and he would never reach an adolescent's mental age. We could do nothing about it, they said. They sympathetically but firmly advised us to find a

115

private institution that would take him. To get him into a public institution, they said, would require a waiting period of five years. To keep him at home for this length of time, they warned, would have a disastrous effect on our family.

That was twenty-seven years ago. In that time, Mark has never been "put away." He has lived at home. The only institution he sees regularly is the workshop he attends, a special workshop for retarded adults. He is as much a part of the family as his mother, his older brother, his younger sister, his father, or our longtime housekeeper and friend, Daisy Rosebourgh.

Mark has contributed to our stability and serenity. His retardation has brought us grief, but we did not go on dwelling on what might have been, and we have been rewarded by finding much good in things the way they are. From the beginning, we have enjoyed Mark for his delightful self. He has never seemed like a burden. He was an "easy" baby, quiet, friendly, and passive; but he needed a baby's care for a long time. It was easy to be patient with him, although I must say that some of his stages, such as his love of making chaos, as we called it, by pulling all the books he could reach off the shelves, lasted much longer than normal children's.

Mark seems more capable of accepting things as they are than his immediate relatives; his mental limitation has given him a capacity for contentment, a focus on the present moment, which is often enviable. His world may be circumscribed, but it is a happy and bright one. His enjoyment of simple experiences—swimming, food, birthday candles, sports-car rides, and cuddly cats—has that directness and intensity so many philosophers recommend to all of us.

Mark's contentment has been a happy contribution to our family, and the challenge of communicating with him, of doing things we can all enjoy, has drawn the family together. And seeing Mark's communicative processes develop in slow motion has taught me much about the process in all children.

Fortunately Mark was born at a time when a whole generation of parents of retarded children had begun to question the accepted dogmas about retardation. Whatever they were told by their physicians about their children, parents began to ask: "Is that so? Let's see." For what is meant by "retarded child"? There are different kinds of retardation. Retarded child No. 1 is not retarded child No. 2, or 3, or 4. Down's syndrome is one condition, while brain damage is something else. There are different degrees of retardation, just as there are different kinds of brain damage. No two retarded children are exactly alike in all respects. Institutional care *does* turn out to be the best answer for some kinds of

retarded children or some family situations. The point is that one observes and reacts to the *specific* case and circumstances rather than to the
generalization.

This sort of attitude has helped public understanding of the nature   8
and problems of retardation to become much deeper and more widespread. It's hard to believe now that it was "definitely known" twenty
years ago that institutionalization was the "only way." We were told that
a retarded child could not be kept at home because "it would not be fair
to the other children." The family would not be able to stand the stress.
"Everybody" believed these things and repeated them, to comfort and
guide the parents of the retarded.

We did not, of course, lightly disregard the well-meant advice of   9
university neurologists and their social-worker teams, for they had had
much experience and we were new at this shattering experience. But our
general semantics, or our parental feelings, made us aware that their
reaction to Mark was to a generalization, while to us he was an individual.
They might have a valid generalization about statistical stresses on statistical families, but they knew virtually nothing about our particular
family and its evaluative processes.

Mark was eight months old before we were told he was retarded.   10
Of course we had known that he was slower than the average child in
smiling, in sitting up, in responding to others around him. Having had
one child who was extraordinarily ahead of such schedules, we simply
thought that Mark was at the other end of the average range.

In the course of his baby checkups, at home and while traveling,   11
we had seen three different pediatricians. None of them gave us the
slightest indication that all was not well. Perhaps they were made uncertain by the fact that Mark, with his part Japanese parentage, had a
right to have "mongolian" features. Or perhaps this news is as hard for
a pediatrician to tell as it is for parents to hear, and they kept putting
off the job of telling us. Finally, Mark's doctor did suggest a neurologist,
indicating what his fears were, and made an appointment.

It was Marge who bore the brunt of the first diagnosis and accom-   12
panying advice, given at the university hospital at a time when I had to
be out of town. Stunned and crushed, she was told: "Your husband is a
professional man. You can't keep a child like this at home."

"But he lives on love," she protested.   13

"Don't your other children live on love, too?" the social worker   14
asked.

Grief-stricken as she was, my wife was still able to recognize a non   15
sequitur. One does not lessen the love for one's children by dividing it
among several.

"What can I read to find out more about his condition and how to   16
take care of him?" Marge asked.

"You can't get help from a book," answered the social worker. "You   17
must put him away."

Today this sounds like dialogue from the Dark Ages. And it *was*   18
the Dark Ages. Today professional advice runs generally in the opposite
direction: "Keep your retarded child at home if it's at all possible."

It was parents who led the way: They organized into parents' groups;   19
they pointed out the need for preschools, schools, diagnostic centers,
work-training centers, and sheltered workshops to serve the children who
were being cared for at home; they worked to get these services, which
are now being provided in increasing numbers. But the needs are a long
way from being fully met.

Yet even now the cost in money—not to mention the cost in   20
human terms—is much less if the child is kept at home than if he is sent
to the institutions in which children are put away. And many of the
retarded are living useful and independent lives, which would never have
been thought possible for them.

But for us at that time, as for other parents who were unknowingly   21
pioneering new ways for the retarded, it was a matter of going along from
day to day, learning, observing, and saying, "Let's see."

There was one more frightening hurdle for our family to get over.   22
On that traumatic day Marge got the diagnosis, the doctor told her that
it was too risky for us to have any more children, that there was a fifty
percent chance of our having another mongoloid child. In those days,
nothing was known of the cause of mongolism. There were many theories. Now, at least, it is known to be caused by the presence of an extra
chromosome, a fault of cell division. But the question "Why does it
happen?" had not yet been answered.

Today, genetic counseling is available to guide parents as to the   23
probabilities of recurrence on a scientific basis. We were flying blind.
With the help of a doctor friend, we plunged into medical books and
discovered that the doctor who gave us the advice was flying just as blind
as we were. No evidence could be found for the fifty percent odds. Although there did seem to be some danger of recurrence, we estimated
that the probabilities were with us. We took the risk and won.

Our daughter, Wynne, is now twenty-five. She started as Mark's   24
baby sister, soon passed him in every way, and really helped bring him
up. The fact that she had a retarded brother must have contributed at
least something to the fact that she is at once delightfully playful and
mature, observant, and understanding. She has a fine relationship with
her two brothers.

Both Wynne and Alan, Mark's older brother, have participated, with patience and delight, in Mark's development. They have shown remarkable ingenuity in instructing and amusing him. On one occasion, when Mark was not drinking his milk, Alan called him to his place at the table and said, "I'm a service station. What kind of car are you?" Mark, quickly entering into the make-believe, said, "Pord." 25

Alan: "Shall I fill her up?" 26

Mark: "Yes." 27

Alan: "Ethyl or regular?" 28

Mark: "Reg'lar." 29

Alan (bringing the glass to Mark's mouth): "Here you are." 30

When Mark finished his glass of milk, Alan asked him, "Do you want your windshield cleaned?" Then, taking a napkin, he rubbed it briskly across Mark's face, while Mark grinned with delight. This routine became a regular game for many weeks. 31

Alan and Wynne interpret and explain Mark to their friends, but never once have I heard them apologize for him or deprecate him. It is almost as if they judge the quality of other people by how they react to Mark. They think he is "great," and expect their friends to think so too. 32

Their affection and understanding were shown when Wynne flew to Oregon with Mark to visit Alan and his wife, Cynthea, who went to college there. Wynne described the whole reunion as "tremendous" and especially enjoyed Mark's delight in the trip. 33

"He was great on the plane," she recalls. "He didn't cause any trouble except that he rang the bell for the stewardess a couple of times when he didn't need anything. He was so great that I was going to send him back on the plane alone. He would have enjoyed that." But she didn't, finally, because she didn't trust others to be able to understand his speech or to know how to treat him without her there to give them clues. 34

Mark looks reasonably normal. He is small for his age (about five feet tall) and childlike. Anyone who is aware of these matters would recognize in him some of the characteristic symptomatic features, but they are not extreme. His almost incomprehensible speech, which few besides his family and teachers can understand, is his most obvious sign of retardation. 35

Mark fortunately does not notice any stares of curiosity he may attract. To imagine how one looks in the eyes of others takes a level of awareness that appears to be beyond him. Hence he is extremely direct and totally without self-consciousness. 36

I have seen him come into our living room, walk up to a woman he has never seen before, and kiss her in response to a genuinely friendly 37 greeting. Since few of us are accustomed to such directness of expression—especially the expression of affection—the people to whom this has happened are deeply moved.

Like other children, Mark responds to the evaluations of others. In 38 our family, he is accepted just as he is. Because others have always treated him as an individual, a valued individual, he feels good about himself, and, consequently, he is good to live with. In every situation between parent and child or between children, evaluations are involved—and these interact on each other. Certainly, having Mark at home has helped us be more aware and be more flexible in our evaluations.

This kind of sensitivity must have carried over into relations be- 39 tween the two normal children, because I cannot remember a single real fight or a really nasty incident between Alan and Wynne. It's as if their readiness to try to understand Mark extended into a general method of dealing with people. And I think Marge and I found the same thing happening to us, so that we became more understanding with Alan and Wynne than we might otherwise have been. If we had time and patience for Mark, why not for the children who were quick and able? We knew we could do serious damage to Mark by expecting too much of him and being disappointed. But how easy it is to expect too much of bright children and how quickly they feel your disappointment! Seeing Mark's slow, slow progress certainly gave us real appreciation of the marvelous perception and quick learning processes of the other two, so that all we had to do was open our eyes and our ears, and listen and enjoy them.

I don't want to sound as if we were never impatient or obtuse as 40 parents. We were, of course. But parents need to be accepted as they are, too. And I think our children—bless their hearts—were reasonably able to do so.

With Mark, it was easy to feel surprise and delight at any of his 41 accomplishments. He cannot read and will never be able to. But he can pick out on request almost any record from his huge collection—Fleetwood Mac, or the Rolling Stones, or Christmas carols—because he knows so well what each record looks like. Once we were discussing the forthcoming marriage of some friends of ours, and Mark disappeared into his playroom to bring out, a few minutes later, a record with the song "A House, a Car, and a Wedding Ring."

His love of music enables him to figure out how to operate almost 42 any record changer or hi-fi set. He never tries to force a piece of machinery because he cannot figure out how it works, as brighter people often do. And in a strange hotel room, with a TV set of unknown make, it is Mark—not Marge or I—who figures out how to turn it on and get a clear picture. As Alan once remarked: "Mark may be retarded, but he's not stupid!"

Of course, it has not all been easy—but when has easiness been 43
the test of the value of anything? To us, the difficult problems that must be faced in the future only emphasize the value of Mark as a person.

What does that future hold for Mark? 44

He will never be able to be independent; he will always have to 45
live in a protected environment. His below-50 IQ reflects the fact that he cannot cope with unfamiliar situations.

Like most parents of the retarded, we are concentrating on provid- 46
ing financial security for Mark in the future, and fortunately we expect to be able to achieve this. Alan and his wife and Wynne have all offered to be guardians for Mark. It is wonderful to know they feel this way. But we hope that Mark can find a happy place in one of the new residence homes for the retarded.

The residence home is something new and promising and it fills an 47
enormous need. It is somewhat like a club, or a family, with a house-mother or manager. The residents share the work around the house, go out to work if they can, share in recreation and companionship. Away from their families, who may be overprotective and not aware of how much the retarded can do for themselves (are we not guilty of this, too!), they are able to live more fully as adults.

An indication that there is still much need for public education 48
about the retarded here in California is that there has been difficulty in renting decent houses for this kind of home. Prospective neighbors have objected. In some ways the Dark Ages are still with us; there are still fear and hostility where the retarded are concerned.

Is Mark able to work? Perhaps. He thrives on routine and enjoys 49
things others despise, like clearing the table and loading the dishwasher. To Mark, it's fun. It has been hard to develop in him the idea of work, which to so many of us is "doing what you don't want to do because you have to." We don't know yet if he could work in a restaurant loading a dishwasher. In school, he learned jobs like sorting and stacking scrap wood and operating a delightful machine that swoops the string around and ties up a bundle of wood to be sold in the supermarket. That's fun, too.

He is now in a sheltered workshop where he can get the kind— 50
the one kind—of pleasure he doesn't have much chance for. That's the pleasure of contributing something productive and useful to the outside world. He does various kinds of assembling jobs, packaging, sorting, and simple machine operations. He enjoys getting a paycheck and cashing it at the bank. He cannot count, but he takes pride in reaching for the

check in a restaurant and pulling out his wallet. And when we thank him for dinner, he glows with pleasure.

It's a strange thing to say, and I am a little startled to find myself   51
saying it, but often I feel that I wouldn't have had Mark any different.

Questions for Study and Discussion

1. The Hayakawas were warned that Mark, if kept at home, would have a "disastrous effect" on the family. Why? What effect did Mark actually have on his parents, his brother, and his sister?

2. What do you believe was Hayakawa's purpose in writing this essay? Apart from what the essay says about Mark, and about Down's syndrome, what important point does it make?

3. How did the Hayakawas' sensitivity to the uses and misuses of language affect their responses to professional advice about Mark?

4. Several times Hayakawa refers to the Dark Ages. What were the Dark Ages? Why are they relevant to Hayakawa's account?

5. Does the essay ever suggest that the Hayakawas may at times have found Mark's behavior irritating, or worse? How does this affect your response to the essay?

Writing Topics

1. Sometimes it is wise to accept and follow expert advice. At other times it may be necessary to disregard such advice and make one's own decision. Have you or another member of your family ever deliberately gone against an authoritative opinion? Recount the episode, and say whether on reflection you still think the decision was a good one.

2. What is now known about Down's syndrome—its cause, its treatment, its risks?

3. According to many books, magazine articles, and television documentaries, the American family is "in trouble." Do you agree? What exactly does such a statement mean to you? Is it a meaningful statement at all?

ANTHONY BRANDT

Anthony Brandt was born in Cranford, New Jersey, in 1936 and studied at Princeton and Columbia. After a brief career in business, he became a free-lance writer and has contributed essays and poems to such magazines as the *Atlantic Monthly, Prairie Schooner,* and the *New York Quarterly.* He published *Reality Police: The Experience of Insanity in America* in 1975 and is presently at work on a book about the American dream, which he says will attempt to define that dream and trace its origins and development.

As a young boy, Brandt was forced to watch his beloved grandmother slowly lose her grip on reality and gradually slide into senility. Thirty years later his mother, too, has had to be consigned to a nursing home, no longer able to take care of herself. In the following memoir, first published in the *Atlantic Monthly,* Brandt describes the two cases and what they have meant to him.

My Grandmother: A Rite of Passage

Some things that happen to us can't be borne, with the paradoxical result that we carry them on our backs the rest of our lives. I have been half obsessed for almost thirty years with the death of my grandmother. I should say with her dying: with the long and terrible changes that came at the worst time for a boy of twelve and thirteen, going through his own difficult changes. It felt like and perhaps was the equivalent of a puberty rite: dark, frightening, aboriginal, an obscure emotional exchange between old and young. It has become part of my character. 1

I grew up in New Jersey in a suburban town where my brother still lives and practices law. One might best describe it as quiet, protected, and green; it was no preparation for death. Tall, graceful elm trees lined both sides of the street where we lived. My father's brother-in-law, a contractor, built our house; we moved into it a year after I was born. My grandmother and grandfather (my mother's parents; they were the only grandparents who mattered) lived up the street "on the hill"; it wasn't much of a hill, the terrain in that part of New Jersey being what it is, but we could ride our sleds down the street after it snowed, and that was hilly enough. 2

Our family lived, or seemed to a young boy to live, in very stable, very ordinary patterns. My father commuted to New York every day, taking the Jersey Central Railroad, riding in cars that had windows you could open, getting off the train in Jersey City and taking a ferry to Manhattan. He held the same job in the same company for more than 3 thirty years. The son of Swedish immigrants, he was a funny man who could wiggle his ears without raising his eyebrows and made up the most dreadful puns. When he wasn't being funny he was quiet, the newspaper his shield and companion, or the *Saturday Evening Post,* which he brought home without fail every Wednesday evening, or *Life,* which he brought home Fridays. It was hard to break through the quiet and the humor, and after he died my mother said, as much puzzled as disturbed, that she hardly knew him at all.

She, the backbone of the family, was fierce, stern, the kind of person who can cow you with a glance. My brother and I, and my cousins, were all a little in awe of her. The ruling passion in her life was to protect her family; she lived in a set of concentric circles, sons and husband the closest, then nieces, nephews, brothers, parents, then more distant relatives, and outside that a few friends, very few. No one and nothing else existed for her; she had no interest in politics, art, history, or even the price of eggs. "Fierce" is the best word for her, or single-minded. In those days (I was born in 1936) polio was every parent's bugbear; she, to keep my brother and me away from places where the disease was supposed to be communicated, particularly swimming pools, took us every summer for the entire summer to the Jersey shore, first to her parents' cottage, later to a little cottage she and my father bought. She did that even though it meant being separated from my father for nearly three months, having nobody to talk to, having to handle my brother and me on her own. She hated it, she told us years later, but she did it: fiercely. Or there's the story of one of my cousins who got pregnant when she was sixteen or seventeen; my mother took her into our house, managed somehow to hide her condition from the neighbors, then, after the birth, arranged privately to have the child adopted by a family the doctor recommended, all this being done without consulting the proper authorities, and for the rest of her life never told a single person how she made these arrangements or where she had placed the child. She was a genuine primitive, like some tough old peasant woman. Yet her name was Grace, her nickname Bunny; if you saw through the fierceness, you understood that it was a version of love.

Her mother, my grandmother, seemed anything but fierce. One of our weekly routines was Sunday dinner at their house on the hill, some five or six houses from ours. When I was very young, before World War II, the house had a mansard roof, a barn in the back, lots of yard space, lots of rooms inside, and a cherry tree. I thought it was a palace. Actually it was rather small, and became smaller when my grandmother insisted on tearing down the mansard roof and replacing it with a conventional peaked roof; the house lost three attic rooms in the process. Sunday dinner was invariably roast beef or chicken or leg of lamb with mashed potatoes and vegetables, standard American fare but cooked by my grandparents' Polish maid, Josephine, not by my grandmother. Josephine made wonderful pies in an old cast-iron coal stove and used to let me tie her with string to the kitchen sink. My grandfather was a gentle man who smoked a pipe, had a bristly reddish moustache, and always seemed to wind up paying everybody else's debts in the family; my mother worshipped him. There were usually lots of uncles at these meals, and they were a playful bunch. I have a very early memory of two of them tossing me back and forth between them, and another of the youngest, whose name was Don, carrying me on his shoulders into the surf. I also remember my grandmother presiding at these meals. She was gray-haired and benign.

Later they sold that house. My benign grandmother, I've been told 6 since, was in fact a restless, unsatisfied woman; changing the roof line, moving from house to house, were her ways of expressing that dissatisfaction. In the next house, I think it was, my grandfather died; my grandmother moved again, then again, and then to a house down the street, at the bottom of the hill this time, and there I got to know her better. I was nine or ten years old. She let me throw a tennis ball against the side of the house for hours at a time; the noise must have been terribly aggravating. She cooked lunch for me and used to make pancakes the size of dinner plates, and corn fritters. She also made me a whole set of yarn figures a few inches long, rolling yarn around her hand, taking the roll and tying off arms, legs, and a head, then sewing a face onto the head with black thread. I played with these and an odd assortment of hand-me-down toy soldiers for long afternoons, setting up wars, football games, contests of all kinds, and designating particular yarn figures as customary heroes. Together we played a spelling game: I'd be on the floor playing with the yarn figures, she'd be writing a letter and ask me how to spell "appreciate" (it was always that word), and I'd spell it for her while she pretended to be impressed with my spelling ability and I pretended that she hadn't asked me to spell that same word a dozen times before. I was good, too, at helping her find her glasses.

One scene at this house stands out. My uncle Bob came home from 7 the war and the whole family, his young wife, other uncles, my mother and father and brother and I, gathered at the house to meet him, and he came in wearing his captain's uniform and looking to me, I swear it, like a handsome young god. In fact he was an ordinary man who spent the rest of his life selling insurance. He had been in New Guinea, a ground officer in the Air Corps, and the story I remember is of the native who came into his tent one day and took a great deal of interest in the scissors my uncle was using. The native asked in pidgin English what my uncle would require for the scissors in trade, and he jokingly said, well, how about a tentful of bananas. Sure enough, several days later two or three hundred natives came out of the jungle, huge bunches of bananas on their shoulders, and filled my uncle's tent.

Things went on this way for I don't know how long, maybe two years, maybe three. I don't want to describe it as idyllic. Youth has its problems. But this old woman who could never find her glasses was wonderful to me, a grandmother in the true likeness of one, and I couldn't understand the changes when they came. She moved again, against all advice, this time to a big, bare apartment on the other side of town. She was gradually becoming irritable and difficult, not much fun to be around. There were no more spelling games; she stopped writing letters. Because she moved I saw her less often, and her home could no longer be a haven for me. She neglected it, too; it grew dirtier and dirtier, until my mother eventually had to do her cleaning for her. 8

Then she began to see things that weren't there. A branch in the back yard became a woman, I remember, who apparently wasn't fully clothed, and a man was doing something to her, something unspeakable. She developed diabetes and my mother learned to give her insulin shots, but she wouldn't stop eating candy, the worst thing for her, and the diabetes got worse. Her face began to change, to slacken, to lose its shape and character. I didn't understand these things; arteriosclerosis, hardening of the arteries, whatever the explanation, it was only words. What I noticed was that her white hair was getting thinner and harder to control, that she herself seemed to be shrinking even as I grew, that when she looked at me I wasn't sure it was me she was seeing anymore. 9

After a few months of this, we brought her to live with us. My mother was determined to take care of her, and certain family pressures were brought to bear too. That private man my father didn't like the idea at all, but he said nothing, which was his way. And she was put in my brother's bedroom over the garage, my brother moving in with me. It was a small house, six rooms and a basement, much too small for what we had to face. 10

What we had to face was a rapid deterioration into senile dementia and the rise from beneath the surface of this smiling, kindly, white-haired old lady of something truly ugly. Whenever she was awake she called for attention, calling, calling a hundred times a day. Restless as always, she picked the bedclothes off, tore holes in sheets and pillows, took off her nightclothes and sat naked talking to herself. She hallucinated more and more frequently, addressing her dead husband, a dead brother, scolding, shouting at their apparitions. She became incontinent and smeared feces 11 on herself, the furniture, the walls. And always calling—"Bunny, where are you? Bunny, I want you!"—scolding, demanding; she could seldom remember what she wanted when my mother came. It became an important event when she fell asleep; to make sure she stayed asleep the radio was kept off, the four of us tiptoed around the house, and when I went out to close the garage door, directly under her window (it was an overhead door and had to be pulled down), I did it so slowly and carefully, half an inch at a time, that it sometimes took me a full fifteen minutes to get it down.

That my mother endured this for six months is a testimony to her strength and determination, but it was really beyond her and almost destroyed her health. My grandmother didn't often sleep through the night; she would wake up, yell, cry, a creature of disorder, a living *memento mori*,[1] and my mother would have to tend to her. The house began to smell in spite of all my mother's efforts to keep my grandmother's room clean. My father, his peace gone, brooded in his chair behind his newspaper. My brother and I fought for *Lebensraum*,[2] each of us trying to grow up in his own way. People avoided us. My uncles were living elsewhere—Miami, Cleveland, Delaware. My grandmother's two surviving sisters, who lived about ten blocks away, never came to see her. Everybody seemed to sense that something obscene was happening, and stayed away. Terrified, I stayed away, too. I heard my grandmother constantly, but in the six months she lived with us I think I went into her room only once. That was as my mother wished it. She was a nightmare, naked and filthy without warning.

After six months, at my father's insistence, after a night nurse had been hired and left, after my mother had reached her limits and beyond, my parents started looking for a nursing home, anyplace they could put her. It became a family scandal; the two sisters were outraged that my mother would consider putting her own mother in a home, there were telephone calls back and forth between them and my uncles, but of course the sisters had never come to see her themselves, and my mother never forgave them. One of my uncles finally came from Cleveland, saw what was happening, and that day they put my grandmother in a car and drove her off to the nearest state mental hospital. They brought her back the same day; desperate as they were, they couldn't leave her in hell. At last, when it had come time to go to the shore, they found a nursing home in the middle of the Pine Barrens, miles from anywhere, and kept

12

13

---

[1] A remembrance of death, usually a work of art with symbols of death or mortality, such as a skull.

[2] Living space, room for growth, development, or the like.

her there for a while. That, too, proving unsatisfactory, they put her in a small nursing home in western New Jersey, about two hours away by car. We made the drive every Sunday for the next six months, until my grandmother finally died. I always waited in the car while my mother visited her. At the funeral I refused to go into the room for one last look at the body. I was afraid of her still. The whole thing had been a subtle act of violence, a violation of the sensibilities, made all the worse by the fact that I knew it wasn't really her fault, that she was a victim of biology, of life itself. Hard knowledge for a boy just turned fourteen. She became the color of all my expectations.

Life is savage, then, and even character is insecure. Call no man   14
happy until he be dead, said the Greek lawgiver Solon. But what would a wise man say to this? In that same town in New Jersey, that town I have long since abandoned as too flat and too good to be true, my mother, thirty year older now, weighing in at ninety-two pounds, incontinent, her white hair wild about her head, sits strapped into a chair in another nursing home talking incoherently to her fellow patients and working her hands at the figures she thinks she sees moving around on the floor. It's enough to make stones weep to see this fierce, strong woman, who paid her dues, surely, ten times over, reduced to this.

Yet she is *cheerful.* This son comes to see her and she quite literally   15
babbles with delight, introduces him (as her father, her husband—the connections are burnt out) to the aides, tells him endless stories that don't make any sense at all, and *shines,* shines with a clear light that must be her soul. Care and bitterness vanish in her presence. Helpless, the victim of numerous tiny strokes—"shower strokes," the doctors call them—that are gradually destroying her brain, she has somehow achieved a radiant serenity that accepts everything that happens and incorporates and transforms it.

Is there a lesson in this? Is some pattern larger than life working   16
itself out; is this some kind of poetic justice on display, a mother balancing a grandmother, gods demonstrating reasons beyond our comprehension? It was a bitter thing to put her into that place, reeking of disinfectant, full of senile, dying old people, and I used to hate to visit her there, but as she has deteriorated she has also by sheer force of example managed to change my attitude. If she can be reconciled to all this, why can't I? It doesn't last very long, but after I've seen her, talked to her for half an hour, helped feed her, stroked her hair, I walk away amazed, as if I had been witness to a miracle.

Questions for Study and Discussion

1. What, for Brandt, is the meaning of his experiences with his grandmother and mother? How have those experiences affected his attitude toward life?

2. A "rite of passage" is a ritual associated with an important change in one's life. Brandt finds an analogy between his experiences with his grandmother and the frightening ritual in primitive societies by which the elders formally initiate the young into adulthood. How are Brandt's experiences like an initiation? How do they differ?

3. Are there any other "rites of passage" (besides Brandt's own) in the essay? Who changes, and how? What rituals, if any, are involved?

4. How much time passes between the onset of the grandmother's senility and her death? How does Brandt indicate this passage of time? As you read, did you feel that events were moving more quickly or slowly than that? Why do you suppose Brandt handles time in this way?

5. What part of this essay struck you most forcefully? Examine the writing of that passage. Can you identify any specific elements that seem to affect the total impact of the passage?

6. Brandt writes in paragraph 13, "The whole thing had been a subtle act of violence, a violation of the sensibilities." What does he mean? You may find it helpful to look up the word *sensibility* in your desk dictionary.

Writing Topics

1. Anthony Brandt describes his grandmother as an elderly, loving, playful companion. What have your grandparents been to you? What do you think a grandparent's role should be?

2. Old age may be a time of great achievement, as in the cases of the cellist Pablo Casals or the artist Georgia O'Keeffe, or it may bring senility, as with Anthony Brandt's grandmother. What is your conception of old age? Describe the people you know, or know about, who are examples of that conception.

FERN KUPFER

Fern Kupfer is the mother of Zachariah, a child severely brain-damaged from birth. She and her husband, knowing that his care precluded any semblance of normal family life, decided to institutionalize their son. Kupfer relates the ordeal of their decision in *Before and After Zachariah: A Family Story About a Different Kind of Courage* (1982). Their decision is not a very popular one currently. In the following essay, which first appeared in the "My Turn" column of *Newsweek* in 1982, Kupfer takes an open and honest look at a subject that is generally considered taboo and dealt with euphemistically if at all.

Institution Is Not a Dirty Word

I watched Phil Donahue recently. He had on mothers of handi- 1 capped children who talked about the pain and blessing of having a "special" child. As the mother of a severely handicapped six-year-old boy who cannot sit, who cannot walk, who will be in diapers all of his days, I understand the pain. The blessing part continues to elude me—notwithstanding the kind and caring people we've met through this tragedy.

What really makes my jaws clench, though, is the use of the word 2 "special." The idea that our damaged children are "special," and that we as parents were somehow picked for the role, is one of the myths that come with the territory. It's reinforced by the popular media, which present us with heartwarming images of retarded people who marry, of quadriplegics who fly airplanes, of those fortunate few who struggle out of comas to teach us about the meaning of courage and love. I like these stories myself. But, of course, inspirational tales are only one side of the story. The other side deals with the daily care of a family member who might need more than many normal families can give. Parents who endure with silent stoicism or chin-up good humor are greeted with kudos and applause. "I don't know how you do it," the well-wishers say, not realizing, of course, that no one has a choice in this matter. No one would consciously choose to have a child anything less than healthy and normal. The other truth is not spoken aloud: "Thank God, it's not me."

One mother on the Donahue show talked about how difficult it was 3 to care for her severely brain-damaged daughter, but in the end, she said serenely, "She gives much more than she takes from our family." And no, she would never institutionalize her child. She would never "put her away." For "she is my child," the woman firmly concluded as the audience clapped in approval. "I would never give her up."

Everyone always says how awful the institutions are. Don't they   4
have bars on the windows and children lying neglected in crowded wards?
Aren't all the workers sadists, taking direction from the legendary Big
Nurse? Indeed, isn't institutionalizing a child tantamount to locking him
away? Signing him out of your life forever? Isn't it proof of your failure
as a parent—one who couldn't quite measure up and love your child, no
matter what?

No, to all of the above. And love is beside the point.   5

Our child Zachariah has not lived at home for almost four years. I   6
knew when we placed him, sorry as I was, that this was the right decision,
for his care precluded any semblance of normal family life for the rest of
us. I do not think that we "gave him up," although he is cared for daily
by nurses, caseworkers, teachers and therapists, rather than by his mother
and father. When we come to visit him at his "residential facility," a
place housing fifty severely physically and mentally handicapped youngsters, we usually see him being held and rocked by a foster grandma who
has spent the better part of the afternoon singing him nursery rhymes. I
do not feel that we have "put him away." Perhaps it is just a question
of language. I told another mother who was going through the difficult
decision regarding placement for her retarded child, "Think of it as going
to boarding school rather than institutionalization." Maybe euphemisms
help ease the pain a little bit. But I've also seen enough to know that
institution need not be a dirty word.

The media still relish those institution horror stories: a page-one   7
photo of a retarded girl who was repeatedly molested by the janitor on
night duty. Oh, the newspapers have a field day with something like
that. And that is how it should be, I suppose. To protect against institutional abuse we need critical reporters with sharpened pencils and a
keen investigative eye. But there are other scenes from the institution
as well. I've seen a young caseworker talk lovingly as she changed the
diapers of a teen-age boy. I've watched as an aide put red ribbons into
the ponytail of a cerebral-palsied woman, wipe away the drool and kiss
her on the cheek. When we bring Zach back to his facility after a visit
home, the workers welcome him with hugs and notice if we gave him a
haircut or a new shirt.

The reporters don't make news out of that simple stuff. It doesn't   8
mesh with the anti-institutional bias prevalent in the last few years, or
the tendency to canonize the handicapped and their accomplishments.
This anti-institutional trend has some very frightening ramifications. We
force mental patients out into the real world of cheap welfare hotels and
call it "community placement." We parole youthful offenders because
"jails are such dangerous places to be," making our city streets dangerous

places for the law-abiding. We heap enormous guilt on the families that need, for their own survival, to put their no-longer-competent elderly in that dreaded last stop: the nursing home.

Another danger is that in a time of economic distress for all of us,   9
funds could be cut for human-service programs under the guise of anti-institutionalization. We must make sure, before we close the doors of those "awful" institutions, that we have alternative facilities to care for the clientele. The humanitarians who tell us how terrible institutions are should be wary lest they become unwilling bedfellows to conservative politicians who want to walk a tight fiscal line. It takes a lot of money to run institutions. No politician is going to say he's against the handicapped, but he can talk in sanctimonious terms about efforts to preserve the family unit, about families remaining independent and self-sufficient. Translated, this means, "You got your troubles, I got mine."

Most retarded people do not belong in institutions any more than   10
most people over sixty-five belong in nursing homes. What we need are options and alternatives for a heterogeneous population. We need group homes and halfway houses and government subsidies to families who choose to care for dependent members at home. We need accessible housing for independent handicapped people; we need to pay enough to foster-care families to show that a good home is worth paying for. We need institutions. And it shouldn't have to be a dirty word.

Questions for Study and Discussion

1. Why do Americans use the word "special" to refer to handicapped children? Why does the use of this word bother Kupfer?

2. In paragraph 5, what does Kupfer mean when she states: "And love is beside the point"?

3. In what ways do "euphemisms help ease the pain" of placing a family member in an institution? Explain the euphemisms "put her away" and "boarding school." Will we always need euphemisms if we can come to accept institutions as a real option or alternative for the care of the handicapped?

4. What arguments does Kupfer have with the media? How, according to Kupfer, have the media helped to make "institution" a dirty word?

5. Why is Kupfer frightened by the current anti-institutional trend in the United States? What solutions does she offer?

6. Where does Kupfer first introduce the issue of institutionalizing the handicapped? Why do you suppose she did not introduce it earlier in the essay? How does she lead up to the statement of her position?

7. What exactly is Kupfer arguing for? Has she managed to change your

thinking? What aspects of her argument do you find most persuasive? Least persuasive?

8. What is Kupfer's tone in this essay? Is it appropriate given her subject and purpose? Why, or why not?

Writing Topics

1. Write an essay in which you discuss to what extent our reactions to and treatment of the handicapped are "just a question of language." Is the public becoming more understanding of the situation, or do we still need to shroud the subject in euphemisms and taboos?

2. The institutionalization of family members is not the only social issue talked about little or not at all. Certainly drugs, venereal disease, divorce, homosexuality, pornography, sexual abuse, rape, and incest have been treated as taboo. Using Kupfer's essay as a model, write an essay in which you advocate a strong position about one of the above topics.

ROBERT HAYDEN

The black experience is the source of some of Robert Hayden's best poetry, from his dramatic evocation of the slave trade in "Middle Passage" to his elegy for Malcolm X in "El-Hajj Malik El-Shabazz." Alongside these, however, are many other poems about his own particular roots, "Pennsylvania gothic, Kentucky homespun, Virginia baroque," and a great-grandmother who was "a Virginia freedman's Indian bride," as he says in "Beginnings." Hayden was born in Detroit in 1913 and went to college there at Wayne State University, which was then Detroit City College. He taught English at Fisk University in Nashville from 1946 to 1969 and then returned to his native state, where he taught at the University of Michigan until his death in 1980. In his last years he was named Consultant in Poetry to the Library of Congress, the only public position by which the United States can honor its leading poets. His own selection of his best poems was published in 1975 as *Angle of Ascent*.

One of Hayden's first published poems, "Obituary," was about his father. Twenty years later, when he was nearly fifty and was himself a parent, he reflected once again on his father in "Those Winter Sundays." One hears often of labors of love; here, Hayden tells of a love that could express itself only through labor.

Those Winter Sundays

Sundays too my father got up early
and put his clothes in the blueblack cold,
then with cracked hands that ached
from labor in the weekday weather made
banked fires blaze. No one ever thanked him.   5

I'd wake and hear the cold splintering, breaking.
When the rooms were warm, he'd call,
and slowly I would rise and dress,
fearing the chronic angers of that house,

Speaking indifferently to him,   10
who had driven out the cold
and polished my good shoes as well.
What did I know, what did I know
of love's austere and lonely offices?

Questions for Study and Discussion

1. What does the speaker of the poem now realize about his father that he did not realize at an earlier age? Why do those "winter Sundays" stand out in his memory?

2. What might Hayden mean when he refers to "the chronic angers of that house"?

3. Does the poem suggest something about the relationship that often exists between parents and children? If so, what?

4. How does the speaker of the poem now view his behavior as a child? How does he feel about it? What lines indicate his feeling?

5. What is the tone of the poem? How would you describe Hayden's diction? What effect does it create?

6. What does Hayden mean by "love's austere and lonely offices"? State the meaning of the phrase in your own words, and explain how it applies to the rest of the poem.

Writing Topics

1. In the last line of the poem, Hayden writes of "love's austere and lonely offices." How can one know that an action is motivated by love, if it is not done in a clearly loving way? Or do actions really speak louder than words? Call on your own experience to support your answer in an essay.

2. Hayden refers to "chronic angers" in the household in which he grew up. What are some of the effects such a situation has on children? Besides your own experience and that of people you know, you may want to consult sources in psychiatry or developmental psychology before writing an essay on this topic.

EUDORA WELTY

The American South has brought forth more than its share of fine writers, and Eudora Welty holds an honored place among them. She was born in 1909 in Jackson, Mississippi, and that is where she has lived for most of her life. Her father was president of an insurance company, and she was able to go away to the University of Wisconsin and then to take a postgraduate course in advertising at Columbia University's business school. By then the Great Depression had set in, and jobs in advertising were scarce, so she returned home to Jackson and began to write. Her published works include many short stories, now available as her *Collected Stories* (1980), five novels, and a collection of her essays, *The Eye of the Story* (1975). In her autobiographical *One Writer's Beginnings*, Welty recounts the events in childhood that influenced her development as a writer. In "A Worn Path" we meet one of Welty's memorable characters, old Phoenix Jackson, on her way to town on a vital errand.

A Worn Path

It was December—a bright frozen day in the early morning. Far out   1
in the country there was an old Negro woman with her head tied in a red rag, coming along a path through the pinewoods. Her name was Phoenix Jackson. She was very old and small and she walked slowly in the dark pine shadows, moving a little from side to side in her steps, with the balanced heaviness and lightness of a pendulum in a grandfather clock. She carried a thin, small cane made from an umbrella, and with this she kept tapping the frozen earth in front of her. This made a grave and persistent noise in the still air, that seemed meditative like the chirping of a solitary little bird.

She wore a dark striped dress reaching down to her shoe tops, and   2
an equally long apron of bleached sugar sacks, with a full pocket: all neat and tidy, but every time she took a step she might have fallen over her shoelaces, which dragged from her unlaced shoes. She looked straight ahead. Her eyes were blue with age. Her skin had a pattern all its own of numberless branching wrinkles and as though a whole little tree stood in the middle of her forehead, but a golden color ran underneath, and the two knobs of her cheeks were illumined by a yellow burning under the dark. Under the red rag her hair came down on her neck in the frailest of ringlets, still black, and with an odor like copper.

Now and then there was a quivering in the thicket. Old Phoenix   3
said, "Out of my way, all you foxes, owls, beetles, jack rabbits, coons

and wild animals! . . . Keep out from under these feet, little bob-whites.
. . . Keep the big wild hogs out of my path. Don't let none of those
come running my direction. I got a long way." Under her small black-
freckled hand her cane, limber as a buggy whip, would switch at the
brush as if to rouse up any hiding things.

On she went. The woods were deep and still. The sun made the   4
pine needles almost too bright to look at, up where the wind rocked.
The cones dropped as light as feathers. Down in the hollow was the
mourning dove—it was not too late for him.

The path ran up a hill. "Seem like there is chains about my feet,   5
time I get this far," she said, in the voice of argument old people keep
to use with themselves. "Something always take a hold of me on this
hill—pleads I should stay."

After she got to the top she turned and gave a full, severe look   6
behind her where she had come. "Up through pines," she said at length.
"Now down through oaks."

Her eyes opened their widest, and she started down gently. But   7
before she got to the bottom of the hill a bush caught her dress.

Her fingers were busy and intent, but her skirts were full and long,   8
so that before she could pull them free in one place they were caught in
another. It was not possible to allow the dress to tear. "I in the thorny
bush," she said. "Thorns, you doing your appointed work. Never want
to let folks pass, no sir. Old eyes thought you was a pretty little *green*
bush."

Finally, trembling all over, she stood free, and after a moment dared   9
to stoop for her cane.

"Sun so high!" she cried, leaning back and looking, while the thick   10
tears went over her eyes. "The time getting all gone here."

At the foot of this hill was a place where a log was laid across the   11
creek.

"Now comes the trial," said Phoenix.   12

Putting her right foot out, she mounted the log and shut her eyes.   13
Lifting her skirt, leveling her cane fiercely before her, like a festival figure
in some parade, she began to march across. Then she opened her eyes
and she was safe on the other side.

"I wasn't as old as I thought," she said.   14

But she sat down to rest. She spread her skirts on the bank around   15
her and folded her hands over her knees. Up above her was a tree in a
pearly cloud of mistletoe. She did not dare to close her eyes, and when
a little boy brought her a plate with a slice of marble-cake on it she spoke
to him. "That would be acceptable," she said. But when she went to
take it there was just her own hand in the air.

So she left that tree, and had to go through a barbed-wire fence. 16
There she had to creep and crawl, spreading her knees and stretching
her fingers like a baby trying to climb the steps. But she talked loudly to
herself: she could not let her dress be torn now, so late in the day, and
she could not pay for having her arm or her leg sawed off if she got caught
fast where she was.

At last she was safe through the fence and risen up out in the 17
clearing. Big dead trees, like black men with one arm, were standing in
the purple stalks of the withered cotton field. There sat a buzzard.

"Who you watching?" 18

In the furrow she made her way along. 19

"Glad this not the season for bulls," she said, looking sideways, 20
"and the good Lord made his snakes to curl up and sleep in the winter.
A pleasure I don't see no two-headed snake coming around that tree,
where it come once. It took a while to get by him, back in the summer."

She passed through the old cotton and went into a field of dead 21
corn. It whispered and shook and was taller than her head. "Through
the maze now," she said, for there was no path.

Then there was something tall, black, and skinny there, moving 22
before her.

At first she took it for a man. It could have been a man dancing 23
in the field. But she stood still and listened, and it did not make a sound.
It was as silent as a ghost.

"Ghost," she said sharply, "who be you the ghost of? For I have 24
heard of nary death close by."

But there was no answer—only the ragged dancing in the wind. 25

She shut her eyes, reached out her hand, and touched a sleeve. 26
She found a coat and inside that an emptiness, cold as ice.

"You scarecrow," she said. Her face lighted. "I ought to be shut up 27
for good," she said with laughter. "My senses is gone. I too old. I the
oldest people I ever know. Dance, old scarecrow," she said, "while I
dancing with you."

She kicked her foot over the furrow, and with mouth drawn down, 28
shook her head once or twice in a little strutting way. Some husks blew
down and whirled in streamers about her skirts.

Then she went on, parting her way from side to side with the cane, 29
through the whispering field. At last she came to the end, to a wagon
track where the silver grass blew between the red ruts. The quail were
walking around like pullets, seeming all dainty and unseen.

"Walk pretty," she said. "This the easy place. This the easy going." 30

She followed the track, swaying through the quiet bare fields, through 31
the little strings of trees silver in their dead leaves, past cabins silver

from weather, with the doors and windows boarded shut, all like old women under a spell sitting there. "I walking in their sleep," she said, nodding her head vigorously.

In a ravine she went where a spring was silently flowing through a hollow log. Old Phoenix bent and drank. "Sweetgum makes the water sweet," she said, and drank more. "Nobody know who made this well, for it was here when I was born." 32

The track crossed a swampy part where the moss hung as white as lace from every limb. "Sleep on, alligators, and blow your bubbles." Then the track went into the road. 33

Deep, deep the road went down between the high green-colored banks. Overhead the live-oaks met, and it was as dark as a cave. 34

A black dog with a lolling tongue came up out of the weeds by the ditch. She was meditating, and not ready, and when he came at her she only hit him a little with her cane. Over she went in the ditch, like a little puff of milkweed. 35

Down there, her senses drifted away. A dream visited her, and she reached her hand up, but nothing reached down and gave her a pull. So she lay there and presently went to talking. "Old woman," she said to herself, "that black dog come up out of the weeds to stall you off, and now there he sitting on his fine tail, smiling at you." 36

A white man finally came along and found her—a hunter, a young man, with his dog on a chain. 37

"Well, Granny!" he laughed. "What are you doing there?" 38

"Lying on my back like a June-bug waiting to be turned over, mister," she said, reaching up her hand. 39

He lifted her up, gave her a swing in the air, and set her down. "Anything broken, Granny?" 40

"No sir, them old dead weeds is springy enough," said Phoenix, when she had got her breath. "I thank you for your trouble." 41

"Where do you live, Granny?" he asked, while the two dogs were growling at each other. 42

"Away back yonder, sir, behind the ridge. You can't even see it from here." 43

"On your way home?" 44

"No sir, I going to town." 45

"Why, that's too far! That's as far as I walked when I come out myself, and I get something for my trouble." He patted the stuffed bag he carried, and there hung down a little closed claw. It was one of the bob-whites, with its beak hooked bitterly to show it was dead. "Now you go on home, Granny!" 46

"I bound to go to town, mister," said Phoenix. "The time come   47
around."

He gave another laugh, filling the whole landscape. "I know you   48
old colored people! Wouldn't miss going to town to see Santa Claus!"

But something held old Phoenix very still. The deep lines in her   49
face went into a fierce and different radiation. Without warning, she had
seen with her own eyes a flashing nickel fall out of the man's pocket
onto the ground.

"How old are you, Granny?" he was saying.   50

"There is no telling, mister," she said, "no telling."   51

Then she gave a little cry and clapped her hands and said, "Git on   52
away from here, dog! Look! Look at that dog!" She laughed as if in
admiration. "He ain't scared of nobody. He a big black dog." She whispered, "Sic him!"

"Watch me get rid of that cur," said the man. "Sic him, Pete! Sic   53
him!"

Phoenix heard the dogs fighting, and heard the man running and   54
throwing sticks. She even heard a gunshot. But she was slowly bending
forward by that time, further and further forward, the lids stretched down
over her eyes, as if she were doing this in her sleep. Her chin was
lowered almost to her knees. The yellow palm of her hand came out
from the fold of her apron. Her fingers slid down and along the ground
under the piece of money with the grace and care they would have in
lifting an egg from under a setting hen. Then she slowly straightened
up, she stood erect, and the nickel was in her apron pocket. A bird
flew by. Her lips moved. "God watching me the whole time. I come to
stealing."

The man came back, and his own dog panted about them. "Well,   55
I scared him off that time," he said, and then he laughed and lifted his
gun and pointed it at Phoenix.

She stood straight and faced him.   56

"Doesn't the gun scare you?" he said, still pointing it.   57

"No, sir, I seen plenty go off closer by, in my day, and for less than   58
what I done," she said, holding utterly still.

He smiled, and shouldered the gun. "Well, Granny," he said, "you   59
must be a hundred years old, and scared of nothing. I'd give you a dime
if I had any money with me. But you take my advice and stay home,
and nothing will happen to you."

"I bound to go on my way, mister," said Phoenix. She inclined her   60
head in the red rag. Then they went in different directions, but she could
hear the gun shooting again and again over the hill.

She walked on. The shadows hung from the oak trees to the road   61
like curtains. Then she smelled wood-smoke, and smelled the river, and
she saw a steeple and the cabins on their steep steps. Dozens of little
black children whirled around her. There ahead was Natchez shining.
Bells were ringing. She walked on.

In the paved city it was Christmas time. There were red and green   62
electric lights strung and crisscrossed everywhere, and all turned on in
the daytime. Old Phoenix would have been lost if she had not distrusted
her eyesight and depended on her feet to know where to take her.

She paused quietly on the sidewalk where people were passing by.   63
A lady came along in the crowd, carrying an armful of red-, green- and
silver-wrapped presents; she gave off perfume like the red roses in hot
summer, and Phoenix stopped her.

"Please, missy, will you lace up my shoe?" She held up her foot.   64

"What do you want, Grandma?"   65

"See my shoe," said Phoenix. "Do all right for out in the country,   66
but wouldn't look right to go in a big building."

"Stand still then, Grandma," said the lady. She put her pack-   67
ages down on the sidewalk beside her and laced and tied both shoes
tightly.

"Can't lace 'em with a cane," said Phoenix. "Thank you, missy. I   68
doesn't mind asking a nice lady to tie up my shoe, when I gets out on
the street."

Moving slowly and from side to side, she went into the big building, 69
and into a tower of steps, where she walked up and around and around
until her feet knew to stop.

She entered a door, and there she saw nailed up on the wall the   70
document that had been stamped with the gold seal and framed in the
gold frame, which matched the dream that was hung up in her head.

"Here I be," she said. There was a fixed and ceremonial stiffness   71
over her body.

"A charity case, I suppose," said an attendant who sat at the desk   72
before her.

But Phoenix only looked above her head. There was sweat on her   73
face, the wrinkles in her skin shone like a bright net.

"Speak up, Grandma," the woman said. "What's your name? We   74
must have your history, you know. Have you been here before? What
seems to be the trouble with you?"

Old Phoenix only gave a twitch to her face as if a fly were bothering 75
her.

"Are you deaf?" cried the attendant.   76

But then the nurse came in.   77

"Oh, that's just old Aunt Phoenix," she said. "She doesn't come   78
for herself—she has a little grandson. She makes these trips just as regular
as clockwork. She lives away back off the Old Natchez Trace." She bent
down. "Well, Aunt Phoenix, why don't you just take a seat? We won't
keep you standing after your long trip." She pointed.

The old woman sat down, bolt upright in the chair.   79

"Now, how is the boy?" asked the nurse.   80

Old Phoenix did not speak.   81

"I said, how is the boy?"   82

But Phoenix only waited and stared straight ahead, her face very   83
solemn and withdrawn into rigidity.

"Is his throat any better?" asked the nurse. "Aunt Phoenix, don't   84
you hear me? Is your grandson's throat any better since the last time you
came for the medicine?"

With her hands on her knees, the old woman waited, silent, erect,   85
and motionless, just as if she were in armor.

"You mustn't take up our time this way, Aunt Phoenix," the nurse   86
said. "Tell us quickly about your grandson, and get it over. He isn't dead,
is he?"

At last there came a flicker and then a flame of comprehension   87
across her face, and she spoke.

"My grandson. It was my memory had left me. There I sat and   88
forgot why I made my long trip."

"Forgot?" The nurse frowned. "After you came so far?"   89

Then Phoenix was like an old woman begging a dignified forgive-   90
ness for waking up frightened in the night. "I never did go to school, I
was too old at the Surrender," she said in a soft voice. "I'm an old woman
without an education. It was my memory fail me. My little grandson, he
is just the same, and I forgot it in the coming."

"Throat never heals, does it?" said the nurse, speaking in a loud,   91
sure voice to old Phoenix. By now she had a card with something written
on it, a little list. "Yes. Swallowed lye. When was it?—January—two-
three years ago—"

Phoenix spoke unasked now. "No, missy, he not dead, he just the   92
same. Every little while his throat begin to close up again, and he not
able to swallow. He not get his breath. He not able to help himself. So
the time come around, and I go on another trip for the soothing medicine."

"All right. The doctor said as long as you came to get it, you could   93
have it," said the nurse. "But it's an obstinate case."

"My little grandson, he sit up there in the house all wrapped up,   94
waiting by himself," Phoenix went on. "We is the only two left in the
world. He suffer and it don't seem to put him back at all. He got a sweet
look. He going to last. He wear a little patch quilt and peep out holding
his mouth open like a little bird. I remembers so plain now. I not going
to forget him again, no, the whole enduring time. I could tell him from
all the others in creation."

"All right." The nurse was trying to hush her now. She brought   95
her a bottle of medicine. "Charity," she said, making a check mark in a
book.

Old Phoenix held the bottle close to her eyes, and then carefully   96
put it into her pocket.

"I thank you," she said.   97

"It's Christmas time, Grandma," said the attendant. "Could I give   98
you a few pennies out of my purse?"

"Five pennies is a nickel," said Phoenix stiffly.   99

"Here's a nickel," said the attendant.   100

Phoenix rose carefully and held out her hand. She received the   101
nickel and then fished the other nickel out of her pocket and laid it
beside the new one. She stared at her palm closely, with her head on
one side.

Then she gave a tap with her cane on the floor.   102

"This is what come to me to do," she said. "I going to the store   103
and buy my child a little windmill they sells, made out of paper. He
going to find it hard to believe there such a thing in the world. I'll march
myself back where he waiting, holding it straight up in this hand."

She lifted her free hand, gave a little nod, turned around, and   104
walked out of the doctor's office. Then her slow step began on the stairs,
going down.

Questions for Study and Discussion

1. Why is Old Phoenix going to Natchez? Who does she tell, and why?

2. What obstacles does Phoenix meet on the way? How, emotionally, does
she cope with those obstacles? What does this reveal about her character?

3. How does Phoenix get the money she plans to spend at the end of the
story? What will she be bringing home to her grandson? What is the significance of this gift?

4. What is the nature of the relationship between Phoenix and her grandson?

5. In paragraph 90 Phoenix says, "I never did go to school, I was too old at
the Surrender." What does this mean?

6. Welty uses many figurative comparisons in this story—for example, "Over she went in the ditch, like a little puff of milkweed." Collect some other examples of metaphor and simile, and explain what each means. Do all of them have something in common? If so, what significance do you find in that?

7. What does the title of the story mean to you? Does it have any metaphorical meaning? Explain.

8. After reading this story, many people have asked: "Is Phoenix Jackson's grandson really dead?" Did this question occur to you? Is an answer to this question important to an understanding of Welty's story? Explain.

Writing Topics

1. Write a character sketch of an old person you know well. If you like, you can organize your sketch by showing your subject engaged in some typical activity.

2. Family obligations can be tiresome chores, or willing acts of love, or even both. What family obligations do you have—or do others have toward you? How do you feel about these obligations? Write an essay in which you explain your thoughts on these obligations.

3. Though brought up in a time and place where racial discrimination and hatred were widespread, Eudora Welty writes of Phoenix Jackson with understanding and love. Is this typical of her? Read some of her other works—perhaps the story "Powerhouse" or the essay "A Pageant of Birds"—and then write an essay in which you assess the image of black people in her work.

The Troubled American Family

MARGARET MEAD

With the publication of *Coming of Age in Samoa* in 1928, Margaret Mead (1901–1978) began a career that would establish her as one of the world's leading cultural anthropologists. Over the course of her lifetime she studied in various fields—family structures, primitive societies, ecology, cultural traditions, and mental health. She served as curator of ethnology at the American Museum of Natural History and as director of Columbia University's Research on Contemporary Cultures. After she retired, she became a contributing editor for *Redbook*, where the following article appeared in 1977. In this essay she examines the problems that are besetting the contemporary American family. Despite the grim picture she paints, Mead remains essentially optimistic. She believes that we can help each other make the family viable for ourselves and future generations.

Can the American Family Survive?

All over the United States, families are in trouble. It is true that there are many contented homes where parents are living in harmony and raising their children responsibly, and with enjoyment in which the children share. Two out of three American households are homes in which a wife and husband live together, and almost seven out of ten children are born to parents living together in their first marriage.

However, though reassuring, these figures are deceptive. A great many of the married couples have already lived through one divorce. And a very large number of the children in families still intact will have to face the disruption of their parents' marriage in the future. The numbers increase every year.

It is also true that the hazards are much greater for some families than for others. Very young couples, the poorly educated, those with few skills and a low income, Blacks and members of other minority groups—particularly if they live in big cities—all these are in danger of becoming high-risk families for whose children a family breakdown is disastrous.

145

But no group, whatever its status and resources, is exempt. This in   4
itself poses a threat to all families, especially those with young children.
For how can children feel secure when their friends in other families so
like their own are conspicuously lost and unhappy? In one way or another
we all are drawn into the orbit of families in trouble.

Surely it is time for us to look squarely at the problems that beset   5
families and to ask what must be done to make family life more viable,
not only for ourselves now but also in prospect for all the children growing
up who will have to take responsibility for the next generation.

The Grim Picture

There are those today—as at various times in the past—who doubt   6
that the family can survive, and some who believe it should not survive.
Indeed, the contemporary picture is grim enough.

• Many young marriages entered into with love and high hopes collapse be-   7
fore the first baby is weaned. The very young parents, on whom the whole
burden of survival rests, cannot make it entirely on their own, and they
give up.

• Families that include several children break up and the children are up-   8
rooted from the only security they have known. Some children of divorce,
perhaps the majority, will grow up as stepchildren in homes that, however
loving, they no longer dare to trust fully. Many—far too many—will grow up
in single-parent homes. Still others will be moved, rootless as rolling stones,
from foster family to foster family until at last they begin a rootless life on
their own.

• In some states a family with a male breadwinner cannot obtain welfare, and   9
some fathers, unable to provide adequately for their children, desert them so
that the mothers can apply for public assistance. And growing numbers of
mothers, fearful of being deserted, are leaving their young families while, as
they hope and believe, they still have a chance to make a different life for
themselves.

• As divorce figures have soared—today the proportion of those currently   10
divorced is more than half again as high as in 1960, and it is predicted that
one in three young women in this generation will be divorced—Americans
have accepted as a truism the myth that from the mistakes made in their first
marriage women and men learn how to do it better the second time around.
Sometimes it does work. But a large proportion of those who have resorted
to divorce once choose this as the easier solution again and again. Easily
dashed hopes become more easily dashed.

• At the same time, many working parents, both of whom are trying hard to   11
care for and keep together the family they have chosen to bring into being,

find that there is no place at all where their children can be cared for safely and gently and responsibly during the long hours of their own necessary absence at their jobs. They have no relatives nearby and there is neither a day-care center nor afterschool care for their active youngsters. Whatever solution they find, their children are likely to suffer.

The Bitter Consequences

The consequences, direct and indirect, are clear. Thousands of young couples are living together in some arrangement and are wholly dependent on their private, personal commitment to each other for the survival of their relationship. In the years from 1970 to 1975 the number of single persons in the 25-to-34-year age group has increased by half. Some couples living together have repudiated marriage as a binding social relationship and have rejected the family as an institution. Others are delaying marriage because they are not sure of themselves or each other; still others are simply responding to what they have experienced of troubled family life and the effects of divorce. 12

At the end of the life span there are the ever-growing numbers of women and men, especially women, who have outlived their slender family relationships. They have nowhere to turn, no one to depend on but strangers in public institutions. Unwittingly we have provided the kind of assistance that, particularly in cities, almost guarantees such isolated and helpless old people will become the prey of social vultures. 13

And at all stages of their adult life, demands are made increasingly on women to earn their living in the working world. Although we prefer to interpret this as an expression of women's wish to fulfill themselves to have the rights that go with money earned and to be valued as persons, the majority of women who work outside their homes do so because they must. It is striking that ever since the 1950s a larger proportion of married women with children than of married but childless women have entered the labor force. According to recent estimates some 14 million women with children—four out of ten mothers of children under six years of age and more than half of all mothers of school-age children—are working, the great majority of them in full-time jobs. 14

A large proportion of these working women are the sole support of their families. Some 10 million children—more than one in six—are living with only one parent, generally with the mother. This number has doubled since 1960. 15

The majority of these women and their children live below the poverty level, the level at which the most minimal needs can be met. Too 16 often the women, particularly the younger ones, having little education and few skills, are at the bottom of the paid work force. Though they and their children are in great need, they are among those least able to demand and obtain what they require merely to survive decently, in good health and with some hope for the future.

But the consequences of family trouble are most desperate as they affect children. Every year, all over the country, over 1 million adolescents, nowadays principally girls, run away from home because they have found life with their families insupportable. Some do not run very far and in the end a great many come home again, but by no means all of them. And we hear about only a handful whose terrifying experiences or whose death happens to come into public view.   17

In homes where there is no one to watch over them, elementary-school children are discovering the obliterating effects of alcohol; a growing number have become hard-case alcoholics in their early teens. Other young girls and boys, wanderers in the streets, have become the victims of corruption and sordid sex. The youngsters who vent their rage and desperation on others by means of violent crimes are no less social victims than are the girls and boys who are mindlessly corrupted by the adults who prey on them.   18

Perhaps the most alarming symptom of all is the vast increase in child abuse, which, although it goes virtually unreported in some groups, is not limited to any one group in our population. What seems to be happening is that frantic mothers and fathers, stepparents or the temporary mates of parents turn on the children they do not know how to care for, and beat them—often in a desperate, inarticulate hope that someone will hear their cries and somehow bring help. We know this, but although many organizations have been set up to help these children and their parents, many adults do not know what is needed or how to ask for assistance or whom they may expect a response from.   19

And finally there are the children who end their own lives in absolute despair. Suicide is now third among the causes of death for youngsters 15 to 19 years old.   20

What Has Gone Wrong?

In recent years, various explanations have been suggested for the breakdown of family life.   21

Blame has been placed on the vast movement of Americans from rural areas and small towns to the big cities and on the continual, restless surge of people from one part of the country to another, so that millions   22 of families, living in the midst of strangers, lack any continuity in their life-style and any real support for their values and expectations.

Others have emphasized the effects of unemployment and under-employment among Blacks and other minority groups, which make their families peculiarly vulnerable in life crises that are exacerbated by economic uncertainty. This is particularly the case where the policies of welfare agencies penalize the family that is poor but intact in favor of the single-parent family.   23

There is also the generation gap, particularly acute today, when parents and their adolescent children experience the world in such very different ways. The world in which the parents grew up is vanishing, unknown to their children except by hearsay. The world into which adolescents are growing is in many ways unknown to both generations—and neither can help the other very much to understand it.   24

Then there is our obvious failure to provide for the children and young people whom we do not succeed in educating, who are in deep trouble and who may be totally abandoned. We have not come to grips with the problems of hard drugs. We allow the courts that deal with juveniles to become so overloaded that little of the social protection they were intended to provide is possible. We consistently underfund and understaff the institutions into which we cram children in need of re-education and physical and psychological rehabilitation, as if all that concerned us was to get them—and keep them—out of our sight.   25

Other kinds of explanations also have been offered.   26

There are many people who, knowing little about child development, have placed the principal blame on what they call "permissiveness"—on the relaxing of parental discipline to include the child as a small partner in the process of growing up. Those people say that children are "spoiled," that they lack "respect" for their parents or that they have not learned to obey the religious prohibitions that were taught to their parents, and that all the troubles plaguing family life have followed.   27

Women's Liberation, too, has come in for a share of the blame. It is said that in seeking self-fulfillment, women are neglecting their homes and children and are undermining men's authority and men's sense of responsibility. The collapse of the family is seen as the inevitable consequence.   28

Those who attribute the difficulties of troubled families to any single cause, whether or not it is related to reality, also tend to advocate panaceas, each of which—they say—should restore stability to the traditional family or, alternatively, supplant the family. Universal day care from birth, communal living, group marriage, contract marriage and open marriage all have their advocates.   29

Each such proposal fastens on some trouble point in the modern   30
family—the lack of adequate facilities to care for the children of working
mothers, for example, or marital infidelity, which, it is argued, would be
eliminated by being institutionalized. Others, realizing the disastrous effects of poverty on family life, have advocated bringing the income of
every family up to a level at which decent living is possible. Certainly
this must be one of our immediate aims. But it is wholly unrealistic to
suppose that all else that has gone wrong will automatically right itself if
the one—but very complex—problem of poverty is eliminated.

A Look at Alternatives

Is there, in fact, any viable alternative to the family as a setting in   31
which children can be successfully reared to become capable and responsible adults, relating to one another and a new generation of children as
well as to the world around them? Or should we aim at some wholly new
social invention?

Revolutionaries have occasionally attempted to abolish the family,   32
or at least to limit its strength by such measures as arranging for marriages
without binding force or for rearing children in different kinds of collec-
tives. But as far as we know, in the long run such efforts have never
worked out satisfactorily.

The Soviet Union, for instance, long ago turned away from the   33
flexible, impermanent unions and collective child-care ideals of the early
revolutionary days and now heavily emphasizes the values of a stable family life. In Israel the kibbutz, with its children's house and carefully planned,
limited contact between parents and children, is losing out to social forms
in which the family is both stronger and more closely knit. In Scandina-
vian countries, where the standards of child care are very high, serious
efforts have been made to provide a viable situation for unmarried mothers and the children they have chosen to bring up alone; but there are
disturbing indices of trouble, expressed, for example, in widespread alcoholism and a high rate of suicide.

Experience suggests that we would do better to look in other direc-   34
tions. Two approaches may be rewarding. First we can look at other kinds
of societies—primitive societies, peasant societies and traditional complex but unindustrialized societies (prerevolutionary China, for example)—to discover whether there are ways in which families are organized
that occur in all societies. This can give us some idea of needs that must
be satisfied for families to survive and prosper.

Second we can ask whether the problems that are besetting Ameri-   35
can families are unique or are instead characteristic of families wherever
modern industrialization, a sophisticated technology and urban living are
drawing people into a new kind of civilization. Placing our own difficulties within a wider context can perhaps help us to assess what our priorities must be as we attempt to develop new forms of stability in keeping
with contemporary expressions of human needs.

Looking at human behavior with all that we know—and can infer—   36
about the life of our human species from earliest times, we have to realize
that the family, as an association between a man and a woman and the
children she bears, has been universal. As far as we know, both primitive
"group" marriage and primitive matriarchy are daydreams—or nightmares, depending on one's point of view—without basis in historical reality. On the contrary, the evidence indicates that the couple, together
with their children, biological or adopted, are everywhere at the core of
human societies, even though this "little family" (as the Chinese called
the nuclear family) may be embedded in joint families, extended families
of great size, clans, manorial systems, courts, harems or other institutions
that elaborate on kin and marital relations.

Almost up to the present, women on the whole have kept close to   37
home and domestic tasks because of the demands of pregnancy and the
nursing of infants, the rearing of children and the care of the disabled
and the elderly. They have been concerned primarily with the conservation of intimate values and human relations from one generation to another over immense reaches of time. In contrast, men have performed
tasks that require freer movement over greater distances, more intense
physical effort and exposure to greater immediate danger; and everywhere
men have developed the formal institutions of public life and the values
on which these are based. However differently organized, the tasks of
women and men have been complementary, mutually supportive. And
where either the family or the wider social institutions have broken down,
the society as a whole has been endangered.

In fact, almost everywhere in the world today societies *are* endan-   38
gered. The difficulties that beset families in the United States are by no
means unique. Families are in trouble everywhere in a world in which
change—kinds of change that in many cases we ourselves proudly initiated—has been massive and rapid, and innovations have proliferated
with only the most superficial concern for their effect on human lives and
the earth itself. One difference between the United States and many
other countries is that, caring so much about progress, Americans have
moved faster. But we may also have arrived sooner at a turning point at

which it becomes crucial to redefine what we most value and where we are headed.

Looking to the past does not mean that we should return to the past   39
or that we can undo the experiences that have brought us where we are now. The past can provide us only with a base for judging what threatens sound family life and for considering whether our social planning is realistic and inclusive enough. Looking to the past is not a way of binding ourselves but of increasing our awareness, so that we are freer to find new solutions in keeping with our deepest human needs.

So the question is not whether women should be forced back into   40
their homes or should have an equal say with men in the world's affairs. We urgently need to draw on the talents women have to offer. Nor is there any question whether men should be deprived of a more intimate family role. We have made a small beginning by giving men a larger share in parenting, and I believe that men and children have been enriched by it.

What we need to be sure of is that areas of caretaking associated in   41
the past with families do not simply drop out of our awareness so that basic human needs go unmet. All the evidence indicates that this is where our greatest difficulties lie. The troubles that plague American families and families all over the industrialized world are symptomatic of the breakdown of the responsible relationship between families and the larger communities of which they are part.

For a long time we have worked hard at isolating the individual   42
family. This has increased the mobility of individuals; and by encouraging young families to break away from the older generation and the home community, we have been able to speed up the acceptance of change and the rapid spread of innovative behavior. But at the same time we have burdened every small family with tremendous responsibilities once shared within three generations and among a large number of people—the nurturing of small children, the emergence of adolescents into adulthood, the care of the sick and disabled and the protection of the aged. What we have failed to realize is that even as we have separated the single family from the larger society, we have expected each couple to take on a range of obligations that traditionally have been shared within a larger family and a wider community.

So all over the world there are millions of families left alone, as it   43
were, each in its own box—parents faced with the specter of what may happen if either one gets sick, children fearful that their parents may end their quarrels with divorce, and empty-handed old people without any role in the life of the next generation.

Then, having pared down to almost nothing the relationship be-   44
tween families and the community, when families get into trouble because they cannot accomplish the impossible we turn their problems over
to impersonal social agencies, which can act only in a fragmented way
because they are limited to patchwork programs that often are too late to
accomplish what is most needed.

Individuals and families do get some kind of help, but what they   45
learn and what those who work hard within the framework of social agencies convey, even as they try to help, is that families should be able to
care for themselves.

What Can We Do?

Can we restore family stability? Can we establish new bonds be-   46
tween families and communities? Perhaps most important of all, can we
move to a firm belief that living in a family is worth a great effort? Can
we move to a new expectation that by making the effort, families can
endure? Obviously the process is circular. Both optimism and action are
needed.

We shall have to distinguish between the things that must be done   47
at once and the relations between families and communities that can be
built up only over time. We shall have to accept willingly the cost of
what must be done, realizing that whatever we do ultimately will be less
costly than our present sorry attempts to cope with breakdown and disaster. And we shall have to care for the failures too.

In the immediate future we shall have to support every piece of   48
Federal legislation through which adequate help can be provided for families, both single-parent families and intact poor families, so that they can
live decently and safely and prepare their children for another kind of
life.

We shall have to support Federal programs for day care and after-   49
school care for the children of working mothers and working parents, and
for facilities where in a crisis parents can safely leave their small children
for brief periods; for centers where the elderly can be cared for without
being isolated from the rest of the world; for housing for young families
and older people in communities where they can actually interact as friendly
grandparents and grandchildren might; and for a national health program
that is concerned not with fleecing the Government but with health care.
And we must support the plea of Vice-President Walter F. Mondale, who,
as chairman of the Senate Subcommittee on Children and Youth, called
for "family impact" statements requiring Government agencies to account

for what a proposed policy would do for families—make them worse off or better able to take care of their needs.

Government-funded programs need not be patchwork, as likely to destroy as to save. We need to realize that problems related to family and community life—problems besetting education, housing, nutrition, health care, child care, to name just a few—are interlocked. To solve them, we need awareness of detail combined with concern for the whole, and a wise use of tax dollars to accomplish our aims.   50

A great deal depends on how we see what is done—whether we value it because we are paying for it and because we realize that the protection given families in need is a protection for all families, including our own. Committing ourselves to programs of care—instead of dissociating ourselves from every effort—is one step in the direction of reestablishing family ties with the community. But this will happen only if we accept the idea that each of us, as part of a community, shares in the responsibility for everyone, and thereby benefits from what is done.   51

The changes that are needed cannot be accomplished by Federal legislation alone. Over a longer time we must support the design and building of communities in which there is housing for three generations, for the fortunate and the unfortunate, and for people of many backgrounds. Such communities can become central in the development of the necessary support system for families. But it will take time to build such communities, and we cannot afford just to wait and hope they will happen.   52

Meanwhile we must act to interrupt the runaway belief that marriages must fail, that parents and children can't help but be out of communication, that the family as an institution is altogether in disarray. There still are far more marriages that succeed than ones that fail; there are more parents and children who live in trust and learn from one another than ones who are out of touch; there are more people who care about the future than we acknowledge.   53

What we need, I think, is nationwide discussion—in magazines, in newspapers, on television panel shows and before Congressional committees—of how people who are happily married can help those who are not, how people who are fortunate can help those who are not and how people who have too little to do can help those who are burdened by too much.   54

Out of such discussions can come a heightened awareness and perhaps some actual help, but above all, fresh thought about what must be done and the determination to begin to do it.   55

It is true that all over the United States, families are in trouble.   56

Realizing this should not make us cynical about the family. It should start us working for a new version of the family that is appropriate to the contemporary world.

Questions for Study and Discussion

1. What types of families, according to Mead, are more prone to breakdown? Why do you suppose this is true? What effect does this breakdown have on the children of so-called secure families?

2. In paragraph 6 Mead draws a grim picture of the contemporary American family. In her analysis of the situation what does she see as the major effects on adults? On children?

3. What for Mead is the "most alarming symptom" of family trouble? What explanation does she offer for why it occurs so often?

4. What according to Mead are the explanations that have been suggested for the breakdown of family life? Which ones do you find most plausible?

5. Mead suggests that it is sometimes helpful to look to the past. Does she advocate returning to the past? Explain.

6. What does Mead mean when she states in paragraph 41, "The troubles that plague American families and families all over the industrialized world are symptomatic of the breakdown of the responsible relationship between families and the larger communities of which they are part"?

7. What solutions to the problem of family breakdown does Mead offer? Do you agree with her on any of these solutions? Wouldn't the dissolution of the family structure be a much easier solution? Why does Mead see this as a viable alternative?

8. Paragraphs 1–5 serve to introduce Mead's essay. What would be gained or lost had Mead combined these paragraphs into a single paragraph?

Writing Topics

1. Write an essay in which you argue for one or more innovative alternatives to the family as a traditional social unit.

2. Write an essay in which you explore the importance of family for you. What benefits do you derive from your family? What do you give your family in return? Do you think the American family is in trouble? Why, or why not?

Lionel Tiger is an anthropologist and sociologist. A Canadian, Tiger was born in Montreal in 1937 and took his B.A. and M.A. degrees at McGill University in that city and his Ph.D. at the University of London in 1962. He is currently a professor of anthropology at Rutgers University, where he has also served as director of graduate studies. A prolific researcher, Tiger has written scores of articles on a wide variety of subjects including the family unit and alternatives to it. Among his published works are *Men in Groups* (1969); *The Imperial Animal* (with Robin Fox, 1971); *Women in the Kibbutz* (with Joseph Shepher, 1975); and *Optimism: The Biology of Hope* (1980).

In the following article, which first appeared in *Psychology Today*, Tiger analyzes what is happening to the traditional family structure as the rate of divorce increases and new family arrangements evolve.

Omnigamy: The New Kinship System

A hapless British cabinet minister responsible for the hapless UK telephone system once complained that the more phones installed in his country, the more there were to call, and so the demand for phones increased: supply creates demand. Somewhat the same thing is happening with marriage in America. The more divorces there are, the more experienced marriers exist, ready to remarry—and many do. The divorce rate has jumped 250 percent in the past 21 years; about 80 percent of the formerly married remarry. With each new marriage, the parents and children involved acquire a whole new set of relatives, friends, and associations—in effect, they stretch their kinship system. Many people are married to people who have been married to other people who are now married to still others to whom the first parties may not have been married, but to whom somebody has likely been married. Our society, once based on the principle of solid monogamy until death do us part, has shifted toward a pattern of serial polygamy, in which people experience more than one spouse, if only one at a time. Thus we appear to be moving to a new and imprecise system we might call omnigamy, in which each will be married to all.

People keep marrying, even though happy marriages are regarded as surprising and much-envied occurrences. The not-so-stately pageant of marriage goes on, heedless of the cautionary cries of pain and the clenched question: Why? Various responsible estimators expect that from a third to a half of the marriages formed in this decade will end in divorce sometime. That is astonishing. It is also astonishing that, under the

156

circumstances, marriage is still legally allowed. If nearly half of anything else ended so disastrously, the government would surely ban it immediately. If half the tacos served in restaurants caused dysentery, if half the people learning karate broke their palms, if only 6 percent of people who went on roller-coasters damaged their middle ears, the public would be clamoring for action. Yet the most intimate of disasters—with consequences that may last a lifetime for both adults and children—happens over and over again. Marriage has not yet gone underground.

To an anthropologist, the emergence of a new kinship system should be as exciting as the discovery of a new comet to an astronomer. But in the case of omnigamy, the developing pattern is still unclear, the forces shaping it unanalyzed, the final structure difficult to predict. We know the numbers of marriages and remarriages, but what about the apparent acceleration of the process? The new system permits—perhaps even demands—that its members repair themselves quickly after crises of vast personal proportion. In the slapdash, overpraised, and sentimental film *An Unmarried Woman*, Jill Clayburgh explains to her (quite nauseating) therapist how agonizing and lonely it was when her husband of umpteen years left her, and how she has been without sexual congress for such a long, long time. When the therapist hears this dreadful fact, she earnestly recommends that this casualty of a massive private accident return immediately to the sexual fray. It has, after all, been *seven weeks*.

The heroine subsequently decides to reject an offer to join an attractive and apparently quite suitable artist. Instead she chooses to lead an independent life as a part-time secretary in a SoHo art gallery, which makes her somewhat radical with respect to the omnigamous system. For her obligation seems clear: she must form some sturdy response, one way or the other, to the ambient fact of marriage and remarriage. To remain haunted by grief and inhibited by a sense of failure is taken as a mere expression of cowardice or restlessness.

When anthropology first started out, the difficult trick in studying any culture was to discover just what the kinship system was—who was married to whom, and why, and what connections counted for inheritance, status, and authority. We found that marriage was the instrument for creating the extended family, which provided for most human needs in the tribal societies. If an anthropologist from the Trobriand Islands came here now, he or she could well conclude that by stimulating further marriages, divorce has come to be an important organizing principle in our society, since kinship alliances among divorced people are so extensive and complex.

When parents divorce and remarry, the new family connections extend the reach of family life to dimensions a Baganda or Trobriander or Hopi could well understand. Take an example: after the divorce of A and B, siblings A1 and B1 live with A and her new husband, C, but visit B and his new wife, D, on weekends. C's children, C1, C2, and C3, like to go to basketball games with A1 and B1. D's children by her first marriage also enjoy the company of A1 and B1, and take them along on visits to their father, E, a former star athlete who becomes an important hero and role model to the children of A, who has never met him and probably never will.

Nor is it only marriage that binds. In a world where all Mom and Dad's companions are potential mates, Dad's live-in girl friend may turn up for parents' night at school when he's out of town. She also may have a brother—a kind of stepuncle to the kids—with a 40-foot sloop. (The spreading network can put children in touch with a dislocating variety of styles.)   7

What this means for children, and how it affects their sense of what is stable, what is optional, what is fast, slow, brisk, or stately, is, of course, difficult to say. The generation of children spawned by the Age of Omnigamy has not yet made its mark on the social system in any clear way; we cannot know whether they are immune, immunized, or carriers of the bug across generational lines. In the old days, people were titillated by the polygamous habits of Hollywood celebrities, but few were tempted to emulate them. Parents, grandparents, aunts, and uncles seem to be more important role models for children. When they keep changing partners, it will likely increase the child's sense of the tentativeness in all relations that the new system reflects.   8

While I am not implying that omnigamous parents set a bad example, they surely set some example. The consequences for their own children and for those others with whom they come in contact must be considerable. Divorce as a recurrent aspect of life may make it relatively easier for children to accept when they are young, but harder to avoid when they become adults. And who has calculated the effect of omnigamy on grandparents, whose connections with their grandchildren suddenly come to be mediated by strangers—stepparents who might even move them to some distant city?   9

I do not mean to be alarmist and implacably negative about all this. The existence of relatively civilized divorce options is as much a sign of human freedom as it is of sanctioned personal confusion and pain. Who, after all, would wish to confirm in their desperate plight the countless real-world descendants of Madame Bovary?   10

Surely, too, there is a value in the extension of personal experience to wider circles of people than strict and permanent monogamy permits.   11

And there is presumably an enhancement of personal vividness, which the new, relatively unstructured world permits—if not coerces.

Omnigamy may have interesting economic implications as well. Adrienne Harris of York University in Toronto has pointed out that each marital separation stimulates the repurchase of those items left in one household and needed in the next. Like amoebas splitting, one dishwasher becomes two, one vacuum cleaner becomes two, one television becomes two; domestic purchases even become imperious ("Why shouldn't I have *my* Cuisinart to do my fish mousse when he/she has *our* Cuisinart for hers/his?"). One can't help speculating that the rapid increase in retail outlets selling cooking equipment reflects the doubled demands of the new kinship system.

And where would the real estate market be without house sales to accommodate people who can no longer accommodate each other? And has anyone wondered why the garage sale has recently become so common? The economic shifts that depend on the breakup and re-forming of marital units are a form of internal colonialism: at the same time that the United States can no longer control foreign markets, it is expanding its internal ones. The family system, which both Engels and Marx saw as the stimulus for the development of capitalism, may even, in the new form, turn out to be one of its props. As with all colonialisms, however, many people come to be exploited. Taking up the options omnigamy offers strains the financial and emotional resources both.

Can it be said that these comments apply mostly to a small group of self-involved persons inhabiting the Upper East and West Sides of Manhattan, where the production of novels and articles about marriage and anguished personal failure is a major cottage industry? No. If the divorce rates persist and cities continue to export their social patterns, as in the past, other communities still complacently conventional and relatively monogamous will make a gradual but perceptible shift to omnigamy. The pattern will broaden unless there is soon—and there could be—a renewed commitment to monogamous fidelity, and possibly even to the importance of virginity as a factor in marital choice (this possibility seems rather remote). What does seem clear is that many changes will derive from these many changes, perhaps even a return to notions of marriage based on economic convenience and an agreement to mount a common assault on loneliness. Marriage could be on its way to becoming a generalized corporate, if small-scale, experience capable of providing some sense of community and some prospect of continuity. But it may also become a relatively planless arrangement and rearrangement of fickle magnets inexplicably and episodically drawn into each other's orbits for varying purposes and periods.

12

13

14

Questions for Study and Discussion

1. What is omnigamy? Where does Tiger define the term? Does the term accurately reflect the social phenomena that he describes?

2. Given the high divorce rate, why do you suppose people continue to marry? Remarry?

3. What are the effects of omnigamy on family members—parents, grandparents, and children?

4. What are some of the benefits of omnigamy that Tiger mentions? Who benefits in each case?

5. In the final paragraph Tiger describes a number of possible scenarios for social change. What are they? Which to you seems most plausible? Is this paragraph an effective way to conclude this essay? Why, or why not?

6. Why does Tiger summarize the plot of the movie *An Unmarried Woman*? Explain Tiger's allusion to Madame Bovary in paragraph 10.

7. What do you believe Tiger is thinking of when he says that "divorce has come to be an organizing principle in our society"?

Writing Topics

1. Tiger says that it is difficult to know what the effects of omnigamy will be on children. In an essay speculate about what you think the social, psychological, and economic effects will be.

2. From your own experience or observation, write an essay about the effects of divorce on family structure.

ELLEN GOODMAN

Ellen Goodman was born in 1941 in Boston. After graduating cum laude from Radcliffe College in 1963, she worked as a reporter and researcher for *Newsweek*. In 1967 she began working at the *Boston Globe* and, since 1974, has been a full-time columnist. Her regular column, "At Large," is syndicated by the *Washington Post* Writers' Group and appears in nearly 400 newspapers across the country. In addition, her writing has appeared in *McCall's*, *Harper's Bazaar*, and *Family Circle*, and her commentaries have been broadcast on radio and television. In 1979 she published *Close to Home*, a collection of her columns; two other collections have appeared since then, *At Large* (1981) and *Keeping in Touch* (1985). In *Turning Points* (1979), Goodman examines the impact of the feminist movement on men's and women's lives. In 1980 Goodman was awarded the Pulitzer Prize for commentary.

The Family that Stretches (Together)

Casco Bay, Maine—The girl is spending the summer with her extended family. She doesn't put it this way. But as we talk on the beach, the ten-year-old lists the people who are sharing the same house this month with the careful attention of a genealogist.   1

First of all there is her father—visitation rights awarded him the month of August. Second of all there is her father's second wife and two children by her first marriage. All that seems perfectly clear. A stepmother and two stepbrothers.   2

Then there are the others, she slowly explains. There is her stepmother's sister for example. The girl isn't entirely sure whether this makes the woman a stepaunt, or whether her baby is a stepcousin. Beyond that, the real puzzle is whether her stepaunt's husband's children by his first marriage have any sort of official relationship to her at all. It does, we both agree, seem a bit fuzzy.   3

Nevertheless, she concludes, with a certainty that can only be mustered by the sort of ten-year-old who keeps track of her own Frequent Flier coupons, "We are in the same family." With that she closes the subject and focuses instead on her peanut butter and jelly.   4

I am left to my thoughts. My companion, in her own unselfconscious way, is a fine researcher. She grasps the wide new family configurations that are neglected by census data takers and social scientists.   5

After all, those of us who grew up in traditional settings remember families which extended into elaborate circles of aunts, uncles, and cous-   6 ins. There were sides to this family, names and titles to be memorized. But they fit together in a biological pattern.

Now, as my young friend can attest, we have fewer children and   7
more divorces. We know that as many as 50 percent of recent marriages may end. About 75 percent of divorced women and 83 percent of divorced men then remarry. Of those marriages, 59 percent include a child from a former marriage.

So, our families often extend along lines that are determined by   8
decrees, rather than genes. If the nucleus is broken, there are still links forged in different directions.

The son of a friend was asked to produce a family tree for his sixth-   9
grade class. But he was dissatisfied with his oak. There was no room on it for his stepgrandfather, though the man had married his widowed grandmother years ago.

More to the point, the boy had to create an offshoot for his new   10
baby half-brother that seemed too distant. He couldn't find a proper place for the uncle—the ex-uncle to be precise—whom he visited last summer with his cousin.

A family tree just doesn't work, he complained. He would have   11
preferred to draw family bushes.

The reality is that divorce has created kinship ties that rival the   12
most complex tribe. These are not always easy relationships. The children and even the adults whose family lives have been disrupted by divorce and remarriage learn that people they love do not necessarily love each other. This extended family does not gather for reunions and Thanksgivings.

But when it works, it can provide a support system of sorts. I have   13
seen the nieces, nephews—even the dogs—of one marriage welcomed as guests into another. There are all sorts of relationships that survive the marital ones, though there are no names for these kinfolk, no nomenclature for this extending family.

Not long ago, when living together first became a common pattern,   14
people couldn't figure out what to call each other. It was impossible to introduce the man you lived with as a "spouse equivalent." It was harder to refer to the woman your son lived with as his lover, mistress, housemate.

It's equally difficult to describe the peculiar membership of this new   15
lineage. Does your first husband's mother become a mother-out-law? Is the woman no longer married to your uncle an ex-aunt? We have nieces and nephews left dangling like participles from other lives and stepfamilies entirely off the family tree.

Our reality is more flexible and our relationships more supportive 16
than our language. But for the moment, my ten-year-old researcher is
right. However accidentally, however uneasily, "We are in the same
family."

Questions for Study and Discussion

1. Explain the meaning of Goodman's title.

2. What for Goodman is a traditional family? What does she mean when
she says "our families often extend along lines that are determined by decrees,
rather than genes"?

3. What is Goodman's attitude toward her "ten-year-old researcher"? How
do you know?

4. What is Goodman's point in this essay? Is she being completely objective
or is she judgmental?

5. What problems does the sixth-grade boy have in drawing his family tree?
How much do you know about your own family tree? Are there any relationships within your family that are difficult to place on the family tree?

Writing Topics

1. Write an essay in which you use the following statement from Goodman's
essay as your thesis: "Our reality is more flexible and our relationships more
supportive than our language." Be sure to use appropriate examples to illustrate your essay.

2. Write an essay in which you compare and contrast the attitudes of Goodman and Tiger (pp. 156–159) about the new kinship systems.

JANE HOWARD

Jane Howard was born in Springfield, Illinois, in 1935. After graduating from the University of Michigan in 1956, she went to work for *Life* magazine, first as a reporter, then as an editor, and later as a staff reporter. Later she taught courses in writing at the University of Georgia, Yale University, the State University of New York at Albany, and Southamptom College. From 1974 to 1983 she served as the book critic for *Mademoiselle.* Her published works include *Please Touch: A Guided Tour of the Human Potential Movement* (1970), *A Different Woman* (1973), *Families* (1978), and *Margaret Mead: A Life* (1984).

The following selection is from *Families,* of which *New York Review of Books* critic Diane Johnson wrote: "All in all, there's comfort in Howard's book for everyone who worries about his family arrangements—that is, for 83.7 percent of us. It's reassuring to read about people who are weirder than you are, and inspiring to read about people who are better."

All Happy Clans Are Alike: In Search of the Good Family

Call it a clan, call it a network, call it a tribe, call it a family. Whatever you call it, whoever you are, you need one. You need one because you are human. You didn't come from nowhere. Before you, around you, and presumably after you, too, there are others. Some of these others must matter a lot—to you, and if you are very lucky, to one another. Their welfare must be nearly as important to you as your own. Even if you live alone, even if your solitude is elected and ebullient, you still cannot do without a clan or a tribe.

The trouble with the clans and tribes many of us were born into is not that they consist of meddlesome ogres but that they are too far away. In emergencies we rush across continents and if need be oceans to their sides, as they do to ours. Maybe we even make a habit of seeing them, once or twice a year, for the sheer pleasure of it. But blood ties seldom dictate our addresses. Our blood kin are often too remote to ease us from our Tuesdays to our Wednesdays. For this we must rely on our families of friends. If our relatives are not, do not wish to be, or for whatever reasons cannot be our friends, then by some complex alchemy we must try to transform our friends into our relatives. If blood and roots don't do the job, then we must look to water and branches, and sort ourselves into new constellations, new families.

These new families, to borrow the terminology of an African tribe   3
(the Bangwa of the Cameroons), may consist either of friends of the
road, ascribed by chance, or friends of the heart, achieved by choice.
Ascribed friends are those we happen to go to school with, work with,
or live near. They know where we went last weekend and whether we
still have a cold. Just being around gives them a provisional importance
in our lives, and us in theirs. Maybe they will still matter to us when we
or they move away; quite likely they won't. Six months or two years will
probably erase us from each other's thoughts, unless by some chance they
and we have become friends of the heart.

Wishing to be friends, as Aristotle wrote, is quick work, but friend-   4
ship is a slowly ripening fruit. An ancient proverb he quotes in his *Ethics*
had it that you cannot know a man until you and he together have eaten
a peck of salt. Now a peck, a quarter of a bushel, is quite a lot of salt—
more, perhaps, than most pairs of people ever have occasion to share.
We must try though. We must sit together at as many tables as we can.
We must steer each other through enough seasons and weathers so that
sooner or later it crosses our minds that one of us, God knows which or
with what sorrow, must one day mourn the other.

We must devise new ways, or revive old ones, to equip ourselves   5
with kinfolk. Maybe such an impulse prompted whoever ordered the cake
I saw in my neighborhood bakery to have it frosted to say "HAPPY BIRTHDAY
SURROGATE." I like to think that this cake was decorated not for a judge
but for someone's surrogate mother or surrogate brother: Loathsome jargon, but admirable sentiment. If you didn't conceive me or if we didn't
grow up in the same house, we can still be related, if we decide we ought
to be. It is never too late, I like to hope, to augment our families in ways
nature neglected to do. It is never too late to choose new clans.

The best-chosen clans, like the best friendships and the best blood   6
families, endure by accumulating a history solid enough to suggest a
future. But clans that don't last have merit too. We can lament them
but we shouldn't deride them. Better an ephemeral clan or tribe than
none at all. A few of my life's most totally joyous times, in fact, have
been spent with people whom I have yet to see again. This saddens me,
as it may them too, but dwelling overlong on such sadness does no good.
A more fertile exercise is to think back on those times and try to figure
out what made them, for all their brevity, so stirring. What can such
times teach us about forming new and more lasting tribes in the future?

New tribes and clans can no more be willed into existence, of   7
course, than any other good thing can. We keep trying, though. To try,
with gritted teeth and girded loins, is after all American. That is what
the two Helens and I were talking about the day we had lunch in a room

up in a high-rise motel near the Kansas City airport. We had lunch there at the end of a two-day conference on families. The two Helens were social scientists, but I liked them even so, among other reasons because they both objected to that motel's coffee shop even more than I did. One of the Helens, from Virginia, disliked it so much that she had brought along homemade whole wheat bread, sesame butter, and honey from her parents' farm in South Dakota, where she had visited before the conference. Her picnic was the best thing that happened, to me at least, those whole two days.

"If you're voluntarily childless and alone," said the other Helen,   8
who was from Pennsylvania by way of Puerto Rico, "it gets harder and harder with the passage of time. It's stressful. That's why you need support systems." I had been hearing quite a bit of talk about "support systems." The term is not among my favorites, but I can understand its currency. Whatever "support systems" may be, the need for them is clearly urgent, and not just in this country. Are there not thriving "megafamilies" of as many as three hundred people in Scandinavia? Have not the Japanese for years had an honored, enduring—if perhaps by our standards rather rigid—custom of adopting nonrelatives to fill gaps in their families? Should we not applaud and maybe imitate such ingenuity?

And consider our own Unitarians. From Santa Barbara to Boston   9
they have been earnestly dividing their congregations into arbitrary "extended families" whose members are bound to act like each other's relatives. Kurt Vonnegut, Jr., plays with a similar train of thought in his fictional *Slapstick*. In that book every newborn baby is assigned a randomly chosen middle name, like Uranium or Daffodil or Raspberry. These middle names are connected with hyphens to numbers between one and twenty, and any two people who have the same middle name are automatically related. This is all to the good, the author thinks, because "human beings need all the relatives they can get—as possible donors or receivers not of love but of common decency." He envisions these extended families as "one of the four greatest inventions by Americans," the others being *Robert's Rules of Order*, the Bill of Rights, and the principles of Alcoholics Anonymous.

This charming notion might even work, if it weren't so arbitrary.   10
Already each of us is born into one family not of our choosing. If we're going to devise new ones, we might as well have the luxury of picking the members ourselves. Clever picking might result in new families whose benefits would surpass or at least equal those of the old. As a member in reasonable standing of six or seven tribes in addition to the one I was born to, I have been trying to figure which characteristics are common to both kinds of families.

1. Good families have a chief, or a heroine, or a founder—someone 11 around whom others cluster, whose achievements, as the Yiddish word has it, let them *kvell,* and whose example spurs them on to like feats. Some blood dynasties produce such figures regularly; others languish for as many as five generations between demigods, wondering with each new pregnancy whether this, at last, might be the messianic baby who will redeem them. Look, is there not something gubernatorial about her footstep, or musical about the way he bangs with his spoon on his cup? All clans, of all kinds, need such a figure now and them. Sometimes clans based on water rather than blood harbor several such personages at one time. The Bloomsbury Group in London six decades ago was not much hampered by its lack of a temporal history.

2. Good families have a switchboard operator—someone who can- 12 not help but keep track of what all the others are up to, who plays Houston Mission Control to everyone else's Apollo. This role is assumed rather than assigned. The person who volunteers for it often has the instincts of an archivist, and feels driven to keep scrapbooks and photograph albums up to date, so that the clan can see proof of its own continuity.

3. Good families are much to all their members, but everything to 13 none. Good families are fortresses with many windows and doors to the outer world. The blood clans I feel most drawn to were founded by parents who are nearly as devoted to what they do outside as they are to each other and their children. Their curiosity and passion are contagious. Everybody, where they live, is busy. Paint is spattered on eyeglasses. Mud lurks under fingernails. Person-to-person calls come in the middle of the night from Tokyo and Brussels. Catcher's mitts, ballet slippers, overdue library books, and other signs of extrafamilial concerns are everywhere.

4. Good families are hospitable. Knowing that hosts need guests as 14 much as guests need hosts, they are generous with honorary memberships for friends, whom they urge to come early and often and to stay late. Such clans exude a vivid sense of surrounding rings of relatives, neighbors, teachers, students, and godparents, any of whom at any time might break or slide into the inner circle. Inside that circle a wholesome, tacit emotional feudalism develops: you give me protection, I'll give you fealty. Such pacts begin with, but soon go far beyond, the jolly exchange of pie at Thanksgiving or cake on a birthday. They mean that you can ask me to supervise your children for the fortnight you will be in the hospital, and that however inconvenient this might be for me, I shall manage to do so. It means I can phone you on what for me is a dreary, wretched Sunday afternoon and for you is the eve of a deadline, knowing you will tell me to come right over, if only to watch you type. It means we need

not dissemble. ("To yield to seeming," as Martin Buber wrote, "is man's essential cowardice, to resist it is his essential courage . . . one must at times pay dearly for life lived from the being, but it is never too dear.")

5. Good families deal squarely with direness. Pity the tribe that 15 doesn't have, and cherish, at least one flamboyant eccentric. Pity too the one that supposes it can avoid for long the woes to which all flesh is heir. Lunacy, bankruptcy, suicide, and other unthinkable fates sooner or later afflict the noblest of clans with an undertow of gloom. Family life is a set of givens, someone once told me, and it takes courage to see certain givens as blessings rather than as curses. It surely does. Contradictions and inconsistencies are givens, too. So is the battle against what the Oregon patriarch Kenneth Babbs calls malarkey. "There's always malarkey lurking, bubbles in the cesspool, fetid bubbles that pop and smell. But I don't put up with malarkey, between my stepkids and my natural ones or anywhere else in the family."

6. Good families prize their rituals. Nothing welds a family more 16 than these. Rituals are vital especially for clans without histories, because they evoke a past, imply a future, and hint at continuity. No line in the seder service at Passover reassures more than the last: "Next year in Jerusalem!" A clan becomes more of a clan each time it gathers to observe a fixed ritual (Christmas, birthdays, Thanksgiving, and so on), grieves at a funeral (anyone may come to most funerals; those who do declare their tribalness), and devises a new rite of its own. Equinox breakfasts can be at least as welding as Memorial Day parades. Several of my colleagues and I used to meet for lunch every Pearl Harbor Day, preferably to eat some politically neutral fare like smorgasbord, to "forgive" our only ancestrally Japanese friend, Irene Kubota Neves. For that and other things we became, and remain, a sort of family.

"Rituals," a California friend of mine said, "aren't just externals 17 and holidays. They are the performances of our lives. They are a kind of shorthand. They can't be decreed. My mother used to try to decree them. She'd make such a goddamn fuss over what we talked about at dinner, aiming at Topics of Common Interest, topics that celebrated our cohesion as a family. These performances were always hollow, because the phenomenology of the moment got sacrificed for the *idea* of the moment. Real rituals are discovered in retrospect. They emerge around constitutive moments, moments that only happen once, around whose memory meanings cluster. You don't choose those moments. They choose themselves." A lucky clan includes a born mythologizer, like my blood sister, who has the gift for apprehending such a moment when she sees it, and who cannot help but invent new rituals everywhere she goes.

7. Good families are affectionate. This of course is a matter of style. I know clans whose members greet each other with gingerly handshakes or, in what pass for kisses, with hurried brushes of jawbones, as if the object were to touch not the lips but the ears. I don't see how such people manage. "The tribe that does not hug," as someone who has been part of many *ad hoc* families recently wrote to me, "is no tribe at all. More and more I realize that everybody, regardless of age, needs to be hugged and comforted in a brotherly or sisterly way now and then. Preferably now." [18]

8. Good families have a sense of place, which these days is not achieved easily. As Susanne Langer wrote in 1957, "Most people have no home that is a symbol of their childhood, not even a definite memory of one place to serve that purpose . . . all the old symbols are gone." Once I asked a roomful of supper guests if anyone felt a strong pull to any certain spot on the face of the earth. Everyone was silent, except for a visitor from Bavaria. The rest of us seemed to know all too well what Walker Percy means in *The Moviegoer* when he tells of the "genie-soul of a place, which every place has or else is not a place [and which] wherever you go, you must meet and master or else be met and mastered." All that meeting and mastering saps plenty of strength. It also underscores our need for tribal bases of the sort which soaring real estate taxes and splintering families have made all but obsolete. [19]

So what are we to do, those of us whose habit and pleasure and doom is our tendency, as a Georgia lady put it, to "fly off at ever other whipstitch?" Think in terms of movable feasts, that's what. Live here, wherever here may be, as if we were going to belong here for the rest of our lives. Learn to hallow whatever ground we happen to stand on or land on. Like medieval knights who took their tapestries along on Crusades, like modern Afghanis with their yurts, we must pack such totems and icons as we can to make short-term quarters feel like home. Pillows, small rugs, watercolors can dispel much of the chilling anonymity of a motel room or sublet apartment. When we can, we should live in rooms with stoves or fireplaces or at least candlelight. The ancient saying is still true: Extinguished hearth, extinguished family. [20]

Round tables help too, and as a friend of mine once put it, so do "too many comfortable chairs, with surfaces to put feet on, arranged so as to encourage a maximum of eye contact." Such rooms inspire good talk, of which good clans can never have enough. [21]

9. Good families, not just the blood kind, find some way to connect with posterity. "To forge a link in the humble chain of being, encircling heirs to ancestors," as Michael Novak has written, "is to walk within a circle of magic as primitive as humans knew in caves." He is talking of [22]

course about babies, feeling them leap in wombs, giving them suck. Parenthood, however, is a state which some miss by chance and others by design, and a vocation to which not all are called. Some of us, like the novelist Richard P. Brickner, look on as others "name their children and their children in turn name their own lives, devising their own flags from their parents' cloth." What are we who lack children to do? Build houses? Plant trees? Write books or symphonies or laws? Perhaps, but even if we do these things, there should be children on the sidelines if not at the center of our lives.

It is a sadly impoverished tribe that does not allow access to, and make much of, some children. Not too much, of course; it has truly been said that never in history have so many educated people devoted so much attention to so few children. Attention, in excess, can turn to fawning, which isn't much better than neglect. Still, if we don't regularly see and talk to and laugh with people who can expect to outlive us by twenty years or so, we had better get busy and find some.

10. Good families also honor their elders. The wider the age range, the stronger the tribe. Jean-Paul Sartre and Margaret Mead, to name two spectacularly confident former children, have both remarked on the central importance of grandparents in their own early lives. Grandparents are now in much more abundant supply than they were a generation or two ago, when old age was more rare. If actual grandparents are not at hand, no family should have too hard a time finding substitute ones to whom to pay unfeigned homage. The Soviet Union's enchantment with day-care centers, I have heard, stems at least in part from the state's eagerness to keep children away from their presumably subversive grandparents. Let that be a lesson to clans based on interest as well as to those based on genes.

Of course there are elders and elders. Most people in America, as David T. Bazelon has written, haven't the slightest idea of what to do with the extra thirty years they have been given to live. Few are as briskly secure as Alice Roosevelt Longworth, who once, when I visited her for tea, showed a recent photograph and asked whether I didn't think it made her look like "a malevolent Eurasian concubine—an *aged* malevolent Eurasian concubine." I admitted that it did, which was just what she wanted to hear. But those of us whose fathers weren't Presidents may not grow old, if at all, with such style.

Sad stories abound. The mother of one friend of mine languished for years, never far from a coma, in a nursing home. Only when her husband and children sang one of her favorite old songs, such as "Lord Jeffrey Amherst," would a smile fleet across her face. But a man I know of in New Jersey, who couldn't stand the state of Iowa or babies, changed his mind on both counts when his daughter, who lived in Iowa, had a baby. Suddenly he took to inventing business trips to St. Louis, by way of Cedar Rapids, phoning to say he would be at the airport there at 11:31 P.M. and "Be sure to bring Jake!" That cheers me. So did part of a talk I had with a woman in Albuquerque, whom I hadn't seen since a trip some years before to the Soviet Union.

"Honey," she said when I phoned her during a short stopover and asked how she was, "if I were any better I'd blow up and *bust!* I can't *tell* you how *neat* it is to put some age on! A lot of it, of course, has to do with going to the shrink, getting uncorked, and of course it doesn't hurt to have money—no, we *don't* have a ranch; it's only 900 acres, so we call it a farm. But every year, as far as age is concerned, I seem to get better, doing more and more stuff I love to do. The only thing I've ever wanted and don't have is a good marriage. Nothing I do ever pleases the men I marry. The only reason I'm still married now is it's too much trouble not to be. But my girls are growing up to be just *neat* humans, and the men they're sharing their lives with are too. They pick nice guys, my girls. I wish I could say the same. But I'm a lot better off than many women my age. I go to parties where sixty-year-olds with blue bouffant hairdos are still telling the same jokes they told twenty-five or thirty years ago. Complacent? No, that's not it, exactly. What they are is sad —sad as the dickens. They don't seem to be *connected*." [27]

Some days my handwriting resembles my mother's, slanting hopefully and a bit extravagantly eastward. Other days it looks more like my father's: resolute, vertical, guardedly free of loops. Both my parents will remain in my nerves and muscles and mind until the day I die, and so will my sister, but they aren't the only ones. If I were to die tomorrow, the obituary would note that my father and sister survived me. True, but not true enough. Like most official lists of survivors, this one would be incomplete. [28]

Several of the most affecting relationships I have ever known of, or been part of, have sprung not from genes or contracts but from serendipitous, uncanny bonds of choice. I don't think enough can be said for the fierce tenderness such bonds can generate. Maybe the best thing to say is nothing at all, or very little. Midwestern preachers used to hold that "a heavy rain doesn't seep into the ground but rolls off—when you preach to farmers, your sermon should be a drizzle instead of a downpour." So too with any cause that matters: shouting and lapel-grabbing and institutionalizing can do more harm than good. A quiet approach works better. [29]

"I wish it would hurry up and get colder," I said one warm afternoon several Octobers ago to a black man with whom I was walking in a park. [30]

"Don't worry," he told me. "Like my grandmother used to say when   31
I was a boy, 'Hawk'll be here soon enough.' "

"What did she mean by 'hawk'?"   32

"Hawk meant winter, cold, trouble. And she was right: the hawk   33
always came."

With regard to families, many would say that the hawk has long   34
been here, hovering. "I'd rather put up with being lonely now than have
to put up with being still more lonely in the future," says a character in
Natsume Soseki's novel *Kokoro*. "We live in an age of freedom, independence, and the self, and I imagine this loneliness is the price we have
to pay for it." Seven decades earlier, in *Either/Or*, Sören Kierkegaard had
written, "Our age has lost all the substantial categories of family, state,
and race. It must leave the individual entirely to himself, so that in a
stricter sense he becomes his own creator."

If it is true that we must create ourselves, maybe while we are about   35
it we can also devise some new kinds of families, new connections to
supplement the old ones. The second verse of a hymn by James Russell
Lowell says,

New occasions bring new duties;
Time makes ancient good uncouth.

Surely one outworn "good" is the maxim that blood relatives are the
only ones who can or should greatly matter. Or look at it another way:
go back six generations, and each one of us has sixty-four direct ancestors.
Go back twenty—only four or five centuries, not such a big chunk of
human history—and we each have more than a million. Does it not
stand to reason, since the world population was then so much smaller,
that we all have a lot more cousins—though admittedly distant ones—
than we were brought up to suspect? And don't these cousins deserve
our attention?

One day after lunch at a friend's apartment I waited in his lobby   36
while he collected his mail. Out of the elevator came two nurses supporting a wizened, staring woman who couldn't have weighed much more
than seventy pounds. It was all the woman could do to make her way
down the three steps to the sidewalk and the curb where a car was
waiting. Those steps must have been to that woman what a steep mountain trail would be to me. The nurses guided her down them with infinite
patience.

"Easy, darlin'," one nurse said to the woman.   37

"That's a good girl," said the other. The woman, my friend's door-   38
man told us, was ninety. That morning she had fallen and hurt herself.
On her forehead was something which, had it not been a bruise, we
might have thought beautiful: a marvel of mauve and lavender and ma-

genta. This woman, who was then being taken to a nursing home, had lived in my friend's apartment for forty years. All her relatives were dead, and her few surviving friends no longer chose to see her.

"But how can that be?" I asked my friend. "*We* could never be that alone, could we?"   39

"Don't be so sure," said my friend, who knows more of such matters   40
than I do. "Even if we were to end up in the same nursing home, if I was in markedly worse shape than you were, you might not want to see me, either."

"But I can't imagine not wanting to see you."   41

"It happens," my friend said.   42

Maybe we can keep it from happening. Maybe the hawk can be   43
kept at bay, if we give more thought to our tribes and our clans and our several kinds of families. No aim seems to me more urgent, nor any achievement more worthy of a psalm. So *hosanna in excelsis,* and blest be the tie that binds. And please pass the salt.

Questions for Study and Discussion

1. As Howard's subtitle indicates, this essay is concerned with the articulation and enumeration of the characteristics of the good family. According to Howard, what is it that all good families have in common?

2. How does Howard organize her essay?

3. What are "friends of the road"? How do they differ from "friends of the heart"?

4. What are some of the problems or difficulties or shortcomings of contemporary life that prompt Jane Howard to search for the "good family"? Why can people no longer count on their biological families?

5. Howard uses a wide variety of examples to support and illustrate her philosophic points. What types of examples has she used? Which examples do you find most effective? Explain.

6. In paragraph 4 Howard refers to an ancient proverb Aristotle quotes in his *Ethics:* "You cannot know a man until you and he together have eaten a peck of salt." How do you interpret this proverb?

Writing Topics

1. Howard says that she belongs to six or seven tribes in addition to her biological family. Write an essay in which you discuss one or more of the various "tribes" of which you are a member.

2. Howard believes that "good families prize their rituals." What are some of the rituals that you and your family share? What personal needs do these rituals satisfy for you? Write an essay in which you argue for the preservation of rituals in the family setting.

What Are Friends?

MARGARET MEAD AND RHODA METRAUX

Margaret Mead (1901–1978) was a noted educator, anthropologist, and author. Educated at Barnard College and Columbia University, she was for many years a professor of anthropology at Columbia. She spent much of her life studying foreign societies and became an expert in such fields as family structure, mental health, drugs, environmental problems, and women's roles in society. Her best-known books include *Coming of Age in Samoa* (1928), *Male and Female* (1949), *The Study of Culture at a Distance* (1953), and *Childhood in Contemporary Cultures* (1955). Rhoda Metraux was born in 1914 and is also an anthropologist. She was educated at Vassar, Yale, and Columbia. Metraux first met Mead while working at the American Museum of Natural History. A contributor to anthropological journals, Metraux collaborated with Mead on *A Way of Seeing* (1970), from which the following selection was taken. As you read this essay, notice the way the authors use examples both to define friendship and to point out the way different cultures regard friendship.

On Friendship

Few Americans stay put for a lifetime. We move from town to city   1
to suburb, from high school to college in a different state, from a job in
one region to a better job elsewhere, from the home where we raise our
children to the home where we plan to live in retirement. With each
move we are forever making new friends, who become part of our new
life at that time.

For many of us the summer is a special time for forming new friend-   2
ships. Today millions of Americans vacation abroad, and they go not
only to see new sights but also—in those places where they do not feel
too strange—with the hope of meeting new people. No one really expects
a vacation trip to produce a close friend. But surely the beginning of a
friendship is possible? Surely in every country people value friendship?

They do. The difficulty when strangers from two countries meet is   3

175

not a lack of appreciation of friendship, but different expectations about what constitutes friendship and how it comes into being. In those European countries that Americans are most likely to visit, friendship is quite sharply distinguished from other, more casual relations, and is differently related to family life. For a Frenchman, a German or an Englishman friendship is usually more particularized and carries a heavier burden of commitment.

But as we use the word, "friend" can be applied to a wide range of   4
relationships—to someone one has known for a few weeks in a new place, to a close business associate, to a childhood playmate, to a man or woman, to a trusted confidant. There are real differences among these relations for Americans—a friendship may be superficial, casual, situational or deep and enduring. But to a European, who sees only our surface behavior, the differences are not clear.

As they see it, people known and accepted temporarily, casually,   5
flow in and out of Americans' homes with little ceremony and often with little personal commitment. They may be parents of the children's friends, house guests of neighbors, members of a committee, business associates from another town or even another country. Coming as a guest into an American home, the European visitor finds no visible landmarks. The atmosphere is relaxed. Most people, old and young, are called by first names.

Who, then, is a friend?   6

Even simple translation from one language to another is difficult.   7
"You see," a Frenchman explains, "if I were to say to you in France, 'This is my good friend,' that person would not be as close to me as someone about whom I said only, 'This is my friend.' Anyone about whom I have to say *more* is really less."

In France, as in many European countries, friends generally are of   8
the same sex, and friendship is seen as basically a relationship between men. Frenchwomen laugh at the idea that "women can't be friends," but they also admit sometimes that for women "it's a different thing." And many French people doubt the possibility of a friendship between a man and a woman. There is also the kind of relationship within a group— men and women who have worked together for a long time, who may be very close, sharing great loyalty and warmth of feeling. They may call one another *copains*—a word that in English becomes "friends" but has more the feeling of "pals" or "buddies." In French eyes this is not friendship, although two members of such a group may well be friends.

For the French, friendship is a one-to-one relationship that de-   9
mands a keen awareness of the other person's intellect, temperament and particular interests. A friend is someone who draws out your own best

qualities, with whom you sparkle and become more of whatever the friendship draws upon. Your political philosophy assumes more depth, appreciation of a play becomes sharper, taste in food or wine is accentuated, enjoyment of a sport is intensified.

And French friendships are compartmentalized. A man may play 10
chess with a friend for thirty years without knowing his political opinions, or he may talk politics with him for as long a time without knowing about his personal life. Different friends fill different niches in each person's life. These friendships are not made part of family life. A friend is not expected to spend evenings being nice to children or courteous to a deaf grandmother. These duties, also serious and enjoined, are primarily for relatives. Men who are friends may meet in a café. Intellectual friends may meet in larger groups for evenings of conversation. Working people may meet at the little *bistro* where they drink and talk, far from the family. Marriage does not affect such friendships; wives do not have to be taken into account.

In the past in France, friendships of this kind seldom were open to 11
any but intellectual women. Since most women's lives centered on their homes, their warmest relations with other women often went back to their girlhood. The special relationship of friendship is based on what the French value most—on the mind, on compatibility of outlook, on vivid awareness of some chosen area of life.

Friendship heightens the sense of each person's individuality. Other 12
relationships commanding as great loyalty and devotion have a different meaning. In World War II the first resistance groups formed in Paris were built on the foundation of *les copains*. But significantly, as time went on these little groups, whose lives rested in one another's hands, called themselves "families." Where each had a total responsibility for all, it was kinship ties that provided the model. And even today such ties, crossing every line of class and personal interest, remain binding on the survivors of these small, secret bands.

In Germany, in contrast with France, friendship is much more 13
articulately a matter of feeling. Adolescents, boys and girls, form deeply sentimental attachments, walk and talk together—not so much to polish their wits as to share their hopes and fears and dreams, to form a common front against the world of school and family and to join in a kind of mutual discovery of each other's and their own inner life. Within the family, the closest relationship over a lifetime is between brothers and sisters. Outside the family, men and women find in their closest friends of the same sex the devotion of a sister, the loyalty of a brother. Appropriately, in Germany friends usually are brought into the family. Children call their father's and their mother's friends "uncle" and "aunt." Between

French friends, who have chosen each other for the congeniality of their point of view, lively disagreement and sharpness of argument are the breath of life. But for Germans, whose friendships are based on mutuality of feeling, deep disagreement on any subject that matters to both is regarded as a tragedy. Like ties of kinship, ties of friendship are meant to be irrevocably binding. Young Germans who come to the United States have great difficulty in establishing such friendships with Americans. We view friendship more tentatively, subject to changes in intensity as people move, change their jobs, marry, or discover new interests.

English friendships follow still a different pattern. Their basis is   14
shared activity. Activities at different stages of life may be of very different kinds—discovering a common interest in school, serving together in the armed forces, taking part in a foreign mission, staying in the same country house during a crisis. In the midst of the activity, whatever it may be, people fall into step—sometimes two men or two women, sometimes two couples, sometimes three people—and find that they walk or play a game or tell stories or serve on a tiresome and exacting committee with the same easy anticipation of what each will do day by day or in some critical situation. Americans who have made English friends comment that, even years later, "you can take up just where you left off." Meeting after a long interval, friends are like a couple who begin to dance again when the orchestra strikes up after a pause. English friendships are formed outside the family circle, but they are not, as in Germany, contrapuntal to the family nor are they, as in France, separated from the family. And a break in an English friendship comes not necessarily as a result of some irreconcilable difference of viewpoint or feeling but instead as a result of misjudgment, where one friend seriously misjudges how the other will think or feel or act, so that suddenly they are out of step.

What, then, is friendship? Looking at these different styles, in-   15
cluding our own, each of which is related to a whole way of life, are there common elements? There is the recognition that friendship, in contrast with kinship, invokes freedom of choice. A friend is someone who chooses and is chosen. Related to this is the sense each friend gives the other of being a special individual, on whatever grounds this recognition is based. And between friends there is inevitably a kind of equality of give-and-take. These similarities make the bridge between societies possible, and the American's characteristic openness to different styles of relationship makes it possible for him to find new friends abroad with whom he feels at home.

Questions for Study and Discussion

1. How, according to Mead and Metraux, do Americans use the term "friend"? Do you agree with their sense of how the word is used? How does our use of the word differ from that of Europeans?

2. What is the authors' purpose in this essay—to tell a story, to explain, to persuade? How do you know?

3. What are the major differences between the way friends are viewed in France, Germany, and England? Do any of these differences surprise you? Explain.

4. What do Mead and Metraux see as the difference between "friendship" and "kinship"?

5. Why do Americans seem to be able to find new "friends" when traveling abroad?

Writing Topics

1. What are your expectations of a friendship? What does the term "best friend" mean to you? How has your conception of friendship changed as you've grown older? Present your responses to these three questions in an essay.

2. Is it possible for men and women to have friendships? What, if any, are the problems that could arise with such a relationship? Your essay may simply reflect on the issue, or it may take the form of an argument for or against the possibility of male-female friendships.

JUDITH VIORST

The American philosopher George Santayana once wrote, "Friendship is almost always the union of a part of one mind with a part of another; people are friends in spots." Judith Viorst would agree. In fact, in this essay, she goes further, mapping the different kinds of spots where her mind achieves union with her friends'. A professional writer, Viorst was born in 1936 and has marked off the periods of her life with books of light verse: *It's Hard to Be Hip over Thirty and Other Tragedies of Married Life* (1970); *How Did I Get to Be Forty and Other Atrocities* (1976). She also writes books for children, has collaborated with her husband on a guide to the restaurants of Washington, D.C., and is a contributing editor of *Redbook*. As you read this essay, which first appeared in her regular column in *Redbook*, see whether your own friends fit into Viorst's categories.

Friends, Good Friends
—and Such Good Friends

Women are friends, I once would have said, when they totally love   1
and support and trust each other, and bare to each other the secrets of their souls, and run—no questions asked—to help each other, and tell harsh truths to each other (no, you can't wear that dress unless you lose ten pounds first) when harsh truths must be told.

Women are friends, I once would have said, when they share the   2
same affection for Ingmar Bergman, plus train rides, cats, warm rain, charades, Camus, and hate with equal ardor Newark and Brussels sprouts and Lawrence Welk and camping.

In other words, I once would have said that a friend is a friend all   3
the way, but now I believe that's a narrow point of view. For the friendships I have and the friendships I see are conducted at many levels of intensity, serve many different functions, meet different needs and range from those as all-the-way as the friendship of the soul sisters mentioned above to that of the most nonchalant and casual playmates.

Consider these varieties of friendship: 4

1. Convenience friends. These are women with whom, if our paths   5
weren't crossing all the time, we'd have no particular reason to be friends: a next-door neighbor, a woman in our car pool, the mother of one of our children's closest friends or maybe some mommy with whom we serve juice and cookies each week at the Glenwood Co-op Nursery.

Convenience friends are convenient indeed. They'll lend us their 6
cups and silverware for a party. They'll drive our kids to soccer when
we're sick. They'll take us to pick up our car when we need a lift to the
garage. They'll even take our cats when we go on vacation. As we will
for them.

But we don't, with convenience friends, ever come too close or tell 7
too much; we maintain our public face and emotional distance. "Which
means," says Elaine, "that I'll talk about being overweight but not about
being depressed. Which means I'll admit being mad but not blind with
rage. Which means that I might say that we're pinched this month but
never that I'm worried sick over money."

But which doesn't mean that there isn't sufficient value to be found 8
in these friendships of mutual aid, in convenience friends.

2. Special-interest friends. These friendships aren't intimate, and 9
they needn't involve kids or silverware or cats. Their value lies in some
interest jointly shared. And so we may have an office friend or a yoga
friend or a tennis friend or a friend from the Women's Democratic Club.

"I've got one woman friend," says Joyce, "who likes, as I do, to 10
take psychology courses. Which makes it nice for me—and nice for her.
It's fun to go with someone you know and it's fun to discuss what you've
learned, driving back from the classes." And for the most part, she says,
that's all they discuss.

"I'd say that what we're doing is *doing* together, not being together," 11
Suzanne says of her Tuesday-doubles friends. "It's mainly a tennis relationship, but we play together well. And I guess we all need to have a
couple of playmates."

I agree. 12

My playmate is a shopping friend, a woman of marvelous taste, a 13
woman who knows exactly *where* to buy *what,* and furthermore is a woman
who always knows beyond a doubt what one ought to be buying. I don't
have the time to keep up with what's new in eyeshadow, hemlines and
shoes and whether the smock look is in or finished already. But since
(oh, shame!) I care a lot about eyeshadows, hemlines and shoes, and
since I don't *want* to wear smocks if the smock look is finished, I'm very
glad to have a shopping friend.

3. Historical friends. We all have a friend who knew us when . . . 14
maybe way back in Miss Meltzer's second grade, when our family lived
in that three-room flat in Brooklyn, when our dad was out of work for
seven months, when our brother Allie got in that fight where they had
to call the police, when our sister married the endodontist from Yonkers
and when, the morning after we lost our virginity, she was the first, the
only, friend we told.

The years have gone by and we've gone separate ways and we've   15
little in common now, but we're still an intimate part of each other's
past. And so whenever we go to Detroit we always go to visit this friend
of our girlhood. Who knows how we looked before our teeth were
straightened. Who knows how we talked before our voice got un-Brook-
lyned. Who knows what we ate before we learned about artichokes. And
who, by her presence, puts us in touch with an earlier part of ourself, a
part of ourself it's important never to lose.

"What this friend means to me and what I mean to her," says   16
Grace, "is having a sister without sibling rivalry. We know the texture
of each other's lives. She remembers my grandmother's cabbage soup. I
remember the way her uncle played the piano. There's simply no other
friend who remembers those things."

4. Crossroads friends. Like historical friends, our crossroads friends   17
are important for *what was*—for the friendship we shared at a crucial,
now past, time of life. A time, perhaps, when we roomed in college
together; or worked as eager young singles in the Big City together; or
went together, as my friend Elizabeth and I did, through pregnancy, birth
and that scary first year of new motherhood.

Crossroads friends forge powerful links, links strong enough to en-   18
dure with not much more contact than once-a-year letters at Christmas.
And out of respect for those crossroads years, for those dramas and dreams
we once shared, we will always be friends.

5. Cross-generational friends. Historical friends and crossroads friends   19
seem to maintain a special kind of intimacy—dormant but always ready
to be revived—and though we may rarely meet, whenever we do connect,
it's personal and intense. Another kind of intimacy exists in the friendships that form across generations in what one woman calls her daughter-
mother and her mother-daughter relationships.

Evelyn's friend is her mother's age—"but I share so much more   20
than I ever could with my mother"—a woman she talks to of music, of
books and of life. "What I get from her is the benefit of her experience.
What she gets—and enjoys—from me is a youthful perspective. It's a
pleasure for both of us."

I have in my own life a precious friend, a woman of 65 who has   21
lived very hard, who is wise, who listens well; who has been where I am
and can help me understand it; and who represents not only an ultimate
ideal mother to me but also the person I'd like to be when I grow up.

In our daughter role we tend to do more than our share of self-   22
revelation; in our mother role we tend to receive what's revealed. It's
another kind of pleasure—playing wise mother to a questing younger
person. It's another very lovely kind of friendship.

6. Part-of-a-couple friends. Some of the women we call our friends   23
we never see alone—we see them as part of a couple at couples' parties.
And though we share interests in many things and respect each other's
views, we aren't moved to deepen the relationship. Whatever the reason,
a lack of time or—and this is more likely—a lack of chemistry, our
friendship remains in the context of a group. But the fact that our feeling
on seeing each other is always, "I'm *so* glad she's here" and the fact that
we spend half the evening talking together says that this too, in its own
way, counts as a friendship.

(Other part-of-a-couple friends are the friends that came with the   24
marriage, and some of these are friends we could live without. But sometimes, alas, she married our husband's best friend; and sometimes, alas,
she *is* our husband's best friend. And so we find ourselves dealing with
her, somewhat against our will, in a spirit of what I'll call *reluctant* friendship.)

7. Men who are friends. I wanted to write just of women friends,   25
but the women I've talked to won't let me—they say I must mention
man-woman friendships too. For these friendships can be just as close
and as dear as those that we form with women. Listen to Lucy's description of one such friendship:

"We've found we have things to talk about that are different from   26
what he talks about with my husband and different from what I talk
about with his wife. So sometimes we call on the phone or meet for
lunch. There are similar intellectual interests—we always pass on to each
other the book that we love—but there's also something tender and
caring too."

In a couple of crises, Lucy says, "he offered himself for talking and   27
for helping. And when someone died in his family he wanted me there.
The sexual, flirty part of our friendship is very small—but *some*—just
enough to make it fun and different." She thinks—and I agree—that the
sexual part, though small, is always *some*, is always there when a man
and a woman are friends.

It's only in the past few years that I've made friends with men, in   28
the sense of a friendship that's *mine,* not just part of two couples. And
achieving with them the ease and the trust I've found with women friends
has value indeed. Under the dryer at home last week, putting on mascara
and rouge, I comfortably sat and talked with a fellow named Peter. Peter,
I finally decided, could handle the shock of me minus mascara under the
dryer. Because we care for each other. Because we're friends.

There are medium friends, and pretty good friends, and very good   29
friends indeed, and these friendships are defined by their level of intimacy. And what we'll reveal at each of these levels of intimacy is cali-

brated with care. We might tell a medium friend, for example, that yesterday we had a fight with our husband. And we might tell a pretty good friend that this fight with our husband made us so mad that we slept on the couch. And we might tell a very good friend that the reason we got so mad in that fight that we slept on the couch had something to do with that girl who works in his office. But it's only to our very best friends that we're willing to tell all, to tell what's going on with that girl in his office.

The best of friends, I still believe, totally love and support and trust each other, and bare to each other the secrets of their souls, and run— no questions asked—to help each other, and tell harsh truths to each other when they must be told. 30

But we needn't agree about everything (only 12-year-old girl friends agree about *everything*) to tolerate each other's point of view. To accept without judgment. To give and to take without ever keeping score. And to *be* there, as I am for them and as they are for me, to comfort our sorrows, to celebrate our joys. 31

Questions for Study and Discussion

1. In the opening paragraphs Viorst explains how she once would have defined friendship. What definition might she have given? Why does she now think differently?

2. What is Viorst's purpose in this essay? How does her extended list of categories serve that purpose?

3. The readership of *Redbook*, where this essay first appeared, consists largely of women between the ages of twenty-five and thirty-five. If Viorst had been writing for an audience of young men, how might her categories have been different? How might her examples have been different?

4. How does Viorst use quotation in her essay? Are her quotations appropriate and credible?

5. Throughout the essay Viorst often uses the word *we*. Why do you think she does this? Does it cause problems? If so, where?

6. What is the tone of this essay? Cite passages that show how Viorst creates the tone.

Writing Topics

1. Some people would say that all the relationships Viorst describes are forms of friendship. Others may feel that most are mere acquaintances, and that true friendship is something different. Write an essay in which you explain

what your idea of friendship is. Illustrate your definition with examples from your experience or your reading.

2. American society holds a much broader notion of friendship than many other societies do, and Americans are quite quick to address each other familiarly—using first names and not using titles, for example. Those who have traveled or lived abroad invariably notice this, as do foreigners visiting the United States. What do you think are the advantages of such "easy" friendship and informality? What might the disadvantages be? Write an essay in which you explain your views.

MARC FEIGEN FASTEAU

Marc Feigen Fasteau is a practicing lawyer in New York City with a specialty in sex-discrimination litigation. While at Harvard Law School he was the editor of the Harvard Law Review, and later he worked in government service in Washington, D.C., his birthplace. Fasteau is a frequent lecturer on topics ranging from sex-discrimination legislation to sexual stereotypes, and is the author of *The Male Machine* (1974). His articles have appeared in scholarly journals as well as in such popular magazines as *Ms*.

In *The Male Machine* Fasteau analyzes the stereotype of the American male and concludes that the prevailing stereotype has, in part, dehumanized American men. The following selection is an excerpt from *The Male Machine* in which Fasteau explains why friendships among men are seemingly unfeeling.

Friendships among Men

There is a long-standing myth in our society that the great friend- 1
ships are between men. Forged through shared experience, male friendship is portrayed as the most unselfish, if not the highest form, of human
relationship. The more traditionally masculine the shared experience
from which it springs, the stronger and more profound the friendship is
supposed to be. Going to war, weathering crises together at school or
work, playing on the same athletic team, are some of the classic experiences out of which friendships between men are believed to grow.

By and large, men do prefer the company of other men, not only 2
in their structured time but in the time they fill with optional, nonoblig-
atory activity. They prefer to play games, drink, and talk, as well as work
and fight together. Yet something is missing. Despite the time men spend
together, their contact rarely goes beyond the external, a limitation which
tends to make their friendships shallow and unsatisfying.

My own childhood memories are of doing things with my friends— 3
playing games or sports, building walkie-talkies, going camping. Other
people and my relationships to them were never legitimate subjects for
attention. If someone liked me, it was an opaque, mysterious occurrence
that bore no analysis. When I was slighted, I felt hurt. But relationships
with people just happened. I certainly had feelings about my friends, but
I can't remember a single instance of trying consciously to sort them out
until I was well into college.

For most men this kind of shying away from the personal continues 4
into adult life. In conversations with each other, we hardly ever use

186

ourselves as reference points. We talk about almost everything except how we ourselves are affected by people and events. Everything is discussed as though it were taking place out there somewhere, as though we had no more felt response to it than to the weather. Topics that can be treated in this detached, objective way become conversational mainstays. The few subjects which are fundamentally personal are shaped into discussions of abstract general questions. Even in an exchange about their reactions to liberated women—a topic of intensely personal interest—the tendency will be to talk in general, theoretical terms. Work, at least its objective aspects, is always a safe subject. Men also spend an incredible amount of time rehashing the great public issues of the day. Until early 1973, Vietnam was the work-horse topic. Then came Watergate. It doesn't seem to matter that we've all had a hundred similar conversations. We plunge in for another round, trying to come up with a new angle as much as to impress the others with what we know as to keep from being bored stiff.

Games play a central role in situations organized by men. I remem- 5
ber a weekend some years ago at the country house of a law-school classmate as a blur of softball, football, croquet, poker, and a dice-and-board game called Combat, with swimming thrown in on the side. As soon as one game ended, another began. Taken one at a time, these "activities" were fun, but the impression was inescapable that the host, and most of his guests, would do anything to stave off a lull in which they would be together without some impersonal focus for their attention. A snapshot of almost any men's club would show the same thing, 90 percent of the men engaged in some activity—ranging from backgammon to watching the tube—other than, or at least as an aid to, conversation. *

My composite memory of evenings spent with a friend at college 6
and later when we shared an apartment in Washington is of conversations punctuated by silences during which we would internally pass over any personal or emotional thoughts which had arisen and come back to the permitted track. When I couldn't get my mind off personal matters, I said very little. Talks with my father have always had the same tone. Respect for privacy was the rationale for our diffidence. His questions to me about how things were going at school or at work were asked as discreetly as he would have asked a friend about someone's commitment to a hospital for the criminally insane. Our conversations, when they

---

*Women may use games as a reason for getting together—bridge clubs, for example. But the show is more for the rest of the world—to indicate that they are doing *something*—and the games themselves are not the only means of communication.

touched these matters at all, to say nothing of more sensitive matters, would veer quickly back to safe topics of general interest.

In our popular literature, the archetypal male hero embodying this personal muteness is the cowboy. The classic mold for the character was set in 1902 by Owen Wister's novel *The Virginian* where the author spelled out, with an explicitness that was never again necessary, the characteristics of his protagonist. Here's how it goes when two close friends the Virginian hasn't seen in some time take him out for a drink: 7

> All of them had seen rough days together, and they felt guilty with emotion.
> "It's hot weather," said Wiggin.
> "Hotter in Box Elder," said McLean. "My kid has started teething."
> Words ran dry again. They shifted their positions, looked in their glasses, read the labels on the bottles. They dropped a word now and then to the proprietor about his trade, and his ornaments.

One of the Virginian's duties is to assist at the hanging of an old friend as a horse thief. Afterward, for the first time in the book, he is visibly upset. The narrator puts his arm around the hero's shoulders and describes the Virginian's reaction:

> I had the sense to keep silent, and presently he shook my hand, not looking at me as he did so. He was always very shy of demonstration.

And, for explanation of such reticence, "As all men know, he also knew that many things should be done in this world in silence, and that talking about them is a mistake."

There are exceptions, but they only prove the rule. 8

One is the drunken confidence: "Bob, ole boy, I gotta tell ya— being divorced isn't so hot. . . . [and see, I'm too drunk to be held responsible for blurting it out]." Here, drink becomes an excuse for exchanging confidences and a device for periodically loosening the restraint against expressing a need for sympathy and support from other men— which may explain its importance as a male ritual. Marijuana fills a similar need. 9

Another exception is talking to a stranger—who may be either someone the speaker doesn't know or someone who isn't in the same social or business world. (Several black friends told me that they have been on the receiving end of personal confidences from white acquaintances that they were sure had not been shared with white friends.) In either case, men are willing to talk about themselves only to other men with whom they do not have to compete or whom they will not have to confront socially later. 10

Finally, there is the way men depend on women to facilitate certain   11
conversations. The women in a mixed group are usually the ones who
make the first personal reference, about themselves or others present.
The men can then join in without having the onus for initiating a discussion of "personalities." Collectively, the men can "blame" the conversation on the women. They can also feel in these conversations that
since they are talking "to" the women instead of "to" the men, they can
be excused for deviating from the masculine norm. When the women
leave, the tone and subject invariably shift away from the personal.

The effect of these constraints is to make it extraordinarily difficult   12
for men to really get to know each other. A psychotherapist who has
conducted a lengthy series of encounter groups for men summed it up:

> With saddening regularity [the members of these groups] described how
> much they wanted to have closer, more satisfying relationships with other
> men: "I'd settle for having one really close man friend. I supposedly have
> some close men friends now. We play golf or go for a drink. We complain
> about our jobs and our wives. I care about them and they care about me.
> We even have some physical contact—I mean we may even give a hug
> on a big occasion. But it's not enough."

The sources of this stifling ban on self disclosure, the reasons why men
hide from each other, lie in the taboos and imperatives of the masculine
stereotype.

To begin with, men are supposed to be functional, to spend their   13
time working or otherwise solving or thinking about how to solve problems. Personal reaction, how one feels about something, is considered
dysfunctional, at best an irrelevant distraction from the expected objec-
tivity. Only weak men, and women, talk about—i.e., "give in," to their
feelings. "I group my friends in two ways," said a business executive:

> those who have made it and don't complain and those who haven't made
> it. And only the latter spend time talking to their wives about their prob-
> lems and how bad their boss is and all that. The ones who concentrate
> more on communicating . . . are those who have realized that they aren't
> going to make it and therefore they have changed the focus of attention.

In a world which tells men they have to choose between expressiveness
and manly strength, this characterization may be accurate. Most of the
men who talk personally to other men *are* those whose problems have
gotten the best of them, who simply can't help it. Men not driven to
despair don't talk about themselves, so the idea that self-disclosure and
expressiveness are associated with problems and weakness becomes a self-
fulfilling prophecy.

Obsessive competitiveness also limits the range of communication   14
in male friendships. Competition is the principal mode by which men
relate to each other—at one level because they don't know how else to
make contact, but more basically because it is the way to demonstrate,
to themselves and others, the key masculine qualities of unwavering
toughness and the ability to dominate and control. The result is that
they inject competition into situations which don't call for it.

In conversations, you must show that you know more about the   15
subject than the other man, or at least as much as he does. For example,
I have often engaged in a contest that could be called My Theory Tops
Yours, disguised as a serious exchange of ideas. The proof that it wasn't
serious was that I was willing to participate even when I was sure that
the participants, including myself, had nothing fresh to say. Convincing
the other person—victory—is the main objective, with control of the
floor an important tactic. Men tend to lecture at each other, insist that
the discussion follow their train of thought, and are often unwilling to
listen. As one member of a men's rap group said,

> When I was talking I used to feel that I had to be driving to a point, that
> it had to be rational and organized, that I had to persuade at all times,
> rather than exchange thoughts and ideas.

Even in casual conversation some men hold back unless they are absolutely sure of what they are saying. They don't want to have to change
a position once they have taken it. It's "just like a woman" to change
your mind, and, more important, it is inconsistent with the approved
masculine posture of total independence.

Competition was at the heart of one of my closest friendships, now   16
defunct. There was a good deal of mutual liking and respect. We went
out of our way to spend time with each other and wanted to work together. We both had "prospects" as "bright young men" and the same
"liberal but tough" point of view. We recognized this about each other,
and this recognition was the basis of our respect and of our sense of
equality. That we saw each other as equals was important—our friendship
was confirmed by the reflection of one in the other. But our constant
and all-encompassing competition made this equality precarious and fragile. One way or another, everything counted in the measuring process.
We fought out our tennis matches as though our lives depended on it.
At poker, the two of us would often play on for hours after the others
had left. These *mano a mano* poker marathons seem in retrospect especially revealing of the competitiveness of the relationship: playing for
small stakes, the essence of the game is in outwitting, psychologically
beating down the other player—the other skills involved are negligible.

Winning is the only pleasure, one that evaporates quickly, a truth that struck me in inchoate form every time our game broke up at four A.M. and I walked out the door with my five-dollar winnings, a headache, and a sense of time wasted. Still, I did the same thing the next time. It was what we did together, and somehow it counted. Losing at tennis could be balanced by winning at poker; at another level, his moving up in the federal government by my getting on the *Harvard Law Review*.

This competitiveness feeds the most basic obstacle to openness be- 17
tween men, the inability to admit to being vulnerable. Real men, we learn early, are not supposed to have doubts, hopes and ambitions which may not be realized, things they don't (or even especially do) like about themselves, fears and disappointments. Such feelings and concerns, of course, are part of everyone's inner life, but a man must keep quiet about them. If others know how you really feel you can be hurt, and that in itself is incompatible with manhood. The inhibiting effect of this imperative is not limited to disclosures of major personal problems. Often men do not share even ordinary uncertainties and half-formulated plans of daily life with their friends. And when they do, they are careful to suggest that they already know how to proceed—that they are not really asking for help or understanding but simply for particular bits of information. Either way, any doubts they have are presented as external, carefully characterized as having to do with the issue as distinct from the speaker. They are especially guarded about expressing concern or asking a question that would invite personal comment. It is almost impossible for men to simply exchange thoughts about matters involving them personally in a comfortable, non-crisis atmosphere. If a friend tells you of his concern that he and a colleague are always disagreeing, for example, he is likely to quickly supply his own explanation—something like "different professional backgrounds." The effect is to rule out observations or suggestions that do not fit within this already reconnoitered protective structure. You don't suggest, even if you believe it is true, that in fact the disagreements arise because he presents his ideas in a way which tends to provoke a hostile reaction. It would catch him off guard; it would be something he hadn't already thought of and accepted about himself and, for that reason, no matter how constructive and well-intentioned you might be, it would put you in control for the moment. He doesn't want that; he is afraid of losing your respect. So, sensing he feels that way, because you would yourself, you say something else. There is no real give-and-take.

It is hard for men to get angry at each other honestly. Anger be- 18
tween friends often means that one has hurt the other. Since the straightforward expression of anger in these situations involves an admission of

vulnerability, it is safer to stew silently or find an "objective" excuse for retaliation. Either way, trust is not fully restored.

Men even try not to let it show when they feel good. We may report the reasons for our happiness, if they have to do with concrete accomplishments, but we try to do it with straight face, as if to say, "Here's what happened, but it hasn't affected my grown-up unemotional equilibrium, and I am not asking for any kind of response." Happiness is a precarious, "childish" feeling, easy to shoot down. Others may find the event that triggers it trivial or incomprehensible, or even threatening to their own self-esteem—in the sense that if one man is up, another man is down. So we tend not to take the risk of expressing it.

What is particularly difficult for men is seeking or accepting help from friends. I, for one, learned early that dependence was unacceptable. When I was eight, I went to a summer camp I disliked. My parents visited me in the middle of the summer and, when it was time for them to leave, I wanted to go with them. They refused, and I yelled and screamed and was miserably unhappy for the rest of the day. That evening an older camper comforted me, sitting by my bed as I cried, patting me on the back soothingly and saying whatever it is that one says at times like that. He was in some way clumsy or funny-looking, and a few days later I joined a group of kids in cruelly making fun of him, an act which upset me, when I thought about it, for years. I can only explain it in terms of my feeling, as early as the age of eight, that by needing and accepting his help and comfort I had compromised myself, and took it out on him.

"You can't express dependence when you feel it," a corporate executive said, "because it's a kind of absolute. If you are loyal 90 percent of the time and disloyal 10 percent, would you be considered loyal? Well, the same happens with independence: you are either dependent or independent; you can't be both." "Feelings of dependence," another explained, "are identified with weakness or 'untoughness' and our culture doesn't accept those things in men." The result is that we either go it alone or "act out certain games or rituals to provoke the desired reaction in the other and have our needs satisfied without having to ask for anything."

Somewhat less obviously, the expression of affection also runs into emotional barriers growing out of the masculine stereotype. When I was in college, I was suddenly quite moved while attending a friend's wedding. The surge of feeling made me uncomfortable and self-conscious. There was nothing inherently difficult or, apart from the fact of being moved by a moment of tenderness, "unmasculine" about my reaction. I just did not know how to deal with or communicate what I felt. "I consider myself a sentimentalist," one man said, "and I think I am quite able to express my feelings. But the other day my wife described a friend of mine to some people as my best friend and I felt embarrassed when I heard her say it."

A major source of these inhibitions is the fear of being, of being thought, homosexual. Nothing is more frightening to a heterosexual man in our society. It threatens, at one stroke, to take away every vestige of his claim to a masculine identity—something like knocking out the foundations of a building—and to expose him to the ostracism, ranging from polite tolerance to violent revulsion, of his friends and colleagues. A man can be labeled as homosexual not just because of an overt sexual act but because of almost any sign of behavior which does not fit the masculine stereotype. The touching of another man, other than shaking hands or, under emotional stress, an arm around the shoulder, is taboo. Women may kiss each other when they meet; men are uncomfortable when hugged even by close friends. Onlookers might misinterpret what they saw, and more important, what would we think of ourselves if we feel a twinge of sensual pleasure from the embrace.

Direct verbal expressions of affection or tenderness are also something that only homosexuals and women engage in. Between "real" men affection had to be disguised in gruff, "you old son-of-a-bitch" style. Paradoxically, in some instances, terms of endearment between men can be used as a ritual badge of manhood, dangerous medicine safe only for the strong. The flirting with homosexuality that characterizes the initiation rites of many fraternities and men's clubs serves this purpose. Claude Brown wrote about black life in New York City in the 1950s:

> The term ["baby"] had a hip ring to it. . . . It was like saying, "Man, look at me. I've got masculinity to spare. . . . I can say 'baby' to another cat and he can say 'baby' to me, and we can say it with strength in our voices." If you could say it, this meant that you really had to be sure of yourself, sure of your masculinity.

Fear of homosexuality does more than inhibit the physical display of affection. One of the major recurring themes in the men's groups led by psychotherapist Don Clark was:

> "A large segment of my feelings about other men are unknown or distorted because I am afraid they might have something to do with homosexuality. Now I'm lonely for other men and don't know how to find what I want with them."

As Clark observes, "The specter of homosexuality seems to be the dragon at the gateway to self-awareness, understanding, and acceptance of male-

male needs. If a man tries to pretend the dragon is not there by turning a blind eye to erotic feelings for all other males, he also blinds himself to the rich variety of feelings that are related."

The few situations in which men do acknowledge strong feelings   25 of affection and dependence toward other men are exceptions which prove the rule. With "cop couples," for example, or combat soldier "buddies," intimacy and dependence are forced on the men by their work—they have to ride in the patrol car or be in the same foxhole with somebody—and the jobs themselves have such highly masculine images that the man can get away with behavior that would be suspect under any other conditions.

Furthermore, even these combat-buddy relationships, when looked   26 at closely, turn out not to be particularly intimate or personal. Margaret Mead has written:

> During the last war English observers were confused by the apparent contradiction between American soldiers' emphasis on the buddy, so grievously exemplified in the break-downs that followed a buddy's death, and the results of detailed inquiry which showed how transitory these buddy relationships were. It was found that men actually accepted their buddies as derivatives from their outfit, and from accidents of association, rather than because of any special personality characteristics capable of ripening into friendship.

One effect of the fear of appearing to be homosexual is to reinforce the practice that two men rarely get together alone without a reason. I once called a friend to suggest that we have dinner together. "O.K.," he said. "What's up?" I felt uncomfortable telling him that I just wanted to talk, that there was no other reason for the invitation.

Men get together to conduct business, to drink, to play games and   27 sports, to re-establish contact after long absences, to participate in heterosexual social occasions—circumstances in which neither person is responsible for actually wanting to see the other. Men are particularly comfortable seeing each other in groups. The group situation defuses any possible assumptions about the intensity of feeling between particular men and provides the safety of numbers—"All the guys are here." It makes personal communication, which requires a level of trust and mutual understanding not generally shared by all members of a group, more difficult and offers an excuse for avoiding this dangerous territory. And it provides what is most sought after in men's friendships: mutual reassurance of masculinity.

Questions for Study and Discussion

1. Why does Fasteau think that the belief that the great friendships are between men is a long-standing myth?

2. Why does Fasteau find male friendships "shallow and unsatisfying"?

3. Why do men tend to shy away from anything that smacks of the personal? How do they rationalize this behavior?

4. Why do games play such an important role in men's lives? What role do they play in women's lives?

5. In what types of situations do men become personal?

6. According to Fasteau, what effect does competition have on male friendships? Do you agree with his analysis? Explain.

7. Fasteau concludes his essay by stating that the group situation "provides what is most sought after in men's friendships: mutual reassurance of masculinity." Why do you suppose men need such reassurance? Do they seem to need it more today than in times past? Explain.

Writing Topics

1. Using your own experiences and observations write an essay in which you argue with Fasteau's position that "despite the time men spend together, their contact rarely goes beyond the external."

2. If you accept Fasteau's analysis of the "reasons why men hide from each other," what can be done to make more meaningful communication possible? Write an essay in which you propose some solutions.

Although she was born in Birmingham, Alabama, the novelist and short story writer Gail Godwin now makes her home in Woodstock, New York. A graduate of the University of North Carolina, Godwin earned her M.A. and Ph.D. degrees in English from the University of Iowa. She has published five novels, *The Perfectionists* (1970), *Glass People* (1972), *The Odd Woman* (1974), *Violet Clay* (1978), and *A Mother and Two Daughters* (1982), and a collection of short stories, *Dream Children* (1976). At the time of its publication the critic Jonathan Yardley wrote, "*Dream Children* is the work of a writer who, though still young and still testing the range of her powers, is moving confidently to the forefront of contemporary fiction."

In "To Noble Companions" Godwin gives food for thought to those of us who believe that a friendship shines brightest when we lend comfort and assistance to a friend in need. After dismissing a rather clichéd definition of the term *friend* Godwin offers up a more subtle definition of her own.

To Noble Companions

The dutiful first answer seems programmed into us by our meager expectations: "A friend is one who will be there in times of trouble." But I believe this is a skin-deep answer to describe skin-deep friends. There is something irresistible about misfortune to human nature, and standbys for setbacks and sicknesses (as long as they are not too lengthy, or contagious) can usually be found. They can be *hired*. What I value is not the "friend" who, looming sympathetically above me when I have been dashed to the ground, appears gigantically generous in the hour of my reversal; more and more I desire friends who will endure my ecstasies with me, who possess wings of their own and who will fly with me. I don't mean this as arrogance (I am too superstitious to indulge long in that trait), and I don't fly all that often. What I mean is that I seek (and occasionally find) friends with whom it is possible to drag out all those beautiful, old, outrageously *aspiring* costumes and rehearse together for the Great Roles; persons whose qualities groom me and train me up for love. It is for these people that I reserve the glowing hours, too good not to share. It is the existence of these people that reminds me that the words "friend" and "free" grew out of each other. (OE *freo*, not in bondage, noble, glad; OE *freon*, to love; OE *freond*, friend.)

When I was in the eighth grade, I had a friend. We were shy and "too serious" about our studies when it was becoming fashionable with our classmates to acquire the social graces. We said little at school, but

196

she would come to my house and we would sit down with pencils and paper, and one of us would say: "Let's start with a train whistle today." We would sit quietly together and write separate poems or stories that grew out of a train whistle. Then we would read them aloud. At the end of that school year, we, too, were transformed into social creatures and the stories and poems stopped.

When I lived for a time in London, I had a friend. He was in   3
despair and I was in despair, but our friendship was based on the small flicker of foresight in each of us that told us we would be sorry later if we did not explore this great city because we had felt bad at the time. We met every Sunday for five weeks and found many marvelous things. We walked until our despairs resolved themselves and then we parted. We gave London to each other.

For almost four years I have had a remarkable friend whose imag-   4
ination illumines mine. We write long letters in which we often discover our strangest selves. Each of us appears, sometimes prophetically, some-times comically, in the other's dreams. She and I agree that, at certain times, we seem to be parts of the same mind. In my most sacred and interesting moments, I often think: "Yes, I must tell _____." We have never met.

It is such exceptional (in a sense divine) companions I wish to   5
salute. I have seen the glories of the world reflected briefly through our encounters. One bright hour with their kind is worth more to me than a lifetime guarantee of the services of a Job's comforter whose "helpful" lamentations will only clutter the healing silence necessary to those dark-est moments in which I would rather be my own best friend.

Questions for Study and Discussion

1. Why does Godwin reject the common definition of a friend: "A friend is one who will be there in times of trouble"? What is her own definition of "friend"? What characteristics does she find essential in a friend?

2. How are paragraphs 2–4 related to paragraph 1? What organizational pat-tern do you see in paragraphs 2–4?

3. Explain the meaning of Godwin's last sentence. What is "Job's com-forter"? How is her last sentence related to what comes before?

4. What is Godwin's purpose in giving the etymology of *friend* and *free* in paragraph 1? Why does she present the etymology in parentheses?

5. Why does Godwin use the word "noble" in her title? Where in her essay does she indicate its meaning?

Writing Topics

1. Write an essay in which you discuss the noble companions in your life. What experiences have they shared with you, and what have you derived from those experiences?

2. Write an essay in which you argue for or against Godwin's position that valued friends are those "who will endure my ecstasies with me."

3. In English we have many words to describe the various types of relationships that might come under the general heading of a friend. For example, consider the following: pal, companion, roomie, the guys, colleague, chum, bosom buddy, and sidekick. Write an essay in which you discuss the terms that you commonly use and the types of relationships they describe.

THEODORE ROETHKE

Theodore Roethke is known among readers and critics as one of the finest American poets of his generation. Among poets, he is also remembered as an inspiring teacher of creative writing, especially during his fourteen years at the University of Washington. He was born in Michigan in 1908 and educated at the University of Michigan; later he had his first teaching job at Michigan State University and also served as the university's public relations director and tennis coach. A complex man, swinging between extremes of egoistic boastfulness and severe depression, he could be both formidable and vulnerable in the classroom, sometimes in the same hour. In 1959 he received the Bollingen Prize for the body of his poetic work, which was published after his death in 1963 as his *Collected Poems* (1966). "Elegy for Jane" presents both Roethke the skillful, sensitive poet and Roethke the loving teacher, one who could be both mentor and friend.

Elegy for Jane

My Student, Thrown by a Horse

I remember the neckcurls, limp and damp as tendrils;
And her quick look, a sidelong pickerel smile;
And how, once startled into talk, the light syllables leaped for her,
And she balanced in the delight of her thought,
A wren, happy, tail into the wind,   5
Her song trembling the twigs and small branches.
The shade sang with her;
The leaves, their whispers turned to kissing;
And the mold sang in the bleached valleys under the rose.

Oh, when she was sad, she cast herself down into such a pure depth,   10
Even a father could not find her;
Scraping her cheek against straw;
Stirring the clearest water.

My sparrow, you are not here,
Waiting like a fern, making a spiny shadow.   15
The sides of wet stones cannot console me,
Nor the moss, wound with the last light.

If only I could nudge you from this sleep,
My maimed darling, my skittery pigeon.
Over this damp grave I speak the words of my love: 20
I, with no rights in this matter,
Neither father nor lover.

Questions for Study and Discussion

1. What is the setting of the poem?

2. How is the poem organized? How does the emphasis shift from stanza to stanza? In what way does the poet lead you gradually to the death that is lamented in the final stanza?

3. Roethke compares Jane with many things through similes and metaphors. Identify several of these. What do these comparisons have in common? What does each contribute to our knowledge of Jane?

4. What do lines 10–14 mean?

5. How would you characterize the relationship between the speaker and Jane? If the speaker is "Neither father nor lover," what then is the "love" that he refers to in line 20? Do you agree with the speaker that he has "no rights in this matter"?

Writing Topics

1. Think of the teacher you believe has taught you the most, and the teacher you have liked the best. Were they the same person? Describe each teacher's qualities, as a person and as a teacher. What is the nature of the relationship between students and teachers? Would friendship adequately characterize it?

2. Have you experienced the death of a loved one or close friend? How did you feel at the news of this death? On reflection, how does this experience affect your understanding of Roethke's poem?

3 Men and Women

I think that implicit in the women's movement is the idea that women will share in the economic burden, and men will share more equally in the home and the family.
BETTY FRIEDAN

Marriage is like a long trip in a tiny rowboat. if one passenger starts to rock the boat, the other has to steady it; otherwise they will go to the bottom together.
DAVID REUBEN

Gender Roles

SUSAN JACOBY

When Susan Jacoby became a newspaper reporter in 1963, at the age of seventeen, she had no intention of writing about "women's subjects." "To write about women was to write about trivia: charity balls, cake sales, and the like," she recalls. "I would have laughed at anyone who tried to tell me that one day I would believe the members of my own sex were important enough to write about." But times have changed. Although the old female stereotypes have not completely disappeared, many people have come to regard them as unfair and unacceptable. And Jacoby has, in fact, written extensively about women's subjects, often in *The New York Times* and *McCall's*. Many of these pieces have been collected in her book *The Possible She* (1979). In the following essay, originally published in the "Hers" column of the *Times* in 1978, Jacoby tells of two experiences when she felt mistreated because she was a woman and describes how she dealt with each situation.

Unfair Game

My friend and I, two women obviously engrossed in conversation, 1 are sitting at a corner table in the crowded Oak Room of the Plaza at ten o'clock on a Tuesday night. A man materializes and interrupts us with the snappy opening line, "A good woman is hard to find."

We say nothing, hoping he will disappear back into his bottle. But 2 he fancies himself as our genie and asks, "Are you visiting?" Still we say nothing. Finally my friend looks up and says, "We live here." She and I look at each other, the thread of our conversation snapped, our thoughts focused on how to get rid of this intruder. In a minute, if something isn't done, he will scrunch down next to me on the banquette and start offering to buy us drinks.

"Would you leave us alone, please," I say in a loud but reasonably 3 polite voice. He looks slightly offended but goes on with his bright social patter. I become more explicit. "We don't want to talk to you, we didn't

203

ask you over here, and we want to be alone. Go away." This time he directs his full attention to me—and he is mad. "All right, all right, *excuse me.*" He pushes up the corners of his mouth in a Howdy Doody smile. "You ought to try smiling. You might even be pretty if you smiled once in a while."

At last the man leaves. He goes back to his buddy at the bar. I   4
watch them out of the corner of my eye, and he gestures angrily at me for at least fifteen minutes. When he passes our table on the way out of the room, this well-dressed, obviously affluent man mutters, "Good-bye, bitch," under his breath.

Why is this man calling me names? Because I have asserted my   5
right to sit at a table in a public place without being drawn into a sexual flirtation. Because he has been told, in no uncertain terms, that two attractive women prefer each other's company to his.

This sort of experience is an old story to any woman who travels,   6
eats, or drinks—for business or pleasure—without a male escort. In Holiday Inns and at the Plaza, on buses and airplanes, in tourist and first class, a woman is always thought to be looking for a man in addition to whatever else she may be doing. The man who barged in on us at the bar would never have broken into the conversation of two men, and it goes without saying that he wouldn't have imposed himself on a man and a woman who were having a drink. But two women at a table are an entirely different matter. Fair game.

This might be viewed as a relatively small flaw in the order of the   7
universe—something in a class with an airline losing luggage or a computer fouling up a bank statement. Except a computer doesn't foul up your bank account every month and an airline doesn't lose your suitcase every time you fly. But if you are an independent woman, you have to spend a certain amount of energy, day in and day out, in order to go about your business without being bothered by strange men.

On airplanes, I am a close-mouthed traveler. As soon as the "No   8
Smoking" sign is turned off, I usually pull some papers out of my briefcase and start working. Work helps me forget that I am scared of flying. When I am sitting next to a woman, she quickly realizes from my monosyllabic replies that I don't want to chat during the flight. Most men, though, are not content to be ignored.

Once I was flying from New York to San Antonio on a plane that   9
was scheduled to stop in Dallas. My seatmate was an advertising executive who kept questioning me about what I was doing and who remained undiscouraged by my terse replies until I ostentatiously covered myself

with a blanket and shut my eyes. When the plane started its descent into Dallas, he made his move.

"You don't really have to get to San Antonio today, do you?" 10

"Yes." 11

"Come on, change your ticket. Spend the evening with me here. 12 I'm staying at a wonderful hotel, with a pool, we could go dancing . . ."

"No." 13

"Well, you can't blame a man for trying." 14

I do blame a man for trying in this situation—for suggesting that a 15 woman change her work and travel plans to spend a night with a perfect stranger in whom she had displayed no personal interest. The "no personal interest" is crucial; I wouldn't have blamed the man for trying if I had been stroking his cheek and complaining about my dull social life.

There is a nice postscript to this story. Several months later, I was 16 walking my dog in Carl Schurz Park when I ran into my erstwhile seatmate, who was taking a stroll with his wife and children. He recognized me, all right, and was trying to avoid me when I went over and courteously reintroduced myself. I reminded him that we had been on the same flight to Dallas. "Oh yes," he said. "As I recall you were going on to somewhere else." "San Antonio," I said. "I was in a hurry that day."

The code of feminine politeness, instilled in girlhood, is no help 17 in dealing with the unwanted approaches of strange men. Our mothers didn't teach us to tell a man to get lost; they told us to smile and hint that we'd be just delighted to spend time with the gentleman if we didn't have other commitments. The man in the Oak Room bar would not be put off by a demure lowering of eyelids; he had to be told, roughly and loudly, that his presence was a nuisance.

Not that I am necessarily against men and women picking each 18 other up in public places. In most instances, a modicum of sensitivity will tell a woman or a man whether someone is open to approaches.

Mistakes can easily be corrected by the kind of courtesy so many 19 people have abandoned since the "sexual revolution." One summer evening, I was whiling away a half hour in the outdoor bar of the Stanhope Hotel. I was alone, dressed up, having a drink before going on to meet someone in a restaurant. A man at the next table asked, "If you're not busy, would you like to have a drink with me?" I told him I was sorry but I would be leaving shortly. "Excuse me for disturbing you," he said, turning back to his own drink. Simple courtesy. No insults and no hurt feelings.

One friend suggested that I might have avoided the incident in the 20

Oak Room by going to the Palm Court instead. It's true that the Palm Court is a traditional meeting place for unescorted ladies. But I don't like violins when I want to talk. And I wanted to sit in a large, comfortable leather chair. Why should I have to hide among the potted palms to avoid men who think I'm looking for something else?

Questions for Study and Discussion

1. What is the main point of Jacoby's essay? Where is it stated most directly? What was her purpose in writing this piece?

2. What solutions, if any, does Jacoby suggest for dealing with the problem she describes?

3. Jacoby complains about the code of feminine politeness. What exactly is this "code"? Does she seem constrained by it?

4. In paragraph 16, why does Jacoby say as her parting shot, "I was in a hurry that day"?

5. What is Jacoby's tone in this essay? How does she achieve this tone? Give several examples from the essay.

Writing Topics

1. Jacoby has written that this article drew a larger response than anything she has ever published. What kinds of responses do you imagine it drew from women? From men? How do you respond to this article? Compose a response as if you were going to send it to *The New York Times* or to Jacoby herself.

2. In one respect, the situations Jacoby describes have mainly to do with courtesy, with good and bad manners. Write an essay in which you define *courtesy*. What purpose does it serve? Should people be expected always to show consideration for others, or should they be free to say and do whatever they please? Why?

3. Write an essay on some aspect of dating. Why do people go on dates? What do people gain from dining together, or going to a movie together? How has dating changed since you started dating? How should one arrange a date with a stranger?

MIKE McGRADY

Born in New York City in 1933, Mike McGrady was educated at Yale University and spent a year as a Neiman Fellow at Harvard. He is a free-lance writer who has taken on many different assignments, from reporting to reviewing to ghostwriting. He has published several books, including *A Dove in Vietnam* (1968) and *The Kitchen Sink Papers—My Life as a Househusband* (1975). He is currently a restaurant critic for Long Island's *Newsday*.

The following essay, which first appeared in a 1976 issue of *Newsweek*, presents McGrady's views on the limitations of housework and offers a somewhat radical proposal.

Let 'em Eat Leftovers

Last year my wife and I traded roles. Every morning she went off ¹ to an office and earned the money that paid the bills. I cooked and cleaned, picked up after three kids, went head-to-head with bargain-hunting shoppers, pleaded for a raise in allowance and lived the generally hellish life that half the human race accepts as its lot.

The year is over now but the memories won't go away. What is ² guaranteed to stir them up is any of those Total Woman or Fascinating Womanhood people singing the praises of the happy housewife—that mythical woman who manages a spotless house, runs herd over half a dozen kids, whips up short-order culinary masterpieces, smells good and still finds time to read Great Books and study Japanese line engraving.

I never qualified. Never even came close. In fact, I never quite ³ mastered that most basic task, the cleaning of the house. Any job that requires six hours to do and can be undone in six minutes by one small child carrying a plate of crackers and a Monopoly set—this is not a job that will long capture my interest. After a year of such futility, I have arrived at a rule of thumb—if the debris accumulates to a point where small animals can be seen to be living there, it should be cleaned up, preferably by someone hired for the occasion.

Housekeeping was just one facet of the nightmare. I think back to ⁴ a long night spent matching up four dozen bachelor socks, all of them wool, most of them gray. Running an all-hours taxi service for subteens. Growing older in orthodontists' waiting rooms. Pasting trading stamps into little booklets. Oh, the nightmare had as many aspects as there were hours in the day.

207

Empress of Domestic Arts

At the heart of my difficulty was this simple fact: for the past two decades I had been paid for my work. I had come to feel my time was valuable. Suddenly my sole payment was a weekly allowance given to me with considerable fanfare by my breadwinning wife. I began to see that as a trap, a many-strings-attached offering that barely survived a single session in the supermarket and never got me through a neighborhood poker game.

The pay was bad and the hours were long but what bothered me most was my own ineptitude, my inability to apply myself to the business of managing a home. No longer do I feel guilty about my failure as a homemaker. I would no more applaud the marvelously efficient and content housewife than I would applaud the marvelously efficient and content elevator operator. The image strikes me as useful on several levels but the point is this: it is always someone else who goes up, someone else who gets off.

Some people seem to feel that the housewife's lot would be bettered if she were given a new title, one that takes into account the full range and complexity of her role, something along the lines of "household engineer" or, perhaps, "domestic scientist." Wonderful. You come and take care of my house and my kids and you can be the Empress of the Domestic Arts, the Maharanee of the Vacuum Cleaner.

Try a Little Neglect

A more intriguing suggestion is that husbands pay their wives salaries for housework. I suggested this to my wife and she said I don't make enough money to pay her to do that job again. Neither, according to her, does J. Paul Getty. I am coming to the feeling that this is a job that should not be done by any one person for love or for money.

This is not to put down the whole experience. By the end of the year, I had succeeded in organizing my time so that there were a few hours for the occasional book, the random round of golf. Then, too, it was a pleasure to be more than a weekend visitor in my kids' lives. While my wife and I are now willing to de-emphasize housekeeping, neither of us would cut back on what some people call parenting and what I look at as the one solid reward in this belated and male motherhood of mine.

Of course, I had it easy—relatively easy anyway. This was my little experiment, not my destiny. There is a considerable difference between a year in prison and a life sentence.

It will be argued: well, *someone* has to do these things. Not neces-   11
sarily. In the first place, some two can do most of these things. Secondly,
I can think of no area in modern life that could more easily sustain a
policy of benign neglect than the home. I'm arguing here in favor of
letting the dust gather where it may; in favor of making greater use of
slow cookers and nearby fish-and-chips stands; of abolishing, as far as
possible, the position of unpaid servant in the family.

Many men surely will find this line of thought threatening. That's   12
just as it should be. Few plantation owners were enthusiastic about the
Emancipation Proclamation. What is more surprising is that these thoughts
will prove equally threatening to many women. OK. Those females who
demand the right to remain in service should not necessarily be discouraged—we all know how hard it is to find decent household help these
days.

I suspect the real reason for many women's reluctance to break bonds   13
is fear of the world that exists outside the home. They sense the enormous
complexity of their husbands' lives, the tremendous skills required to head
up a team of salesmen or to write cigarette commercials or to manufacture
lawn fertilizer. The mind that feels these fears may be beyond the reach
of change. It is another sort of mind, the mind that finds itself in constant
rebellion against the limitations of housewifery, that concerns me more
here.

The Life You Save

To this mind, this person, we should say: go ahead. There is a world   14
out here, a whole planet of possibilities. The real danger is that you won't
do it. If Gutenberg had been a housewife, I might be writing these words
with a quill pen. And if Edison had been a housewife, you might be
reading them by candlelight.

No escape is simple and a certain amount of toughness will be re-   15
quired. How do you do it? You might start by learning how to sweep
things under the rug. You might have to stop pampering the rest of the
family—let 'em eat leftovers. And be prepared for the opposition that will
surely develop. Even the most loving family hates to lose that trusted
servant, that faithful family retainer, that little old homemaker, you. No
one enjoys it when the most marvelous appliance of them all breaks down.
But if it will be any comfort to you, the life you save will surely be your
own.

Questions for Study and Discussion

1. How does McGrady respond to the concept of "the happy housewife"? What does he think about "those 'Total Woman' or 'Fascinating Womanhood' people"?

2. What is so distressing about cleaning a house, as far as McGrady is concerned? What other aspects of being a homemaker are central to McGrady's dissatisfaction? Why does McGrady not feel guilty about being a bad homemaker?

3. What is the "one solid reward" McGrady sees in being a homemaker?

4. What, in McGrady's view, keeps some housewives from breaking free of their positions? What suggestions does he offer to those who *are* in rebellion?

5. In paragraph 7, McGrady writes, "Some people seem to feel that the housewife's lot would be bettered if she were given a new title, one that takes into account the full range and complexity of her role. . . ." What is his opinion of this proposal? Do you agree with him? Why, or why not?

6. Who, do you suppose, is McGrady's audience? To what belief and/or action is he trying to persuade his audience? What, if anything, did you find particularly persuasive about his method of development?

7. Upon being informed that the poor people of France were without bread and starving, Marie Antoinette allegedly said, "Let them eat cake." The reply is now justly famous for its apparent callousness. Is McGrady's title callous? What connection does it bear to his essay?

8. McGrady's tone might often be called sarcastic. Find at least three examples of sarcasm in his essay and describe your response. Has McGrady made his point effectively?

9. Does McGrady need the headings "Empress of Domestic Arts," "Try a Little Neglect," and "The Life You Save"? What effect do they have on you as a reader?

Writing Topics

1. Choose from your local newspaper or from a national newsmagazine an editorial about a controversial issue. First, outline the argument made in the editorial. Then, assume that you have been given equal space in the publication to present an opposing viewpoint. Consider the types of evidence you will need; then write a counterargument, trying as much as possible to respond to each point made in the editorial.

2. Write an essay in which you examine how traditional roles—husband as breadwinner, wife as homemaker—are giving way to other arrangements in many modern marriages. In addition to your own experiences and observations, you may wish to consult the *Reader's Guide to Periodical Literature* and books like *Megatrends* and *Future Shock* for discussions of current societal trends.

NOEL PERRIN

Noel Perrin is a New Yorker by birth and has spent much of his life in the academic world, yet he is most widely known as an essayist on the demands and rewards of country life. He was born in 1927, attended Williams College, Duke University, and Cambridge University, England, and is now a professor of English at Dartmouth College in New Hampshire. He lives in neighboring Vermont and wrote about his home state in *Vermont in All Weathers* (1973). His country pieces, which he calls "essays of a sometime farmer," have been collected in *First Person Rural* (1978), *Second Person Rural* 1980, and *Third Person Rural* (1982).

In "The Androgynous Man" Perrin addresses the restrictive roles that sexual stereotyping casts us into and the impact that these roles have on our personality and behavior. In keeping with the independent spirit of his other writings, he argues for freedom from such restrictive sex roles.

The Androgynous Man

The summer I was 16, I took a train from New York to Steamboat Springs, Colo., where I was going to be assistant horse wrangler at a camp. The trip took three days, and since I was much too shy to talk to strangers, I had quite a lot of time for reading. I read all of *Gone With the Wind*. I read all of the interesting articles in a couple of magazines I had, and then I went back and read all the dull stuff. I also took all the quizzes, a thing of which magazines were even fuller then than now. 1

The one that held my undivided attention was called "How Masculine/Feminine Are You?" It consisted of a large number of inkblots. The reader was supposed to decide which of four objects each blot most resembled. The choices might be a cloud, a steam-engine, a caterpillar and a sofa. 2

When I finished the test, I was shocked to find that I was barely masculine at all. On a scale of 1 to 10, I was about 1.2. Me, the horse wrangler? (And not just wrangler, either. That summer, I had to skin a couple of horses that died—the camp owner wanted the hides.) 3

The results of that test were so terrifying to me that for the first time in my life I did a piece of original analysis. Having unlimited time on the train, I looked at the "masculine" answers over and over, trying to find what it was that distinguished real men from people like me— and eventually I discovered two very simple patterns. It was "masculine" to think the blots looked like man-made objects, and "feminine" to think they looked like natural objects. It was masculine to think they looked 4

211

like things capable of causing harm, and feminine to think of innocent things.

Even at 16, I had the sense to see that the compilers of the test   5
were using rather limited criteria—maleness and femaleness are both more complicated than that—and I breathed a huge sigh of relief. I wasn't necessarily a wimp, after all.

That the test did reveal something other than the superficiality of   6
its makers I realized only many years later. What it revealed was that there is a large class of men and women both, to which I belong, who are essentially androgynous. That doesn't mean we're gay, or low in the appropriate hormones, or uncomfortable performing the jobs traditionally assigned our sexes. (A few years after that summer, I was leading troops in combat and, unfashionable as it now is to admit this, having a very good time. War is exciting. What a pity the 20th century went and spoiled it with high-tech weapons.)

What it does mean to be spiritually androgynous is a kind of free-   7
dom. Men who are all-male, or he-man, or 100% red-blooded Ameri-cans, have a little biological set that causes them to be attracted to physical power, and probably also to dominance. Maybe even to watching football. I don't say this to criticize them. Completely masculine men are quite often wonderful people: good husbands, good (though some-times overwhelming) fathers, good members of society. Furthermore, they are often so unself-consciously at ease in the world that other men seek to imitate them. They just aren't as free as androgynes. They pretty nearly have to be what they are; we have a range of choices open.

The sad part is that many of us never discover that. Men who are   8
not 100% red-blooded Americans—say those who are only 75% red-blooded—often fail to notice their freedom. They are too busy trying to copy the he-men ever to realize that men, like women, come in a wide variety of acceptable types. Why this frantic imitation? My answer is mere speculation, but not casual. I have speculated on this for a long time.

Partly they're just envious of the he-man's unconscious ease. Mostly   9
they're terrified of finding that there may be something wrong with them deep down, some weakness at the heart. To avoid discovering that, they spend their lives acting out the role that the he-man naturally lives. Sad.

One thing that men owe to the women's movement is that this   10
kind of failure is less common than it used to be. In releasing themselves from the single ideal of the dependent woman, women have more or less incidentally released a lot of men from the single ideal of the dominant male. The one mistake the feminists have made, I think, is in supposing

that all men need this release, or that the world would be a better place if all men achieved it. It wouldn't. It would just be duller.

So far I have been pretty vague about just what the freedom of the androgynous man is. Obviously it varies with the case. In the case I know best, my own, I can be quite specific. It has freed me most as a parent. I am, among other things, a fairly good natural mother. I like the nurturing role. It makes me feel good to see a child eat—and it turns me to mush to see a 4-year-old holding a glass with both small hands, in order to drink. I even enjoyed sewing patches on the knees of my daughter Amy's Dr. Dentons when she was at the crawling stage. All that pleasure I would have lost if I had made myself stick to the notion of the paternal role that I started with.

Or take a smaller and rather ridiculous example. I feel free to kiss cats. Until recently it never occurred to me that I would want to, though my daughters have been doing it all their lives. But my elder daughter is now 22, and in London. Of course, I get to look after her cat while she is gone. He's a big, handsome farm cat named Petrushka, very unsentimental, though used from kittenhood to being kissed on the top of the head by Elizabeth. I've gotten very fond of him (he's the adventurous kind of cat who likes to climb hills with you), and one night I simply felt like kissing him on the top of the head, and did. Why did no one tell me sooner how silky cat fur is?

Then there's my relation to cars. I am completely unembarrassed by my inability to diagnose even minor problems in whatever object I happen to be driving, and don't have to make some insider's remark to mechanics to try to establish that I, too, am a "Man With His Machine."

The same ease extends to household maintenance. I do it, of course. Service people are expensive. But for the last decade my house has functioned better than it used to because I have had the aid of a volume called "Home Repairs Any Woman Can Do," which is pitched just right for people at my technical level. As a youth, I'd as soon have touched such a book as I would have become a transvestite. Even though common sense says there is really nothing sexual whatsoever about fixing sinks.

Or take public emotion. All my life I have easily been moved by certain kinds of voices. The actress Siobhan McKenna's, to take a notable case. Give her an emotional scene in a play, and within ten words my eyes are full of tears. In boyhood, my great dread was that someone might notice. I struggled manfully, you might say, to suppress this weakness. Now, of course, I don't see it as a weakness at all, but as a kind of fulfillment. I even suspect that the true he-men feel the same way, or one kind of them does, at least, and it's only the poor imitators who have to struggle to repress themselves.

11
12
13
14
15

Let me come back to the inkblots, with their assumption that mas-   16
culine equates with machinery and science, and feminine with art and
nature. I have no idea whether the right pronoun for God is He, She,
or It. But this I'm pretty sure of. If God could somehow be induced to
take that test, God would not come out macho and not feminismo,
either, but right in the middle. Fellow androgynes, it's a nice thought.

Questions for Study and Discussion

1. What does Perrin mean by androgyny? Where does he present his definition? Why does he present it at that point? Is he using the term in the strict
dictionary sense? Explain.

2. State Perrin's thesis in your own words. What do you think his purpose is
in writing the essay?

3. What does Perrin believe are the benefits of androgyny? Are all his examples equally convincing to you? Explain.

4. Perrin's essay first appeared in a weekly column called "About Men." Do
you think Perrin intended his essay primarily for male readers or readers of
both sexes?

5. Explain the meaning of Perrin's last paragraph. How effective is it as a
conclusion? Explain.

Writing Topics

1. Write an essay in which you establish your own definition of masculinity
or femininity. What are its identifying characteristics? How does your definition differ, if at all, from prevailing stereotypes?

2. Using Perrin's essay as a model, recount experiences you have had in
growing up in which gender roles have been a significant factor. For example,
were there ever summer jobs you felt you could not apply for? Or, were you
ever made to feel inadequate in certain athletic and/or social situations? How
were you able to resolve the problem?

BRIGID BROPHY

Brigid Brophy is an English novelist and essayist who was born in London in 1929. She attended St. Paul's Girls' School and St. Hugh's College, Oxford. Although few, if any, of her published novels would be known to American readers, she won the Cheltenham Literary Festival First Prize for a first novel for *Hackenfeller's Ape*. She is, however, recognized as perhaps the most outspoken and prolific of contemporary women writers. One critic found her "quick-witted, sharp-tongued, keenly intelligent, and consistently feminine. She does not try to think and write like a man." In her regular contributions to popular magazines, both here and in England, Brophy has established a reputation as an advocate of sexual freedom, a denouncer of the hypocrisies of marriage, and a debunker of the macho, tough-guy stereotype.

The following selection is taken from *Don't Never Forget: Collected Views and Reviews* (1963). Brophy makes the point that women, just like animals in cages, are restrained by subtle forces at work in our society. Freeing women would also free men, she argues, and a better civilization would be the result.

Women: Invisible Cages

1   All right, nobody's disputing it. Women are free. At least, they *look* free. They even feel free. But in reality women in the western, industrialised world today are like the animals in a modern zoo. There are no bars. It appears that cages have been abolished. Yet in practice women are still kept in their place just as firmly as the animals are kept in their enclosures. The barriers which keep them in now are invisible.

2   It is about forty years since the pioneer feminists, several of whom were men, raised such a rumpus by rattling the cage bars—or created such a conspicuous nuisance by chaining themselves to them—that society was at last obliged to pay attention. The result was that the bars were uprooted, the cage thrown open: whereupon the majority of the women who had been held captive decided they would rather stay inside anyway.

3   To be more precise, they *thought* they decided; and society, which can with perfect truth point out "Look, no bars," *thought* it was giving them the choice. There are no laws and very little discrimination to prevent western, industrialised women from voting, being voted for or entering the professions. If there are still comparatively few women lawyers and engineers, let alone women presidents of the United States,

215

what are women to conclude except that this is the result either of their own free choice or of something inherent in female nature?

Many of them do draw just this conclusion. They have come back   4
to the old argument of the anti-feminists, many of whom were women, that women are unfit by nature for life outside the cage. And in letting this old wheel come full cycle women have fallen victim to one of the most insidious and ingenious confidence tricks ever perpetrated.

In point of fact, neither female nature nor women's individual free   5
choice has been put to the test. As American Negroes have discovered, to be officially free is by no means the same as being actually and psychologically free. A society as adept as ours has become at propaganda— whether political or commercial—should know that "persuasion," which means the art of launching myths and artificially inducing inhibitions, is every bit as effective as force of law. No doubt the reason society eventually agreed to abolish its anti-women laws was that it had become confident of commanding a battery of hidden dissuaders which would do the job just as well. Cage bars are clumsy methods of control, which excite the more rebellious personalities inside to rattle them. Modern society, like the modern zoo, has contrived to get rid of the bars without altering the fact of imprisonment. All the zoo architect needs to do is run a zone of hot or cold air, whichever the animal concerned cannot tolerate, round the cage where the bars used to be. Human animals are not less sensitive to social climate.

The ingenious point about the new-model zoo is that it deceives   6
both sides of the invisible barrier. Not only can the animal not see how it is imprisoned; the visitor's conscience is relieved of the unkindness of keeping animals shut up. He can say "Look, no bars round the animals," just as society can say "Look, no laws restricting women" even while it keeps women rigidly in place by zones of fierce social pressure.

There is, however, one great difference. A woman, being a think-   7
ing animal, may actually be more distressed because the bars of her cage cannot be seen. What relieves society's conscience may afflict hers. Unable to perceive what is holding her back, she may accuse herself and her whole sex of craven timidity because women have not jumped at what has the appearance of an offer of freedom. Evidently quite a lot of women have succumbed to guilt of this sort, since in recent years quite an industry has arisen to assuage it. Comforting voices make the air as thick and reassuring as cotton wool while they explain that there is nothing shameful in not wanting a career, that to be intellectually unadventurous is no sin, that taking care of home and family may be personally "fulfilling" and socially valuable.

This is an argument without a flaw: except that it is addressed 8
exclusively to women. Address it to both sexes and instantly it becomes
progressive and humane. As it stands, it is merely anti-woman prejudice
revamped.

That many women would be happier not pursuing careers or intel- 9
lectual adventures is only part of the truth. The whole truth is that many
people would be. If society had the clear sight to assure men as well as
women that there is no shame in preferring to stay non-competitively
and non-aggressively at home, many masculine neuroses and ulcers would
be avoided, and many children would enjoy the benefit of being brought
up by a father with a talent for the job instead of by a mother with no
talent for it but a sense of guilt about the lack.

But society does nothing so sensible. Blindly it goes on insisting on 10
the tradition that men are the ones who go out to work and adventure—
an arrangement which simply throws talent away. All the home-making
talent which happens to be born inside male bodies is wasted; and our
businesses and governments are staffed quite largely by people whose
aptitude for the work consists solely of their being what is, by tradition,
the right sex for it.

The pressures society exerts to drive men out of the house are very 11
nearly as irrational and unjust as those by which it keeps women in. The
mistake of the early reformers was to assume that men were emancipated
already and that therefore reform need ask only for the emancipation of
women. What we ought to do now is go right back to scratch and demand
the emancipation of both sexes. It is only because men are not free
themselves that they have found it necessary to cheat women by the
deception which makes them appear free when they are not.

The zones of hot and cold air which society uses to perpetuate its 12
uneconomic and unreasonable state of affairs are the simplest and most
effective conceivable. Society is playing on our sexual vanity. Just as the
sexual regions are the most vulnerable part of the body, sexuality is the
most vulnerable part of the Ego. Tell a man that he is not a real man,
or a woman that she is not one hundred per cent woman, and you are
threatening both with not being attractive to the opposite sex. That is
the climate which the human animal cannot tolerate.

So society has us all at its mercy. It has only to murmur to the man 13
that staying at home is a feminine characteristic, and he will be out of
the house like a bullet. It has only to suggest to the woman that logic
and reason are the province of the masculine mind, whereas "intuition"
and "feeling" are the female *forte,* and she will throw her physics textbooks out of the window, barricade herself into the house and give herself
up to having wishy-washy poetical feelings while she arranges the flowers.

She will, incidentally, take care that her feelings *are* wishy-washy. 14
She has been persuaded that to have cogent feelings, of the kind which
really do go into great poems (most of which are by men), would make
her an unfeminine woman, a woman who imitates men. In point of fact,
she would not be imitating men as such, most of whom have never
written a line of great poetry, but poets, most of whom so far happen to
be men. But the bad logic passes muster with her because part of the
mythology she has swallowed ingeniously informs her that logic is not
her *forte*.

Should a woman's talent or intelligence be so irrepressible that she 15
insists on producing cogent works of art or watertight meshes of argument, she will be said to have "a mind like a man's." This is simply
current idiom; translated, it means "a good mind." The use of the idiom
contributes to an apparently watertight proof that all good minds are
masculine, since whenever they occur in women they are described as
"like a man's."

What is more, this habit of thought actually contributes to perpet- 16
uating a state of affairs where most good minds really do belong to men.
It is difficult for a woman to *want* to be intelligent when she has been
told that to be so will make her like a man. She inclines to think an
intelligence would be as unbecoming to her as a moustache; and many
women have tried in furtive privacy to disembarrass themselves of intellect as though it were facial hair.

Discouraged from growing "a mind like a man's," women are en- 17
couraged to have thoughts and feelings of a specifically feminine tone.
For society is cunning enough not to place its whole reliance on threatening women with blasts of icy air. It also flatters them with a zone of
hot air. The most deceptive and cynical of its blandishments is the notion
that women have some specifically feminine contribution to make to
culture. Unfortunately, as culture had already been shaped and largely
built up by men before the invitation was issued, this leaves women little
to do. Culture consists of reasoned thought and works of art composed
of cogent feeling and imagination. There is only one way to be reasonable, and that is to reason correctly; and the only kind of art which is
any good is good art. If women are to eschew reason and artistic imagination in favour of "intuition" and "feeling," it is pretty clear what is
meant. "Intuition" is just a polite name for bad reasoning, and "feeling"
for bad art.

In reality, the whole idea of a specifically feminine—or, for the 18
matter of that, masculine—contribution to culture is a contradiction of
culture. A contribution to culture is not something which could not have
been made by the other sex—it is something which could not have been

made by any other *person*. Equally, the notion that anyone, of either sex, can create good art out of simple feeling, untempered by discipline, is a philistine one. The arts are a sphere where women seem to have done well; but really they have done *too* well—too well for the good of the arts. Instead of women sharing the esteem which ought to belong to artists, art is becoming smeared with femininity. We are approaching a philistine state of affairs where the arts are something which it is nice for women to take up in their spare time—men having slammed out of the house to get on with society's "serious" business, like making money, administering the country and running the professions.

In that "serious" sphere it is still rare to encounter a woman. A man sentenced to prison would probably feel his punishment was redoubled by indignity if he were to be sentenced by a woman judge under a law drafted by a woman legislator—and if, on admission, he were to be examined by a woman prison doctor. If such a thing happened every day, it would be no indignity but the natural course of events. It has never been given the chance to become the natural course of events and never will be so long as women remain persuaded it would be unnatural of them to want it.   19

So brilliantly has society contrived to terrorise women with this threat that certain behaviour is unnatural and unwomanly that it has left them no time to consider—or even sheerly observe—what womanly nature really is. For centuries arrant superstitions were accepted as natural law. The physiological fact that only women can secrete milk for feeding babies was extended into the pure myth that it was women's business to cook for and wait on the entire family. The kitchen became woman's "natural" place because, for the first few months of her baby's life, the nursery really was. To this day a woman may suspect that she is unfeminine if she can discover in herself no aptitude or liking for cooking. Fright has thrown her into such a muddle that she confuses having no taste for cookery with having no breasts, and conversely assumes that nature has endowed the human female with a special handiness with frying pans.   20

Even psycho-analysis, which in general has been the greatest benefactor of civilisation since the wheel, has unwittingly reinforced the terrorisation campaign. The trouble was that it brought with it from its origin in medical therapy a criterion of normality instead of rationality. On sheer statistics every pioneer, genius and social reformer, including the first woman who demanded to be let out of the kitchen and into the polling booth, is abnormal, along with every lunatic and eccentric. What distinguishes the genius from the lunatic is that the genius's abnormality is justifiable by reason or aesthetics. If a woman who is irked by confine-   21 ment to the kitchen merely looks round to see what other women are doing and finds they are accepting kitchens, she may well conclude that she is abnormal and had better enlist her psycho-analyst's help towards "living with" her kitchen. What she ought to ask is whether it is rational for women to be kept in the kitchen, and whether nature really does insist on that in the way it insists women have breasts. And in a far-reaching sense to ask that question is much more normal and natural than learning to "live with" the handicap of women's inferior social status. The normal and natural thing for human beings is not to tolerate handicaps but to reform society and to circumvent or supplement nature. We don't learn to live minus a leg; we devise an artificial limb.

That, indeed, is the crux of the matter. Not only are the distinc- 22
tions we draw between male nature and female nature largely arbitrary and often pure superstition: they are completely beside the point. They ignore the essence of *human* nature. The important question is not whether women are or are not less logical by nature than men, but whether education, effort and the abolition of our illogical social pressures can improve on nature and make them (and, incidentally, men as well) *more* logical. What distinguishes human from any other animal nature is its ability to be unnatural. Logic and art are not natural or instinctive activities; but our nature includes a propensity to acquire them. It is not natural for the human body to orbit the earth; but the human mind has a natural adventurousness which enables it to invent machines whereby the body can do so. There is, in sober fact, no such creature as a natural man. Go as far back as they will, the archaeologists cannot come on a wild man in his natural habitat. At his most primitive, he has already constructed himself an artificial habitat, and decorated it not by a standardised instinctual method, as birds build nests, but by individualised—that is, abnormal—works of art or magic. And in doing so he is not limited by the fingers nature gave him; he has extended their versatility by making tools.

Civilisation consists not necessarily in defying nature but in making 23
it possible for us to do so if we judge it desirable. The higher we can lift our noses from the grindstone of nature, the wider the area we have of choice; and the more choices we have freely made, the more individualised we are. We are at our most civilised when nature does not dictate to us, as it does to animals and peasants, but when we can opt to fall in with it or better it. If modern civilisation has invented methods of education which make it possible for men to feed babies and for women to think logically, we are betraying civilisation itself if we do not set both sexes free to make a free choice.

Questions for Study and Discussion

1. What is Brophy's thesis, and where is it stated?

2. Brophy uses the analogy of the zoo to explain the plight of women in contemporary society. What are the elements of her analogy? How does the analogy work? Did you find the analogy effective? Why, or why not?

3. According to Brophy, women are not the only victims of society's pressures. In what ways does she believe men have been victimized as well?

4. On what grounds does Brophy criticize psychoanalysis? Do you agree with her argument? Why, or why not?

5. Brophy uses a number of italicized words in her essay. Why do you suppose she uses them? Did you find their use effective? Explain.

6. What does Brophy see as a solution to sex-role stereotypes? Does her solution seem reasonable? What specific suggestions if any does she give to implement?

Writing Topics

1. Brophy's essay is rather theoretical; that is, it does not make use of specific examples or case studies. Do your experiences and observations bear out the truth of Brophy's view of the situation with regard to women? It may be helpful to recount Brophy's points as a way to both think about and organize your examples.

2. Write an essay in which you argue for or against the following proposition: Traditional gender roles serve to protect people and to make them secure in their positions, whereas the women's movement has created a chaotic situation in which both men and women are unsure of who they are and how they are supposed to act.

Marriage and Its Alternatives

BLACK ELK

Black Elk was a *wickasha wakon,* a kind of preacher or holy man of the Oglala Sioux of South Dakota. He was born in 1863 on the Little Powder River and was a second cousin to Crazy Horse. In 1930 the poet John G. Neihardt happened upon Black Elk while doing research for his narrative poem *Cycle of the West.* For Black Elk this was more than a chance meeting. As he told Neihardt, "There is so much to teach you. What I know was given to me for men and it is true and it is beautiful. Soon I shall be under the grass and it will be lost. You were sent to save it, and you must come back so that I can teach you." Neihardt did return the following spring to listen to Black Elk's life story and to record his sacred "Great Vision" for men. In 1932 Neihardt published the book *Black Elk Speaks.*

In general, Black Elk paints a bleak picture of the Indians' condition at the end of the nineteenth century and the beginning of this century, but in "High Horse's Courting" he not only provides a bit of humor but also a firsthand account of the courting customs of the Sioux. Black Elk died in 1950.

High Horse's Courting

You know, in the old days, it was not very easy to get a girl when you wanted to be married. Sometimes it was hard work for a young man and he had to stand a great deal. Say I am a young man and I have seen a young girl who looks so beautiful to me that I feel all sick when I think about her. I cannot just go and tell her about it and then get married if she is willing. I have to be a very sneaky fellow to talk to her at all, and after I have managed to talk to her, that is only the beginning.

Probably for a long time I have been feeling sick about a certain girl because I love her so much, but she will not even look at me, and her parents keep a good watch over her. But I keep feeling worse and worse all the time; so maybe I sneak up to her tepee in the dark and wait

1

2

until she comes out. Maybe I just wait there all night and don't get any sleep at all and she does not come out. Then I feel sicker than ever about her.

Maybe I hide in the brush by a spring where she sometimes goes   3
to get water, and when she comes by, if nobody is looking, then I jump out and hold her and just make her listen to me. If she likes me too, I can tell that from the way she acts, for she is very bashful and maybe will not say a word or even look at me the first time. So I let her go, and then maybe I sneak around until I can see her father alone, and I tell him how many horses I can give him for his beautiful girl, and by now I am feeling so sick that maybe I would give him all the horses in the world if I had them.

Well, this young man I am telling about was called High Horse,   4
and there was a girl in the village who looked so beautiful to him that he was just sick all over from thinking about her so much and he was getting sicker all the time. The girl was very shy, and her parents thought a great deal of her because they were not young any more and this was the only child they had. So they watched her all day long, and they fixed it so that she would be safe at night too when they were asleep. They thought so much of her that they had made a rawhide bed for her to sleep in, and after they knew that High Horse was sneaking around after her, they took rawhide thongs and tied the girl in bed at night so that nobody could steal her when they were asleep, for they were not sure but that their girl might really want to be stolen.

Well, after High Horse had been sneaking around a good while and   5
hiding and waiting for the girl and getting sicker all the time, he finally caught her alone and made her talk to him. Then he found out that she liked him maybe a little. Of course this did not make him feel well. It made him sicker than ever, but now he felt as brave as a bison bull, so he went right to her father and said he loved the girl so much that he would give two good horses for her—one of them young and the other one not so very old.

But the old man just waved his hand, meaning for High Horse to   6
go away and quit talking foolishness like that.

High Horse was feeling sicker than ever about it; but there was   7
another young fellow who said he would loan High Horse two ponies and when he got some more horses, why, he could just give them back for the ones he had borrowed.

Then High Horse went back to the old man and said he would give   8
four horses for the girl—two of them young and the other two not hardly old at all. But the old man just waved his hand and would not say anything.

So High Horse sneaked around until he could talk to the girl again,   9
and he asked her to run away with him. He told her he thought he would
just fall over and die if she did not. But she said she would not do that;
she wanted to be bought like a fine woman. You see she thought a great
deal of herself too.

That made High Horse feel so sick that he could not eat a bite,   10
and he went around with his head hanging down as though he might
just fall down and die any time.

Red Deer was another young fellow, and he and High Horse were   11
great comrades, always doing things together. Red Deer saw how High
Horse was acting, and he said: "Cousin, what is the matter? Are you
sick in the belly? You look as though you were going to die."

Then High Horse told Red Deer how it was, and said he thought   12
he could not stay alive much longer if he could not marry the girl pretty
quick.

Red Deer thought awhile about it, and then he said: "Cousin, I   13
have a plan, and if you are man enough to do as I tell you, then everything will be all right. She will not run away with you; her old man will
not take four horses; and four horses are all you can get. You must steal
her and run away with her. Then afterwhile you can come back and the
old man cannot do anything because she will be your woman. Probably
she wants you to steal her anyway."

So they planned what High Horse had to do, and he said he loved   14
the girl so much that he was man enough to do anything Red Deer or
anybody else could think up. So this is what they did.

That night late they sneaked up to the girl's tepee and waited until   15
it sounded inside as though the old man and the old woman and the girl
were sound asleep. Then High Horse crawled under the tepee with a
knife. He had to cut the rawhide thongs first, and then Red Deer, who
was pulling up the stakes around that side of the tepee, was going to help
drag the girl outside and gag her. After that, High Horse could put her
across his pony in front of him and hurry out of there and be happy all
the rest of his life.

When High Horse had crawled inside, he felt so nervous that he   16
could hear his heart drumming, and it seemed so loud he felt sure it
would 'waken the old folks. But it did not, and afterwhile he began
cutting the thongs. Every time he cut one it made a pop and nearly
scared him to death. But he was getting along all right and all the thongs
were cut down as far as the girl's thighs, when he became so nervous
that his knife slipped and stuck the girl. She gave a big, loud yell. Then
the old folks jumped up and yelled too. By this time High Horse was
outside, and he and Red Deer were running away like antelope. The old

man and some other people chased the young men but they got away in the dark and nobody knew who it was.

Well, if you ever wanted a beautiful girl you will know how sick   17
High Horse was now. It was very bad the way he felt, and it looked as though he would starve even if he did not drop over dead sometime.

Red Deer kept thinking about this, and after a few days he went   18
to High Horse and said: "Cousin, take courage! I have another plan, and I am sure, if you are man enough, we can steal her this time." And High Horse said: "I am man enough to do anything anybody can think up, if I can only get that girl."

So this is what they did.   19

They went away from the village alone, and Red Deer made High   20
Horse strip naked. Then he painted High Horse solid white all over, and after that he painted black stripes all over the white and put black rings around High Horse's eyes. High Horse looked terrible. He looked so terrible that when Red Deer was through painting and took a good look at what he had done, he said it scared even him a little.

"Now," Red Deer said, "if you get caught again, everybody will be   21
so scared they will think you are a bad spirit and will be afraid to chase you."

So when the night was getting old and everybody was sound asleep,   22
they sneaked back to the girl's tepee. High Horse crawled in with his knife, as before, and Red Deer waited outside, ready to drag the girl out and gag her when High Horse had all the thongs cut.

High Horse crept up by the girl's bed and began cutting at the   23
thongs. But he kept thinking, "If they see me they will shoot me because I look so terrible." The girl was restless and kept squirming around in bed, and when a thong was cut, it popped. So High Horse worked very slowly and carefully.

But he must have made some noise, for suddenly the old woman   24
awoke and said to her old man: "Old Man, wake up! There is somebody in this tepee!" But the old man was sleepy and didn't want to be bothered. He said: "Of course there is somebody in this tepee. Go to sleep and don't bother me." Then he snored some more.

But High Horse was so scared by now that he lay very still and as   25
flat to the ground as he could. Now, you see, he had not been sleeping very well for a long time because he was so sick about the girl. And while he was lying there waiting for the old woman to snore, he just forgot everything, even how beautiful the girl was. Red Deer who was lying outside ready to do his part, wondered and wondered what had happened in there, but he did not dare call out to High Horse.

Afterwhile the day began to break and Red Deer had to leave with   26
the two ponies he had staked there for his comrade and girl, or somebody
would see him.

So he left.   27

Now when it was getting light in the tepee, the girl awoke and the   28
first thing she saw was a terrible animal, all white with black stripes on
it, lying asleep beside her bed. So she screamed, and then the old woman
screamed and the old man yelled. High Horse jumped up, scared almost
to death, and he nearly knocked the tepee down getting out of there.

People were coming running from all over the village with guns   29
and bows and axes, and everybody was yelling.

By now High Horse was running so fast that he hardly touched the   30
ground at all, and he looked so terrible that the people fled from him
and let him run. Some braves wanted to shoot at him, but the others
said he might be some sacred being and it would bring bad trouble to
kill him.

High Horse made for the river that was near, and in among the   31
brush he found a hollow tree and dived into it. Afterwhile some braves
came there and he could hear them saying that it was some bad spirit
that had come out of the water and gone back in again.

That morning the people were ordered to break camp and move   32
away from there. So they did, while High Horse was hiding in his hollow
tree.

Now Red Deer had been watching all this from his own tepee and   33
trying to look as though he were as much surprised and scared as all the
others. So when the camp moved, he sneaked back to where he had seen
his comrade disappear. When he was down there in the brush, he called,
and High Horse answered, because he knew his friend's voice. They
washed off the paint from High Horse and sat down on the river bank
to talk about their troubles.

High Horse said he never would go back to the village as long as   34
he lived and he did not care what happened to him now. He said he
was going to go on the war-path all by himself. Red Deer said: "No,
cousin, you are not going on the war-path alone, because I am going
with you."

So Red Deer got everything ready, and at night they started out   35
on the war-path all alone. After several days they came to a Crow camp
just about sundown, and when it was dark they sneaked up to where the
Crow horses were grazing, killed the horse guard, who was not thinking
about enemies because he thought all the Lakotas were far away, and
drove off about a hundred horses.

They got a big start because all the Crow horses stampeded and it   36
was probably morning before the Crow warriors could catch any horses
to ride. Red Deer and High Horse fled with their herd three days and
nights before they reached the village of their people. Then they drove
the whole herd right into the village and up in front of the girl's tepee.
The old man was there, and High Horse called out to him and asked if
he thought maybe that would be enough horses for his girl. The old man
did not wave him away that time. It was not the horses that he wanted.
What he wanted was a son who was a real man and good for something.

So High Horse got his girl after all, and I think he deserved her.   37

Questions for Study and Discussion

1. What seems to be Black Elk's purpose in telling the story of High Horse?

2. What does Black Elk mean by High Horse's "sickness"? What are its characteristics?

3. Briefly describe the courtship ritual that High Horse participates in. What is the role of the girl? The parents? Red Deer?

4. Why did the girl refuse to run away with High Horse?

5. How do the first three paragraphs function in the context of this narrative?

6. Many readers find Black Elk's narrative humorous. What, if anything, makes the story humorous? Why do you suppose Black Elk chose to be humorous?

Writing Topics

1. Examine American courtship rituals, and write an essay in which you describe a typical courtship. Is there anything humorous about our own rituals? Is there anything about our rituals that foreigners would be unlikely to understand?

2. Discuss courtship practices with your parents or grandparents or with people of their generations. Write an essay in which you compare and/or contrast their practices with those that are prevalent today.

LOUISE MONTAGUE

The sexual revolution of the sixties brought about a dramatic increase in the number of unmarried couples who chose to live together. This social phenomenon continues to cause a great upheaval and debate in our society. Proponents of this new living-together arrangement cite a variety of reasons to justify their behavior—a way to test marriage, to sustain romantic spontaneity, to reap financial benefits, or, quite simply, to make life convenient. Louise Montague was born in 1931 and is the author of two books on divorce and the novel *Sand Castles*. She believes that the living-together arrangement is not as attractive as it may appear to be on the surface and that it "can actually spoil a good relationship between two people who should eventually marry." Because, as she writes, "you cannot hope to find love by experimenting biologically," she advocates a more traditional courtship period before marriage.

Montague's essay first appeared in *Reader's Digest* in 1970.

Straight Talk about the Living-Together Arrangement

As the author of two books on divorce, I try to accept as many   1
speaking engagements in high-school and college classes as I can. For it is my feeling that one answer to the soaring divorce rate is "preventive thinking"—the time to face many of the problems of divorce is *before* marriage. Lately, however, I find that at every session someone will stand up and state that marriage is outmoded and that the answer to the divorce problem is to live with a partner without the legal commitment of marriage.

Unhappily, "living together" is a modern phenomenon, a national   2
trend today. Between 1960 and 1970, according to the U.S. Department of the Census, there was an eightfold increase in the Living-Together Arrangement (LTA). Why are so many people opting for this arrangement? And how do they get into it?

Certainly it's a very attractive idea sexually. But many young people   3
also say it's a good way to "test" marriage. Others claim it's a terrific financial boon. And some don't even know how they ended up together. He started staying over or she began to leave clothes in his closet. These young people feel that by not making their relationship permanent they can maintain the spontaneous atmosphere of new love. By eliminating the legal commitment, they feel they have eliminated the "bad" part of marriage.

But the phenomenon is not limited to young people. Many divorced persons burned in marriage are trying it. Some have religious convictions forbidding a second marriage. Divorced men who are financially strapped feel they can't take on the responsibility of a new wife. Or the divorced woman may be reluctant to give up the alimony which would stop with her remarriage.

With all these "pluses" why do so many people engaged in an LTA write to me about the problems they have encountered? Why *is* the Living-Together Arrangement a detriment to those involved? Let's first consider the college students who decide on or slide into an LTA. You'd be surprised, once the subject comes up for discussion in a classroom, how many youngsters tell unhappy stories about themselves or their best friends.

Take the case of the young couple at Stanford. After they moved in together, the boy lost his scholarship and was not able to meet the high tuition costs from his part-time job. The girl quit school in order to work and let him finish his education. When he graduated, he applied for—and received—a scholarship to do graduate work in England. The girl was extremely hurt and angry; she felt he owed it to her to stay and help her finish *her* education. They argued bitterly for a day, and then the young man packed and left!

This situation is typical of dozens I have heard. The LTA simply can't work when it breeds the mutual dependency of marriage without the mutual responsibility.

Another example is a young couple at Georgetown University who moved into an apartment together. The girl's parents, shocked and hurt, cut off all their daughter's funds. The boy suggested they split up and go back to their dorms, but the girl, having had a terrible row with her family, insisted that it was now his responsibility to take care of her! Both got jobs, and the young man, not a strong student, fell behind and was unable to graduate.

Certainly it's difficult to think in realistic terms when a couple imagine themselves in love. But it is unfair to expect parental values to be dropped at a whim. The censure of family and friends is one of the greatest burdens the LTA carries. Young people who need the support of family are very foolish to chuck their long-term goals for short-term pleasures.

To be sure, intimate relationships are widely accepted today, but any resourceful couple can find ways of being together without moving in together. Moreover, living alone at times and developing individuality should be a prime concern of young people. For few can handle the LTA until they have learned to live with themselves.

Some of the most heartbreaking stories I hear about LTA's concern   11
children. Whatever life-style a single male or female chooses is that
individual's responsibility. But to bring a child into this atmosphere is to
involve an innocent third party in an experiment that can leave all
parties damaged. Although the law generally requires a father to support
his children, it is often difficult to enforce these laws. Women are frequently left with the burden of support while the air of illegitimacy hangs
heavy on the child.

A divorced or widowed woman who involves her children in an   12
LTA may also be subjecting them to undue stress. Children experience
great pressures to conform. What the mother and her companion view
as a marvelous, free life-style, a child could see as a freaky embarrassment.
The man in question, not being either father or stepfather, has no social
definition as to the role he should play in the child's life. In some states,
a divorced mother in an LTA stands a good chance of losing not only
support payments but custody of her children.

Even a highly motivated working couple should be aware of the   13
consequences of their actions. How you present yourself to the world is
how you will be judged. A young petroleum engineer, living with a dental
hygienist, applied for a much-wanted overseas job with an oil company.
When the company conducted its routine investigation, and found that
the young woman with whom he was living was not his wife, he was
turned down; the firm felt that his LTA smacked of indecisiveness, instability, and failure on his part to accept responsibility. Who is to say
if the oil company made the right decision? But, judging from a great
many instances, it happens to be the way things are. What a couple may
view as a sophisticated way to live, the business community may see as
a career impediment.

Heartbreak and setback are also in the cards for a woman who   14
moves in with a man in the hope of getting married. My advice is to
avoid this strategy. When you demand nothing of a relationship, that's
often exactly what you get. The very impermanence of the LTA suggests
that that is what each partner has settled for. If marriage is what you
want, marriage is what you should have. So why commit youself to a
shaky arrangement that keeps you out of the mainstream of life where
you quite possibly will meet someone who shares your views?

Many divorced women with a great need for a little security, and   15
with little faith in themselves, seek an LTA as a temporary answer to
help them get on their feet. All this does is prolong their adjustment and
reinforce their self-doubts. I'm reminded of one such woman who told
me she had been living with a man for four years and wanted out but
was afraid to leave. "Why?" I asked. Because, she said, she feared to give

up the free rent and all that "security" she had with him. "Wrong," I said. "You have no security of any kind. You stand a good chance of being replaced by a younger version of yourself. And as for free rent, that's no security either. Security is owning the building."

Probably the greatest single hazard of the LTA is that it can actually spoil a good relationship between two people who should eventually marry. Because it is entered into out of weakness rather than strength, doubt rather than conviction, drift rather than decision, it offers unnecessary obstacles. Knowing this, you shouldn't casually toss aside those inherited institutions that have had a history of success.   16

If I were asked to give one reason only why I am opposed to the LTA, I would state quite simply that I am morally against it. As Barbara Tuchman wrote in *McCall's*: "Standards of taste, as well as morality, need continued reaffirmation to stay alive, as liberty needs eternal vigilance." There are valid standards of judgment which come from confidence in yourself and your values. To accept a living pattern that goes against your better judgment is to chip away at your personal freedom.   17

And what of love? You cannot hope to find love by experimenting biologically. You don't build love by creating a living situation designed to test it. You don't create love by setting up a forced proximity. Love *is*. And when you love you commit to it—for better or for worse. When we finally realize that all our experiments in alternate life-styles, communal marriage and open-ended covenants are simply a means of running *from* responsibility and love, not *to* them, we will have reached the beginning of maturity.   18

Questions for Study and Discussion

1. Why does Montague begin by stating that she is the author of two books on divorce and a regular speaker on high-school and college campuses?

2. What are some of the reasons people give Montague for living together?

3. Where does Montague reveal her attitude about LTA's? What reason does she give in arguing against such arrangements?

4. What, according to Montague, is the "greatest single hazard of the LTA"? Do you agree? Why, or why not?

5. Take another look at the examples that Montague uses to illustrate the disadvantages of LTA's. How persuasive do you find them? Explain.

6. Summarize Montague's thinking about love. What is it? What is its relationship to responsibility?

Writing Topics

1. In an essay present your views about the LTA. What do you see as its main advantages? Disadvantages? Are your views shared by your peers?

2. Write an essay in which you argue for a courtship period (as opposed to an LTA) as a "test" for a permanent relationship.

3. Montague states that "few can handle the LTA until they have learned to live with themselves." Write an essay in which you argue that a sense of individuality, responsibility, and maturity are necessary before entering an LTA or a marriage.

ERNEST VAN DEN HAAG

Ernest van den Haag is a practicing psychoanalyst and lecturer in sociology and psychology at both New York University and the New School for Social Research. He was born in The Hague in 1914, and after attending the universities of Naples and Florence, and the Sorbonne, University of Paris, came to the United States in 1940. He subsequently earned his M.A. from the State University of Iowa and his Ph.D. from New York University. A much sought after lecturer at colleges and universities across the country, van den Haag has written many books, including *The Fabric of Society* (1967), and has contributed articles to popular magazines both here and abroad.

In "Love and Marriage," which first appeared in *Harper's Magazine* in 1962, van den Haag takes a look at the history of marriage and concludes that romantic love is exerting unrealistic pressures on the institution as it exists in the United States today.

Love and Marriage

If someone asks, "Why do people marry?" he meets indignation or astonishment. The question seems absurd if not immoral: the desirability of marriage is regarded as unquestionable. Divorce, on the other hand, strikes us as a problem worthy of serious and therapeutic attention. Yet marriage precedes divorce as a rule, and frequently causes it. 1

What explains marriage? People divorce often but they marry still more often. Lately they also marry—and divorce, of course—younger than they used to, particularly in the middle classes (most statistics understate the change by averaging all classes). And the young have a disproportionate share of divorces. However, their hasty exertions to get out of wedlock puzzle me less than their eagerness to rush into it in the first place. 2

A hundred years ago there was every reason to marry young— though middle-class people seldom did. The unmarried state had heavy disadvantages for both sexes. Custom did not permit girls to be educated, to work, or to have social, let alone sexual, freedom. Men were free but since women were not, they had only prostitutes for partners. (When enforced, the double standard is certainly self-defeating.) And, though less restricted than girls shackled to their families, single men often led a grim and uncomfortable life. A wife was nearly indispensable, if only to darn socks, sew, cook, clean, take care of her man. Altogether, both sexes needed marriage far more than now—no TV, cars, dates, drip-dry 3 shirts, cleaners, canned foods—and not much hospital care, insurance, or social security. The family was all-important.

Marriage is no longer quite so indispensable a convenience; yet we find people marrying more than ever, and earlier. To be sure, prosperity makes marriage more possible. But why are the young exploiting the possibility so sedulously? Has the yearning for love become more urgent and widespread?   4

What has happened is that the physical conveniences which reduced the material usefulness of marriage have also loosened the bonds of family life. Many other bonds that sustained us psychologically were weakened as they were extended: beliefs became vague; associations impersonal, discontinuous, and casual. Our contacts are many, our relationships few: our lives, externally crowded, often are internally isolated; we remain but tenuously linked to each other and our ties come easily undone. One feels lonely surrounded by crowds and machines in an unbounded, abstract world that has become morally unintelligible; and we have so much time now to feel lonely in. Thus one longs, perhaps more acutely than in the past, for somebody to be tangibly, individually, and definitely one's own, body and soul.   5

This is the promise of marriage. Movies, songs, TV, romance magazines, all intensify the belief that love alone makes life worthwhile, is perpetual, conquers the world's evils, and is fulfilled and certified by marriage. "Science" hastens to confirm as much. Doesn't popular psychology, brandishing the banner of Freud with more enthusiasm than knowledge, tell us, in effect, that any male who stays single is selfish or homosexual or mother-dominated and generally neurotic? and any unmarried female frustrated (or worse, not frustrated) and neurotic? A "normal" person, we are told, must love and thereupon marry. Thus love and marriage are identified with each other and with normality, three thousand years of experience notwithstanding. The yearning for love, attended by anxiety to prove oneself well-adjusted and normal, turns into eagerness to get married.   6

The young may justly say that they merely practice what their parents preached. For, indeed, the idea that "love and marriage go together like a horse and carriage" has been drummed into their heads, so much that it finally has come to seem entirely natural. Yet, nothing could be less so. Love has long delighted and distressed mankind, and marriage has comforted us steadily and well. Both, however, are denatured—paradoxically enough, by their staunchest supporters—when they are expected to "go together." For love is a very unruly horse, far more apt to run away and overturn the carriage than to draw it. That is why,   7 in the past, people seldom thought of harnessing marriage to love. They felt that each has its own motive power: one primed for a lifelong journey; the other for an ardent improvisation, a voyage of discovery.

More than a Frenzy?

Though by no means weaker, the marital bond is quite different 8 from the bond of love. If you like, it is a different bond of love—less taut, perhaps, and more durable. By confusing these two related but in many ways dissimilar bonds, we stand to lose the virtues and gain the vices of both: the spontaneous passion of love and the deliberate permanence of marriage are equally endangered as we try to live up to an ideal which bogs down one and unhinges the other.

Marriage is an immemorial institution which, in some form, exists 9 everywhere. Its main purpose always was to unite and to continue the families of bride and groom and to further their economic and social position. The families, therefore, were the main interested parties. Often marriages were arranged (and sometimes they took place) before the future husbands or wives were old enough to talk. Even when they were grown up, they felt, as did their parents, that the major purpose of marriage was to continue the family, to produce children. Certainly women hoped for kind and vigorous providers and men for faithful mothers and good housekeepers; both undoubtedly hoped for affection, too; but love did not strike either of them as indispensable and certainly not as sufficient for marriage.

Unlike marriage, love has only recently come to be generally accepted as something more than a frenzied state of pleasure and pain. It is a welcome innovation—but easily ruined by marriage; which in turn has a hard time surviving confusion with love. Marriage counselors usually recognize this last point, but people in love seldom consult them. Perhaps their limited clientele colors the views of too many marriage counselors: instead of acknowledging that love and marriage are different but equally genuine relationships, they depict love as a kind of dependable wheel horse that can be harnessed to the carriage of married life. For them, any other kind of love must be an "immature" or "neurotic" fantasy, something to be condemned as Hollywood-inspired, "unrealistic" romanticism. It is as though a man opposed to horse racing—for good reasons perhaps—were to argue that race horses are not real, that all real horses are draft horses. Thus marriage counselors often insist that the only "real" and "true" love is "mature"—it is the comfortable workaday relation

Mommy and Daddy have. The children find it hard to believe that there is nothing more to it.

They are quite right. And they have on their side the great litera-   11
ture of the world, and philosophers from Plato to Santayana. What is wrong with Hollywood romance surely is not that it is romantic, but that its romances are shoddy clichés. And since Hollywood shuns the true dimensions of conflict, love in the movies is usually confirmed by marriage and marriage by love, in accordance with wishful fantasy, though not with truth.

Was the love Tristan bore Isolde "mature" or "neurotic"? They loved   12
each other before and after Isolde was married—to King Mark. It never occurred to them to marry each other; they even cut short an extramarital idyll together in the forest. (And Tristan too, while protesting love for Isolde, got married to some other girl.) Dante saw, but never actually met, Beatrice until he reached the nether world, which is the place for permanent romance. Of course, he was a married man.

It is foolish to pretend that the passionate romantic longing doesn't   13
exist or is "neurotic," i.e., shouldn't exist; it is as foolish to pretend that romantic love can be made part of a cozy domesticity. The truth is simple enough, though it can make life awfully complicated: there are two things, love and affection (or marital love), not one; they do not usually pull together as a team; they tend to draw us in different directions, if they are present at the same time. God nowhere promised to make this a simple world.

In the West, love came to be socially approved around the twelfth   14
century. It became a fashionable subject of discussion then, and even of disputation, in formal "courts of love" convoked to argue its merits and to elaborate its true characteristics. Poets and singers created the models and images of love. They still do—though mass production has perhaps affected the quality; what else makes the teen-age crooners idols to their followers and what else do they croon about? In medieval times, as now, manuals were written, codifying the behavior recommended to lovers. With a difference though. Today's manuals are produced not by men of letters, but by doctors and therapists, as though love, sex, and marriage were diseases or therapeutic problems—which they promptly become if one reads too many of these guidebooks (any one is one too many). To-day's manuals bear titles like "Married Love" (unmarried lovers can manage without help, I guess); but regardless of title, they concentrate on sex. In handbooks on dating they tell how to avoid it; in handbooks on marriage, how to go about it. The authors are sure that happiness depends

on the sexual mechanics they blueprint. Yet, one doesn't make love better by reading a book any more than one learns to dance, or ride a bicycle, by reading about it.

The Use of "Technique"

The sexual engineering (or cookbook) approach is profitable only   15 for the writer: in an enduring relationship, physical gratification is an effect and not a cause. If a person does not acquire sexual skill from experience, he is not ready for it. Wherever basic inhibitions exist, no book can remove them. Where they do not, no book is necessary. I have seen many an unhappy relationship in my psychoanalytic practice, but none ever in which sexual technique or the lack of it was more than a symptom and an effect. The mechanical approach never helps.

The troubadours usually took sex and marriage for granted and dealt   16 with love—the newest and still the most surprising and fascinating of all relationships. And also the most unstable. They conceived love as a longing, a tension between desire and fulfillment. This feeling, of course, had been known before they celebrated it. Plato described love as a desire for something one does not have, implying that it is a longing, not a fulfillment. But in ancient Greece, love was regarded diffidently, as rather undesirable, an intoxication, a bewitchment, a divine punishment—usually for neglecting sex. The troubadours thought differently, although, unlike many moderns, they did not deny that love is a passion, something one suffers.* But they thought it a sweet suffering to be cultivated, and they celebrated it in song and story.

The troubadours clearly distinguished love and sex. Love was to   17 them a yearning for a psychic gratification which the lover feels only the beloved can give: sex, an impersonal desire anybody possessing certain fairly common characteristics can gratify by physical actions. Unlike love, sex can thrive without an intense personal relationship and may erode it if it exists. Indeed, the Romans sometimes wondered if love would not

---

*. . . I am in love
And that is my shame.
What hurts the soul
My souls adores,
No better than a beast
Upon all fours.

So says W. B. Yeats. About eight centuries earlier, Chrestien de Troyes expressed the same sentiment. [van den Haag's note]

blunt and tame their sexual pleasures, whereas the troubadours fretted lest sex abate the fervor of love's longing. They never fully resolved the contest between love and sex; nor has anyone else. (To define it away is, of course, not to solve it.)

We try to cope with this contest by fusing love and sex. (Every high-school student is taught that the two go together.) This, as Freud pointed out, does not always succeed and may moderate both, but, as he also implied, it is the best we can hope for. In the words of William Butler Yeats, "Desire dies because every touch consumes the myth and yet, a myth that cannot be consumed becomes a specter. . . ." 18

Romantics, who want love's desiring to be conclusive, though endless, often linked it to death: if nothing further can happen and rival its significance, if one dies before it does, love indeed is the end. But this is ending the game as much as winning it—certainly an ambiguous move. The religious too perpetuate longing by placing the beloved altogether out of physical reach. The "bride of Christ" who retires to a convent longs for her Redeemer —and she will continue to yearn, as long as she lives, for union with a God at once human and divine, incarnating life and love everlasting. In its highest sense, love is a reaching for divine perfection, an act of creation. And always, it is a longing. 19

Since love is longing, experts in the Middle Ages held that one could not love someone who could not be longed for—for instance, one's wife. Hence, the Comtesse de Champagne told her court in 1174: "Love cannot extend its rights over two married persons." If one were to marry one's love, one would exchange the sweet torment of desire, the yearning, for that which fulfills it. Thus the tension of hope would be replaced by the comfort of certainty. He who longs to long, who wants the tension of desire, surely should not marry. In former times, of course, he married—the better to love someone else's wife. 20

When sexual objects are easily and guiltlessly accessible, in a society that does not object to promiscuity, romantic love seldom prospers. For example, in imperial Rome it was rare and in Tahiti unknown. And love is unlikely to arouse the heart of someone brought up in a harem, where the idea of uniqueness has a hard time. Love flowers best in a monogamous environment morally opposed to unrestrained sex, and interested in cultivating individual experience. In such an environment, longing may be valued for itself. Thus, love as we know it is a Christian legacy, though Christianity in the main repudiates romantic love where the object is worldly, and accepts passion only when transcendent, when God is the object—or when muted into affection: marital love. 21

Shifting the Object

Let me hazard a Freudian guess about the genesis of the longing we   22
call love. It continues and reproduces the child's first feeling for his parent—the original source of unconditioned and unconditional love. But
what is recreated is the child's image, the idealized mother or father,
young and uniquely beautiful, and not the empirical parent others see.
The unconsummated love for this ideal parent (and it could be someone
else important in the child's experience) remains as an intense longing.
Yet any fulfillment now must also become a disappointment—a substitute,
cheating the longing that wants to long. Nonetheless most of us marry
and replace the ideal with an imperfect reality. We repudiate our longing
or we keep it but shift its object. If we don't, we may resent our partners
for helping us "consume the myth," and leaving us shorn of longing—
which is what Don Giovanni found so intolerable, and what saddens many
a faithful husband.

Sexual gratification, of course, diminishes sexual desire for the time   23
being. But it does more. It changes love. The longing may become gratitude; the desire tenderness; love may become affectionate companionship—"After such knowledge, what forgiveness?" Depending on character and circumstance, love may also be replaced by indifference or hostility.

One thing is certain though: if the relationship is stabilized, love is   24
replaced by other emotions. (Marriage thus has often been recommended
as the cure for love. But it does not always work.) The only way to keep
love is to try to keep up—or re-establish—the distance between lovers
that was inevitably shortened by intimacy and possession, and thus, possibly, regain desire and longing. Lovers sometimes do so by quarreling.
And some personalities are remote enough, or inexhaustible enough, to
be longed for even when possessed. But this has disadvantages as well.
And the deliberate and artificial devices counseled by romance magazines
and marriage manuals ("surprise your husband . . .")—even when they
do not originate with the love of pretense—are unlikely to yield more
than the pretense of love.

The sexual act itself may serve as a vehicle for numberless feelings: 25
lust, vanity, and self-assertion, doubt and curiosity, possessiveness, anxiety, hostility, anger, or indifferent release from boredom. Yet, though seldom the only motive, and often absent altogether, love nowadays is given
as the one natural and moral reason which authorizes and even ordains
sexual relations. What we have done is draw a moral conclusion from a
rule of popular psychology: that "it is gratifying, and therefore healthy
and natural, to make love when you love, and frustrating, and therefore

unhealthy and unnatural, not to; we must follow nature; but sex without love is unnatural and therefore immoral."

Now, as a psychological rule, this is surely wrong; it can be as healthy   26
to frustrate as it is to gratify one's desires. Sometimes gratification is very unhealthy; sometimes frustration is. Nor can psychological health be accepted as morally decisive. Sanity, sanitation, and morality are all desirable, but they are not identical; our wanting all of them is the problem, not the solution. It may be quite "healthy" to run away with your neighbor's wife, but not, therefore, right. And there is nothing unhealthy about wishing to kill someone who has injured you—but this does not morally justify doing so. Finally, to say "we must follow nature" is always specious: we follow nature in whatever we do—we can't ever do what nature does not let us do. Why then identify nature only with the nonintellectual, the sensual, or the emotional possibilities? On this view, it would be unnatural to read: literacy is a gift of nature only if we include the intellect and training in nature's realm. If we do, it makes no sense to call a rule unnatural merely because it restrains an urge: the urge is no more natural than the restraint.

The combination of love and sex is no more natural than the sepa-   27
ration. Thus, what one decides about restraining or indulging an emotion, or a sexual urge, rests on religious, social, or personal values, none of which can claim to be more natural than any other.

Not that some indulgences and some inhibitions may not be health-   28
ier than others. But one cannot flatly say which are good or bad for every man. It depends on their origins and effects in the personalities involved. Without knowing these, more cannot be said—except, perhaps, that we should try not to use others, or even ourselves, merely as means—at least not habitually and in personal relations. Sex, unalloyed, sometimes leads to this original sin which our moral tradition condemns. Psychologically, too, the continued use of persons merely as instruments ultimately frustrates both the user and the used. This caution, though it justifies no positive action, may help perceive problems; it does not solve them; no general rule can.

How Long Does It Last?

What about marriage? In our society, couples usually invite the fam-   29
ilies to their weddings, although the decision to marry is made exclusively by bride and groom. However, a license must be obtained and the marriage registered; and it can be dissolved only by a court of law. Religious ceremonies state the meaning of marriage clearly: The couple are asked

to promise "forsaking all others, [to] keep thee only unto her [him], so long as ye both shall live." The vow does not say, "as long as ye both shall want to," because marriage is a promise to continue even when one no longer wishes to. If marriage were to end when love does, it would be redundant: why solemnly ask two people to promise to be with each other for as long as they want to be with each other?

Marriage was to cement the family by tying people together "till death do us part" in the face of the fickleness of their emotions. The authority of state and church was to see to it that they kept a promise voluntarily made, but binding, and that could not be unmade. Whether it sprang from love did not matter. Marriage differed from a love affair inasmuch as it continued regardless of love. Cupid shoots his arrows without rhyme or reason. But marriage is a deliberate rational act, a public institution making the family independent of Cupid's whims. Once enlisted, the volunteers couldn't quit, even when they didn't like it any longer. That was the point.

The idea that marriage must be synchronous with love or even affection nullifies it altogether. (That affection should coincide with marriage is, of course, desirable, though it does not always happen.) We would have to reword the marriage vow. Instead of saying, "till death do us part," we might say, "till we get bored with each other"; and, instead of "forsaking all others," "till someone better comes along." Clearly, if the couple intend to stay "married" only as long as they want to, they only pretend to be married: they are having an affair with legal trimmings. To marry is to vow fidelity regardless of any future feeling, to vow the most earnest attempt to avoid contrary feelings altogether, but, at any rate, not to give in to them.

Perhaps this sounds grim. But it needn't be if one marries for affection more than for love. For affection, marital love may grow with knowledge and intimacy and shared experience. Thus marriage itself, when accepted as something other than a love affair, may foster affection. Affection differs from love as fulfillment differs from desire. Further, love longs for what desire and imagination make uniquely and perfectly lovable. Possession erodes it. Affection, however—which is love of a different, of a perhaps more moral and less aesthetic kind—cares deeply also for what is unlovable without transforming it into beauty. It cares for the unvarnished person, not the splendid image. Time can strengthen it. But the husband who wants to remain a splendid image must provide a swan to draw him away, or find a wife who can restrain her curiosity about his real person—something that Lohengrin did not succeed in doing. Whereas love stresses the unique form perfection takes in the lover's mind, affection stresses the uniqueness of the actual person.

One may grow from the other. But not when this other is expected   33
to remain unchanged. And affection probably grows more easily if not
preceded by enchantment. For the disenchantment which often follows
may turn husband and wife against each other, and send them looking
elsewhere for re-enchantment—which distance lends so easily. Indeed,
nothing else does.

Questions for Study and Discussion

1. In his opening paragraph van den Haag states "the desirability of marriage
is regarded as unquestionable." While this may accurately reflect the situation in 1962 when this essay was written, is it accurate today? What, if anything, has changed?

2. According to van den Haag, why is marriage "no longer quite so
indispensable a convenience" as it was, say, one hundred years ago? Why do
people get married today?

3. What are the defining characteristics of romantic love according to the
author? What does he see as the relationship between romantic love and
marriage?

4. How did the ancients and the troubadours view love and sex? Does a
knowledge of their views have relevance for us today? Explain

5. What is the author's attitude toward sexual engineering or the cookbook
approach to sex?

6. What does van den Haag mean when he says, "it can be as healthy to
frustrate as to gratify one's desires"? Do you find his explanation convincing?
Explain.

7. What, according to the author, is affection? What is its role in marriage?
How does it differ from love?

Writing Topics

1. If you were to marry, what would you expect from marriage as an institution? Write an essay in which you explain what you are prepared to bring to
a marriage and what ideally you would like to receive from it.

2. Write an essay in which you try to explain why people continue to get
married in spite of the obvious problems that are facing the institution. What
is there about marriage that people find so attractive or appealing?

3. Recently Stephen Morris, a student at the University of Pennsylvania,
wrote an essay entitled "But Why Are You Getting Married." He begins:
"When I told my roommate that I was getting married, his reaction was,
quite simply, stupefied disbelief. Reactions from other friends ran the gamut,

244 Ernest van den Haag

from 'Surely you jest!' to 'You are insane!' My wife, Eden, encountered the same incredulity and ambivalence wherever she broke the news." Do you believe the response the Morrises received are typical of college students? If so, how do you account for this cynical attitude toward marriage? If not, what is the prevailing attitude on your campus? Write an essay in which you examine the issue, expressing as well your own attitudes about marriage.

ANNE ROIPHE

Born in New York City in 1935, Anne Roiphe is a 1957 graduate of Sarah Lawrence College. After graduation, she pursued further study in Munich, Germany, before starting a career as a writer. Roiphe is best known as a novelist; her novels include *Digging Out* (1967), *Long Division* (1972), and *Torch Song* (1977). *Up the Sandbox* (1970) was well received and later made into a popular motion picture. Each of her novels deals with human relationships and some aspect of a woman's search for identity. Her articles have appeared in *Vogue* and *The New York Times Magazine*. Roiphe is the mother of three children and stepmother of two.

In "Why Marriages Fail" Roiphe attempts to look beyond individual differences and particular circumstances for the underlying reasons that so many marriages end in divorce. In the process of analyzing the causes of marriage failure, Roiphe tells what, for her, is necessary to make a marriage work and endure.

Why Marriages Fail

These days so many marriages end in divorce that our most sacred   1
vows no longer ring with truth. "Happily ever after" and "Till death do us part" are expressions that seem on the way to becoming obsolete. Why has it become so hard for couples to stay together? What goes wrong? What has happened to us that close to one-half of all marriages are destined for the divorce courts? How could we have created a society in which 42 percent of our children will grow up in single-parent homes? If statistics could only measure loneliness, regret, pain, loss of self-confidence and fear of the future, the numbers would be beyond quantifying.

Even though each broken marriage is unique, we can still find the   2
common perils, the common causes for marital despair. Each marriage has crisis points and each marriage tests endurance, the capacity for both intimacy and change. Outside pressures such as job loss, illness, infertility, trouble with a child, care of aging parents and all the other plagues of life hit marriage the way hurricanes blast our shores. Some marriages survive these storms and others don't. Marriages fail, however, not simply because of the outside weather but because the inner climate becomes too hot or too cold, too turbulent or too stupefying.

When we look at how we choose our partners and what expecta-   3
tions exist at the tender beginnings of romance, some of the reasons for disaster become quite clear. We all select with unconscious accuracy a mate who will recreate with us the emotional patterns of our first homes.

245

Dr. Carl A. Whitaker, a marital therapist amd emeritus professor of psychiatry at the University of Wisconsin, explains, "From early childhood on, each of us carried models for marriage, femininity, masculinity, motherhood, fatherhood and all the other family roles." Each of us falls in love with a mate who has qualities of our parents, who will help us rediscover both the psychological happiness and miseries of our past lives. We may think we have found a man unlike Dad, but then he turns to drink or drugs, or loses his job over and over again or sits silently in front of the T.V. just the way Dad did. A man may choose a woman who doesn't like kids just like his mother or who gambles away the family savings just like his mother. Or he may choose a slender wife who seems unlike his obese mother but then turns out to have other addictions that destroy their mutual happiness.

A man and a woman bring to their marriage bed a blended concoction of conscious and unconscious memories of their parents' lives together. The human way is to compulsively repeat and recreate the patterns of the past. Sigmund Freud so well described the unhappy design that many of us get trapped in: the unmet needs of childhood, the angry feelings left over from frustrations of long ago, the limits of trust and the reoccurrence of old fears. Once an individual senses this entrapment, there may follow a yearning to escape, and the result could be a broken, splintered marriage. 4

Of course people can overcome the habits and attitudes that developed in childhood. We all have hidden strengths and amazing capacities for growth and creative change. Change, however, requires work—observing your part in a rotten pattern, bringing difficulties out into the open—and work runs counter to the basic myth of marriage: "When I wed this person all my problems will be over. I will have achieved success and I will become the center of life for this other person and this person will be my center, and we will mean everything to each other forever." This myth, which every marriage relies on, is soon exposed. The coming of children, the pulls and tugs of their demands on affection and time, place a considerable strain on that basic myth of meaning everthing to each other, of merging together and solving all of life's problems. 5

Concern and tension about money take each partner away from the other. Obligations to demanding parents or still-depended-upon parents create further strain. Couples today must also deal with all the cultural changes brought on in recent years by the women's movement and the sexual revolution. The altering of roles and the shifting of responsibilities have been extremely trying for many marriages. 6

These and other realities of life erode the visions of marital bliss the way sandstorms eat at rock and the ocean nibbles away at the dunes. 7

Those euphoric, grand feelings that accompany romantic love are really self-delusions, self-hypnotic dreams that enable us to forge a relationship. Real life, failure at work, disappointments, exhaustion, bad smells, bad colds and hard times all puncture the dream and leave us stranded with our mate, with our childhood patterns pushing us this way and that, with our unfulfilled expectations.

The struggle to survive in marriage requires adaptability, flexibility,   8
genuine love and kindness and an imagination strong enough to feel what the other is feeling. Many marriages fall apart because either partner cannot imagine what the other wants or cannot communicate what he or she needs or feels. Anger builds until it erupts into a volcanic burst that buries the marriage in ash.

It is not hard to see, therefore, how essential communication is for   9
a good marriage. A man and a woman must be able to tell each other how they feel and why they feel the way they do; otherwise they will impose on each other roles and actions that lead to further unhappiness. In some cases, the communication patterns of childhood—of not talking, of talking too much, of not listening, of distrust and anger, of withdrawal—spill into the marriage and prevent a healthy exchange of thoughts and feelings. The answer is to set up new patterns of communication and intimacy.

At the same time, however, we must see each other as individuals.   10
"To achieve a balance between separateness and closeness is one of the major psychological tasks of all human beings at every stage of life," says Dr. Stuart Bartle, a psychiatrist at the New York University Medical Center.

If we sense from our mate a need for too much intimacy, we tend   11
to push him or her away, fearing that we may lose our identities in the merging of marriage. One partner may suffocate the other partner in a childlike dependency.

A good marriage means growing as a couple but also growing as   12
individuals. This isn't easy. Richard gives up his interest in carpentry because his wife, Helen, is jealous of the time he spends away from her. Karen quits her choir group because her husband dislikes the friends she makes there. Each pair clings to each other and are angry with each other as life closes in on them. This kind of marital balance is easily thrown as one or the other pulls away and divorce follows.

Sometimes people pretend that a new partner will solve the old   13
problems. Most often extramarital sex destroys a marriage because it allows an artificial split between the good and the bad—the good is projected on the new partner and the bad is dumped on the head of the old. Dishonesty, hiding and cheating create walls between men and women.

Infidelity is just a symptom of trouble. It is a symbolic complaint, a weapon of revenge, as well as an unraveler of closeness. Infidelity is often that proverbial last straw that sinks the camel to the ground.

All right—marriage has always been difficult. Why then are we seeing so many divorces at this time? Yes, our modern social fabric is thin, and yes the permissiveness of society has created unrealistic expectations and thrown the family into chaos. But divorce is so common because people today are unwilling to exercise the self-discipline that marriage requires. They expect easy joy, like the entertainment on TV, the thrill of a good party.   14

Marriage takes some kind of sacrifice, not dreadful self-sacrifice of the soul, but some level of compromise. Some of one's fantasies, some of one's legitimate desires have to be given up for the value of the marriage itself. "While all marital partners feel shackled at times, it is they who really choose to make the marital ties into confining chains or supporting bonds," says Dr. Whitaker. Marriage requires sexual, financial and emotional discipline. A man and a woman cannot follow every impulse, cannot allow themselves to stop growing or changing.   15

Divorce is not an evil act. Sometimes it provides salvation for people who have grown hopelessly apart or were frozen in patterns of pain or mutual unhappiness. Divorce can be, despite its initial devastation, like the first cut of the surgeon's knife, a step toward new health and a good life. On the other hand, if the partners can stay past the breaking up of the romantic myths into the development of real love and intimacy, they have achieved a work as amazing as the greatest cathedrals of the world. Marriages that do not fail but improve, that persist despite imperfections, are not only rare these days but offer a wondrous shelter in which the face of our mutual humanity can safely show itself.   16

Questions for Study and Discussion

1. What, according to Roiphe, are the main reasons why marriages fail? Which of these are "external" and which are "internal"?
2. What is "the basic myth about marriage"? How is this myth usually exposed?
3. How has Roiphe organized her essay?
4. How, according to Dr. Carl A. Whitaker, do most of us choose our partners? What are the usual consequences of such choices? How can a person minimize the effects of such choices?
5. What does Roiphe think is required for one to "survive" in marriage? Add any character traits that you think she has overlooked.
6. Why is divorce so common today, according to Roiphe? What is her attitude toward divorce? How do you know?

Writing Topics

1. Write an essay in which you discuss the implications of Dr. Stuart Bartle's statement: "To achieve a balance between separateness and closeness is one of the major psychological tasks of all human beings at every stage of life." Use examples from your own experiences and observations to illustrate your essay.

2. We always seem to hear reasons why so many marriages end in divorce. We never seem to hear about those marriages that succeed. Write an essay in which you present your ideas of what makes for a successful, enduring marriage.

KATHERINE ANNE PORTER

Born in 1890 in Texas, and a resident of Mexico for several years, Katherine Anne Porter knew first hand the sunburnt, wide-open land in which her short story "Rope" is set. She also knew first hand the tensions of marriage, which the story depicts in convincing detail. Educated in convent schools, she eloped from one of them at sixteen and between 1933 and 1942 was twice married and twice divorced. As she put it, her problem was that writing came before everything else. Even so, her collected short fiction consists of only twenty-seven stories and novellas, and she wrote only one full-length novel, *Ship of Fools* (1962). Her last book, reflecting her continuing concern with politics and social issues, is a remembrance of the Sacco-Vanzetti trial of the 1920s (*The Never-Ending Wrong*, 1977). She died in 1980.

"Rope" comes from Porter's first collection of short stories, *Flowering Judas* (1930). Without making grand statements, she uses a short, sharp quarrel between a husband and wife to reveal something of the risks and rewards of marriage.

Rope

On the third day after they moved to the country he came walking   1
back from the village carrying a basket of groceries and a twenty-four-yard coil of rope. She came out to meet him, wiping her hands on her green smock. Her hair was tumbled, her nose was scarlet with sunburn; he told her that already she looked like a born country woman. His gray flannel shirt stuck to him, his heavy shoes were dusty. She assured him he looked like a rural character in a play.

Had he brought the coffee? She had been waiting all day long for   2
coffee. They had forgot it when they ordered at the store the first day.

Gosh, no, he hadn't. Lord, now he'd have to go back. Yes, he   3
would if it killed him. He thought, though, he had everything else. She reminded him it was only because he didn't drink coffee himself. If he did he would remember it quick enough. Suppose they ran out of cigarettes? Then she saw the rope. What was that for? Well, he thought it might do to hang clothes on, or something. Naturally she asked him if he thought they were going to run a laundry? They already had a fifty-foot line hanging right before his eyes? Why, hadn't he noticed it, really? It was a blot on the landscape to her.

He thought there were a lot of things a rope might come in handy   4
for. She wanted to know what, for instance. He thought a few seconds,

250

but nothing occurred. They could wait and see, couldn't they? You need all sorts of strange odds and ends around a place in the country. She said, yes, that was so; but she thought just at that time when every penny counted, it seemed funny to buy more rope. That was all. She hadn't meant anything else. She hadn't just seen, not at first, why he felt it was necessary.

Well, thunder, he had bought it because he wanted to, and that was all there was to it. She thought that was reason enough, and couldn't understand why he hadn't said so, at first. Undoubtedly it would be useful, twenty-four yards of rope, there were hundreds of things, she couldn't think of any at the moment, but it would come in. Of course. As he had said, things always did in the country.

But she was a little disappointed about the coffee, and oh, look, look, look at the eggs! Oh, my, they're all running! What had he put on top of them? Hadn't he known eggs mustn't be squeezed? Squeezed, who had squeezed them, he wanted to know. What a silly thing to say. He had simply brought them along in the basket with the other things. If they got broke it was the grocer's fault. He should know better than to put heavy things on top of eggs.

She believed it was the rope. That was the heaviest thing in the pack, she saw him plainly when he came in from the road, the rope was a big package on top of everything. He desired the whole wide world to witness that this was not a fact. He had carried the rope in one hand and the basket in the other, and what was the use of her having eyes if that was the best they could do for her?

Well, anyhow, she could see one thing plain: no eggs for breakfast. They'd have to scramble them now, for supper. It was too damned bad. She had planned to have steak for supper. No ice, meat wouldn't keep. He wanted to know why she couldn't finish breaking the eggs in a bowl and set them in a cool place.

Cool place! if he could find one for her, she'd be glad to set them there. Well, then, it seemed to him they might very well cook the meat at the same time they cooked the eggs and then warm up the meat for tomorrow. The idea simply choked her. Warmed-over meat, when they might as well have had it fresh. Second best and scraps and makeshifts, even to the meat! He rubbed her shoulder a little. It doesn't really matter so much, does it, darling? Sometimes when they were playful, he would rub her shoulder and she would arch and purr. This time she hissed and almost clawed. He was getting ready to say that they could surely manage somehow when she turned on him and said, if he told her they could manage somehow she would certainly slap his face.

He swallowed the words red hot, his face burned. He picked up the 10
rope and started to put it on the top shelf. She would not have it on the
top shelf, the jars and tins belonged there; positively she would not have
the top shelf cluttered up with a lot of rope. She had borne all the clutter
she meant to bear in the flat in town, there was space here at least and
she meant to keep things in order.

Well, in that case, he wanted to know what the hammer and nails 11
were doing up there? And why had she put them there when she knew
very well he needed that hammer and those nails upstairs to fix the
window sashes? She simply slowed down everything and made double
work on the place with her insane habit of changing things around and
hiding them.

She was sure she begged his pardon, and if she had had any reason 12
to believe he was going to fix the sashes this summer she would have left
the hammer and nails right where he put them; in the middle of the
bedroom floor where they could step on them in the dark. And now if
he didn't clear the whole mess out of there she would throw them down
the well.

Oh, all right, all right—could he put them in the closet? Naturally 13
not, there were brooms and mops and dustpans in the closet, and why
couldn't he find a place for his rope outside her kitchen? Had he stopped
to consider there were seven God-forsaken rooms in the house, and only
one kitchen?

He wanted to know what of it? And did she realize she was making 14
a complete fool of herself? And what did she take him for, a three-year-
old idiot? The whole trouble with her was she needed something weaker
than she was to heckle and tyrannize over. He wished to God now they
had a couple of children she could take it out on. Maybe he'd get some
rest.

Her face changed at this, she reminded him he had forgot the coffee 15
and had bought a worthless piece of rope. And when she thought of all
the things they actually needed to make the place even decently fit to
live in, well, she could cry, that was all. She looked so forlorn, so lost
and despairing he couldn't believe it was only a piece of rope that was
causing all the racket. What *was* the matter, for God's sake?

Oh, would he please hush and go away, and *stay* away, if he could, 16
for five minutes? By all means, yes, he would. He'd stay away indefinitely
if she wished. Lord, yes, there was nothing he'd like better than to clear
out and never come back. She couldn't for the life of her see what was
holding him, then. It was a swell time. Here she was, stuck, miles from
a railroad, with a half-empty house on her hands, and not a penny in
her pocket, and everything on earth to do; it seemed the God-sent mo-

ment for him to get out from under. She was surprised he hadn't stayed in town as it was until she had come out and done the work and got things straightened out. It was his usual trick.

It appeared to him that this was going a little far. Just a touch out   17 of bounds, if she didn't mind his saying so. Why the hell had he stayed in town the summer before? To do a half-dozen extra jobs to get the money he had sent her. That was it. She knew perfectly well they couldn't have done it otherwise. She had agreed with him at the time. And that was the only time so help him he had ever left her to do anything by herself.

Oh, he could tell that to his great-grandmother. She had her notion   18 of what had kept him in town. Considerably more than a notion, if he wanted to know. So, she was going to bring all that up again, was she? Well, she could just think what she pleased. He was tired of explaining. It may have looked funny but he had simply got hooked in, and what could he do? It was impossible to believe that she was going to take it seriously. Yes, yes, she knew how it was with a man: if he was left by himself a minute, some woman was certain to kidnap him. And naturally he couldn't hurt her feelings by refusing!

Well, what was she raving about? Did she forget she had told him   19 those two weeks alone in the country were the happiest she had known for four years? And how long had they been married when she said that? All right, shut up! If she thought that hadn't stuck in his craw.

She hadn't meant she was happy because she was away from him.   20 She meant she was happy getting the devilish house nice and ready for him. That was what she had meant, and now look! Bringing up something she had said a year ago simply to justify himself for forgetting her coffee and breaking the eggs and buying a wretched piece of rope they couldn't afford. She really thought it was time to drop the subject, and now she wanted only two things in the world. She wanted him to get that rope from underfoot, and go back to the village and get her coffee, and if he could remember it, he might bring a metal mitt for the skillets, and two more curtain rods, and if there were any rubber gloves in the village, her hands were simply raw, and a bottle of milk of magnesia from the drugstore.

He looked out at the dark blue afternoon sweltering on the slopes,   21 and mopped his forehead and sighed heavily and said, if only she could wait a minute for *anything*, he was going back. He had said so, hadn't he, the very instant they found he had overlooked it?

Oh, yes, well . . . run along. She was going to wash windows. The   22 country was so beautiful! She doubted they'd have a moment to enjoy it. He meant to go, but he could not until he had said that if she wasn't such a hopeless melancholiac she might see that this was only for a few days. Couldn't she remember anything pleasant about the other summers? Hadn't they ever had any fun? She hadn't time to talk about it, and now would he please not leave that rope lying around for her to trip on? He picked it up, somehow it had toppled off the table, and walked out with it under his arm.

Was he going this minute? He certainly was. She thought so. Sometimes it seemed to her he had second sight about the precisely perfect moment to leave her ditched. She had meant to put the mattresses out to sun, if they put them out this minute they would get at least three hours, he must have heard her say that morning she meant to put them out. So of course he would walk off and leave her to it. She supposed he thought the exercise would do her good. 23

Well, he was merely going to get her coffee. A four-mile walk for two pounds of coffee was ridiculous, but he was perfectly willing to do it. The habit was making a wreck of her, but if she wanted to wreck herself there was nothing he could do about it. If he thought it was coffee that was making a wreck of her, she congratulated him: he must have a damned easy conscience. 24

Conscience or no conscience, he didn't see why the mattresses couldn't very well wait until tomorrow. And anyhow, for God's sake, were they living *in* the house, or were they going to let the house ride them to death? She paled at this, her face grew livid about the mouth, she looked quite dangerous, and reminded him that housekeeping was no more her work than it was his: she had other work to do as well, and when did he think she was going to find time to do it at this rate? 25

Was she going to start on that again? She knew as well as he did that his work brought in the regular money, hers was only occasional, if they depended on what *she* made—and she might as well get straight on this question once for all! 26

That was positively not the point. The question was, when both of them were working on their own time, was there going to be a division of the housework, or wasn't there? She merely wanted to know, she had to make her plans. Why, he thought that was all arranged. It was understood that he was to help. Hadn't he always, in summers? 27

Hadn't he, though? Oh, just hadn't he? And when, and where, and doing what? Lord, what an uproarious joke! 28

It was such a very uproarious joke that her face turned slightly purple, and she screamed with laughter. She laughed so hard she had to sit down, and finally a rush of tears spurted from her eyes and poured down into the lifted corners of her mouth. He dashed towards her and dragged her up to her feet and tried to pour water on her head. The 29 dipper hung by a string on a nail and he broke it loose. Then he tried to pump water with one hand while she struggled in the other. So he gave it up and shook her instead.

She wrenched away, crying for him to take his rope and go to hell, 30 she had simply given him up: and ran. He heard her high-heeled bedroom slippers clattering and stumbling on the stairs.

He went out around the house into the lane; he suddenly realized 31 he had a blister on his heel and his shirt felt as if it were on fire. Things broke so suddenly you didn't know where you were. She could work herself into a fury about simply nothing. She was terrible, damn it: not an ounce of reason. You might as well talk to a sieve as that woman when she got going. Damned if he'd spend his life humoring her! Well, what to do now? He would take back the rope and exchange it for something else. Things accumulated, things were mountainous, you couldn't move them or sort them out or get rid of them. They just lay and rotted around. He'd take it back. Hell, why should he? He wanted it. What was it anyhow? A piece of rope. Imagine anybody caring more about a piece of rope than about a man's feelings. What earthly right had she to say a word about it? He remembered all the useless, meaningless things she bought for herself: Why? because I wanted it, that's why! He stopped and selected a large stone by the road. He would put the rope behind it. He would put it in the tool-box when he got back. He'd heard enough about it to last him a life-time.

When he came back she was leaning against the post box beside 32 the road waiting. It was pretty late, the smell of broiled steak floated nose high in the cooling air. Her face was young and smooth and fresh-looking. Her unmanageable funny black hair was all on end. She waved to him from a distance, and he speeded up. She called out that supper was ready and waiting, was he starved?

You bet he was starved. Here was the coffee. He waved it at her. 33 She looked at his other hand. What was that he had there?

Well, it was the rope again. He stopped short. He had meant to 34 exchange it but forgot. She wanted to know why he should exchange it, if it was something he really wanted. Wasn't the air sweet now, and wasn't it fine to be here?

She walked beside him with one hand hooked into his leather belt. 35 She pulled and jostled him a little as he walked, and leaned against him. He put his arm clear around her and patted her stomach. They exchanged wary smiles. Coffee, coffee for the Ootsum-Wootsums! He felt as if he were bringing her a beautiful present.

He was a love, she firmly believed, and if she had had her coffee 36 in the morning, she wouldn't have behaved so funny . . . There was a whippoorwill still coming back, imagine, clear out of season, sitting in the crab-apple tree calling all by himself. Maybe his girl stood him up. Maybe she did. She hoped to hear him once more, she loved whippoorwills . . . He knew how she was, didn't he?

Sure, he knew how she was.   37

Questions for Study and Discussion

1. Discuss the circumstances of the couple's move to the country. Why are they so disorganized?

2. How would you characterize the man and woman in this story? What exactly do they seem to be quarreling about? What do you think is the underlying cause of their disagreement? Why does the man offer to go back to town?

3. The story is told by an impersonal third-person narrator. How would it be different if told from the wife's point of view? From the husband's point of view?

4. Though most of the story consists of conversation, Porter has chosen not to use any dialogue. What is the advantage of presenting the quarrel indirectly, instead of making the characters speak directly for themselves? How do you account for the large number of questions in the story?

5. At several points in the story the tone changes. Locate the places where this occurs. How do the changes in tone affect the development of the story?

6. Why do you think Porter introduces the whippoorwill in the concluding scene?

7. What is the significance of the story's title?

Writing Topics

1. Couples, like the people in Porter's story, often get into quarrels over seemingly trivial matters. From your own experience and observation, what can such quarrels do to a relationship? What can they signify? When are they destructive, and when are they constructive? Write an essay in which you present your views of "lovers' " quarrels.

2. Like the man in the story, do you sometimes buy things without any particular reason for buying them? Or are you a person who buys things wisely and purposefully? Write an essay in which you analyze your own buying habits.

4 The Aims of Education

By the age of six the average child will have completed the basic American education and will be ready to enter school.
RUSSELL BAKER

There may be a tendency to mistake data for wisdom, just as there has always been a tendency to confuse logic with values, and intelligence with insight.
NORMAN COUSINS

Must all sports teach that success is "beating" some other person or group?
JEFFREY SCHRANK

Education Under Scrutiny

DAVID P. GARDNER

David P. Gardner was born in 1933 in Berkeley, California, and graduated from Brigham Young University. After a two-year stint in the army, he returned to the University of California, Berkeley, where he received his M.A. and Ph.D. His interests as a professor of higher education and as a university administrator prepared him for the presidency of the University of Utah. He is now the president of the University of California and has written widely on the purposes, functions, and problems of public education. In 1981 President Reagan appointed Gardner chairman of a commission to study the condition of public education in the United States. The commission published its report, A *Nation at Risk*, in 1983.

In the following excerpt from this report, Gardner and his fellow commission members sharply criticized certain trends in public education and called for a renewed emphasis on excellence.

A Nation at Risk

Our Nation is at risk. Our once unchallenged preeminence in com-   1
merce, industry, science, and technological innovation is being over-
taken by competitors throughout the world. This report is concerned
with only one of the many causes and dimensions of the problem, but it
is the one that undergirds American prosperity, security, and civility.
We report to the American people that while we can take justifiable
pride in what our schools and colleges have historically accomplished
and contributed to the United States and the well-being of its people,
the educational foundations of our society are presently being eroded by
a rising tide of mediocrity that threatens our very future as a Nation and
a people. What was unimaginable a generation ago has begun to occur—
others are matching and surpassing our educational attainments.

If an unfriendly foreign power had attempted to impose on America   2
the mediocre educational performance that exists today, we might well

have viewed it as an act of war. As it stands, we have allowed this to happen to ourselves. We have even squandered the gains in student achievement made in the wake of the Sputnik challenge. Moreover, we have dismantled essential support systems which helped make those gains possible. We have, in effect, been committing an act of unthinking, unilateral educational disarmament.

Our society and its educational institutions seem to have lost sight   3
of the basic purposes of schooling, and of the high expectations and disciplined effort needed to attain them. This report, the result of 18 months of study, seeks to generate reform of our educational system in fundamental ways to renew the Nation's commitment to schools and colleges of high quality throughout the length and breadth of our land.

That we have compromised this commitment is, upon reflection,   4
hardly surprising, given the multitude of often conflicting demands we have placed on our Nation's schools and colleges. They are routinely called on to provide solutions to personal, social, and political problems that the home and other institutions either will not or cannot resolve. We must understand that these demands on our schools and colleges often exact an educational cost as well as a financial one.

On the occasion of the Commission's first meeting President Reagan   5
noted the central importance of education in American life when he said: "Certainly there are few areas of American life as important to our society, to our people, and to our families as our schools and colleges." This report, therefore, is as much an open letter to the American people as it is a report to the Secretary of Education. We are confident that the American people, properly informed, will do what is right for their children and for the generations to come.

The Risk

History is not kind to idlers. The time is long past when America's   6
destiny was assured simply by an abundance of natural resources and inexhaustible human enthusiasm, and by our relative isolation from the malignant problems of older civilizations. The world is indeed one global village. We live among determined, well-educated, and strongly motivated competitors. We compete with them for international standing and markets, not only with products but also with the ideas of our laboratories and neighborhood workshops. America's position in the world may once have been reasonably secure with only a few exceptionally well-trained men and women. It is no longer.

The risk is not only that the Japanese make automobiles more effi-   7
ciently than Americans and have government subsidies for development
and export. It is not just that the South Koreans recently built the world's
most efficient steel mill, or that American machine tools, once the pride
of the world, are being displaced by German products. It is also that these
developments signify a redistribution of trained capability throughout the
globe. Knowledge, learning, information, and skilled intelligence are the
new raw materials of international commerce and are today spreading
throughout the world as vigorously as miracle drugs, synthetic fertilizers,
and blue jeans did earlier. If only to keep and improve on the slim competitive edge we still retain in world markets, we must dedicate ourselves
to the reform of our educational system for the benefit of all—old and
young alike, affluent and poor, majority and minority. Learning is the
indispensable investment required for success in the "information age" we
are entering.

Our concern, however, goes well beyond matters such as industry   8
and commerce. It also includes the intellectual, moral, and spiritual
strengths of our people which knit together the very fabric of our society.
The people of the United States need to know that individuals in our   .
society who do not possess the levels of skill, literacy, and training essential to this new era will be effectively disenfranchised, not simply from
the material rewards that accompany competent performance, but also
from the chance to participate fully in our national life. A high level of
shared education is essential to a free, democratic society and to the fos-
tering of a common culture, especially in a country that prides itself on
pluralism and individual freedom.

For our country to function, citizens must be able to reach some   9
common understandings on complex issues, often on short notice and on
the basis of conflicting or incomplete evidence. Education helps form
these common understandings, a point Thomas Jefferson made long ago
in his justly famous dictum:

> I know no safe depository of the ultimate powers of the society but the
> people themselves; and if we think them not enlightened enough to exer-
> cise their control with a wholesome discretion, the remedy is not to take
> it from them but to inform their discretion.

Part of what is at risk is the promise first made on this continent: 10
All, regardless of race or class or economic status, are entitled to a fair
chance and to the tools for developing their individual powers of mind
and spirit to the utmost. This promise means that all children by virtue
of their own efforts, competently guided, can hope to attain the mature

and informed judgment needed to secure gainful employment and to manage their own lives, thereby serving not only their own interests but also the progress of society itself.

Indicators of the Risk

The educational dimensions of the risk before us have been amply documented in testimony received by the Commission. For example: 11

• International comparisons of student achievement, completed a decade ago, reveal that on 19 academic tests American students were never first or second and, in comparison with other industrialized nations, were last seven times.

• Some 23 million American adults are functionally illiterate by the simplest tests of everyday reading, writing, and comprehension.

• About 13 percent of all 17-year-olds in the United States can be considered functionally illiterate. Functional illiteracy among minority youth may run as high as 40 percent.

• Average achievement of high school students on most standardized tests is now lower than 26 years ago when Sputnik was launched.

• Over half the population of gifted students do not match their tested ability with comparable achievement in school.

• The College Board's Scholastic Aptitude Tests (SAT) demonstrate a virtually unbroken decline from 1963 to 1980. Average verbal scores fell over 50 points and average mathematics scores dropped nearly 40 points.

• College Board achievement tests also reveal consistent declines in recent years in such subjects as physics and English.

• Both the number and proportion of students demonstrating superior achievement on the SATs (i.e., those with scores of 650 or higher) have also dramatically declined.

• Many 17-year-olds do not possess the "higher order" intellectual skills we should expect of them. Nearly 40 percent cannot draw inferences from written material; only one-fifth can write a persuasive essay; and only one-third can solve a mathematics problem requiring several steps.

• There was a steady decline in science achievement scores of U.S. 17-year-olds as measured by national assessments of science in 1969, 1973, and 1977.

• Between 1975 and 1980, remedial mathematics courses in public 4-year colleges increased by 72 percent and now constitute one-quarter of all mathematics courses taught in those institutions.

• Average tested achievement of students graduating from college is also lower.

• Business and military leaders complain that they are required to spend millions of dollars on costly remedial education and training programs in such basic skills as reading, writing, spelling, and computation. The Department of the Navy, for example, reported to the Commission that one-quarter of its recent recruits cannot read at the ninth grade level, the minimum needed simply to understand written safety instructions. Without remedial work they cannot even begin, much less complete, the sophisticated training essential in much of the modern military.

These deficiencies come at a time when the demand for highly skilled workers in new fields is accelerating rapidly. For example: 12

• Computers and computer-controlled equipment are penetrating every aspect of our lives—homes, factories, and offices.

• One estimate indicates that by the turn of the century millions of jobs will involve laser technology and robotics.

• Technology is radically transforming a host of other occupations. They include health care, medical science, energy production, food processing, construction, and the building, repair, and maintenance of sophisticated scientific, educational, military, and industrial equipment.

Analysts examining these indicators of student performance and the demands for new skills have made some chilling observations. Educational researcher Paul Hurd concluded at the end of a thorough national survey of student achievement that within the context of the modern scientific revolution, "We are raising a new generation of Americans that is scientifically and technologically illiterate." In a similar vein, John Slaughter, a former Director of the National Science Foundation, warned of "a growing chasm between a small scientific and technological elite and a citizenry ill-informed, indeed uninformed, on issues with a science component." 13

But the problem does not stop there, nor do all observers see it the same way. Some worry that schools may emphasize such rudiments as reading and computation at the expense of other essential skills such as comprehension, analysis, solving problems, and drawing conclusions. Still others are concerned that an over-emphasis on technical and occupational skills will leave little time for studying the arts and humanities that so enrich daily life, help maintain civility, and develop a sense of community. Knowledge of the humanities, they maintain, must be harnessed to science and technology if the latter are to remain creative and humane, just as the humanities need to be informed by science and technology if they are to remain relevant to the human condition. Another analyst, Paul Copperman, has drawn a sobering conclusion. Until now, he has noted: 14

> Each generation of Americans has outstripped its parents in education, in literacy, and in economic attainment. For the first time in the history of

our country, the educational skills of one generation will not surpass, will not equal, will not even approach, those of their parents.

It is important, of course, to recognize that *the average citizen* today   15
is better educated and more knowledgeable than the average citizen of a generation ago—more literate, and exposed to more mathematics, literature, and science. The positive impact of this fact on the well-being of our country and the lives of our people cannot be overstated. Nevertheless, *the average graduate* of our schools and colleges today is not as well-educated as the average graduate of 25 or 35 years ago, when a much smaller proportion of our population completed high school and college. The negative impact of this fact likewise cannot be overstated.

Hope and Frustration

Statistics and their interpretation by experts show only the surface   16
dimension of the difficulties we face. Beneath them lies a tension between hope and frustration that characterizes current attitudes about education at every level.

We have heard the voices of high school and college students, school   17
board members, and teachers; of leaders of industry, minority groups, and higher education; of parents and State officials. We could hear the hope evident in their commitment to quality education and in their descriptions of outstanding programs and schools. We could also hear the intensity of their frustration, a growing impatience with shoddiness in many walks of American life, and the complaint that this shoddiness is too often reflected in our schools and colleges. Their frustration threatens to overwhelm their hope.

What lies behind this emerging national sense of frustration can be   18
described as both a dimming of personal expectations and the fear of losing a shared vision for America.

On the personal level the student, the parent, and the caring teacher   19
all perceive that a basic promise is not being kept. More and more young people emerge from high school ready neither for college nor for work. This predicament becomes more acute as the knowledge base continues its rapid expansion, the number of traditional jobs shrinks, and new jobs demand greater sophistication and preparation.

On a broader scale, we sense that this undertone of frustration has   20
significant political implications, for it cuts across ages, generations, races, and political and economic groups. We have come to understand that the public will demand that educational and political leaders act forcefully and effectively on these issues. Indeed, such demands have already ap-

peared and could well become a unifying national preoccupation. This unity, however, can be achieved only if we avoid the unproductive tendency of some to search for scapegoats among the victims, such as the beleaguered teachers.

On the positive side is the significant movement by political and educational leaders to search for solutions—so far centering largely on the nearly desperate need for increased support for the teaching of mathematics and science. This movement is but a start on what we believe is a larger and more educationally encompassing need to improve teaching and learning in fields such as English, history, geography, economics, and foreign languages. We believe this movement must be broadened and directed toward reform and excellence throughout education. 21

Excellence in Education

We define "excellence" to mean several related things. At the level of the *individual learner*, it means performing on the boundary of individual ability in ways that test and push back personal limits, in school and in the workplace. Excellence characterizes a *school or college* that sets high expectations and goals for all learners, then tries in every way possible to help students reach them. Excellence characterizes a *society* that has adopted these policies, for it will then be prepared through the education and skill of its people to respond to the challenges of a rapidly changing world. Our Nation's people and its schools and colleges must be committed to achieving excellence in all these senses. 22

We do not believe that a public commitment to excellence and educational reform must be made at the expense of a strong public commitment to the equitable treatment of our diverse population. The twin goals of equity and high-quality schooling have profound and practical meaning for our economy and society, and we cannot permit one to yield to the other either in principle or in practice. To do so would deny young people their chance to learn and live according to their aspirations and abilities. It also would lead to a generalized accommodation to mediocrity in our society on the one hand or the creation of an undemocratic elitism on the other. 23

Our goal must be to develop the talents of all to their fullest. Attaining that goal requires that we expect and assist all students to the limits of their capabilities. We should expect schools to have genuinely high standards rather than minimum ones, and parents to support and encourage their children to make the most of their talents and abilities. 24

The search for solutions to our educational problems must also in-   25
clude a commitment to life-long learning. The task of rebuilding our system of learning is enormous and must be properly understood and taken
seriously: Although a million and a half new workers enter the economy
each year from our schools and colleges, the adults working today will
still make up about 75 percent of the workforce in the year 2000. These
workers, and new entrants into the workforce, will need further education and retraining if they—and we as a Nation—are to thrive and prosper.

The Learning Society

In a world of ever-accelerating competition and change in the con-   26
ditions of the workplace, of ever-greater danger, and of ever-larger opportunities for those prepared to meet them, educational reform should
focus on the goal of creating a Learning Society. At the heart of such a
society is the commitment to a set of values and to a system of education
that affords all members the opportunity to stretch their minds to full
capacity, from early childhood through adulthood, learning more as the
world itself changes. Such a society has as a basic foundation the idea
that education is important not only because of what it contributes to
one's career goals but also because of the value it adds to the general
quality of one's life. Also at the heart of the Learning Society are educational opportunities extending far beyond the traditional institutions of
learning, our schools and colleges. They extend into homes and work-
places; into libraries, art galleries, museums, and science centers; indeed,
into every place where the individual can develop and mature in work
and life. In our view, formal schooling in youth is the essential foundation
for learning throughout one's life. But without life-long learning, one's
skills will become rapidly dated.

In contrast to the ideal of the Learning Society, however, we find   27
that for too many people education means doing the minimum work necessary for the moment, then coasting through life on what may have been
learned in its first quarter. But this should not surprise us because we tend
to express our educational standards and expectations largely in terms of
"minimum requirements." And where there should be a coherent contin-
uum of learning, we have none, but instead an often incoherent, outdated patchwork quilt. Many individual, sometimes heroic, examples of
schools and colleges of great merit do exist. Our findings and testimony
confirm the vitality of a number of notable schools and programs, but
their very distinction stands out against a vast mass shaped by tensions

and pressures that inhibit systematic academic and vocational achievement for the majority of students. In some metropolitan areas basic literacy has become the goal rather than the starting point. In some colleges maintaining enrollments is of greater day-to-day concern than maintaining rigorous academic standards. And the ideal of academic excellence as the primary goal of schooling seems to be fading across the board in American education.

Thus, we issue this call to all who care about America and its future: 28
to parents and students; to teachers, administrators, and school board members; to colleges and industry; to union members and military leaders; to governors and State legislators; to the President; to members of Congress and other public officials; to members of learned and scientific societies; to the print and electronic media; to concerned citizens everywhere. America is at risk.

Questions for Study and Discussion

1. What is the main point that the commission is trying to get across in their report? What are the assumptions underlying their argument? In your opinion, do they have a valid point? Explain.

2. What exactly is the purpose of the commission's report?

3. What does Gardner mean when he refers to a "rising tide of mediocrity"? To the "Sputnik challenge"? To the "information age"?

4. The report states that our nation's schools are "routinely called upon to provide solutions to personal, social, and political problems that the home and other institutions either will not or cannot resolve." From your own experience in high school, what types of programs and services do you think the commission is referring to? Do you believe that these programs and services should be the school's responsibilities? Explain.

5. In paragraph 11, the commission summarizes what they call the "indicators of the risk." How convincing do you find their documentation? Explain.

6. The commission concludes that "educational reform should focus on the goal of creating a Learning Society." What are the main characteristics of this Learning Society? Are the means already in place to achieve it? Explain.

7. How would you characterize the tone of the report? What in the diction of the report led you to this conclusion? Is the tone appropriate for both the subject of the report and the audience? Explain.

8. How does the commission define *excellence*? Is this definition helpful in the context of the report?

Writing Topics

1. Analyze and evaluate your high school in light of the commission's report. Then write a report of your own pointing out both areas of excellence and areas that could be improved.

2. Write an essay in which you examine the relationship between individual motivations and academic challenges. How do we as a society encourage our young people to aspire to excellence? Which comes first, the motivation or the challenges? Explain.

3. In the past twenty years computers have begun what futurist and science fiction writer Arthur C. Clarke calls "one of the swiftest and most momentous revolutions in the entire history of technology." How has this affected your life? Try to make your own educated guess as to how computers will affect the future.

CAROLINE BIRD

Caroline Bird was born in New York City, attended Vassar College for three years, and received her B.A. from the University of Toledo and her M.A. from the University of Wisconsin. A feminist writer throughout most of her career, Bird has focused her attention on women's roles in the business world. She has published such influential and well-reviewed books as *The Invisible Scar: The Great Depression and What It Did to American Life, from Then Until Now* (with Sarah Welles Briller) (1966), *Born Female: The High Cost of Keeping Women Down* (1968), *Everything a Woman Needs to Know to Get Paid What She's Worth* (1973), *Enterprising Women: Their Contribution to the American Economy, 1776–1976* (1976), *What Women Want* (1978), and *The Two-Paycheck Marriage: How Women at Work Are Changing Life in America* (1979).

In the following selection Bird turns her attention away from feminist issues and asks whether or not a college education is a worthwhile financial investment. What would be the result, for example, if you were to take the money that you will spend on your college education and invest it and become gainfully employed instead of attending school?

College Is a Waste of Time and Money

A great majority of our nine million college students are not in 1 school because they want to be or because they want to learn. They are there because it has become the thing to do or because college is a pleasant place to be; because it's the only way they can get parents or taxpayers to support them without working at a job they don't like; because Mother wanted them to go, or some other reason entirely irrelevant to the course of studies for which college is supposedly organized.

As I crisscross the United States lecturing on college campuses, I 2 am dismayed to find that professors and administrators, when pressed for a candid opinion, estimate that no more than 25 percent of their students are turned on by classwork. For the rest, college is at best a social center or aging vat, and at worst a young folks' home or even a prison that keeps them out of the mainstream of economic life for a few more years.

The premise—which I no longer accept—that college is the best 3 place for all high-school graduates grew out of a noble American ideal. Just as the United States was the first nation to aspire to teach every small child to read and write, so, during the 1950s, we became the first and only great nation to aspire to higher education for all. During the '60s, we damned the expense and built great state university systems as

269

fast as we could. And adults—parents, employers, high-school counselors—began to push, shove, and cajole youngsters to "get an education."

It became a mammoth industry, with taxpayers footing more than   4
half the bill. By 1970, colleges and universities were spending more than
30 billion dollars annually. But still only half our high-school graduates
were going on. According to estimates made by the economist Fritz
Machlup, if we had been educating every young person until age 22 in
that year of 1970, the bill for higher education would have reached 47.5
billion dollars, 12.5 billion more than the total corporate profits for the
year.

Figures such as these have begun to make higher education for all   5
look financially prohibitive, particularly now when colleges are squeezed
by the pressures of inflation and a drop-off in the growth of their traditional market.

Predictable demography has caught up with the university empire   6
builders. Now that the record crop of postwar babies has graduated from
college, the rate of growth of the student population has begun to decline.
To keep their mammoth plants financially solvent, many institutions
have begun to use hard-sell, Madison-Avenue techniques to attract students. They sell college like soap, promoting features they think students
want: innovative programs, an environment conducive to meaningful
personal relationships, and a curriculum so free that it doesn't sound like
college at all.

Pleasing the customers is something new for college administrators.   7
Colleges have always known that most students don't like to study, and
that at least part of the time they are ambivalent about college, but
before the student riots of the 1960s educators never thought it either
right or necessary to pay any attention to student feelings. But when
students rebelling against the Vietnam war and the draft discovered they
could disrupt a campus completely, administrators had to act on some
student complaints. Few understood that the protests had tapped the
basic discontent with college itself, a discontent that did not go away
when the riots subsided.

Today students protest individually rather than in concert. They   8
turn inward and withdraw from active participation. They drop out to
travel to India or to feed themselves on subsistence farms. Some refuse
to go to college at all. Most, of course, have neither the funds nor the
self-confidence for constructive articulation of their discontent. They
simply hang around college unhappily and reluctantly.

All across the country, I have been overwhelmed by the prevailing   9
sadness on American campuses. Too many young people speak little, and
then only in drowned voices. Sometimes the mood surfaces as diffidence,

wariness, or coolness, but whatever its form, it looks like a defense mechanism, and that rings a bell. This is the way it used to be with women, and just as society had systematically damaged women by insisting that their proper place was in the home, so we may be systematically damaging 18-year-olds by insisting that their proper place is in college.

Campus watchers everywhere know what I mean when I say students are sad, but they don't agree on the reason for it. During the Vietnam war some ascribed the sadness to the draft; now others blame affluence or say it has something to do with permissive upbringing. 10

Not satisfied with any of these explanations, I looked for some answers with the journalistic tools of my trade—scholarly studies, economic analyses, the historical record, the opinions of the especially knowledgeable, conversations with parents, professors, college administrators, and employers, all of whom spoke as alumni too. Mostly I learned from my interviews with hundreds of young people on and off campuses all over the country. 11

My unnerving conclusion is that students are sad because they are not needed. Somewhere between the nursery and the employment office, they become unwanted adults. No one has anything in particular against them. But no one knows what to do with them either. We already have too many people in the world of the 1970s, and there is no room for so many newly minted 18-year-olds. So we temporarily get them out of the way by sending them to college where in fact only a few belong. 12

To make it more palatable, we fool ourselves into believing that we are sending them there for their own best interests, and that it's good for them, like spinach. Some, of course, learn to like it, but most wind up preferring green peas. 13

Educators admit as much. Nevitt Sanford, distinguished student of higher education, says students feel they are "capitulating to a kind of voluntary servitude." Some of them talk about their time in college as if it were a sentence to be served. I listened to a 1970 Mount Holyoke graduate: "For two years I was really interested in science, but in my junior and senior years I just kept saying, 'I've done two years; I'm going to finish.' When I got out I made up my mind that I wasn't going to school anymore because so many of my courses had been bullshit." 14

But bad as it is, college is often preferable to a far worse fate. It is better than the drudgery of an uninspiring nine-to-five job, and better than doing nothing when no jobs are available. For some young people, it is a graceful way to get away from home and become independent without losing the financial support of their parents. And sometimes it is the only alternative to an intolerable home situation. 15

It is difficult to assess how many students are in college reluctantly.   16
The conservative Carnegie Commission estimates from 5 to 30 percent.
Sol Linowitz, who was once chairman of a special committee on campus
tension of the American Council on Education, found that "a significant
number were not happy with their college experience because they felt
they were there only in order to get the 'ticket to the big show' rather
than to spend the years as productively as they otherwise could."

Older alumni will identify with Richard Baloga, a policeman's son,   17
who stayed in school even thought he "hated it" because he thought it
would do him some good. But fewer students each year feel this way.
Daniel Yankelovich has surveyed undergraduate attitudes for a number
of years, and reported in 1971 that 74 percent thought education was
"very important." But just two years earlier, 80 percent thought so.

The doubters don't mind speaking up. Leon Lefkowitz, chairman   18
of the department of social studies at Central High School in Valley
Stream, New York, interviewed 300 college students at random, and
reports that 200 of them didn't think that the education they were getting
was worth the effort. "In two years I'll pick up a diploma," said one
student, "and I can honestly say it was a waste of my father's bread."

Nowadays, says one sociologist, you don't have to have a reason   19
for going to college; it's an institution. His definition of an institution is
an arrangement everyone accepts without question; the burden of proof
is not on why you go, but why anyone thinks there might be a reason
for not going. The implication is that an 18-year-old is too young and
confused to know what he wants to do, and that he should listen to
those who know best and go to college.

I don't agree. I believe that college has to be judged not on what   20
other people think is good for students, but on how good it feels to the
students themselves.

I believe that people have an inside view of what's good for them.   21
If a child doesn't want to go to school some morning, better let him stay
at home, at least until you find out why. Maybe he knows something
you don't. It's the same with college. If high-school graduates don't want
to go, or if they don't want to go right away, they may perceive more
clearly than their elders that college is not for them. It is no longer
obvious that adolescents are best off studying a core curriculum that was
constructed when all educated men could agree on what made them
educated, or that professors, advisors, or parents can be of any particular
help to young people in choosing a major or a career. High-school graduates see college graduates driving cabs and decide it's not worth going.
College students find no intellectual stimulation in their studies and drop
out.

If students believe that college isn't necessarily good for them, you   22
can't expect them to stay on for the general good of mankind. They don't
go to school to beat the Russians to Jupiter, improve the national defense,
increase the GNP, or create a new market for the arts—to mention some
of the benefits taxpayers are supposed to get for supporting higher education.

Nor should we expect to bring about social equality by putting all   23
young people through four years of academic rigor. At best, it's a roundabout and expensive way to narrow the gap between the highest and
lowest in our society anyway. At worst, it is unconsciously elitist. Equalizing opportunity through universal higher education subjects the whole
population to the intellectual mode natural only to a few. It violates the
fundamental egalitarian principle of respect for the differences between
people.

Of course, most parents aren't thinking of the "higher" good at all.   24
They send their children to college because they are convinced young
people benefit financially from those four years of higher education. But
if money is the only goal, college is the dumbest investment you can
make. I say this because a young banker in Poughkeepsie, New York,
Stephen G. Necel, used a computer to compare college as an investment
with other investments available in 1974, and college did not come out
on top.

For the sake of argument, the two of us invented a young man   25
whose rich uncle gave him, in cold cash, the cost of a four-year education
at any college he chose, but the young man didn't have to spend the
money on college. After bales of computer paper, we had our mythical
student write to his uncle: "Since you said I could spend the money
foolishly if I wished, I am going to blow it all on Princeton."

The much respected financial columnist Sylvia Porter echoed the   26
common assumption when she said last year, "A college education is
among the very best investments you can make in your entire life." But
the truth is not quite so rosy, even if we assume that the Census Bureau
is correct when it says that as of 1972, a man who completed four years
of college would expect to earn $199,000 more between the ages of 22
and 64 than a man who had only a high-school diploma.

However, If a 1972 Princeton-bound high-school graduate had put the $34,181   27
that his four years of college would have cost him into a savings bank at
7.5 percent interest compounded daily, he would have had at age 64 a
total of $1,129,200, or $528,200 more than the earnings of a male college
graduate, and more than five times as much as the $199,000 extra the
more educated man could expect to earn between 22 and 64.

The big advantage of getting your college money in cash now is   28
that you can invest it in something that has a higher return than a
diploma. For instance, a Princeton-bound high-school graduate of 1972
who liked fooling around with cars could have banked his $34,181, and
gone to work at the local garage at close to $1,000 more per year than
the average high-school graduate. Meanwhile, as he was learning to be
an expert auto mechanic, his money would be ticking away in the bank.
When he became 28, he would have earned $7,199 less on his job from
age 22 to 28 than his college-educated friend, but he would have had
$73,113 in his passbook—enough to buy out his boss, go into the used-
car business, or acquire his own new-car dealership. If successful in business, he could expect to make more than the average college graduate.
And if he had the brains to get into Princeton, he would be just as likely
to make money without the four years spent on campus. Unfortunately,
few college-bound high-school graduates get the opportunity to bank such
a large sum of money and then wait for it to make them rich. And few
parents are sophisticated enough to understand that in financial returns
alone, their children would be better off with the money than with the
education.

Rates of return and dollar signs on education are fascinating brain   29
teasers, but obviously there is a certain unreality to the game. Quite aside
from the noneconomic benefits of college, and these should loom larger
once the dollars are cleared away, there are grave difficulties in assigning
a dollar value to college at all.

In fact there is no real evidence that the higher income of college   30
graduates is due to college. College may simply attract people who are
slated to earn more money anyway; those with higher IQs, better family
backgrounds, a more enterprising temperament. No one who has wrestled
with the problem is prepared to attribute all of the higher income to the
impact of college itself.

Christopher Jencks, author of *Inequality*, a book that assesses the   31
effect of family and schooling in America, believes that education in
general accounts for less than half of the difference in income in the
American population. "The biggest single source of income differences,"
writes Jencks, "seems to be the fact that men from high-status families
have higher incomes than men from low-status families even when they
enter the same occupations, have the same amount of education, and
have the same test scores."

Jacob Mincer of the National Bureau of Economic Research and   32
Columbia University states flatly that of "20 to 30 percent of students at
any level, the additional schooling has been a waste, at least in terms of
earnings." College fails to work its income-raising magic for almost a

third of those who go. More than half of those people in 1972 who earned $15,000 or more reached that comfortable bracket without the benefit of a college diploma. Jencks says that financial success in the U.S. depends a good deal on luck, and the most sophisticated regression analyses have yet to demonstrate otherwise.

But most of today's students don't go to college to earn more money anyway. In 1968, when jobs were easy to get, Daniel Yankelovich made his first nationwide survey of students. Sixty-five percent of them said they "would welcome less emphasis on money." By 1973, when jobs were scarce, that figure jumped to 80 percent.   33

The young are not alone. Americans today are all looking less to the pay of a job than to the work itself. They want "interesting" work that permits them "to make a contribution," "express themselves" and "use their special abilities," and they think college will help them find it.   34

Jerry Darring of Indianapolis knows what it is to make a dollar. He worked with his father in the family plumbing business, on the line at Chevrolet, and in the Chrysler foundry. He quit these jobs to enter Wright State University in Dayton, Ohio, because "in a job like that a person only has time to work, and after that he's so tired that he can't do anything else but come home and go to sleep."   35

Jerry came to college to find work "helping people." And he is perfectly willing to spend the dollars he earns at dull, well-paid work to prepare for lower-paid work that offers the reward of service to others.   36

Jerry's case is not unusual. No one works for money alone. In order to deal with the nonmonetary rewards of work, economists have coined the concept of "psychic income," which according to one economic dictionary means "income that is reckoned in terms of pleasure, satisfaction, or general feelings of euphoria."   37

Psychic income is primarily what college students mean when they talk about getting a good job. During the most affluent years of the late 1960s and early 1970s college students told their placement officers that they wanted to be researchers, college professors, artists, city planners, social workers, poets, book publishers, archeologists, ballet dancers, or authors.   38

The psychic income of these and other occupations popular with students is so high that these jobs can be filled without offering high salaries. According to one study, 93 percent of urban university professors would choose the same vocation again if they had the chance, compared with only 16 percent of unskilled auto workers. Even though the monetary gap between college professor and auto worker is now surprisingly small, the difference in psychic income is enormous.   39

But colleges fail to warn students that jobs of these kinds are hard   40
to come by, even for qualified applicants, and they rarely accept the
responsibility of helping students choose a career that will lead to a job.
When a young person says he is interested in helping people, his coun-
selor tells him to become a psychologist. But jobs in psychology are
scarce. The Department of Labor, for instance, estimates there will be
4,300 new jobs for psychologists in 1975 while colleges are expected to
turn out 58,430 B.A.s in psychology that year.

Of thirty psych majors who reported back to Vassar what they were   41
doing a year after graduation in 1973, only five had jobs in which they
could possibly use their courses in psychology, and two of these were
working for Vassar.

The outlook isn't much better for students majoring in other psychic-   42
pay disciplines: sociology, English, journalism, anthropology, forestry,
education. Whatever college graduates want to do, most of them are
going to wind up doing what there is to do.

John Shingleton, director of placement at Michigan State Univer-   43
sity, accuses the academic community of outright hypocrisy. "Educators
have never said, 'Go to college and get a good job,' but this has been
implied, and now students expect it. . . . If we care what happens to
students after college, then let's get involved with what should be one
of the basic purposes of education: career preparation."

In the 1970s, some of the more practical professors began to see   44
that jobs for graduates meant jobs for professors too. Meanwhile, students
themselves reacted to the shrinking job market, and a "new vocationalism" exploded on campus. The press welcomed the change as a return
to the ethic of achievement and service. Students were still idealistic,
the reporters wrote, but they now saw that they could best make the
world better by healing the sick as physicians or righting individual wrongs
as lawyers.

But there are no guarantees in these professions either. The Amer-   45
ican Enterprise Institute estimated in 1971 that there would be more
than the target ratio of 100 doctors for every 100,000 people in the
population by 1980. And the odds are little better for would-be lawyers.
Law schools are already graduating twice as many new lawyers every year
as the Department of Labor thinks will be needed, and the oversupply is
growing every year.

And it's not at all apparent that what is actually learned in a   46
"professional" education is necessary for success. Teachers, engineers,
and others I talked to said they find that on the job they rarely use what
they learned in school. In order to see how well college prepared engineers and scientists for actual paid work in their fields, The Carnegie

Commission queried all the employees with degrees in these fields in two large firms. Only one in five said the work they were doing bore a "very close relationship" to their college studies, while almost a third saw "very little relationship at all." An overwhelming majority could think of many people who were doing their same work, but had majored in different fields.

Majors in nontechnical fields report even less relationship between   47
their studies and their jobs. Charles Lawrence, a communications major
in college and now the producer of "Kennedy & Co.," the Chicago morning television show, says, "You have to learn all that stuff and you never use it again. I learned my job doing it." Others employed as architects, nurses, teachers, and other members of the so-called learned professions report the same thing.

Most college administrators admit that they don't prepare their   48
graduates for the job market. "I just wish I had the guts to tell parents that when you get out of this place you aren't prepared to do anything," the academic head of a famous liberal-arts college told us. Fortunately, for him, most people believe that you don't have to defend a liberal-arts education on those grounds. A liberal-arts education is supposed to provide you with a value system, a standard, a set of ideas, not a job. "Like Christianity, the liberal arts are seldom practiced and would probably be hated by the majority of the populace if they were," said one defender.

The analogy is apt. The fact is, of course, that the liberal arts are   49
a religion in every sense of that term. When people talk about them, their language becomes elevated, metaphorical, extravagant, theoretical and reverent. And faith in personal salvation by the liberal arts is professed in a creed intoned on ceremonial occasions such as commencements.

If the liberal arts are a religious faith, the professors are its priests.   50
But disseminating ideas in a four-year college curriculum is slow and most expensive. If you want to learn about Milton, Camus, or even Margaret Mead you can find them in paperback books, the public library, and even on television.

And when most people talk about the value of a college education,   51
they are not talking about great books. When at Harvard commencement, the president welcomes the new graduates into "the fellowship of educated men and women," what he could be saying is, "Here is a piece of paper that is a passport to jobs, power, and instant prestige." As Glenn Bassett, a personnel specialist at G.E., says, "In some parts of G.E., a college degree appears completely irrelevant to selection to, say, a manager's job. In most, however, it is a ticket of admission."

But now that we have doubled the number of young people at- 52
tending college, a diploma cannot guarantee even that. The most charitable conclusion we can reach is that college probably has very little, if
any, effect on people and things at all. Today, the false premises are easy
to see:

First, college doesn't make people intelligent, ambitious, happy, or 53
liberal. It's the other way around. Intelligent, ambitious, happy, liberal
people are attracted to higher education in the first place.

Second, college can't claim much credit for the learning experi- 54
ences that really change students while they are there. Jobs, friends,
history, and most of all the sheer passage of time, have as big an impact
as anything even indirectly related to the campus.

Third, colleges have changed so radically that a freshman entering 55
in the fall of 1974 can't be sure to gain even the limited value research
studies assigned to colleges in the '60s. The sheer size of undergraduate
campuses of the 1970s makes college even less stimulating now than it
was 10 years ago. Today even motivated students are disappointed with
their college courses and professors.

Finally, a college diploma no longer opens as many vocational doors. 56
Employers are beginning to realize that when they pay extra for someone
with a diploma, they are paying only for an empty credential. The fact
is that most of the work for which employers now expect college training
is now or has been capably done in the past by people without higher
educations.

College, then, may be a good place for those few young people who 57
are really drawn to academic work, who would rather read than eat, but
it has become too expensive, in money, time, and intellectual effort, to
serve as a holding pen for large numbers of our young. We ought to make
it possible for those reluctant, unhappy students to find alternative ways
of growing up and more realistic preparation for the years ahead.

Questions for Study and Discussion

1. What reasons does Bird give for believing that college is a waste of time
and money? Which reasons, if any, do you find most compelling? Explain
why.

2. Why, according to Bird, do people go to college? Do you agree with her
assessment? Why, or why not?

3. In the 1960s and early 1970s students protested en masse on campuses
across the country. How, according to Bird, do students protest today? Is this
true of students on your campus? Explain.

4. In traveling to college campuses across the country Bird was struck by the

"prevailing sadness." Why does she believe students are sad? Do you think she's right? Why, or why not?

5. Why, after going through the exercises of showing the economic advantages of investing money instead of spending it on a college education, does Bird admit that "there is a certain unreality to the game"? Do you agree with her when she says, "few parents are sophisticated enough to understand that in financial returns alone, their children would be better off with the money than with the education"?

6. What, according to Bird, is psychic income? How can a person estimate the value of psychic income? How important is such income to you and your peers?

7. What is the "new vocationalism" of the 1970s that Bird refers to? Is this still a campus reality in the late 1980s? Explain.

8. What types of sources does Bird use to substantiate her argument? In what ways do these sources help her to avoid the charges of being opinionated, cynical, or sensational?

9. How are paragraphs 52–57 related to what comes before? Does the paragraph block function as an appropriate conclusion? Explain.

Writing Topics

1. Bird says that college is "at best a social center or aging vat, and at worst a young folks' home or even a prison that keeps them out of the mainstream of economic life for a few more years." She concludes her essay by saying "We ought to make it possible for those reluctant, unhappy students to find alternative ways of growing up and more realistic preparation for the years ahead." Write an essay in which you explore different possible learning experiences and opportunities for personal growth to prepare our youth for the years ahead.

2. The selections by David P. Gardner (pp. 259–267) and Caroline Bird concern educational issues at the college level, and approach the subject from different vantage points. Gardner's report sounds an alarm because the nation's post-secondary schools are not striving for excellence, and Bird claims that college is a waste of time and money. One is concerned with the nation's welfare and future, the other with students' potential financial gains. Compare and contrast the arguments made by each author. Are the issues raised really two different ones or are they actually different sides of the same problem? If the nation's colleges were able to achieve the excellence Gardner's commission calls for, do you think Caroline Bird would still believe that college is a waste of time and money? Can the issues be resolved in some way?

3. College is, or at least should be, something more than a place to get the credentials necessary to earn more money in the job market. Write an essay in which you explain what you hope to gain intellectually, morally, and socially from your college education.

Norman Cousins was born in New Jersey in 1915, and after attending Columbia University he began a long and industrious career as a journalist and writer. Cousins has taught at a number of universities and colleges and has won many awards for his service to education and the world community. He is perhaps best known, however, as the editor of *Saturday Review*, a position he held for thirty-eight years. In the pages of the *Saturday Review* he championed the importance of education and argued forcefully for the centrality of the humanities in higher education.

His numerous books include *The Last Defense in a Nuclear Age*, *The Celebration of Life*, *The Quest for Immortality*, and most recently *Anatomy of An Illness as Perceived by the Patient: Reflections on Healing and Regeneration*, his widely read account of how he coped with a nearly fatal illness.

Cousins believes that today "Education is being measured more by the size of the benefits the individual can extract from society than by the extent to which the individual can come into possession of his or her full powers." In the following essay, one of Cousins's last *Saturday Review* columns, he argues for more emphasis on the liberal arts, especially in an age that seems enamored of professional training.

How to Make People Smaller Than They Are

Three months ago in this space we wrote about the costly retreat from the humanities on all the levels of American education. Since that time, we have had occasion to visit a number of campuses and have been troubled to find that the general situation is even more serious than we had thought. It has become apparent to us that one of the biggest problems confronting American education today is the increasing vocationalization of our colleges and universities. Throughout the country, schools are under pressure to become job-training centers and employment agencies.

The pressure comes mainly from two sources. One is the growing determination of many citizens to reduce taxes—understandable and even commendable in itself, but irrational and irresponsible when connected to the reduction or dismantling of vital public services. The second source of pressure comes from parents and students who tend to scorn courses of study that do not teach people how to become attractive to employers in a rapidly tightening job market.

It is absurd to believe that the development of skills does not also 3
require the systematic development of the human mind. Education is
being measured more by the size of the benefits the individual can extract
from society than by the extent to which the individual can come into
possession of his or her full powers. The result is that the life-giving juices
are in danger of being drained out of education.

Emphasis on "practicalities" is being characterized by the subordi- 4
nation of words to numbers. History is seen not as essential experience
to be transmitted to new generations, but as abstractions that carry dank
odors. Art is regarded as something that calls for indulgence or patronage
and that has no place among the practical realities. Political science is
viewed more as a specialized subject for people who want to go into
politics than as an opportunity for citizens to develop a knowledgeable
relationship with the systems by which human societies are governed.
Finally, literature and philosophy are assigned the role of add-ons—intellectual adornments that have nothing to do with "genuine" education.

Instead of trying to shrink the liberal arts, the American people 5
ought to be putting pressure on colleges and universities to increase the
ratio of the humanities to the sciences. Most serious studies of medical-
school curricula in recent years have called attention to the stark gaps
in the liberal education of medical students. The experts agree that the
schools shouldn't leave it up to students to close those gaps.

The irony of the emphasis being placed on careers is that nothing 6
is more valuable for anyone who has had a professional or vocational
education than to be able to deal with abstractions or complexities, or
to feel comfortable with subtleties of thought or language, or to think
sequentially. The doctor who knows only disease is at a disadvantage
alongside the doctor who knows at least as much about people as he does
about pathological organisms. The lawyer who argues in court from a
narrow legal base is no match for the lawyer who can connect legal
precedents to historical experience and who employs wide-ranging intellectual resources. The business executive whose competence in general
management is bolstered by an artistic ability to deal with people is of
prime value to his company. For the technologist, the engineering of
consent can be just as important as the engineering of moving parts. In
all these respects, the liberal arts have much to offer. Just in terms of
career preparation, therefore, a student is shortchanging himself by short-
cutting the humanities.

But even if it could be demonstrated that the humanities contribute 7
nothing directly to a job, they would still be an essential part of the
educational equipment of any person who wants to come to terms with
life. The humanities would be expendable only if human beings didn't

have to make decisions that affect their lives and the lives of others; if the human past never existed or had nothing to tell us about the present; if thought processes were irrelevant to the achievement of purpose; if creativity was beyond the human mind and had nothing to do with the joy of living; if human relationships were random aspects of life; if human beings never had to cope with panic or pain, or if they never had to anticipate the connection between cause and effect; if all the mysteries of mind and nature were fully plumbed; and if no special demands arose from the accident of being born a human being instead of a hen or a hog.

Finally, there would be good reason to eliminate the humanities if a free society were not absolutely dependent on a functioning citizenry. If the main purpose of a university is job training, then the underlying philosophy of our government has little meaning. The debates that went into the making of American society concerned not just institutions or governing principles but the capacity of humans to sustain those institutions. Whatever the disagreements were over other issues at the American Constitutional Convention, the fundamental question sensed by everyone, a question that lay over the entire assembly, was whether the people themselves would understand what it meant to hold the ultimate power of society, and whether they had enough of a sense of history and destiny to know where they had been and where they ought to be going.

Jefferson was prouder of having been the founder of the University of Virginia than of having been President of the United States. He knew that the educated and developed mind was the best assurance that a political system could be made to work—a system based on the informed consent of the governed. If this idea fails, then all the saved tax dollars in the world will not be enough to prevent the nation from turning on itself.

Questions for Study and Discussion

1. What is the "vocationalization" of colleges and universities that Cousins speaks of? What evidence of this do you find at your own school?

2. According to Cousins, what are the two sources of pressure on colleges and universities to become more vocational?

3. In paragraph 4, Cousins states that the "emphasis on 'practicalities' " has resulted in the "subordination of words to numbers." What does he mean? How does Cousins characterize traditional liberal arts courses? Do you agree with his assessment? Explain.

4. What are Cousins's arguments in favor of the humanities? How has he

organized his arguments? Could paragraphs 6–8 be reordered? What would be gained or lost if they were reordered?

5. What is the meaning of Cousins's title? What does it imply about human nature? Is the title effective?

6. What for Cousins is the relationship between education and democracy?

Writing Topics

1. Compelling as Cousins's arguments may be, many liberal arts undergraduates complain that their course of study could be more career-oriented without any loss of integrity. Write an argument either for or against career-oriented courses in your area of study.

2. Write an essay in which you explain how you think your college education will help you grow as a person. For example, will it provide you with what Cousins calls "an artistic ability to deal with people"?

3. Can you identify one feature of your education that has done the most for you? What would that feature be, and why do you consider it so valuable? Has there been anything in your education that you feel has held you back? If so, what?

LAURENCE J. PETER

Laurence J. Peter is currently professor of education at the University of Southern California, where he coordinates programs for emotionally disturbed children. Born in 1919 in Canada, Peter is a prolific writer and is perhaps best known for his books *Prescriptive Teaching* (1965), *The Peter Principle* (1969), *The Peter Plan* (1977), and *Why Things Go Wrong* (1985). He is described by his co-worker Raymond Hull as "the Newton of incompetence theory,"

The following selection from Peter's most recent book, *Why Things Go Wrong*, reflects his career-long pursuit of competence, especially in the teaching profession. Here he explores the intriguing question "What is it that teachers do that causes children to learn?"

A Quest for Competence

The first phase of my pursuit of competence began in 1938, when I took my first teacher education course, and continued until 1963—a period in which I took professional or higher-education courses each year. Did those twenty-five years of study mean I was the ultimate incompetent scholar or simply that I had been confused for longer than anyone else? I'll never know, but my explanation for my persistent search for knowledge is that early in my career I became intrigued with the question "What is it that teachers do that causes children to learn?"

This question entered my consciousness during a World War II teacher shortage. I had taken education courses and had obtained a credential that designated me a qualified teacher. I assumed this meant I had acquired special knowledge and skills not possessed by nonmembers of the profession.

> I prefer the company of peasants because they have not been educated sufficiently to reason incorrectly.
>
> Montaigne

Because of the shortage of certificated high school teachers, temporary teaching permits were granted to persons qualified in a particular subject but lacking specific teacher education. Ben E. Fitz,[1] a co-worker in my department, was teaching on a temporary (war emergency) permit. When I became aware that his teaching was much like mine and that student achievement was similar in both our classes, I was somewhat disconcerted. What had I learned in all those teacher-education classes?

---

[1]Names of some persons have been changed to protect the innocent and the guilty.

Why was I not a better teacher than Ben, who had not set foot in a teacher-education institution? Had I been fooling myself into believing education courses were important and relevant to the teaching function? These questions sparked my interest in teacher competence and how it is acquired.

> Successful teachers are effective in spite of the psychological theories they suffer under.
>
> Educational proverb

A Supercompetent

In 1943, I taught in a basement room in Central Elementary School in Chilliwack, British Columbia, Canada. In the other basement room, Mrs. Abel taught first grade. My first impression of Mrs. Abel was of a short, plump, middle-aged woman with gray hair combed up into a large neat bun on top of her head. She wore black walking shoes and was dressed, as always, in a navy-blue skirt and white blouse. Her most impressive characteristics were her manner and speech. She had an aura of complete calm and she looked directly at whomever she spoke to. I had been warned by the principal that the other teachers found her impossible to get along with but that she was a wonderful teacher and the children and their parents loved and admired her. Later, he told me of a problem he had: All the parents of first-graders wanted their children to be in Mrs. Abel's class because she was known throughout the district as the best teacher of beginning reading and writing.

It was not long before I understood why she did not get along with the school staff. She attended only the first staff meeting of the school year and did not go to in-service meetings or school social functions. She preferred to eat her lunch in her classroom with her pupils rather than in the staff lunchroom. She told me she was the best first-grade teacher in the district and the other teachers didn't know what they were doing. When they sought her help or advice, she replied, "I have developed techniques that work for me. Why don't you develop techniques that work for you?" Asked how her pupils all learned to read in the first few weeks of school, when other teachers took all year to achieve the same results, she answered, "Because my techniques are superior to theirs."

> A teacher affects eternity; no one can tell where his influence stops.
>
> Henry Adams

When the principal realized that my interest in Mrs. Abel was motivated not by idle curiosity about her idiosyncratic behavior, but by my admiration for her ability, he shared some background information with me. She had graduated from the local high school forty-four years earlier and had attended the Provincial Normal School for one year of teacher training. She returned home to Chilliwack and became a first-grade teacher. Except for three years—during which she was married, had a daughter, and became a widow—she had remained a first-grade teacher. In spite of the promptings of the superintendent and others, she steadfastly refused to upgrade her qualifications or to take in-service courses. When pressed, she said, "Do they know any more than I about teaching?" When urged to get a degree so she would be eligible for promotion, she replied, "I don't want a promotion. I don't want to be an administrator. I like working with children, not adults."

> Why in the world are salaries higher for administrators when the basic mission is teaching?
>
> Governor Jerry Brown

I can only speculate on why Mrs. Abel invited me into her classroom and shared her ideas with me, but my first visit convinced me I was in the presence of genius. Although my observations, over a two-year period, were merely glimpses of a brilliantly conceived and effectively implemented teaching program, I offer here some of my perceptions along with Mrs. Abel's explanations of her methods.   7

The First Day. In the 1940's there were no kindergarten or preschool programs in this rural area, so Mrs. Abel began by introducing her pupils to school routines. After the children were settled and eager for their first lesson, she hung a chart at the front of the room picturing three red apples. She said, "We are going to learn a rhyme about these apples." She chanted slowly: "How many apples do you see? You can count them, one, two, three." She then had the class recite the poem in unison, following the beat she marked with her hand. When she was certain that all the children were participating, she turned over the picture, revealing: 8

She pointed to the words and beat time as before while the children chanted the words. As the final activity of the day, she passed out mimeographed copies of the rhyme and the children recited it as they pointed to the words. It was a happy group of children who left school that first day, and I expect that families throughout the district were surprised when their one-day scholars pointed to the words and "read" the apple poem.

> The mediocre teacher tells. The good teacher explains. The superior teacher demonstrates. The great teacher inspires.
>
> William Arthur Ward

Mrs. Abel explained: "I start with words and objects with which the children are familiar. Children accomplish the most complex learning achievement of their lives—to speak their native tongue—without formal instruction. The sound of the word *apple* is a symbol that in no way resembles an apple. Neither does the visual representation of the word: APPLE. If the child can speak the word, reading the word should present no problems. Therefore I teach the children to say the words, and then show them the words." 9

I was in no position to question her theory, but I was certainly impressed with the results she achieved. Systematically she progressed to longer rhymes and then used the words from them in other contexts. The children read from the first day and progressed rapidly. Their joy of accomplishment was obvious. When they used the prescribed readers, they completed them in less than half the usual time and were able to engage in substantial supplemental reading. 10

In every detail of teaching, Mrs. Abel seemed to have a system that worked. Her program was developmentally sequenced to assure that every child acquired each component skill required for reading, writing, and elementary arithmetic. Her ability to observe each child, so that no essential accomplishment was missed, was phenomenal. In answer to my questions, she gave precise and lucid explanations: 11

"There is an old saying, 'The eye of the farmer fattens the flock.' I can believe that. Much of my success is because I detect when any child is having difficulty. That's why no child in my class gets left behind. Once a child is left behind, the problems of cumulative error can result in development of a learning disability. The eye of the teacher strengthens the child's learning." 12

And another: "The reading experts are divided into two camps. One group promotes phonics as the royal road to learning, and the other believes that the look-and-say method will produce more happy little readers. Can you believe that intelligent adults would waste their time on such a silly argument? Good teaching includes both methods, but not 13 as separate approaches. Take the word *can* in the apple rhyme. The children see the word and say the word. Then we play a game on one of my charts, changing only the last letter, starting with *can* and going on to *cat, cab, car, cap*. Then we start with *can* and change only the first letter: *an, fan, man, tan, pan, van*. After they have worked with all the vowels and consonants in this way, they can read phonetically many one-syllable words. Then we combine some of these words and they read *hatbox, dustpan, dishpan, tomcat, fishpond, handbag, bathtub, lipstick*, and so forth. I just keep increasing their sight vocabulary, their word-analysis skills, and phonics by building on their experience and the poems and stories we read. These techniques are an integrated process in my teaching and are not competitive techniques, as the experts like to believe."

She told me that years ago the superintendent had encouraged her 14
to take courses in psychology. She said, "When I asked why, he told me it might help me to understand the children better. I told him that as a teacher I was more concerned that the children understand me.

For a number of years she had resolutely declined invitations to 15
demonstrate her methods for other teachers, but in her last year before retirement she weakened. She and I shared a storeroom. A few days before the teachers' convention I discovered that she had moved some teaching material out of storage and had replaced it with material she used in the classroom. When I asked her why, she said, "I'm storing the things that work best for me and showing them the stuff that I no longer use. It's taken me forty years to develop my technique and they're not getting it for nothing."

Educational authorities would give Mrs. Abel very low marks for 16
attitude, cooperation with co-workers, in-service education, professional advancement, use of new audiovisual materials, and application of approved teaching methods. I wish that she had shared her teaching techniques more freely, that she had been more open to new ideas, and that she had improved her own education background. The fact remains, in spite of her idiosyncrasies and lack of "professionalism," she was one of that select group of super teachers. Her students had great enthusiasm for school and read better and learned more than any other first-graders I have encountered.

Teaching is not a lost art, but regard for it is a lost tradition.
Jacques Barzun

Probably the key to Mrs. Abel's success was her sensitivity to feed- 17
back. She was acutely aware of her students' responses to her instruction. The children's learning told her which of her methods was effective. Her experience showed her which things to reject and which to retain for

future lessons. Her sensitivity to her own effectiveness shaped her teaching performance. Each teaching experience was a learning experience for her, so that she grew in competence throughout her whole career.

> Most educators would continue to lecture on navigation while the ship is going down.
>
> James H. Boren

More Competents

During the next ten years I met many outstanding teachers—including Mr. Julius, who had developed a system of simulation games that taught retarded children practical self-care, traffic safety, housekeeping, and other socially valuable skills. He enriched the life of every child in his classes at the provincial residential school for retarded children. I admired the work of Mr. Query, who taught gifted high school students. He stimulated their superior mental abilities by his powerful challenges and his tenacious questioning. Ann Cestery taught social studies by having her students research their own homes and community. They did so well they were given awards by the British Columbia Historical Society and the British Columbia Research Council. I studied what these and other highly successful teachers did to achieve their outstanding results. In almost every case their effectiveness was the result of original or unorthodox methods, and not those acquired in teacher education.   18

Years later, I was not surprised when I read the results of a research project conducted by Dr. James Popham of UCLA in which he studied teacher effectiveness.[2] More than two thousand students were instructed by fully qualified, certificated teachers, and by persons educated in relevant subject matter who had not taken any courses in teacher education. He called the former group *teachers*, and the latter, *nonteachers*. There was no statistically significant difference, in the amount the students learned, between teachers and nonteachers.   19

Questions for Study and Discussion

1. What question became the focal point of Peter's pursuit of competence? How does he answer this question?

2. What for Peter is the relationship between teacher-education classes and effective teaching?

---

[2]W. J. Popham, "Performance Tests of Teaching Proficiency: Rationale, Development, and Validation," *American Educational Research Journal* (January 1971).

3. What, according to Peter, is the key to Mrs. Abel's success? Why do you suppose Mrs. Abel is reluctant to share her techniques with her fellow teachers? Is she selfish? Does she have an ulterior motive? Explain.

4. Briefly summarize Mrs. Abel's good qualities as a teacher. Does Peter believe that she had any faults as a teacher? How important was her interaction with her colleagues in terms of teacher effectiveness?

5. Discuss Peter's use of Mrs. Abel as an extended example of competence. What is he able to accomplish through his use of her that he would not be able to do with a series of short examples?

6. What does the old saying "The eye of the farmer fattens the flock" mean? How does Mrs. Abel apply it to her classroom?

7. What do you suppose helped Mrs. Abel to survive forty-one years of teaching? Why wasn't she interested in additional courses, degrees, or promotions?

Writing Topics

1. If you had the opportunity to talk with people preparing to become high-school teachers, what advice would you give them based upon your own experience as a high-school student?

2. Using Peter's analysis of Mrs. Abel as a model, write an essay in which you explain what it takes to be successful in a particular endeavor or career.

3. Reflect on the teachers that you've had during the past two or three years. What teaching traits have distinguished each one? Write an essay in which you classify your teachers according to the traits that you've discovered.

4. Write an essay in which you answer the following question: "Why do people love to hate teachers?"

Teaching and Testing

ALEXANDER CALANDRA

Tests in school and college are usually designed so that each question has only one correct answer, especially in disciplines such as the natural sciences. Yet many important discoveries have been made by individuals who have reached beyond the obvious and "known" answers—take Galileo, Columbus, and Einstein, for example. Alexander Calandra, a professor of physics at Washington University in St. Louis, once came across a college student who insisted on giving every answer but the expected one to a physics exam question. In this essay, originally published in *Saturday Review*, he tells what happened.

Angels on a Pin

Some time ago, I received a call from a colleague who asked if I would be the referee on the grading of an examination question. He was about to give a student a zero for his answer to a physics question, while the student claimed he should receive a perfect score and would if the system were not set up against the student. The instructor and the student agreed to submit this to an impartial arbiter, and I was selected.

I went to my colleague's office and read the examination question: "Show how it is possible to determine the height of a tall building with the aid of a barometer."

The student had answered: "Take the barometer to the top of the building, attach a long rope to it, lower the barometer to the street, and then bring it up, measuring the length of the rope. The length of the rope is the height of the building."

I pointed out that the student really had a strong case for full credit, since he had answered the question completely and correctly. On the other hand, if full credit were given, it could well contribute to a high grade for the student in his physics course. A high grade is supposed to certify competence in physics, but the answer did not confirm this. I

291

suggested that the student have another try at answering the question. I was not surprised that my colleague agreed, but I was surprised that the student did.

I gave the student six minutes to answer the question, with the warning that his answer should show some knowledge of physics. At the end of five minutes, he had not written anything. I asked if he wished to give up, but he said no. He had many answers to this problem; he was just thinking of the best one. I excused myself for interrupting him, and asked him to please go on. In the next minute, he dashed off his answer, which read:

"Take the barometer to the top of the building and lean over the edge of the roof. Drop the barometer, timing its fall with a stopwatch. Then, using the formula $S = \frac{1}{2} at^2$, calculate the height of the building."

At this point, I asked my colleague if *he* would give up. He conceded, and I gave the student almost full credit.

In leaving my colleague's office, I recalled that the student had said he had other answers to the problem, so I asked him what they were. "Oh, yes," said the student. "There are many ways of getting the height of a tall building with the aid of a barometer. For example, you could take the barometer out on a sunny day and measure the height of the barometer, the length of its shadow, and the length of the shadow of the building, and by the use of a simple proportion, determine the height of the building."

"Fine," I said. "And the others?"

"Yes," said the student. "There is a very basic measurement method that you will like. In this method, you take the barometer and begin to walk up the stairs. As you climb the stairs, you mark off the length of the barometer along the wall. You then count the number of marks, and this will give you the height of the building in barometer units. A very direct method.

"Of course, if you want a more sophisticated method, you can tie the barometer to the end of a string, swing it as a pendulum, and determine the value of 'g' at the street level and at the top of the building. From the difference between the two values of 'g,' the height of the building can, in principle, be calculated."

Finally he concluded, there are many other ways of solving the problem. "Probably the best," he said, "is to take the barometer to the basement and knock on the superintendent's door. When the superintendent answers, you speak to him as follows: 'Mr. Superintendent, here I have a fine barometer. If you will tell me the height of this building, I will give you this barometer.'"

5

6

7

8

9

10

11

12

At this point, I asked the student if he really did not know the   13
conventional answer to this question. He admitted that he did, but said
that he was fed up with high school and college instructors trying to
teach him how to think, to use the "scientific method," and to explore
the deep inner logic of the subject in a pedantic way, as is often done
in the new mathematics, rather than teaching him the structure of the
subject. With this in mind, he decided to revive scholasticism as an
academic lark to challenge the Sputnik-panicked classrooms of America.

Questions for Study and Discussion

1. What is the point of this essay? What makes the narrative more than a
humorous story about a student and his physics exam?

2. What was the exam question supposed to test? Why did the question fail?
How might the actual wording have caused this failure? How would you rewrite the question so that it would do what it was meant to do?

3. Why do you think the student gave the answer in paragraph 6 as the best
one? Do you agree? What motivated him to avoid the conventional answer?

4. Why do you think the teacher accepted the answer in paragraph 6 but did
not give the student full credit? Was he right to do so? Explain.

5. What relevant information does Calandra leave out of the essay? Why do
you think he does this?

6. The scholastic philosophers of the Middle Ages used to debate theological
questions that seem pointless to us today, such as how many angels could
dance on the head of a pin. In this context, what do you think is meant by
the reference to scholasticism in the last sentence of the essay? What does
the title contribute to the essay?

7. How would you characterize all of the student's answers? Granting their
imaginativeness, what other quality did they all possess?

Writing Topics

1. History and everyday life are full of examples of what Edward de Bono
calls "lateral thinking," going outside the conventional limits of a problem
to find an unexpected but effective answer. The student in Calandra's essay
is obviously an imaginative lateral thinker. What examples of lateral thinking
can you find in your own experience, or from other sources? How can one set
about thinking laterally? Write an essay in which you discuss the benefits of
lateral thinking.

2. What are tests and exams normally used for? What should they be used
for? How can you tell a good examination question from a bad one? Based
upon exams that you have taken, write an essay that examines the function
of testing in the educational process.

ANDREW WARD

Photographer, former art teacher, and humorist, Andrew Ward was born in Chicago in 1946. He attended Oberlin College in Ohio and the Rhode Island School of Design and now makes his home in New Haven, Connecticut. His writing has appeared in a wide variety of publications including *Horizon, Inquiry, American Heritage,* and *Fantasy and Science Fiction Magazine.* He also published two collections of his essays: *Fits and Starts: The Premature Memoirs of Andrew Ward* (1978), and *Bits and Pieces* (1980). In 1980 he also published *Baby Bear and the Long Sleep,* a book for very young children.

"Pencils Down," taken from *Fits and Starts,* recounts with pity, pathos, nostalgia, and abrupt humor the many fearful testing situations Ward has faced throughout his school years.

Pencils Down

Everything will be going fine and then suddenly I will have that 1 dream again, the one in which I am walking across a campus and a classmate runs by me, waving his arms and shouting, "Come on! You're late!"

"Late?" I call after him. "Late for what?" 2

"Late for what?!" he exclaims. "Late for Bretko's final!" 3

In spite of myself, I begin to lope after him. "Bretko? Who's Bretko?" 4

"Jesus Christ!" he says as we dash toward the classroom building, 5 "where have you *been* all semester?"

It is just when we reach the classroom, where the final in a course 6 I have never heard of on a subject I know nothing about is already in progress, that I wake up in a tangle of bedding, my eyes bulging like eggs.

The first real test I remember taking was at a solemn little pedagogic 7 enterprise called the Lab School, to which the faculty of the University of Chicago sent its children and in which it tested out some of its educational theories. I spent four years guinea-pigging my way through the Lab School, but I don't remember very much about it. I do remember a wide, saintly kindergarten teacher who cured my stuttering ("Now, take your time, Andy," she would say as I stammered before her, "we have all the time in the world."). And I remember Miss Mums, a siren of a second-grade teacher with a flamboyant bust who used to hop up and down whenever one of us answered her correctly. I still think the University was on to something when it hired Miss Mums; most of us did our best to keep her perpetually hopping before us.

In any case, sometime during the second grade a group of pale young men with attaché cases arrived at the school and established themselves in a little room which was usually devoted to hearing tests. We were called in one by one "to have a little fun," as Miss Mums put it, "with some nice big men." Some of us didn't want to have a little fun. One boy, whose mother made him wear some sort of prophylactic powder in his hair, fainted in the hallway when his turn came, and had to spend the rest of the day with the nurse. 8

When it came my turn, I walked down to the testing room and stood silently in the doorway, waiting to be noticed, which was my way of announcing myself in those days. I was finally beckoned in by a man with thick glasses that made his eyes look like fish suspended in ice. 9

"Now, Mark," he said brightly, "if you'll just take your seat right here, we can all start playing with blocks." 10

Much too polite to correct him about my name, I took my seat at a table around which four men with note pads loomed attentively. I was given six red plastic cubes and told, with many winks and nods, to do whatever I felt like doing with them. In truth, I didn't feel like doing anything with them. I was old enough to know that you couldn't build anything with six cubes. But the men looked so eager that I decided to do what I could, which was to line them all up into a row, then into two rows of three, then into three rows of two. The three rows of two seemed to go over very big. I could see out of the corner of my eye that they had begun to jot furiously, nodding to themselves as if entire life philosophies were being confirmed before their eyes. 11

I shoved the blocks around a while longer and finally leaned back. There was a pause, and then suddenly one of the men rose to his feet agitatedly and jabbed his pencil into the fish-eyed man's ribs. 12

"See?" he exclaimed. "See? What did I tell you?" 13

"You never told me *anything!*" the fish-eyed man hissed back, shoving the pencil aside. There was a scene, and in the confusion I got down off my chair and made my way back to Miss Mums' room. "Now," she asked me as I sat down at my desk, "wasn't that fun?" 14

"Yes," I said, and she gave a little hop. 15

My parents seemed to have had me down for college *in utero*. I remember working on a geography report about Bolivia when I was in the third grade and my mother standing over me with an anxious look and declaring, "They're going to count this for college." 16

As far as she was concerned, they were going to count everything for college. She used college in her disciplinary warnings the way some 17

mothers used Santa Claus. This had the effect of simultaneously trivial-
izing and exalting my academic labors. On the one hand, I could not
believe that my knowledge that Bolivia was the only country in the world
to lynch two successive heads of state from the same lamp post was going
to count for anything in college. On the other hand, I could sometimes
imagine a tweedy admissions officer leaning back and asking, "By the
way, Andrew, what country was it that lynched two successive heads of
state from the same lamp post?"

"I believe that was Bolivia, sir."   18

"Excellent! Oh, excellent! Andrew, I believe you and Harvard are   19
going to get along very nicely."

I never did very well in school; in fact, the further along I got the   20
worse I did, until by senior year in high school I was just squeaking
through. I ascribe this to a diffficulty I've always had with admitting to
ignorance. It is hard to learn anything when you are constantly trying
to look as though you know it already. I would rarely ask a question, for
instance, unless it was designed to demonstrate a precocious knowledge
of the subject under discussion. I would always start off my questions
with, "Wouldn't you say that . . . , " knowing full well that the teacher
would, and congratulate me for my insight. In math and science it got
me nowhere.

My parents were perplexed by my performance in high school, to   21
the point of commissioning a university testing center in New York City
to determine what my problem was. Every Saturday for four weeks I made
my way into the Village to undergo batteries of five or six tests at a
sitting. I went in with my parents the first day, and we all sat around
with a cheerful man who kept asking me what I thought of myself. I told
him I wanted to be an artist, and had trouble studying. He smiled in-
dulgently and said we would see about that.

I guess I've blocked out a lot of the tests I took in the following   22
weeks. One of them was to check out my suitability for cost accounting.
Another consisted of a series of paintings depicting ambiguous scenes
which I was to interpret using multiple choice.

The man and woman in the picture above have just: 23
A. Had an argument.
B. Made love.
C. Poisoned themselves.
D. Filed a joint return.

Another was a tricky test for artistic ability. There would be four   24
drawings of, say, a circle placed in a square. In one the circle would be
centered, in another it would be to one side, in another it would be to

another side, and so on. The idea was to select the one which was most sound compositionally. I say this was tricky because at the time every artistic convention was up for grabs, and I could have whipped up a convincing aesthetic argument for any one of them. I decided, however, that the centered circle was most likely to suit the testing center's artistic soul, and my high score bore this out.

One of the exams was an oral I.Q. test. The tester was an earnest   25
man in shirt sleeves who repeatedly told me to relax. "We're just going to kick around a few things," he said. "There's absolutely nothing to be afraid of."

He had me push blocks through holes, do something simple with   26
some checkers, and perform various other tasks, and then we came to a part of the test where I was to explain to him the derivation of different sayings. This proved a bumpier ride than he had expected, because I had never heard a lot of the sayings he read to me. "One swallow does not make a summer," for instance, troubled me deeply. I had never heard it, knew nothing about ornithology, and stammered along for several minutes, operating on the theory that he meant the act of swallowing. I think I said something about the wine of life and the flask of spring, and I could see from the way my tester fidgeted that he had not been provided with contingencies covering my interpretation.

I can't say I didn't get anything out of all this. I was given some   27
instruction on the ukelele by an old man in Washington Square during a testing break, and discovered a newsstand near the subway where I could buy *Gent* and *Nugget* without raising an eyebrow. When my parents and I were called back to hear the results, we were told that I was sharp as a tack, had trouble motivating myself to study, and should consider art as a profession. The cheerful man accepted my father's check for $125.00, and we all silently rode the train back to where I'd started.

I did pretty well on my English and history College Boards, and   28
miserably in math and science, as was my pattern. My parents had me sign up for every testing date there was, and I swung at the ball in such varying locales as Danbury State Teachers' College, Tom's School of Business Success, and most of the high school auditoriums in southwestern Connecticut. One day, my mother saw an ad in the back of the *Times* for a College Board preparation class at a private school in the city, and in no time I was commuting again. It turned out that I was the only one in the class who did not come from midtown Manhattan, and the only male who didn't wear a yarmulke. The course turned out to be a fraud. The teacher, a shaky old fellow in gold framed bifocals, started off by informing us that there was no secret to doing well on College Boards, went on to talk a little about a sister of his who was about to

undergo surgery, and then had us spend the rest of the time taking mock College Boards in exercise books we bought from the school for five dollars apiece.

Oberlin College was my first choice, naturally enough, because my   29 parents went there, and my brother, and all my aunts and uncles, because my grandfather was head of its art department, and my father was one of its trustees. Oberlin had strict admissions standards in those days, and there was considerable doubt on my parents' part that I would gain admittance.

When I had my admissions interview in a hotel suite in New York,   30 I had just received a D in chemistry, a course I had to pass in order to meet the science requirement, since I had flunked biology the year before. After several genial inquiries as to my family's health and whereabouts, the admissions officer proved remarkably encouraging. He hinted that I would be admitted under what he called Oberlin's "Tom Sawyer Program," which permitted students with "asymmetrical aptitudes," as he put it, to get in. He could not keep from wincing as his eyes descended row upon row of D's and C's in my high-school record, but he emphasized and reemphasized the positive side: high marks in art and English, soloist in the chorus, good attendance; and as the interview drew to a close, I got the impression that he was even more eager for me to go to Oberlin College than I was. As he waited with me for the elevator in the foyer outside his suite, he held my coat for me as I attempted, in vain, to get my second arm into its sleeve. We waltzed around in this way for some time, and as I finally stepped into the elevator, still lunging about for my elusive sleeve, he looked at me with the game, pained expression of a man at a dinner party who must smack his lips over something repugnant.

Oberlin didn't turn out to be quite what I had in mind, and vice   31 versa. As I went along, I had more and more trouble getting to class, until eventually I lost all track of where I was supposed to be, and when. Sometimes I would catch a glimpse of someone dimly familiar and follow him to his next class, in the hope that it would turn out to be one of my own. It never did turn out to be one of my own, but in this way I attended some fascinating lectures on subjects ranging from a historical review of the Albanian nation-state to the topical poetry of Po Chü-i.

I was well into my third, last-ditch semester at Oberlin College   32 before I finally managed to pinpoint my problem. I couldn't read. Not that I couldn't have stood up before a Wednesday Assembly and read aloud from my geology text in a clear, authoritative voice, making myself heard unto the last rows of Finney Chapel. It was just that to my own ears I wouldn't have been making any sense.

As finals week approached, I tried to overcome this disability by locking myself into my room in the dormitory, laying out my study materials in the lone beam of my Tensor desk lamp, and sitting there, hunched over my open textbook with a yellow felt-tip pen ready to underline important passages. I sat that way for hours at a time, waiting for the words over which my eyes passed to form phrases, sentences, ideas, and managing only an occasional flicker of recognition, enough to link perhaps twenty words together—"The exercise begins a rather extensive study to be continued in later sections of Chapter XXI"—never enough to gain me a foothold.

I was reduced to hoping that it was all penetrating my mind subconsciously, and I would tidily underline what I could only assume was important—headings, captions, opening and closing sentences, numbers, anything resembling a list, and sometimes a central sentence, a few of which, I figured, were probably important, too.

Underlining accomplished several purposes. It gave me something to do, demarcated the pages I had already gone through (I had no other way of knowing), and it hid from whoever might duck into my room the fact that I was, in effect, an illiterate, and had no business being in college in the first place.

My last final at Oberlin was in Geology I, a course I took because it was touted to have been designed for the scientifically inept. This touting did not, however, seem to have originated with the Geology Department. If there is more to know about rocks than was included in Geology I, I don't want to hear about it. By the time I took the final, I had missed all but seven of my classes, and had received an F on my research paper, a study of the Greenwich, Connecticut, reservoir system which I had based on a water company comic book starring a character made out of drain-pipe named Wally Water.

I took the exam with some fifty other geology cadets in a dark, gothic room overlooking Tappan Square. The proctor, a work-booted geology major, handed out the test sheet and bluebooks, and, stop-watch raised, signalled to us to begin.

The questions must have been mimeographed minutes before, because the ink still smelled sweet and dizzying. The first and second questions rang no bells at all, and as I read them my pen felt icy and useless in my fingers. In the third question I could barely make out the following: ". . . bituminous coal and discuss its suitability as a fuel. Use illustrations to explain your answer where necessary."

It was as if I had stumbled into someone else's identity. I didn't know anything about rocks. I didn't know anything about science. Why were they asking me these things? I stared up at the blackboard, where the proctor was already chalking up how much time we had left. He squinted back at me with suspicion, and I swerved my gaze ceilingward, as if searching for the appropriate phrasing with which to set down my brimming knowledge.

Coal. What did I know about coal? I thought of black lung, carbon paper, the heap of coal in my parents' basement in Chicago. Then, for a moment, a phrase sprang to my mind from an eighth-grade science text: "Coal results from the deterioration and mineralization of prehistoric tropical rainforests." 40

Quickly, before it sank back out of reach, I opened my bluebook and began to write. "Coal results from the deterioration and mineralization of prehistoric tropical rainforests. Coal deposits are apt to be found in those places where prehistoric tropical rainforests once stood. Thus, coal mines in present use are located in these places. 41

"Coal," I continued boldly, "contains some of the chemical elements of prehistoric tropical rainforests, but usually not all of them. Those that remain are those which have survived and, in a sense, resulted from, the deterioration and mineralization of prehistoric tropical rainforests." 42

That got me through three pages of large, loopy script. All around me, my classmates were filling one bluebook after another. One girl across the room wrote the ink out of one ballpoint, hurled it to the floor, and furiously scrawled on with another. All I could hear in the room was the steady scrape of pens and the rapid flutter of pages. 43

To drive home my point, I decided to deliver on a few illustrations. Carefully, but with a certain graphic flair, I drew: 44

1. a rainforest with arrows pointing to "trees," "scrub vegetation," "sun," and "topsoil,"
2. a rainforest deteriorating,
3. a deteriorated rainforest making its way underground,
4. a coal mine in full operation labelled "Thousands of years later," and,
5. a black lump labelled "resultant coal ore fragment."

These led to another drawing illustrating the chemical breakup of coal. I drew a circle and divided it into three parts, labelled "sulfur," "carbon," and "other." Coal was suitable as a fuel, I noted, because it burned. 45

As I underlined all my headings and captions I wondered about my alternatives. I could claim that I had overdosed on NoDoz, that I was reeling, hallucinating, unable to think. I could hand in a blank bluebook, 46 copy out a C-level set of answers in another bluebook that evening, hand it in the next morning, and elegantly apologize for the mixup. I could feign a fainting spell or an epileptic fit or psychosomatic paralysis of my right hand. I could accuse the earnest, chalk-faced girl beside me of cheating and storm out the door, or punch out the proctor in a rebellious frenzy, becoming, overnight, a campus legend.

But it gradually became obvious to me that the college simply wanted   47
me to answer these questions. Otherwise, I reasoned, they would not be asking them. And it was just as obvious that if I couldn't answer their questions, I had no business being there. Somehow, in the rustle of the testing room, this hit me like a revelation. I wanted to get up then, find the professor, and exclaim, "Say, sir, I didn't *realize* any of this." He would understand. It must have happened before.

I looked at two of my friends a few rows away, both busily writing.   48
At these times my friends seemed distant and unfamiliar. They were each into their third or fourth bluebooks. What in God's name were they writing about?

The hinge of my jaw ached and trembled and as I yawned, the floor   49
took on a soft, inviting look. I put down my pen and stretched out my legs and wondered if it would be all right if I just curled up for a little while on the scuffed, hardwood floor, closed my eyes, and slept.

"Pencils down," the proctor commanded, chopping at the air with   50
his hand.

A resolute, perspiring girl in the front row raised her hand and   51
asked if she could "just finish one last sentence."

The proctor nodded and a score of heads and hands ducked back   52
down to finish sentences. I sat still for a moment, and then scribbled one last sentence, "Coal remains one of the most popular forms of fuel in use today."

"All right, that's it," the proctor declared, and everyone groaned   53
and stretched and stacked their bluebooks. I signed mine with a bold hand, but glancing over my five pages I knew it was at last all over for me at Oberlin College. All that remained was one last explosion of red-inked exclamations expressing regrets, alarm, and grave concern for my future.

Questions for Study and Discussion

1. At what point in the essay were you first aware of Ward's humor? Examine several humorous passages and explain how the humor works in each case.

2. What point does Ward make about the examination or testing experience? How does humor help to make that point?

3. What role do Ward's parents play in his education? What does Ward mean when he says, "My parents seemed to have me down for college *in utero*"?

4. In paragraph 32 Ward says that he pinpointed his problem—he discovered he couldn't read. What does he mean when he says he "couldn't read," and how does the problem manifest itself?

5. Reread paragraphs 38–52. How would you characterize Ward's answer to the question of the Geology 1 final exam? What in particular about his answer is inadequate? Would he have fared better with this type of writing in a nonscientific course? Explain.

6. How has Ward organized his essay? How do paragraphs 1–6 fit into that organizational structure?

7. Discuss the extent to which examinations are specific to the academic environment. Are we ever tested elsewhere in life?

Writing Topics

1. Ward vividly remembers taking the College Boards and being enrolled in class to prepare for these examinations. Write an essay either for or against the use of College Board exams in the admissions process. You may want to interview your admissions director to determine how College Boards are used at your institution and how effective they are at predicting academic success.

2. It's a well known fact that many students suffer from the anxiety of studying for and taking examinations. Write an essay in which you propose and describe one or more alternatives to traditional academic testing. What problems would your proposal address? Can your proposal be readily or easily implemented? Explain.

3. Write an essay in which you analyze examination trauma and account for the major causes of it.

SAMUEL H. SCUDDER

Samuel H. Scudder (1837–1911) was a graduate of Williams College and Harvard University and was a university professor and leading scientist of his day. His special field of study was butterflies, grasshoppers, and crickets, and in 1888–1889 he published the result of his thirty years of research on butterflies in *The Butterflies of the Eastern United States and Canada with Special Reference to New England.*

Although the following article about the famous zoologist and geologist Louis Agassiz was first published in 1874, the approach Agassiz took with Scudder and the lesson he imparted to him are as valid for us today as when Scudder first met this great teacher.

Learning to See

It was more than fifteen years ago that I entered the laboratory of   1
Professor Agassiz, and told him I had enrolled my name in the Scientific
School as a student of natural history. He asked me a few questions about
my object in coming, my antecedents generally, the mode in which I
afterwards proposed to use the knowledge I might acquire, and, finally,
whether I wished to study any special branch. To the latter I replied
that, while I wished to be well grounded in all departments of zoology,
I purposed to devote myself specially to insects.

"When do you wish to begin?" he asked.   2

"Now," I replied.   3

This seemed to please him, and with an energetic "Very well!" he   4
reached from a shelf a huge jar of specimens in yellow alcohol.

"Take this fish," said he, "and look at it; we call it a haemulon; by   5
and by I will ask what you have seen."

With that he left me, but in a moment returned with explicit   6
instructions as to the care of the object entrusted to me.

"No man is fit to be a naturalist," said he, "who does not know   7
how to take care of specimens."

I was to keep the fish before me in a tin tray, and occasionally   8
moisten the surface with alcohol from the jar, always taking care to
replace the stopper tightly. Those were not the days of ground-glass
stoppers and elegantly shaped exhibition jars; all the old students will
recall the huge neckless glass bottles with their leaky, wax-besmeared
corks, half eaten by insects, and begrimed with cellar dust. Entomology
was a cleaner science than ichthyology, but the example of the Professor,

who had unhesitatingly plunged to the bottom of the jar to produce the fish, was infectious; and though this alcohol had a "very ancient and fishlike smell," I really dared not show any aversion within these sacred precincts, and treated the alcohol as though it were pure water. Still I was conscious of a passing feeling of disappointment, for gazing at a fish did not commend itself to an ardent entomologist. My friends at home, too, were annoyed when they discovered that no amount of eau-de-Cologne would drown the perfume which haunted me like a shadow.

In ten minutes I had seen all that could be seen in that fish, and 9 started in search of the Professor—who had, however, left the Museum; and when I returned, after lingering over some of the odd animals stored in the upper apartment, my specimen was dry all over. I dashed the fluid over the fish as if to resuscitate the beast from a fainting-fit, and looked with anxiety for a return of the normal sloppy appearance. This little excitement over, nothing was to be done but to return to a steadfast gaze at my mute companion. Half an hour passed—an hour—another hour; the fish began to look loathsome. I turned it over and around; looked it in the face—ghastly; from behind, beneath, above, sideways, at a three-quarters' view—just as ghastly. I was in despair; at an early hour I concluded that lunch was necessary; so, with infinite relief, the fish was carefully replaced in the jar, and for an hour I was free.

On my return, I learned that Professor Agassiz had been at the 10 Museum, but had gone, and would not return for several hours. My fellow-students were too busy to be disturbed by continued conversation. Slowly I drew forth that hideous fish, and with a feeling of desperation again looked at it. I might not use a magnifying-glass; instruments of all kinds were interdicted. My two hands, my two eyes, and the fish; it seemed a most limited field. I pushed my finger down its throat to feel how sharp the teeth were. I began to count the scales in the different rows, until I was convinced that that was nonsense. At last a happy thought stuck me—I would draw the fish; and now with surprise I began to discover new features in the creature. Just then the Professor returned.

"That is right," said he; "a pencil is one of the best of eyes. I am 11 glad to notice, too, that you keep your specimen wet, and your bottle corked."

With these encouraging words, he added: 12

"Well, what is it like?" 13

He listened attentively to my brief rehearsal of the structure of parts 14 whose names were still unknown to me: the fringed gill-arches and movable operculum; the pores of the head, fleshy lips and lidless eyes; the lateral line, the spinous fins and forked tail; the compressed and arched body. When I had finished, he waited as if expecting more, and then, with an air of disappointment:

"You have not looked very carefully; why," he continued more 15 earnestly, "you haven't even seen one of the most conspicuous features of the animal, which is as plainly before your eyes as the fish itself; look again, look again!" and he left me to my misery.

I was piqued; I was mortified. Still more of that wretched fish! But 16 now I set myself to my task with a will, and discovered one new thing after another, until I saw how just the Professor's criticism had been. The afternoon passed quickly; and when, toward its close, the Professor inquired:

"Do you see it yet?" 17

"No," I replied, "I am certain I do not, but I see how little I saw 18 before."

"That is next best," said he, earnestly, "but I won't hear you now; 19 put away your fish and go home; perhaps you will be ready with a better answer in the morning. I will examine you before you look at the fish."

This was disconcerting. Not only must I think of my fish all night, 20 studying, without the object before me, what this unknown but most visible feature might be; but also, without reviewing my discoveries, I must give an exact account of them the next day. I had a bad memory; so I walked home by Charles River in a distracted state, with my two perplexities.

The cordial greeting from the Professor the next morning was reas- 21 suring; here was a man who seemed to be quite as anxious as I that I should see for myself what he saw.

"Do you perhaps mean," I asked, "that the fish has symmetrical 22 sides with paired organs?"

His thoroughly pleased "Of course! of course!" repaid the wakeful 23 hours of the previous night. After he had discoursed most happily and enthusiastically—as he always did—upon the importance of this point, I ventured to ask what I should do next.

"Oh, look at your fish!" he said, and left me again to my own 24 devices. In a little more than an hour he returned, and heard my new catalogue.

"That is good, that is good!" he repeated; "but that is not all; go 25 on"; and so for three long days he placed that fish before my eyes, for-bidding me to look at anything else, or to use any artificial aid. "Look, look, look," was his repeated injunction.

This was the best entomological lesson I ever had—a lesson whose 26 influence has extended to the details of every subsequent study; a legacy the Professor has left to me, as he has left it to many others, of inestimable value, which we could not buy, with which we cannot part.

A year afterward, some of us were amusing ourselves with chalking   27
outlandish beasts on the Museum blackboard. We drew prancing star-fishes; frogs in mortal combat; hydra-headed worms; stately crawfishes, standing on their tails, bearing aloft umbrellas; and grotesque fishes with gaping mouths and staring eyes. The Professor came in shortly after, and was as amused as any at our experiments. He looked at the fishes.

"Haemulons, every one of them," he said; "Mr. ——— drew them."   28

True; and to this day, if I attempt a fish, I can draw nothing but   29
haemulons.

The fourth day, a second fish of the same group was placed beside   30
the first, and I was bidden to point out the resemblances and differences between the two; another and another followed, until the entire family lay before me, and a whole legion of jars covered the table and surrounding shelves; the odor had become a pleasant perfume; and even now, the sight of an old, six-inch, worm-eaten cork brings fragrant memories.

The whole group of haemulons was thus brought in review; and,   31
whether engaged upon the dissection of the internal organs, the preparation and examination of the bony framework, or the description of the various parts, Agassiz's training in the method of observing facts and their orderly arrangement was ever accompanied by the urgent exhortation not to be content with them.

"Facts are stupid things," he would say, "until brought into con-   32
nection with some general law."

At the end of eight months, it was almost with reluctance that I   33
left these friends and turned to insects; but what I had gained by this outside experience has been of greater value than years of later investigation in my favorite groups.

Questions for Study and Discussion

1. What important lesson does Scudder learn from his experience with Professor Agassiz? Where is the lesson referred to in the essay?

2. Briefly describe Professor Agassiz's teaching technique or method. What about his style made it effective with Scudder? Would it be as effective today? Explain.

3. How much time did Scudder spend studying haemulons? Was it necessary to spend this amount of time? Could the process have been speeded up with the use of lectures and/or textbooks? Explain.

4. How did Scudder happen to draw the fish? How did his drawing the fish

help him better to understand or know the fish? What does Agassiz mean when he says "a pencil is one of the best of eyes"?

5. What is Scudder's diction indicates his attitude toward the experience? What in Scudder's style and diction show that this essay was written in the nineteenth century and not the twentieth?

6. What did Agassiz mean when he said, "Facts are stupid things until brought into connection with some general law"?

Writing Topics

1. Using Scudder's essay as a model, write about a teacher who had a significant impact or influence on you and your education. What was there in the way this particular teacher approached learning that has stayed with you?

2. Professor Agassiz's comment "a pencil is one of the best of eyes" has been echoed by many writers over the years. For example, Anne Morrow Lindbergh has said "I think best with a pencil in my hand." What for you is the relationship between writing, thinking, and learning? Does your understanding of a subject increase when you write about it? Do you see relationships or connections that you didn't see when reading and talking about a subject?

3. In education, how important do you think it is to find good answers to other people's questions, and how important to learn to ask good questions yourself? Where has the emphasis been in your education so far? Can good question-asking be taught and learned? If so, how? If not, why not?

GARY PAVELA

Gary Pavela is a lawyer and the director of judicial programs at the College Park campus of the University of Maryland. The University of Maryland, like other college campuses across the country, was troubled by an increasing incidence of academic dishonesty, and decided to do something about it. In "Cheating on the Campus: Who's Really to Blame?" Pavela gives some historical perspective on the problem and some suggestions for combating cheating based on the program that his institution developed. His essay appeared in the *Chronicle of Higher Education* on February 9, 1981. The *Chronicle* is a weekly publication aimed at college and university faculty and administration.

Cheating on the Campus: Who's Really to Blame?

A faculty member generated national publicity for the University of Maryland last year by apprehending several students who had taken examinations for others. The story that was not adequately told, however, was that lethargy and confusion among many university administrators and faculty members were major contributors to problems of academic dishonesty that were being blamed exclusively on the deficient moral standards of our students.

Academic dishonesty is nothing new. In 1930, F. W. Parr observed in the *Journal of Higher Education* that more than 40 per cent of students were "likely to be dishonest in the college classroom." Similar warnings were issued in subsequent decades, including William Bower's widely publicized report in 1964, which contained the "alarming finding" that "at least half the students in the [nationwide] sample have engaged in some form of academic dishonesty." In short, the willingness of students to engage in academic dishonesty seems to have remained relatively constant over the years, partly because, as Mr. Parr wrote, "any individual will or could be made to deviate from what is considered 'proper' conduct if confronted with a sufficiently potent incentive."

The incentives to engage in academic dishonesty on our campus included a lack of attention to even rudimentary precautions in the preparation and proctoring of examinations, vague and cumbersome policies and procedures that discouraged faculty members from reporting cases, and lenient penalties that suggested to the campus community that academic dishonesty was not regarded as a serious offense. The consequences were predictable. Students systematically stole and distributed examinations, forged dozens of "grade change" forms and related documents, infiltrated an administrative office (where over 40 grades for the members of a campus fraternity were falsified), and engaged in open and rampant cheating during examinations in several large lecture courses.

Moral condemnation and sociological generalizations were not suf- 4 ficient responses to the serious incidents we were encountering. What was also needed was careful attention to the ways in which our own policies and procedures were compounding the problem of academic dishonesty on the campus. Some of our efforts in this direction have progressed to the point that we can share a few suggestions with others:

Develop a definition of "academic dishonesty." It is difficult to dis- 5 courage academic dishonesty effectively if students and faculty members don't know what the term means. At Maryland, for example, we simply had prohibited all "academic irregularities," which, if taken literally, could have included chewing gum in class. As a result, we frequently wasted a considerable amount of energy in protracted and frustrating debates about whether or not academic dishonesty included negligent as well as intentional acts, or whether or not it was improper to submit portions of the same academic work in more than one class. The board of regents recently resolved these and several other dilemmas by adopting a document that divides academic dishonesty into four categories: "cheating," "fabrication," "facilitating academic dishonesty," and "plagiarism," with specific definitions for each.

Reaffirm the importance of academic integrity. Academic dishonesty 6 has had relatively strong peer support and acceptance among some students, partly because we did not make a serious effort to explain why such behavior is contemptible. It is imperative to remind ourselves and our students that the university is dedicated to learning and that academic dishonesty undermines the very foundation of that enterprise. Furthermore, academic dishonesty deceives those who may eventually depend upon our knowledge and integrity, even to the point of jeopardizing their lives or property. A recent study reported in the *Journal of Medical Education*, for example, found a "positive correlation between cheating in school and cheating in patient care" by young physicians.

Reduce temptation. We normally recognize that certain forms of neg- 7 ligence may tempt otherwise decent people to be dishonest. Why is it, then, when we hear of students cheating in insufficiently proctored examinations, or misusing official forms left carelessly outside administrative offices, that we are so inclined to make pronouncements about the decadence of youth and the decline of Western civilization? Instead, we should review the procedures followed by administrators and faculty members and eliminate those that encourage academic dishonesty.

Eliminate proceduralism. Many administrators, paralyzed by a mis- 8 conception of "due process," have erroneously assumed that full adversarial hearing, technical rules of evidence, multiple appeals, and the like are required "by law" in student disciplinary cases. Not surprisingly, faculty members are reluctant to involve themselves in such proceedings. As a consequence, some of them ignore academic dishonesty altogether, thereby putting honest students at a competitive disadvantage. Others simply lower the grades of students whom they presume guilty of cheating or plagiarism. Both practices injure students without any due process at all, and prevent the university from identifying repeat offenders.

Colleges and universities across the country are now revising dis- 9 ciplinary regulations. It is important to develop equitable procedures that are compatible with the needs of the academic community. For example, the new *Code of Student Conduct* at our institution provides for streamlined "disciplinary conferences" rather than formal hearings in most cases.

Impose strict penalties. Last year's report by the Carnegie Council on 10 Policy Studies in Higher Education contained the observation that "colleges and their faculties have generally tended to be lax in punishing students for academic dishonesty." The most common example, on our campus and elsewhere, has been the practice of simply giving the offending student a failing grade. Such a policy misleads other schools to which the student might apply, and does not deter those students already in danger of failing the course. Instead, if clear definitions of academic dishonesty have been developed, and if a reasonable effort has been made to inform students that such offenses are treated seriously, the appropriate punishment for a willful offense should be some form of separation from the university, a permanent notation on the student's official transcript, or both. It is often painful to impose such sanctions in a specific case, but it is imperative to do so if we wish to eliminate a campus climate that not only is tolerant of academic dishonesty, but may also have the perverse effect of encouraging students who did not cheat at home or in secondary school to adopt such practices in college and throughout their lives.

One of the journalists who visited our campus stopped taking notes 11 when I shifted the topic of our conversation from the moral values of contemporary students to the shortcomings at the university. The article that he later wrote was not inaccurate, but his primary focus upon student attitudes did not encompass the full scope of the problem. Academic dishonesty does indeed reveal the moral deficiencies of those students who engage in it. Responsibility also lies, however, with administrators and faculty members who knowingly tolerate conditions that would allow academic dishonesty to flourish in any generation of students.

Questions for Study and Discussion

1. What is Pavela's thesis, and where is it stated?

2. What measures does Pavela suggest for colleges and universities to take in order to try to eliminate the conditions that are favorable to cheating? Are these conditions presented randomly or do you discern an order in Pavela's solutions? Explain.

3. How does Pavela answer the question raised in his title?

4. What does Pavela find wrong with lenient penalties for academic dishonesty? Do you agree with his arguments?

5. Pavela's essay was published in the *Journal of Higher Education*. In what ways is his argument particularly suited to this publication?

6. Reread Pavela's final paragraph. Is it a fitting conclusion to his essay? Explain.

Writing Topics

1. In his essay Pavela tells college administrators and teachers what they can do to attack the problem of academic dishonesty. Write an essay in which you offer suggestions for how students can reduce the temptation and incidence of academic dishonesty.

2. Pavela believes that "it is difficult to discourage academic dishonesty effectively if students and faculty members don't know what the term means." In an essay develop your own definition of academic dishonesty, using examples as you see fit. You may want to consider the University of Maryland's four categories of dishonesty in writing your definition.

3. Research the question of academic dishonesty on your campus, and report your findings in an essay.

LANGSTON HUGHES

Born in Joplin, Missouri, Langston Hughes (1902–1967) wrote poetry, fiction, and drama and regularly contributed a column to the *New York Post*. An important figure in the Harlem Renaissance, he is best known for *Weary Blues*, *The Negro Mother*, *Shakespeare in Harlem*, and *Ask Your Mama*, volumes of poetry which reflect his racial pride, his familiarity with the traditions of black people, and his knowledge of jazz rhythms. The speaker of "Theme for English B" is a student at Columbia University, where Hughes had enrolled for a year in 1921. The poem, though quite short, embodies the two great themes of Hughes's work and indeed of the Harlem Renaissance: the celebration of black culture and the demand for equal treatment and respect.

Theme for English B

The instructor said,

> *Go home and write*
> *a page tonight.*
> *And let that page come out of you—*
> *Then, it will be true.*   5

I wonder if it's that simple?
I am twenty-two, colored, born in Winston-Salem.
I went to school there, then Durham, then here
to this college on the hill above Harlem.[1]
I am the only colored student in my class.   10

The steps from the hill lead down into Harlem,
through a park, then I cross St. Nicholas,
Eighth Avenue, Seventh, and I come to the Y,
the Harlem Branch Y, where I take the elevator
up to my room, sit down, and write this page: 15

It's not easy to know what is true for you or me
at twenty-two, my age. But I guess I'm what
I feel and see and hear, Harlem, I hear you:
hear you, hear me—we two—you, me, talk on this page.
(I hear New York, too.) Me—who?   20

---

[1]Refers to Columbia University, which is located next to Harlem.

Well, I like to eat, sleep, drink, and be in love.
I like to work, read, learn, and understand life.
I like a pipe for a Christmas present,
or records—Bessie,[2] bop, or Bach.
I guess being colored doesn't make me *not* like   25
the same things other folks like who are other races.
So will my page be colored that I write?
Being me, it will not be white.
But it will be
a part of you, instructor.   30
You are white—
yet a part of me, as I am a part of you.
That's American.
Sometimes perhaps you don't want to be a part of me.
Nor do I often want to be a part of you.   35
But we are, that's true!
As I learn from you,
I guess you learn from me—
although you're older—and white—
and somewhat more free.   40

This is my page for English B.

Questions for Study and Discussion

1. What does the instructor mean when he tells the student that the writing should "come out of you"? Why would it then be "true"?

2. Is the student in the poem Hughes himself? Why, or why not?

3. What is the significance of the student's speaking of Columbia as "on the hill above Harlem"?

4. The student says that he is a part of his instructor, and that his instructor is a part of him. What does he mean? Are we all part of each other? If so, in what way? If not, why not?

5. The student ends by saying, "This is my page for English B." Is the "page" what the instructor asked for or wanted? Why, or why not?

[2]Bessie Smith (1898?–1937), American blues singer, considered by many critics to be the greatest jazz singer of her time.

Writing Topics

1. The poem says, "As I learn from you, / I guess you learn from me." What do you think teachers learn from their students, if anything? What should they learn? Write an essay in which you describe what for you is the ideal student-teacher relationship.

2. What constitutes a good writing assignment? Compose one or two essay assignments for your class, keeping in mind the purpose of the course and other students' backgrounds and interests.

JOYCE CAROL OATES

Like many a writer, Joyce Carol Oates draws on her own observations and experiences for her fiction. Born in 1938 to a Roman Catholic family in Lockport, New York, she earned a bachelor's degree from Syracuse University and a master of arts degree in English from the University of Wisconsin. She has taught English, first at the University of Detroit, and since 1967 at the University of Windsor in Ontario, Canada. A prodigious and versatile writer, Oates has published thirteen novels, including *Them* (1969), *Bellefleur* (1980), and *Angel of Light* (1981); dozens of short stories; eight books of poems; six plays; and four volumes of literary criticism. "In the Region of Ice" is from her third collection of stories, *The Wheel of Love* (1971). In it Sister Irene, a nun and a professor of literature at a Jesuit university, struggles to be true to her vocation when she is confronted by a searching and troubled student.

In the Region of Ice

Sister Irene was a tall, deft woman in her early thirties. What one could see of her face made a striking impression — serious, hard gray eyes, a long slender nose, a face waxen with thought. Seen at the right time, from the right angle, she was almost handsome. In her past teaching positions she had drawn a little upon the fact of her being young and brilliant and also a nun, but she was beginning to grow out of that.

This was a new university and an entirely new world. She had heard—of course it was true—that the Jesuit administration of this school had hired her at the last moment to save money and to head off the appointment of a man of dubious religious commitment. She had prayed for the necessary energy to get her through this first semester. She had no trouble with teaching itself; once she stood before a classroom she felt herself capable of anything. It was the world immediately outside the classroom that confused and alarmed her, though she let none of this show—the cynicism of her colleagues, the indifference of many of the students, and, above all, the looks she got that told her nothing much would be expected of her because she was a nun. This took energy, strength. At times she had the idea that she was on trial and that the excuses she made to herself about her discomfort were only the common excuses made by guilty people. But in front of a class she had no time to worry about herself or the conflicts in her mind. She became, once and for all, a figure existing only for the benefit of others, an instrument by which facts were communicated.

315

About two weeks after the semester began, Sister Irene noticed a   3
new student in her class. He was slight and fair-haired, and his face was
blank, but not blank by accident, blank on purpose, suppressed and
restricted into a dumbness that looked hysterical. She was prepared for
him before he raised his hand, and when she saw his arm jerk, as if he
had at last lost control of it, she nodded to him without hesitation.

"Sister, how can this be reconciled with Shakespeare's vision in   4
Hamlet? How can these opposing views be in the same mind?"

Students glanced at him, mildly surprised. He did not belong in   5
the class, and this was mysterious, but his manner was urgent and blind.

"There is no need to reconcile opposing views," Sister Irene said,   6
leaning forward against the podium. "In one play Shakespeare suggests
one vision, in another play another; the plays are not simultaneous creations, and even if they were, we never demand a logical—"

"We must demand a logical consistency," the young man said. "The   7
idea of education is itself predicated upon consistency, order, sanity—"

He had interrupted her, and she hardened her face against him—   8
for his sake, not her own, since she did not really care. But he noticed
nothing. "Please see me after class," she said.

After class the young man hurried up to her.   9

"Sister Irene, I hope you didn't mind my visiting today. I'd heard   10
some things, interesting things," he said. He stared at her, and something
in her face allowed him to smile. "I . . . could we talk in your office?
Do you have time?"

They walked down to her office. Sister Irene sat at her desk, and   11
the young man sat facing her; for a moment they were self-conscious and
silent.

"Well, I suppose you know—I'm a Jew," he said.   12

Sister Irene stared at him. "Yes?" she said.   13

"What am I doing at a Catholic university, huh?" He grinned.   14
"That's what you want to know."

She made a vague movement of her hand to show that she had no   15
thoughts on this, nothing at all, but he seemed not to catch it. He was
sitting on the edge of the straight-backed chair. She saw that he was
young but did not really look young. There were harsh lines on either
side of his mouth, as if he had misused that youthful mouth somehow.
His skin was almost as pale as hers, his eyes were dark and not quite in
focus. He looked at her and through her and around her, as his voice
surrounded them both. His voice was a little shrill at times.

"Listen, I did the right thing today—visiting your class! God, what   16
a lucky accident it was; some jerk mentioned you, said you were a *good*
teacher—I thought, what a laugh! These people know about good teach-

ers here? But yes, listen, yes, I'm not kidding—you are good. I mean that."

Sister Irene frowned. "I don't quite understand what all this means." 17

He smiled and waved aside her formality, as if he knew better. 18
"Listen, I got my B.A. at Columbia, then I came back here to this crappy city. I mean, I did it on purpose, I wanted to come back. I wanted to. I have my reasons for doing things. I'm on a three-thousand-dollar fellowship," he said, and waited for that to impress her. "You know, I could have gone almost anywhere with that fellowship, and I came back home here—my home's in the city—and enrolled here. This was last year. This is my second year. I'm working on a thesis, I mean I was, my master's thesis—but the hell with that. What I want to ask you is this: Can I enroll in your class, is it too late? We have to get special permission if we're late."

Sister Irene felt something nudging her, some uneasiness in him 19
that was pleading with her not to be offended by his abrupt, familiar manner. He seemed to be promising another self, a better self, as if his fair, childish, almost cherubic face were doing tricks to distract her from what his words said.

"Are you in English studies?" she asked. 20

"I was in history. Listen," he said, and his mouth did something 21
odd, drawing itself down into a smile that made the lines about it deepen like knives, "listen, they kicked me out."

He sat back, watching her. He crossed his legs. He took out a 22
package of cigarettes and offered her one. Sister Irene shook her head, staring at his hands. They were small and stubby and might have belonged to a ten-year-old, and the nails were a strange near-violet color. It took him awhile to extract a cigarette.

"Yeah, kicked me out. What do you think of that?" 23

"I don't understand." 24

"My master's thesis was coming along beautifully, and then this 25
bastard—I mean, excuse me, this professor, I won't pollute your office with his name—he started making criticisms, he said some things were unacceptable, he—" The boy leaned forward and hunched his narrow shoulders in a parody of secrecy. "We had an argument. I told him some frank things, things only a broad-minded person could hear about himself. That takes courage, right? He didn't have it! He kicked me out of the master's program, so now I'm coming into English. Literature is greater than history; European history is one big pile of garbage. Sky-high. Filth and rotting corpses, right? Aristotle says that poetry is higher than history; he's right; in your class today I suddenly realized that this is my field, Shakespeare, only Shakespeare is—"

Sister Irene guessed that he was going to say that only Shake- 26
speare was equal to him, and she caught the moment of recognition
and hesitation, the half-raised arm, the keen, frowning forehead, the
narrowed eyes; then he thought better of it and did not end the sentence. "The students in your class are mainly negligible, I can tell you
that. You're new here, and I've been here a year—I would have finished my studies last year but my father got sick, he was hospitalized, I
couldn't take exams and it was a mess—but I'll make it through English
in one year or drop dead. I can do it, I can do anything. I'll take six
courses at once—" He broke off, breathless. Sister Irene tried to smile.
"All right then, it's settled? You'll let me in? Have I missed anything
so far?"

He had no idea of the rudeness of his question. Sister Irene, feeling 27
suddenly exhausted, said, "I'll give you a syllabus of the course."

"Fine! Wonderful!" 28

He got to his feet eagerly. He looked through the schedule, mut- 29
tering to himself, making favorable noises. It struck Sister Irene that she
was making a mistake to let him in. There were these moments when
one had to make an intelligent decision. . . . But she was sympathetic
with him, yes. She was sympathetic with something about him.

She found out his name the next day: Allen Weinstein. 30

After this she came to her Shakespeare class with a sense of ex- 31
citement. It became clear to her at once that Weinstein was the most
intelligent student in the class. Until he had enrolled, she had not understood what was lacking, a mind that could appreciate her own. Within
a week his jagged, protean mind had alienated the other students, and
though he sat in the center of the class, he seemed totally alone, encased
by a miniature world of his own. When he spoke of the "frenetic humanism of the High Renaissance," Sister Irene dreaded the raised eyebrows and mocking smiles of the other students, who no longer bothered
to look at Weinstein. She wanted to defend him, but she never did,
because there was something rude and dismal about his knowledge; he
used it like a weapon, talking passionately of Nietzsche and Goethe and
Freud until Sister Irene would be forced to close discussion.

In meditation, alone, she often thought of him. When she tried to 32
talk about him to a young nun, Sister Carlotta, everything sounded gross.
"But no, he's an excellent student," she insisted. "I'm very grateful to
have him in class. It's just that . . . he thinks ideas are real." Sister
Carlotta, who loved literature also, had been forced to teach grade-school
arithmetic for the last four years. That might have been why she said, a
little sharply, "You don't think ideas are real?"

Sister Irene acquiesced with a smile, but of course she did not think   33
so: only reality is real.

When Weinstein did not show up for class on the day the first   34
paper was due, Sister Irene's heart sank, and the sensation was somehow
a familiar one. She began to lecture and kept waiting for the door to
open and for him to hurry noisily back to his seat, grinning an apology
toward her—but nothing happened.

If she had been deceived by him, she made herself think angrily,   35
it was as a teacher and not as a woman. He had promised her nothing.

Weinstein appeared the next day near the steps of the liberal arts   36
building. She heard someone running behind her, a breathless exclamation: "Sister Irene!" She turned and saw him, panting and grinning
in embarrassment. He wore a dark-blue suit with a necktie, and he looked,
despite his childish face, like a little old man; there was something oddly
precarious and fragile about him. "Sister Irene, I owe you an apology,
right?" He raised his eyebrows and smiled a sad, forlorn, yet irritatingly
conspiratorial smile. "The first paper—not in on time, and I know what
your rules are. . . . You won't accept late papers, I know—that's good
discipline, I'll do that when I teach too. But, unavoidably, I was unable
to come to school yesterday. There are many—many—" He gulped for
breath, and Sister Irene had the startling sense of seeing the real Weinstein stare out at her, a terrified prisoner behind the confident voice.
"There are many complications in family life. Perhaps you are unaware—
I mean—"

She did not like him, but she felt this sympathy, something tugging   37
and nagging at her the way her parents had competed for her love so
many years before. They had been whining, weak people, and out of
their wet need for affection, the girl she had been (her name was Yvonne)
had emerged stronger than either of them, contemptuous of tears because
she had seen so many. But Weinstein was different; he was not simply
weak—perhaps he was not weak at all—but his strength was confused
and hysterical. She felt her customary rigidity as a teacher begin to falter.
"You may turn your paper in today if you have it," she said, frowning.

Weinstein's mouth jerked into an incredulous grin. "Wonderful!   38
Marvelous!" he said. "You are very understanding, Sister Irene, I must
say. I must say . . . I didn't expect, really . . ." He was fumbling in a
shabby old briefcase for the paper. Sister Irene waited. She was prepared
for another of his excuses, certain that he did not have the paper, when
he suddenly straightened up and handed her something. "Here! I took
the liberty of writing thirty pages instead of just fifteen," he said. He was
obviously quite excited; his cheeks were mottled pink and white. "You
may disagree violently with my interpretation—I expect you to, in fact

I'm counting on it—but let me warn you, I have the exact proof, right here in the play itself!" He was thumping at a book, his voice growing louder and shriller. Sister Irene, startled, wanted to put her hand over his mouth and soothe him.

"Look," he said breathlessly, "may I talk with you? I have a class 39
now I hate, I loathe, I can't bear to sit through! Can I talk with you instead?"

Because she was nervous, she stared at the title page of the paper: 40
" 'Erotic Melodies in *Romeo and Juliet*' by Allen Weinstein, Jr."

"All right?" he said. "Can we walk around here? Is it all right? I've 41
been anxious to talk with you about some things you said in class."

She was reluctant, but he seemed not to notice. They walked slowly 42
along the shaped campus paths. Weinstein did all the talking, of course, and Sister Irene recognized nothing in his cascade of words that she had mentioned in class. "The humanist must be committed to the totality of life," he said passionately. "This is the failing one finds everywhere in the academic world! I found it in New York and I found it here and I'm no ingénu, I don't go around with my mouth hanging open—I'm experienced, look, I've been to Europe, I've lived in Rome! I went everywhere in Europe except Germany, I don't talk about Germany . . . Sister Irene, think of the significant men in the last century, the men who've changed the world! Jews, right? Marx, Freud, Einstein! Not that I believe Marx, Marx is a madman . . . and Freud, no, my sympathies are with spiritual humanism. I believe that the Jewish race is the exclusive . . . the exclusive, what's the word, the exclusive means by which humanism will be extended . . . Humanism begins by excluding the Jew, and now," he said with a high, surprised laugh, "the Jew will perfect it. After the Nazis, only the Jew is authorized to understand humanism, its limitations and its possibilities. So, I say that the humanist is committed to life in its totality and not just to his profession! The religious person is totally religious, he is his religion! What else? I recognize in you a humanist and a religious person—"

But he did not seem to be talking to her or even looking at her. 43

"Here, read this," he said. "I wrote it last night." It was a long 44
free-verse poem, typed on a typewriter whose ribbon was worn out.

"There's this trouble with my father, a wonderful man, a lovely 45
man, but his health—his strength is fading, do you see? What must it be to him to see his son growing up? I mean, I'm a man now, he's getting old, weak, his health is bad—it's hell, right? I sympathize with him. I'd do anything for him, I'd cut open my veins, anything for a father—right? That's why I wasn't in school yesterday," he said, and his voice dropped for the last sentence, as if he had been dragged back to earth by a fact.

Sister Irene tried to read the poem, then pretended to read it. A 46
jumble of words dealing with "life" and "death" and "darkness" and
"love." "What do you think?" Weinstein said nervously, trying to read
it over her shoulder and crowding against her.

"It's very . . . passionate," Sister Irene said. 47

This was the right comment; he took the poem back from her in 48
silence, his face flushed with excitement. "Here, at this school, I have
few people to talk with. I haven't shown anyone else that poem." He
looked at her with his dark, intense eyes, and Sister Irene felt them focus
upon her. She was terrified at what he was trying to do—he was trying
to force her into a human relationship.

"Thank you for your paper," she said, turning away. 49

When he came the next day, ten minutes late, he was haughty and 50
disdainful. He had nothing to say and sat with his arms folded. Sister
Irene took back with her to the convent a feeling of betrayal and confusion. She had been hurt. It was absurd, and yet—She spent too much
time thinking about him, as if he were somehow a kind of crystallization
of her own loneliness; but she had no right to think so much of him.
She did not want to think of him or of her loneliness. But Weinstein
did so much more than think of his predicament: he embodied it, he
acted it out, and that was perhaps why he fascinated her. It was as if he
were doing a dance for her, a dance of shame and agony and delight,
and so long as he did it, she was safe. She felt embarrassment for him,
but also anxiety; she wanted to protect him. When the dean of the
graduate school questioned her about Weinstein's work, she insisted that
he was an "excellent" student, though she knew the dean had not wanted
to hear that.

She prayed for guidance, she spent hours on her devotions, she was 51
closer to her vocation than she had been for some years. Life at the
convent became tinged with unreality, a misty distortion that took its
tone from the glowering skies of the city at night, identical smokestacks
ranged against the clouds and giving to the sky the excrement of the
populated and successful earth. This city was not her city, this world was
not her world. She felt no pride in knowing this, it was a fact. The little
convent was not like an island in the center of this noisy world, but
rather a kind of hole or crevice the world did not bother with, something
of no interest. The convent's rhythm of life had nothing to do with the
world's rhythm, it did not violate or alarm it in any way. Sister Irene
tried to draw together the fragments of her life and synthesize them
somehow in her vocation as a nun: she was a nun, she was recognized
as a nun and had given herself happily to that life, she had a name, a
place, she had dedicated her superior intelligence to the Church, she

worked without pay and without expecting gratitude, she had given up pride, she did not think of herself but only of her work and her vocation, she did not think of anything external to these, she saturated herself daily in the knowledge that she was involved in the mystery of Christianity.

A daily terror attended this knowledge, however, for she sensed herself being drawn by that student, that Jewish boy, into a relationship she was not ready for. She wanted to cry out in fear that she was being forced into the role of a Christian, and what did that mean? What could her studies tell her? What could the other nuns tell her? She was alone, no one could help; he was making her into a Christian, and to her that was a mystery, a thing of terror, something others slipped on the way they slipped on their clothes, casually and thoughtlessly, but to her a magnificent and terrifying wonder.

For days she carried Weinstein's paper, marked A, around with her; he did not come to class. One day she checked with the graduate office and was told that Weinstein had called in to say his father was ill and that he would not be able to attend classes for a while. "He's strange, I remember him," the secretary said. "He missed all his exams last spring and made a lot of trouble. He was in and out of here every day."

So there was no more of Weinstein for a while, and Sister Irene stopped expecting him to hurry into class. Then, one morning, she found a letter from him in her mailbox.

He had printed it in black ink, very carefully, as if he had not trusted handwriting. The return address was in bold letters that, like his voice, tried to grab onto her: Birchcrest Manor. Somewhere north of the city. "Dear Sister Irene," the block letters said, "I am doing well here and have time for reading and relaxing. The Manor is delightful. My doctor here is an excellent, intelligent man who has time for me, unlike my former doctor. If you have time, you might drop in on my father, who worries about me too much I think, and explain to him what my condition is. He doesn't seem to understand. I feel about this new life the way that boy, what's his name, in *Measure for Measure*, feels about the prospects of a different life; you remember what he says to his sister when she visits him in prison, how he is looking forward to an escape into another world. Perhaps you could *explain* this to my father and he would stop worrying." The letter ended with his father's name and address, in letters that were just a little too big. Sister Irene, walking slowly down the corridor as she read the letter, felt her eyes cloud over with tears. She was cold with fear, it was something she had never experienced before. She knew what Weinstein was trying to tell her, and the desperation of his attempt made it all the more pathetic; he did not deserve this, why did God allow him to suffer so?

She read through Claudio's speech to his sister, in *Measure for* 56
Measure:

> Ay, but to die, and go we know not where;
> To lie in cold obstruction and to rot;
> This sensible warm motion to become
> A kneaded clod; and the delighted spirit
> To bathe in fiery floods, or to reside
> In thrilling region of thick-ribbed ice,
> To be imprison'd in the viewless winds
> And blown with restless violence round about
> The pendent world; or to be worse than worst
> Of those that lawless and incertain thought
> Imagines howling! 'Tis too horrible!
> The weariest and most loathed worldly life
> That age, ache, penury, and imprisonment
> Can lay on nature is a paradise
> To what we fear of death.

Sister Irene called the father's number that day. "Allen Weinstein 57
residence; who may I say is calling?" a woman said, bored. "May I speak to Mr. Weinstein? It's urgent—about his son," Sister Irene said. There was a pause at the other end. "You want to talk to his mother, maybe?" the woman said. "His mother? Yes, his mother, then. Please. It's very important."

She talked with this strange, unsuspected woman, a disembodied 58
voice that suggested absolutely no face, and insisted upon going over that afternoon. The woman was nervous, but Sister Irene, who was a university professor, after all, knew enough to hide her own nervousness. She kept waiting for the woman to say, "Yes, Allen has mentioned you . . ." but nothing happened.

She persuaded Sister Carlotta to ride over with her. This urgency 59
of hers was something they were all amazed by. They hadn't suspected that the set of her gray eyes could change to this blurred, distracted alarm, this sense of mission that seemed to have come to her from nowhere. Sister Irene drove across the city in the late afternoon traffic, with the high whining noises from residential streets where trees were being sawed down in pieces. She understood now the secret, sweet wildness that Christ must have felt, giving himself for man, dying for the billions of men who would never know of him and never understand the sacrifice. For the first time she approached the realization of that great act. In her troubled mind the city traffic was jumbled and yet oddly

coherent, an image of the world that was always out of joint with what was happening in it, its inner history struggling with its external spectacle. This sacrifice of Christ's, so mysterious and legendary now, almost lost in time—it was that by which Christ transcended both God and man at one moment, more than man because of his fate to do what no other man could do, and more than God because no god could suffer as he did. She felt a flicker of something close to madness.

She drove nervously, uncertainly, afraid of missing the street and afraid of finding it too, for while one part of her rushed forward to confront these people who had betrayed their son, another part of her would have liked nothing so much as to be waiting as usual for the summons to dinner, safe in her room. . . . When she found the street and turned onto it, she was in a state of breathless excitement. Here lawns were bright green and marred with only a few leaves, magically clean, and the houses were enormous and pompous, a mixture of styles: ranch houses, colonial houses, French country houses, white-bricked wonders with curving glass and clumps of birch trees somehow encircled by white concrete. Sister Irene stared as if she had blundered into another world. This was a kind of heaven, and she was too shabby for it.

The Weinsteins' house was the strangest one of all: it looked like a small Alpine lodge, with an inverted-V-shaped front entrance. Sister Irene drove up the black-topped driveway and let the car slow to a stop; she told Sister Carlotta she would not be long.

At the door she was met by Weinstein's mother, a small, nervous woman with hands like her son's. "Come in, come in," the woman said. She had once been beautiful, that was clear, but now in missing beauty she was not handsome or even attractive but looked ruined and perplexed, the misshapen swelling of her white-blond professionally set hair like a cap lifting up from her surprised face. "He'll be right in. Allen?" she called, "our visitor is here." They went into the living room. There was a grand piano at one end and an organ at the other. In between were scatterings of brilliant modern furniture in conversational groups, and several puffed-up white rugs on the polished floor. Sister Irene could not stop shivering.

"Professor, it's so strange, but let me say when the phone rang I had a feeling—I had a feeling," the woman said, with damp eyes. Sister Irene sat, and the woman hovered about her. "Should I call you Professor? We don't . . . you know . . . we don't understand the technicalities that go with—Allen, my son, wanted to go here to the Catholic school; I told my husband why not? Why fight? It's the thing these days, they do anything they want for knowledge. And he had to come home, you know. He couldn't take care of himself in New York, that was the beginning of the trouble. . . . Should I call you Professor?"

"You can call me Sister Irene." 64

"Sister Irene?" the woman said, touching her throat in awe, as if 65 something intimate and unexpected had happened.

Then Weinstein's father appeared, hurrying. He took long, impa- 66 tient strides. Sister Irene stared at him and in that instant doubted every- thing—he was in his fifties, a tall, sharply handsome man, heavy but not fat, holding his shoulders back with what looked like an effort, but hold- ing them back just the same. He wore a dark suit and his face was flushed, as if he had run a long distance.

"Now," he said, coming to Sister Irene and with a precise wave of 67 his hand motioning his wife off, "now, let's straighten this out. A lot of confusion over that kid, eh?" He pulled a chair over, scraping it across a rug and pulling one corner over, so that its brown underside was ex- posed. "I came home early just for this, Libby phoned me. Sister, you got a letter from him, right?"

The wife looked at Sister Irene over her husband's head as if trying 68 somehow to coach her, knowing that this man was so loud and impatient that no one could remember anything in his presence.

"A letter—yes today—" 69

"He says what in it? You got the letter, eh? Can I see it?" 70

She gave it to him and wanted to explain, but he silenced her with 71 a flick of his hand. He read through the letter so quickly that Sister Irene thought perhaps he was trying to impress her with his skill at reading. "So?" he said, raising his eyes, smiling, "so what is this? He's happy out there, he says. He doesn't communicate with us any more, but he writes to you and says he's happy—what's that? I mean, what the hell is that?"

"But he isn't happy. He wants to come home," Sister Irene said. 72 It was so important that she make him understand that she could not trust her voice; goaded by this man, it might suddenly turn shrill, as his son's did. "Someone must read their letters before they're mailed, so he tried to tell me something by making an allusion to—"

"What?" 73

"—an allusion to a play, so that I would know. He may be thinking 74 suicide, he must be very unhappy—"

She ran out of breath. Weinstein's mother had begun to cry, but 75 the father was shaking his head jerkily back and forth. "Forgive me, Sister, but it's a lot of crap, he needs the hospital, he needs help—right? It costs me fifty a day out there, and they've got the best place in the state, I figure it's worth it. He needs help, that kid, what do I care if he's unhappy? He's unbalanced!" he said angrily. "You want us to get him out again? We argued with the judge for two hours to get him in, an acquaintance of mine. Look, he can't control himself—he was smashing things here, he was hysterical. They need help, lady, and you do something about it fast! You do something! We made up our minds to do something and we did it! This letter—what the hell is this letter? He never talked like that to us!"

"But he means the opposite of what he says—"   76

"Then he's crazy! I'm the first to admit it." He was perspiring and   77
his face had darkened. "I've got no pride left this late. He's a little
bastard, you want to know? He calls me names, he's filthy, got a filthy
mouth—that's being smart, huh? They give him a big scholarship for his
filthy mouth? I went to college too, and I got out and knew something,
and I for Christ's sake did something with it; my wife is an intelligent
woman, a learned woman, would you guess she does book reviews for
the little newspaper out here? Intelligent isn't crazy—crazy isn't intelligent. Maybe for you at the school he writes nice papers and gets an A,
but out here, around the house, he can't control himself, and we got
him committed!"

"But—"   78

"We're fixing him up, don't worry about it!" He turned to his wife.   79
"Libby, get out of here, I mean it. I'm sorry, but get out of here, you're
making a fool of yourself, go stand in the kitchen or something, you and
the goddamn maid can cry on each other's shoulders. That one in the
kitchen is nuts too, they're all nuts. Sister," he said, his voice lowering,
"I thank you immensely for coming out here. This is wonderful, your
interest in my son. And I see he admires you—that letter there. But
what about that letter? If he did want to get out, which I don't admit—
he was willing to be committed, in the end he said okay himself—if he
wanted out I wouldn't do it. Why? So what if he wants to come back?
The next day he wants something else, what then? He's a sick kid, and
I'm the first to admit it."

Sister Irene felt that sickness spread to her. She stood. The room   80
was so big it seemed it must be a public place; there had been nothing
personal or private about their conversation. Weinstein's mother was
standing by the fireplace, sobbing. The father jumped to his feet and
wiped his forehead in a gesture that was meant to help Sister Irene on
her way out. "God, what a day," he said, his eyes snatching at hers for
understanding, "you know—one of those days all day long? Sister, I thank
you a lot. There should be more people in the world who care about
others, like you. I mean that."

On the way back to the convent, the man's words returned to her,   81
and she could not get control of them; she could not even feel anger.

She had been pressed down, forced back, what could she do? Weinstein might have been watching her somehow from a barred window, and he surely would have understood. The strange idea she had had on the way over, something about understanding Christ, came back to her now and sickened her. But the sickness was small. It could be contained.

About a month after her visit to his father, Weinstein himself showed up. He was dressed in a suit as before, even the necktie was the same. He came right into her office as if he had been pushed and could not stop.

"Sister," he said, and shook her hand. He must have seen fear in her because he smiled ironically. "Look, I'm released. I'm let out of the nut house. Can I sit down?"

He sat. Sister Irene was breathing quickly, as if in the presence of an enemy who does not know he is an enemy.

"So, they finally let me out. I heard what you did. You talked with him, that was all I wanted. You're the only one who gave a damn. Because you're a humanist and a religious person, you respect . . . the individual. Listen," he said, whispering, "it was hell out there! Hell Birchcrest Manor! All fixed up with fancy chairs and *Life* magazines lying around—and what do they do to you? They locked me up, they gave me shock treatments! Shock treatments, how do you like that, it's discredited by everybody now—they're crazy out there themselves, sadists. They locked me up, they gave me hypodermic shots, they didn't treat me like a human being! Do you know what that is," Weinstein demanded savagely, "not to be treated like a human being? They made me an animal—for fifty dollars a day! Dirty filthy swine! Now I'm an outpatient because I stopped swearing at them. I found somebody's bobby pin, and when I wanted to scream I pressed it under my fingernail and it stopped me—the screaming went inside and not out—so they gave me good reports, those sick bastards. Now I'm an outpatient and I can walk along the street and breathe in the same filthy exhaust from the buses like all you normal people! Christ," he said, and threw himself back against the chair.

Sister Irene stared at him. She wanted to take his hand, to make some gesture that would close the aching distance between them. "Mr. Weinstein—"

"Call me Allen!" he said sharply.

"I'm very sorry—I'm terribly sorry—"

"My own parents committed me, but of course they didn't know what it was like. It was hell," he said thickly, "and there isn't any hell except what other people do to you. The psychiatrist out there, the main shrink, he hates Jews too, some of us were positive of that, and he's got

82

83

84

85

86

87

88

89

a bigger nose than I do, a real beak." He made a noise of disgust. "A dirty bastard, a sick, dirty, pathetic bastard—all of them. Anyway, I'm getting out of here, and I came to ask you a favor."

"What do you mean?"　　90

"I'm getting out. I'm leaving. I'm going up to Canada and lose　91 myself. I'll get a job, I'll forget everything, I'll kill myself maybe—what's the difference? Look, can you lend me some money?"

"Money?"　　92

"Just a little! I have to get to the border, I'm going to take a　93 bus."

"But I don't have any money—"　　94

"No money?" He stared at her. "You mean—you don't have any?　95 Sure you have some!"

She stared at him as if he had asked her to do something obscene.　96 Everything was splotched and uncertain before her eyes.

"You must . . . you must go back," she said, "you're making a—"　97

"I'll pay it back. Look, I'll pay it back, can you go to where you　98 live or something and get it? I'm in a hurry. My friends are sons of bitches: one of them pretended he didn't see me yesterday—I stood right in the middle of the sidewalk and yelled at him, I called him some appropriate names! So he didn't see me, huh? You're the only one who understands me, you understand me like a poet, you—"

"I can't help you, I'm sorry—I . . ."　　99

He looked to one side of her and flashed his gaze back, as if he　100 could control it. He seemed to be trying to clear his vision.

"You have the soul of a poet," he whispered, "you're the only one.　101 Everybody else is rotten! Can't you lend me some money, ten dollars maybe? I have three thousand in the bank, and I can't touch it! They take everything away from me, they make me into an animal. . . . You know I'm not an animal, don't you? Don't you?"

"Of course," Sister Irene whispered.　　102

"You could get money. Help me. Give me your hand or something,　103 touch me, help me—please. . . ." He reached for her hand and she drew back. He stared at her and his face seemed about to crumble, like a child's. "I want something from you, but I don't know what—I want something!" he cried. "Something real! I want you to look at me like I was a human being, is that too much to ask? I have a brain, I'm alive, I'm suffering—what does that mean? Does that mean nothing? I want something real and not this phony Christian love garbage—it's all in the books, it isn't personal—I want something real—look. . . ."

He tried to take her hand again, and this time she jerked away.　104 She got to her feet. "Mr. Weinstein," she said, "please—"

"You! You nun!" he said scornfully, his mouth twisted into a mock   105
grin. "You nun! There's nothing under that ugly outfit, right? And you're
not particularly smart even though you think you are; my father has more
brains in his foot than you—"

He got to his feet and kicked the chair.   106

"You bitch!" he cried.   107

She shrank back against her desk as if she thought he might hit   108
her, but he only ran out of the office.

Weinstein: the name was to become disembodied from the figure,   109
as time went on. The semester passed, the autumn drizzle turned into
snow, Sister Irene rode to school in the morning and left in the afternoon, four days a week, anonymous in her black winter cloak, quiet and
stunned. University teaching was an anonymous task, each day disso-
ciated from the rest, with no necessary sense of unity among the teachers:
they came and went separately and might for a year just miss a colleague
who left his office five minutes before they arrived, and it did not matter.

She heard of Weinstein's death, his suicide by drowning, from the   110
English Department secretary, a handsome white-haired woman who kept
a transistor radio on her desk. Sister Irene was not surprised, she had
been thinking of him as dead for months. "They identified him by some
special television way they have now," the secretary said. "They're shipping the body back. It was up in Quebec. . . ."

Sister Irene could feel a part of herself drifting off, lured by the   111
plains of white snow to the north, the quiet, the emptiness, the sweep
of the Great Lakes up to the silence of Canada. But she called that part
of herself back. She could only be one person in her lifetime. That was
the ugly truth, she thought, that she could not really regret Weinstein's
suffering and death; she had only one life and had already given it to
someone else. He had come too late to her. Fifteen years ago, perhaps,
but not now.

She was only one person, she thought, walking down the corridor   112
in a dream. Was she safe in this single person, or was she trapped? She
had only one identity. She could make only one choice. What she had
done or hadn't done was the result of that choice, and how was she
guilty? If she could have felt guilt, she thought, she might at least have
been able to feel something.

Questions for Study and Discussion

1. How does Sister Irene view her responsibilities as a teacher? As a nun? In
paragraph 51, she refers to her vocation; what exactly is this vocation?

2. What profession is Allen preparing for? What does he say that suggests

why he might be attracted to that profession? Does he seem suited for it? Why, or why not?

3. Does Oates make it clear whether or not Allen is really insane? If so, where? How does this affect your reading of the story?

4. What do you learn about Allen and the source of his disturbance from Sister Irene's visit to his family? How does what we know of Sister Irene's own upbringing help to explain her attitudes and behavior?

5. Why does Sister Irene think that Allen is "making her into a Christian"? Why is it a "terrifying wonder" for her to assume the role of a Christian?

6. Sister Irene says of Allen that he thinks ideas are real, but she thinks that only reality is real. What is the issue here? For example, what does it mean to speak of *ideas* that change the world?

7. Where does Oates draw the title of the story from? What does the title contribute to your understanding of the story?

8. What is the meaning of the last paragraph of the story?

Writing Topics

1. Sister Irene believes that teachers exist "only for the benefit of others" and that she is "an instrument by which facts [are] communicated." Allen, on the other hand, claims that humanists, including academics, must be "committed to life in its totality and not just to [their] profession." What can you say in support of each view? Can the two views be reconciled? Write an essay in which you present your conclusions.

2. Write an essay in which you explain how your attitudes toward school and your classmates relate to your ambitions and your view of life.

The Student Athlete in Crisis

MARK NAISON

In recent years many college athletic programs have come under fire for illegal and unethical practices. Talented high school athletes have been heavily recruited by college coaches to bolster their football and basketball programs and perhaps gain national recognition for themselves and their schools. With the growing commercialization of athletic programs, many college student athletes feel cheated and victimized by promises of an education and perhaps even a professional sports career. Mark Naison, an associate professor of Afro-American studies and the director of the Urban Studies program at Fordham University, is concerned about the impact of the college sports scandal on higher education.

In the following article, which first appeared in *Commonweal* magazine, Naison traces the history of college sports scandals in order to give us perspective on the current situation. He concludes his article by offering some practical suggestions for alleviating the exploitation of college athletes.

Scenario for Scandal

During the last few years, a series of scandals has rocked college   1
athletics. Many educators, coaches, and sportswriters have become convinced that the dilution of educational standards, the exploitation of
student athletes, and the proliferation of illegal recruiting practices are
now *normal* features of revenue-producing sports at American universities. Although a national coaches committee survey, completed in 1976,
claimed that only twelve percent of the schools cheat (a figure which
may be plausible if one includes schools that do not give athletic scholarships), many players and coaches have insisted that the figure should
be raised to ninety percent if one concentrates on Division I institutions
which field nationally competitive football and basketball programs.

So many athletes have come forward with tales of transcript forging,   2
bribes, and under-the-table payments that even sports journalists, a no-

toriously hard-bitten and cynical crew, have been shaken. "Boxing has always been typecast as . . . 'the red light district of sports,' " wrote Dave Anderson, a sports columnist for the *New York Times*. "But boxing is almost a boys choir now in contrast to the garbage dump that so much of college athletics has become. Call college athletics the 'green light district of sports' now."

The contrast between the allegedly high moral ideals of American education and the dynamics of commercialized college sports was highlighted by a study undertaken by the American Council on Education in the mid 1970s. After finding that the governance of athletic departments at many institutions had become separated from the control of faculties and college presidents, the Council tried to develop guidelines and procedures that would help universities subject athletic departments to greater fiscal and academic accountability. But not a single coach, faculty member, or administrator who participated in the Council's study expressed confidence that such procedures would significantly reduce abuses at schools where commercialized sports programs were well established. Indeed, all predicted that the ethical and educational problems connected with college sports would become *more*, rather than less troublesome in subsequent years.

"The combined effects of the movement toward equality in sports for women," George Hanford, President of the College Board wrote, "declining student enrollments, and tax reduction legislation are bound to keep the economic squeeze on all facets of higher education, which will in turn put even greater premium on television dollars for sports and so exacerbate the ethical problems in the recruitment and subsidy of television revenue-producing athletes."

The disparity between the breadth of the abuses revealed, and the admitted insufficiency of strategies for reform, suggests the need to develop new ways of looking at the role of sports in higher education. Let me try to present a framework that will explain why college sports scandals have been endemic since the late nineteenth century and why they are becoming particularly blatant and visible now, followed by proposals for some solutions to the problems faced by athletes in revenue-producing sports.

When I first began reviewing the history of college sports, what immediately attracted my attention was how quickly American universities became involved in providing sports entertainment for their students and the general public. According to Frederick Rudolph, discussing the rise of college football in the late nineteenth century, "few movements so captured the colleges and universities. . . . At last, the American college and university had discovered something that all sorts of people cared about passionately." So quickly did the general public seize upon college football as a subject of enthusiasm and identification (aided by the proliferation of mass circulation newspapers) that university presidents, operating in a climate not always conducive to intellectual concerns, began consciously to use the sport as a vehicle for attracting financial and political support, whether from alumni, state legislators, or prospective students and contributors.

At some institutions, especially private colleges in the East, the tendency to exploit public interest in football to the fullest was partially checked by efforts to attract academically and financially elite student bodies, and to develop internationally respected research faculties and graduate schools. But at land-grant colleges in the midwestern and southern states, founded to provide practical training to farmers or specialized technical education conducive to the expansion of local industries, university administrators "often discovered that athletic victories were more important than anything else in convincing reluctant legislators to open the public purse." Indeed, the very features of the state institutions which made them most democratic—their responsiveness to public opinion, their commitment to making higher education available to broad sections of the populace, their insistence on a practical justification for the universities' existence— led them to assume major responsibility for the provision of sports entertainment for their states and regions.

"Football became the major instrument of publicity," Frederick Rudolph writes, "because both on and off the campus, it was the sport that inspired the most enthusiasm, elicited the most interest, and brought into the camp of college and university supporters people for whom the idea of going to college was out of the question, but for whom the idea of supporting the team was a matter of course. . . . By 1900, the relationship between football and public relations had been firmly established and almost everywhere acknowledged as one of the sport's major justifications." In states where populist suspicions of "higher learning" were deeply rooted, fielding a football team sometimes came to be regarded as the university's most important single cultural activity.

One consequence of the university's entry into the sphere of sports entertainment was professionalism; explicitly, in the case of coaches, and implicitly, in the recruitment and maintenance of athletes. Under-the-table payments, illegal recruiting, and fictional class attendance by athletes had become visible in many institutions by the 1890s. But though strong voices for reform were raised by many college presidents and one president of the United States (Theodore Roosevelt), efforts to assure that athletes functioned as parts of the normal student population suc-

ceeded primarily at institutions which did not need sports as a primary
fund-raising mechanism.

    At the Ivy League colleges, which assumed the mission of training   10
a social elite, popular sports programs managed to survive without the
recruitment of semi-literate athletes or illegal cash payments for their
services. But in the large state universities, where the faculty often lacked
the authority to challenge professionalization or insist on high standards
of admission, the business and entertainment dimension of college football grew virtually unchecked, inspiring the construction of huge football
stadiums on many campuses in the boom years of the 1920s and producing
a chain of scandals that provoked the Carnegie Commission to issue a
report in 1929 recommending the de-emphasis of college sports.

    As this brief account suggests, the university's role in providing   11
sports entertainment reflected the democratic outlook and hard-nosed
practicality of many university constituents and supporters, especially in
frontier and developing regions of the country. But despite the egalitarian
ethos that pervaded college sports, athletic departments proved far more
vulnerable to the domination of "special interests" and powerful local
elites than the academic divisions of the universities.

    By the 1890s, college athletics had come largely under the domi-   12
nation of the alumni, who alone possessed the funds and the business
expertise to promote a spectacle possessing consistent mass appeal. At
institutions where faculty power and self-confidence were limited, the
alumni take-over of sports was particularly pronounced, at once superseding and shaping the professionalization of coaching and athletic management. By the mid 1920s, athletic departments with large football
programs, with few exceptions, had evolved almost entirely autono-
mously of the academic divisions of the university, and commanded impressive political power and financial backing.

    Nevertheless, alumni domination of sports, reinforced by the par-   13
ticipation of local business and legislators, did not go completely unchallenged. As faculty members launched a generally successful struggle
to upgrade their status and reduce the involvement of nonacademicians
(particularly businessmen and politicians) in the day-to-day life of the
university, their efforts helped create a climate, at least at some institutions, conducive to a reduced emphasis on big-time sports. Even the
land-grant colleges were partially affected by this trend. Many state institutions, responding to the technical and cultural needs of their regions,
undertook impressive upgrading of the faculties and research bodies, creating
constituencies within the faculties, and within the community at large,
who pressed for the raising of academic standards.

College presidents, in the post-World War II years, found them- 14
selves having to mediate between complex arrays of interest groups, some
with a stake in producing winning teams, some with a stake in attracting
more skilled and sophisticated students and faculty members. The cross
pressures had highly varied results. In the early 1950s and '60s, some
institutions de-emphasized big-time sports (particularly after a series of
damaging basketball scandals), some placed them under tighter supervi-
sion, others let them evolve virtually unchecked. The result seems to
have been a system in which the majority of institutions kept commercialism in check, while the big powers ran semi-professional programs
with as much discretion as competitive conditions would allow.

In the late sixties and early seventies, however, dramatic cultural 15
and demographic changes within American universities, coincident with
a rapidly expanding television market for college sports, loosened existing
constraints on the professionalization of college athletics. The recruitment of black students by major universities, the rapid expansion of
university enrollment among all sections of the population, and a climate
of student activism inspired by the war in Vietnam, limited the faculty's
power to maintain and enforce academic standards, and temporarily loosened administrative control at many institutions.

Athletic departments took advantage of the "liberalized" climate 16
to pursue the best athletes available, irrespective of racial background or
level of academic preparation, and to reap the financial rewards to be
won from expanded television coverage. Insensitive to many of the black
athletes they recruited, who came from more impoverished backgrounds
than most of their white players, coaches and administrators sometimes
insulated black athletes from the mainstream of the campus experience,
creating elaborate subterfuges to maintain their eligibility.

Black athletes, after an initial period of accommodation, engaged 17
in protests that effectively eliminated double standards of treatment at
most schools. But what they were not able to counteract, in the revenue-
producing programs, was an intensification of training and competition
for all athletes, a process that rendered the academic rewards of the
athletic scholarship problematical indeed. To put the matter bluntly,
coaches and athletic administrators, with virtually no opposition from
the NCAA, launched a "speed-up" in college athletics which made it
increasingly difficult to participate in revenue-producing programs and
graduate in four years.

By the early 1970s, bowl games, post-season tournaments and "hol- 18
iday classics" had multiplied to the point where almost every player in a
revenue-producing sport had to miss more than ten days of classes and
their entire Christmas reading period (in addition to practicing three

hours a day all year round). How athletes with limited academic skills and poor high school preparation were supposed to maintain "normal academic progress," while enduring this kind of regimen is an issue no NCAA halftime show has ever satisfactorily explained.

It took some time for deteriorating educational prospects for athletes   19
to capture the attention of educators and civil rights leaders. But thanks to the efforts of people like Dr. Harry Edwards and Dr. Roscoe Browne, Jr., low graduation rates of athletes, particularly black athletes, have become a major public issue. The phenomenon itself is not new; Dave Meggysey, attending Syracuse University in the early 1960s, was one of only three varsity football players in his entering class who graduated in four years. But the seriousness of the problem has intensified in recent years because of the gradual evolution of the American economy away from a dependence on heavy industry into high technology enterprises and an advanced service sector requiring a professionally trained, literate labor force. Athletes not graduating in the late seventies and eighties increasingly lacked the option of working in mines, factories, or construction jobs at decent, trade union wages. If they failed to graduate, or acquire quantitative and communicative skills, they were often forced to resort to a combination of "hustling" (selling drugs, running numbers, etc.), low-paying service jobs, and public assistance to make ends meet.

Stories in the media documenting the tragic fate of athletes who   20
have completed their eligibility without receiving their degree have proliferated. Despite this fact, neither the American Council on Education, nor the NCAA, nor any other important body in higher education has offered a realistic plan to protect athletes from exploitation or to reduce corruption in college sports. Indeed, several developments in the economy, the media, and in higher education itself suggest that professionalization in college sports will accelerate in coming years, placing pressures on college athletes fundamentally incompatible with educational achievement.

First of all, shrinking enrollments, sparked by a large decline in the   21
college age population and strapped state budgets, have created a grave fiscal crisis for many universities. Not only have universities become desperate for new sources of revenue, but they have increasingly resorted to sophisticated "marketing" strategies to try to maintain enrollment levels and a high degree of public visibility. For many institutions, especially those without strong academic reputations, developing a nationally competitive sports program, especially in basketball, represents a quick way to get public exposure and free advertising, along with the associated benefits of improved campus morale and increased alumni interest.

Secondly, the growth of cable television promises to bring about a   22
vast increase in revenue to schools fielding successful sports programs,
offering powerful temptations to institutions battered by inflation, budget
cuts, and declining enrollments. "No one can predict with any confidence how much money will be raised now that cable and pay-for-view
television have begun to compete with the networks to show football
and basketball games," a *New York Times* reporter observed. "But those
connected with sports, television, and academia do not doubt that a
huge windfall is on the horizon." Resistance to professionalization, largely
centered in the faculty, is likely to weaken when sports-generated revenues are presented as an alternative to layoffs, increased course-loads,
and assaults on tenure.

Finally, deteriorating conditions of life among the poorer strata of   23
the American population, from which a disproportionate share of successful athletes derives, renders the college athletic work force even more
vulnerable to exploitation. Not only has the percentage of Americans
living in poverty gone up in the late 1970s and 1980s, but urban school
systems have sharply deteriorated, resulting in astronomical levels of unemployment among minority teenagers.

Sports, perhaps now more than ever, are perceived by youngsters   24
in poor communities as their best chance of getting into the mainstream
of the economy and are approached with a desperate, single-minded
intensity. The result is a huge pool of highly skilled athletes, without
the education, training, and sophistication to survive in most college
environments, and who are thus totally dependent on coaches and athletic administrators for income and psychological support. The very few
of them who are superstars can work out a good bargain; but most are at
the mercy of far wealthier and sophisticated adults who know that good
players are a dime a dozen in the rubble-strewn lots and schoolyards of
"The Other America."

What can be done? The first thing is to dispense with all illusions   25
about "amateurism" in big-time college sports.

The provision of sports entertainment for the general public has   26
been an important function of the American university system for over
one hundred years. At some state institutions (many of which are the
leading powers in the College Football Association) this function has
historically been perceived by legislators and the general public as equaling, if not superseding, academic training. Such a pattern is impossible
to reverse, especially when it has resulted in huge investments of fixed
and liquid capital (stadiums, fieldhouses, athletic dormitories, weight
rooms, scholarship funds, coaches' salaries, etc.) and the acquisition of
lucrative television contracts.

Then there is the fiscal crisis of the universities. That and the 27
anticipated windfall in revenue from televised sports will accelerate tendencies toward professionalism even further in schools where it is already
established, and will encourage new institutions to pursue that route.

Educators must therefore shift the focus of their reform efforts. The 28
major problem in college sports today is not commercialism—it is the
exploitation of athletes and the proliferation of illicit practices which
dilute educational standards.

Many universities are currently deriving substantial benefits from 29
sports programs that depend on the labor of athletes drawn from the
poorest sections of America's population. It is the responsibility of educators, civil rights leaders, and concerned citizens to see that these young
people get a fair return for their labor both in terms of direct remuneration, and in terms of career preparation for a life outside sports.

Minimally, scholarships in revenue-producing sports should be de- 30
signed to extend until graduation, rather than covering only four years
of athletic eligibility, and should include guarantees of tutoring, counseling, and proper medical care. At institutions where the profits are
particularly large (such as Texas A & M, which can afford to pay its
football coach $280,000 a year) scholarships should also provide salaries
that extend beyond room, board, and tuition. The important thing is
that the athlete be remunerated fairly and have the opportunity to gain
skills from a university environment without undue competition from a
physically and psychologically demanding full-time job. This may well
require that scholarships be extended over five or six years, including
summers.

Such a proposal, I suspect, will not be easy to implement. The 31
current amateur system, despite its moral and educational flaws, enables
universities to hire their athletic labor at minimal cost. But solving the
fiscal crisis of the universities on the backs of America's poor and minorities is not, in the long run, a tenable solution. With the support of
concerned educators, parents, and civil rights leaders, and with the help
from organized labor, the college athlete, truly a sleeping giant, will
someday speak out and demand what is rightly his—and hers—a fair
share of the revenue created by their hard work.

Questions for Study and Discussion

1. According to George Hanford, what are the causes of the ethical problems
in recruiting and subsidizing student athletes?

2. What did Naison learn when he began to review the history of college
sports?

3. Why did land-grant colleges in the Midwest and South come to place a high premium on sports programs?

4. How has Naison organized his essay? Does he explain the organization of his essay so that you can follow it easily? Explain.

5. What, according to Naison, is the relationship between television and college sports?

6. What three reasons does Naison give to support his belief that "professionalization in college sports will accelerate in coming years"?

7. What is the function of paragraph 25 within the context of Naison's essay?

8. What for Naison is the major problem in college sports today? And what does he offer as a solution?

Writing Topics

1. Since the time of the writing of this essay, the NCAA no longer negotiates television rights for all its member colleges. Colleges are free to negotiate their own deals with the networks and the media. Argue for or against this new development in college sports.

2. Using examples from your own experience or observation, write an essay arguing for or against the following statement: "Today's college athletes are not part of the student population."

3. After sixteen seasons in the National Basketball Association, Elvin Hayes returned to the University of Houston to complete his senior year of college. In a recent article he explains why after a highly successful career in professional sports he has returned to complete his education:

> As an athlete, I would not consider facing my opponent without being thoroughly prepared. I now realize that the toughest competition I'll ever face is in the "game of life." Today, more than ever, the stakes are high, and in order for a person to remain a winner, an education is no longer optional—but essential. Fellow athletes, take heed—a career in athletics is finite, but the benefits from your education last a lifetime.

Write an essay in which you explain what you believe to be the function and place of sports within the context of higher education.

4. Study the athletic programs available to students on your campus. Where does the emphasis seem to be in the programs? Do you see any evidence of the professionalization of sports that Naison talks about? Are there any differences between programs for men and women? What do the student athletes themselves think of your college's programs? Write a well-organized report of your findings.

GRACE LICHTENSTEIN

Grace Lichtenstein was born in 1941 in New York City, and graduated from Brooklyn College of the City University of New York in 1962. She started her career in journalism as an advertising copy writer and a radio news script writer before becoming a reporter and national correspondent for the *New York Times* in 1970. She is currently on the faculty of the Graduate School of Journalism at Columbia University. Her own interests in skiing and tennis are reflected in her books on women in sports: *A Long Way Baby: Behind the Scenes in Women's Pro Tennis* (1874) and *Machisma: Women and Daring* (1981). Lichtenstein has had articles on women in sports in such popular magazines as *Esquire, Redbook, Ms., Seventeen,* and *Cosmopolitan.*

First published in *Rolling Stone* in 1982, the following essay takes a critical look at athletes and their institutions when money has been introduced into college sports.

Playing for Money

Big-time college sports have become a gross perversion of a concept dear to the ivory-tower crowd. The issue of student-athletes—along with the alleged transgressions of coaches, recruiters and university officials—has leaped beyond mere controversy to the level of all-American scandal. In the process, educational institutions have covered themselves with mud. And lives have been ruined.

During the past year, more than two dozen colleges—prestige and jock schools alike—have been hit by charges ranging from illegal recruiting, to cash payoffs, ticket scalping, phony transcripts, medical mistreatment and point fixing. Many schools, including the University of Southern California, UCLA, Boston College and Clemson University, have in effect become farm systems for pro football, baseball and basketball teams. Coaches, who sometimes command higher salaries than university presidents, cry that they're forced to break amateur-athletics rules because if they don't they can't build winning teams and will be fired. And television continues to fuel this overheated system by pumping millions into the coffers of the National Collegiate Athletic Association (NCAA) for TV rights to big games.

Now, the athletes have begun to fight back. Their biggest supporters are not the pro-team owners who have a future interest in them, but the pro-basketball and pro-football players' unions. "Owners are in a better position to take advantage of a youngster if he doesn't have a degree," says one union organizer. "The kid doesn't have as many options, so the owners don't have to pay him as much as he's worth."

Individually and collectively, athletes are charging that colleges   4
prevented them from getting their degrees, injected them with needless
painkillers and even bribed them. Unfortunately, for every James Worthy
(the former University of North Carolina basketball star drafted by the
Los Angeles Lakers after his junior year), there are thousands of Saturday's heroes who have turned into Sunday's chumps—bounced off campus
without an education, unable to find work, left only with arthritic legs
to stand on. They were lured, as athletes have been for years, by the
dream of one day reaching the pros. But of the 10,000 football players
who come out of college each year, barely 100 to 200 make it to a pro
club. In the long run, even those who do may not really be lucky. More
than two-thirds of today's pro players lack a college degree.

"I've been to dinner with fellow players who earn $300,000 a year   5
and can't read the menu," says Kermit Alexander, past president and
current field representative of the National Football League (NFL) Players
Association.

That's one reason Alexander has joined a small cadre of reformers   6
intent on helping young athletes cope with a system that could be dangerous to their physical and emotional health. These reformers are themselves ex-jocks who know how sweet Final Four, Rose Bowl or Olympic
glory can be, and how bitter is the aftertaste.

Alexander has doubled as field coordinator for the Center for Athletes' Rights and Education (CARE), a year-old organization originally   7
sponsored by the NFL Players Association and the National Conference
of Black Lawyers. Another reformist group, Athletes for Better Education
(AFBE), was formed in Chicago six years ago and is sponsored by the
National Basketball (NBA) Players Association.

AFBE is guided by Arthur "Chick" Sherrer Jr., who was a bench   8
warmer on the Princeton basketball squad that was led by Bill Bradley
in the early Sixties. The group sponsors free basketball camps at which
high-school students are tutored as much in reading and recruitment as
they are in pick-and-rolls. To raise money, AFBE holds auctions of jock
memorabilia (Walter Payton's jersey fetched a thousand dollars). It also
conducts "profile scrimmages" in Chicago, New York and Los Angeles
to showcase high-school players who need athletic and academic scholarships and who may have been overlooked by some recruiters. According
to the AFBE score card, the group has helped hundreds of players get
some kind of scholarship since 1978. "We tell them, chase the dream
but catch an education. Don't just go through four years of college and

be totally exploited," explains Charles Grantham, AFBE adviser and NBA Players Association executive vice-president.

Both AFBE and CARE have drawn up lists of tough questions that they urge student-athletes, parents and high-school administrators to pose to fast-talking recruiters. Among the questions: "If I perform well in the classroom but fall short of my coach's expectations in athletics, will my scholarship be renewed every year?" "If I'm injured badly enough to require surgery, will the school pay for a second opinion by a doctor of my choice?" "Do the athletes take courses that prepare them for a career, or do they take 'softer' courses designed to keep them eligible?" "Do coaches use physical activity as punishment and discipline rather than as a source of fitness and human development?"   9

Full-ride scholarships (including room, board, tuition and books) are limited at even the biggest schools, and the competition is fierce. NCAA Division 1-A schools—the 137 elite football factories—are each allowed a maximum of 95 full-ride football scholarships at any one time, while the 276 Division I basketball schools are permitted only fifteen full-rides a year in basketball. And the NCAA itself does not know how many full-ride athletes get their scholarships renewed.   10

From its office on New York's East 156th Street, a teeming bazaar surrounded by the desert of the city's premier slum, the South Bronx, CARE dispenses a stream of speakers, pamphlets and position papers on the abuses of the current system. While CARE's staff has undergone changes, its leaders have included Cary Goodman, former Colgate player and long-time sports activist; Phil Shinnick, former Olympic long jumper; and Allen Sack, former Notre Dame football star. (All three happen to be Ph.D.'s as well.) The organization's largest financial backer is currently the U.S. Department of Education.   11

Last winter, CARE put Florida State University basketball star James Bozeman in front of the national media to tell how his school mishandled his injuries until he could hardly walk, how it plied athletes with cash, how one coach used a female cheerleader to recruit a high schooler, and how students who did not play ball up to expectations found themselves in academic trouble. (A review committee at FSU rejected most of Bozeman's contentions, to no one's surprise.)   12

But the Bozeman case is a small skirmish in CARE's attack on the college sports establishment. Through the school systems in New York City, Detroit and other cities, the group is distributing an "Athletes' Bill of Rights" guaranteed to nettle the NCAA. It advises would-be scholarship students (if indeed they can be viewed as employees) that although they virtually turn over total control of their lives when they sign a "letter of intent" to attend a college on a full-ride, they should still be entitled   13 to a share of a school's sports revenues, to workman's compensation if injured and to a student-athletes' union.

"Student-athletes are workers. A scholarship athlete is the em- 14 ployee of the university," says Alan Sack, current director of CARE. "If he decides to give up sports for books, he loses his pay. If he doesn't perform on the athletic field, he gets fired."

Recently, another Florida State basketball player, Pernell Tookes, 15 filed a workman's compensation claim against the university on the grounds that a knee injury had been caused by his "employment." The Tookes case could set a precedent for claims in other college sports as well.

Perhaps more radical is CARE's lobbying to get the NCAA to set 16 up an academic trust fund that would finance the education of injured athletes or those who have used up their playing eligibility but are short of a degree. The fund would be financed by about fifteen percent of the fees paid by networks to televise NCAA games—or nearly $40 million alone from the latest two-network football pact.

Goodman argues that the NCAA is not actually a rules-enforce- 17 ment agency anyway, but rather a big-business "cartel" whose purpose is to protect member colleges and collect TV riches for them.

Why all this fuss about campus jocks, the envy of so many of their 18 fellow students? Because Goodman, Sherrer and others maintain that the vast majority of high-school student-athletes don't have the slightest idea about the reality of college recruiting . . . or of the college jock's life afterward.

Recruiting is "one of the most pressurized, distorted, sophisticated 19 processes," declares Dick Versace, head basketball coach at Illinois' Bradley University. Blue-chip prospects "absolutely wack out. They become numb. Even the most sophisticated, intelligent parent trips out. I haven't met one who can handle it."

Norm Ellenberger, former basketball coach at the University of 20 New Mexico, thinks a list of questions for recruiters might allow the athletes to recognize unscrupulous headhunters. "If you're a used-car salesman and you're trying to sell me a clunker, you don't want me to see the busted engine, you want me to see the shiny new paint job. Let's face it: when you're a seventeen-year-old kid and you've got a dozen coaches dangling a full ride and a promise to lead you off into glory, it's hard to know what questions to ask."

Several top high-school stars remember well what a typical re- 21 cruiter's pitch sounded like, whether it came from a head coach or an assistant whose primary role was recruitment:

"William," they would say, always careful to be courteous, "with 22 your size and speed, you'll be a starter your first year, no question. Know the last guy I scouted with talent like yours? O.J., that's who! You're a blue-chipper, William, and with you, we've got the makings of a top-ten team. Mrs. Johnson, wouldn't it be great to see your son here on TV in the Mango Bowl? Did I mention that all our full-ride freshmen get Sony color consoles for their folks? Our boosters are very generous about flying parents to Podunk for the weekend of a big home game, Mrs. Johnson. And we don't want you or your son to worry about the little things. You've got a tough English course, William? We've got tutors helping all our boys. Now I know you also want walking-around money, and we've got part-time jobs for all our blue-chippers, William, so you can count on ten dollars an hour for putting out the practice gear in the afternoon. . . ."

Often, though, it's what is left out of the pitch that matters.   23

According to Nancy Lieberman, a former basketball star at Old   24
Dominion University in Virginia, the most important promise not kept by recruiters is that a student-athlete will have the time for both halves of his or her hyphenated life. "You learn that you've got to choose between really studying or playing ball," she says. "No way can you do both."

Curtis Taliaferro would certainly agree. Last spring in Pittsburgh,   25
the Ohio University football player told an athletes conference of eleventh- and twelfth-graders that "recruiters hate a person who asks too many questions." He had not asked enough. He had had few clues that he would be pressured to play when hurt, and that coaches would discourage his academic studies because they interfered with football practice.

In truth, long before he probably knew how to spell *interference*,   26
Curtis Taliaferro was being scouted by recruiters.

"The road starts not with your senior year, not with your sophomore   27
year, but in junior high school," he warned an audience brought together by the Urban League and a social-service agency called the Kingsley Association. "You're winning, you're getting certificates, you're so great, okay? Coaches pat you on the back, get you out of class, tell you that you need to go over plays for upcoming games. Your books are right there in your hand. They just stay there."

Wooed by such legendary football schools as Southern Cal, Notre   28
Dame, Penn State, Tulane and Syracuse, Taliaferro accepted a full-ride scholarship at Ohio. Suddenly, as a freshman on the varsity team, he realized how that defined him: "nothing but a paycheck, 185 pounds' worth of beef." His schedule each afternoon was "two to six, practice. Seven to eight, watch films. Eight to 10:30, go to study hall—where you just get plays from coaches." He thought he was going crazy. "To become

a human being, I had to learn how to leave my sweats in the locker room. You ask yourself if it's worth it."

By his second year, Taliaferro found the burden too heavy. "You're spending most of your time uptown, drinking beer, trying to see how many women you can hold or just sleeping." Finally one day, he quit and came home to his mother. "It was the first time in my life I was not on a winning football team. I cried because I wasn't playing." 29

Why don't athletes like Taliaferro get better guidance on handling the pressure? Often because administrators can't keep track of slick recruiters—or because ambitious high-school coaches are in the recruiters' pockets. 30

In Detroit not long ago, several in a group of six black high-school principals (three of whom had gone to college on athletic scholarships themselves) admitted to NFL Players Association field representative Kermit Alexander that they did not know that most full rides were not complete four-year scholarships but "one-year renewables," contingent upon a student-athlete's performance. Moreover, they said they were inundated by recruiters from across the country who roamed their hallways, keeping blue-chippers out of class in order to pitch them. 31

"We've developed a monster here," said James Soloman of Detroit's Martin L. King High School. "We produce so many quality athletes, we're almost not able to live with it." It was noted that when one gifted basketball star was slightly injured, recruiters literally lined up beside his hospital bed. Another principal bemoaned the "new breed" of high-school coach, who figures, "If I keep sending enough good kids to Michigan, they'll hire me on as an assistant coach." 32

Alexander—a charming man who lasted fourteen seasons in the pros as a defensive back, earning his bachelor's degree from UCLA eight years after his eligibility ended—did not mince words. Since Detroit was such fertile athletic territory, he argued, the principals were in a position to dictate rules to recruiters rather than be swamped by them. Indeed, a school-system-wide recruiter-screening process is going into effect this fall. 33

In terms of power and money, Alexander and the other reformers appear to be in the position of a peewee football team scrimmaging against the San Francisco 49ers. They're up against a multimillion-dollar operation that feeds the universities' hunger for instant recognition from sports, as well as the hunger of talented young men who are convinced they can be the next O. J. Simpson. The enforcement of regulations designed to prevent abuses is in the hands of a fourteen-member NCAA committee; still another committee negotiates and promotes the immensely profitable television packages. 34

"It comes down to a dollars-and-cents situation," says Ellenberger. 35
"There are more and more schools finding that basketball is a profitable
business. It's awfully easy for a college administrator to put subtle pressure
on a coach to win at all costs, and to hide under his desk when the thing
is overturned." He scoffs at the notion that athletes and parents are pawns
who are "raped, pillaged and plundered." On the contrary, "There are
plenty with their palms up," he says.

Norm Ellenberger knows whereof he speaks. As New Mexico's head 36
coach from 1972 to 1979, he compiled a remarkable win-loss average of
.684, consistently filling "the Pit" in Albuquerque with players recruited
from all over the nation—until a scandal of mammoth proportions caved
in on the Lobos. The saga of New Mexico's "Lobogate," as it was dubbed,
illustrates how corrupt college sports can become.

A successful high-school and college coach in the Midwest, Ellen- 37
berger joined the Lobos in 1967 as an assistant coach. The team had
played only one exhibition game in 1979 when a state wiretap that
recorded an Ellenberger conversation with his assistant, Manny Gold-
stein, set in motion a federal investigation into racketeering, illegal travel
vouchers and other irregularities within the Lobo ranks.

The university fired Ellenberger. Eventually, he stood trial in state 38
court on twenty-two counts of fraud and filing false travel vouchers. He
was convicted on twenty-one of them, which could have meant incar-
ceration for twenty-one years. Yet, in a dramatic courtroom denouement,
the judge refused to sentence the popular Ellenberger to a single day
behind bars. The coach, thundered the judge, was "one cog" in a rotten
system, and he'd done "what almost everybody in this community wanted
him to do"—win games. "The real hypocrisy," the judge added, "is that
colleges and universities across this country . . . maintain and establish
what amounts to professional ball clubs. At the same time, they purport
to operate under amateur rules." An NCAA investigation, however,
found the university guilty of thirty-four rules violations and ordered it
to suspend one player and declare five others ineligible, suffer three years
of NCAA probation and return $36,000 in gate receipts.

University of New Mexico president William "Bud" Davis was ac- 39
cused of knowing about many of the violations. He denied it.

Lobogate has since died down in Albuquerque. Ellenberger is now 40
part owner of a racquet club called Supreme Courts. Davis (who refused
to speak to *Rolling Stone*) also emerged unscathed and left the university
to become the state of Oregon's chancellor for higher education. One of
Ellenberger's stars, Michael Cooper, is a fixture with the Los Angeles
Lakers. But not all his recruits fared as well. Willie Howard, for example.
He's in prison.

Howard was born in Chicago and raised in Los Angeles. He blos-   41
somed as a basketball player while at Cerritos College, a two-year institution in California. After proving his worth there, Howard was pursued
by excited recruiters from seventy-five senior colleges. He chose to transfer to New Mexico, partly because "they filled the arena every night,"
partly because a team assistant promised to arrange "special loans" for a
new car.

The six-foot-eight forward was on probation in California on a   42
charge of assault with a firearm. During his two years with the Lobos,
however, he became quite a favorite. Before a big game, "prominent"
community members would ask him to deliver a pep talk about "incentive," a talk sealed with cash gifts, Howard said recently. Sometimes it
was a token for extra rebounds, but before a crucial game against the
University of Nevada at Las Vegas, Howard says he got $200.

Howard was soon envisioning a career in the NBA, although his   43
schoolwork left something to be desired. People were "basketball crazy,
not interested in an education," said Howard. He did not pass many
required courses, but someone always "talked to an instructor to make
sure I got an incomplete." During the summer, he says, it was arranged
for him to be enrolled in an out-of-state college to make up the credits
necessary for him to maintain his eligibility as a player. "I never went,"
he said, "but I got credit anyway."

He claims the "special loan" was delivered to him in the form of a   44
check at a local Albuquerque bank. Howard had himself a brand-new
Impala.

His eligibility ran out in 1978. Howard was the seventh-round draft   45
choice of the New Orleans Jazz. For Willie Howard, the classic jock's
dream seemed ready to come true.

Then, bit by bit, his life began to unravel. The Jazz, he recalls,   46
released him before the exhibition season. Confused, he went to California and, for a year and a half, worked as a furniture delivery man. By
1979, wanting to be near his family and engaged to a local woman, he
returned to Albuquerque. The homecoming was rough. He was out of
work for months before he landed another furniture-moving job. The
"prominent" people who he alleged had once slipped him C-notes no
longer knew him.

In January 1981, there was a break-in at the apartment of a former   47
Lobo football player, reportedly involving a fight over a tape deck. Willie
Howard, it was alleged, tried to smash one man's head with a sledge-
hammer. Howard was convicted of residential burglary this past May and
marched off to the state penitentiary for three years.

But Willie Howard, with a wife and infant daughter, maintains he's 48 a good family man. The "burglary," he says, was simply a disagreement among friends who called the cops to get even. The judge, however, did not show Howard the kind of understanding that his counterpart had shown in the Ellenberger case. And the prosecutor, who once had season tickets to watch the Lobos play, now thinks it's a disgrace that his alma mater suited up "criminals." These attitudes are of little consequence to Willie Howard. "They only call me a star now when I'm in trouble," he says.

At the time of his arrest, Howard listed his occupation as "unem- 49 ployed athlete." The Impala was long gone, sold to pay grocery bills.

Norm Ellenberger optioned the movie rights to his life story to Ray 50 Stark Television for an undisclosed sum.

It is not necessary to be poor, gifted and black to be exploited by 51 college athletics. Take the case of Kevin Rutledge, a gifted white football player from a middle-income Phoenix family.

Several years ago, Rutledge enrolled at his hometown school, Ar- 52 izona State University, eager to play Pac-10 football under the coach who was revered throughout the state, Frank Kush. Like many of his successful colleagues, Kush was known as a stern taskmaster. In his sopho- more year, Rutledge found out just how stern. That fall, ASU was behind by twenty-one points in the third quarter of a game against Washington. Rutledge, a punter, got off a thirty-yard kick. Kush, recalled the punter, "didn't like it." When Rutledge got to the sidelines, he claimed the coach punched him in the face.

Later, Rutledge testified it was not the first time Kush had abused 53 a player. "He was like a god," the young man says now. "The players were all afraid of him; the coaches were all afraid of him." But Rutledge was not afraid, and he filed a multimillion-dollar lawsuit against the god of the Sun Devils. Soon thereafter, Kush, accused of trying to cover up the incident, was fired. A month after *that*, Arizona State became em- broiled in a transcript scandal similar to the one in New Mexico, and the football team was forced to forfeit several victories from a previous season.

Kush denied both the punching incident and the transcript scam. 54 When Rutledge's suit finally came to trial in 1981, such blue-chip defense witnesses as former Sun Devil Danny White, who was by then a Dallas Cowboys quarterback, and Olympic hockey coach Herb Brooks testified on Kush's stalwart behalf.

Rutledge had already transferred to another college out of Arizona 55 and believed that no one in his family was safe. After his suit had been filed, Rutledge's younger brother, a high-school football player, received death threats. His father's insurance office in Phoenix had been torched. The police officially labeled it arson and denied it had anything to do with the trial.

In court, Kush was acquitted in the punching incident. His legal bills were paid by the state, because he had been an employee of its university at the time the suit occurred. "It's hard to believe," Rutledge says now, "but Kush could do no wrong. You didn't see how much power he had. It went right to the judicial structure of the state." 56

(Various appeals are now being considered, and the American Civil Liberties Union is planning to file an amicus brief on Rutledge's behalf.) 57

By the fall of 1981, Kevin Rutledge had played out his eligibility at his new university and had gotten married. Still some credits shy of a degree, he worked for a time as a laborer in Las Vegas, then moved to a small island off South Carolina, hoping to start a new life, perhaps as a shrimp-boat captain. Rutledge says he would like to try out as a free agent for a pro-football team, but he suspects his notoriety might handicap him. This fall, he is reentering college to finish his degree work. 58

Frank Kush? He's head coach of the Baltimore Colts.[1] 59

The Arizona State athletic director who fired Kush was himself demoted. Recently, the former director, Fred L. Miller, wrote that cheating by coaches was a "cancer" preventing governance of college sports, and that many university presidents go out of their way to make sure "not to be in the direct firing line should athletic problems erupt." 60

And erupt they have. Last spring, the University of Southern California—alma mater of O. J. Simpson and Tom Seaver, and one of the five leading television football drawing cards—was slapped with a heavy NCAA penalty: it seems that for ten years, assistant football coaches had been selling athletes' free-game tickets to willing boosters. And two years ago, Southern Cal exposed, on its own, an admissions procedure under which hundreds of star athletes, among others, were enrolled despite high-school grades lower than USC standards. "It was a system gone awry," admitted the president, James H. Zumberge, at the time. Yet, when the latest sanctions were announced (including a two-year ban on telecasts of Southern Cal games), Zumberge expressed outrage. The NCAA was being "vindictive" against his school. Besides, he said, "ethical standards often come into conflict." One element that upset the president was that the school would lose an enormous amount of money from TV. 61

However, because the NCAA penalties were imposed for the 1983 and 1984 seasons, the biggest nonbowl game of the 1982 TV schedule, 62

---

[1]The Colts have since moved to Indianapolis.

Southern Cal versus Notre Dame, won't be affected. Furthermore, since Pac-10 schools share revenues from telecasts of any member school's games, Southern Cal will collect some money in 1983 and 1984.

The litany of scandals goes on and on. In Tennessee, two former   63
high-school blue-chip football stars brought a lawsuit against Clemson (an Atlantic Coast Conference school and the number-one college-football team in 1981) charging that they were handed money to sign letters of intent and then denied the opportunity to go to a Southeastern Conference school; it is now in the appeals stage. Rick Kuhn, a former Boston College basketball player, was sentenced to ten years in jail on a point-shaving charge. Wichita State's basketball team was hit with a three-year NCAA probation, giving that school the dubious distinction of having the most frequent sanctions in the country.

Louisiana State released a confidential report showing that major-   64
sport athletes were admitted despite low testing scores, and that many athletes were funneled into laughable courses designed solely to keep them academically eligible. (The most popular course was called Know Louisiana, also known as "the bus course," in which student athletes, among others, received college credit for traveling around the state.) In addition, Louisiana State forced the departure last May of two assistant athletic directors after a general audit of the athletics department. At about the same time, a Louisiana State assistant basketball coach reported that his briefcase had been stolen on a recruiting trip—with $2000 in cash inside. A chancellor's investigation cleared him of any improprieties.

Seven former athletes at California State University at Los Angeles   65
have filed a multimillion-dollar lawsuit charging that they had been guided into courses that kept them from getting a meaningful education. One of the top women's basketball coaches, Pam Parsons, left the University of South Carolina amid a scandal that involved, among other things, allegations of drug use and sexual relations with players.

There are signs that important sports personalities are beginning to   66
see the need for drastic change, perhaps along the very lines outlined by CARE. Senator Bill Bradley of New Jersey, who knows a bit about college sports, said not long ago that "college athletic programs should simply operate on two different tracks," amateur and semipro. The latter schools "would accept and pay star athletes. . . . The colleges would not have to compromise their academic ideals. The athletes would not have to pretend that their basic interest is a quality education." Cary Goodman would like to go even further. He wants a congressional investigation into the colleges' misuse of federal grants-in-aid to students.

There are also signs that some young athletes are heeding the message of Chick Sherrer, who says that "basketball should be a means to an end." At AFBE's New York profile scrimmage last spring, Louis "Stuntman" Stitzer, a high-school guard from North Bergen, New Jersey, said he had come to the showcase for a single reason: "I want a free education. Anywhere. I'll take Whatsamatta U!"

67

Of course, Stitzer hoped North Carolina's Dean Smith was waiting with a full ride in hand. But when the offers he received boiled down to half rides at obscure Southern colleges, Stitzer was content to accept a job as a lifeguard and a straight student grant from Ramapo College, an hour from his home. "Sure, I thought this was gonna be Joe Notre Dame, the 280-Z car, the works. It didn't turn out that way. Hey, I wouldn't mind being paid $10,000 to play ball in school. But you only stay in college a few years," Stitzer reasoned. "Then, if you don't have a degree, you're a bum."

68

Cary Goodman knows the reformers have their work cut out for them. "When we're going at college sports, it's like knocking mom's apple pie. But the evidence is mounting. Six months from now, something will produce a spark to change things. We'll just keep punching, punching, punching."

69

Questions for Study and Discussion

1. What percentage of professional football players has a college degree? What advantage do these players have in negotiating with club owners?

2. What are the organizations CARE and AFBE? How did they come into being? In your opinion what is the likelihood of their success in reforming college sports?

3. What are some of the problems that are plaguing college sports? How effective has the NCAA been in dealing with rules violations?

4. Norman Ellenberger and Willie Howard were both convicted of criminal charges. How are their cases related? What does their differing treatment at the hands of our judicial system tell us? Explain. What is Lichtenstein's attitude toward these two cases?

5. Lichtenstein's essay is filled with illustrative examples. What purpose do these examples serve? Would fewer examples have served this purpose as well? Why, or why not?

6. What's wrong with many recruiting practices today? According to Nancy Lieberman, what's the "most important promise not kept by recruiters"?

Writing Topics

1. Write an essay using the following idea as your thesis: In order to understand the problems that are affecting college sports, it is necessary to see them in the context of the American Dream and the lure of big money.

2. Are student-athletes workers? Are they entitled to workman's compensation, a share of college sports revenues, and to unionize? What responsibilities should colleges have for their student-athletes? Discuss what you believe should be the normal or typical relationship between a college and its student-athletes.

THOMAS TUTKO AND WILLIAM BRUNS

Born in Gallitzin, Pennsylvania, in 1931, Thomas A. Tutko was educated at Pennsylvania State University and Northwestern University. A professor of psychology at San Jose State University, Tutko is a specialist in sports psychology. The titles of some of his books reflect his far-ranging interests: *Problem Athletes and How to Handle Them* (1968), *Motivation and Play, Game, and Sports* (1970), *Coaching Girls and Women: Psychological Perspectives* (1975), *Sports Psyching: Playing Your Best Game All the Time* (1976). In 1976 Tutko teamed up with William Bruns to write *Winning Is Everything and Other American Myths*. Born in 1935 in Pasadena, California, Bruns was educated at the University of Redlands, Harvard University, and the University of California, Berkeley. Currently he is a professor of business at Harvard's Graduate School of Business Administration.

In the following selection from their book, Tutko and Bruns look at Americans' unquenchable thirst for winning and reflect on how we have somehow managed to take the fun out of it.

To Win or Not to Win: That Is the Question

One effect of this country's sports craze is that the owners, coaches, players, and fans all suffer from the same delusions. We thirst for whatever tangible evidence we can find that says, "We're a winner. We're Number One!" The athlete or coach who is near the bottom always feels, "I'll win and that'll mean something. I'll be worthwhile, loved, honored, and obeyed." This fundamental faith in the goodness of sports was typified by George Raveling when he took over as head basketball coach at Washington State in 1972 with the goal of helping to end UCLA's dominance in the Pacific Eight conference and in the country. When Raveling was asked how he thought he could succeed where so many had fallen short before, he answered: "I just rely on that saying that the struggle to the top is a rugged one but the view from the top is beautiful. I want that view, and we'll work as hard as we can to get there."

I like Raveling; I think he's a model young coach. But what realistically will happen if, by chance, he knocks off UCLA in 1982 and wins the NCAA title? What happens when *anybody* reaches the top in sports? Can they relax and savor that moment? Of course not. They have to do it again the next year, and the year after that. When the San Francisco Warriors won the NBA title in 1975, a newspaper headline the next afternoon read: "Are the Warriors Going to be One Year Champions?" No longer is it even, "Did you win?" but "How long are you going to keep winning?" Even if you are John Wooden and you win seven consecutive NCAA championships, your fans grumble when you fail to win an eighth. In individual sports like swimming and track and field, breaking records only leaves new records to be broken. No matter at what level we compete and in what sport, when we attain a goal we simply move it up another notch, hunting for a perfection that is always just out of reach.

Winning, in fact, is like drinking salt water; it will never quench   3
your thirst. It is an insatiable greed. There are never enough victories, never enough championships or records. If we win, we take another gulp and have even greater fantasies.

From their inception in 1960, the Dallas Cowboys went twelve   4
frustrating years without winning the National Football League championship. They had outstanding talent and they came close on several occasions, but they never could win "the big one." When they finally did win the Super Bowl in 1972, owner Tex Schramm went on television in the midst of his celebrating players and boasted that Dallas would now build a *dynasty!* That's what happens when you drink salt water instead of champagne.

Individual athletes are caught up in the same competitive madness.   5
In 1974, 22-year-old Jimmy Connors suddenly blasted his way to the top of the tennis world by winning Wimbledon and Forest Hills and over $200,000. By September there was no denying his number one ranking. Yet he was never able to relax and enjoy his time on top, something he had trained for from the time he was three years old. A week after winning at Forest Hills he won a tournament in Los Angeles and then was practically forced into playing in San Francisco, two nights later. Furthermore, reporters began asking him what he would do for an encore in 1975. "Well, I plan to just have another great year," he told them. "Do it all over again. Pancho Gonzales told me the other day, 'Jim, you proved this year you're a *good* player. But you'll have to do it a lot of times to prove you're a great one.' "

Added one of Connors' tennis rivals, Alex Mayer: "You have to   6
say he's at a peak. The question now is can he stay there. To be immortalized, he has to keep winning."

Freud would have clearly defined our behavior as a repetition com-   7
pulsion because there is no moment where the winner can feel, "I've made it." In *Meat on the Hoof*, Texas football player Gary Shaw wrote: "A clear-cut victory leads only to another challenge in a perpetual rat race. As long as there is an attempt to hold on to this simple view of

life as a series of challenges and victories with a few winners and many losers, then we will be trapped in an anxious and basically frustrating existence."

In pro football, the elation of a Sunday victory might last until   8
Monday morning. But then the coach and his players begin to worry about next Sunday's game. Counting exhibition games and the play-offs, a team can be consumed by Sunday preparation for nearly six months. Is it any wonder most head coaches seem preoccupied? Only one—the Super Bowl winner—is allowed to be happy for the other six months of the year. Even then, a coach like Don Shula, whose Miami Dolphins were winners in 1973 and 1974, is never allowed to be content where he is. He must set new goals: "We can't rest on our laurels; we want to win three in a row. No other team has ever done that." I can't blame Shula for challenging a team that had already enjoyed extraordinary success. But the point is that two straight Super Bowl victories are really only temporary in his mind. There has to be a third.

Let's speculate for a moment. What if Shula, before the 1974–75   9
season, had told reporters: "We're not really worrying about winning the title this year. We're still enjoying last year"? Not only would his sanity have been questioned, he would have been investigated by a Senate subcommittee on insatiable competitiveness.

The craze in this country that demands that your success in sports   10
is measured only by winning, that you are nothing until you're Number One, was crystallized by Vince Lombardi's dictum "Winning isn't everything. It's the only thing." Years later, the famous football coach claimed he had been misquoted, that what he had actually said was, "Winning is not everything—but making the effort to win is."

In fact, the "winning" quote apparently originated with another   11
football coach, the late Red Sanders, when he was at Vanderbilt in 1940. The phrase later surfaced, inevitably, in a John Wayne movie, *Trouble Along the Way*. Wayne plays a tough ex-professional football coach who is trying to keep custody of his only daughter while at the same time whipping a small college team into a national powerhouse. Donna Reed, an employee of the child welfare bureau, asks him one day, "Is winning everything to you?" The Duke replies, "No, ma'am. Winning isn't everything. It's the only thing."

This drive to compete and to be a "winner" has always been part   12
of the American psyche. Our early ancestors were aggressive and competitive to begin with. They knew they were pitted against amazing odds, but they also felt they were a select and chosen group. They defied their mother country and were successful. Later came the "frontier spirit," the belief in survival of the fittest, and the growing American fetish for

figures, statistics, records, and winners. Over forty years ago, John R. Tunis wrote, in *The American Way in Sport:* "We worship the victors. But why? The Dutch don't especially, nor the Swedes, neither do the Danes, the Swiss, or the English, and they all seem fairly civilized people." We devised an international "scoreboard" to chart our successes in the Olympics as well as in our wars, an obsession that was tragically reflected in our approach to Vietnam, where both President Johnson and President Nixon vowed that they were not going down in history as "the first American President who lost a war."

The competitive instinct that permeates the American spirit is one of the most highly prized values in the country, emanating from our presidents on down. But it is not just competition that is important—it is who *wins* that really matters. When Gerald Ford was vice-president, he wrote in *Sports Illustrated:* "It has been said that we are losing our competitive spirit in this country, the thing that made us great, the guts of the free-enterprise system. I don't agree with that; the competitive urge is deep-rooted in the American character." Fair enough, but then he goes on to say: "We have been asked to swallow a lot of home-cooked psychology in recent years that winning isn't all that important anymore, whether on the athletic field or in any other field, national and international. I don't buy that for a minute. It is not enough to just compete. Winning is very important. Maybe more important than ever." Later, when he was president, Ford continued to plug winning as a great American tradition. "What about winning?" he asked. "How about a good word for the ultimate reason any of us have for going into a competitive sport? As much as I enjoyed the physical and emotional dividends that college athletics brought me, I sincerely doubt if I ever suited up, put on my helmet . . . without the total commitment of going out there to win, not to get exercise, gold or glory, but simply to win."

President Ford is just one of many defenders of the winning creed, as the following quotations will show.

Washington Redskins coach George Allen: "The winner is the only individual who is truly alive. I've said this to our ball club: 'Every time you win, you're reborn; when you lose, you die a little.' " (Allen has a career won-lost record that most coaches would envy. But by his own definition he is a loser, because although he has made the play-offs six times, he has failed to win the Super Bowl.)

Texas football coach Darrel Royal: "The only way I know how to keep football fun is to win. That's the only answer. There is no laughter in losing." (Read *Meat on the Hoof* to confirm that Royal is not joking.)

Former Kansas City Chiefs coach Hank Stram: "It's only a game when you win. When you lose it's hell." (Especially when it costs you your job.)

Former Boston Bruins coach Bep Guidolin: "Winning is the name of the game. The more you win the less you get fired." (This statement was made before Guidolin lost his job when his Bruins lost in the seventh game of the 1974 Stanley Cup play-off finals to Philadelphia.) 18

Alabama football coach Bear Bryant, asked what he most wanted to be remembered for: "I'd like if it'd be for winning . . . That's our approach: If it's worth playing, it's worth paying the price to win." 19

Ohio State coach Woody Hayes: "Winners are men who have dedicated their whole lives to winning." (That's why you don't find Ohio State playing Alabama.) 20

Dallas quarterback Roger Staubach: "In pro football winning is all there is. If you don't win, you haven't done what the game is about." (Staubach is an active member of the Fellowship for Christian Athletes. Does he feel that Christ was a winner or a loser?) 21

Norman Vincent Peale: "I once asked Ty Cobb, 'Why do you put such an emphasis on winning? It's only a game.' He said, 'That's the reason I'm out there. Why play if you don't play to win?' " (What about camaraderie and the joy of simply playing a game?) 22

Baseball manager Billy Martin: "The players may not like you some of the time but I've always made the statement I'd play Adolph Hitler to win." (Yes, but Hitler was a loser.) 23

Pro basketball guard Pete Maravich: "Personal things like leading the league [in scoring] don't get you a cup of coffee. My obsession is to be on a championship team. As soon as I am, I'll retire. Definitely. Right then. Because then I will have been successful. I'm really only happy when I'm winning. Losses always bother me." (Playing for an expansion team in New Orleans, he should enjoy a long, unhappy career.) 24

Hubert Humphrey, in the Minnesota Vikings dressing room, after a club official pointed out he never shows up after a losing game: "That's true. Frankly, I love being around winners. When you win, you win. And when you lose, you lose. And winning is a lot more fun." 25

Why has winning taken on such importance? Why have we become obsessed with winning at all costs? For one thing, we play our games against the backdrop of an intensely competitive culture. A high premium is placed on achievement and success. Americans measure everything in terms of progress, or pseudo progress; we always have to feel that we're moving up. In a society that is preoccupied with competition, the average person needs something to latch on to that says, "I'm really *worthwhile*, too." Winning can provide that boost, even if it means that 26 a person is living vicariously through a sports team like the old Green Bay Packers or basking in the triumphs of a once-heroic Arnold Palmer.

Secondly, we are heirs to the Judeo-Christian ethic, which states   27
in principle that man should work hard to succeed, that if a person does his best, works unceasingly, and makes the right sacrifices, he will win. The assumption is that somehow the winner does everything right and the loser does everything wrong. All too often, the message that comes through to those who lose or who fail to reach the top is that obviously they didn't work hard enough and that they're not as worthwhile as the winners. Our tendency is to excuse the shortcomings of a winner—to gloss over his human frailties. But when a person starts to lose, we begin to question his character. Winners and losers are actually seen as good and bad people. If the athlete manifests certain behavior that leads to success, we say he has "courage," he's a "competitor," he's "mentally tough." Those who fail to demonstrate the same behavior are "losers," "flakes," "gutless," or "chokers." Our winning sports heroes even begin to appear sexually superior; they are "better looking" and more appealing. Their faces sell products on television, although it's interesting to note that the faces change as the level of success changes.

A study by one of my students, Seth Brody, clearly supports the   28
"halo effect" of winners. Individuals were asked to make personality ratings of amateur boxers viewed on film. The winner was seen as more mature, better looking, more valuable, more potent, and more active than the loser. These findings are reinforced by successful sports figures who are quoted in newspapers and magazines. For example, Pete Newell, general manager of the Los Angeles Lakers, commented on Oregon coach Dick Harter and his efforts to produce a team that could end the UCLA basketball dynasty: "I'm encouraged to see young men go through the demanding process of building a winner. You make it and you look around at the others who have made it and you say, 'He's a man, and I'm a man.' It can be an educating experience."

Perhaps we could justify this obsession with winning if, at the end   29
of the road, it led to a better and more wholesome life. If when you won a trophy or the championship or set a record, you became a more contented person. Or people used you as a mature model. Or something meaningful happened to you beyond making $100,000 a year and being in demand on the meat loaf circuit. Unfortunately, when you finally do win the whole ball of wax, not only do you have to win it again, but you become a marked man. Everybody wants to beat you. You accumulate enemies simply because you have won. When U.S. backstroke swimmer John Naber handed East Germany's Roland Matthes his first defeat in seven years, Naber acknowledged his dilemma: "I wanted his record more

than anything. Now all I'll get is the headache of people trying to beat me simply because I was the one who beat him."

Countless other athletes have struggled to the top only to find that winning is a hollow trip. In fact, the higher up the scale they go, the worse the pressures become: the incredible strain to keep winning; the clamoring public that demands autographs; banquet appearances and business deals; the insatiable news media that hunger for "fresh" quotes and every possible insight into the athlete's personal life, and the athlete's own internal demands to maintain the conditioning and training that brought him to the top in the first place. Small wonder that many top athletes finally confide, "What the hell is it all about?" Said tennis heroine Chris Evert: "It's tough being on top. It's lonely there. It's lonely because the other players are so competitive. If you want to be the best, you can't be best friends with everybody."

Another contributing pressure is the realization that an athlete can be a winner one day and a complete bum the next. Unless he is consistent, he runs the risk of being classified as a loser and facing the wrath of all his "loyal" fans. Ferguson Jenkins won 20 games or more for seven consecutive seasons. When he finally came up short—winning "only" 14 games in 1973—his fans in Chicago started booing him, and his owner proceeded to trade him to one of the worst teams in baseball (where, ironically, he won 25 games the following season).

The final irony is that if an athlete or a team wins *too* consistently, many of their fans will start getting bored if records are not broken or the winning margin is not overwhelming. Let a team win too much, like the New York Yankees of old or the UCLA basketball team, and many people are unhappy—from the critics who lament, "Break up the dynasty! They're ruining the game" to disgruntled players who have to ride the bench when they could be starting on any other team. Fans begin to form a strange alliance. It is not that they are *for* a team but against the other team. I know a number of basketball fans who are clearly against UCLA whenever they play, simply because they win too often. Even when John Wooden was in the midst of UCLA's 88-game winning streak, he and his wife, Nell, found very little contentment. More often it was a life of aggravation and smoldering pressure. Late in the streak, Mrs. Wooden told a reporter:

> These should have been the best years of our lives. But they haven't been. Nine national championships in ten years is great. So are the winning streaks. But the fans are so greedy. They've reached the point where they are unhappy if John wins a championship game by five points. If he ever loses a game they're going to say that he's too old and he's lost his touch. They can stretch the rules and let him stay until he's sixty-seven, but I

wonder if it would be worth it. What more does my husband have to prove?

The UCLA fans were indeed voracious winners. Yet by this stage   33
in John Wooden's career, his own drive for success had become an obsession. Four months later, after UCLA had been upset by North Carolina State in the NCAA finals, Wooden made an unprecedented three
recruiting trips to Salt Lake City in order to finally tie down seven-foot
Brett Vroman, a player he felt the Bruins needed to win even more
championships in the coming years. Here was the greatest basketball
coach in college history, a 64-year-old man with a heart problem, pursuing a 17-year-old hotshot who might help keep a basketball machine
humming for another three or four years. Is any clearer testimony needed
to show us where our fanaticism has brought us?

Questions for Study and Discussion

1. What point about winning do Tutko and Bruns make in this essay? In what way is winning "like drinking salt water"?

2. How, according to Tutko and Bruns, is the drive to compete particularly American? Are you convinced by their presentation? Does your experience with people in other cultures bear out John R. Tunis's assessment?

3. In paragraphs 15–25 the authors quote a number of prominent Americans with strong beliefs about winning. What is the function of the parenthetical comment or question that follows each of the quotations? Explain each one.

4. Why, according to the authors, has winning taken on such importance in America? How could we justify this obsession?

5. Explain what Tutko and Bruns mean by the "halo effect" of winners. How does it fuel the winning syndrome?

6. Why do you suppose Tutko and Bruns save the example of John Wooden for their conclusion? What is ironic about his career as head coach of basket-ball at UCLA? Explain.

Writing Topics

1. Write an essay in which you argue with Tutko and Bruns's position. Care-fully explain why you believe that winning is so important.

2. Write an essay in which you demonstrate that for better or worse the values of the sporting world are a mere reflection of our national culture and character.

JOHN UPDIKE

John Updike was born in 1932 and grew up in Shillington, Pennsylvania, a small town where his father taught high school. His childhood, described in a sketch called "The Dogwood Tree" (1965), was much like that of millions of other middle-class Americans, and these are typically the characters of his short stories, novels, and poems. Updike went to Harvard, where he became editor of its undergraduate humor magazine *The Lampoon*. Since graduation he has published many short stories as well as poems, plays, and ten novels. Three of his best known novels are about a high-school basketball player, Harry "Rabbit" Angstrom: *Rabbit, Run* (1961), *Rabbit Redux* (1971), and *Rabbit Is Rich* (1981). In the following poem, first published in *The New Yorker*, Updike draws a sad portrait of a former high-school basketball star whose career seemed to stand still after graduation.

Ex-Basketball Player

Pearl Avenue runs past the high-school lot,
Bends with the trolley tracks, and stops, cut off
Before it has a chance to go two blocks,
At Colonel McComsky Plaza. Berth's Garage
Is on the corner facing west, and there,   5
Most days, you'll find Flick Webb, who helps Berth out.

Flick stands tall among the idiot pumps—
Five on a side, the old bubble-head style,
Their rubber elbows hanging loose and low.
One's nostrils are two S's, and his eyes   10
An E and O. And one is squat, without
A head at all—more of a football type.

Once Flick played for the high-school team, the Wizards.
He was good: in fact, the best. In '46
He bucketed three hundred ninety points,   15
A county record still. The ball loved Flick.
I saw him rack up thirty-eight or forty
In one home game. His hands were like wild birds.

He never learned a trade, he just sells gas,
Checks oil, and changes flats. Once in a while,   20

As a gag, he dribbles an inner tube.
But most of us remember anyway.
His hands are fine and nervous on the lug wrench.
It makes no difference to the lug wrench, though.

Off work, he hangs around Mae's Luncheonette.   25
Grease-grey and kind of coiled, he plays pinball,
Sips lemon cokes, and smokes those thin cigars;
Flick seldom speaks to Mae, just sits and nods
Beyond her face towards bright applauding tiers
Of Necco Wafers, Nibs, and Juju Beads.   30

Questions for Study and Discussion

1. What is the relation of the speaker in the poem to Flick Webb? What is
the speaker's attitude toward Flick as a basketball player? As a gas-station
attendant?

2. How in stanza one does the narrator suggest that Flick's career as a basketball player did not mature?

3. In stanza two Updike uses personification. What precisely is personified
and to what end?

4. Why do you suppose Updike said "The ball loved Flick" instead of "Flick
loved the ball"? In contrast, what is Flick's relationship to the lug wrench?

5. Why does the narrator bother to tell us about Flick's off-work hours? Explain the metaphor in the last two lines. How well does it work for you?

Writing Topics

1. Write an essay in which you explore the expectations that Americans
have for their sports heroes. Can we reasonably expect them to perform in
all aspects of life? Or, are the former sports heroes given special treatment by
the public, treatment that they sometimes don't deserve?

2. Write an essay in which you compare and contrast Flick Webb, high
school basketball hero, with an athletic star from your high school.

5 Work

His job must not only feed his body; it must sustain his spirit.
DANIEL BELL

I'm not going to get away with being a curious unique female for long. I'll have to be judged on my performance.
ANNE ARMSTRONG

Job Satisfaction

LANCE MORROW

What are our attitudes toward our work, and toward work in general? What has become of the once-compelling American "work ethic"? Lance Morrow, writing in *Time* magazine for Labor Day, 1981, approaches these questions from the vantage point of our history as well as of our contemporary society. Morrow was born 1939 in Philadelphia and attended Harvard College, where he graduated in 1963. Shortly thereafter he joined the staff of *Time* and has been one of that magazine's regular contributors since 1965, writing on a wide range of topics of current interest.

The American work ethic had its origins in the beliefs of ascetic Protestants who held that God approves of strict discipline and hard work and shows His approval through worldly success and prosperity. Many non-Protestant immigrants also found justification for hard labor in an effort to make a better life for their families. But what is the value of work now, in the eighties? Morrow suggests some answers.

The Value of Working

During the 19th century industrialization of America, the idea of work's inherent virtue may have seemed temporarily implausible to generations who labored in the mines and mills and sweatshops. The century's huge machinery of production punished and stunned those who ran it.   1

And yet for generations of immigrants, work *was* ultimately availing: the numb toil of an illiterate grandfather got the father a foothold and a high school education, and the son wound up in college or even law school. A woman who died in the Triangle Shirtwaist Co. fire in lower Manhattan had a niece who made it to the halcyon Bronx, and another generation on, the family went to Westchester County.[1] So for   2

[1] The Triangle Shirtwaist Company was a sweatshop employing European immigrants, mostly women, at very low wages. In a 1911 fire there 145 people were killed.

millions of Americans, as they labored through the complexities of generations, work worked, and the immigrant work ethic came at last to
merge with the Protestant work ethic.

The motive of work was all. To work for mere survival is desperate.   3
To work for a better life for one's children and grandchildren lends the
labor a fierce dignity. That dignity, an unconquerably hopeful energy and
aspiration—driving, persisting like a life force—is the American quality
that many find missing now.

The work ethic is not dead, but it is weaker now. The psychology   4
of work is much changed in America. The acute, painful memory of the
Great Depression used to enforce a disciplined and occasionally docile
approach to work—in much the way that older citizens in the Soviet
Union do not complain about scarce food and overpopulated apartments,
because they remember how much more horrible everything was during
the war. But the generation of the Depression is retiring and dying off,
and today's younger workers, though sometimes laid off and kicked around
by recessions and inflation, still do not keep in dark storage that residual
apocalyptic memory of Hoovervilles and the Dust Bowl[2] and banks cap-
sizing.

Today elaborate financial cushions—unemployment insurance, union   5
benefits, welfare payments, food stamps and so on—have made it less
catastrophic to be out of a job for a while. Work is still a profoundly
respectable thing in America. Most Americans suffer a sense of loss, of
diminution, even of worthlessness if they are thrown out on the street.
But the blow seldom carries the life-and-death implications it once had,
the sense of personal ruin. Besides, the wild and notorious behavior of
the economy takes a certain amount of personal shame out of joblessness;
if Ford closes down a plant in New Jersey and throws 3,700 workers into
the unemployment lines, the guilt falls less on individuals than on Japanese imports or American car design or an extortionate OPEC.[3]

Because today's workers are better educated than those in the past,   6
their expectations are higher. Many younger Americans have rearranged
their ideas about what they want to get out of life. While their fathers
and grandfathers and great-grandfathers concentrated hard upon plow
and drill press and pressure gauge and tort, some younger workers now

---

[2]Hooverville was the name of any shantytown of unemployed, dispossessed people
during the early years of the Great Depression. The name came from President Her-
bert Hoover because it was during his administration that they existed. The Dust
Bowl was a region including Oklahoma and parts of neighboring states that was afflicted by severe drought and high winds.

[3]Organization of Petroleum-exporting Countries, the international price- and quota-
setting cartel.

ask previously unimaginable questions about the point of knocking themselves out. For the first time in the history of the world, masses of people in industrially advanced countries no longer have to focus their minds upon work as the central concern of their existence.

In the formulation of Psychologist Abraham Maslow, work functions in a hierarchy of needs: first, work provides food and shelter, basic human maintenance. After that, it can address the need for security and then for friendship and "belongingness." Next, the demands of the ego arise, the need for respect. Finally, men and women assert a larger desire for "self-actualization." That seems a harmless and even worthy enterprise but sometimes degenerates into self-infatuation, a vaporously selfish discontent that dead-ends in isolation, the empty face that gazes back from the mirror.

Of course in patchwork, pluralistic America, different classes and ethnic groups are perched at different stages in the work hierarchy. The immigrants—legal and illegal—who still flock densely to America are fighting for the foothold that the jogging tribes of self-actualizers achieved three generations ago. The zealously ambitious Koreans who run New York City's best vegetable markets, or boat people trying to open a restaurant, or Chicanos who struggle to start a small business in the *barrio* are still years away from est and the Sierra Club.[4] Working women, to the extent that they are new at it, now form a powerful source of ambition and energy. Feminism—and financial need—have made them, in effect, a sophisticated-immigrant wave upon the economy.

Having to work to stay alive, to build a future, gives one's exertions a tough moral simplicity. The point of work in that case is so obvious that it need not be discussed. But apart from the sheer necessity of sustaining life, is there some inherent worth in work? Carlyle believed that "all work, even cotton spinning, is noble; work is alone noble." Was he right?

It is seigneurial cant to romanticize work that is truly detestable and destructive to workers. But misery and drudgery are always comparative. Despite the sometimes nostalgic haze around their images, the preindustrial peasant and the 19th century American farmer did brutish work far harder than the assembly line. The untouchable who sweeps excrement in the streets of Bombay would react with blank incomprehension to the malaise of some $17-an-hour workers on a Chrysler assembly line. The Indian, after all, has passed from "alienation" into a degradation

7

8

9

10

---

[4]*Barrio*, Spanish for "neighborhood" and here used to refer to a Hispanic area. *Est*, Latin for "is," refers to a self-realization program and group founded by Werner Erhard. The Sierra Club is an organization for enjoying and protecting the wilderness of America.

that is almost mystical. In Nicaragua, the average 19-year-old peasant has worked longer and harder than most Americans of middle age. Americans prone to restlessness about the spiritual disappointments of work should consult unemployed young men and women in their own ghettos: they know with painful clarity the importance of the personal dignity that a job brings.

Americans often fall into fallacies of misplaced sympathy. Psychologist Maslow, for example, once wrote that he found it difficult "to conceive of feeling proud of myself, self-loving and self-respecting, if I were working, for example, in some chewing-gum factory . . ." Well, two weeks ago, Warner-Lambert announced that it would close down its gum-manufacturing American Chicle factory in Long Island City, N.Y.: the workers who had spent years there making Dentyne and Chiclets were distraught. "It's a beautiful place to work," one feeder-catcher-packer of chewing gum said sadly. "It's just like home." There is a peculiar elitist arrogance in those who discourse on the brutalizations of work simply because they cannot imagine themselves performing the job. Certainly workers often feel abstracted out, reduced sometimes to dreary robotic functions. But almost everyone commands endlessly subtle systems of adaptation; people can make the work their own and even cherish it against all academic expectations. Such adaptations are often more important than the famous but theoretical alienation from the process and product of labor.

Work is still the complicated and crucial core of most lives, the occupation melded inseparably to the identity; Freud said that the successful psyche is one capable of love and of work. Work is the most thorough and profound organizing principle in American life. If mobility has weakened old blood ties, our co-workers often form our new family, our tribe, our social world; we become almost citizens of our companies, living under the protection of salaries, pensions and health insurance. Sociologist Robert Schrank believes that people like jobs mainly because they need other people; they need to gossip with them, hang out with them, to schmooze. Says Schrank: "The workplace performs the function of community."

Unless it is dishonest or destructive—the labor of a pimp or a hit man, say—all work is intrinsically honorable in ways that are rarely understood as they once were. Only the fortunate toil in ways that express them directly. There is a Renaissance splendor in Leonardo's effusion: "The works that the eye orders the hands to make are infinite."[5] But most of us labor closer to the ground. Even there, all work expresses the

11

12

13

---

[5]Refers to Leonardo da Vinci (1452–1519), Italian artist and scientist.

laborer in a deeper sense: all life must be worked at, protected, planted, replanted, fashioned, cooked for, coaxed, diapered, formed, sustained. Work is the way that we tend the world, the way that people connect. It is the most vigorous, vivid sign of life—in individuals and in civilizations.

Questions for Study and Discussion

1. In Morrow's view, what does work do for people? How does he support his view?

2. Morrow says, "The work ethic is not dead, but it is weaker now." How does he support that statement? In your own view, what reasons are there for believing or disbelieving his statement?

3. What kinds of workers does Morrow approve of? What workers does he disapprove of? How does he reveal his attitudes? What specific words reveal his attitudes?

4. What is "self-actualization"? What does Morrow think of it? How does his opinion relate to his views on the value of working?

5. Morrow says "Work is still a profoundly respectable thing in America." What reasons does Morrow give for believing this? How does he qualify his assertion?

6. Morrow asks, "Is there some inherent worth in work?" How does he (not Carlyle) answer his question?

Writing Topics

1. Think about what you would like your life's work to be. What are your expectations of such work? What satisfaction and rewards do you hope to get from your work? Write an essay in which you discuss your career aspirations.

2. Morrow quotes the nineteenth-century British writer Thomas Carlyle as saying, "All work, even cotton-spinning, is noble; work is alone noble. . . ." Write an essay in which you support or oppose Carlyle's view. If you consider work noble, how would you define *noble*? If not, how would you characterize work? What other pursuits might be as noble as work? more noble?

3. Read several accounts people have written about what they do and how they feel about their work. (One excellent source is Studs Terkel's *Working*.) Or, interview people you know personally who are working, such as teachers, grocery clerks, and the like. Now write an essay about people's expectations and attitudes about their work.

Most people want their work to be satisfying and admire or envy those who are happy in their work. But what if work becomes an obsession? Marilyn Machlowitz, a management psychologist, has studied obsessive workers for some years and has published her findings in *Workaholics* (1980). She was born in 1952 and graduated from Princeton. Later she earned her doctorate in psychology at Yale. She is currently at work on a study of the consequences of succeeding at an early age.

The word *workaholics* was formed by analogy with *alcoholic,* and suggests that those who live for their work are victims of an unfortunate addiction. But are they? In this selection from her book, Machlowitz defines workaholism and describes how some typical over-achievers behave.

Workaholics

To rest is to rust.
LESTER LANIN

When I interviewed Dr. Stuart Berger, who is now an associate   1
professor of psychiatry at Harvard, he was 25 and wrapping up his final days at New York City's Bellevue Hospital. A tall, good-looking man with dark, curly hair, Berger was wearing jeans and Adidas, almost as much a part of the uniform of a young doctor as the beeper attached to his belt. We met in his small apartment, which was dominated by both its imposing view of the New York skyline and a large, well-stocked wine rack. The interview was interrupted by incessant phone calls, for which Berger apologized, explaining, "My life has been a bit busy."

And indeed it had. Besides seeing private patients, teaching psy-   2
chiatry and law, directing an institute for the study of law and medicine, consulting for a drug-free therapeutic community, seeing clinic patients, supervising medical students and junior residents, and writing a book, Berger had been flying around the country to lecture and appear on television talk shows.

"My average week is about 100 hours long and very fast-paced. I   3
get up about 6 A.M., shower, and have coffee; start reading journals at 6:30; see my first patients at 8:00; teach; never eat lunch—I just have garbage food all day. Three-quarters of the time I have a work-related dinner, and it's not uncommon on private days[1] to see patients until

[1]That is, days reserved for seeing patients in his office rather than at the hospital.

8:00, 8:30 at night. Of course, there's something very important to say about this horrendous-sounding schedule: I adore it!"

What makes him go and what keeps him going? "Give me a good goal. Give me something I can get excited about, that I can fantasize about, that I can live. I don't need any thank you's. I don't need any appreciation. I just need something I can get excited about. . . . I absolutely crave psychiatry and love developing better systems for providing patient care. And these are things I can work on for months at a time at this pace. The goals are never accomplishable. There are always going to be more social problems. There'll never be an end. No matter how much I accomplish, it'll always be trivial compared to what's left to be done." 4

When asked what he does when he's not working, he paused and was hard-pressed to come up with anything. "What kinds of things do I like? I have to think of them. I've given up collecting coins and I'd always been a great reader before I went to college." Having just bought a summer home, he was planning to spend time there. "I'm taking three-day weekends. People who know me don't believe it. I'll read the books that have been piling up for seven years, sail, lose some weight, jog, and make myself healthy before I go into hibernation again." 5

But even as he spoke, Berger began to doubt his words. Smiling sheepishly, he said, "Call me up at the end of the summer and I'll tell you if I did it." 6

[Berger] has most of the earmarks of the workaholic: He is intense and driven, he doesn't sleep much, he works almost all of his waking hours, and vacations and time off remain firmly in the realm of fantasy. Berger's workaholic tendencies seem to fit well with his job and with his single, busy life-style. He is what I call a fulfilled workaholic, one who gets great enjoyment from his work and who has successfully shaped the rest of his life around his central passion. 7

Others, especially those with families, have more difficulty accomplishing such a feat. Alex Loukides (a pseudonym) is a typical example. Brought up in a lower class Greek community in Connecticut, Loukides graduated from college and served in the Marines before he joined the Manhattan firm where he still works. Loukides is 41, his wife is a few years younger, and their two children are 12 and 14. Loukides is now a senior partner in the firm. Whereas most of his colleagues commute from lush suburbs, he still lives in the town where he grew up, despite his substantial six-figure income. 8

• • • •

His present position is, he says, more "unpredictable" and therefore 9
more "exhilarating" than any of the many he has held since his trainee
days. Still, he says, "I feel the same getting off the elevator as I did
twenty years ago. There's no sense of power or anything like that." He
cites his success in business as his main source of satisfaction, explaining,
"I don't think you can separate yourself from what you do. I don't think
your concept of yourself can be separated from what you do."

Loukides is frequently in his Manhattan office six days a week. He 10
arrives home around 8 P.M. His travel schedule is less time-consuming
than it could be, however, for when he travels, he resorts to turnaround
trips: "I've been to Paris thirteen times for a total of twelve days."

Nor are vacations a temptation. "Vacations bore me. I don't really 11
enjoy them. . . . In the past few years, I've made a real effort to take
them. We bought a house by the shore. This was an effort on my part
to force me to spend time with my family."

Not surprisingly, he feels guilty about "not having been as good a 12
husband and a father as I'd like to be. . . . I don't think the kids resent
my working [hard]. . . . I think my wife does. . . . she's a housewife and
she's going through the same thing every other woman's going through.
'Should I go back to school? Should I get a job?' I don't try to discourage
her, but I find it kind of threatening, too. It's sort of comfortable for me
to have her in the house."

• • • •

When I asked him if he was a workaholic, Loukides said, "I don't 13
know. If you asked my wife, she would say 'Definitely.' And probably a
lot of other people would, too. . . . If being a workaholic means you're
dependent on work and you have to work in order to function, well, I
think that's true for everybody."

Loukides seemed vaguely aware of some rumblings both in the office 14
(his "unpredictable" position) and at home. Yet he either doesn't see
clearly or chooses not to accept that some of these problems could be
tied to his addiction for work.

Both Loukides and Berger share six basic characteristics that set all 15
workaholics apart. These "traits" indicate that workaholism is considerably more paradoxical than the stereotype would lead us to believe. Still,
my research shows that these characteristics are common to each and
every workaholic that I interviewed. Let's take a look at them.

Workaholics are intense, energetic, competitive, and driven. The inten- 16
sity of a workaholic is inspiring. Eileen Ford, founder and head of the
New York modeling agency, skips much of the weekend social scene.

"It's not the good life that interests me so much as the good job." She explains that she spends her weekends working. "I lock myself in my bedroom on Saturday and Sunday with shades drawn and work until I accomplish what I wish to accomplish."

Part of the ability to work so hard, finds Mrs. Ford, comes from working at what one enjoys. "If I'm working, that's just what I am doing, nothing else. I'm not thinking about what else I would like to do, only what I'm doing. My mind doesn't wander. I am capable of tremendous concentration. I am never tired."

Workaholics also have an overwhelming zest for life. They are people who wake up and can't wait to get going. A banker explained, "I have a tremendous amount of energy. . . . my father says Con Ed should have plugged into me during the energy crisis." Already energetic, workaholics are energized rather than enervated by their work— their energy paradoxically expands as it is expended. This relationship between energy and work is somewhat circular. As an advertising executive explained, "My energy contributes to my job and my job contributes to my energy."

Workaholics compete fiercely with others. However, the most stringent standards are internal and the strongest competition is with themselves. As one man explained, "I live on ten-year goals. . . . I set my own goals, make my own challenges, and compete with myself." They live life as a game—better yet, a race—to be won for fear that others will gain on them unless they keep getting ahead. One workaholic delighted in getting to work hours before anyone else because, "by 9.00 I had done a day's work. . . . I was already a day ahead of everybody."

Not surprisingly, the number one topic for comparison in this competition is hours of work. A young physician explained that the main obsession among his medical school classmates, the residents who supervised them in hospital wards, and the physicians who taught them the courses wasn't money, sex, or knowledge, but how hard they worked. Five-minute lunches never left much time for conversation, but this topic was always discussed.

Workaholics are driven. While waiting for the critical and commercial success that will permit him to move from Manhattan and television to Hollywood and the movies, a young screenwriter holds a full-time job as a staff writer for a mundane trade magazine. He considers himself a workaholic "because I totally define myself in terms of my work. . . . I'm so used to its directing my life. It's directing me. I'm not directing it. . . . But it's gone too far. I can't not do it. I get physically sick if I don't do something on a script each day. . . ."

His drive is not derived from a sense of self-discipline. Rather, his   22
seeming self-discipline stems from his drive. "Writing gives me discipline.
You have to be home at a certain time to write." He is not one to do
nothing. "Intellectually, I realize there's a value to rest, [to] 'hanging
out,' 'bumming around,' but emotionally, I can't."

Workaholics have strong self-doubts. Although they appear assured to   23
the point of arrogance, they secretly suspect that they are inadequate.
No matter how undeserved and/or suppressed these suspicions are, they
still inspire insecurities. Working hard can be a way of concealing or
compensating for such suspected shortcomings.

Shelly Gross is a producer, novelist, and co-founder of Music Fair   24
Enterprises, Inc., an organization that produces shows and concerts
throughout the United States and Canada. Gross' workweek typically
includes commuting between suburban Philadelphia, where he lives and
works, and Manhattan, where partner Lee Guber lives and works; catching new acts; and throwing cast suppers in each city. His strategy, like
that of most workaholics, is to organize his time. "I try my best compulsively not to waste time." Gross feels uneasy when forced to waste
time, so he makes sure that he's seldom put in that position: He fills his
time with surf fishing and writing; he's finished five novels so far. What
makes Shelly run? "Deep down inside, there's the feeling that I'm trading
sweat for talent."

This concern is not uncommon. One man felt he wasn't quite the   25
intellectual equal of his peers, despite his Harvard degrees. Therefore,
he thought the only way to keep up would be by doing more. Others
maintain that their work isn't just the thing they're best at, but the only
thing they're even good at. Barbara Walters, for instance, squelches claims
that she is an all-around Wonder Woman with an appealing combination
of honesty and modesty. She told *Vogue* magazine, "I flunked gym, flunked
home economics. I am not visual and can't draw. But I'm compulsive. Whatever it is, I must do it today. And must do it over until it's
right."

Workaholics prefer labor to leisure. With respect to weekends and   26
vacations, the ways of workaholics once again appear to be at odds with
those of the rest of society. Either because of position or personality,
they have blended or reversed the customary roles, preferring labor to
leisure. What they do for a living has evolved into an endlessly fascinating endeavor. They have no use for and little need of free time.
They find inactivity intolerable and pressure preferable. Workaholics
never say "Thank God it's Friday" for they prefer weekdays to week-

ends. Mondays, in fact, offer welcome relief from the "Sunday neurosis," a syndrome of anxiety and depression stimulated by weekend's tranquility.

Workaholics can—and do—work anytime and anywhere. They are heedless of holidays, slow seasons, and weekends. Many maintain that they save time this way. Explains Senator William Proxmire "I find that by working on weekends or evenings or times when the phone is not ringing and others are not present, it is possible to accomplish a lot in a short time." Nor are they likely to turn off after hours. As a securities analyst said, "I'm forever thinking about new companies and new industries and, to a degree, this puts me in my office twenty-four hours a day." [27]

As a result, their homes often become but branch offices of their businesses and both airplanes and commuter trains are pressed into service as substitute offices. Mary Wells Lawrence, who heads Wells, Rich, Greene, a New York ad agency, was once asked by a reporter when she stops, slows down, turns off, tunes out. She replied, "Never. I am either digesting new material or looking for new solutions to a client's problem. When I'm on a plane, I don't waste a minute. I cover all the magazines— I demolish them. I see a picture of a yacht we could photograph, read about a restaurant to take clients to or a new take-out place for chili because there's a client who likes chili." [28]

Workaholics make the most of their time. Their attitude toward time and its use is their most telling trait: The quest to conquer time is constant. They glance at their watches continually, as though calculating how to fit the most work into the least amount of time. Saving time becomes a goal in itself as they put to good use the spare seconds others seem not to notice. As Stanley Marcus, the department store magnate, stated in *Minding the Store,* "Time is a precious possession and I attempt to make the most of it by not wasting it, for it is irreplaceable. One of the ways I cover so much ground is by using time judiciously. . . . we all have time to do everything we want to do if we organize our time properly." [29]

For workaholics, "killing time" would seem tantamount to committing suicide. . . . So they sleep six hours a night (at most) and get up and get going early. Their meals are typically functional (breakfast business meetings) or fast (lunch at the desk). They use lists, appointment books, and gadgets—the dictating devices, lighted pens for darkened rooms, and even car telephones that enable them to work wherever they are—to master every minute. Indeed, workaholics are so conscious of and compulsive about using every minute that they struggle to save [30] seconds. They are the ones who continually punch the elevator button and then take the stairs because they don't want to wait. They rush through the day and into the night. As one harried woman reported, "I feel I even have to sleep fast."

They fill their Daytimers months in advance. And as Mary Wells   31
Lawrence told *Vogue*, "I run my life the way a lot of people run their businesses; I have to. I don't literally draw charts and graphs, but it's how I think. Everything is written down, planned in advance. I plan the year, I plan the month, I plan the week, I plan the day." Workaholics will win whenever being booked up becomes something of a status game. And a game it is. Jack Lenor Larsen, the New York fabric designer, cheerfully concedes that "to do ten things in one day would be too much, but to try for fifteen becomes an interesting game."

Workaholics blur the distinctions between business and pleasure. Louis   32
L'Amour, the prolific novelist, maintains that "the things I would do for fun are the things necessary to my work anyway. My work is also my hobby. I am happiest when working." One workaholic told me, "I don't think of work as any different from play. I mean, I do enjoy it—I'd rather do that than anything else. I'd rather do that than play—at anything else. I don't know why one has to draw the distinction."

As a result, the professional and personal lives of these work addicts   33
become intertwined. "Some of my best friends are people I've met over a conference table . . . and some of my clients are people I've met at parties," explained Laurel Cutler, senior vice-president for marketing planning at Leber Katz Partners in New York.

Although each and every workaholic exhibits these characteristics,   34
workaholics do differ from one another. The variation involves their attitude toward nonwork activities. Some workaholics, as the stereotype suggests, eschew these entirely. Others incorporate them into their work in one of several ways.

My research revealed four distinct types of workaholics.   35

The Dedicated Workaholic. The first type of workaholic is single-   36
minded and one-dimensional. These people fit the stereotype to a "T." They don't expand "job descriptions" to include their other interests because they simply have no other interests. They often seem humorless and brusque—and they are. As one executive recruiter confessed, "I'm so single-minded. I have to work very hard at not working twenty-four hours a day." Lew Wasserman, chairman of M.C.A., Inc., the entertainment conglomerate, has no hobbies. According to *Fortune*, "he admits with seeming pride that he has never played a set of tennis or round

of golf, and that in his forty-year career with M.C.A. he has taken but a single vacation." And Leda Sanford, a magazine editor, reportedly hates sports, spurns theatre and ballet, and is never without her briefcase.

Similarly, Revlon's Charles Revson was said to be particularly single-minded and exclusively devoted to his business. One of his associates once wished to interrupt a meeting momentarily to glance out the window as the Pope's motorcade passed by on Fifth Avenue. Revson was said to be indignant and totally uninterested in the historic procession below. The Vatican, after all, was not a prime purchaser of nail polish and lipstick.

The Integrated Workaholic. For the second type of workaholics, work is also "everything," but their work includes outside interests as well. By virtue of their job's purpose or their own personalities, they incorporate outside activities into the job itself. The president of one management consulting firm claimed to do little but work. Yet he reeled off trips and accomplishments ("I've published two books and have three more written in my head") that he merely considered to be part of his job.

David Rockefeller, chairman of The Chase Manhattan Bank, told *The New Yorker* "I can't imagine a more interesting job than mine. . . . The bank has dealings with everything. There is no field of activity it isn't involved in. It's a springboard for whatever interests one may have in any direction." And Barbara Walters once told a reporter, "I'm doing what I absolutely love. . . . I have the best job that anyone could have. . . . I have the opportunity to meet everyone, to interview everyone."

The Diffuse Workaholic. This third kind of workaholic is likely to have "fingers in lots of pies" and "several balls in the air" whether at work or not. These people may change jobs and fields fairly frequently. Their pursuits are more scattered than those of integrated workaholics. One Wall Street executive exemplified this approach particularly well. "I'm hyper during the day," he explained. "I have a kind of short attention span where a lot of things turn me on, and then, after a short period of time, I will drop them."

Similarly, one woman concedes "this job doesn't fill my time." So she resorts to filling her twenty-hour days with work for over a dozen committees, task forces, charitable organizations, civic groups, and community boards.

The Intense Workaholic. The fourth type of workaholic pursues leisure activities with the same passion, sense of purpose, and pace as he pursues work. A hobby just becomes "a job of a different kind." Recognizing this, one writer has warned that hobbies can be dangerous because workaholics will pursue them with "the same intensity and preoccupation as they do their work." As one woman workaholic told me, "I love sports. . . . I'm as avid about those as I am about working." She believes that "anybody who's very intense in business is also intense in their other pursuits." For example, more than one person in my sample was a marathoner, applying the same energy and exactitude toward training, clocking times, and completing difficult courses as toward their careers.

Alex Lewyt, who founded the vacuum cleaner company that bears his name, was profiled by *The New York Times.* Since Lewyt never took vacations, his doctor told him that he was a prime candidate for a heart attack and urged him to get a hobby. But he began collecting watches and clocks so obsessively that the doctor finally told him to lay off the timepieces, too.

43

Questions for Study and Discussion

1. What general definition of a workaholic does Machlowitz provide in this essay? How does she construct her definition?

2. Why do you think Machlowitz begins her essay with the anecdotes of Dr. Stuart Berger and Alex Loukides? How else might she have begun her essay?

3. Machlowitz is an authority on her subject. In what ways does she reveal the breadth and depth of her knowledge?

4. In what way is a workaholic different from other workers? What behavioral patterns characterize the workaholic? How does a workaholic relate to his or her job, family, friends, leisure time, and so forth?

5. Machlowitz divides workaholics into four types. What are they? What are the essential differences between these types? Do you know anyone you would call a workaholic? Which type is that person, and why?

6. Does any particular section of the essay strike you with unusual force? Which part? Why do you think you respond so strongly to it?

Writing Topics

1. Machlowitz's essay seems to imply that workaholics themselves may be very happy, but that those who live with them often suffer some deprivation. Do you think this is true or not? Why do you think so? Write an essay in which you support your view, using examples and anecdotes from your own experiences and observations.

2. Machlowitz explains what workaholism is and what workaholics do, but she does not discuss how a person becomes addicted to work. Write an essay

in which you speculate about some reasons for such an addiction. How might workaholism be avoided? Or should it be?

3. In "The Value of Working" (pages 365–369), Lance Morrow discusses various needs that work can fill in people's lives. How does Morrow's essay contribute to an understanding of workaholism? What does Machlowitz's essay add to Morrow's discussion of the work ethic and the value of working? Write an essay in which you discuss your answers to these questions.

PATRICK FENTON

Patrick Fenton was born in Brooklyn in 1941, and at the age of sixteen dropped out of school to go to work in a local factory before entering the army. After a two-year hitch in Germany, he went to work as an airport cargo handler at John F. Kennedy Airport in New York. At the same time he started to write articles for local publications. Eight years as a cargo handler proved to be too much. Fenton took a civil-service job and continued to work as a free-lance writer. He is now working toward a college degree he began some years ago.

While working as a cargo handler for Seaboard World Airlines, Fenton wrote "Confessions of a Working Stiff," in which he tells us how he makes his living and how physically and spiritually debilitating such a job is. The essay was first published in the April 1975 issue of *New York* magazine.

Confessions of a Working Stiff

The Big Ben is hammering out its 5:45 alarm in the half-dark of another Tuesday morning. If I'm lucky, my car down in the street will kick over for me. I don't want to think about that now; all I want to do is roll over into the warm covers that hug my wife. I can hear the wind as it whistles up and down the sides of the building. Tuesday is always the worst day—it's the day the drudgery, boredom, and fatigue start all over again. I'm off from work on Sunday and Monday, so Tuesday is my blue Monday.

I make my living humping cargo for Seaboard World Airlines, one of the big international airlines at Kennedy Airport. They handle strictly all cargo. I was once told that one of the Rockefellers is the major stockholder for the airline, but I don't really think about that too much. I don't get paid to think. The big thing is to beat that race with the time clock every morning of your life so the airline will be happy. The worst thing a man could ever do is to make suggestions about building a better airline. They pay people $40,000 a year to come up with better ideas. It doesn't matter that these ideas never work; it's just that they get nervous when a guy from South Brooklyn or Ozone Park acts like he actually has a brain.

I throw a Myadec high-potency vitamin into my mouth to ward off one of the ten colds I get every year from humping mailbags out in the cold rain at Kennedy. A huge DC-8 stretch jet waits impatiently for the 8,000 pounds of mail that I will soon feed its empty belly. I wash the Myadec down with some orange juice and grab a brown bag filled with

380

bologna and cheese. Inside the lunch bag there is sometimes a silly note from my wife that says, "I Love You—Guess Who?" It is all that keeps me going to a job that I hate.

I've been going there for seven years now and my job is still the same. It's weary work that makes a man feel used up and worn out. You push and you pull all day long with your back. You tie down pallets loaded with thousands of pounds of freight. You fill igloo-shaped containers with hundreds of boxes that look the same. If you're assigned to work the warehouse, it's really your hard luck. This is the job all the men hate most. You stack box upon box until the pallet resembles the exact shape of the inside of the plane. You get the same monotonous feeling an adult gets when he plays with a child's blocks. When you finish one pallet, you find another and start the whole dull process over again.

The airline pays me $192 a week for this. After they take out taxes and $5.81 for the pension, I go home with $142. Once a month they take out $10 for term life insurance, and $5.50 for union dues. The week they take out the life insurance is always the worst. I go home with $132. My job will never change. I will fill up the same igloos with the same boxes for the next 34 years of my life, I will hump the same mailbags into the belly of the plane, and push the same 8,000-pound pallets with my back. I will have to do this until I'm 65 years old. Then I'll be free, if I don't die of a heart attack before that, and the airline will let me retire.

In winter the warehouse is cold and damp. There is no heat. The large steel doors that line the warehouse walls stay open most of the day. In the cold months, wind, rain and snow blow across the floor. In the summer the warehouse becomes an oven. Dust and sand from the runways mix with the toxic fumes of fork lifts, leaving a dry, stale taste in your mouth. The high windows above the doors are covered with a thick, black dirt that kills the sun. The men work in shadows with the constant roar of jet engines blowing dangerously in their ears.

Working the warehouse is a tedious job that leaves a man's mind empty. If he's smart he will spend his days wool-gathering. He will think about pretty girls that he once knew, or some other daydream of warm, dry places where you never had a chill. The worst thing he can do is to think about his problems. If he starts to think about how he is going to pay the mortgage on the $30,000 home that he can't afford, it will bring him down. He will wonder why he comes to the cargo airline every morning of his life, and even on Christmas Day. He will start to wonder why he has to listen to the deafening sound of the jets as they rev up their engines. He will wonder why he crawls on his hands and knees, breaking his back a little bit more every day.

To keep his kids in that great place in the country in the summer,   8
that great place far away from Brooklyn and the South Bronx, he must
work every hour of overtime that the airline offers him. If he never turns
down an hour, if he works some 600 hours over, he can make about
$15,000. To do this he must turn against himself, he must pray that the
phone rings in the middle of the night, even though it's snowing out and
he doesn't feel like working. He must hump cargo late into the night,
eat meatball heroes for supper, drink coffee that starts to taste like oil,
and then hope that his car starts when it's time to go home. If he gets
sick—well, he better not think about that.

All over Long Island, Ozone Park, Brooklyn, and as far away as   9
the Bronx, men stir in the early morning hours as a new day begins.
Every morning is the same as the last. Some of the men drink beer for
breakfast instead of coffee. Way out in Bay Shore a cargoman snaps open
a can of Budweiser. It's 6 A.M., and he covers the top of the can with
his thumb in order to keep down the loud hiss as the beer escapes. He
doesn't want to awaken his children as they dream away the morning in
the next room. Soon he will swing his Pinto wagon up onto the crowded
Long Island Expressway and start the long ride to the job. As he slips
the car out of the driveway he tucks another can of beer between his
legs.

All the men have something in common: they hate the work they   10
are doing and they drink a little too much. They come to work only to
punch a timecard that has their last name on it. At the end of the week
they will pick up a paycheck with their last name on it. They will never
receive a bonus for a job well done, or even a party. At Christmastime
a card from the president of the airline will arrive at each one of their
houses. It will say Merry Christmas and have the president's name printed
at the bottom of it. They know that the airline will be there long after
they are dead. Nothing stops it. It runs non-stop, without sleep, through
Christmas Day, New Year's Eve, Martin Luther King's birthday, even
the deaths of Presidents.

It's seven in the morning and the day shift is starting to drift in.   11
Huge tractors are backing up to the big-mouth doors of the warehouse.
Cattle trucks bring in tons of beef to feed its insatiable appetite for cargo.
Smoke-covered trailers with refrigerated units packed deep with green
peppers sit with their diesel engines idling. Names like White, Mack,
and Kenworth are welded to the front of their radiators, which hiss and
moan from the overload. The men walk through the factory-type gates
of the parking lot with their heads bowed, oblivious of the shuddering
diesels that await them.

Once inside the warehouse they gather in groups of threes and fours   12
like prisoners in an exercise yard. They stand in front of the two time
clocks that hang below a window in the manager's office. They smoke
and cough in the early morning hour as they await their work assignments. The manager, a nervous-looking man with a stomach that is
starting to push out at his belt, walks out with the pink work sheets in
his hand.

Eddie, a young Irishman with a mustache, has just bolted in through   13
the door. The manager has his timecard in his hand, holding it so no
one else can hit Eddie in. Eddie is four minutes late by the time clock.
His name will now go down in the timekeeper's ledger. The manager
hands the card to him with a "you'll be up in the office if you don't
straighten out" look. Eddie takes the card, hits it in, and slowly takes
his place with the rest of the men. He has been out till four in the
morning drinking beer in the bars of Ozone Park; the time clock and the
manager could blow up, for all he cares. "Jesus," he says to no one in
particular, "I hope to Christ they don't put me in the warehouse this
morning."

Over in another group, Kelly, a tall man wearing a navy knit hat,   14
talks to the men. "You know, I almost didn't make it in this morning.
I passed this green VW on the Belt Parkway. The girl driving it was
singing. Jesus, I thought to myself, it must be great going somewhere at
6:30 in the morning that makes you want to sing." Kelly is smiling as
he talks. "I often think, why the hell don't you keep on going, Kelly?
Don't get off at the cargo exit, stay on. Go anywhere, even if it's only
Brooklyn. Christ, if I was a single man I think I would do just that.
Some morning I'd pass this damn place by and drive as far away as
Riverhead. I don't know what I'd do when I got there—maybe I'd pick
up a pound of beefsteak tomatoes from one of those roadside stands or
something."

The men laugh at Kelly but they know he is serious. "I feel the   15
same way sometimes," the man next to him says. "I find myself daydream-
ing a lot lately; this place drives you to do that. I get up in the morning
and I just don't want to come to work. I get sick when I hit that parking
lot. If it wasn't for the kids and the house I'd quit." The men then talk
about how hard it is to get work on "the outside." They mention "outside" as if they were in a prison.

Each morning there is an Army-type roll call from the leads. The   16
leads are foremen who must keep the men moving; if they don't, it could
mean their jobs. At one time they had power over the men but as time
went by the company took away their little bit of authority. They also
lost the deep interest, even enjoyment, for the hard work they once did.

As the cargo airline grew, it beat this out of them, leaving only apathy. The ramp area is located in the backyard of the warehouse. This is where the huge jets park to unload their 70,000-pound payloads. A crew of men fall in behind the ramp lead as he mopes out of the warehouse. His long face shows the hopelessness of another day.

A brutal rain has started to beat down on the oil-covered concrete of the ramp as the 306 screeches in off the runway. Its engines scream as they spit off sheets of rain and oil. Two of the men cover their ears as they run to put up a ladder to the front of the plane. The airline will give them ear covers only if they pay for half of them. A lot of the men never buy them. If they want, the airline will give them two little plugs free. The plugs don't work and hurt the inside of the ears.   17

The men will spend the rest of the day in the rain. Some of them will set up conveyor belts and trucks to unload the thousands of pounds of cargo that sit in the deep belly of the plane. Then they will feed the awkward bird until it is full and ready to fly again. They will crawl on their hands and knees in its belly, counting and humping hundreds of mailbags. The rest of the men will work up topside on the plane, pushing 8,000-pound pallets with their backs. Like Egyptians building a pyramid, they will pull and push until the pallet finally gives in and moves like a massive stone sliding through sand. They don't complain too much; they know that when the airline comes up with a better system some of them will go.   18

The old-timers at the airline can't understand why the younger men stay on. They know what the cargo airline can do to a man. It can work him hard but make him lazy at the same time. The work comes in spurts. Sometimes a man will be pushed for three hours of sweat, other times he will just stand around bored. It's not the hard work that breaks a man at the airline, it's the boredom of doing the same job over and over again.   19

At the end of the day the men start to move in off the ramp. The rain is still beating down at their backs but they move slowly. Their faces are red and raw from the rain-soaked wind that has been snapping at them for eight hours. The harsh wind moves in from the direction of the city. From the ramp you can see the Manhattan skyline, gray- and blue-looking, as it peeks up from the west wall of the warehouse. There is nothing to block the winter weather as it rolls in like a storm across a prairie. They head down to the locker room, heads bowed, like a football team that never wins.   20

With the workday almost over, the men move between the narrow, gray rows of lockers. Up on the dirty walls that surround the lockers someone has written a couple of four-letter words. There is no wit to the   21 words; they just say the usual. As they strip off their wet gear the men seem to come alive.

"Hey, Arnie! You want to stay four hours? They're asking for over-   22
time down in Export," one of the men yells over the lockers.

Arnie is sitting about four rows over, taking off his heavy winter   23
clothing. He thinks about this for a second and yells back, "What will we be doing?"

"Working the meat trailer." This means that Arnie will be humping   24
huge sides of beef off rows of hooks for four hours. Blood will drip down onto his clothes as he struggles to the front of the trailer. Like most of the men, he needs the extra money, and knows that he should stay. He has Master Charge, Korvettes, Times Square Stores, and Abraham & Straus to pay.

"Nah, I'm not staying tonight. Not if it's working the meat trailer.   25
Don wanted to stop for a few beers at The Owl; maybe I'll stay tomorrow night."

It's four o'clock in the afternoon now—the men have twelve min-   26
utes to go before they punch out. The airline has stopped for a few seconds as the men change shifts. Supervisors move frantically across the floor pushing the fresh lot of new men who have just started to come in. They hand out work sheets and yell orders: "Jack, get your men into their rain gear. Put three men in the bellies to finish off the 300 flight. Get someone on the pepper trailers, they've been here all morning."

The morning shift stands around the time clock with three minutes   27
to go. Someone says that Kevin Delahunty has just been appointed to the Fire Department. Kevin, a young Irishman from Ozone Park, has been working the cargo airline for six years. Like most of the men, he has hated every minute of it. The men are openly proud of him as they reach out to shake his hand. Kevin has found a job on "the outside." "Ah, you'll be leaving soon," he tells Pat. "I never thought I'd get out of here either, but you'll see, you're going to make it."

The manager moves through the crowd handing out timecards and   28
stops when he comes to Kevin. Someone told him Kevin is leaving. "Is that right, Delahunty? Well I guess we won't expect you in tomorrow, will we? Going to become a fireman, eh? That means you'll be jumping out of windows like a crazy man. Don't act like you did around here," he adds as he walks back to his office.

The time clock hits 4:12 and the men pour out of the warehouse.   29
Kevin will never be back, but the rest of them will return in the morning to grind out another eight hours. Some of them will head straight home to the bills, screaming children, and a wife who tries to understand them.

They'll have a Schaefer or two, then they'll settle down to a night of television.

Some of them will start to fill up the cargo bars that surround 30 Kennedy Airport. They will head to places like Gaylor's on Rockaway Boulevard or The Dew Drop Inn down near Farmers Boulevard. They will drink deep glasses of whiskey and cold mugs of Budweiser. The Dew Drop has a honky-tonk mood of the Old West to it. The barmaid moves around like a modern-day Katie Elder. Like Brandy, she's a fine girl, but she can out-curse any cargoman. She wears a low-cut blouse that reveals most of her breasts. The jukebox will beat out some Country & Western as she says, "Ah, hell, you played my song." The cargomen will hoot and holler as she substitutes some of her own obscene lyrics.

They will drink late into the night, forgetting time clocks, Master 31 Charge, First National City, Korvettes, mortgages, cars that don't start, and jet engines that hurt their ears. They will forget about damp, cold warehouses, winters that get longer and colder every year, minutes that drift by like hours, supervisors that harass, and the thought of growing old on a job they hate. At midnight they will fall dangerously into their cars and make their way up onto the Southern State Parkway. As they ride into the dark night of Long Island they will forget it all until 5:45 the next morning—when the Big Ben will start up the whole grind all over again.

Questions for Study and Discussion

1. What is Fenton's attitude toward the airline company he works for? What in particular does Fenton dislike about his job? What are the immediate causes for his dissatisfaction? Why does he continue to work for the airline company?

2. Why, in your opinion, does the airline not do something to improve working conditions for its employees? Why does the airline company "get nervous when a guy from South Brooklyn or Ozone Park acts like he actually has a brain"?

3. What are "leads," and why does Fenton feel it is important to define and to discuss them?

4. For Fenton and his co-workers, working for the airline is a regimented, prison-like existence. How do Fenton's diction and imagery help to establish this motif?

5. Fenton uses concrete details and specific incidents to show rather than merely tell us how awful a job with the airline is. Identify several paragraphs that rely heavily on concrete detail and two or three revealing incidents that dramatize the plight of the workers. Explain how these passages make the cause-and-effect relationship that Fenton sees real for the reader.

6. Comment on the appropriateness of the following similes, which Fenton uses to describe the workers:
   a. "like prisoners in an exercise yard" (12)
   b. "like Egyptians building a pyramid" (18)
   c. "like a football team that never wins" (20)

7. In the title of his essay, Fenton refers to himself as a "working stiff." What does he mean?

8. What is it, according to Fenton, that breaks a man at the airline?

Writing Topics

1. In "Confessions of a Working Stiff," Patrick Fenton discusses the reasons why he hates his job. Not all people, of course, dislike their work. In fact, many people derive considerable satisfaction from the work they do. In an essay, discuss the reasons why some jobs are more satisfying than others. Why is it possible for a job to be satisfying for one person and not for another?

2. You are a manager who supervises a crew of Patrick Fentons. What do you think you could do as a manager to address the problems he raises in his essay? Write an essay in which you make proposals for such changes, explain how they would work, and argue for their acceptance.

ROBERT L. VENINGA and JAMES P. SPRADLEY

Robert L. Veninga, born in 1941 in Milwaukee, Wisconsin, is professor of health education at the University of Minnesota, where he earlier received his Ph.D. He writes and lectures frequently on topics relating to health administration and education. Coauthor James P. Spradley, born in 1933 in Baker, Oregon, received his Ph.D. in anthropology from the University of Washington. The author of more than a dozen scholarly books and one textbook, *Conformity and Conflict: Readings in Cultural Anthropology*, Spradley was DeWitt Wallace Professor of Anthropology at Macalester College, St. Paul, Minnesota, at the time of his death in 1982. Together Veninga and Spradley wrote *The Work/Stress Connection: How to Cope with Job Burnout*, from which the following selection was taken. First they define job burnout, that "debilitating psychological condition brought about by unrelieved work stress," and then consider the four major signs of it.

What Is Job Burnout?

We wanted to identify the range of job pressures, trace out their consequences, and find out how people managed stress on the job.

1

One of the most important facts revealed by our data, though not new, struck us with new urgency. It is simply that *your job can be hazardous to your health.* Stress in the workplace can give you negative fringe benefits you never bargained for. Physical illness. Emotional exhaustion. Ulcers. High blood pressure. Drinking too much. Headaches. Depression. In short, your job can burn you out. It can leave you listless and angry, upset with your spouse and kids, unable to enjoy your evenings and weekends. Like a thief in the night, work stress robs millions of workers of their health and happiness, then goes scot-free while the blame is laid elsewhere.

2

But we learned an equally important lesson from the people we studied: *you can avoid job burnout.* You can prevent the damage caused by unrelieved work stress. You can find ways to release the pressure. It's possible to humanize the workplace, to match people with jobs, to equip workers to cope with stress. Again and again we talked with people who had learned to live with high levels of stress in their jobs. They knew how to identify and avoid the hazard and had discovered ways to renew themselves. They were workers who lived in pressure-cooker jobs from eight to five, yet remained free from job-burnout symptoms.

3

We will have a great deal to say about both of these findings. Drawing on the data from our own studies of job burnout, we hope to

4

provide you with a clear understanding of this malady, as well as show you how to avoid it altogether or recover if you become a casualty. From time to time we will draw on the literally thousands of recent scientific studies related to work, stress, and health. Let's begin with a definition of job burnout.

Job Burnout: A Definition

Job burnout refers to *a debilitating psychological condition brought about*   5
by unrelieved work stress, which results in:

1. depleted energy reserves
2. lowered resistance to illness
3. increased dissatisfaction and pessimism
4. increased absenteeism and inefficiency at work.

This condition is debilitating because it has the power to weaken,   6
even devastate, otherwise healthy, energetic, and competent individuals. Its primary cause is unrelieved stress, the kind that goes on day after day, month after month, year after year. It manifests itself in these four major symptom areas, ones we will look at briefly here.

Every kind of work creates some type of stress. You must work   7
overtime to complete a report by a deadline imposed by someone else. You have to stand in the same two-by-three-foot area for eight hours a day, packaging tiny computer parts that come down the assembly line. You sit at your desk with nothing to do, watching the clock, unable to leave, unable to do what you would like. Each of these situations can place special demands on you—a stress to which you must respond. Some workers will find these stresses a challenge, even enjoyable, while others evaluate them in more negative terms.

For Sally Swanson, in her job as a bank teller, it was the unrelenting   8
criticism of her supervisor that became a chronic irritant and stress. Bob Mackler's stress came, in part, from the fifty-five to sixty hours a week he spent at Wendy's. But more important, he continued to feel responsible even when not at work. On his day off he found himself calling in to see how things were going. The chronic nature of the pressure took its toll and, as Bob freely admitted, "I just burned out from that job." Both Bill Hansen and Liz Keifer felt the continuing stress that came from feeling trapped in jobs they had outgrown. Liz Keifer's frustration centered on an unchallenging job. Bill Hansen had come to doubt his own

ability to find another church: "I feel used up here but don't see any hope of [being assigned to] another parish."

One of the first consequences of unrelieved work stress takes the form of depleted energy reserves. When people talk about burning out, they usually report feelings of exhaustion, weariness, loss of enthusiasm. They feel bone tired, when they go to bed and also when they wake up. A nurse told us, "I'm constantly preoccupied with the problems at work. I require more sleep and cannot drag myself out of bed in the morning." A purchasing agent confided, "I become emotionally exhausted and I just can't face going to work. I've even called in sick, just because I couldn't stand the thought of facing that place. I get depressed and forgetful." When your energy runs low, it can affect leisure-time activities. Bob Mackler loved to read books, but job burnout took away his interest, made his mind wander, and robbed him of his pleasure." In three months I've only finished reading a couple chapters," he said, shaking his head.

Depleted energy reserves also can spoil your time with other people or wipe it out altogether. As the nurse mentioned above remarked, "I'm no fun to be with anymore." A middle-aged veterinarian said, "I used to enjoy playing with my son in the evening. Now I'm too tired. I get impatient with him. I just want to get alone."

The second result of the stress that causes job burnout is *lowered resistance to illness.* "I began to get more colds," said a school principal, reflecting on the start of his own experience of job burnout. This is a common complaint among those who suffer from job burnout, but more serious problems can follow. Dr. Carroll Brodsky, a physician at the University of California Medical School in San Francisco, studied the way work stress led to illness in prison guards and teachers. He found that two-thirds of those he studied suffered from diseases such as ulcers, hypertension, arthritis, and depression.

Dr. Walter Menninger, senior staff psychiatrist at the Menninger Foundation, Topeka, Kansas, believes there is a clear relationship between stress and the aches and pains of everyday life. He says, "A chronic backache may signal the load is getting too heavy; the ulcer may suggest dealing with a situation you can't stomach. . . . Some degree of exhaustion is observed along with the development of other symptoms such as migraine headache, gastrointestinal upset, canker sores, and flu."

The exact manner in which work stress lowers your resistance to illness and contributes to disease is not fully understood. Yet we do know that scientific studies have shown that stress is implicated in many serious illnesses. Take the nation's number-one killer: coronary heart disease. In one investigation, a group of experts rated overall stress of specialties in

9

10

11

12

13

medicine, dentistry, and law, then studied the health records of professionals in these fields. They discovered that people in high-pressure jobs, such as trial lawyer and oral surgeon, not only smoked more (a stress-related activity), but had a higher incidence of coronary heart problems. In another study, tax accountants' cholesterol levels increased as the income-tax deadline drew near and their workloads increased. After work tapered off, cholesterol levels also declined. What they ate made little difference in this fluctuation. Another scientific study, this one of NASA personnel working on space flights, showed a direct relation between coronary-artery disease and stressful jobs. Researchers studied the health and work stress of managers, scientists, and engineers. The managers had to cope with the most work stress, especially in the form of conflict and overload. Among these three groups, the managers had a significantly higher incidence of coronary heart disease than the others.

The stress of job burnout also leads to *increased dissatisfaction and* 14 *pessimism.* Again and again we found that as people lived with unrelieved stress, the jobs they once enjoyed turned sour. Many looked back wistfully to an earlier era of contentment with their work. A housewife suffering from job burnout said, "For the first five years I loved being a housewife. It was meaningful and fun, but that seems like a long time ago. Now when my husband comes home I'm ready to climb the walls. I get headaches almost every day. I feel guilty, but I just hate the feeling of being a trapped housewife." The head of personnel in a large company, who recognized his own symptoms of job stress, said, "I started noticing a definite change in how I felt about my job. Like staff meetings. I used to look forward to them eagerly, but now I dread them like the plague. I'm just too tired to put up with the hassles."

With amazing regularity we found that when people did learn to 15 cope with work pressures, when they recovered from job burnout, their satisfaction level went up dramatically. A college professor is typical of many others. "I used to go around angry all the time at the administration of this college. I had lost my first love for students and for teaching. I came within a hair's breadth of giving it all up and trying some other career. I know now it was a case of burnout, and when I got that under control, my old enthusiasm returned. This college is a great place—and it really hasn't changed. But I sure have."

For many of those we studied, dissatisfaction had slowly turned to 16 dark pessimism. We asked one sample of workers in a variety of occupations, "How would you feel if you had to continue your present job for the rest of your life?" Here are some of their candid answers, which reveal the tragedy of unrelieved stress:

- "I would be worn out at fifty."

- "Very depressed. Would probably require professional help."

- "I couldn't face it. I would be very depressed."

- "If my position were not to improve . . . I don't feel that I could stand it much longer, let alone for the rest of my life."

- "Horrible, I would feel pinned down, locked into a position where there would be very little sense of achievement."

- "I'd kill myself. I could not take it."

- "Totally defeated. There would be little to look forward to."

Finally, job burnout leads to *increased absenteeism and inefficiency at work*. This may occur because of actual stress-related illness or simply lowered morale. As Jerome Rosow, head of the Work in America Institute, says, "Workers who are turned off will stay out under any pretext." In 1976, the Bureau of Labor Statistics reported that Americans lose 3.5 percent of work hours through absenteeism. It has been estimated that one out of three workers on any particular day has called in sick because of a stress-related problem. And when job burnout sets in, even those days on the job are less efficiently spent. Workers under stress take longer coffee breaks, take longer to accomplish tasks, make more mistakes, and put off tasks that require immediate attention. Many observers see a direct link between job burnout and our national decline in worker productivity.

17

Questions for Study and Discussion

1. In your own words, what is job burnout?

2. According to Veninga and Spradley, what are the four major symptoms of job burnout?

3. What is the ultimate effect of job burnout on the individual, corporations, institutions, and the people that they serve? Do you agree with those who believe that there is "a direct link between job burnout and our national decline in worker productivity"? Explain.

4. While the authors do not offer specific suggestions in their essay for alleviating job burnout, they do nonetheless suggest areas in which solutions can be found. What are those areas?

5. What is the function of the many examples that Veninga and Spradley use in their essay? Do the examples help to establish their authority on the subject? Explain.

Writing Topics

1. What is stress? Write an essay in which you define the term, using examples from your own experiences and observations as a student and worker.

2. Much attention has been focused on the nature of job burnout and the people who suffer from it. Little has been done to try to understand the consequences of job burnout beyond the immediate situation. Write an essay in which you speculate about the possible far-reaching effects of job burnout on our society.

3. Write an essay in which you analyze student burnout. What is it? How is it different from job burnout? Why do you believe student burnout exists? What can be done to alleviate the condition?

JAN HALVORSEN

Like death and taxes, unemployment seems to be a nagging problem even in the best of economic times. Indeed, some experts believe that we as a nation will never be 100 percent fully employed. Yet most working Americans do not give serious thought to what it would be like to be unemployed. Such was the case with Jan Halvorsen, who in 1980 quite unexpectedly found herself without a job. The experience was devastating for her, and she felt compelled to share her feelings in the following essay, which first appeared in *Newsweek*. In explaining what it felt like to lose her job Halvorsen accomplishes something more. As she writes, "You've gained something—a little more knowledge and a lot more compassion. You've learned the value of the routine you scorned and the importance of the job you took for granted." Shortly after this essay appeared, Jan Halvorsen was back on the job, this time as an assistant editor for the *Twin Cities Courier* in St. Paul, Minnesota.

How It Feels to Be Out of Work

Layoffs, unemployment and recession have always affected Walter   1
Cronkite's tone of voice and the editorial page. And maybe they affected a neighborhood business or a friend's uncle. But these terms have always been just words, affecting someone else's world, like a passing ambulance. At least they were until a few weeks ago, when the ambulance came for me.

Even as I sat staring blankly at my supervisor, hearing, "I've got   2
bad news: we're going to have to let you go," it all still seemed no more applicable to my daily life than a "60 Minutes" exposé. I kept waiting for the alternative—"but you can come back after a couple of months," or "you could take a salary cut, a different position," or even, "April fool." But none of these came. This was final. There was no mistake and no alternative.

You find yourself going back over it in your idle moments. There   3
wasn't so much as a "Thank you" for the long nights working alone, the "Sure, no problem, I'll have it tomorrow," the "Let me know if I can help," the "I just went ahead and did it this weekend" and, especially, for the "You forgot to tell me it changed? Oh, that's all right, I'll just do it over. No big deal."

No big deal. How it all echoes through your evenings and awakens   4
you in the morning. The mornings are probably the worst—waking up with a habitual jar, for the first two weeks, thinking, "I'm late!" Late for what? The dull ache in your lower stomach reminds you: late for nothing.

Depression

Again, you face the terms. "Loss of self-esteem and security, fear of 5
the future, stress, depression." You wonder dully if eating a dozen chocolate-chip cookies, wearing a bathrobe until 4, combing your hair at 5,
cleaning behind the stove (twice) and crying in an employment-agency
parking lot qualify as symptoms of stress or maybe loss of self-esteem.
Fighting with your spouse/boyfriend? Aha—tension in personal relationships.

The loss of a job is rejection, resulting in the same hurt feelings as 6
if a friend had told you to "bug off." Only this "friend" filled up 40 to 60
(or more) hours of your week. Constant references to the staff as "family"
only accentuate the feeling of desertion and deception. You picture yourself going home to your parents or spouse and being informed, "Your services
as our daughter/my wife are no longer required. Pick up your baby pictures
as you leave."

Each new affirmation of unemployment renews the pain: the first 7
trip to the employment agency, the first friend you tell, the first interview
and, most dreaded of all, the first trip to the unemployment office.

Standing in line at the unemployment office makes you feel very 8
much the same as you did the first time you ever flunked a class or a test—
as if you had a big red "F" for "Failure" printed across your forehead. I
fantasize myself standing at the end of the line in a crisp and efficient blue
suit, chin up, neat and straight as a corporate executive. As I move down
the line I start to come unglued and a half hour later, when I finally reach
the desk clerk, I am slouching and sallow in torn jeans, tennis shoes and
a jacket from the Salvation Army, carrying my wordly belongings in a
shopping bag and unable to speak.

You do eventually become accustomed to being unemployed, in the 9
way you might accept a bad limp. And you gradually quit beating yourself
for not having been somehow indispensable—or for not having become
an accountant. You tire of straining your memory for possible infractions.
You recover some of the confidence that always told you how good you
were at your job and accept what the supervisor said: "This doesn't reflect
on your job performance; sales are down 30 per cent this month."

But each time you recover that hallowed self-esteem, you renew a 10
fight to maintain it. Each time you go to a job interview and give them
your best and they hire someone else, you go another round with yourself
and your self-esteem. Your unemployment seems to drag on beyond all
justification. You start to glimpse a stranger in your rearview mirror. The

stranger suddenly looks like a bum. You look at her with clinical curiosity. Hmmm. Obviously into the chronic stages. Definitely not employable.

We unemployed share a social stigma similar to that of the rape   11
victim. Whether consciously or subconsciously, much of the work-ethic-driven public feels that you've somehow "asked for it," secretly wanted to lose your job and "flirted" with unemployment through your attitude—probably dressed in a way to invite it (left the vest unbuttoned on your three-piece suit).

Satisfaction

But the worst of it isn't society's work-ethic morality; it's your own,   12
which you never knew you had. You find out how much self-satisfaction was gained from even the most simple work-related task: a well-worded letter, a well-handled phone call—even a clean file. Being useful to yourself isn't enough.

But then almost everyone has heard about the need to be a useful   13
member of society. What you didn't know about was the loneliness. You've spent your life almost constantly surrounded by people, in classes, in dorms and at work. To suddenly find yourself with only your cat to talk to all day distorts your sense of reality. You begin to worry that flights of fancy might become one way.

But you always were, and still are, stronger than that. You maintain   14
balance and perspective, mainly through resorting frequently to sarcasm and irreverence. Although something going wrong in any aspect of your life now seems to push you into temporary despair much more easily than before, you have some very important things to hang on to—people who care, your sense of humor, your talents, your cat and your hopes.

And beyond that, you've gained something—a little more knowl-   15
edge and a lot more compassion. You've learned the value of the routine you scorned and the importance of the job you took for granted. But most of all, you've learned what a "7.6 per cent unemployment rate" really means.

Questions for Study and Discussion

1. Briefly summarize Halvorsen's feelings about being unemployed. What important discovery does she make about the value of work?

2. What is her purpose in writing this essay? Why do you suppose she doesn't explain why she lost her job?

3. What does Halvorsen see as the relationship between employment and self-worth? Explain.

4. Do you think that Halvorsen's audience is people who are currently employed or people who are unemployed like herself? What clues did you base your decision on?

5. Where does Halvorsen find solace and relief from the temporary despair of being unemployed?

6. How does Halvorsen's concluding paragraph bring her essay to closure? In what ways is it related to her introductory paragraphs?

7. Halvorsen states: "We unemployed share a social stigma similar to that of the rape victim." What does she mean? Is it a fair comparison?

Writing Topics

1. Think of a situation in which you experienced rejection. How did you feel about being rejected? How did you cope? What did you learn from the experience? Write an essay in which you offer specific advice for people who have suffered similar rejection.

2. Write an essay using the thesis: "Who you are is what you do." How important is a job or activity to your identity and self-esteem? What are some of the major benefits you get from working?

DONALD HALL

Donald Hall, born in New Haven, Connecticut, in 1928, is a poet and a teacher of writing. After graduating from Harvard College and earning a degree at Oxford University, he became poetry editor of the *Paris Review* for nine years, and also joined the faculty of the University of Michigan, where he taught until 1975. Hall then left the university to devote his efforts wholly to writing. An acquaintance writes: "Donald Hall lives with his wife, the poet Jane Kenyon, in his ancestral farm house in New Hampshire. Through the zero winters they burn wood in ancestral woodstoves—eight cords, cut, split, delivered in the fall. Don rises in the night to stoke the fires. In the summers Jane grows a garden. . . . The barn is dilapidated now, the old buggy still inside which Don's grandfather drove to church three-quarters of a century ago. In New England no one throws much away."[1] A selection of his best poems is available as *A Blue Tit Tilts at the Edge of the Sea: Selected Poems 1964–1974* (1975), and his most recent book of poems is *Kicking the Leaves* (1979), from which "Ox Cart Man" is taken.

Ox Cart Man

In October of the year,
he counts potatoes dug from the brown field,
counting the seed, counting
the cellar's portion out,
and bags the rest on the cart's floor.   5

He packs wool sheared in April, honey
in combs, linen, leather
tanned from deerhide,
and vinegar in a barrel
hooped by hand at the forge's fire.   10

He walks by ox's head, ten days
to Portsmouth Market, and sells potatoes,
and the bag that carried potatoes,
flaxseed, birch brooms, maple sugar, goose
feathers, yarn.   15

---

[1]Edward B. Germain, "Donald Hall," in *Contemporary Poets*, ed. James Vinson, 3rd ed. (New York: St. Martin's Press, 1980), p. 625.

When the cart is empty he sells the cart.
When the cart is sold he sells the ox,
harness and yoke, and walks
home, his pockets heavy
with the year's coin for salt and taxes,   20

and at home by fire's light in November cold
stitches new harness
for next year's ox in the barn,
and carves the yoke, and saws planks
building the cart again.   25

Questions for Study and Discussion

1. Why does the farmer sell the cart and the ox? How would you describe his philosophy of life, especially his attitude toward work?

2. In the first stanza (lines 1–5), what is the farmer doing with the potatoes?

3. How does Hall organize the events in the poem? What principle does he follow in dividing it into its five five-line stanzas?

4. Though the poem includes no rhymes, what evidence do you find that Hall has been careful to choose words for their sound as well as their meaning? How does the "sound" of the poem affect your response?

5. What point does Hall make in this poem? How does his choice of words enhance his point?

Writing Topics

1. Farmers like Hall's ox cart man are obliged to live in harmony with the seasons, but much of modern life is based on the conquest and exploitation of nature, rather than a respectful cooperation with it. What are some of the advantages of and dangers in our exploitation of nature? Is a simple life like the ox cart man's still possible—or desirable? Why or why not?

2. In an essay, appraise the ox cart man's attitude toward work in light of the essays by Lance Morrow (pp. 365–369) and/or Gloria Steinem (pp. 411–416).

JAMES JOYCE

Poet, dramatist, and novelist James Joyce was born in Dublin, Ireland, in 1882 and educated at the Jesuit Clongowes Wood College and Belvedere College, and at University College. After his mother's death in 1904, he left Ireland for the Continent, where he taught English at the Berlitz school in Trieste and wrote. *Dubliners*, a book of short stories, was published in 1914, and two years later Joyce's first novel *A Portrait of the Artist as a Young Man* appeared. After World War I, Joyce and his family left Zurich and settled in Paris, where he completed his famous novel *Ulysses* (1922). In later years, Joyce suffered from glaucoma which caused pain both while reading and writing. Two years before his death in 1941, *Finnegans Wake*, a daring and influential experiment in prose, was published.

In the following story from *Dubliners*, Joyce exhibits his sensitivity to both language and detail that enables him to tell his tale of human tragedy. "Counterparts" is the story of Farrington, a man whose job seems to control or dictate his behavior both on and off the job. Joyce seems particularly interested in exploring the causal relationships between events and determining the reasons why people behave toward each other the way they do.

Counterparts

The bell rang furiously and, when Miss Parker went to the tube, a furious voice called out in a piercing North of Ireland accent: 1

—Send Farrington here! 2

Miss Parker returned to her machine, saying to a man who was writing at a desk: 3

—Mr Alleyne wants you upstairs. 4

The man muttered *Blast him!* under his breath and pushed back his chair to stand up. When he stood up he was tall and of great bulk. He had a hanging face, dark wine-coloured, with fair eyebrows and moustache: his eyes bulged forward slightly and the whites of them were dirty. He lifted up the counter and, passing by the clients, went out of the office with a heavy step. 5

He went heavily upstairs until he came to the second landing, where a door bore a brass plate with the inscription *Mr Alleyne*. Here he halted, puffing with labour and vexation, and knocked. The shrill voice cried: 6

—Come in! 7

The man entered Mr Alleyne's room. Simultaneously Mr Alleyne, a little man wearing gold-rimmed glasses on a cleanshaven face, shot his head up over a pile of documents. The head itself was so pink and hairless that it seemed like a large egg reposing on the papers. Mr Alleyne did not lose a moment: 8

—Farrington? What is the meaning of this? Why have I always to complain of you? May I ask you why you haven't made a copy of that contract between Bodley and Kirwan? I told you it must be ready by four o'clock.   9

—But Mr Shelley said, sir—   10

—*Mr Shelley said, sir.* . . . Kindly attend to what I say and not to what *Mr Shelley says, sir.* You have always some excuse or another for shirking work. Let me tell you that if the contract is not copied before this evening I'll lay the matter before Mr Crosbie. . . . Do you hear me now?   11

—Yes, sir.   12

—Do you hear me now? . . . Ay and another little matter! I might as well be talking to the wall as talking to you. Understand once for all that you get a half an hour for your lunch and not an hour and a half. How many courses do you want, I'd like to know. . . . Do you mind me, now?   13

Yes, sir.   14

Mr Alleyne bent his head again upon his pile of papers. The man stared fixedly at the polished skull which directed the affairs of Crosbie & Alleyne, gauging its fragility. A spasm of rage gripped his throat for a few moments and then passed, leaving after it a sharp sensation of thirst. The man recognised the sensation and felt that he must have a good night's drinking. The middle of the month was passed and, if he could get the copy done in time, Mr Alleyne might give him an order on the cashier. He stood still, gazing fixedly at the head upon the pile of papers. Suddenly Mr Alleyne began to upset all the papers, searching for something. Then, as if he had been unaware of the man's presence till that moment, he shot up his head again, saying: 15

—Eh? Are you going to stand there all day? Upon my word, Farrington, you take things easy!   16

—I was waiting to see . . .   17

—Very good, you needn't wait to see. Go downstairs and do your work.   18

The man walked heavily towards the door and, as he went out of the room, he heard Mr Alleyne cry after him that if the contract was not copied by evening Mr Crosbie would hear of the matter.   19

He returned to his desk in the lower office and counted the sheets   20
which remained to be copied. He took up his pen and dipped it in the
ink but he continued to stare stupidly at the last words he had written:
In no case shall the said Bernard Bodley be . . . The evening was falling
and in a few minutes they would be lighting the gas: then he could write.
He felt that he must slake the thirst in his throat. He stood up from his
desk and, lifting the counter as before, passed out of the office. As he
was passing out the chief clerk looked at him inquiringly.

—It's all right, Mr Shelley, said the man, pointing with his finger   21
to indicate the objective of his journey.

The chief clerk glanced at the hat-rack but, seeing the row com-   22
plete, offered no remark. As soon as he was on the landing the man
pulled a shepherd's plaid cap out of his pocket, put it on his head and
ran quickly down the rickety stairs. From the street door he walked on
furtively on the inner side of the path towards the corner and all at once
dived into a doorway. He was now safe in the dark snug of O'Neill's
shop, and, filling up the little window that looked into the bar with his
inflamed face, the colour of dark wine or dark meat, he called out:

—Here, Pat, give us a g.p., like a good fellow.   23

The curate brought him a glass of plain porter. The man drank it   24
at a gulp and asked for a caraway seed. He put his penny on the counter
and, leaving the curate to grope for it in the gloom, retreated out of the
snug as furtively as he had entered it.

Darkness, accompanied by a thick fog, was gaining upon the dusk   25
of February and the lamps in Eustace Street had been lit. The man went
up by the houses until he reached the door of the office, wondering
whether he could finish his copy in time. On the stairs a moist pungent
odour of perfumes saluted his nose: evidently Miss Delacour had come
while he was out in O'Neill's. He crammed his cap back again into his
pocket and reentered the office, assuming an air of absent-mindedness.

—Mr Alleyne has been calling for you, said the chief clerk severely.   26
Where were you?

The man glanced at the two clients who were standing at the   27
counter as if to intimate that their presence prevented him from answering. As the clients were both male the chief clerk allowed himself a
laugh.

—I know that game, he said. Five times in one day is a little bit   28
. . . . Well, you better look sharp and get a copy of our correspondence
in the Delacour case for Mr Alleyne.

This address in the presence of the public, his run upstairs and the   29
porter he had gulped down so hastily confused the man and, as he sat
down at his desk to get what was required, he realised how hopeless was

the task of finishing his copy of the contract before half past five. The dark damp night was coming and he longed to spend it in the bars, drinking with his friends amid the glare of gas and the clatter of glasses. He got out the Delacour correspondence and passed out of the office. He hoped Mr Alleyne would not discover that the last two letters were missing.

The moist pungent perfume lay all the way up to Mr Alleyne's room. Miss Delacour was a middle-aged woman of Jewish appearance. Mr Alleyne was said to be sweet on her or on her money. She came to the office often and stayed a long time when she came. She was sitting beside his desk now in an aroma of perfumes, smoothing the handle of her umbrella and nodding the great black feather in her hat. Mr Alleyne had swivelled his chair round to face her and thrown his right foot jauntily upon his left knee. The man put the correspondence on the desk and bowed respectfully but neither Mr Alleyne nor Miss Delacour took any notice of his bow. Mr Alleyne tapped a finger on the correspondence and then flicked it towards him as if to say: *That's all right: you can go.*

The man returned to the lower office and sat down again at his desk. He stared intently at the incomplete phrase: *In no case shall the said Bernard Bodley be . . .* and thought how strange it was that the last three words began with the same letter. The chief clerk began to hurry Miss Parker, saying she would never have the letters typed in time for post. The man listened to the clicking of the machine for a few minutes and then set to work to finish his copy. But his head was not clear and his mind wandered away to the glare and rattle of the public-house. It was a night for hot punches. He struggled on with his copy, but when the clock struck five he had still fourteen pages to write. Blast it! He couldn't finish it in time. He longed to execrate aloud, to bring his fist down on something violently. He was so enraged that he wrote *Bernard Bernard* instead of *Bernard Bodley* and had to begin again on a clean sheet.

He felt strong enough to clear out the whole office singlehanded. His body ached to do something, to rush out and revel in violence. All the indignities of his life enraged him. . . . Could he ask the cashier privately for an advance? No, the cashier was no good, no damn good: he wouldn't give an advance. . . . He knew where he would meet the boys: Leonard and O'Halloran and Nosey Flynn. The barometer of his emotional nature was set for a spell of riot.

His imagination has so abstracted him that his name was called twice before he answered. Mr Alleyne and Miss Delacour were standing outside the counter and all the clerks had turned round in anticipation of something. The man got up from his desk. Mr Alleyne began a tirade of abuse, saying that two letters were missing. The man answered that

30

31

32

33

he knew nothing about them, that he had made a faithful copy. The tirade continued: it was so bitter and violent that the man could hardly restrain his fist from descending upon the head of the manikin before him.

—I know nothing about any other two letters, he said stupidly.   34

—*You—know—nothing*. Of course you know nothing, said Mr Al-   35
leyne. Tell me, he added, glancing first for approval to the lady beside him, do you take me for a fool? Do you think me an utter fool?

The man glanced from the lady's face to the little egg-shaped head   36
and back again; and, almost before he was aware of it, his tongue had found a felicitous moment:

—I don't think, sir, he said, that that's a fair question to put to   37
me.

There was a pause in the very breathing of the clerks. Everyone   38
was astounded (the author of the witticism no less than his neighbours) and Miss Delacour, who was a stout amiable person, began to smile broadly. Mr Alleyne flushed to the hue of a wild rose and his mouth twitched with a dwarf's passion. He shook his fist in the man's face till it seemed to vibrate like the knob of some electric machine:

—You impertinent ruffian! You impertinent ruffian! I'll make short   39
work of you! Wait till you see! You'll apologise to me for your imperti-
nence or you'll quit the office instanter! You'll quit this, I'm telling you, or you'll apologise to me!

• • • •

He stood in a doorway opposite the office watching to see if the   40
cashier would come out alone. All the clerks passed out and finally the cashier came out with the chief clerk. It was no use trying to say a word to him when he was with the chief clerk. The man felt that his position was bad enough. He had been obliged to offer an abject apology to Mr Alleyne for his impertinence but he knew what a hornet's nest the office would be for him. He could remember the way in which Mr Alleyne had hounded little Peake out of the office in order to make room for his own nephew. He felt savage and thirsty and revengeful, annoyed with himself and with everyone else. Mr Alleyne would never give him an hour's rest; his life would be a hell to him. He had made a proper fool of himself this time. Could he not keep his tongue in his cheek? But they had never pulled together from the first, he and Mr Alleyne, ever since the day Mr Alleyne had overheard him mimicking his North of Ireland accent to amuse Higgins and Miss Parker: that had been the beginning of it. He might have tried Higgins for the money, but sure Higgins never had

anything for himself. A man with two establishments to keep up, of course he couldn't. . . .

He felt his great body again aching for the comfort of the public-house. The fog had begun to chill him and he wondered could he touch Pat in O'Neill's. He could not touch him for more than a bob—and a bob was no use. Yet he must get money somewhere or other: he had spent his last penny for the g.p. and soon it would be too late for getting money anywhere. Suddenly, as he was fingering his watch chain, he thought of Terry Kelly's pawn-office in Fleet Street. That was the dart! Why didn't he think of it sooner?

He went through the narrow alley of Temple Bar quickly, muttering to himself that they could all go to hell because he was going to have a good night of it. The clerk in Terry Kelly's said *A crown!* but the con-signor held out for six shillings; and in the end the six shillings was allowed him literally. He came out of the pawn-office joyfully, making a little cylinder of the coins between his thumb and fingers. In Westmore-land Street the footpaths were crowded with young men and women returning from business and ragged urchins ran here and there yelling out the names of the evening editions. The man passed through the crowd, looking on the spectacle generally with proud satisfaction and staring masterfully at the office-girls. His head was full of the noises of tram-gongs and swishing trolleys and his nose already sniffed the curling fumes of punch. As he walked on he preconsidered the terms in which he would narrate the incident to the boys.

—So, I just looked at him—coolly, you know, and looked at her. Then I looked back at him again—taking my time, you know. *I don't think that that's a fair question to put to me,* says I.

Nosey Flynn was sitting up in his usual corner of Davy Byrne's and, when he heard the story, he stood Farrington a half-one, saying it was as smart a thing as ever he heard. Farrington stood a drink in his turn. After a while O'Halloran and Paddy Leonard came in and the story was repeated to them. O'Halloran stood tailors of malt, hot, all round and told the story of the retort he had made to the chief clerk when he was in Callan's of Fownes's Street; but, as the retort was after the manner of the liberal shepherds in the eclogues, he had to admit that it was not so clever as Farrington's retort. At this Farrington told the boys to polish off that and have another.

Just as they were naming their poisons who should come in but Higgins! Of course he had to join in with the others. The men asked him to give his version of it, and he did so with great vivacity for the sight of five small hot whiskies was very exhilarating. Everyone roared laughing when he showed the way in which Mr Alleyne shook his fist in Farrington's face. Then he imitated Farrington, saying, *And here was my nabs, as cool as you please,* while Farrington looked at the company out of his heavy dirty eyes, smiling and at times drawing forth stray drops of liquor from his moustache with the aid of his lower lip.

When that round was over there was a pause. O'Halloran had money but neither of the other two seemed to have any; so the whole party left the shop somewhat regretfully. At the corner of Duke Street Higgins and Nosey Flynn bevelled off to the left while the other three turned back towards the city. Rain was drizzling down on the cold streets and, when they reached the Ballast Office, Farrington suggested the Scotch House. The bar was full of men and loud with the noise of tongues and glasses. The three men pushed past the whining match-sellers at the door and formed a little party at the corner of the counter. They began to exchange stories. Leonard introduced them to a young fellow named Weathers who was performing at the Tivoli as an acrobat and knockabout *artiste*. Farrington stood a drink all round. Weathers said he would take a small Irish and Apollinaris. Farrington, who had definite notions of what was what, asked the boys would they have an Apollinaris too; but the boys told Tim to make theirs hot. The talk became theatrical. O'Halloran stood a round and then Farrington stood another round, Weathers protesting that the hospitality was too Irish. He promised to get them in behind the scenes and introduce them to some nice girls. O'Halloran said that he and Leonard would go but that Farrington wouldn't go because he was a married man; and Farrington's heavy dirty eyes leered at the company in token that he understood he was being chaffed. Weathers made them all have just one little tincture at his expense and promised to meet them later on at Mulligan's in Poolbeg Street.

When the Scotch House closed they went round to Mulligan's. They went into the parlour at the back and O'Halloran ordered small hot specials all round. They were all beginning to feel mellow. Farrington was just standing another round when Weathers came back. Much to Farrington's relief he drank a glass of bitter this time. Funds were running low but they had enough to keep them going. Presently two young women with big hats and a young man in a check suit came in and sat at a table close by. Weathers saluted them and told the company that they were out of the Tivoli. Farrington's eyes wandered at every moment in the direction of one of the young women. There was something striking in her appearance. An immense scarf of peacock-blue muslin was wound round her hat and knotted in a great bow under her chin; and she wore bright yellow gloves, reaching to the elbow. Farrington gazed admiringly at the plump arm which she moved very often and with much grace; and when, after a little time, she answered his gaze he admired still more her

46

47

large dark brown eyes. The oblique staring expression in them fascinated him. She glanced at him once or twice and, when the party was leaving the room, she brushed against his chair and said O, *pardon!* in a London accent. He watched her leave the room in the hope that she would look back at him, but he was disappointed. He cursed his want of money and cursed all the rounds he had stood, particularly all the whiskies and Apollinaris which he had stood to Weathers. If there was one thing that he hated it was a sponge. He was so angry that he lost count of the conversation of his friends.

When Paddy Leonard called him he found that they were talking about feats of strength. Weathers was showing his biceps muscle to the company and boasting so much that the other two had called on Farrington to uphold the national honour. Farrington pulled up his sleeve accordingly and showed his biceps muscle to the company. The two arms were examined and compared and finally it was agreed to have a trial of strength. The table was cleared and the two men rested their elbows on it, clasping hands. When Paddy Leonard said *Go!* each was to try to bring down the other's hand on to the table. Farrington looked very serious and determined. 48

The trial began. After about thirty seconds Weathers brought his opponent's hand slowly down on to the table. Farrington's dark wine-coloured face flushed darker still with anger and humiliation at having been defeated by such a stripling. 49

—You're not to put the weight of your body behind it. Play fair, he said. 50

— Who's not playing fair? said the other. 51

—Come on again. The two best out of three. 52

The trial began again. The veins stood out on Farrington's forehead, and the pallor of Weathers' complexion changed to peony. Their hands and arms trembled under the stress. After a long struggle Weathers again brought his opponent's hand slowly on to the table. There was a murmur of applause from the spectators. The curate, who was standing beside the table, nodded his red head towards the victor and said with loutish familiarity: 53

—Ah! that's the knack! 54

—What the hell do you know about it? said Farrington fiercely, turning on the man. What do you put in your gab for? 55

—Sh, sh! said O'Halloran, observing the violent expression of Farrington's face. Pony up, boys. We'll have just one little smahan more and then we'll be off. 56

A very sullen-faced man stood at the corner of O'Connell Bridge waiting for the little Sandymount tram to take him home. He was full 57

of smouldering anger and revengefulness. He felt humiliated and discon-
tented; he did not even feel drunk; and he had only twopence in his
pocket. He cursed everything. He had done for himself in the office,
pawned his watch, spent all his money; and he had not even got drunk.
He began to feel thirsty again and he longed to be back again in the hot
reeking public-house. He had lost his reputation as a strong man, having
been defeated twice by a mere boy. His heart swelled with fury and,
when he thought of the woman in the big hat who had brushed against
him and said *Pardon!* his fury nearly choked him.

His tram let him down at Shelbourne Road and he steered his great   58
body along in the shadow of the wall of the barracks. He loathed returning to his home. When he went in by the side-door he found the
kitchen empty and the kitchen fire nearly out. He bawled upstairs:

—Ada! Ada!   59

His wife was a little sharp-faced woman who bullied her husband   60
when he was sober and was bullied by him when he was drunk. They
had five children. A little boy came running down the stairs.

—Who is that? said the man, peering through the darkness.   61

—Me, pa.   62

—Who are you? Charlie?   63

—No, pa. Tom.   64

—Where's your mother?   65

—She's out at the chapel.   66

—That's right. . . . Did she think of leaving any dinner for me?   67

—Yes, pa. I—   68

—Light the lamp. What do you mean by having the place in dark-   69
ness? Are the other children in bed?

The man sat down heavily on one of the chairs while the little boy   70
lit the lamp. He began to mimic his son's flat accent, saying half to
himself: *At the chapel. At the chapel, if you please!* When the lamp was lit
he banged his fist on the table and shouted:

—What's for my dinner?   71

—I'm going . . . to cook it, pa, said the little boy.   72

The man jumped up furiously and pointed to the fire.   73

—On that fire! You let the fire out! By God, I'll teach you to do   74
that again!

He took a step to the door and seized the walking-stick which was   75
standing behind it.

—I'll teach you to let the fire out! he said, rolling up his sleeve in   76
order to give his arm free play.

The little boy cried O, *pa!* and ran whimpering round the table,   77 but the man followed him and caught him by the coat. The little boy looked about him wildly but, seeing no way of escape fell upon his knees.

—Now, you'll let the fire out the next time! said the man, striking   78
at him viciously with the stick. Take that, you little whelp!

The boy uttered a squeal of pain as the stick cut his thigh. He   79
clasped his hands together in the air and his voice shook with fright.

—O, pa! he cried. Don't beat me, pa! And I'll . . . I'll say a *Hail*   80
Mary for you. . . . I'll say a *Hail Mary* for you, pa, if you don't beat
me. . . . I'll say a *Hail Mary*. . . .

Questions for Study and Discussion

1. What is Farrington's job within the law office? What does he find grating about his job? Would you call Farrington burned out?

2. What is Mr. Alleyne's atttitude toward Farrington? Is he justified in his criticism? Explain.

3. Do Farrington's fellow workers support him? Or do they feel he's getting what he deserves? How do you know?

4. Like many of the stories in *Dubliners*, "Counterparts" makes reference to the antagonism between the people of the north and south of Ireland. How important is this antagonism to the story? Cite details that led you to your conclusion.

5. Why does Farrington feel the need to impress his drinking buddies? What is the effect of the arm-wrestling incident on Farrington? Explain.

6. Explain the significance of Joyce's title "Counterparts."

Writing Topics

1. "Don't take your job home with you" is an old saying that many people live by. What exactly does the saying mean? What are its implications? Why is it such difficult advice to follow? Write an essay in which you document the wisdom of the saying.

2. Imagine yourself in a managerial position such as Mr. Alleyne's. How would you have dealt with Farrington? Do you think that it would be possible to make a worker like Farrington more productive? If so, how would you go about it?

3. One essential element of short fiction is conflict—a character may have a conflict with himself, with another character, or with his situation, for example. Write an essay of critical analysis in which you discuss the element(s) of conflict in "Counterparts."

Women in the Workplace

GLORIA STEINEM

Gloria Steinem is a political activist, editor, lecturer, writer, and one of this country's leading feminists. She was born in Toledo, Ohio, in 1934 and graduated from Smith College in 1956. After college she traveled to India to study and then returned to New York, where she later helped to found two important magazines, *New York* and *Ms.* Steinem has published many articles and three books: *The Thousand Indias* (1957), *The Beach Book* (1963), and *Outrageous Acts and Everyday Rebellions* (1983), from which the following article is taken.

In "The Importance of Work" Steinem argues that the standard answer that women give to the question of why they work, "Womenworkbecausewehaveto," is inadequate and a self-deception. Women should be able, she claims, to admit openly that they work because it is a human right and because it is an activity that is both natural and pleasurable.

The Importance of Work

Toward the end of the 1970s, The *Wall Street Journal* devoted an eight-part, front-page series to "the working woman"—that is, the influx of women into the paid-labor force—as the greatest change in American life since the Industrial Revolution.

Many women readers greeted both the news and the definition with cynicism. After all, women have always worked. If all the productive work of human maintenance that women do in the home were valued at its replacement cost, the gross national product of the United States would go up by 26 percent. It's just that we are now more likely than ever before to leave our poorly rewarded, low-security, high-risk job of homemaking (though we're still trying to explain that it's a perfectly good one and that the problem is male society's refusal both to do it and to give it an economic value) for more secure, independent, and better-paid jobs outside the home.

411

Obviously, the real work revolution won't come until all productive   3
work is rewarded—including child rearing and other jobs done in the
home—and men are integrated into so-called women's work as well as
vice versa. But the radical change being touted by the *Journal* and other
media is one part of that long integration process: the unprecedented
flood of women into salaried jobs, that is, into the labor force as it has
been male-defined and previously occupied by men. We are already more
than 41 percent of it—the highest proportion in history. Given the fact
that women also make up a whopping 69 percent of the "discouraged
labor force" (that is, people who need jobs but don't get counted in the
unemployment statistics because they've given up looking), plus an official female unemployment rate that is substantially higher than men's,
it's clear that we could expand to become fully half of the national work
force by 1990.

Faced with this determination of women to find a little indepen-   4
dence and to be paid and honored for our work, experts have rushed to
ask: "Why?" It's a question rarely directed at male workers. Their basic
motivations of survival and personal satisfaction are taken for granted.
Indeed, men are regarded as "odd" and therefore subjects for sociological
study and journalistic reports only when they *don't* have work, even if
they are rich and don't need jobs or are poor and can't find them. Nonetheless, pollsters and sociologists have gone to great expense to prove
that women work outside the home because of dire financial need, or if
we persist despite the presence of a wage-earning male, out of some desire
to buy "little extras" for our families, or even out of good old-fashioned
penis envy."

Job interviewers and even our own families may still ask salaried   5
women the big "Why?" If we have small children at home or are in some
job regarded as "men's work," the incidence of such questions increases.
Condescending or accusatory versions of "What's a nice girl like you
doing in a place like this?" have not disappeared from the workplace.

How do we answer these assumptions that we are "working" out of   6
some pressing or peculiar need? Do we feel okay about arguing that it's
a natural for us to have salaried jobs as for our husbands—whether or
not we have young children at home? Can we enjoy strong career ambitions without worrying about being thought "unfeminine"? When we
confront men's growing resentment of women competing in the work
force (often in the form of such guilt-producing accusations as "You're
taking men's jobs away" or "You're damaging your children"), do we
simply state that a decent job is a basic human right for everybody?

I'm afraid the answer is often no. As individuals and as a movement,   7
we tend to retreat into some version of a tactically questionable defense:

"Womenworkbecausewehaveto." The phrase has become one word, one key on the typewriter—an economic form of the socially "feminine" stance of passivity and self-sacrifice. Under attack, we still tend to present ourselves as creatures of economic necessity and familial devotion. "Womenworkbecausewehaveto" has become the easiest thing to say.

Like most truisms, this one is easy to prove with statistics. Economic need *is* the most consistent work motive—for women as well as men. In 1976, for instance, 43 percent of all women in the paid-labor force were single, widowed, separated, or divorced, and working to support themselves and their dependents. An additional 21 percent were married to men who had earned less than ten thousand dollars in the previous year, the minimum then required to support a family of four. In fact, if you take men's pensions, stocks, real estate, and various forms of accumulated wealth into account, a good statistical case can be made that there are more women who "have" to work (that is, who have neither the accumulated wealth, nor husbands whose work or wealth can support them for the rest of their lives) than there are men with the same need. If we were going to ask one group "Do you really need this job?" we should ask men.

But the first weakness of the whole "have to work" defense is its deceptiveness. Anyone who has ever experienced dehumanized life on welfare or any other confidence-shaking dependency knows that a paid job may be preferable to the dole, even when the handout is coming from a family member. Yet the will and self-confidence to work on one's own can diminish as dependency and fear increase. That may explain why—contrary to the "have to" rationale—wives of men who earn less than three thousand dollars a year are actually *less* likely to be employed than wives whose husbands make ten thousand dollars a year or more.

Furthermore, the greatest proportion of employed wives is found among families with a total household income of twenty-five to fifty thousand dollars a year. This is the statistical underpinning used by some sociologists to prove that women's work is mainly important for boosting families into the middle or upper middle class. Thus, women's incomes are largely used for buying "luxuries" and "little extras": a neat double-whammy that renders us secondary within our families, and makes our jobs expendable in hard times. We may even go along with this interpretation (at least, up to the point of getting fired so a male can have our job). It preserves a husbandly ego-need to be seen as the primary breadwinner, and still allows us a safe "feminine" excuse for working.

But there are often rewards that we're not confessing. As noted in *The Two-Career Couple*, by Francine and Douglas Hall: "Women who hold jobs by choice, even blue-collar routine jobs, are more satisfied with their lives than are the full-time housewives."

In addition to personal satisfaction, there is also society's need for all its members' talents. Suppose that jobs were given out on only a "have to work" basis to both women and men—one job per household. It would be unthinkable to lose the unique abilities of, for instance, Eleanor Holmes Norton, the distinguished chair of the Equal Employment Opportunity Commission. But would we then be forced to question the important work of her husband, Edward Norton, who is also a distinguished lawyer? Since men earn more than twice as much as women on the average, the wife in most households would be more likely to give up her job. Does that mean the nation could do as well without millions of its nurses, teachers, and secretaries? Or that the rare man who earns less than his wife should give up his job?   12

It was this kind of waste of human talents on a society-wide scale that traumatized millions of unemployed or underemployed Americans during the Depression. Then, a one-job-per-household rule seemed somewhat justified, yet the concept was used to displace women workers only, create intolerable dependencies, and waste female talent that the country needed. That Depression experience, plus the energy and example of women who were finally allowed to work during the manpower shortage created by World War II, led Congress to reinterpret the meaning of the country's full-employment goal in its Economic Act of 1946. Full employment was officially defined as "the employment of those who want to work, without regard to whether their employment is, by some definition, necessary. This goal applies equally to men and to women." Since bad economic times are again creating a resentment of employed women— as well as creating more need for women to be employed—we need such a goal more than ever. Women are again being caught in a tragic double bind: We are required to be strong and then punished for our strength.   13

Clearly, anything less than government and popular commitment to this 1946 definition of full employment will leave the less powerful groups, whoever they may be, in danger. Almost as important as the financial penalty paid by the powerless is the suffering that comes from being shut out of paid and recognized work. Without it, we lose much of our self-respect and our ability to prove that we are alive by making some difference in the world. That's just as true for the suburban woman as it is for the unemployed steel worker.   14

But it won't be easy to give up the passive defense of "weworkbecausewehaveto."   15

When a women who is struggling to support her children and grandchildren on welfare sees her neighbor working as a waitress, even though   16 that neighbor's husband has a job, she may feel resentful; and the waitress (of course, not the waitress's husband) may feel guilty. Yet unless we establish the obligation to provide a job for everyone who is willing and able to work, that welfare woman may herself be penalized by policies that give out only one public-service job per household. She and her daughter will have to make a painful and divisive decision about which of them gets that precious job, and the whole household will have to survive on only one salary.

A job as a human right is a principle that applies to men as well   17
as women. But women have more cause to fight for it. The phenomenon of the "working woman" has been held responsible for everything from an increase in male impotence (which turned out, incidentally, to be attributable to medication for high blood pressure) to the rising cost of steak (which was due to high energy costs and beef import restrictions, not women's refusal to prepare the cheaper, slower-cooking cuts). Unless we see a job as part of every citizen's right to autonomy and personal fulfillment, we will continue to be vulnerable to someone else's idea of what "need" is, and whose "need" counts the most.

In many ways, women who do not have to work for simple survival,   18
but who choose to do so nonetheless, are on the frontier of asserting this right for all women. Those with well-to-do husbands are dangerously easy for us to resent and put down. It's easier still to resent women from families of inherited wealth, even though men generally control and benefit from that wealth. (There is no Rockefeller Sisters Fund, no J. P. Morgan & Daughters, and sons-in-law may be the ones who really sleep their way to power.) But to prevent a woman whose husband or father is wealthy from earning her own living, and from gaining the self-confidence that comes with that ability, is to keep her needful of that unearned power and less willing to disperse it. Moreover, it is to lose forever her unique talents.

Perhaps modern feminists have been guilty of a kind of reverse   19
snobbism that keeps us from reaching out to the wives and daughters of wealthy men; yet it was exactly such women who refused the restrictions of class and financed the first wave of feminist revolution.

For most of us, however, "womenworkbecausewehaveto" is just true   20
enough to be seductive as a personal defense.

If we use it without also staking out the larger human right to a   21
job, however, we will never achieve that right. And we will always be subject to the false argument that independence for women is a luxury affordable only in good economic times. Alternatives to layoffs will not be explored, acceptable unemployment will always be used to frighten those with jobs into accepting low wages, and we will never remedy the

real cost, both to families and to the country, of dependent women and a massive loss of talent.

Worst of all, we may never learn to find productive, honored work   22
as a natural part of ourselves and as one of life's basic pleasures.

Questions for Study and Discussion

1. In your own words, what is Gloria Steinem's thesis in this essay?

2. Why did many women readers greet *The Wall Street Journal*'s definition of "the working woman" with cynicism? What was Steinem's response?

3. Steinem states that many women use the "Womenworkbecausewehaveto" defense when asked why they work. Why does Steinem believe they use this defense? Why does she object to it? And what does she gain from turning the sentence "Women work because we have to" into a single word? Explain.

4. How does Steinem dismiss the claim that women who enter the workplace are robbing men of their jobs and damaging their children?

5. What is Steinem's attitude toward women who work even though they don't need to financially? Does she believe they should be applauded or resented?

6. How is "full employment" defined in the Economic Recovery Act of 1946? Is it a definition that Steinem supports? How, according to Steinem, do attitudes toward working women change during bad economic times?

7. How does society benefit from the full employment of men and women? How do individuals benefit?

8. On the basis of the article—tone, diction, and evidence—how would you characterize Gloria Steinem as a persuasive writer?

9. For what audience do you believe Steinem intended her article? What assumptions does she make about her audience? Would this audience find her argument convincing? Would a different audience be persuaded as well? Explain.

Writing Topics

1. Steinem believes that "a decent job is a basic human right for everybody." Is such a position realistic? Does America have an obligation to provide such a job for every citizen? Write an essay in which you argue pro or con.

2. In preparation for an essay on working parents, analyze your own family situation. Did only one or both of your parents work outside the home? What was the effect on the fabric of your family life? Would you have preferred the alternative situation?

CASEY MILLER AND KATE SWIFT

Casey Miller and Kate Swift are free-lance writers, editors, and photographers. Together they have written many articles on sexism and language for national newspapers and magazines. Their interest in language has grown out of editorial work in a wide range of fields, including science, religion, history, and the arts. A graduate of Smith College, Miller studied graphic arts at Yale and was for ten years an editor at Seabury Press. Swift received a degree in journalism from the University of North Carolina and then worked as a science writer and editor with the American Museum of Natural History and the Yale School of Medicine. Free-lance partners since 1970, they explore questions of sexual prejudice in the language in *Words and Women: New Language in New Times* (1976).

Miller and Swift are well aware of the power of language to shape our thinking and to discriminate against women. In the following chapter from *The Handbook of Nonsexist Writing* (1980), they examine the language used to describe women working at home or outside the home and offer many practical suggestions on how to replace exclusive, distorting, ambiguous, and injurious words.

Women and Work

"Do you talk to a working woman any differently than a housewife?"
ADVERTISING EXECUTIVE

What are housewives if not working women? According to a recent   1
study, the average housewife works 99.6 hours a week at a variety of jobs (purchasing agent, cook, cleaner, economist, chauffeur, etc.) for which the combined hourly pay scales would have earned her an annual salary of $17,351.88 in the 1978 job market.

Advertisers, along with other speakers and writers, might achieve   2
better communication with women who are full-time homemakers if they used terms like *salaried women, wage-earning women,* or *women employed outside the home* when referring to women in the paid work force. The executive quoted above might have said

> Do you talk to a woman who works outside the home any differently than to a housewife?

It is interesting and probably significant that many women do not   3
use the term *work* to describe their housekeeping or homemaking activities. Nor, in general, do members of their families. A woman "stays

417

home" rather than "works at home." She "fixes dinner" rather than "works in the kitchen." In contrast, activities men traditionally undertake around the house are usually dignified by the name *work*. A man "works on the car" or "does his own electrical work." He may have a "workshop" in the basement.

Housewife

While the job a housewife performs is greatly undervalued, the word   4
housewife itself is overworked and often used with disparaging connotations. An insurance agency advertises that its agents take the time to explain homeowners' insurance

> in terms even a housewife can understand.

The patronizing tone of the ad would be softened if it were revised to read

> in terms the average householder can understand.

A newspaper article on the making of an animated motion picture   5
described the vast amount of work required to produce 250,000 separate images on celluloid transparencies:

> On four floors of a Los Angeles office building, more than 150 artists did the actual animating. Two hundred housewives with steady hands did the routine work of painting the images onto cels.

Since steady hands and an aptitude for routine work are less characteristic of housewives as a class than they are of, say, watch repairers, the use of the term *housewives* here is either irrelevant or insulting: this chore is so simple even a housewife can do it. Or was the writer trying to say that after the salaried artists had completed the animation, another 200 people finished the routine painting at home on a piecework basis? If so, why not say so? If not, a better alternative would have been

> Two hundred assistants selected for their steady hands did the routine work. . . .

Housewife is also usually out of place as a primary descriptive for a   6
woman who does something newsworthy.

> The counterfeit credit cards were traced to a 47-year-old Denver housewife

gives no more pertinent information than would have been conveyed by "a 47-year-old Denver woman," and it could leave some readers with the impression that a connection exists between housewifery and the use of counterfeit credit cards.

The misuse of *housewife* was epitomized a few years ago when Margaret Thatcher, who had just been elected head of the Conservative Party in Great Britain, was regularly identified in the news media as "a housewife." As it happens Thatcher, a tax lawyer and former cabinet minister, ran her own household and so was in fact a housewife. To single out that term in describing her, however, was to imply that homemaking was her chief or only skill and the primary reason the Conservatives chose her to be their leader. It is hard to imagine any circumstance in which a comparable reference would be made to a man. 7

Perhaps the Thatcher example should be taken as evidence of the high esteem in which the Western world holds the homemaker's job. On the contrary. About the same time Thatcher was being described as "a housewife" an American newspaper ran an article about the growing number of men who are now full-time homemakers and headed it "The Nonworkers." If in the eyes of society *housework* and *nonwork* are equated, no wonder so many women whose chosen job is to maintain a home feel obliged to describe their occupation as "just housewife." 8

Working Wife, Working Mother

"What is a working wife? One whose arms and legs move?"

An editor

"Working mothers? Are there any other kind?"

A Little Leary cartoon

In a series of articles entitled "Women at Work," a financial newspaper presented much well-researched factual information about women's increased participation in the labor market. But the series also reinforced some common assumptions: first, that it is always preferable in a marriage for the husband to be the breadwinner, the wife to be the homemaker and chief parent; second, that although it is acceptable for a man to hold a paid job even when he has other, adequate sources of income, a married woman who works outside the home for satisfaction rather than necessity contributes both to the unemployment of others and to growing inequities between rich and poor. Yet by omitting any consideration of the monetary value of homemaking—a figure that can be reckoned according to its replacement cost in the gross national product—the articles strengthened the widespread attitude that the unpaid work homemakers do is not an essential factor in the economy. 9

Whatever the merits of these assumptions, the language of the series   10
demonstrated how deeply they have become ingrained in our thinking—
and therefore in our patterns of writing and speech. This was particularly
apparent in the use throughout the series of the terms *working wives* and
working mothers.

When used to describe someone employed in a paying job, such   11
phrases define a woman primarily in terms of her domestic role; they
imply that her main responsibilities are toward something other than her
employment. Though the implication is often true, it can be equally true
of many men. Yet in the articles men were rarely identified as *working
husbands* or *working fathers*.

> Armed with surveys showing that working wives tend to get more help
> around the house from husbands . . .

and, quoting a husband,

> Working wives offer their husbands the flexibility to do what they want
> with their lives.

would have been more accurately phrased

> Armed with surveys showing that wives who work outside the home tend
> to get more help around the house from husbands . . .

and

> Wives who bring home a paycheck offer their husbands the flexibility to
> do what they want with their lives.

(In the first instance housework is still assumed to be the wife's responsibility, and in the second she is still assigned a secondary, supporting
role; but the language itself is no longer ambiguous.)

An eight-part series on the subject of women in the work force,   12
especially one which drew on many interviews, could probably not be
expected to avoid terms like *working wife* or *women who work* completely,
and to their credit the writers of the series used many alternatives such
as "women holding jobs," "women who work for pay," "job-holding wife,"
"working parents," and "the husband-wife working family." Phrases like
"women who work at home" also indicated that work done by full-time
homemakers was not being ignored. Nevertheless, the underlying assumption that women belong at home was reinforced both by the language of the writers themselves and of the people they quoted.

For example, one woman who works for a tree-spraying company   13
was described by the writer as doing

> a man's job for equal pay,

implying that when women compete for better-paid jobs they are invading male territory. However, a later reference in the same article used quotation marks to reflect an awareness—at least on the part of the writer and the women being interviewed—that men do not have exclusive rights to certain jobs:

> But many working women say they still have to walk softly on the job, particularly if they're doing "man's work."

Women tended to be seen as wives, whereas men were called "men"   14
more often than "husbands." In each of the following sentences, for example, *husband* (or *husbands*) would have been the appropriate parallel to *wife* (or *wives*).

> It can be an uncomfortable feeling for a man when his wife goes to work.

> There are some less obvious benefits as well that men might gain through their working wives.

> With a working wife, a man can refuse a transfer, quit his job or just tell his boss to go to hell. . . . A wife's job provides a lot of freedom if men are just willing to accept it.

And so ingrained is the image of woman as wife that she continues to be seen as a wife even when she is divorced:

> Mrs. Doe, 53, was divorced three years ago. . . . As head of a household, [she] is a member of the most underprivileged group of working wives.

Married women are seen as blameworthy in a manner not shared   15
by men, whatever their marital, economic, or job status, or by unmarried women:

> Also disturbing are the tensions now arising between wives who work because of strict financial need and those who work because they want the status, satisfaction and adventure of carving a niche in the labor market.

Not surprisingly, wives, even when employed full time, are responsible for the smooth running of the household, as in the example already quoted and in the following:

> Local repairmen . . . get frequent requests nowadays to fix broken appliances after 5 P.M. or on Saturdays, because the customers are working wives.

Actually the reason no one is at home is

> . . . because both the husband and wife have jobs,

and

the day-time absence of employed wives

is every bit as much

the day-time absence of husband and wife, both of whom are employed.

Even the children tend to be more the mother's children than the father's. Following a description of youngsters waiting outside an elementary school before it opens in the morning, the copy reads   16

Occasionally, a teacher or the principal also will come early to mind these offspring of working mothers.

Since the implication was not that these particular children are from single-parent families, but families in which both mother and father are employed, the sentence might have been phrased more equitably:

Occasionally, a teacher or the principal also will come early to mind these children whose parents both have jobs.

When the financial contribution of both spouses is the focus of attention, there is no more reason to single out women as workers (*working mothers, working wives*) than to single out men: 17

Most of the houses in the new development are being built by two-income families.

A two-paycheck family usually has less trouble getting a mortgage.

Homemaking and Parenting

In the small percentage of one-parent families where the parent is a man, and in two-parent families where both parents are employed, fathers increasingly perform or share the work traditionally done by mothers. In addition, the Internal Revenue Service lists some 200,000 men in the United States who are full-time homemakers. Thus the disparity in the once commonly understood meanings of the verbs *to mother* (the social act of nurturance) and *to father* (the biological act of insemination) is disappearing. *Fathering*, too, has acquired the meaning "caring for or looking after someone" previously ascribed only to *mothering*, and a new word, *parenting*, is gaining acceptance.   18

New words come into being because enough people feel a need for them. *Parenting* serves two purposes: it describes the role of single parents who have to try to be both mother and father to their children, and it de-emphasizes the stereotypes so frequently found in two-parent families   19 that only mothers are responsible for "mothering." Like the familiar word *parenthood, parenting* conveys a sense of mutuality and shared responsibility.

> Parents can help each other learn the arts of mothering and fathering

makes an arbitrary distinction between two prescribed roles. A father's ability to nurture and a mother's experiences in a world wider than the home are not denied when the sentence is rephrased

> Mothers and fathers can help each other learn the art of parenting.

Questions for Study and Discussion

1. What seems to be the problematic confusion between "working woman" and "housewife"? What alternatives do Miller and Swift suggest for "working woman" that are not demeaning to housewives?

2. What for you are the connotations of "housewife"? How do you think the word came to acquire these associations?

3. How, according to Miller and Swift, is the word *housewife* misused?

4. Why are Miller and Swift concerned about the language of the "Women at Work" series, which appeared in the *Wall Street Journal* between August 28 and September 22, 1978? How does the language of the articles reflect the major assumptions behind the series?

5. On what grounds do Miller and Swift object to the terms "working wives" and "working mothers"? What alternatives do the writers of the "Women at Work" series use? Explain why each alternative is preferable.

6. Why is the word *parenting* gaining widespread acceptance? What purposes does this word fulfill?

7. What is the tone of this essay? Does the tone influence the way you react to Miller and Swift's suggestions for changing exclusive, distorting, ambiguous, and injurious words? Explain.

Writing Topics

1. Carefully read each of the following sentences.
   a. The average person finds it no problem at all to have three head colds, one sunburn, twenty headaches, and two hangovers, and still get in his sixty-one hours of shaving.
   b. Man can do several things which the animal cannot do. . . . His vital interests are not only life, food, access to females, but also. . . .
   c. A three-year-old may be able to feed and dress himself.

d. The dolphin, a friendly and talkative creature, has a built-in sonar system of his own.

e. It's the great secret among doctors, known only to their wives, that most things get better by themselves.

f. . . . explained in terms even a housewife can understand.

g. With a working wife, a man can refuse a transfer, quit his job. . . .

h. The salutation Dear Sir is always permissible when addressing a person not known to the writer.

i. The author exerts his magnetism on the small boy in all of us.

j. James Brown will serve as chairperson of the Planning Commission and Catherine Roe will serve as chairperson of the Zoning Board.

k. TV listing: Powerful lady attorney and confident young lawyer team up to defend wealthy contractor.

Did you recognize the sexism in each one? Write an essay in which you describe your own speech and writing. Is it sexist? Can you always recognize the sexism in your own language? When you try to avoid or circumvent sexism, what difficulties do you encounter? Does the attempt make you feel uncomfortable?

2. Miller and Swift state that "new words come into being because enough people feel a need for them." Using examples from your own experiences or observations, write an essay in which you show the basic truth of this generalization.

MARY MEBANE

Mary E. Mebane was born in 1933 in Durham, North Carolina. After earning her B.A. at North Carolina State College, she went on to receive her M.A. and Ph.D. from the University of North Carolina and to teach, most recently at the University of Wisconsin at Milwaukee. Her writing has appeared in *A Galaxy of Black Writers* and *The Eloquence of Protest*; her play "Take a Sad Song" was produced in 1975. She has published two widely acclaimed autobiographical books, *Mary* (1981) and *Mary, Wayfarer* (1983). About her own work Mebane has said, "My writings center on the black folk of the South, post-1960. It is my belief that the black folk are the most creative, viable people that America has produced. They just don't know it."

In "Summer Job," taken from *Mary*, Mebane describes the process of getting a job in a southern tobacco factory. And in so doing, she also introduces us to the plight of black women workers in the years preceding the Civil Rights Act of 1964.

Summer Job

It was summer 1949, and I needed a job. Everybody tried to "get on" at the tobacco factory during "green season," when lots of extra workers were hired to "work up" new tobacco—that is, process it for cigarettes. Some people made their chief money of the year during the ten-to-twelve-week green season. The factory paid more money than days work, so lots of women gladly left their housekeeping jobs and went to the factories. In Durham there were two major factories and several smaller ones. The major factories worked up tobacco, but they also made cigarettes and had a shipping department and research laboratories. The smaller factories mainly worked up tobacco for the larger ones, in Durham and in other cities. Of the two major factories in Durham, Liggett and Myers did relatively little hiring in green season; it had a stable year-round force and gave preference to its former workers during the season. My mother worked there. The American Tobacco Company, the other factory, hired a great many temporary workers.

I was told that my best bet was the American. I wasn't eighteen, but I was tall and stocky and could pass for older, and besides, they never asked to see your birth certificate; so, a few months short of my sixteenth birthday, I went to get work at the American, makers of Lucky Strike cigarettes and other brands. From the start, I knew that I wouldn't get a job on the "cigarette side." That was easy work, and I was told that mostly whites worked over there. I would get a chance on the belt on the "tobacco side." Several women in the neighborhood who had worked at the American during the green season instructed me about how to get on. I was told to get there early and stand on the sidewalk in front of the employment office and just as close as possible to it, so that when they came out to select workers I would be easily seen. Also I was told to say, if they asked me, that I had worked there before. Nobody ever checked the records. So, on the morning that hiring began for green season, I went to Durham.

I accompanied neighbors who had received postcards informing them   3
they could come to work. They left me outside while they went in. I was dismayed, for the whole street in front of the employment office was filled with black women. They crowded around the brick porch leading to the employment office; they were on the sidewalk; they overflowed the street and covered the sidewalk behind. They were directly in front of the office, spreading out fanwise in both directions from it. Nobody was allowed on the porch except those who already had cards.

A pudgy white man with a cigar in his mouth came and stood on   4
the porch and said, "All those who have cards, come forward." Those who had cards held them up over their heads and started pushing through the crowd. Sometimes they had to remonstrate with some stubborn woman who refused to give way: "Let me pass, please! Move out of my way!" Slowly the one blocking her path would grudgingly give ground. Others quickly surged forward, trying to fill the space that was left, taking advantage of the confusion to try to push even nearer the office. When the favored ones got in, there began the long wait for the man to come back and start selecting more "hands" from the crowd of women left standing there. The crowd continued to grow bigger by the minute as new arrivals came.

You could tell the veterans from the rookies by the way they were   5
dressed. The knowledgeable ones had their heads covered by kerchiefs, so that if they were hired, tobacco dust wouldn't get in their hair; they had on clean dresses that by now were faded and shapeless, so that if they were hired they wouldn't get tobacco dust and grime on their best clothes. Those who were trying for the first time had their hair freshly done and wore attractive dresses; they wanted to make a good impression. But the dresses couldn't be seen at the distance that many were standing from the employment office, and they were crumpled in the crush.

Some women looked as if they had large families; they looked tired   6
and anxious, but determined. Some looked single; they had on lipstick and eyebrow pencil, and some even wore black patent-leather pumps with stockings.

The morning passed and the sun got hotter; there was no shade on   7
the sidewalks or in the street. The street stayed full, except when trucks
edged their way in and the crowd gave way slowly.

After a while, the pudgy white man with the big cigar came to the   8
door and stood and looked. Instantly the whole mass surged forward. The
shorter ones tried to stand on tiptoe to be seen over the heads of their
taller sisters. Hands shot up in the air, trying to make him notice them.
Those at the front who'd gotten shoved against the brick porch shouted,
"Stop pushing, stop pushing, ya'll! You're hurting me!"

Finally the pudgy man spoke, standing on the porch with his cigar   9
in his mouth. "Until ya'll stop pushing and shoving I'm not gonna hire
none of ya'll." Then he stood for a moment to see what effect his words
were having on the crowd. Sensing that they were having no discernible
effect, the man went back inside, and the surge forward stopped for the
time being.

The women stood and stood; the sun grew hotter. Some grew tired   10
of waiting: "I left my baby with a neighbor. I told her that if I didn't get
on I'd be back before twelve. I gotta go." Others left, saying that they
were "tired of this mess." One woman said, "All ya'll might as well go
home. He's got his number for today. Come back tomorrow when they'll
know how many more they'll need." At that, even more women faded
away. The mass shrunk, but it was still a mass.

Finally, shortly before noon, the pudgy man came quietly to the   11
porch and pointed quickly to two women standing close by. Before the
crowd knew people were getting on, the two women were on the porch
and in the hall, following him. The crowd surged forward but the man
was gone. "What time is it?" someone said. "Nigh noon" was the answer
and everyone seemed to agree that there would be no more hiring until
one or two o'clock, after lunch.

Some sat right down on the sidewalk up against the building and   12
took out their sandwiches. Others drifted away from the crowd and down
to a nearby luncheonette for cold drinks and sandwiches. I had a tomato
sandwich that had become soggy in the press and the heat. I went with
some other women far down the street to sit on the grass and eat my
sandwich. They talked in front of me as if I were grown, so I knew that
I would have no trouble if I got hired. What they said was so interesting
that the crowd was re-forming in front of the employment office in the
hot, boiling sun before I knew it.

Word came over the grapevine that they needed some more helpers   13
and would hire some more today. This gave everybody courage, so the
crowd grew calm. Then the pudgy man came again. He made an announcement: "Any shoving, any pushing, and there'll be no more hiring

today." The women grew quiet. Those who had been impatient hadn't come back from lunch, leaving those who were determined to get on.

The man selected two more women; the crowd gave a little surge   14 forward, but nothing like the shoving and pushing of the morning. In another hour he came back for one more, and soon the word came over the grapevine that we might as well go home. The crowd started fading away, but not the diehards. They didn't believe the grapevine and were determined to stay to see what was going to happen. I had no choice; I was staying until the people I rode with got off from work. It was now three o'clock and we all had been standing in the sun since eight o'clock in the morning. When the neighbors I was waiting for came, they said, "Don't worry. You'll get on tomorrow." Besides, they would go in earlier now that they were on.

I lay in bed that night, too tired to do anything else, and thought   15 about the day. Hundreds of women had stood in the hot sun for seven or eight hours under really bad conditions. There was no bathroom, no drinking fountain, no place to sit down. Those who had to leave lost their place in line and, thus, their chance for a job. Why was this? Because they needed work and the factory didn't need them. The factory had more hands available than it could use. That is why they could treat the surplus as they chose, and there was nothing that the women could do about it.

The next day I was there early and standing in place by the steps   16 before the employment office opened. I recognized some of the faces from the day before, and there were some that looked new to me. The crowd stretched out as far as it had the previous day. The sun was already hot when the pudgy man came to the platform with his cigar in his mouth. "Anyone here with a card?" he called. A few women who hadn't come in yesterday came forward. He went back inside.

I was close enough to see into the hall inside and the glass-faced   17 side of the employment office. It was shut off from the hall by glass because it was air-conditioned. There was a man, so slim and shapely that he looked like a girl, who came to the door and watched as the pudgy man came back and stood over the crowd. He watched the crowd surge forward, and he stepped back a little as if all the energy would wash over him. It seemed to give him great satisfaction to see the sea of black women struggling forward, trying to get a job in his factory; he'd stand and watch for a while, then turn and go into the air-conditioned office. At first the women thought that he was going to do some of the hiring and they pressed close to him and looked up. But once they'd determined that he had nothing to do with the hiring, he ceased to exist for them and they paid him no more attention.

More and more women were hired; the pudgy man would point here and there, then take them off. In an hour or so, he'd come back and hire one or two more. Lunch came and the crowd scattered. I'd brought a meat sandwich, hoping that it wouldn't get crumpled and soggy like my tomato sandwich the day before. I knew enough not to leave my good place near the porch, so I ate standing in the hot sun, along with the rest of the women who had good places. I had been listening to the crowd for two days, so now I knew the words and phrases that would make me sound like a veteran, and I employed them. Evidently nothing was wrong with what I said, for no one looked at me "funny." 18

Around two o'clock the pudgy man came back and his eye fell on me and the woman standing beside me. He motioned us in. I was now a factory hand. 19

The air-conditioning in the office chilled me after the heat of the street as I gave the necessary information. I made up a birthday and nobody questioned it. Then I was taken to a "line" on the first floor. 20

It was a cavernous room, long and tall. The man who led me there called to the boss, who came over to tell me what to do, but the machinery was so loud that I couldn't hear him and I was so startled by my new surroundings that I didn't really concentrate on what he said. I was afraid to take a deep breath, for the room was so cloudy with tobacco dust that brown particles hung in the air. I held my breath as long as I could and then took a deep breath. I started to cough and my eyes watered. I saw lots of women and some men, each doing a task seemingly unrelated to the others', but I knew that there must be a plan. 21

My job had something to do with a conveyor belt. It was shaped like a child's sliding board, only it had a deep trough and it moved. Shredded tobacco was on this belt—I think that it came from upstairs—and my job was to sit by the belt and pick out the pieces whose stems was too large. I tried to determine what kind of stem was too large, for the belt was constantly moving, and obviously I couldn't pick out every single stem on the belt. I looked at the others, but I couldn't see what method they were using. I was in misery, for this was my first "public" job and I didn't want to do badly on it. I did the best that I could, but soon the boss came and told me he was going to put me on the belt upstairs. I was glad, for my back hurt from bending over, trying to pick out stems. Maybe I could do better upstairs. 22

The air was full of tobacco dust there, too, but not as much as it had been downstairs; also, it was quieter. This belt moved horizontally, from right to left; women stood parallel to it, two women facing each other on the same side of the belt, with a barrel of tied tobacco leaves in front of them. They worked in pairs, taking the tobacco from the 23 barrel, the hogshead, and putting it on the belt. The important thing, as my partner explained to me, was to make sure that the tied ends faced me, for the belt was on its way to the cutter and the machine would cut off the hard tied end—which would not go into the making of cigarettes—while the leaves went another way.

The job seemed easy enough as I picked up bundle after bundle of tobacco and put it on the belt, careful to turn the knot end toward me so that it would be placed right to go under the cutting machine. Gradually, as we worked up our tobacco, I had to bend more, for as we emptied the hogshead we had to stoop over to pick up the tobacco, then straighten up and put it on the belt just right. Then I discovered the hard part of the job: the belt kept moving at the same speed all the time and if the leaves were not placed on the belt at the same tempo there would be a big gap where your bundle should have been. So that meant that when you got down lower, you had to bend down, get the tobacco, straighten up fast, make sure it was placed knot end toward you, place it on the belt, and bend down again. Soon you were bending down, up; down, up; down, up. All along the line, heads were bobbing—down, up; down, up—until you finished the barrel. Then you could rest until the men brought you another one. 24

To make sure that you kept the belt filled, there was a line boss, a little blond man who looked scared most of the time. He'd walk up and down behind you, saying, "Put the tobacco on the belt, girls. Put the tobacco on the belt. Too many empty spaces, girls. Too many empty spaces." You'd be working away, when suddenly behind you you'd hear this voice: "Put the tobacco on the belt, girls. Put the tobacco on the belt. No empty spaces, girls. No empty spaces." I noticed that no one paid him any mind. He could be standing right by the belt talking, and it was as if he were invisible. The line kept moving, and the women kept bending and putting tobacco on the belt. 25

Over him was the floor boss. He had charge of all the operations on the floor. He was the line boss's boss, and the line boss was clearly afraid of him. Over the floor boss was the big boss, who seldom came on the floor unless there was real trouble. Most of the women had never seen him, but some had and said that he was mean as the devil. 26

I bent and straightened and bent and straightened and thought that my back would break. Once in the afternoon I got a ten-minute break in the "house" (toilet). I went there and collapsed into a chair. 27

That evening on the way home I tried to talk cheerfully to my neighbors about the new job. They were quite pleased that I had gotten on. That was the one thing that kept me from quitting. I didn't want to let them down by telling them that I found the work killing. So I made up my mind to stay, no matter what, for I knew it was a short season. 28

Questions for Study and Discussion

1. What expectations did Mebane have of work at the American Tobacco Company? How did she come to have these expectations? Mebane devotes the first two-thirds of her essay to the "hiring process." What would have been gained or lost had she shortened this drastically?

2. What jobs did Mebane perform once she was hired? What did she think about the work she performed?

3. Why did everybody seek work at the tobacco factories during the season? Why do you think the work force was made up mostly of women?

4. Mebane's narrative is built upon a series of contrasts. What contrasts did you notice? Explain how they help her convey her experiences.

5. After only one day, Mebane found the work in the factory "killing." Why did she decide not to quit?

6. Mebane uses a great number of details in her writing to give the reader an accurate sense of where she is and what's going on. Cite several instances of her use of details that impressed you and attempt to explain the effect they had on your understanding of her situation.

7. How does Mebane's narrative help her to establish the time, place, and circumstances of her narrative? Cite several examples to document your points.

Writing Topics

1. Write an essay in which you describe the process of seeking summer employment. What steps are generally involved? Offer some tips or suggestions that would enhance a person's chances of getting a summer job.

2. Using your own experiences or observations of summer jobs, write an essay in which you discuss the major differences and similarities between summer work and full-time employment. Is a summer job a fair and accurate introduction to what full-time work is really like? Explain. Write an essay in which you talk about your first summer job. What impressed you the most? The least? What did you think of your fellow workers? Of the working conditions? The pay? Did the job in any way affect your attitude toward education?

LEWIS THOMAS

Lewis Thomas was born in 1913 in New York and attended Princeton and the Harvard Medical School. Thomas has had a distinguished career as a physician, administrator, researcher, teacher, and writer. Having been affiliated with a number of institutions, including the Yale University Medical School, Thomas is currently president of the Memorial Sloan-Kettering Cancer Center. He began his writing career in 1971 with a series of essays for the *New England Journal of Medicine;* many of these were collected in *The Lives of a Cell: Notes of a Biology Watcher,* winner of a National Book Award in 1974. Two further collections of essays have followed: *The Medusa and the Snail: More Notes of a Biology Watcher* and *Late Night Thoughts on Listening to Mahler's Ninth Symphony.*

"Nurses" is a chapter from *The Youngest Science: Notes of a Medicine-Watcher* (1983), Thomas's personal account of the development of the medical profession in this century. Here he examines the ways in which nurses' roles have changed in the last forty years and helps us to realize that the nursing staff is what really holds any hospital together.

Nurses

When my mother became a registered nurse at Roosevelt Hospital, in 1903, there was no question in anyone's mind about what nurses did as professionals. They did what the doctors ordered. The attending physician would arrive for his ward rounds in the early morning, and when he arrived at the ward office the head nurse would be waiting for him, ready to take his hat and coat, and his cane, and she would stand while he had his cup of tea before starting. Entering the ward, she would hold the door for him to go first, then his entourage of interns and medical students, then she followed. At each bedside, after he had conducted his examination and reviewed the patient's progress, he would tell the nurse what needed doing that day, and she would write it down on the part of the chart reserved for nursing notes. An hour or two later he would be gone from the ward, and the work of the rest of the day and the night to follow was the nurse's frenetic occupation. In addition to the stipulated orders, she had an endless list of routine things to do, all learned in her two years of nursing school: the beds had to be changed and made up with fresh sheets by an exact geometric design of folding and tucking impossible for anyone but a trained nurse; the patients had to be washed head to foot; bedpans had to be brought, used, emptied, and washed; temperatures had to be taken every four hours and meticulously recorded

432

on the chart; enemas were to be given; urine and stool samples collected, labeled, and sent off to the laboratory; throughout the day and night, medications of all sorts, usually pills and various vegetable extracts and tinctures, had to be carried on trays from bed to bed. At most times of the year about half of the forty or so patients on the ward had typhoid fever, which meant that the nurse couldn't simply move from bed to bed in the performance of her duties; each typhoid case was screened from the other patients, and the nurse was required to put on a new gown and wash her hands in disinfectant before approaching the bedside. Patients with high fevers were sponged with cold alcohol at frequent intervals. The late-evening back rub was the rite of passage into sleep.

In addition to the routine, workaday schedule, the nurse was re- 2 sponsible for responding to all calls from the patients, and it was expected that she would do so on the run. Her rounds, scheduled as methodical progressions around the ward, were continually interrupted by these calls. It was up to her to evaluate each situation quickly: a sudden abdominal pain in a typhoid patient might signify intestinal perforation; the abrupt onset of weakness, thirst, and pallor meant intestinal hemorrhage; the coughing up of gross blood by a tuberculous patient was an emergency. Some of the calls came from neighboring patients on the way to recovery; patients on open wards always kept a close eye on each other: the man in the next bed might slip into coma or seem to be dying, or be indeed dead. For such emergencies the nurse had to get word immediately to the doctor on call, usually the intern assigned to the ward, who might be off in the outpatient department or working in the diagnostic laboratory (interns of that day did all the laboratory work themselves; technicians had not yet been invented) or in his room. Nurses were not allowed to give injections or to do such emergency procedures as spinal punctures or chest taps, but they were expected to know when such maneuvers were indicated and to be ready with appropriate trays of instruments when the intern arrived on the ward.

It was an exhausting business, but by my mother's accounts it was the 3 most satisfying and rewarding kind of work. As a nurse she was a low person in the professional hierarchy, always running from place to place on orders from the doctors, subject as well to strict discipline from her own administrative superiors on the nursing staff, but none of this came through in her recollections. What she remembered was her usefulness.

Whenever my father talked to me about nurses and their work, he 4 spoke with high regard for them as professionals. Although it was clear in his view that the task of the nurses was to do what the doctor told them to, it was also clear that he admired them for being able to do a lot of things he couldn't possibly do, had never been trained to do. On his own rounds later on, when he became an attending physician himself, he consulted the ward nurse for her opinion about problem cases and paid careful attention to her observations and chart notes. In his own days of intern training (perhaps partly under my mother's strong influence, I don't know) he developed a deep and lasting respect for the whole nursing profession.

I have spent all of my professional career in close association with, and close dependency on, nurses, and like many of my faculty colleagues, I've done a lot of worrying about the relationship between medicine and nursing. During most of this century the nursing profession has been having a hard time of it. It has been largely, although not entirely, an occupation for women, and sensitive issues of professional status, complicated by the special issue of the changing role of women in modern society, have led to a standoffish, often adversarial relationship between nurses and doctors. Already swamped by an increasing load of routine duties, nurses have been obliged to take on more and more purely administrative tasks: keeping the records in order; making sure the supplies are on hand for every sort of ward emergency; supervising the activities of the new paraprofessional group called LPNs (licensed practical nurses), who now perform much of the bedside work once done by RNs (registered nurses); overseeing ward maids, porters, and cleaners; seeing to it that patients scheduled for X rays are on their way to the X-ray department on time. Therefore, they have to spend more of their time at desks in the ward office and less time at the bedsides. Too late maybe, the nurses have begun to realize that they are gradually being excluded from the one duty which had previously been their most important reward but which had been so taken for granted that nobody mentioned it in listing the duties of a nurse: close personal contact with patients. Along with everything else nurses did in the long day's work, making up for all the tough and sometimes demeaning jobs assigned to them, they had the matchless opportunity to be useful friends to great numbers of human beings in trouble. They listened to their patients all day long and through the night, they gave comfort and reassurance to the patients and their families, they got to know them as friends, they were depended on. To contemplate the loss of this part of their work has been the deepest worry for nurses at large, and for the faculties responsible for the curricula of the nation's new and expanding nursing schools. The issue lies at the center of the running argument between medical school and nursing school administrators, but it is never clearly stated. Nursing education has been upgraded in recent years. Almost all the former hospital schools, which took in highschool graduates and provided an RN certificate after two or three years, have been replaced by schools attached to colleges

5

and universities, with a four-year curriculum leading simultaneously to a bachelor's degree and an RN certificate.

The doctors worry that nurses are trying to move away from their 6 historical responsibilities to medicine (meaning, really, to the doctors' orders). The nurses assert that they are their own profession, responsible for their own standards, coequal colleagues with physicians, and they do not wish to become mere ward administrators or technicians (although some of them, carrying the new and prestigious title of "nurse practitioner," are being trained within nursing schools to perform some of the most complex technological responsibilities in hospital emergency rooms and intensive care units). The doctors claim that what the nurses really want is to become substitute psychiatrists. The nurses reply that they have unavoidable responsibilities for the mental health and wellbeing of their patients, and that these are different from the doctors' tasks. Eventually the arguments will work themselves out, and some sort of agreement will be reached, but if it is to be settled intelligently, some way will have to be found to preserve and strengthen the traditional and highly personal nurse-patient relationship.

I have had a fair amount of firsthand experience with the issue, 7 having been an apprehensive patient myself off and on over a three-year period on the wards of the hospital for which I work. I am one up on most of my physician friends because of this experience. I know some things they do not know about what nurses do.

One thing the nurses do is to hold the place together. It is an 8 astonishment, which every patient feels from time to time, observing the affairs of a large, complex hospital from the vantage point of his bed, that the whole institution doesn't fly to pieces. A hospital operates by the constant interplay of powerful forces pulling away at each other in different directions, each force essential for getting necessary things done, but always at odds with each other. The intern staff is an almost irresistible force in itself, learning medicine by doing medicine, assuming all the responsibility within reach, pushing against an immovable attending and administrative staff, and frequently at odds with the nurses. The attending physicians are individual entrepreneurs trying to run small cottage industries at each bedside. The diagnostic laboratories are feudal fiefdoms, prospering from the insatiable demands for their services from the interns and residents. The medical students are all over the place, learning as best they can and complaining that they are not, as they believe they should be, at the epicenter of everyone's concern. Each individual worker in the place, from the chiefs of surgery to the dieticians to the ward maids, porters, and elevator operators, lives and works in the conviction that the whole apparatus would come to a standstill without his or her individual contribution, and in one sense or another each of them is right.

My discovery, as a patient first on the medical service and later in surgery, is that the institution is held together, *glued* together, enabled to function as an organism, by the nurses and by nobody else. 9

The nurses, the good ones anyway (and all the ones on my floor were good), make it their business to know everything that is going on. They spot errors before errors can be launched. They know everything written on the chart. Most important of all, they know their patients as unique human beings, and they soon get to know the close relatives and friends. Because of this knowledge, they are quick to sense apprehensions and act on them. The average sick person in a large hospital feels at risk of getting lost, with no identity left beyond a name and a string of numbers on a plastic wristband, in danger always of being whisked off on a litter to the wrong place to have the wrong procedure done, or worse still, *not* being whisked off at the right time. The attending physician or the house officer, on rounds and usually in a hurry, can murmur a few reassuring words on his way out the door, but it takes a confident, competent, and cheerful nurse, there all day long and in and out of the room on one chore or another through the night, to bolster one's confidence that the situation is indeed manageable and not about to get out of hand. 10

Knowing what I know, I am all for the nurses. If they are to continue their professional feud with the doctors, if they want their professional status enhanced and their pay increased, if they infuriate the doctors by their claims to be equal professionals, if they ask for the moon, I am on their side. 11

Questions for Study and Discussion

1. What is Thomas's thesis, and where is it stated? Could it have been placed elsewhere? Explain.

2. What was nursing like when Thomas's mother was practicing? What is the profession like today? How does Thomas account for the changes?

3. In what ways is comparison and contrast a useful strategy for Thomas in accomplishing his purpose?

4. What job reward does Thomas believe nurses are missing out on today?

5. How has nursing education changed over the years? What effects have these changes had on the nursing profession and its relationship to the medical profession?

6. What specifically does Thomas mean when he says, "One thing the nurses

do is to hold the place together"? Why does Thomas believe he has a better understanding of the role of nurses than his fellow physicians?

7. What influence did Thomas's father have on his view of nurses? Who influenced his father?

Writing Topics

1. Argue for or against the proposition that women are better suited than men to be nurses.

2. Explore the problem that a person encounters when he or she enters a profession largely dominated by the opposite sex. For example, men who choose to be elementary school teachers, nurses, or secretaries or women who choose to go into the clergy, engineering, or police work. Your essay should consider not only problems associated with the job, but also those concerned with education, training, and even the reaction of family and friends to entering a certain line of work.

LESTER C. THUROW

Lester C. Thurow, one of the nation's leading economists, was born in Livingston, Montana, in 1938. He received his B.A. from Williams College, an M.A. from Balliol College, Oxford University, where he was a Rhodes scholar, and an M.A. and Ph.D. from Harvard University. After several years of teaching at Harvard in the department of economics and the Kennedy School of Government, Thurow became professor of economics at the Massachusetts Institute of Technology. A prolific writer and researcher, Thurow has contributed more than sixty articles to scholarly journals and popular magazines, including *The Nation, Newsweek, Challenge, Dissent,* and *Daedalus.* His published books include *Fiscal Policy: Experiment for Prosperity* (1967), *Poverty and Discrimination* (1969), *Investment in Human Capital* (1970), *The Impact of Taxes on the American Economy* (1971), and *The Political Economy of Income Redistribution Policies* (1977).

"Why Women Are Paid Less Than Men" first appeared in the *New York Times.* Thurow explains why there is a pay differential and tells what is needed before male and female earnings can be equalized.

Why Women Are Paid Less Than Men

In the 40 years from 1939 to 1979 white women who work full time   1
have with monotonous regularity made slightly less than 60 percent as
much as white men. Why?

Over the same time period, minorities have made substantial progress   2
in catching up with whites, with minority women making even more
progress than minority men.

Black men now earn 72 percent as much as white men (up 16   3
percentage points since the mid-1950's) but black women earn 92 percent
as much as white women. Hispanic men make 71 percent of what their
white counterparts do, but Hispanic women make 82 percent as much
as white women. As a result of their faster progress, fully employed black
women make 75 percent as much as fully employed black men while
Hispanic women earn 68 percent as much as Hispanic men.

This faster progress may, however, end when minority women fi-   4
nally catch up with white women. In the bible of the New Right, George
Gilder's "Wealth and Poverty," the 60 percent is just one of Mother
Nature's constants like the speed of light or the force of gravity.

Men are programmed to provide for their families economically   5
while women are programmed to take care of their families emotionally
and physically. As a result men put more effort into their jobs than

438

women. The net result is a difference in work intensity that leads to that 40 percent gap in earnings. But there is no discrimination against women— only the biological facts of life.

The problem with this assertion is just that. It is an assertion with   6
no evidence for it other than the fact that white women have made 60 percent as much as men for a long period of time.

"Discrimination against women" is an easy answer but it also has   7
its problems as an adequate explanation. Why is discrimination against women not declining under the same social forces that are leading to a lessening of discrimination against minorities? In recent years women have made more use of the enforcement provisions of the Equal Employment Opportunities Commission and the courts than minorities. Why do the laws that prohibit discrimination against women and minorities work for minorities but not for women?

When men discriminate against women, they run into a problem.   8
To discriminate against women is to discriminate against your own wife and to lower your own family income. To prevent women from working is to force men to work more.

When whites discriminate against blacks, they can at least think   9
that they are raising their own incomes. When men discriminate against women they have to know that they are lowering their own family income and increasing their own work effort.

While discrimination undoubtedly explains part of the male-female   10
earnings differential, one has to believe that men are monumentally stupid or irrational to explain all of the earnings gap in terms of discrimination. There must be something else going on.

Back in 1939 it was possible to attribute the earnings gap to large   11
differences in educational attainments. But the educational gap between men and women has been eliminated since World War II. It is no longer possible to use education as an explanation for the lower earnings of women.

Some observers have argued that women earn less money since they   12
are less reliable workers who are more apt to leave the labor force. But it is difficult to maintain this position since women are less apt to quit one job to take another and as a result they tend to work as long, or longer, for any one employer. From any employer's perspective they are more reliable, not less reliable, than men.

Part of the answer is visible if you look at the lifetime earnings   13
profile of men. Suppose that you were asked to predict which men in a group of 25-year-olds would become economically successful. At age 25 it is difficult to tell who will be economically successful and your predictions are apt to be highly inaccurate.

But suppose that you are asked to predict which men in a group of   14
35-year-olds would become economically successful. If you are successful
at age 35, you are very likely to remain successful for the rest of your
life. If you have not become economically successful by age 35, you are
very unlikely to do so later.

The decade between 25 and 35 is when men either succeed or fail.   15
It is the decade when lawyers become partners in the good firms, when
business managers make it onto the "fast track," when academics get
tenure at good universities, and when blue collar workers find the job
opportunities that will lead to training opportunities and the skills that
will generate high earnings.

If there is any one decade when it pays to work hard and to be   16
consistently in the labor force, it is the decade between 25 and 35. For
those who succeed, earnings will rise rapidly. For those who fail, earnings
will remain flat for the rest of their lives.

But the decade between 25 and 35 is precisely the decade when   17
women are most apt to leave the labor force or become part-time workers
to have children. When they do, the current system of promotion and
skill acquisition will extract an enormous lifetime price.

This leaves essentially two avenues for equalizing male and female   18
earnings.

Families where women who wish to have successful careers, com-   19
pete with men, and achieve the same earnings should alter their family
plans and have their children either before 25 or after 35. Or society can
attempt to alter the existing promotion and skill acquisition system so
that there is a longer time period in which both men and women can
attempt to successfully enter the labor force.

Without some combination of these two factors, a substantial frac-   20
tion of the male-female earnings differentials are apt to persist for the
next 40 years, even if discrimination against women is eliminated.

Questions for Study and Discussion

1. Comment on Thurow's opening paragraphs as an introduction. Did you
find the introduction effective? Why or why not?

2. What is Thurow's thesis?

3. How does his discussion of minorities support his thesis?

4. What problems does Thurow have with the argument that discrimination
is at the heart of the pay differences between men and women? Do you accept
his reasoning in paragraphs 8 and 9? Why or why not?

5. What other reasons have people put forth to explain why women earn
less than men? How does Thurow counter each?

6. What is Thurow's own explanation for the discrepancy in pay? What suggestions does he offer to equalize the pay of men and women? Are his suggestions realistic? Explain.

Writing Topics

1. Write an essay in which you present your own explanation of and solution for the pay discrepancy problem.

2. What problems are created in the workplace when people are paid different salaries for the same work? What would you personally do, if anything, to address the problem? Does differing pay on the basis of seniority make sense to you?

6 *Language in America*

A thing is not necessarily true because badly uttered, nor false because spoken magnificently.
ST. AUGUSTINE

It isn't language that is sexist, it is society.
VICTORIA FROMKIN AND ROBERT RODMAN

If language be not in accordance with the truth of things, affairs cannot be carried on to success.
CONFUCIUS

Is There a Language Crisis?

ALVIN P. SANOFF AND LUCIA SOLORZANO

Many educators have singled out illiteracy as the most pressing problem of the 1980s because the inability of millions of Americans to read or write threatens the very foundation of American democracy. People wonder how a nation like ours with all its wealth, computers, and advanced communications technology can also be home to 27 million adults who cannot read a newspaper ad or a product label and more than a million children in their teens who read at or below the third-grade level. Many colleges have responded to the problem by offering more remedial reading and writing courses. In addition, some textbooks are being "dumbed-down," that is, are being written with simplified vocabulary and style. This, unfortunately, compounds the problem because students find such texts both insulting and boring once the challenge is gone.

Alvin P. Sanoff and Lucia Solorzano are both on the staff of *U.S. News and World Report*; Sanoff is a senior editor in charge of social trends and Solorzano associate editor for education. They teamed up to explore the problem of literacy in America, and their findings were published in the February 18, 1985, issue of *U.S. News and World Report*. In this report they describe the dimensions of the illiteracy problem and try to determine its causes. Specifically, they see our educational system, the swelling tide of immigrants, and television as the three major culprits.

It's at Home Where Our Language Is in Distress

English may be the toast of Paris and Peking, but back here in River City it's got trouble, trouble, trouble—

• Trouble because some 27 million adult Americans are functionally illiterate—unable to read a newspaper ad or a product label—and the total grows by the day.

• Trouble in that millions of other adults read barely well enough to scrape by, and 1 million children age 12 to 17 cannot read above a third-grade level.

• Trouble shown by the verbal scores of college-bound high-school seniors on the Scholastic Aptitude Test, which fell from an average of 466 in 1967 to 424 in 1981 and have risen only 2 points since then.

• Trouble documented in a survey by the National Opinion Research Center that finds the language ability of the U.S. population has dropped ever since the 1950s.

Doubly worrisome is that the ranks of the illiterate and marginally literate are swelling at the very time that rapid technological change makes proficiency with words and concepts more and more important.   2

The most seriously crippled are condemned to live in poverty or its shadow because they cannot fill out a simple application form or read a job manual. The nation spends up to 6 billion dollars annually on welfare and jobless aid for the illiterate, who account for as many as three fourths of the unemployed, one study estimates.   3

But the literacy problem goes far beyond this hard core. It also afflicts millions who, as college graduates, are considered well educated. In fact, many graduates have a weaker command of English than their parents.   4

Analytic ability is waning. The National Assessment of Educational Progress, a federally supported research organization, finds "little evidence of well-developed problem-solving strategies or critical-thinking skills" among youngsters. Richard Mitchell, an English professor at Glassboro (N.J.) State College and editor of the *Underground Grammarian*, says that if literacy is defined as the ability to fathom complex ideas, then "many very highly schooled people today are essentially illiterate."   5

The Rise of "Bonehead English"

Why is a country in which English took root more than 360 years ago facing mounting difficulties in passing on to its young this rich linguistic heritage?   6

Much of the blame is laid at the doorstep of the education establishment. Analysts say that in reaction to the student unrest of the '60s— and the chorus of demands that students be allowed to "do their own thing"—schools and colleges watered down their curricula and ended up giving short shrift to reading, writing and critical thinking.   7

In its 1983 report, "A Nation at Risk," the National Commission on Excellence in Education concluded that "secondary-school curricula have been homogenized, diluted and diffused to the point that they no   8 longer have a central purpose. In effect, we have a cafeteria-style curriculum in which the appetizers and desserts can easily be mistaken for the main courses."

One sign of the dilution: In the late 1960s, 85 percent of high-school graduates received four years of English; a decade later, only 41 percent were getting that much. At the same time, enrollment shot up in less demanding remedial courses—"bonehead English"—in high school as well as in college.

The discipline of writing helps to develop and refine thought, yet many teachers cut back on time devoted to the principles of composition. The upshot: A dismaying number of high-school and college students write prose that is next to incomprehensible.

A recent sampling of high-school writing included this from a New York senior: "Teachers don't have enough energy to keep the kids interesting, and they don't explain their selves enough." A junior in Iowa wrote: "I think that students should not be able to particapat to extra activities if failing in school."

Students frequently dash off only a single draft of a short piece. Writing is checked more for spelling and grammar than for grace or logic—and checking often is done by a poorly paid teacher not well equipped for the job. The average college-bound high-school senior planning to major in education scored 28 points below the national average on the verbal part of the SAT in 1984.

In his book *The Leaning Tower of Babel*, Richard Mitchell shows why some educators are poor teachers of writing. He quotes from an article shot through with errors in spelling and grammar: "The Cheerleaders cheered the Drill Team performaned. The motivation and the momentous was there. It worked as clock word or a puzzle each part fell in place at the right time. If you were at the statium with me. I am sure you would have been satisfied with the performance."

The author of those words? A high-school principal.

Legacy of "Look-Say"

Another setback to literacy, say many experts, grew out of an experiment in reading instruction that went awry. In the 1930s, schools shifted substantially to a "look-say" approach. Pupils were made to learn each new word by reciting it aloud, without breaking it into vowel-and-consonant combinations.

Advocates saw look-say as a way to make reading less mechanical, but it now appears that it left many children ill-prepared to cope with unknown words and made them poor spellers. Before this problem was documented convincingly in the late 1960s, a few generations were taught by this method.

Also working against the development of reading skills are text- 17
books that have been "dumbed down" to the point of repelling young people from the printed word. "The moment textbooks started wooing students by giving them the poetry of Bob Dylan and not that of Dylan Thomas, then what did the language have to look forward to?" asks John Simon, author of *Paradigms Lost: Reflections on Literacy and Its Decline.*

Many analysts also fault a system of permissive promotions in which 18
students who cannot read properly are nevertheless passed to the next grade. In a report on the American high school, Ernest Boyer, president of the Carnegie Foundation for the Advancement of Teaching, contends that schools that advance language-deficient students without providing special help perpetuate "a cruel hoax." Eventually, he argues, the students "drop out or get a piece of paper that is worthless."

Many of these young people end up among the ranks of the func- 19
tionally illiterate, whose numbers are growing by more than 2 million every year.

The increase in English-language illiteracy stems as well from the 20
swelling tide of immigrants entering the United States—530,000 or more legally and an unknown number illegally each year. According to the Census Bureau, about 11 percent of the population now reports speaking a language other than English at home, with Spanish predominant by far.

The spread of non-English speakers has been accompanied by ex- 21
pansion of bilingual education. Teachers give instruction in major subjects such as math and science in the students' native languages, most commonly Spanish, while limiting English training primarily to language classes.

Defenders of bilingualism argue that it allows students to advance 22
academically in other subjects while they are learning English, in contrast to the old "sink or swim" approach in which all instruction was in English. At one point, arguments were also mustered on behalf of classroom use of the dialect called "black English," which gained a temporary foothold in a few schools and then fizzled.

As the debate over bilingual education continues, critics insist that 23
it discourages children from learning English. "The primacy of English is being challenged," argues Gerda Bikales, executive director of U.S. English, a group that seeks to give the language official status in the Constitution. "There is a general belief, nurtured to some extent by bilingual education, that English is not all that necessary."

Even so, most experts warn against making bilingualism a scape-   24
goat for the nation's literacy problem. Jonathan Kozol, author of *Illiterate
America*, says illiteracy is not "a consequence of U.S. 'generosity' in im-
migration policies. It would remain a serious problem even if we had no
immigrants."

TV Makes "Rich Kids Dumber"

Next to the shortcomings of the schoolhouse, television comes in   25
for the biggest share of the criticism. For some analysts, in fact, it looms
as the chief culprit. "In its short lifetime, television has become the major
stumbling block to literacy in America," argues Jim Trelease, author of
The Read-Aloud Handbook.

Statistics show that young people spend hours vegetating, as critics   26
see it, before the television screen, while the time children devote to
recreational reading keeps shrinking as they get older.

Although many analysts treat television viewing as a uniform evil,   27
some studies suggest that its effect varies with intelligence and social class.
Researcher Michael Morgan of the University of Massachusetts at Amherst has found that youngsters from affluent families who watch a lot of
TV do less well on tests of reading and language skills than youngsters
from similar backgrounds who are light viewers.

At the same time, however, youngsters from low-income families   28
who watch a lot of TV do better on standardized tests than low-income
children who are light viewers. "Poor kids get smarter and rich kids get
dumber," says George Gerbner, one of the nation's leading television researchers. "TV represents a limitation for those who have had the advantages of our civilization."

Television affects adults as well. Researchers have found that heavy   29
TV viewers do less well than light viewers on tests of verbal intelligence.

Indeed, the whole range of electronic communications offered by   30
modern life often serves to blunt formal language skills. Where individuals used to write letters, they now frequently make telephone calls. Even
most business executives no longer really write letters. Instead, they talk
into a dictating machine.

In the face of widespread concern about the state of U.S. literacy,   31
some analysts take a more measured view. They argue that, although real
problems exist, Americans age 25 or older are more literate than those
who preceded them in that age group. In 1910, fewer than 14 percent
had graduated from high school and fewer than 3 percent from college,

the analysts point out. By 1984, 73 percent had graduated from high school, 19 percent from college.

With fewer marginal students dropping out and more high-school   32
graduates going to college, those regarded as educated are a less elite group now than in the past. One hundred years ago, says School Superintendent Jack French of Bristol, Va., "by the fourth or fifth grade, many of the poorer students had quit school to go behind the plow, and only the better students stayed. Today, we are teaching all levels."

This democratization of education has had a leveling effect, pulling   33
the bottom up and the top down, scholars acknowledge. One indication of decline at the top: The proportion of students scoring above 600 on the verbal portion of the SAT dropped from 10 percent to 7 percent between 1973 and 1983.

Still, publishers are selling more books today per capita than at any   34
time in U.S. history. "People are reading more than ever," insists John Dessauser, director of the Center for Book Research at the University of Scranton.

"The collective intellectual capital of the United States is greater   35
than it has ever been," argues Arthur Wise, senior social scientist at the Rand Corporation. "Average test-score performance masks the fact that higher percentages of our population are attaining greater levels of knowledge."

The Wellsprings of Reform

Even those who hold an upbeat view concede there is a lot of room   36
for improvement. Now, in the face of public pressures generated by poor student performance and reports proclaiming U.S. education to be in a dismal state, schools are taking action.

Many are overhauling the way reading is taught. In most schools,   37
the look-say method has given way to phonics, with youngsters taught to break words into letter sounds. The return to phonics is credited with a recent rise in reading scores among 9-year-olds.

Television, too, is in the phonics act. "Electric Company," a Public   38
Broadcasting Service program now seen by 3 million children in school and 5 million at home, has for some time been teaching youngsters how various combinations of letters create new words.

School systems are putting more stress on writing as they begin to   39
shift from emphasizing just spelling and grammar. Increasingly, they call on students to write short stories and essays.

Teachers in Brooklyn and Birmingham elementary schools get chil-   40
dren to take more care with writing by discussing ideas in advance and
then having them revise their drafts several times. In Montgomery County,
Md., youngsters are encouraged to write as early as the kindergarten year,
during which they keep journals filled with pictures and letters. Educators
believe that starting early promotes better writing in succeeding years.

The close relationship between reading and writing was demon-   41
strated in a special program, "Writing to Read," tested by the International Business Machines Corporation. About 22,000 kindergartners and
first graders, aided by a computer that can mimic a human voice, learned
42 sounds contained in 30 words. The children practiced writing the
sounds in workbooks and then combined them into new words, from which
they composed stories. Their reading performance surpassed national norms.

Many teachers acknowledge that the computer is an important lit-   42
eracy tool. The word processor makes writing easier by allowing a student
to edit a composition on the screen without having to start over on a
clean sheet of paper with each revision.

The new focus on developing basic skills has been accompanied by   43
widespread competence testing throughout the nation. Many states require students to pass tests of basic skills before they can graduate from
high school, and some school systems take such results into account in
making decisions on other promotions.

Yet educators insist that schools can do only part of the job, that   44
help from parents is vital in producing children who can read, write and
think well. Analysts contend that Japanese and Chinese first graders have
higher reading-achievement scores than first graders in the U.S. partly
because parents in those countries spend more time reading to their children.

Adult illiteracy is also drawing increasing attention. As part of an   45
Adult Literacy Initiative begun by President Reagan in 1983, 50 colleges
and universities are using federal funds to train and pay students to teach
adults to read. In December, 11 national organizations launched a campaign, in cooperation with the Advertising Council, to recruit volunteers
to work with illiterate adults and direct people to literacy clinics.

Corporations are spending hundreds of millions of dollars to estab-   46
lish basic-skills programs for their employees. The Business Council for
Effective Literacy has been set up to get corporations more involved.

The B. Dalton book chain has pledged 3 million dollars to help   47
combat adult illiteracy, an effort that includes grants to literacy organizations.

Experts see all of those steps, from kindergarten through adulthood,   48 as significant strides. But there is concern that the efforts may not be enough to meet the constantly growing demands.

"The advent of the Information Age raises to new levels of urgency   49
the need for all students to be effective in their use of the written and the spoken word," says Boyer of the Carnegie Foundation for the Advancement of Teaching.

This Is War

Some specialists warn that illiteracy is so widespread that nothing   50
less than crash programs at all levels of society can cope with the problem. "We need an all-out literacy war in the United States," declares author Kozol.

Scholars warn that if the battle is not won the nation's very survival   51
as a democracy could be jeopardized. Says a Library of Congress report: "We must face and defeat the twin menaces of illiteracy and aliteracy— the inability to read and the lack of will to read—if our citizens are to remain free and qualified to govern themselves."

Questions for Study and Discussion

1. When analysts say that 27 million adult Americans are "functionally illiterate," what exactly do they mean? In what ways can many college graduates be considered illiterate?

2. How did the education establishment react to student unrest in the 1960s? What were the results, according to education analysts?

3. Briefly explain the "look-say" approach to reading. How, according to Sanoff and Solorzano, did this approach to reading instruction contribute to the literacy problem?

4. What exactly is "bilingual education"? On what grounds do supporters of bilingualism defend it? What do the critics see as its chief disadvantages?

5. What, according to the studies cited in this article, have been the effects of television on children in the United States? Were you surprised by any of the findings? Explain.

6. According to Sanoff and Solorzano, what are schools now doing to help students improve their reading and writing skills? What can parents, corporations, and others do to join in the fight against illiteracy?

7. In paragraphs 11 and 13 the authors use examples of the writings of students and educators. What point do the authors make with the help of these examples? Explain what the problems are in each writing sample.

Writing Topics

1. The National Commission on Excellence in Education concluded in 1983 that "secondary-school curricula have been homogenized, diluted and diffused to the point that they no longer have a central purpose. In effect, we have a cafeteria-style curriculum in which the appetizers and desserts can easily be mistaken for the main courses." What was the curriculum like in your high school? Was it the same for college-bound students and those not planning to go on? Write an essay in which you evaluate your high school curriculum in light of the commission's remarks.

2. Write an essay in which you describe the writing instruction you received in school. What kind of assignments were you given? When can you remember first being taught to write? Did your teachers emphasize correctness or content? Were you ever encouraged to write more than one draft of an essay? How did your teachers respond to and/or evaluate your writing? And finally, how would you rate your abilities as a writer today?

3. How important is good spelling to you? There are some people who equate good spelling with literacy. Has your spelling ever caused you any embarrassing moments? How do you react to people who have trouble with spelling or constantly misspell your name, for example? Write a well-organized essay in which you summarize your beliefs about spelling.

Edwin Newman was born in New York City in 1919. After graduating from the University of Wisconsin in 1940, he became a news commentator, first for International News Service and later with CBS. In 1952 he started his long affiliation with NBC both as a television newsman and as the narrator for such television specials as "Who Shall Live?" (1965), "Violence in America" (1977), "Spying for Uncle Sam" (1978), and "Oil and American Power" (1979). Newman is also the author of *Strictly Speaking: Will America Be the Death of English?* (1974) and *A Civil Tongue* (1976)—two very popular books that have established his reputation as an advocate of correct usage and as a guardian of American English.

In "Language on the Skids," first published in the *Naval War College Review* and later reprinted in *Reader's Digest*, Newman provides numerous examples of redundant, flabby, and self-important language. He believes the English language is being abused and strongly argues for the responsible use of language by us all.

Language on the Skids

It is typical of the English spoken on this side of the Atlantic that enough is almost never enough. Cecil Smith, television critic of the Los Angeles *Times*, considered CBS's "Bicentennial Minutes" not merely unique but singularly unique. Sen. Abraham Ribicoff of Connecticut was worried not only about nuclear proliferation but about the spread of nuclear proliferation. And Reggie Jackson, the *New York Times* advised its readers, "stole second successfully," which is better than stealing it unsuccessfully. 1

All of this is redundancy, to which we have become addicted. A large part of our speech and writing is unnecessary and boring, which makes reading and conversation a chore. We slog through the repetitious, and tarry when we should be moving on. Redundancy triumphs. 2

One reason for our extravagant use of words is the feeling that an idea is more effective if it is repeated and reinforced. That is why Jimmy Carter once described the international situation as very dormant. (Those were the days!) It is why he said that the place where he would meet Leonid Brezhnev would depend not merely on a mutual decision but on "a mutual decision between us." You can't be too careful when dealing with the Russians. 3

Another cause is a failure to understand what words mean. The New York *Daily News* would not have said of a motion picture that it 4 "extolled the evils of the advertising business" if it knew what extolled meant. The weather forecaster at the CBS station in Washington, D.C., would not have said, "Tomorrow afternoon, the temperature will gradually plummet. . . ." And what could have led the New Bedford, Mass., *Standard Times* to run this headline: "Tie vote kills bottle bill, but not fatally"?

There is a third reason for our extravagant use of words—a desire   5 to make what is being done, however simple and routine it may be, sound grand and complicated. Thus, two newspapers in Nevada announce that they intend to put up a building. Do they call it a building? No. It is to be "a community-information center." The Postal Service issues statements about "sortation" of mail. Not sorting. Sortation. The Los Angeles City Teachers' Mathematics Association, at its Annual Recognition Dinner, schedules an associative hour rather than a cocktail hour. What does one do during an associative hour? Get acquainted? Not since computer language has descended on us. One interfaces on a personal basis. By the way, if any well-dressed women are present, it is possible that their dress reflects "Executive Wardrobe Engineering."

Why is such language used? Self-importance, of course, but also   6 because it serves as a fence that keeps others outside and respectful, or leads them to ignore what is going on inside because it is too much trouble to find out. So you may hear about "a horizontal analysis spanning the formal vertical department structure" intended to "identify multipurpose citizen contacts requiring timely responses." Or you may hear of a California school district that closes schools not because there are fewer pupils than expected but because of "accelerated enrollment slippage."

This sort of language is increasingly characteristic of a society where   7 engaged couples are said to be in a commitment situation, and where an economist may refer to work as labor-force participation. In Boston, the Metropolitan District commission did not want to say, "Keep off the ice." It urged that "all persons terminate using any body of water under MDC control for any ice-related recreation." It could have been worse. It could have been ice-related recreation-oriented activity.

There is, of course, a technique involved, but it is easy to grasp.   8 Never say that a tank may spring a leak. Say there may be a "breach of containment." Never say of a product that people won't buy it. Say that it "met consumer resistance." In Knoxville, Tenn., a nurse won a product-naming contest with the suggestion that dust covers for medical equipment be called instead "sterility maintenance covers." That was worth $500 and a lunch at the Hyatt Regency Hotel.

I want to turn now to what I take to be the new pastime. It is   9 "izing." A reporter I know, covering a Presidential visit to Boston, asked the Secret Service where he could park his car. The Secret Service could not help. What should he do, then? "If I were you," the Secret Service man replied, "I would put myself in a chauffeurized situation." The head of the United States Professional Tennis Association proposed "to focalize all major USPTA activities and programs from a single site." Would he be the focalist? Some plastic surgeons, advertising a customized approach, promise "wrinkles youthfulized." This, apparently, leaves the patient with young wrinkles.

Sports broadcasters often have only a shaky grip on grammar and on the connection between words and meaning. During one football game, the announcer told viewers that because of the way some of the boxes in the Superdome were placed, he could not visually see them. This sort of thing is by no means confined to the sports world. For example, we have all heard about alleged victims. They have become confused in some journalistic minds with intended victims, but intended victims are sometimes rendered as would-be-victims, who apparently go out in the hope of being robbed.

An ironic thing is happening now. As we demand more and more openness from those in public life—unwisely, it seems to me—our language becomes more and more obscure, turgid, ponderous and overblown. The candor expected of public officials about their health, their money, their private lives is offset in public matters by language that conceals more than it tells, and often conceals the fact that there is little or nothing worth telling.

We ought to demand that our leaders speak better English, so that we know what they are talking about and, incidentally, so that they do. Some safety does lie in more sensible public attitudes, especially toward the public-relations and advertising techniques now widely used by politicians. It lies also in independent reporting by those of us in the news business, and in greater skepticism on the part of the public, and in an unremitting puncturing of the overblown. In all of this, language is crucial.

I have been told that my view is cranky and pedantic, that I want to keep the language from growing, and to impose a standard and rigid English. Far from it. Our language should be specific and concrete, eloquent where possible, playful where possible, and personal so that we don't all sound alike. Instead, high crimes and misdemeanors are visited upon it, and those who commit them do not understand that the crimes are crimes against themselves. The language belongs to all of us. We have no more valuable possession.

Questions for Study and Discussion

1. In his opening paragraph Newman gives three examples of our extravagant use of words: "singularly unique," "the spread of nuclear proliferation," and "stole second successfully." Explain what the problem is in each case.

2. Newman believes that for most Americans "enough is almost never enough" (1). What does he see as the causes of our extravagance with words?

3. Why, according to Newman, do people use language that promotes self-importance? Is such usage ever appropriate or legitimate in your opinion? Explain.

4. What relationship does Newman see between society and the language used?

5. What does Newman believe we can do to correct the situation he describes?

6. In his final paragraph Newman admits that people sometimes find him "cranky and pedantic." What do you think? Are the language abuses that he cites really "high crimes and misdemeanors" against American English? Explain.

7. What is Newman's thesis in the essay? Where is it stated?

8. Discuss Newman's use of irony in paragraph 8.

9. Without his many examples, how persuasive would Newman's argument be? Did you think that he could have used more examples at any points in the essay? If so, where?

Writing Topics

1. One area of language abuse that Newman discusses is sports. Carefully read the sports section of your local or school newspaper and/or listen to the broadcast of several sports events, collecting examples for an essay on the language abuses of sports broadcasters and writers. Do you agree with Newman's assessment of their language?

2. Write an essay in which you discuss the redundant, highfalutin', and obscure language that you regularly encounter. Where in your experience is such language most common? What effect has this language abuse had on you?

JIM QUINN

Unlike Edwin Newman, Jim Quinn is a liberal on matters of the English language. A journalist by trade, Quinn is the author of several books including *Word of Mouth* (1971) and writes regularly for a number of popular magazines. He is particularly intrigued by our language and the growing number of conservative language watchers whom he fondly calls "pop grammarians." In his book *American Tongue and Cheek* (1981), Quinn directly attacks these pop grammarians—including Edwin Newman, John Simon, and William and Mary Morris—for their belief that the deplorable condition of our language is a direct reflection of the condition of the American society that uses it.

The following essay first appeared in *Newsweek*. As Quinn's title indicates, he has little patience for today's language crusaders. Here he points out some of the errors in their thinking about language.

Hopefully, They Will Shut Up

Almost everybody in America has an illiteracy they love to hate   1
because it makes them feel superior to other Americans: "Anyone can do what they like," "between you and I," "input," "different than," "hopefully." Sometimes the list seems endless. We are in the middle of a great national crusade to protect the language from the people who speak it.

The crusaders certainly seem to be having fun. Though they claim   2
to see the Death of English approaching at any moment, there's a kind of rosy romantic glow to their despair. You get a picture of this gallant little band of the last literates going down to defeat with *Warriner's Grade Four Grammar* in one hand and *Best Loved Poems of College English Departments* in the other. There are only two things wrong with this great conservative crusade of correctors: it is not conservative, and it is not correct. Though our popularizers of good grammar (let's call them pop grammarians for short) think they are defending standards and traditions, they keep attacking idioms that are centuries old. Here are a few examples:

Anyone Can Do What They Like. We must never combine *anyone*   3
with *they*, says John Simon in his book, *Paradigms Lost*: "that way madness lies." Simon seems to think this madness is brand-new, produced in part at least by feminists who want to overturn the old male grammar of "anyone can do what *he* wants" (and *she* better shut up about it). In fact, a wholesale confusion of number and case in pronouns has been a feature of standard English since Elizabethan times. This never hurt the writing

458

of Shakespeare, Marlowe, Ben Jonson, Defoe, Swift, Jane Austen, Dickens, George Bernard Shaw and Oscar Wilde ("Experience is the name that everyone gives to their mistakes"). The use of *they* instead of *he*, in cases where both men and women are meant, is defended by such conservative, pre-liberation authorities as the *Oxford English Dictionary (OED)*, our greatest historical dictionary, and Otto Jespersen, the distinguished scholarly grammarian of our language. If that be madness, as Simon says, it is a venerable and literary lunacy.

Between You and I. "Horrible!" wrote poet W. H. Auden, giving   4
his expert opinion in *The Harper Dictionary of Contemporary Usage*. "All debts are cleared between you and I," wrote poet William Shakespeare (*Merchant of Venice*, Act III, Scene 2). Whom are we to trust? D. H. Lawrence points the way for us here. Never trust the artist, said Lawrence; always trust the art. A poet's idea of how language works is as likely to be correct as his idea of how a typewriter works. "You and I" in the accusative is an ancient (and indestructible) idiom. See the opening line of T. S. Eliot's *The Love Song of J. Alfred Prufrock*: "Let us go then, you and I."

Input. "Computer cant," said Theodore Bernstein in *Dos, Don'ts*   5
& Maybes of English Usage; "laymen sometimes take it over to sound impressive." In fact, "input" has been around since the eighteenth century. Sir Walter Scott used it to mean "contribution" in *The Heart of Midlothian* (1818). The Supplement to the *OED* shows noncant uses in such fields as economics long before the first computer use (1948). Input is not a computer word—it's an old word borrowed by computer scientists. No harm in borrowing it back.

Different Than. "*Different than* rather than *different from* is wrong,"   6
wrote Edwin Newman in *Strictly Speaking*. Short, simple, to the point and utterly without foundation. H. W. Fowler, in *Modern English Usage* (the bible of most pop grammarians), classes insistence on "different from" as a superstition. The *OED* notes that "different than" is considered by many to be incorrect, but that "different than" can be found in writers of all ages. Among them: Addison, Steele, Defoe, DeQuincey, Coleridge, Carlyle, and Thackeray. Use "different from" if you want—but criticize "different than" and you're messing with the big guys.

Rhetoric. "Not so long ago," says William Safire, in his book *On*   7
Language, "the predominant meaning of rhetoric was *the science of persuasion*." Now we tend to use rhetoric to mean empty talk. Safire would like to rescue this good old word from our abuse and has a cure: use "bloviation," an old slang word dating back before 1851, for empty talk. The abuse of "rhetoric" dates back before 1851, too—to the sixteenth century. Among users cited in the *OED*: Spenser, Milton, Swift, and

Swinburne, who warns against "the limp loquacity of long-winded rhetoric, so natural to men and soldiers in an hour of emergency." And so natural, also, to pop grammarians when they invent cures for which there is no disease.

Hopefully, Better-Coordinated Programs Will Result. To John 8 Simon, that use of "hopefully" is an infallible sign of illiteracy. " 'Hopefully' so used is an abomination, its adherents should be lynched," says poet Phyllis McGinley. Adherents include Theodore Bernstein, William Safire, and the editors of the *Concise Oxford, Random House, Merriam-Webster, Webster's New World* and *Standard College* dictionaries. Did Phyllis McGinley really want all of them lynched? The author of the sentence that begins this paragraph was Dr. Nathan Pusey, the former president of Harvard. Does John Simon really believe that Dr. Pusey cannot read or write? Of course not. Both Simon and McGinley were merely using the limp and fuzzy rhetoric of pop grammar, where "illiterate" means only "hasn't read my stylebook."

A New Non-Worry: The Danger From the Right. Should we all 9 worry that the pop grammarians will succeed and that someday soon we'll have to talk what they call Good English? Not at all. Wrongheaded objections to idioms are as much a part of the history of English as the idioms themselves—and probably always will be. There will always be gallant little bands to fling themselves, and their violent rhetoric, in front of some age-old word they have made a fad of trying to stop. And there will always be the rest of us to run right over them. That's why English is still alive.

Questions for Study and Discussion

1. What is Quinn's attitude toward the people who want to "protect the language"? Why does he call them "pop grammarians"?

2. Who, according to Quinn, are the pop grammarians? Have you ever read anything by one of them? If so, what was your reaction to it?

3. Quinn states that "there are only two things wrong with this great conservative crusade of correctors: it is not conservative, and it is not correct." How does he document this claim? What authorities and/or types of evidence does he present to argue with the pop grammarians?

4. Did you find Quinn's argument convincing? Explain.

5. In what ways is the opening paragraph a good introduction to this essay? Do you have an illiteracy you "love to hate"? If so, what is it, and why does it bother you?

6. What is the meaning of Quinn's title? How do you suppose Phyllis Mc-
Ginley would react to it if she were alive today?

7. Is Quinn concerned about the efforts of pop grammarians to reform us and
our language? Do you agree with his position? Why, or why not?

Writing Topics

1. Each of the following items is normally discussed as a question of usage by
usage guides and dictionaries. Consult three or four usage guides and/or dictionaries in the reference section of your library for information about each
item. What advice does each book offer? Is the advice always consistent from
book to book? What conclusions can you draw about the usefulness of such
usage guides and the whole debate about correctness?
   a. fewer/less
   b. nauseous
   c. imply/infer
   d. contact (as a verb)
   e. ain't
   f. enthuse
   g. irregardless
   h. lie/lay
   i. since/because
   j. uninterested/disinterested

2. Write an essay in which you take issue with Quinn's position. Isn't there
a real need to insist upon correctness, to maintain standards and traditions?
Have you even been in situations where you seemed to be judged on the basis
of the correctness of your English as much as on the quality of your ideas?

For the last ten or fifteen years writers like Edwin Newman have warned of the widespread corruption of our language and the demise of Standard English. Such language critics complain that "jargon is rampant; the kids talk funny; politicians brutalize the language in their endless attempts to mislead us; bureaucrats pollute the environment with obfuscation and bluster; the verbal test scores of our schoolchildren are plunging; substandard dialects are often accepted or even encouraged in the schools; non-English speakers are infiltrating our cities; and no one in school or business can write a simple English sentence correctly." In his book *Famous Last Words: The American Language Crisis Reconsidered* (1983), Daniels refutes the idea that a literacy crisis rages throughout the United States and discredits the belief that our language is deteriorating. Daniels has taught at Rosary College and is currently a professor at the National College of Education in Illinois. Much of Daniels's thinking is based in part on his experience in the front lines of today's "language crisis" as the director of the Illinois Writing Project for the state's public school students.

In the following chapter from his book *Famous Last Words*, Daniels takes issue with the "trivial obsessions" of the current language critics. He believes that much of their "scolding and fussing about language focuses on redpenciling the superficial niceties of written and spoken utterances, rather than on understanding where they come from and what they might mean."

Is There Really a Language Crisis?

The deathwatch over American English has begun again. After all the shocks and assaults of her long life, and after all of her glorious recoveries, the Mother Tongue now faces the final hour. Around the bedside cluster the mourners: Edwin Newman, John Simon, Clifton Fadiman, Tony Randall, and Ann Landers. In darkened ranks behind stand somber professors of freshman composition, a few school board members, a representative from the National Assessment of Educational Progress, and the entire usage panel of the *American Heritage Dictionary*. Like all deaths, this one evokes in the bereaved the whole range of human feeling: anger, frustration, denial, despair, confusion, and grim humor. It has been a long, degenerative disease and not pretty to watch.

Is there room for hope? Is it really, uh, terminal? The specialists leave no room for miracles—the prognosis is firm. The obituaries have been prepared and, in some cases, already published. Services will be announced. Memorials are referred to the Educational Testing Service. *Requiescat in pace* American English.

Yet, curiously, the language clings to life. She even weakly speaks   3
from time to time, in delirium no doubt, for her words are in jargon,
cant, argot, doublespeak, and various substandard dialects. She splits
infinitives and dangles participles, and one of the watchers actually thought
he heard her begin a sentence with *hopefully*. How can one so ill survive?
It is torture to see this. It must end.

But it won't. If this is death in life, it is still the normal condition   4
of American English and of all other human languages. As compelling
as the medical metaphors may be, languages really are not very much
like people, healthy or sick, and make poor candidates for personification.
The illnesses, the abuses, the wounds, the sufferings of a language reside
in the minds and hearts of its users, as do its glories, triumphs, and eras
of progress. Our language is an essentially neutral instrument with which
we communicate, more or less, and into which we pour an abundance
of feeling. It is our central cultural asset and our cherished personal
friend, but it is not, in many ways, what we think it is or would like it
to be.

But here is another story about death which I believe does tell us   5
something important about the present state of American English. In
Chicago, during the Christmas season of 1978, twenty-six Spanish-speak-
ing people were killed in a series of tragic fires. Many of them perished
because they could not understand the instructions that firemen shouted
in English. When the city promptly instituted a program to teach the
firefighters a few emergency phrases in Spanish, a storm of protest arose.
"This is America," proclaimed the head of the Chicago Firefighters Union,
"let them speak English." A local newspaper columnist suggested, with
presumably innocent irony: "Let's stop catering to the still-flickering nationalistic desires to perpetuate the Latin heritage." The city's top-rated
television newscaster used his bylined editorial minute to inveigh against
the Spanish-teaching program in the firehouse.

An exasperated resident wrote to the letters column of the *Chicago*   6
Tribune: "I object to bilingual everything. It is a pretty low sort of person
who wants to enjoy the benefits of this country while remaining apart
from it, hiding in an ethnic ghetto." Another letter writer huffed: "What
does it take to bring home to these stiff-necked Latinos that when they
move to a foreign country the least they can do is learn the language? I,
for one, am fed up with the ruination of the best country in the world."
Still another correspondent was even more succinct: "If they can't understand two words—don't jump—they should go back where they came
from." And after my own brief article on the language controversy appeared, an angry firefighter's wife wrote me to explain her husband's awful
dilemma in being stationed in the Latino community. "Why should he
risk his life for nothing?" she wondered.

What does this story, which concerns speakers of Spanish, tell us   7
about the current state of English? It reminds us that our attitudes about
the speechways of other people are as much a part of the linguistic environment as nouns, verbs, and adjectives—and that today these attitudes appear unusually harsh and unforgiving. In the Chicago controversy, some otherwise decent people were willing to imply—and some
plainly stated—that people who don't talk right can damn well take their
chances in a burning building. And while the underlying hostilities that
give rise to such sentiments may not begin with language, it is clear that
we frequently use language as both a channel and an excuse for expressing
some of our deepest prejudices. Admittedly, our unforgiving attitudes
about certain kinds of language do not often decide matters of life and
death. Judging by the angry reaction to the fire crisis in Chicago, it is a
good thing that they don't.

It seems worth noting that this particular outpouring of linguistic   8
intolerance occurred in the midst of a period of more general concern
about the fate of the English language. For the last decade we have been
increasingly hearing about the sudden and widespread corruption of our
native tongue. Standard English is supposedly becoming an endangered
species; jargon is rampant; the kids talk funny; politicians brutalize the
language in their endless attempts to mislead us; bureaucrats pollute the
environment with obfuscation and bluster; the verbal test scores of our
schoolchildren are plunging; substandard dialects are often accepted or
even encouraged in the schools; non-English speakers are infiltrating our
cities; and no one in school or business can write a simple English sentence correctly.

We have been having a "literacy crisis"—a panic about the state   9
of our language in all of its uses, reading and writing and speaking.
Predictions of linguistic doom have become a growth industry. *Time*
magazine asks: "Can't Anyone Here Speak English?" while *Newsweek*
explains "Why Johnny Can't Write." *TV Guide* warns of "The New
Illiteracy," *Saturday Review* bemoans "The Plight of the English Language," and even United Airline's *Mainliner Magazine* blusters "Who's
Been Messing Around with Our Mother Tongue?" Pop grammarians and
language critics appear in every corner of the popular media, relentlessly
detailing the latest abuses of language and pillorying individual abusers.

Blue-ribbon commissions are impaneled to study the declining lan-   10
guage skills of the young, and routinely prescribe strong doses of "The
Basics" as a remedy. Astute educational publishers crank out old-fangled
grammar books. English professors offer convoluted explanations of the
crisis and its causes, most of which lay the blame on public school English
teachers. *The New York Times Magazine* adds Spiro Agnew's former

speechwriter to its roster as a weekly commentator "On Language." The president of the United States goes on record as encouraging the "back-to-basics" movement generally and the rebirth of grammar instruction in particular. Scores of books on illiteracy are published, but none outsells *Strictly Speaking*. Edwin Newman, house grammarian of the National Broadcasting Company had posed the question first, and apparently most frighteningly: "Will America be the death of English?" His answer was frightening too: "My mature, considered judgment is that it will."

It was in the midst of this ripening language panic that the Spanish   11
courses were begun in a few Chicago firehouses. The resulting controversy and debate would surely have happened anyway, since the expression of linguistic prejudice is one of humankind's most beloved amusements. But I also believe that the dispute was broadened, extended, and made more explicitly cruel by the prevailing climate of worry about the overall deterioration of American English.

The public had repeatedly been informed that the language was in   12
a mess, that it was time to draw the line, time to clean up the tongue, time to toughen our standards, time to quit coddling inadequate speakers. In Chicago, that line was drawn in no uncertain terms. Obviously, the connections between the "language crisis," with its mythical Mother Tongue writhing on her deathbed, and the all-too-real events of that recent Chicago winter are subtle and indirect.

Language is changing, yes. People "misuse" language constantly—   13
use it to lie, mislead, and conceal. Few of us write very well. Young people do talk differently from grownups. Our occupations do generate a lot of jargon. We do seem to swear more. I do not personally admire each of these phenomena. But reports of the death of the English language are greatly exaggerated.

English is not diseased, it has not been raped and ravaged, it is not   14
in peril. A language cannot, by its very nature, suffer in such ways. In fact, it cannot suffer at all. One of the sternest of the pop grammarians, Richard Mitchell, has said in one of his calmer moments:

> There is nothing wrong with English. We do not live in the twilight of a dying language. To say that our English is outmoded or corrupt makes as much sense as to say that multiplication has been outmoded by Texas Instruments and corrupted because we've all forgotten the times tables. You may say as often as you please that six times seven is forty-five, but arithmetic will not suffer.

Mitchell goes on to say that the real problem we face lies not in the language itself but in the ignorance and stupidity of its users. I agree, although my definition of ignorance and stupidity is quite different from his.

At least some of the ignorance from which we suffer is ignorance   15
of the history of language and the findings of linguistic research. History shows us that language panics, some just as fierce as our present one, are as familiar a feature of the human chronicle as wars. In fact, one of the persistent characteristics of past crises has been the inevitable sense that everything was fine until the moment at hand, 1965, or 1789, or 2500 B.C., when suddenly the language (be it American English, British English, or Sumerian) began the final plunge to oblivion. Looking at the history of prior language crises gives us a reassuring perspective for evaluating the current one.

But we need more than reassurance—we need facts, or at least the   16
closest thing to them, about the nature of language and how it works. The study of linguistics, which has emerged only during the present century, provides just such crucial information. The fact that the sponsors of the language crisis almost unanimously condemn modern linguistics suggests the irreconcilable difference between the critic's and the lin-guist's views of language. The linguist's work is not to ridicule poor speakers and praise good ones; not to rank various languages according to their supposed superiority in expressing literary or scientific concepts; not to defend the Mother Tongue from real or imagined assaults. Instead, the linguist tries to understand and explain some of the wonderfully complex mechanisms which allow human beings to communicate with each other. This does not mean that linguists don't have opinions about good and bad language, or even that some of them won't cringe at a dangling *hopefully*. But their main business is not evaluative but explan-atory, not prescriptive but descriptive—an orientation which is utterly alien to the work of the contemporary language critics.

Even if a review of the story of language and linguistic research   17
does tend to deflate our sense of crisis, this does not mean that the widespread fear of linguistic corruption is meaningless. Far from it. Some-thing is indeed going on, and the wordsmiths of our society have been able to spread their concern about it quite easily to people who do not make their living by teaching, writing, or editing English. In order to understand what is at stake, we will need to look closely at the assump-tions of contemporary language criticisms and the ways in which they have been shared with the public.

All this worry about a decline extends well beyond the speaking   18
and writing of American English. It represents a much wider concern

about the direction of our society, our culture, as a whole. We have displaced (to use some jargon) much of our anxiety about current cultural changes into concern for the language which of necessity reflects them. Today, as at certain other moments in the past, talking about language has become a way of talking about ourselves, and about what we mean by knowledge, learning, education, discipline, intelligence, democracy, equality, patriotism, and truth.

But there are problems, serious ones. Language itself cannot be asked to carry the weight of such grave issues alone. To the extent that we assign our problems mainly to language, and explain them mostly by reference to aspects of language, we often defeat our own purposes. The critics, in this sense, are actually compounding the problems they profess to solve. First, they are promulgating or reinforcing ideas about language that are just plain wrong. If language is as important as the critics unanimously claim, then we should at least try to tell the truth about it, even if the facts run counter to our favorite prejudices. Second, the ministrations of the critics, with their inaccurate notions about the workings of language, threaten to bring back old—or to inspire new—teaching curricula and techniques that will hinder, rather than enhance, our children's efforts to develop their reading and writing and speaking skills. 19

Third, the critics, ironically enough, often trivialize the study of language. Through their steadfast preoccupation with form—with spelling and punctuation and usage and adolescent jargon and bureaucratic bluster and political doublespeak—they deflect us from meaning. Of course we know that form and content are intimately related, as the study of political propaganda reveals. Yet the real study of propaganda involves penetrating beyond the surface features to the message which is being sent, to the messages unsent, and to the purposes of the senders. But much of the current scolding and fussing about language focuses on redpenciling the superficial niceties of written and spoken utterances, rather than on understanding where they come from and what they might mean. 20

For all their trivial obsessions, the critics do also offer a deeper, more general message. As they advise us to strengthen our democracy by cleaning up the language, they also encourage us to continue using minor differences in language as ways of identifying, classifying, avoiding, or punishing anyone whom we choose to consider our social or intellectual inferior. And this is the gravest problem which the language crisis has given us: it has reinforced and occasionally glorified some of the basest hatreds and flimsiest prejudices in our society. Surely this unfortunate side effect has been mainly inadvertent—but just as surely, it affects us all. 21

Questions for Study and Discussion

1. What, according to Daniels, is the "normal condition" of American English? Why isn't he concerned about all the so-called abuses cited by language watchdogs and pop grammarians?

2. In paragraphs 5 and 6 Daniels relates the story of the 1978 fires in Chicago. What does this story have to do with the current state of English in the United States? Why does Daniels think that it is more than coincidence that the Chicago incident happened at the same time that there was growing public awareness of and concern about the decline of the English language?

3. What solutions have been offered for the "literacy crisis"? What is Daniels's attitude toward these solutions?

4. Daniels states that there are several irreconcilable differences between language critics and linguists. What exactly are these differences?

5. Daniels believes that the pop grammarians and language critics are "actually compounding the problems they profess to solve". What reasons does he give for his opinion? Do you find yourself agreeing or disagreeing with Daniels?

6. What does Daniels think is the "gravest problem" that the current language crisis has strapped us with?

7. How would you characterize Daniels's tone in this essay? What is his attitude toward pop grammarians? toward the current language crisis?

8. Why does Daniels find "medical metaphors" used to describe the language crisis generally unsatisfactory?

Writing Topics

1. After reading what both Newman ("Language on the Skids," pp. 454–456) and Daniels have to say about the language crisis in America, what is your position? Are you more in agreement with watchdog Newman or with linguist Daniels? Explain.

2. While you were in high school you were probably exposed to the "back to basics" movement. What exactly did "back to basics" mean in your area? How did it affect the curriculum? Did this approach adequately address students' language problems in writing, reading, and speaking?

3. Daniels believes that by insisting upon correctness, pop grammarians "encourage us to continue using minor differences in language as ways of identifying, classifying, avoiding, or punishing anyone whom we choose to consider our social or intellectual inferior". Have you ever reacted to anyone negatively or positively on the basis of the English that he or she used, or have you ever been judged on that same basis? Write an essay in which you recount one such incident and discuss how language prejudiced opinion.

Prejudice

GORDON ALLPORT

When Gordon Allport was writing *The Nature of Prejudice,* the influential book from which the following essay is taken, much of the United States was still racially segregated and Senator Joseph McCarthy was at the height of his sensational career, chasing suspected communists and subversives from the national government. Allport's book appeared in 1954, the year in which things began to change. McCarthy's influence was finally ended by Senate censure. That same year the Supreme Court ruled against racial segregation in public schools, and in 1955 Martin Luther King, Jr., led the boycott against Montgomery's segregated bus system that began the modern civil rights movement.

Allport himself was not one to join the picket lines. He was born in 1897 in Montezuma, Indiana, attended Harvard University, and ultimately returned there as a professor of psychology; he retired in 1962 and died five years later. His articles and books on personality established him as a leading authority in his field. *The Nature of Prejudice* remains his most widely-read book, however, as readable and relevant today as it was when first published. In this selection, Allport identifies and discusses some of the ways in which language itself, often very subtly, can express prejudice and even cause it.

The Language of Prejudice

Without words we should scarcely be able to form categories at all. 1 A dog perhaps forms rudimentary generalizations, such as small-boys-are-to-be-avoided—but this concept runs its course on the conditioned reflex level, and does not become the object of thought as such. In order to hold a generalization in mind for reflection and recall, for identification and for action, we need to fix it in words. Without words our world would be, as William James said, an "empirical sand-heap."

Nouns That Cut Slices

In the empirical world of human beings there are some [four] billion   2
grains of sand corresponding to our category "the human race." We cannot possibly deal with so many separate entities in our thought, nor can
we individualize even among the hundreds whom we encounter in our
daily round. We must group them, form clusters. We welcome, therefore,
the names that help us to perform the clustering.

The most important property of a noun is that it brings many grains   3
of sand into a single pail, disregarding the fact that the same grains might
have fitted just as appropriately into another pail. To state the matter
technically, a noun *abstracts* from a concrete reality some one feature and
assembles different concrete realities only with respect to this one feature.
The very act of classifying forces us to overlook all other features, many
of which might offer a sounder basis than the rubric we select. Irving Lee
gives the following example:

> I knew a man who had lost the use of both eyes. He was called a "blind
> man." He could also be called an expert typist, a conscientious worker, a
> good student, a careful listener, a man who wanted a job. But he couldn't
> get a job in the department store order room where employees sat and typed
> orders which came over the telephone. The personnel man was impatient
> to get the interview over. "But you're a blind man," he kept saying, and
> one could almost feel his silent assumption that somehow the incapacity in
> one aspect made the man incapable in every other. So blinded by the label
> was the interviewer that he could not be persuaded to look beyond it.

Some labels, such as "blind man," are exceedingly salient and pow-   4
erful. They tend to prevent alternative classification, or even cross-clas-
sification. Ethnic labels are often of this type, particularly if they refer to
some highly visible feature, e.g., Negro, Oriental. They resemble the
labels that point to some outstanding incapacity—*feeble-minded, cripple,
blind man*. Let us call such symbols "labels of primary potency." These
symbols act like shrieking sirens, deafening us to all finer discriminations
that we might otherwise perceive. Even though the blindness of one man
and the darkness of pigmentation of another may be defining attributes
for some purposes, they are irrelevant and "noisy" for others.

Most people are unaware of this basic law of language—that every   5
label applied to a given person refers properly only to one aspect of his
nature. You may correctly say that a certain man is *human, a philanthropist,
a Chinese, a physician, an athlete*. A given person may be all of these; but
the chances are that *Chinese* stands out in your mind as the symbol of

primary potency. Yet neither this nor any other classificatory label can refer to the whole of a man's nature. (Only his proper name can do so.)

Thus each label we use, especially those of primary potency, distracts our attention from concrete reality. The living, breathing, complex individual—the ultimate unit of human nature—is lost to sight. As in Figure 1, the label magnifies one attribute out of all proportion to its true significance, and masks other important attributes of the individual. . . .

A category, once formed with the aid of a symbol of primary potency, tends to attract more attributes than it should. The category labeled *Chinese* comes to signify not only ethnic membership but also reticence, impassivity, poverty, treachery. To be sure, . . . there may be genuine ethnic-linked traits, making for a certain *probability* that the member of an ethnic stock may have these attributes. But our cognitive process is not cautious. The labeled category, as we have seen, includes indiscriminately the defining attribute, probable attributes, and wholly fanciful, nonexistent attributes.

Even proper names—which ought to invite us to look at the individual person—may act like symbols of primary potency, especially if they arouse ethnic associations. Mr. Greenberg is a person, but since his name is Jewish, it activates in the hearer his entire category of Jews-as-a-whole. An ingenious experiment performed by Razran shows this point clearly, and at the same time demonstrates how a proper name, acting like an ethnic symbol, may bring with it an avalanche of stereotypes.

> Thirty photographs of college girls were shown on a screen to 150 students. The subjects rated the girls on a scale from one to five for *beauty, intelligence, character, ambition, general likability*. Two months later the same subjects were asked to rate the same photographs (and fifteen additional ones introduced to complicate the memory factor). This time five of the original photographs were given Jewish surnames (Cohen, Kantor, etc.), five Italian (Valenti, etc.), and five Irish (O'Brien, etc.); and the remaining girls were given names chosen from the signers of the Declaration of Independence and from the Social Register (Davis, Adams, Clark, etc.).
>
> When Jewish names were attached to photographs there occurred the following changes in ratings:
> decrease in liking
> decrease in character
> decrease in beauty
> increase in intelligence
> increase in ambition
> For those photographs given Italian names there occurred:

6

7

8

decrease in liking
decrease in character
decrease in beauty
decrease in intelligence

Thus a mere proper name leads to prejudgments of personal attributes.
The individual is fitted to the prejudice ethnic category, and not judged in
his own right.

While the Irish names also brought about depreciated judgment, the
depreciation was not as great as in the case of the Jews and Italians. The
falling of likability of the "Jewish girls" was twice as great as for "Italians"
and five times as great as for "Irish." We note, however, that the "Jewish"
photographs caused higher ratings in *intelligence* and in *ambition*. Not all
stereotypes of out-groups are unfavorable.

The anthropologist, Margaret Mead, has suggested that labels of   9
primary potency lose some of their force when they are changed from
nouns into adjectives. To speak of a Negro soldier, a Catholic teacher, or
a Jewish artist calls attention to the fact that some other group classifica-
tions are just as legitimate as the racial or religious. If George Johnson is
spoken of not only as a Negro but also as a *soldier*, we have at least two
attributes to know him by, and two are more accurate than one. To depict
him truly as an individual, of course, we should have to name many more
attributes. It is a useful suggestion that we designate ethnic and religious
membership where possible with *adjectives* rather than with *nouns*.

Emotionally Toned Labels

Many categories have two kinds of labels—one less emotional and   10
one more emotional. Ask yourself how you feel, and what thoughts you
have, when you read the words *school teacher,* and then *school marm.*
Certainly the second phrase calls up something more strict, more ridiculous, more disagreeable than the former. Here are four innocent letters:
m-a-r-m. But they make us shudder a bit, laugh a bit, and scorn a bit.
They call up an image of a spare, humorless, irritable old maid. They do
not tell us that she is an individual human being with sorrows and troubles of her own. They force her instantly into a rejective category.

In the ethnic sphere even plain labels such as Negro, Italian, Jew,   11
Catholic, Irish-American, French-Canadian may have emotional tone
for a reason that we shall soon explain. But they all have their higher key
equivalents: nigger, wop, kike, papist, harp, canuck. When these labels
are employed we can be almost certain that the speaker *intends* not only
to characterize the person's membership, but also to disparage and reject
him.

Quite apart from the insulting intent that lies behind the use of   12
certain labels, there is also an inherent ("physiognomic") handicap in
many terms designating ethnic membership. For example, the proper names
characteristic of certain ethnic memberships strike us as absurd. (We
compare them, of course, with what is familiar and therefore "right.")
Chinese names are short and silly; Polish names intrinsically difficult and
outlandish. Unfamiliar dialects strike us as ludicrous. Foreign dress (which,
of course, is a visual ethnic symbol) seems unnecessarily queer.

But of all these "physiognomic" handicaps the reference to color,   13
clearly implied in certain symbols, is the greatest. The word Negro comes
from the Latin *niger* meaning black. In point of fact, no Negro has a black
complexion, but by comparison with other blonder stocks, he has come
to be known as a "black man." Unfortunately *black* in the English language is a word having a preponderance of sinister connotations: the outlook is black, blackball, blackguard, blackhearted, black death, blacklist,
blackmail, Black Hand. In his novel *Moby Dick,* Herman Melville considers at length the remarkably morbid connotations of black and the
remarkably virtuous connotations of white.

Nor is the ominous flavor of black confined to the English language.   14
A cross-cultural study reveals that the semantic significance of black is
more or less universally the same. Among certain Siberian tribes, members of a privileged clan call themselves "white bones," and refer to all
others as "black bones." Even among Uganda Negroes there is some evidence for a white god at the apex of the theocratic hierarchy; certain it
is that a white cloth, signifying purity, is used to ward off evil spirits and
disease.

There is thus an implied value-judgment in the very concept of   15
white race and *black race.* One might also study the numerous unpleasant
connotations of *yellow,* and their possible bearing on our conception of
the people of the Orient.

Such reasoning should not be carried too far, since there are un-   16
doubtedly, in various contexts, pleasant associations with both black and
yellow. Black velvet is agreeable; so too are chocolate and coffee. Yellow
tulips are well liked; the sun and moon are radiantly yellow. Yet it is true
that "color" words are used with chauvinistic overtones more than most

people realize. There is certainly condescension indicated in many familiar phrases: dark as a nigger's pocket, darktown strutters, white hope (a term originated when a white contender was sought against the Negro heavyweight champion, Jack Johnson), the white man's burden, the yellow peril, black boy. Scores of everyday phrases are stamped with the flavor of prejudice, whether the user knows it or not.

We spoke of the fact that even the most proper and sedate labels for   17
minority groups sometimes seem to exude a negative flavor. In many contexts and situations the very terms *French-Canadian, Mexican,* or *Jew,* correct and nonmalicious though they are, sound a bit opprobrious. The reason is that they are labels of social deviants. Especially in a culture where uniformity is prized, the name of *any* deviant carries with it *ipso facto* a negative value-judgment. Words like *insane, alcoholic, pervert* are presumably neutral designations of a human condition, but they are more: they are finger-pointings at deviance. Minority groups are deviants, and for this reason, from the very outset, the most innocent labels in many situations imply a shading of disrepute. When we wish to highlight the deviance and denigrate it still further we use words of a higher emotional key: crackpot, soak, pansy, greaser, Okie, nigger, harp, kike.

Members of minority groups are often understandably sensitive to   34
names given• them. Not only do they object to deliberately insulting epithets, but sometimes see evil intent where none exists. Often the word Negro is spelled with a small *n*, occasionally as a studied insult, more often from ignorance. (The term is not cognate with white, which is not capitalized, but rather with Caucasian, which is.) Terms like "mulatto," or "octoroon" cause hard feeling because of the condescension with which they have often been used in the past. Sex differentiations are objectionable, since they seem doubly to emphasize ethnic difference: why speak of Jewess and not of Protestantess, or of Negress and not of whitess? Similar overemphasis is implied in the terms like Chinaman or Scotchman; why not American man? Grounds for misunderstanding lie in the fact that minority group members are sensitive to such shadings, while majority members may employ them unthinkingly.

The Communist Label

Until we label an out-group it does not clearly exist in our minds.   35
Take the curiously vague situation that we often meet when a person wishes to locate responsibility on the shoulders of some out-group whose nature he cannot specify. In such a case he usually employs the pronoun "they" without an antecedent. "Why don't they make these sidewalks

wider?" "I hear they are going to build a factory in this town and hire a lot of foreigners." "I won't pay this tax bill; they can just whistle for their money." If asked "who?" the speaker is likely to grow confused and embarrassed. The common use of the orphaned pronoun *they* teaches us that people often want and need to designate out-groups (usually for the purpose of venting hostility) even when they have no clear conception of the out-group in question. And so long as the target of wrath remains vague and ill-defined specific prejudice cannot crystallize around it. To have enemies we need labels.

Until relatively recently—strange as it may seem—there was no 36 agreed-upon symbol for *communist*. The word, of course, existed but it had no special emotional connotation, and did not designate a public enemy. Even when, after World War I, there was a growing feeling of economic and social menace in this country, there was no agreement as to the actual source of the menace.

A content analysis of the *Boston Herald* for the year 1920 turned up 37 the following list of labels. Each was used in a context implying some threat. Hysteria had overspread the country, as it did after World War II. Someone must be responsible for the postwar malaise, rising prices, uncertainty. There must be a villain. But in 1920 the villain was impartially designated by reporters and editorial writers with the following symbols:

> alien, agitator, anarchist, apostle of bomb and torch, Bolshevik, communist, communist laborite, conspirator, emissary of false promise, extremist, foreigner, hyphenated-American, incendiary, IWW, parlor anarchist, parlor pink, parlor socialist, plotter, radical, red, revolutionary, Russian agitator, socialist, Soviet, syndicalist, traitor, undesirable.[1]

From this excited array we note that the *need* for an enemy (some- 38 one to serve as a focus for discontent and jitters) was considerably more apparent than the precise *identity* of the enemy. At any rate, there was no clearly agreed upon label. Perhaps partly for this reason the hysteria abated. Since no clear category of "communism" existed there was no true focus for the hostility.

But following World War II this collection of vaguely interchange- 39 able labels became fewer in number and more commonly agreed upon. The out-group menace came to be designated almost always as *communist* or *red*. In 1920 the threat, lacking a clear label, was vague; after 1945 both symbol and thing became more definite. Not that people knew precisely what they meant when they said "communist," but with the aid of

---

[1]The IWW, or Industrial Workers of the World, was a radical labor organization that advocated violence. Syndicalism advocated that labor unions take over the government and industry.

the term they were at least able to point consistently to *something* that inspired fear. The term developed the power of signifying menace and led to various repressive measures against anyone to whom the label was rightly or wrongly attached.

Logically, the label should apply to specifiable defining attributes, such as members of the Communist Party, or people whose allegiance is with the Russian system, or followers, historically, of Karl Marx. But the label came in for far more extensive use. 40

What seems to have happened is approximately as follows. Having suffered through a period of war and being acutely aware of devastating revolutions abroad, it is natural that most people should be upset, dreading to lose their possessions, annoyed by high taxes, seeing customary moral and religious values threatened, and dreading worse disasters to come. Seeking an explanation for this unrest, a single identifiable enemy is wanted. It is not enough to designate "Russia" or some other distant land. Nor is it satisfactory to fix blame on "changing social conditions." What is needed is a human agent near at hand: someone in Washington, someone in our schools, in our factories, in our neighborhood. If we *feel* an immediate threat, we reason, there must be a near-lying danger. It is, we conclude, communism, not only in Russia but also in America, at our doorstep, in our government, in our churches, in our colleges, in our neighborhood. 41

Are we saying that hostility toward communism is prejudice? Not necessarily. There are certainly phases of the dispute wherein realistic social conflict is involved. American values (e.g., respect for the person) and totalitarian values as represented in Soviet practice are intrinsically at odds. A realistic opposition in some form will occur. Prejudice enters only when the defining attributes of "communist" grow imprecise, when anyone who favors any form of social change is called a communist. People who fear social change are the ones most likely to affix the label to any persons or practices that seem to them threatening. 42

For them the category is undifferentiated. It includes books, movies, preachers, teachers who utter what for them are uncongenial thoughts. If evil befalls—perhaps forest fires or a factory explosion—it is due to communist saboteurs. The category becomes monopolistic, covering almost anything that is uncongenial. On the floor of the House of Representatives in 1946, Representative Rankin called James Roosevelt a communist. Congressman Outland replied with psychological acumen, "Apparently everyone who disagrees with Mr. Rankin is a communist." 43

When differentiated thinking is at a low ebb—as it is in times of social crises—there is a magnification of two-valued logic. Things are perceived as either inside or outside a moral order. What is outside is 44 likely to be called "communist." Correspondingly—and here is where damage is done—whatever is called communist (however erroneously) is immediately cast outside the moral order.

This associative mechanism places enormous power in the hands of   45
a demagogue. For several years Senator McCarthy managed to discredit many citizens who thought differently from himself by the simple device of calling them communist. Few people were able to see through this trick and many reputations were ruined. But the famous senator has no monopoly on the device. As reported in the *Boston Herald* on November 1, 1946, Representative Joseph Martin, Republican leader in the House, ended his election campaign against his Democratic opponent by saying, "The people will vote tomorrow between chaos, confusion, bankruptcy, state socialism or communism, and the preservation of our American life, with all its freedom and its opportunities." Such an array of emotional labels placed his opponent outside the accepted moral order. Martin was re-elected. . . .

Not everyone, of course, is taken in. Demagogy, when it goes too   46
far, meets with ridicule. Elizabeth Dilling's book, *The Red Network*, was so exaggerated in its two-valued logic that it was shrugged off by many people with a smile. One reader remarked, "Apparently if you step off the sidewalk with your left foot you're a communist." But it is not easy in times of social strain and hysteria to keep one's balance, and to resist the tendency of a verbal symbol to manufacture large and fanciful categories of prejudiced thinking.

Verbal Realism and Symbol Phobia

Most individuals rebel at being labeled, especially if the label is   47
uncomplimentary. Very few are willing to be called *fascistic, socialistic,* or *anti-Semitic.* Unsavory labels may apply to others, but not to us.

An illustration of the craving that people have to attach favorable   48
symbols to themselves is seen in the community where white people banded together to force out a Negro family that had moved in. They called themselves "Neighborly Endeavor" and chose as their motto the Golden Rule.[2] One of the first acts of this symbol-sanctified band was to sue the man who sold property to Negroes. They then flooded the house which another Negro couple planned to occupy. Such were the acts performed under the banner of the Golden Rule.

---

[2]"Do unto others as you would have others do unto you."

Studies made by Stagner and Hartmann show that a person's polit-   49
ical attitudes may in fact entitle him to be called a fascist or a socialist,
and yet he will emphatically repudiate the unsavory label, and fail to
endorse any movement or candidate that overtly accepts them. In short,
there is a *symbol phobia* that corresponds to *verbal realism*. We are more
inclined to the former when we ourselves are concerned, though we are
much less critical when epithets of "fascist," "communist," "blind man,"
"school marm" are applied to others.

When symbols provoke strong emotions they are sometimes re-   50
garded no longer as symbols, but as actual things. The expressions "son
of a bitch" and "liar" are in our culture frequently regarded as "fighting
words." Softer and more subtle expressions of contempt may be accepted.
But in these particular cases, the epithet itself must be "taken back." We
certainly do not change our opponent's attitude by making him take back
a word, but it seems somehow important that the word itself be eradi-
cated.

Such verbal realism may reach extreme length.   51

> The City Council of Cambridge, Massachusetts, unanimously passed a res-
> olution (December, 1939) making it illegal "to possess, harbor, sequester,
> introduce or transport, within the city limits, any book, map, magazine,
> newspaper, pamphlet, handbill or circular containing the words Lenin or
> Leningrad."

Such naiveté in confusing language with reality is hard to comprehend
unless we recall that word-magic plays an appreciable part in human
thinking. The following examples, like the one preceding, are taken from
Hayakawa.[3]

> The Malagasy soldier must eschew kidneys, because in the Malagasy lan-
> guage the word for kidney is the same as that for "shot"; so shot he would
> certainly be if he ate a kidney.

> In May, 1937, a state senator of New York bitterly opposed a bill for the
> control of syphilis because "the innocence of children might be corrupted
> by a widespread use of the term. . . . This particular word creates a shudder
> in every decent woman and decent man."

This tendency to reify words underscores the close cohesion that   52
exists between category and symbol. Just the mention of "communist,"
"Negro," "Jew," "England," "Democrats," will send some people into a
panic of fear or a frenzy of anger. Who can say whether it is the word
or the thing that annoys them? The label is an intrinsic part of any

---

[3]S.I. Hayakawa, author of *Language in Thought and Action.*

monopolistic category. Hence to liberate a person from ethnic or political prejudice it is necessary at the same time to liberate him from *word fetishism*. This fact is well known to students of general semantics who tell us that prejudice is due in large part to verbal realism and to symbol phobia. Therefore any program for the reduction of prejudice must include a large measure of semantic therapy.

Questions for Study and Discussion

1. Where does Allport state his main point? How does he support and develop that point in this essay?

2. Names and nouns are essential if we are to make sense of the world, as Allport suggests in his opening paragraph, yet he goes on to say that nouns are inherently unfair. Why is this so?

3. Why are "labels of primary potency" so important? Should we always avoid the use of such labels? Does Allport suggest any ways in which the force of these labels can be diminished? If so, what are they?

4. In paragraphs 10–18, Allport observes that different words with approximately the same literal meaning often express different attitudes. What about this passage had the greatest impact on you? Did any of it seem no longer valid? Why? What does the passage, and your response to it, suggest about the relation between language and prejudice?

5. Paragraphs 19–30 deal with an attitude that was widespread in the early 1950s but is much rarer now. Is Allport's point nonetheless still relevant? Why? If so, what present-day examples would you give to make its relevance plain?

6. What does Allport mean by "symbol phobia" and "verbal realism"? Give your own examples of each.

Writing Topics

1. Everyone belongs to various categories according to sex, race, religion, cultural background, and even appearance. How would you categorize yourself? What is your own image of the categories to which you belong? How do outsiders view these categories? In what ways has language been used to stigmatize you or the categories to which you belong? How do you feel about it?

2. In recent years, members of various groups have sought to have new labels applied to themselves, labels that express their own views rather than those of outsiders. Two prominent examples are women and blacks. Choose a group and trace how it has named itself and how this has influenced the labels others use. What conclusions can you draw from that history?

CASEY MILLER AND KATE SWIFT

Casey Miller was born in Toledo, Ohio, in 1919 and graduated from Smith College in 1940. She has worked in various editorial positions at the Seabury Press and elsewhere before becoming a free-lance writer and editor in 1964. Kate Swift, born in Yonkers, New York, in 1923, attended Connecticut College and graduated from the University of North Carolina in 1944. She started work as a newsroom copy runner with NBC and later became an editorial assistant at *Time* magazine. Since 1948 she has served as a public relations writer for the Girl Scouts of the U.S.A., as a science writer for the American Museum of Natural History, and most recently as the director of the news bureau for the Yale University School of Medicine. In 1970 she formed a free-lance editorial partnership with Casey Miller. Together they have written numerous articles for such popular magazines as *New York, Ms.,* and *The New York Times Magazine* and several books, including *Words and Women* (1976) and *The Handbook of Nonsexist Writing* (1980).

Since the early 1970s, Miller and Swift have been pioneers in the study of sexism and language. "It was out of our work as free-lance editors that we became interested in the effect of language on women," they stated in a recent interview. "We document many changes occurring in English today as a result of women's changing perception of themselves." "One Small Step for Genkind," first published in 1972 in *The New York Times Magazine,* was one of the first articles to bring widespread attention to the ways in which language discriminates against women. Here they discuss traditional gender words, prefixes, suffixes, and pronouns that reveal deep-seated biases against women in our male-dominated English language. Their analysis raises important questions about the possibility of establishing equal rights for women in this country.

One Small Step for Genkind

A riddle is making the rounds that goes like this: A man and his young son were in an automobile accident. The father was killed and the son, who was critically injured, was rushed to a hospital. As attendants wheeled the unconscious boy into the emergency room, the doctor on duty looked down at him and said, "My God, it's my son!" What was the relationship of the doctor to the injured boy? 1

If the answer doesn't jump to your mind, another riddle that has been around a lot longer might help: The blind beggar had a brother. The blind beggar's brother died. The brother who died had no brother. What relation was the blind beggar to the blind beggar's brother? 2

As with all riddles, the answers are obvious once you see them: 3
The doctor was the boy's mother and the beggar was her brother's sister.
Then why doesn't everyone solve them immediately? Mainly because our
language, like the culture it reflects, is male oriented. To say that a
woman in medicine is an exception is simply to confirm that statement.
Thousands of doctors are women, but in order to be seen in the mind's
eye, they must be called women doctors.

Except for words that refer to females by definition (mother, actress, 4
Congresswoman), and words for occupations traditionally held by females
(nurse, secretary, prostitute), the English language defines everyone as
male. The hypothetical person ("If a man can walk 10 miles in two hours
. . ."), the average person ("the man in the street") and the active person
("the man on the move") are male. The assumption is that unless otherwise identified, people in general—including doctors and beggars—are
men. It is a semantic mechanism that operates to keep women invisible:
man and *mankind* represent everyone; *he* in generalized use refers to either
sex; the "land where our fathers died" is also the land of our mothers—
although they go unsung. As the beetle-browed and mustachioed man
in a Steig cartoon says to his two male drinking companions, "When I
speak of mankind, one thing I *don't* mean is womankind."

Semantically speaking, woman is not one with the species of man, 5
but a distinct subspecies. "Man," says the 1971 edition of the Britannica
Junior Encyclopedia, "is the highest form of life on earth. His superior
intelligence, combined with certain physical characteristics, have enabled man to achieve things that are impossible for other animals." (The
prose style has something in common with the report of a research team
describing its studies on "the development of the uterus in rats, guinea
pigs and men.") As though quoting the Steig character, still speaking to
his friends in McSorley's, the Junior Encyclopedia continues: "Man must
invent most of his behavior, because he lacks the instincts of lower
animals. . . . Most of the things he learns have been handed down from
his ancestors by language and symbols rather than by biological inheritance."

Considering that for the last 5,000 years society has been patriar- 6
chal, that statement explains a lot. It explains why Eve was made from
Adam's rib instead of the other way around, and who invented all those
Adam-rib words like *female* and *woman* in the first place. It also explains
why, when it is necessary to mention woman, the language makes her a
lower caste, a class separate from the rest of man; why it works to "keep
her in her place."

This inheritance through language and other symbols begins in the 7
home (also called a man's castle) where man and wife (not husband and

wife, or man and woman) live for a while with their children. It is reinforced by religious training, the educational system, the press, government, commerce and the law. As Andrew Greeley wrote not long ago in his magazine, "man is a symbol-creating animal. He orders and interprets his reality by his symbols, and he uses the symbols to reconstruct that reality."

Consider some of the reconstructed realities of American history. When school children learn from their textbooks that the early colonists gained valuable experience in governing themselves, they are not told that the early colonists who were women were denied the privilege of self-government; when they learn that in the 18th century the average man had to manufacture many of the things he and his family needed, they are not told that this "average man" was often a woman who manufactured much of what she and her family needed. Young people learn that intrepid pioneers crossed the country in covered wagons with their wives, children and cattle; they do not learn that women themselves were intrepid pioneers rather than part of the baggage.   8

In a paper published this year in Los Angeles as a guide for authors and editors of social-studies textbooks, Elizabeth Burr, Susan Dunn and Norma Farquhar document unintentional skewings of this kind that occur either because women are not specifically mentioned as affecting or being affected by historical events, or because they are discussed in terms of outdated assumptions. "One never sees a picture of women captioned simply 'farmers' or 'pioneers,' " they point out. The subspecies nomenclature that requires a caption to read "women farmers" or "women pioneers" is extended to impose certain jobs on women by definition. The textbook guide gives as an example the word *housewife*, which it says not only "suggests that domestic chores are the exclusive burden of females," but gives "female students the idea that they were born to keep house and teaches male students that they are automatically entitled to laundry, cooking and housecleaning services from the women in their families."   9

Sexist language is any language that expresses such stereotyped attitudes and expectations, or that assumes the inherent superiority of one sex over the other. When a woman says of her husband, who has drawn up plans for a new bedroom wing and left out closets, "Just like a man," her language is as sexist as the man's who says, after his wife has changed her mind about needing the new wing after all, "Just like a woman."   10

Male and female are not sexist words, but masculine and feminine almost always are. Male and female can be applied objectively to individual people and animals and, by extension, to things. When electricians and plumbers talk about male and female couplings, everyone knows   11 or can figure out what they mean. The terms are graphic and culture free.

Masculine and feminine, however, are as sexist as any words can be, since it is almost impossible to use them without invoking cultural stereotypes. When people construct lists of "masculine" and "feminine" traits they almost always end up making assumptions that have nothing to do with innate differences between the sexes. We have a friend who happens to be going through the process of pinning down this very phenomenon. He is 7 years old and his question concerns why his coats and shirts button left over right while his sister's button the other way. He assumes it must have something to do with the differences between boys and girls, but he can't see how.

12

What our friend has yet to grasp is that the way you button your coat, like most sex-differentiated customs, has nothing to do with real differences but much to do with what society wants you to feel about yourself as a male or female person. Society decrees that it is appropriate for girls to dress differently from boys, to act differently, and to think differently. Boys must be masculine, whatever that means, and girls must be feminine.

13

Unabridged dictionaries are a good source for finding out what society decrees to be appropriate, though less by definition than by their choice of associations and illustrations. Words associated with males— *manly, virile* and *masculine,* for example—are defined through a broad range of positive attributes like strength, courage, directness and independence, and they are illustrated through such examples of contemporary usage as "a manly determination to face what comes," "a virile literary style," "a masculine love of sports." Corresponding words associated with females are defined with fewer attributes (though weakness is often one of them) and the examples given are generally negative if not clearly pejorative: "feminine wiles," "womanish tears," "a womanlike lack of promptness," "convinced that drawing was a waste of time, if not downright womanly."

14

Male-associated words are frequently applied to females to describe something that is either incongruous ("a mannish voice") or presumably commendable ("a masculine mind," "she took it like a man"), but female-associated words are unreservedly derogatory when applied to males, and are sometimes abusive to females as well. The opposite of "masculine" is "effeminate," although the opposite of "feminine" is simply "unfeminine."

15

One dictionary, after defining the word *womanish* as "suitable to or resembling a woman," further defines it as "unsuitable to a man or to a strong character of either sex." Words derived from "sister" and "brother"

16

provide another apt example, for whereas "sissy," applied either to a male or female, conveys the message that sisters are expected to be timid and cowardly, "buddy" makes clear that brothers are friends.

The subtle disparagement of females and corresponding approbation of males wrapped up in many English words is painfully illustrated by "tomboy." Here is an instance where a girl who likes sports and the out-of-doors, who is curious about how things work, who is adventurous and bold instead of passive, is defined in terms of something she is not—a boy. By denying that she can be the person she is and still be a girl, the word surreptitiously undermines her sense of identity: it says she is unnatural. A "tomboy," as defined by one dictionary, is a "girl, especially a young girl, who behaves like a spirited boy." But who makes the judgment that she is acting like a spirited boy, not a spirited girl? Can it be a coincidence that in the case of the dictionary just quoted the editor, executive editor, managing editor, general manager, all six members of the Board of Linguists, the usage editor, science editor, all six general editors of definitions, and 94 out of the 104 distinguished experts consulted on usage—are men? 17

It isn't enough to say that any invidious comparisons and stereotypes lexicographers perpetuate are already present in the culture. There are ways to define words like womanly and tomboy that don't put women down, though the tradition has been otherwise. Samuel Johnson, the lexicographer, was the same Dr. Johnson who said, "A woman preaching is like a dog's walking on his hind legs. It is not done well; but you are surprised to find it done at all." 18

Possibly because of the negative images associated with womanish and womanlike, and with expressions like "woman driver" and "woman of the street," the word woman dropped out of fashion for a time. The women at the office and the women on the assembly line and the women one first knew in school all became ladies or girls or gals. Now a countermovement, supported by the very term women's liberation, is putting back into words like woman and sister and sisterhood the meaning they were losing by default. It is as though, in the nick of time, women had seen that the language itself could destroy them. 19

Some long-standing conventions of the news media add insult to injury. When a woman or girl makes news, her sex is identified at the beginning of a story, if possible in the headline or its equivalent. The assumption, apparently, is that whatever event or action is being reported, a woman's involvement is less common and therefore more newsworthy than a man's. If the story is about achievement, the implication is: "pretty good for a woman." And because people are assumed to be male unless otherwise identified, the media have developed a special and 20 extensive vocabulary to avoid the constant repetition of "woman." The results, "Grandmother Wins Nobel Prize," "Blonde Hijacks Airliner," "Housewife to Run for Congress," convey the kind of information that would be ludicrous in comparable headlines if the subjects were men. Why, if "Unsalaried Husband to Run for Congress" is unacceptable to editors, do women have to keep explaining that to describe them through external or superficial concerns reflects a sexist view of women as decorative objects, breeding machines and extensions of men, not real people?

Members of the Chicago chapter of the National Organization for 21 Women recently studied the newspapers in their area and drew up a set of guidelines for the press. These include cutting out descriptions of the "clothes, physical features, dating life and marital status of women where such references would be considered inappropriate if about men"; using language in such a way as to include women in copy that refers to home-owners, scientists and business people where "newspaper descriptions often convey the idea that all such persons are male"; and displaying the same discretion in printing generalizations about women as would be shown toward racial, religious and ethnic groups. "Our concern with what we are called may seem trivial to some people," the women said, "but we regard the old usages as symbolic of women's position within this society."

The assumption that an adult woman is flattered by being called a 22 girl is matched by the notion that a woman in a menial or poorly paid job finds compensation in being called a lady. Ethel Strainchamps has pointed out that since lady is used as an adjective with nouns designating both high and low occupations (lady wrestler, lady barber, lady doctor, lady judge), some writers assume they can use the noun form without betraying value judgments. Not so, Strainchamps says, rolling the issue into a spitball: "You may write, 'He addressed the Republican ladies,' or 'The Democratic ladies convened' . . . but I have never seen 'the Communist ladies' or 'the Black Panther ladies' in print."

Thoughtful writers and editors have begun to repudiate some of the 23 old usages. "Divorcée," "grandmother" and "blonde," along with "vivacious," "pert," "dimpled" and "cute," were dumped by the Washington Post in the spring of 1970 by the executive editor, Benjamin Bradlee. In a memo to his staff, Bradlee wrote, "The meaningful equality and dignity of women is properly under scrutiny today . . . because this equality has been less than meaningful and the dignity not always free of stereotype and condescension."

What women have been called in the press—or at least the part 24 that operates above ground—is only a fraction of the infinite variety of alternatives to "women" used in the subcultures of the English-speaking world. Beyond "chicks," "dolls," "dames," "babes," "skirts" and "broads" are the words and phrases in which women are reduced to their sexuality and nothing more. It would be hard to think of another area of language in which the human mind has been so fertile in devising and borrowing abusive terms. In "The Female Eunuch," Germaine Greer devotes four pages to anatomical terms and words for animals, vegetables, fruits, baked goods, implements and receptacles, all of which are used to dehumanize the female person. Jean Faust, in an article aptly called "Words That Oppress," suggests that the effort to diminish women through language is rooted in a male fear of sexual inadequacy. "Woman is made to feel guilty for and akin to natural disasters," she writes; "hurricanes and typhoons are named after her. Any negative or threatening force is given a feminine name. If a man runs into bad luck climbing up the ladder of success (a male-invented game), he refers to the 'bitch goddess' success."

The sexual overtones in the ancient and no doubt honorable custom 25
of calling ships "she" have become more explicit and less honorable in an age of air travel: "I'm Karen. Fly me." Attitudes of ridicule, contempt and disgust toward female sexuality have spawned a rich glossary of insults and epithets not found in dictionaries. And the usage in which four-letter words meaning copulate are interchangeable with cheat, attack and destroy can scarcely be unrelated to the savagery of rape.

In her updating of Ibsen's "A Doll's House," Clare Booth Luce has 26
Nora tell her husband she is pregnant—"In the way only men are supposed to get pregnant." "Men, pregnant?" he says, and she nods; "With ideas. Pregnancies there [*she taps his head*] are masculine. And a very superior form of labor. Pregnancies here [*taps her tummy*] are feminine—a very inferior form of labor."

Public outcry followed a revised translation of the New Testament 27
describing Mary as "pregnant" instead of "great with child." The objections were made in part on esthetic grounds: there is no attractive adjective in modern English for a woman who is about to give birth. A less obvious reason was that replacing the euphemism with a biological term undermined religious teaching. The initiative and generative power in the conception of Jesus are understood to be God's; Mary, the mother, was a vessel only.

Whether influenced by this teaching or not, the language of human 28
reproduction lags several centuries behind scientific understanding. The male's contribution to procreation is still described as though it were the entire seed from which a new life grows: the initiative and generative power involved in the process are thought of as masculine, receptivity and nurturance as feminine. "Seminal" remains a synonym for "highly original," and there is no comparable word to describe the female's equivalent contribution.

An entire mythology has grown from this biological misunderstand-   29
ing and its semantic legacy; its embodiment in laws that for centuries
made women nonpersons was a key target of the 19th-century feminist
movement. Today, more than 50 years after women finally won the basic
democratic right to vote, the word "liberation" itself, when applied to
women, means something less than when used of other groups of people.
An advertisement for the N.B.C. news department listed Women's Liberation along with crime in the streets and the Vietnam war as "bad
news." Asked for his views on Women's Liberation, a highly placed
politician was quoted as saying, "Let me make one thing perfectly clear.
I wouldn't want to wake up next to a lady pipe-fitter."

One of the most surprising challenges to our male-dominated cul-   30
ture is coming from within organized religion, where the issues are being
stated, in part, by confronting the implications of traditional language.
What a growing number of theologians and scholars are saying is that
the myths of the Judeo-Christian tradition, being the products of patriar-
chy, must be reexamined, and that the concept of an exclusively male
ministry and the image of a male god have become idolatrous.

Women are naturally in the forefront of this movement, both in   31
their efforts to gain ordination and full equality and through their contributions to theological reform, although both these efforts are often
subtly diminished. When the Rev. Barbara Anderson was ordained by
the American Lutheran Church, one newspaper printed her picture over
a caption headed "Happy Girl." *Newsweek's* report of a protest staged
last December by women divinity students at Harvard was jocular ("another tilt at the windmill") and sarcastic: "Every time anyone in the
room lapsed into what [the students] regarded as male chauvinism—such
as using the word 'mankind' to describe the human race in general—the
outraged women . . . drowned out the offender with earpiercing blasts
from party-favor kazoos. . . . What annoyed the women most was the
universal custom of referring to God as 'He.' "

The tone of the report was not merely unfunny; it missed the con-   32
nection between increasingly outmoded theological language and the
accelerating number of women (and men) who are dropping out of organized religion, both Jewish and Christian. For language, including pronouns, can be used to construct a reality that simply mirrors society's
assumptions. To women who are committed to the reality of religious
faith, the effect is doubly painful. Professor Harvey Cox, in whose classroom the protest took place, stated the issue directly: The women, he
said, were raising the "basic theological question of whether God is more
adequately thought of in personal or suprapersonal terms."

Toward the end of Don McLean's remarkable ballad "American   33
Pie," a song filled with the imagery of abandonment and disillusion, there

is a stanza that must strike many women to the quick. The church bells are broken, the music has died; then:

And the three men I admire most,
The Father, Son and the Holy Ghost,
They caught the last train for the Coast—
The day the music died.

Three men I admired most. There they go, briefcases in hand and topcoats buttoned left over right, walking down the long cold platform under the city, past the baggage wagons and the hissing steam onto the Pullman. Bye, bye God—all three of you—made in the image of male supremacy. Maybe out there in L.A. where the weather is warmer, someone can believe in you again. 34

The Roman Catholic theologian Elizabeth Farians says "the bad theology of an overmasculinized church continues to be one of the root causes of women's oppression." The definition of oppression is "to crush or burden by abuse of power or authority; burden spiritually or mentally as if by pressure." 35

When language oppresses, it does so by any means that disparage and belittle. Until well into the 20th century, one of the ways English was manipulated to disparage women was through the addition of feminine endings to nonsexual words. Thus a woman who aspired to be a poet was excluded from the company of real poets by the label poetess, and a women who piloted an airplane was denied full status as an aviator by being called an aviatrix. At about the time poetess, aviatrix, and similar Adam-ribbisms were dropping out of use, H. W. Fowler was urging that they be revived. "With the coming expansion of women's vocations," he wrote in the first edition (1926) of "Modern English Usage," "feminines for vocation-words are a special need of the future." There can be no doubt he subsconsciously recognized the relative status implied in the -ess designations. His criticism of a woman who wished to be known as an author rather than an authoress was that she had no need "to raise herself to the level of the male author by asserting her right to his name." 36

Who has the prior right to a name? The question has an interesting bearing on words that were once applied to men alone, or to both men and women, but now, having acquired abusive associations, are assigned to women exclusively. Spinster is a gentle case in point. Prostitute and many of its synonyms illustrate the phenomenon better. If Fowler had chosen to record the changing usage of harlot from hired man (in Chaucer's time) through rascal and entertainer to its present definition, would he have maintained that the female harlot is trying to raise herself to 37 the level of the male harlot by asserting her right to his name? Or would he have plugged for harlotress?

The demise of most *-ess* endings came about before the start of the new feminist movement. In the second edition of "Modern English Usage," published in 1965, Sir Ernest Gowers frankly admitted what his predecessors had been up to. "Feminine designations," he wrote, "seem now to be falling into disuse. Perhaps the explanation of this paradox is that it symbolizes the victory of women in their struggle for equal rights; it reflects the abandonment by men of those ideas about women in the professions that moved Dr. Johnson to his rude remark about women preachers." 38

If Sir Ernest's optimism can be justified, why is there a movement back to feminine endings in such words as chairwoman, councilwoman and congresswoman? Betty Hudson, of Madison, Conn., is campaigning for the adoption of "selectwoman" as the legal title for a female member of that town's executive body. To have to address a woman as "Selectman," she maintains, "is not only bad grammar and bad biology, but it implies that politics is still, or should be, a man's business." A valid argument, and one that was, predictably, countered by ridicule, the sure-fire weapon for undercutting achievement. When the head of the Federal Maritime Commission, Helen D. Bentley, was named "Man of the Year" by an association of shipping interests, she wisely refused to be drawn into light-hearted debate with interviewers who wanted to make the award's name a humorous issue. Some women, of course, have yet to learn they are invisible. An 8-year-old who visited the American Museum of Natural History with her Brownie scout troop went through the impressive exhibit on pollution and overpopulation called "Can Man Survive?" Asked afterward, "Well, can he?" she answered, "I don't know about him, but we're working on it in Brownies." 39

Nowhere are women rendered more invisible by language than in politics. The United States Constitution, in describing the qualifications for Representative, Senator and President, refers to each as *he*. No wonder Shirly Chisholm, the first woman since 1888 to make a try for the Presidential nomination of a major party, has found it difficult to be taken seriously. 40

The observation by Andrew Greeley already quoted—that "man" uses "his symbols" to reconstruct "his reality"—was not made in reference to the symbols of language but to the symbolic impact the "nomination of a black man for Vice-Presidency" would have on race relations in the United States. Did the author assume the generic term "man" would of course be construed to include "woman"? Or did he deliberately use a 41

semantic device to exclude Shirley Chisholm without having to be explicit?

Either way, his words construct a reality in which women are ig-   42
nored. As much as any other factor in our language, the ambiguous
meaning of *man* serves to deny women recognition as people. In a recent
magazine article, we discussed the similar effect on women of the generic
pronoun *he*, which we proposed to replace by a new common gender
pronoun *tey*. We were immediately told, by a number of authorities, that
we were dabbling in the serious business of linguistics, and the message
that reached us from these scholars was loud and clear: It - is - absolutely
- impossible - for - anyone - to - introduce - a - new - word - into - the - language
- just - because - there - is - a - need - for - it, so - stop - wasting - your - time.

When words are suggested like "herstory" (for history), "sportsone-   43
ship" (for sportsmanship) and "mistresspiece" (for the work of a Virginia
Woolf) one suspects a not-too-subtle attempt to make the whole language
problem look silly. But unless Alexander Pope, when he wrote "The
proper study of mankind is man," meant that women should be relegated
to the footnotes (or, as George Orwell might have put it, "All men are
equal, but men are more equal than women"), viable new words will
surely someday supersede the old.

Without apologies to Freud, the great majority of women do not   44
wish in their hearts that they were men. If having grown up with a
language that tells them they are at the same time men and not men
raises psychic doubts for women, the doubts are not of their sexual identity but of their human identity. Perhaps the present unrest surfacing in
the Women's Movement is part of an evolutionary change in our particular form of life—the one form of all in the animal and plant kingdoms
that orders and interprets its reality by symbols. The achievements of the
species called man have brought us to the brink of self-destruction. If
the species survives into the next century with the expectation of going
on, it may only be because we have become part of what Harlow Shapley
calls the psychozoic kingdom, where brain overshadows brawn and rationality has replaced superstition.

Searching the roots of Western civilization for a word to call this   45
new species of man and woman, someone might come up with *gen*, as
in genesis and generic. With such a word, *man* could be used exclusively
for males as *woman* is used for females, for gen would include both sexes.
Like the words deer and bison, gen would be both plural and singular.
Like progenitor, progeny, and generation, it would convey continuity.
Gen would express the warmth and generalized sexuality of generous,

gentle, and genuine; the specific sexuality of genital and genetic. In the new family of gen, girls and boys would grow to genhood, and to speak of genkind would be to include all the people of the earth.

Questions for Study and Discussion

1. What is the authors' thesis, and where is it stated?

2. How, according to Miller and Swift, does the English language operate to "keep women invisible"?

3. Miller and Swift believe that language works to keep women in their place. They argue that this is "reinforced by religious training, the educational system, the press, government, commerce, and the law." What evidence do they present to document this assertion? What examples can you add from your own experience or observations?

4. What, according to the authors, is sexist language? What do they mean when they say, "Male and female are not sexist words, but masculine and feminine are"?

5. In paragraph 17 Miller and Swift present the lengthy example of the word "tomboy." What point about language is this example meant to illustrate?

6. According to Miller and Swift, how important is it to eliminate the automatic use of *he* and *his* and *him* when the person referred to could just as easily be *female*? How important an issue is it for you? Explain.

7. Why do you suppose Miller and Swift use so many examples and quotations? What effect did they have on you as you read the essay?

8. What is the tone of this essay? How do Miller and Swift maintain this tone? Is their tone appropriate for their subject and audience? Explain.

9. Explain the meaning of the essay's title. To what, if anything, are the authors alluding, and how is the allusion related to their thesis?

Writing Topics

1. Write an essay in which you discuss the power of language to shape society's attitudes toward women, or another minority.

2. Miller and Swift provide us with an extensive catalogue of words that reveal a disparaging attitude toward women. They argue that changes must be made in our language if we are going to eliminate sexist language. Write an essay in which you discuss the possible things that you as a user of language, lexicographers as makers of dictionaries, and women and men as leaders of the equal-rights movement can do to bring about change and improve the lot of women in this country.

3. Miller and Swift believe that "the usage in which four-letter words mean-

ing copulate are interchangeable with cheat, attack and destroy can scarcely be unrelated to the savagery of rape." What exactly do they mean here? Do you commonly use sexual obscenities and feel justified in doing so? Or do such words offend you when you hear them? How would you describe your feelings about such words? Write an essay in which you defend your feelings to someone who does not share them.

4. Miller and Swift wrote this essay for *The New York Times Magazine* in the spring of 1972. Certainly, the world has changed greatly in the intervening years. But much has remained unchanged. Write an essay describing the progress that has been made to eliminate sexist language from English. What areas have remained problems and still need attention? Do we have reason to be optimistic or pessimistic about the future? Why?

CYRA McFADDEN

Born in Great Falls, Montana, in 1937, Cyra McFadden earned both her B.A. and M.A. from San Francisco State University. Before becoming a professional writer in 1976, she taught English at her alma mater. Over the years she has contributed articles to magazines like *McCall's, The New York Times Magazine,* the *Nation,* and *Smithsonian* and written the best-selling novel *The Serial* (1977). "My book is social satire," McFadden once remarked. "So is much of my other published writing. I think seeing things at a slant is an involuntary reflex for me, like a tic in the eyelid."

For almost two decades now, feminist linguists have spearheaded the movement to change language that discriminates against women. Although their attempts to eradicate sexism have been largely applauded, some people, including McFadden, do not like what has happened to English in the process. In the following essay, she argues that the expressions resulting from the "neutering" of English are awkward and ludicrous in both speech and writing.

In Defense of Gender

So pervasive is the neutering of the English language on the progressive West Coast, we no longer have people here, only persons: male persons and female persons, chairpersons and doorpersons, waitpersons, mailpersons—who may be either male or female mailpersons—and refuse-collection persons. In the classified ads, working mothers seek childcare persons, though one wonders how many men (archaic for "male person") take care of child persons as a full-time occupation. One such ad, fusing nonsexist language and the most popular word in the California growth movement, solicits a "nurtureperson."

Dear gents and ladies, as I might have addressed you in less troubled times, this female person knows firsthand the reasons for scourging sexist bias from the language. God knows what damage was done me, at fifteen, when I worked in my first job—as what is now known as a newspaper copyperson—and came running to the voices of men barking, "Boy!"

No aspirant to the job of refuse-collection person myself, I nonetheless take off my hat (a little feathered number, with a veil) to those of my own sex who may want both the job and a genderless title with it. I argue only that there must be a better way, and I wish person or persons unknown would come up with one.

Defend it on any grounds you choose; the neutering of spoken and written English, with its attendant self-consciousness, remains ludicrous. In print, those "person" suffixes and "he/she's" jump out from the page,

493

as distracting as a cloud of gnats, demanding that the reader note the writer's virtue. "Look what a nonsexist writer person I am, voiding the use of masculine forms for the generic."

Spoken, they leave conversation fit only for the Coneheads on "Saturday Night Live." "They have a daily special," a woman at the next table told her male companion in Perry's, a San Francisco restaurant. "Ask your waitperson." In a Steig cartoon, the words would have marched from her mouth in the form of a computer printout.

In Berkeley, Calif., the church to which a friend belongs is busy stripping its liturgy of sexist references. "They've gone berserk," she writes, citing a reading from the pulpit of a verse from 1 Corinthians. Neutered, the once glorious passage becomes "Though I speak with the tongues of persons and of angels. . . ." So much for sounding brass and tinkling cymbals.

The parson person of the same church is now referring to God as "He/She" and changing all references accordingly—no easy undertaking if he intends to be consistent. In the following, the first pronoun would remain because at this primitive stage of human evolution, male persons do not give birth to babies: "And she brought forth her first-born son/daughter, and wrapped him/her in swaddling clothes, and laid him/her in a manger; because there was no room for them in the inn. . . ."

As the after-dinner speaker at a recent professional conference, I heard a text replete with "he/she's" and "his/her's" read aloud for the first time. The hapless program female chairperson stuck with the job chose to render these orally as "he-slash-she" and "his-slash-her," turning the following day's schedule for conference participants into what sounded like a replay of the Manson killings.

Redress may be due those of us who, though female, have answered to masculine referents all these years, but slashing is not the answer; violence never is. Perhaps we could right matters by using feminine forms as the generic for a few centuries, or simply agree on a per-woman lump-sum payment.

Still, we would be left with the problem of referring, without bias, to transpersons. These are not bus drivers or Amtrack conductors but persons in transit from one gender to the other—or so I interpret a fund-driven appeal asking me to defend their civil rights, along with those of female and male homosexuals.

Without wishing to step on anyone's civil rights, I hope transpersons are not the next politically significant pressure group. If they are, count on it, they will soon want their own pronouns.

In the tradition of the West, meanwhile, feminists out here wrestle the language to the ground, plant a foot on its neck and remove its masculine appendages. Take the local art critic Beverly Terwoman.

She is married to a man surnamed Terman. She writes under "Ter- 13
woman," presumably in the spirit of *vive la différence*. As a letter to the editor of the paper for which she writes noted, however, "Terwoman" is not ideologically pure. It still contains "man," a syllable reeking of all that is piggy and hairy-chested.

Why not Beverly Terperson? Or better, since "Terperson" contains 14
"son," "Terdaughter"? Or a final refinement, Beverly Ter?

Beverly Terwoman did not dignify this sexist assault with a reply. 15
The writer of the letter was a male person, after all, probably the kind who leaves his smelly sweat socks scattered around the bedroom floor.

No one wins these battles anyway. In another letter to the same 16
local weekly, J. Seibert, female, lets fire at the printing of an interview with Phyllis Schlafly. Not only was the piece "an offense to everything that Marin County stands for," but "it is even more amusing that your interview was conducted by a male.

"This indicates your obvious assumption that men understand wom- 17
en's issues better than women since men are obviously more intelligent (as no doubt Phyllis would agree)."

A sigh suffuses the editor's note that follows: "The author of the 18
article, Sydney Weisman, is a female."

So the war of the pronouns and suffixes rages, taking no prisoners 19
except writers. Neuter your prose with all those clanking "he/she's," and no one will read you except Alan Alda. Use masculine forms as the generic, and you have joined the ranks of the oppressor. None of this does much to encourage friendly relations between persons, transpersons or—if there are any left—people.

I also have little patience with the hyphenated names more and 20
more California female persons adopt when they marry, in the interests of retaining their own personhood. These accomplish their intention of declaring the husband separate but equal. They are hell on those of us who have trouble remembering one name, much less two. They defeat answering machines, which can't handle "Please call Gwendolyn Grunt-Messerschmidt." And in this culture, they retain overtones of false gentility.

Two surnames, to me, still bring to mind the female writers of bad 21
romances and Julia Ward Howe.

It's a mug's game, friends, this neutering of a language already fat, 22
bland and lethargic, and it's time we decide not to play it. This female person is currently writing a book about rodeo. I'll be dragged behind a saddle bronc before I will neuter the text with "cowpersons."

Questions for Study and Discussion

1. Why does McFadden object to the "neutering" of English? Does she think that this neutering process is just another language fad? How do you know?

2. How does McFadden react to "person" suffixes and "he/she's" in print? In speech? Do you have similar reactions? She claims that "person" suffixes and "he/she's" are both awkward and ridiculous. In what ways does her essay itself illustrate this point?

3. On what grounds does McFadden object to hyphenated names? Do you share her objections? Why, or why not?

4. What does McFadden mean when she says "so the war of the pronouns and suffixes rages, taking no prisoners except writers"?

5. McFadden believes there must be a "better way" to eliminate sexism than to "slash" English to death. Does she offer any solutions? Can you think of any solutions?

6. In paragraph 2 McFadden says that "this female person knows firsthand the reasons for scourging sexist bias from the language." How does this claim function in the context of her argument? Did you find it effective? Why, or why not?

7. Identify several metaphors and similes that McFadden uses and explain how each one works.

8. Why do you think McFadden chose to use the word "neuter" to describe the process of eliminating sexism from English? What are the connotations of this word? Is it an appropriate choice? Explain.

Writing Topics

1. When McFadden wrote her essay in 1981, she believed that the neutering of English was largely a West Coast phenomenon. How widespread is it today? Do you come into contact with neutered English on a daily basis? Or, has such usage started to die out? Write an essay in which you discuss neutering as a language fad or as a "here-to-stay" change. Feel free to take issue with McFadden and show the serious intent of the changes that have occurred. You might also want to consider other negative reactions to feminist "over-zealousness."

2. Select a passage from the Bible, an essay in this book, or a legal document and rewrite it so as to eliminate all sexist language. What do you think of the revised version? What has been lost in the rewriting? Which version do you prefer?

Language That Manipulates

GEORGE ORWELL

In the totalitarian state of George Orwell's novel *1984* (1949), the government has imposed on its subjects a simplified language, Newspeak, which is continually revised to give them fewer and fewer words with which to express themselves. Words like *terrible, abhorrent,* and *evil,* for example, have all been replaced by the single expression, *double-plus-ungood.* The way people use language, Orwell maintained, is both a result of the way they think and an important influence on their thought as well. This is also the point of his classic essay, "Politics and the English Language." Though published in 1946, the essay is as accurate and relevant now as it was then. Indeed, during the war in Vietnam various American officials were still using euphemisms such as "pacification" and "transfer of population," as if Orwell hadn't long since exposed those phrases as doubletalk. But Orwell goes beyond exposé. He not only holds up to public view and ridicule some choice examples of political language at its worst, but also offers a few short, simple, and effective rules for writers who want to do better. (For biographical information about Orwell, see page 45.)

Politics and the English Language

Most people who bother with the matter at all would admit that the English language is in a bad way, but it is generally assumed that we cannot by conscious action do anything about it. Our civilization is decadent and our language—so the argument runs—must inevitably share in the general collapse. It follows that any struggle against the abuse of language is a sentimental archaism, like preferring candles to electric light or hansom cabs to aeroplanes. Underneath this lies the half-conscious belief that language is a natural growth and not an instrument which we shape for our own purposes. 1

Now, it is clear that the decline of a language must ultimately have political and economic causes: it is not due simply to the bad influence 2 of this or that individual writer. But an effect can become a cause, reinforcing the original cause and producing the same effect in an intensified form, and so on indefinitely. A man may take to drink because he feels himself to be a failure, and then fail all the more completely because he drinks. It is rather the same thing that is happening to the English language. It becomes ugly and inaccurate because our thoughts are foolish, but the slovenliness of our language makes it easier for us to have foolish thoughts. The point is that the process is reversible. Modern English, especially written English, is full of bad habits which spread by imitation and which can be avoided if one is willing to take the necessary trouble. If one gets rid of these habits one can think more clearly, and to think clearly is a necessary first step toward political regeneration: so that the fight against bad English is not frivolous and is not the exclusive concern of professional writers. I will come back to this presently, and I hope that by that time the meaning of what I have said here will have become clearer. Meanwhile, here are five specimens of the English language as it is now habitually written.

These five passages have not been picked out because they are especially bad—I could have quoted far worse if I had chosen—but because they illustrate various of the mental vices from which we now suffer. They are a little below the average, but are fairly representative samples. I number them so that I can refer back to them when necessary: 3

> (1) I am not, indeed, sure whether it is not true to say that the Milton who once seemed not unlike a seventeenth-century Shelley had not become, out of an experience even more bitter in each year, more alien [*sic*] to the founder of that Jesuit sect which nothing could induce him to tolerate.
>
> Professor Harold Laski (Essay in *Freedom of Expression*)

> (2) Above all, we cannot play ducks and drakes with[1] a native battery of idioms which prescribes such egregious collocations of vocables as the Basic *put up with* for *tolerate* or *put at a loss* for *bewilder*.
>
> Professor Lancelot Hogben (*Interglossa*)

> (3) On the one side we have the free personality: by definition it is not neurotic, for it has neither conflict nor dream. Its desires, such as they are, are transparent, for they are just what institutional approval keeps in the forefront of consciousness; another institutional pattern would alter their number and intensity; there is little in them that is natural, irreducible, or culturally dangerous. But *on the other side*, the social bond itself is nothing but the mutual reflection of these self-secure integrities. Recall the definition of love. Is not this the very picture of a small academic?

---

[1]Squander.

Where is there a place in this hall of mirrors for either personality or fraternity?

Essay on psychology in *Politics* (New York)

(4) All the "best people" from the gentlemen's clubs, and all the frantic fascist captains, united in common hatred of Socialism and bestial horror of the rising tide of the mass revolutionary movement, have turned to acts of provocation, to foul incendiarism, to medieval legends of poisoned wells, to legalize their own destruction of proletarian organizations, and rouse the agitated petty-bourgeoisie to chauvinistic fervor on behalf of the fight against the revolutionary way out of the crisis.

Communist pamphlet

(5) If a new spirit *is* to be infused into this old country, there is one thorny and contentious reform which must be tackled, and that is the humanization and galvanization of the B.B.C.[2] Timidity here will bespeak canker and atrophy of the soul. The heart of Britain may be sound and of strong beat, for instance, but the British lion's roar at present is like that of Bottom in Shakespeare's *Midsummer Night's Dream*—as gentle as any sucking dove. A virile new Britain cannot continue indefinitely to be traduced in the eyes or rather ears, of the world by the effete languors of Langham Place, brazenly masquerading as "standard English." When the Voice of Britain is heard at nine o'clock, better far and infinitely less ludicrous to hear altches honestly dropped than the present priggish, inflated, inhibited, school-ma'amish arch braying of blameless bashful mewing maidens!

Letter in *Tribune*

Each of these passages has faults of its own, but, quite apart from avoidable ugliness, two qualities are common to all of them. The first is staleness of imagery; the other is lack of precision. The writer either has a meaning and cannot express it, or he inadvertently says something else, or he is almost indifferent as to whether his words mean anything or not. This mixture of vagueness and sheer incompetence is the most marked characteristic of modern English prose, and especially of any kind of political writing. As soon as certain topics are raised, the concrete melts into the abstract and no one seems able to think of turns of speech that are not hackneyed: prose consists less and less of *words* chosen for the sake of their meaning, and more and more of *phrases* tacked together like the sections of a prefabricated henhouse. I list below, with notes and examples, various of the tricks by means of which the work of prose-construction is habitually dodged:

4

---

[2]British Broadcasting Corporation, the government-run radio and television network. "B.B.C. English" is meant to reflect standard pronunciation in England.

Dying Metaphors

A newly invented metaphor assists thought by evoking a visual image, while on the other hand a metaphor which is technically "dead" (e.g., *iron resolution*) has in effect reverted to being an ordinary word and can generally be used without loss of vividness. But in between these two classes there is a huge dump of worn-out metaphors which have lost all evocative power and are merely used because they save people the trouble of inventing phrases for themselves. Examples are: *Ring the changes on, take up the cudgels for, toe the line, ride roughshod over, stand shoulder to shoulder with, play into the hands of, no axe to grind, grist to the mill, fishing in troubled waters, on the order of the day, Achilles' heel, swan song, hotbed.* Many of these are used without knowledge of their meaning (what is a "rift," for instance?), and incompatible metaphors are frequently mixed, a sure sign that the writer is not interested in what he is saying. Some metaphors now current have been twisted out of their original meaning without those who use them even being aware of the fact. For example, *toe the line* is sometimes written *tow the line.* Another example is *the hammer and the anvil,* now always used with the implication that the anvil gets the worst of it. In real life it is always the anvil that breaks the hammer, never the other way about: a writer who stopped to think what he was saying would be aware of this, and would avoid perverting the original phrase.

Operators or Verbal False Limbs

These save the trouble of picking out appropriate verbs and nouns, and at the same time pad each sentence with extra syllables which give it an appearance of symmetry. Characteristic phrases are *render inoperative, militate against, make contact with, be subjected to, give rise to, give grounds for, have the effect of, play a leading part (role) in, make itself felt, take effect, exhibit a tendency to, serve the purpose of,* etc., etc. The keynote is the elimination of simple verbs. Instead of being a single word, such as *break, stop, spoil, mend, kill,* a verb becomes a *phrase,* made up of a noun or adjective tacked on to some general-purpose verb such as *prove, serve, form, play, render.* In addition, the passive voice is wherever possible used in preference to the active, and noun constructions are used instead of gerunds (*by examination of* instead of *by examining*). The range of verbs is further cut down by means of the *-ize* and *de-* formations, and the banal statements are given an appearance of profundity by means of the *not un-* formation. Simple conjunctions and prepositions are replaced by such phrases as *with respect to, having regard to, the fact that, by dint of, in view of, in the interests of, on the hypothesis that;* and the ends of sentences are saved from anticlimax by such resounding commonplaces as *greatly to be desired, cannot be left out of account, a development to be expected in the near future, deserving of serious consideration, brought to a satisfactory conclusion,* and so on and so forth.

Pretentious Diction

Words like *phenomenon, element, individual* (as noun), *objective, categorical, effective, virtual, basic, primary, promote, constitute, exhibit, exploit, utilize, eliminate, liquidate,* are used to dress up simple statement and give an air of scientific impartiality to biased judgments. Adjectives like *epoch-making, epic, historic, unforgettable, triumphant, age-old, inevitable, inexorable, veritable,* are used to dignify the sordid processes of international politics, while writing that aims at glorifying war usually takes on an archaic color, its characteristic words being: *realm, throne, chariot, mailed fist, trident, sword, shield, buckler, banner, jackboot, clarion.* Foreign words and expressions such as *cul de sac, ancien régime, deus ex machina, mutatis mutandis, status quo, gleichschaltung, weltanschauung,* are used to give an air of culture and elegance. Except for the useful abbreviations *i.e., e.g.,* and *etc.,* there is no real need for any of the hundreds of foreign phrases now current in English. Bad writers, and especially scientific, political, and sociological writers, are nearly always haunted by the notion that Latin or Greek words are grander than Saxon ones, and unnecessary words like *expedite, ameliorate, predict, extraneous, deracinated, clandestine, subaqueous,* and hundreds of others constantly gain ground from their Anglo-Saxon opposite numbers.[3] The jargon peculiar to Marxist writing (*hyena, hangman, cannibal, petty bourgeois, these gentry, lackey, flunkey, mad dog, White Guard,* etc.) consists largely of words and phrases translated from Russian, German, or French; but the normal way of coining a new word is to use a Latin or Greek root with the appropriate affix and, where necessary, the size formation. It is often easier to make up words of this kind (*deregionalize, impermissible, extramarital, nonfragmentary* and so forth) than to think up the English words that will cover one's meaning. The result, in general, is an increase in slovenliness and vagueness.

7

---

[3] An interesting illustration of this is the way in which the English flower names which were in use till very recently are being ousted by Greek ones, *snapdragon* becoming *antirrhinum, forget-me-not* becoming *myosotis,* etc. It is hard to see any practical reason for this change of fashion: it is probably due to an instinctive turning away from the more homely word and a vague feeling that the Greek word is scientific. [Orwell's note]

Meaningless Words

In certain kinds of writing, particularly in art criticism and literary   8
criticism, it is normal to come across long passages which are almost completely lacking in meaning.[4] Words like *romantic, plastic, values, human,
dead, sentimental, natural, vitality,* as used in art criticism, are strictly
meaningless, in the sense that they not only do not point to any discov-
erable object, but are hardly ever expected to do so by the reader. When
one critic writes, "The outstanding feature of Mr. X's work is its living
quality," while another writes, "The immediately striking thing about
Mr. X's work is its peculiar deadness," the reader accepts this as a simple
difference of opinion. If words like *black* and *white* were involved, instead
of the jargon words *dead* and *living,* he would see at once that language
was being used in an improper way. Many political words are similarly
abused. The word *Fascism* has now no meaning except in so far as it
signifies "something not desirable." The words *democracy, socialism, freedom, patriotic, realistic, justice,* have each of them several different meanings which cannot be reconciled with one another. In the case of a word
like *democracy,* not only is there no agreed definition, but the attempt to
make one is resisted from all sides. It is almost universally felt that when
we call a country democratic we are praising it: consequently the defenders of every kind of régime claim that it is a democracy, and fear that they
might have to stop using the word if it were tied down to any one meaning. Words of this kind are often used in a consciously dishonest way.
That is, the person who uses them has his own private definition, but
allows his hearer to think he means something quite different. Statements
like *Marshal Pétain was a true patriot,*[5] *The Soviet press is the freest in the
world, The Catholic Church is opposed to persecution,* are almost always made
with intent to deceive. Other words used in variable meanings, in most
cases more or less dishonestly, are: *class, totalitarian, science, progressive,
reactionary, bourgeois, equality.*

Now that I have made this catalogue of swindles and perversions,   9
let me give another example of the kind of writing that they lead to.
This time it must of its nature be an imaginary one. I am going to

---

[4]Example: "[Alex] Comfort's catholicity of perception and image, strangely Whit-
manesque in range, almost the exact opposite in aesthetic compulsion, continues to
evoke that trembling atmospheric accumulative hinting at a cruel, an inexorably
serene timelessness. . . . Wrey Gardiner scores by aiming at simple bull's-eyes with
precision. Only they are not so simple, and through this contented sadness runs more
than the surface bittersweet of resignation." (*Poetry Quarterly.*) [Orwell's note]

[5]In fact, Pétain was the Nazi-supported ruler of much of France from 1940 to 1944,
and was convicted of treason in 1945.

translate a passage of good English into modern English of the worst sort. Here is a well-known verse from *Ecclesiastes*:

> I returned and saw under the sun, that the race is not to the swift, nor the battle to the strong, neither yet bread to the wise, nor yet riches to men of understanding, nor yet favour to men of skill; but time and chance happeneth to them all.

Here it is in modern English:

> Objective considerations of contemporary phenomena compels the conclusion that success or failure in competitive activities exhibits no tendency to be commensurate with innate capacity, but that a considerable element of the unpredictable must invariably be taken into account.

This is a parody, but not a very gross one. Exhibit (3), above, for instance, contains several patches of the same kind of English. It will be seen that I have not made a full translation. The beginning and ending of the sentence follow the original meaning fairly closely, but in the middle the concrete illustrations—race, battle, bread—dissolve into the vague phrase "success or failure in competitive activities." This had to be so, because no modern writer of the kind I am discussing—no one capable of using phrases like "objective consideration of contemporary phenomena"—would ever tabulate his thoughts in that precise and detailed way. The whole tendency of modern prose is away from concreteness. Now analyze these two sentences a little more closely. The first contains forty-nine words but only sixty syllables, and all its words are those of everyday life. The second contains thirty-eight words of ninety syllables: eighteen of its words are from Latin roots, and one from Greek. The first sentence contains six vivid images, and only one phrase ("time and chance") that could be called vague. The second contains not a single fresh, arresting phrase, and in spite of its ninety syllables it gives only a shortened version of the meaning contained in the first. Yet without a doubt it is the second kind of sentence that is gaining ground in modern English. I do not want to exaggerate. This kind of writing is not yet universal, and outcrops of simplicity will occur here and there in the worst-written page. Still, if you or I were told to write a few lines on the uncertainty of human fortunes, we should probably come much nearer to my imaginary sentence than to the one from *Ecclesiastes*. 10

As I have tried to show, modern writing at its worst does not consist in picking out words for the sake of their meaning and inventing images in order to make the meaning clearer. It consists in gumming together long strips of words which have already been set in order by someone else, and making the results presentable by sheer humbug. The attraction 11 of this way of writing is that it is easy. It is easier—even quicker, once you have the habit—to say *In my opinion it is not an unjustifiable assumption that* than to say *I think*. If you use ready-made phrases, you not only don't have to hunt about for words; you also don't have to bother with the rhythms of your sentences, since these phrases are generally so arranged as to be more or less euphonious. When you are composing in a hurry— when you are dictating to a stenographer, for instance, or making a public speech—it is natural to fall into a pretentious, Latinized style. Tags like *a consideration which we should do well to bear in mind* or *a conclusion to which all of us would readily assent* will save many a sentence from coming down with a bump. By using stale metaphors, similes, and idioms, you save much mental effort, at the cost of leaving your meaning vague, not only for your reader but for yourself. This is the significance of mixed metaphors. The sole aim of a metaphor is to call up a visual image. When these images clash—as in *The Fascist octopus has sung its swan song, the jackboot is thrown into the melting pot*—it can be taken as certain that the writer is not seeing a mental image of the objects he is naming; in other words he is not really thinking. Look again at the examples I gave at the beginning of this essay. Professor Laski (1) uses five negatives in fifty-three words. One of these is superfluous, making nonsense of the whole passage, and in addition there is the slip—*alien* for akin—making further nonsense, and several avoidable pieces of clumsiness which increase the general vagueness. Professor Hogben (2) plays ducks and drakes with a battery which is able to write prescriptions, and, while disapproving of the everyday phrase *put up with*, is unwilling to look *egregious* up in the dictionary and see what it means; (3), if one takes an uncharitable attitude towards it, is simply meaningless: probably one could work out its intended meaning by reading the whole of the article in which it occurs. In (4), the writer knows more or less what he wants to say, but an accumulation of stale phrases chokes him like tea leaves blocking a sink. In (5), words and meaning have almost parted company. People who write in this manner usually have a general emotional meaning— they dislike one thing and want to express solidarity with another—but they are not interested in the detail of what they are saying. A scrupulous writer, in every sentence that he writes, will ask himself at least four questions, thus: What am I trying to say? What words will express it? What image or idiom will make it clearer? Is this image fresh enough to have an effect? And he will probably ask himself two more: Could I put it more shortly? Have I said anything that is avoidably ugly? But you are not obliged to go to all this trouble. You can shirk it by simply throwing your mind open and letting the ready-made phrases come crowding in. They will construct your sentences for you—even think your thoughts for you, to a certain extent—and at need they will perform the important service of partially concealing your meaning even from yourself. It is at this point that the special connection between politics and the debasement of language becomes clear.

In our time it is broadly true that political writing is bad writing. 12
Where it is not true, it will generally be found that the writer is some kind of rebel, expressing his private opinions and not a "party line." Orthodoxy, of whatever color, seems to demand a lifeless, imitative style. The political dialects to be found in pamphlets, leading articles, manifestoes, White Papers and the speeches of undersecretaries do, of course, vary from party to party, but they are all alike in that one almost never finds in them a fresh, vivid, homemade turn of speech. When one watches some tired hack on the platform mechanically repeating the familiar phrases—*bestial atrocities, iron heel, bloodstained tyranny, free peoples of the world, stand shoulder to shoulder*—one often has a curious feeling that one is not watching a live human being but some kind of dummy: a feeling which suddenly becomes stronger at moments when the light catches the speaker's spectacles and turns them into blank discs which seem to have no eyes behind them. And this is not altogether fanciful. A speaker who uses that kind of phraseology has gone some distance toward turning himself into a machine. The appropriate noises are coming out of his larynx, but his brain is not involved as it would be if he were choosing his words for himself. If the speech he is making is one that he is accustomed to make over and over again, he may be almost unconscious of what he is saying, as one is when one utters the responses in church. And this reduced state of consciousness, if not indispensable, is at any rate favorable to political conformity.

In our time, political speech and writing are largely the defense of 13
the indefensible. Things like the continuance of British rule in India, the Russian purges and deportations, the dropping of the atom bombs on Japan, can indeed be defended, but only by arguments which are too brutal for most people to face, and which do not square with the professed aims of political parties. Thus political language has to consist largely of euphemism, question-begging and sheer cloudy vagueness. Defenseless villages are bombarded from the air, the inhabitants driven out into the countryside, the cattle machine-gunned, the huts set on fire with incendiary bullets: this is called *pacification*. Millions of peasants are robbed of their farms and sent trudging along the roads with no more than they can carry: this is called *transfer of population* or *rectification of frontiers*. People are imprisoned for years without trial, or shot in the back of the neck or sent to die of scurvy in Arctic lumber camps: this is called *elimination of unreliable elements*. Such phraseology is needed if one wants

to name things without calling up mental pictures of them. Consider for instance some comfortable English professor defending Russian totalitarianism. He cannot say outright, "I believe in killing your opponents when you can get good results by doing so." Probably, therefore, he will say something like this:

"While freely conceding that the Soviet régime exhibits certain   14
features which the humanitarian may be inclined to deplore, we must, I think, agree that a certain curtailment of the right to political opposition is an unavoidable concomitant of transitional periods, and that the rigors which the Russian people have been called upon to undergo have been amply justified in the sphere of concrete achievement."

The inflated style is itself a kind of euphemism. A mass of Latin   15
words falls upon the facts like soft snow, blurring the outlines and covering up all the details. The great enemy of clear language is insincerity. When there is a gap between one's real and one's declared aims, one turns as it were instinctively to long words and exhausted idioms, like a cuttlefish squirting out ink. In our age there is no such thing as "keeping out of politics." All issues are political issues, and politics itself is a mass of lies, evasions, folly, hatred, and schizophrenia. When the general atmosphere is bad, language must suffer. I should expect to find—this is a guess which I have not sufficient knowledge to verify—that the German, Russian and Italian languages have all deteriorated in the last ten or fifteen years, as a result of dictatorship.

But if thought corrupts language, language can also corrupt thought.   16
A bad usage can spread by tradition and imitation, even among people who should and do know better. The debased language that I have been discussing is in some ways very convenient. Phrases like *a not unjustifiable assumption, leaves much to be desired, would serve no good purpose, a consideration which we should do well to bear in mind,* are a continuous temptation, a packet of aspirins always at one's elbow. Look back through this essay, and for certain you will find that I have again and again committed the very faults I am protesting against. By this morning's post I have received a pamphlet dealing with conditions in Germany. The author tells me that he "felt impelled" to write it. I open it at random, and here is almost the first sentence that I see: "[The Allies] have an opportunity not only of achieving a radical transformation of Germany's social and political structure in such a way as to avoid a nationalistic reaction in Germany itself, but at the same time of laying the foundations of a co-operative and unified Europe." You see, he "feels impelled" to write—feels, presumably, that he has something new to say—and yet his words, like cavalry horses answering the bugle, group themselves automatically into the familiar dreary pattern. This invasion of one's mind

by ready-made phrases (*lay the foundations, achieve a radical transformation*) can only be prevented if one is constantly on guard against them, and every such phrase anaesthetizes a portion of one's brain.

I said earlier that the decadence of our language is probably curable. 17 Those who deny this would argue, if they produced an argument at all, that language merely reflects existing social conditions, and that we cannot influence its development by any direct tinkering with words and constructions. So far as the general tone or spirit of a language goes, this may be true, but it is not true in detail. Silly words and expressions have often disappeared, not through any evolutionary process but owing to the conscious action of a minority. Two recent examples were *explore every avenue* and *leave no stone unturned,* which were killed by the jeers of a few journalists. There is a long list of flyblown metaphors which could similarly be got rid of if enough people would interest themselves in the job; and it should also be possible to laugh the *not un-* formation out of existence,[6] to reduce the amount of Latin and Greek in the average sentence, to drive out foreign phrases and strayed scientific words, and, in general, to make pretentiousness unfashionable. But all these are minor points. The defense of the English language implies more than this, and perhaps it is best to start by saying what it does *not* imply.

To begin with it has nothing to do with archaism, with the sal- 18 vaging of obsolete words and turns of speech, or with the setting up of a "standard English" which must never be departed from. On the contrary, it is especially concerned with the scrapping of every word or idiom which has outworn its usefulness. It has nothing to do with correct grammar and syntax, which are of no importance so long as one makes one's meaning clear, or with the avoidance of Americanisms, or with having what is called a "good prose style." On the other hand it is not concerned with fake simplicity and the attempt to make written English colloquial. Nor does it even imply in every case preferring the Saxon word to the Latin one, though it does imply using the fewest and shortest words that will cover one's meaning. What is above all needed is to let the meaning choose the word, and not the other way about. In prose, the worst thing one can do with words is to surrender to them. When you think of a concrete object, you think wordlessly, and then, if you want to describe the thing you have been visualizing you probably hunt about till you find the exact words that seem to fit it. When you think of something abstract you are more inclined to use words from the start, and unless you make a conscious effort to prevent it, the existing dialect will come rushing in

---

[6]One can cure oneself of the *not un-* formation by memorizing this sentence: A *not unblack dog was chasing a not unsmall rabbit across a not ungreen field.*

and do the job for you, at the expense of blurring or even changing your meaning. Probably it is better to put off using words as long as possible and get one's meaning as clear as one can through pictures or sensations. Afterward one can choose—not simply *accept*—the phrases that will best cover the meaning, and then switch round and decide what impression one's words are likely to make on another person. This last effort of the mind cuts out all stale or mixed images, all prefabricated phrases, needless repetitions, and humbug and vagueness generally. But one can often be in doubt about the effect of a word or a phrase, and one needs rules that one can rely on when instinct fails. I think the following rules will cover most cases:

(i) Never use a metaphor, simile, or other figure of speech which you are used to seeing in print.

(ii) Never use a long word where a short one will do.

(iii) If it is possible to cut a word out, always cut it out.

(iv) Never use the passive where you can use the active.

(v) Never use a foreign phrase, a scientific word, or a jargon word if you can think of an everyday English equivalent.

(vi) Break any of these rules sooner than say anything outright barbarous.

These rules sound elementary, and so they are, but they demand a deep change of attitude in anyone who has grown used to writing in the style now fashionable. One could keep all of them and still write bad English, but one could not write the kind of stuff that I quoted in those five specimens at the beginning of this article.

I have not here been considering the literary use of language, but merely language as an instrument for expressing and not for concealing or preventing thought. Stuart Chase and others have come near to claiming that all abstract words are meaningless, and have used this as a pretext for advocating a kind of political quietism. Since you don't know what Fascism is, how can you struggle against Fascism? One need not swallow such absurdities as this, but one ought to recognize that the present political chaos is connected with the decay of language, and that one can probably bring about some improvement by starting at the verbal end. If you simplify your English, you are freed from the worst follies of orthodoxy. You cannot speak any of the necessary dialects, and when you make a stupid remark its stupidity will be obvious, even to yourself. Political language—and with variations this is true of all political parties, from Conservatives to Anarchists—is designed to make lies sound truthful and murder respectable, and to give an appearance of solidity to pure

19

wind. One cannot change this all in a moment, but one can at least change one's own habits, and from time to time one can even, if one jeers loudly enough, send some worn-out and useless phrase—some *jackboot, Achilles' heel, hotbed, melting pot, acid test, veritable inferno,* or other lump of verbal refuse—into the dustbin where it belongs.

Questions for Study and Discussion

1. In your own words, explain the relationship Orwell sees between politics and the English language. Do you agree with him? Why or why not?

2. What terms and concepts does Orwell define in his essay? What is his purpose in defining them? How does he go about it?

3. Our world is becoming increasingly prefabricated. In what way does the concept of prefabrication relate to Orwell's observations about the prevalence of habitual and trite phrases?

4. Orwell uses the following comparisons in his essay. How does each of them reinforce or clarify his meaning?

    a. "But in between these two classes there is a huge dump of worn-out metaphors which have lost all evocative power. . . ." (paragraph 5)

    b. "The writer knows more or less what he wants to say, but an accumulation of stale phrases chokes him like tea leaves blocking a sink. . . ." (paragraph 11)

    c. "A mass of Latin words falls upon the facts like soft snow, blurring the outlines and covering up all the details." (paragraph 15)

    d. "When there is a gap between one's real and one's declared aims, one turns as it were instinctively to long words and exhausted idioms, like a cuttlefish squirting out ink." (paragraph 15)

    e. "He 'feels impelled' to write—feels, presumably, that he has something new to say—and yet his words, like cavalry horses answering the bugle, group themselves automatically into the familiar dreary pattern." (paragraph 16)

5. Orwell confesses that he himself is guilty, in this essay, of some of the errors he is pointing out. Can you detect any of them? What is the effect on you of these "errors," and of Orwell's confession?

6. The last of Orwell's six rules for better English reads, "Break any of these rules sooner than say anything outright barbarous." What do you think he means by this?

Writing Topics

1. As some of Orwell's examples suggest, language is sometimes used not to express our meanings but to conceal them. Is this true only of politics? Can you think of any situations in which you, or others you know, have been

under pressure to say something yet had nothing you were ready or willing to say? What happened? How can one handle such situations honestly?

2. Gather five examples of recent American political English that you consider, in Orwell's words, "ugly and inaccurate." Can you analyze them using Orwell's terms? If not, what new terms would you invent to classify them?

3. Read Orwell's discussion of Newspeak in *1984*. What is the relation between politics and language in Oceania? How does it connect with Orwell's views in "Politics and the English Language"?

DONNA WOOLFOLK CROSS

Most people are opposed to propaganda in principle, but few know exactly what it is and how it works. Donna Woolfolk Cross has looked closely at the subject, and her observations have been published in *Word Abuse: How the Words We Use, Use Us* (1979). She was born in New York City in 1947, and graduated from the University of Pennsylvania and UCLA. She now teaches at Onondaga Community College in New York State. For several years prior to teaching she worked in publishing and advertising, practicing as well as observing some of the techniques she writes about in her book *Mediaspeak* (1981).

Propaganda is a Latin term meaning "that which is to be made known" and is basically a means of persuasion. As such, it can be used "for good causes as well as bad." In the following essay, adapted by the author from *Word Abuse*, she discusses thirteen fallacies that propagandists can use to trick and mislead us and offers advice on how we can avoid being manipulated by the propaganda that is part of our everyday lives.

Propaganda: How Not to Be Bamboozled

Propaganda. If an opinion poll were taken tomorrow, we can be 1 sure that nearly everyone would be against it because it *sounds* so bad. When we say, "Oh, that's just propaganda," it means, to most people, "That's a pack of lies." But really, propaganda is simply a means of persuasion and so it can be put to work for good causes as well as bad— to persuade people to give to charity, for example, or to love their neighbors, or to stop polluting the environment.

For good or evil, propaganda pervades our daily lives, helping to 2 shape our attitudes on a thousand subjects. Propaganda probably determines the brand of toothpaste you use, the movies you see, the candidates you elect when you get to the polls. Propaganda works by tricking us, by momentarily distracting the eye while the rabbit pops out from beneath the cloth. Propaganda works best with an uncritical audience. Joseph Goebbels, Propaganda Minister in Nazi Germany, once defined his work as "the conquest of the masses." The masses would not have been conquered, however, if they had known how to challenge and to question, how to make distinctions between propaganda and reasonable argument.

People are bamboozled mainly because they don't recognize prop- 3 aganda when they see it. They need to be informed about the various devices that can be used to mislead and deceive—about the propagandist's overflowing bag of tricks. The following, then, are some common pitfalls for the unwary.

511

1. Name-Calling

As its title suggests, this device consists of labeling people or ideas   4
with words of bad connotation, literally, "calling them names." Here the
propagandist tries to arouse our contempt so we will dismiss the "bad
name" person or idea without examining its merits.

Bad names have played a tremendously important role in the history   5
of the world. They have ruined reputations and ended lives, sent people
to prison and to war, and just generally made us mad at each other for
centuries.

Name-calling can be used against policies, practices, beliefs and ideals,   6
as well as against individuals, groups, races, nations. Name-calling is at
work when we hear a candidate for office described as a "foolish idealist"
or a "two-faced liar" or when an incumbent's policies are denounced as
"reckless," "reactionary," or just plain "stupid." Some of the most effective names a public figure can be called are ones that may not denote
anything specific: "Congresswoman Jane Doe is a *bleeding heart!*" (Did she
vote for funds to help paraplegics?) or "The Senator is a *tool of Washington!*" (Did he happen to agree with the President?) Senator Yakalot uses
name-calling when he denounces his opponent's "radical policies" and
calls them (and him) "socialist," "pinko," and part of a "heartless plot."
He also uses it when he calls small cars "puddle-jumpers," "canopeners,"
and "motorized baby buggies."

The point here is that when the propagandist uses name-calling, he   7
doesn't want us to think—merely to react, blindly, unquestioningly. So
the best defense against being taken in by name-calling is to stop and ask,
"Forgetting the bad name attached to it, what are the merits of the idea
itself? What does this name really mean, anyway?"

2. Glittering Generalities

Glittering generalities are really name-calling in reverse. Name-calling   8
uses words with bad connotations; glittering generalities are words with
good connotations—"virtue words," as the Institute for Propaganda Analysis
has called them. The Institute explains that while name-calling tries to
get us to *reject* and *condemn* someone or something without examining the
evidence, glittering generalities try to get us to *accept* and *agree* without
examining the evidence.

We believe in, fight for, live by "virtue words" which we feel deeply   9
about: "justice," "motherhood," "the American way," "our Constitutional rights," "our Christian heritage." These sound good, but when we

examine them closely, they turn out to have no specific, definable meaning. They just make us feel good. Senator Yakalot uses glittering generalities when he says, "I stand for all that is good in America, for our American way and our American birthright." But what exactly *is* "good for America"? How can we define our "American birthright"? Just what parts of the American society and culture does "our American way" refer to?

We often make the mistake of assuming we are personally unaffected by glittering generalities. The next time you find yourself assuming that, listen to a political candidate's speech on TV and see how often the use of glittering generalities elicits cheers and applause. That's the danger of propaganda; it *works*. Once again, our defense against it is to ask questions: Forgetting the virtue words attached to it, what are the merits of the idea itself? What does "Americanism" (or "freedom" or "truth") really *mean* here? . . .

Both name-calling and glittering generalities work by stirring our emotions in the hope that this will cloud our thinking. Another approach that propaganda uses is to create a distraction, a "red herring," that will make people forget or ignore the real issues. There are several different kinds of "red herrings" that can be used to distract attention.

3. Plain Folks Appeal

"Plain folks" is the device by which a speaker tries to win our confidence and support by appearing to be a person like ourselves—"just one of the plain folks." The plain-folks appeal is at work when candidates go around shaking hands with factory workers, kissing babies in supermarkets, and sampling pasta with Italians, fried chicken with Southerners, bagels and blintzes with Jews. "Now I'm a businessman like yourselves" is a plain-folks appeal, as is "I've been a farm boy all my life." Senator Yakalot tries the plain-folks appeal when he says, "I'm just a small-town boy like you fine people." The use of such expressions once prompted Lyndon Johnson to quip, "Whenever I hear someone say, 'I'm just an old country lawyer,' the first thing I reach for is my wallet to make sure it's still there."

The irrelevancy of the plain-folks appeal is obvious: even if the man *is* "one of us" (which may not be true at all), that doesn't mean his ideas and programs are sound—or even that he honestly has our best interests at heart. As with glittering generalities, the danger here is that we may mistakenly assume we are immune to this appeal. But propagandists wouldn't use it unless it had been proved to work. You can protect yourself by asking, "Aside from his 'nice guy next door' image, what does this man stand for? Are his ideas and his past record really supportive of my best interests?"

4. Argumentum ad Populum (Stroking)

Argumentum ad populum means "argument to the people" or "telling   14
the people what they want to hear." The colloquial term from the Watergate era is "stroking," which conjures up pictures of small animals or
children being stroked or soothed with compliments until they come to
like the person doing the complimenting—and, by extension, his or her
ideas.

We all like to hear nice things about ourselves and the group we   15
belong to—we like to be liked—so it stands to reason that we will respond
warmly to a person who tells us we are "hard-working taxpayers" or "the
most generous, free-spirited nation in the world." Politicians tell farmers
they are the "backbone of the American economy" and college students
that they are the "leaders and policy makers of tomorrow." Commercial
advertisers use stroking more insidiously by asking a question which invites a flattering answer: "What kind of a man reads *Playboy*?" (Does he
really drive a Porsche and own $10,000 worth of sound equipment?) Sen-
ator Yakalot is stroking his audience when he calls them the "decent law-
abiding citizens that are the great pulsing heart and the life blood of this,
our beloved country," and when he repeatedly refers to them as "you fine
people," "you wonderful folks."

Obviously, the intent here is to sidetrack us from thinking critically   16
about the man and his ideas. Our own good qualities have nothing to do
with the issue at hand. Ask yourself, "Apart from the nice things he has
to say about me (and my church, my nation, my ethnic group, my neighbors), what does the candidate stand for? Are his or her ideas in my best
interests?"

5. Argumentum ad Hominem

Argumentum ad hominem means "argument to the man" and that's   17
exactly what it is. When a propagandist uses *argumentum ad hominem*, he
wants to distract our attention from the issue under consideration with
personal attacks on the people involved. For example, when Lincoln issued the Emancipation Proclamation, some people responded by calling
him the "baboon." But Lincoln's long arms and awkward carriage had

nothing to do with the merits of the Proclamation or the question of whether or not slavery should be abolished.

Today *argumentum ad hominem* is still widely used and very effective. 18 You may or may not support the Equal Rights Amendment, but you should be sure your judgment is based on the merits of the idea itself, and not the result of someone's denunciation of the people who support the ERA as "fanatics" or "lesbians" or "frustrated old maids." Senator Yakalot is using *argumentum ad hominem* when he dismisses the idea of using smaller automobiles with a reference to the personal appearance of one of its supporters, Congresswoman Doris Schlepp. Refuse to be waylaid by *argumentum ad hominem* and ask, "Do the personal qualities of the person being discussed have anything to do with the issues at hand? Leaving him or her aside, how good is the idea itself?"

6. *Transfer (Guilt or Glory by Association)*

In *argumentum ad hominem*, an attempt is made to associate negative 19 aspects of a person's character or personal appearance with an issue or idea he supports. The transfer device uses this same process of association to make us accept or condemn a given person or idea.

A better name for the transfer device is guilt (or glory) by associa- 20 tion. In glory by association, the propagandist tries to transfer the positive feelings of something we love and respect to the group or idea he wants us to accept. "This bill for a new dam is in the best tradition of this country, the land of Lincoln, Jefferson, and Washington," is glory by association at work. Lincoln, Jefferson, and Washington were great leaders that most of us revere and respect, but they have no logical connection to the proposal under consideration—the bill to build a new dam. Senator Yakalot uses glory by association when he says full-sized cars "have always been as American as Mom's apple pie or a Sunday drive in the country."

The process works equally well in reverse, when guilt by association 21 is used to transfer our dislike or disapproval of one idea or group to some other idea or group that the propagandist wants us to reject and condemn. "John Doe says we need to make some changes in the way our government operates; well, that's exactly what the Ku Klux Klan has said, so there's a meeting of great minds!" That's guilt by association for you; there's no logical connection between John Doe and the Ku Klux Klan apart from the one the propagandist is trying to create in our minds. He wants to distract our attention from John Doe and get us thinking (and worrying) about the Ku Klux Klan and its politics of violence. (Of course, there are sometimes legitimate associations between the two things; if John Doe had been a *member* of the Ku Klux Klan, it would be reasonable and fair to draw a connection between the man and his group.) Senator Yakalot tries to trick his audience with guilt by association when he remarks that "the words 'Community' and 'Communism' look an awful lot alike!" He does it again when he mentions that Mr. Stu Pott "sports a Fidel Castro beard."

How can we learn to spot the transfer device and distinguish be- 22
tween fair and unfair associations? We can teach ourselves to *suspend judgment* until we have answered these questions: "Is there any legitimate connection between the idea under discussion and the thing it is associated with? Leaving the transfer device out of the picture, what are the merits of the idea by itself?"

7. Bandwagon

Ever hear of the small, ratlike animal called the lemming? Lem- 23
mings are arctic rodents with a very odd habit: periodically, for reasons no one entirely knows, they mass together in a large herd and commit suicide by rushing into deep water and drowning themselves. They all run in together, blindly, and not one of them ever seems to stop and ask, "*Why* am I doing this? Is this really what I want to do?" and thus save itself from destruction. Obviously, lemmings are driven to perform their strange mass suicide rites by common instinct. People choose to "follow the herd" for more complex reasons, yet we are still all too often the unwitting victims of the bandwagon appeal.

Essentially, the bandwagon urges us to support an action or an opin- 24
ion because it is popular—because "everyone else is doing it." This call to "get on the bandwagon" appeals to the strong desire in most of us to be one of the crowd, not to be left out or alone. Advertising makes extensive use of the bandwagon appeal ("join the Pepsi people"), but so do politicians ("Let us join together in this great cause"). Senator Yakalot uses the bandwagon appeal when he says that "More and more citizens are rallying to my cause every day," and asks his audience to "join them— and me—in our fight for America."

One of the ways we can see the bandwagon appeal at work is in the 25
overwhelming success of various fashions and trends which capture the interest (and the money) of thousands of people for a short time, then disappear suddenly and completely. For a year or two in the fifties, every child in North America wanted a coonskin cap so they could be like Davy Crockett; no one wanted to be left out. After that there was the hula-

hoop craze that helped to dislocate the hips of thousands of Americans. More recently, what made millions of people rush out to buy their very own "pet rocks"?

The problem here is obvious: just because everyone's doing it doesn't   26
mean that *we* should too. Group approval does not prove that something is true or is worth doing. Large numbers of people have supported actions we now condemn. Just a generation ago, Hitler and Mussolini rose to absolute and catastrophically repressive rule in two of the most sophisticated and cultured countries of Europe. When they came into power they were welled up by massive popular support from millions of people who didn't want to be "left out" at a great historical moment.

Once the mass begins to move—on the bandwagon—it becomes   27
harder and harder to perceive the leader *riding* the bandwagon. So don't be a lemming, rushing blindly on to destruction because "everyone else is doing it." Stop and ask, "Where is this bandwagon headed? Never mind about everybody else, is this what is best for *me?*" . . .

As we have seen, propaganda can appeal to us by arousing our   28
emotions or distracting our attention from the real issues at hand. But there's a third way that propaganda can be put to work against us—by the use of faulty logic. This approach is really more insidious than the other two because it gives the appearance of reasonable, fair argument. It is only when we look more closely that the holes in the logical fiber show up. The following are some of the devices that make use of faulty logic to distort and mislead.

8. Faulty Cause and Effect

As the name suggests, this device sets up a cause-and-effect rela-   29
tionship that may not be true. The Latin name for this logical fallacy is *post hoc ergo propter hoc,* which means "after this, therefore because of this." But just because one thing happened after another doesn't mean that one *caused* the other.

An example of false cause-and-effect reasoning is offered by the story   30
(probably invented) of the woman aboard the ship *Titanic.* She woke up from a nap and, feeling seasick, looked around for a call button to summon the steward to bring her some medication. She finally located a small button on one of the walls of her cabin and pushed it. A split second later, the *Titanic* grazed an iceberg in the terrible crash that was to send the entire ship to its destruction. The woman screamed and said, "Oh, God, what have I done? What have I done?" The humor of that anecdote comes from the absurdity of the woman's assumption that pushing the

small red button resulted in the destruction of a ship weighing several hundred tons: "It happened after I pushed it, therefore it must be *because* I pushed it"—*post hoc ergo propter hoc* reasoning. There is, of course, no cause-and-effect relationship there.

The false cause-and-effect fallacy is used very often by political can-   31 didates. "After I came to office, the rate of inflation dropped to 6 per- cent." But did the person do anything to cause the lower rate of inflation or was it the result of other conditions? Would the rate of inflation have dropped anyway, even if he hadn't come to office? Senator Yakalot uses false cause and effect when he says "our forefathers who made this country great never had free hot meal handouts! And look what they did for our country!" He does it again when he concludes that "driving full-sized cars means a better car safety record on our American roads today."

False cause-and-effect reasoning is terribly persuasive because it seems   32 so logical. Its appeal is apparently to experience. We swallowed X prod- uct—and the headache went away. We elected Y official and unemploy- ment went down. Many people think, "There *must* be a connection." But causality is an immensely complex phenomenon; you need a good deal of evidence to prove that an event that follows another in time was "therefore" caused by the first event.

Don't be taken in by false cause and effect; be sure to ask, "Is there   33 enough evidence to prove that this cause led to that effect? Could there have been any *other* causes?"

9. False Analogy

An analogy is a comparison between two ideas, events, or things.   34 But comparisons can be fairly made only when the things being compared are alike in significant ways. When they are not, false analogy is the result.

A famous example of this is the old proverb "Don't change horses   35 in the middle of a stream," often used as an analogy to convince voters not to change administrations in the middle of a war or other crisis. But the analogy is misleading because there are so many differences between the things compared. In what ways is a war or political crisis like a stream? Is the President or head of state really very much like a horse? And is a nation of millions of people comparable to a man trying to get across a stream? Analogy is false and unfair when it compares two things that have little in common and assumes that they are identical. Senator Yakalot tries to hoodwink his listeners with false analogy when he says, "Trying to take Americans out of the kind of cars they love is as undemocratic as trying to deprive them of the right to vote."

Of course, analogies can be drawn that are reasonable and fair. It 36 would be reasonable, for example, to compare the results of busing in one small Southern city with the possible results in another, *if* the towns have the same kind of history, population, and school policy. We can decide for ourselves whether an analogy is false or fair by asking, "Are the things being compared truly alike in significant ways? Do the differences between them affect the comparison?"

10. Begging the Question

Actually, the name of this device is rather misleading, because it 37 does not appear in the form of a question. Begging the question occurs when, in discussing a questionable or debatable point, a person assumes as already established the very point that he is trying to prove. For example, "No thinking citizen could approve such a completely unacceptable policy as this one." But isn't the question of whether or not the policy *is* acceptable the very point to be established? Senator Yakalor begs the question when he announces that his opponent's plan won't work "because it is unworkable."

We can protect ourselves against this kind of faulty logic by asking, 38 "What is assumed in this statement? Is the assumption reasonable, or does it need more proof?"

11. The Two Extremes Fallacy (False Dilemma)

Linguists have long noted that the English language tends to view 39 reality in sets of two extremes or polar opposites. In English, things are either black or white, tall or short, up or down, front or back, left or right, good or bad, guilty or not guilty. We can ask for a "straightforward yes-or-no answer" to a question, the understanding being that we will not accept or consider anything in between. In fact, reality cannot always be dissected along such strict lines. There may be (usually are) *more* than just two possibilities or extremes to consider. We are often told to "listen to both sides of the argument." But who's to say that every argument has only two sides? Can't there be a third—even a fourth or fifth—point of view?

The two-extremes fallacy is at work in this statement by Lenin, the 40 great Marxist leader: "You cannot eliminate *one* basic assumption, one substantial part of this philosophy of Marxism (it is as if it were a block of steel), without abandoning truth, without falling into the arms of bourgeois-reactionary falsehood." In other words, if we don't agree 100 percent with every premise of Marxism, we must be placed at the opposite end of the political-economic spectrum—for Lenin, "bourgeois-reactionary falsehood." If we are not entirely *with* him, we must be against him; those are the only two possibilities open to us. Of course, this is a logical fallacy; in real life there are any number of political positions one can maintain *between* the two extremes of Marxism and capitalism. Senator Yakalot uses the two-extremes fallacy in the same way as Lenin when he tells his audience that "in this world a man's either for private enterprise or he's for socialism."

One of the most famous examples of the two-extremes fallacy in recent history is the slogan, "America: Love it or leave it," with its implicit suggestion that we either accept everything just as it is in America today without complaint—or get out. Again, it should be obvious that there is a whole range of action and belief between those two extremes. 41

Don't be duped; stop and ask, "Are those really the only two options I can choose from? Are there other alternatives not mentioned that deserve considerations?" 42

12. Card Stacking

Some questions are so multifaceted and complex that no one can make an intelligent decision about them without considering a wide variety of evidence. One selection of facts could make us feel one way and another selection could make us feel just the opposite. Card stacking is a device of propaganda which selects only the facts that support the propagandist's point of view, and ignores all the others. For example, a candidate could be made to look like a legislative dynamo if you say, "Representative McNerd introduced more new bills than any other member of the Congress," and neglect to mention that most of them were so preposterous that they were laughed off the floor. 43

Senator Yakalot engages in card stacking when he talks about the proposal to use smaller cars. He talks only about jobs without mentioning the cost to the taxpayers or the very real—though still denied—threat of depletion of resources. He says he wants to help his countrymen keep their jobs, but doesn't mention that the corporations that offer the jobs will also make large profits. He praises the "American chrome industry," overlooking the fact that most chrome is imported. And so on. 44

The best protection against card stacking is to take the "Yes, but   45
. . ." attitude. This device of propaganda is not untrue, but then again it
is not the *whole* truth. So ask yourself, "Is this person leaving something
out that I should know about? Is there some other information that should
be brought to bear on this question?" . . .

So far, we have considered three approaches that the propagandist   46
can use to influence our thinking: appealing to our emotions, distracting
our attention, and misleading us with logic that may appear to be reasonable but is in fact faulty and deceiving. But there is a fourth approach
that is probably the most common propaganda trick of them all.

13. Testimonial

The testimonial device consists in having some loved or respected   47
person give a statement of support (testimonial) for a given product or
idea. The problem is that the person being quoted may *not* be an expert
in the field; in fact, he may know nothing at all about it. Using the name
of a man who is skilled and famous in one field to give a testimonial for
something in another field is unfair and unreasonable.

Senator Yakalot tries to mislead his audience with testimonial when   48
he tells them that "full-sized cars have been praised by great Americans
like John Wayne and Jack Jones, as well as by leading experts on car safety
and comfort."

Testimonial is used extensively in TV ads, where it often appears in   49
such bizarre forms as Joe Namath's endorsement of a pantyhose brand.
Here, of course, the "authority" giving the testimonial not only is no
expert about pantyhose, but obviously stands to gain something (money!)
by making the testimonial.

When celebrities endorse a political candidate, they may not be   50
making money by doing so, but we should still question whether they are
in any better position to judge than we ourselves. Too often we are willing
to let others we like or respect make our decisions *for us*, while we follow
along acquiescently. And this is the purpose of testimonial—to get us to
agree and accept *without* stopping to think. Be sure to ask, "Is there any
reason to believe that this person (or organization or publication or whatever) has any more knowledge or information than I do on this subject?
What does the idea amount to on its own merits, without the benefit of
testimonial?"

The cornerstone of democratic society is reliance upon an informed   51
and educated electorate. To be fully effective citizens we need to be able
to challenge and to question wisely. A dangerous feeling of indifference

toward our political processes exists today. We often abandon our right, our duty, to criticize and evaluate by dismissing *all* politicians as "crooked," *all* new bills and proposals as "just more government bureaucracy." But there are important distinctions to be made, and this kind of apathy can be fatal to democracy.

If we are to be led, let us not be led blindly, but critically, intelligently, with our eyes open. If we are to continue to be a government "by the people," let us become informed about the methods and purposes of propaganda, so we can be the masters, not the slaves of our destiny.

52

Questions for Study and Discussion

1. What are the four general types of propaganda devices that Cross discusses?

2. What, according to Cross, is the most common propaganda trick of them all? Give some examples from your experience.

3. What organization does Cross use for each of her discussions of a propaganda device? Do you see any purpose for the order in which she presents the thirteen devices?

4. Who is Senator Yakalot? What is his significance in Cross's essay?

5. Cross uses an analogy in her discussion of bandwagon appeal. How does this analogy work? Is it a true or a false analogy, according to Cross's own definitions? Explain.

Writing Topics

1. As Cross says in the beginning of her essay, propaganda "can be put to work for good causes as well as bad". Using materials from the Red Cross, United Way, or some other public service organization, write an essay in which you discuss the propaganda used by such organizations. How would you characterize their appeals? Do you ever find such propaganda objectionable? Does the end always justify the means?

2. In an effort to better understand the thought processes involved in propaganda, try writing a piece yourself. Using the devices described by Cross, try to persuade your classmates to (a) join a particular campus organization, (b) support, either spiritually or financially, a controversial movement or issue on campus, or (c) vote for one candidate and not another in a campus election.

PAUL STEVENS

Paul Stevens is the pen name of Carl P. Wrighter, a former advertising copywriter who worked for a major advertising firm in New York City. Born in 1937, Stevens, a graduate of Syracuse University, was a teacher of English and music before pursuing a career in advertising. In 1972 he wrote *I Can Sell You Anything,* a bristling exposé of questionable advertising language and techniques.

Most of us are already aware that commercials are a very real part of our daily lives. What we are not aware of, however, is how commercials work on us, how language devices play such a big role in successful advertising. Advertisers really don't have to substantiate their claims, as Stevens points out in this chapter from his book, because they can use "weasel words" to make customers hear things that aren't being said. As consumers, we need to understand what's really being said in the ads we read and hear. Stevens shows how devious the effects of advertising can be, as he classifies ad slogans according to the ways they mislead us.

Weasel Words

Advertising has power, all right. And advertising works, all right. 1
And what it really boils down to is that advertising works because you believe it. You're the one who believes Josephine the Plumber really knows about stains. You're the one who believes Winston tastes good like a cigarette should. You're the one who believes Plymouth is coming through. The real question is, why do you believe all these things? And the answer is, because you don't yet understand how advertising makes you believe. You don't understand what to believe, or even how to believe advertising. Well, if you're ready to learn how to separate the wheat from the chaff, if you're ready to learn how to make advertising work *for* you, if you're ready to learn how to stop being a sucker, then you're ready to go to work.

First of all, you know what a weasel is, right? It's a small, slimy 2
animal that eats small birds and other animals, and is especially fond of devouring vermin. Now, consider for a moment the kind of winning personality he must have. I mean, what kind of a guy would get his jollies eating rats and mice? Would you invite him to a party? Take him home to meet your mother? This is one of the slyest and most cunning of all creatures; sneaky, slippery, and thoroughly obnoxious. And so it is with great and warm personal regard for these attributes that we humbly award

this King of All Devious the honor of bestowing his name upon our golden sword: the weasel word.

A weasel word is "a word used in order to evade or retreat from a direct or forthright statement or position" (Webster). In other words, if we can't say it, we'll weasel it. And, in fact, a weasel word has become more than just an evasion or retreat. We've trained our weasels. They can do anything. They can make you hear things that aren't being said, accept as truths things that have only been implied, and believe things that have only been suggested. Come to think of it, not only do we have our weasels trained, but they, in turn, have got you trained. When *you* hear a weasel word, you automatically hear the implication. Not the real meaning, but the meaning *it* wants *you* to hear. So if you're ready for a little reeducation, let's take a good look under a strong light at the two kinds of weasel words.

Words That Mean Things They Really Don't Mean

HELP

That's it. "Help." It means "aid" or "assist." Nothing more. Yet, "help" is the one single word which, in all the annals of advertising, has done the most to say something that couldn't be said. Because "help" is the great qualifier; once you say it, you can say almost anything after it. In short, "help" has helped help us the most.

Helps keep you young
Helps prevent cavities
Help keep your house germ-free

"Help" qualifies everything. You've never heard anyone say, "This product will keep you young," or "This toothpaste will positively prevent cavities for all time." Obviously, we can't say anything like that, because there aren't any products like that made. But by adding that one little word, "help," in front, we can use the strongest language possible afterward. And the most fascinating part of it is, you are immune to the word. You literally don't hear the word "help." You only hear what comes after it. Any why not? That's strong language, and likely to be much more important to you than the silly little word at the front end.

I would guess that 75 percent of all advertising uses the word "help." Think, for a minute, about how many times each day you hear these phrases:

Helps stop . . .
Helps prevent . . .

Helps fight . . .
Helps overcome . . .
Helps you feel . . .
Helps you look . . .

I could go on and on, but so could you. Just as a simple exercise, call it homework if you wish, tonight when you plop down in front of the boob tube for your customary three and a half hours of violence and/or situation comedies, take a pad and pencil, and keep score. See if you can count how many times the word "help" comes up during the commercials. Instead of going to the bathroom during the pause before Marcus Welby operates, or raiding the refrigerator prior to witnessing the Mod Squad wipe out a nest of dope pushers, stick with it. Count the "helps," and discover just how dirty a four-letter word can be.

LIKE

Coming in second, but only losing by a nose, is the word "like,"   7
used in comparison. Watch:

It's like getting one bar free
Cleans like a white tornado
It's like taking a trip to Portugal

Okay. "Like" is a qualifier, and is used in much the same way as   8
"help." But "like" is also a comparative element, with a very specific purpose; we use "like" to get you to stop thinking about the product per se, and to get you thinking about something that is bigger or better or different from the product we're selling. In other words, we can make you believe that the product is more than it is by likening it to something else.

Take a look at that first phrase, straight out of recent Ivory Soap   9
advertising. On the surface of it, they tell you that four bars of Ivory cost about the same as three bars of most other soaps. So, if you're going to spend a certain amount of money on soap, you can buy four bars instead of three. Therefore, it's like getting one bar free. Now, the question you have to ask yourself is, "Why the weasel? Why do they say 'like'? Why don't they just come out and say, 'You get one bar free'?" The answer is, of course, that for one reason or another, you really don't. Here are two possible reasons. One: sure, you get four bars, but in terms of the actual amount of soap that you get, it may very well be the same as in three bars of another brand. Remember, Ivory has a lot of air in it— that's what makes it float. And air takes up room. Room that could otherwise be occupied by more soap. So, in terms of pure product, the

amount of actual soap in four bars of Ivory may be only as much as the actual amount of soap in three bars of most others. That's why we can't— or won't—come out with a straightforward declaration such as, "You get 25 percent more soap," or "Buy three bars, and get the fourth one free."

Reason number two: the actual cost and value of the product. Did 10 it ever occur to you that Ivory may simply be a cheaper soap to make and, therefore, a cheaper soap to sell? After all, it doesn't have any perfume or hexachlorophene, or other additives that can raise the cost of manufacturing. It's plain, simple, cheap soap, and so it can be sold for less money while still maintaining a profit margin as great as more expensive soaps. By way of illustrating this, suppose you were trying to decide whether to buy a Mercedes-Benz or a Ford. Let's say the Mercedes cost $7,000, and the Ford $3,500. Now the Ford salesman comes up to you with this deal: as long as you're considering spending $7,000 on a car, buy my Ford for $7,000 and I'll give you a second Ford, free! Well, the same principle can apply to Ivory: as long as you're considering spending 35 cents on soap, buy my cheaper soap, and I'll give you more of it.

I'm sure there are other reasons why Ivory uses the weasel "like." 11 Perhaps you've thought of one or two yourself. That's good. You're starting to think.

Now, what about that wonderful white tornado? Ajax pulled that 12 one out of the hat some eight years ago, and you're still buying it. It's a classic example of the use of the word "like" in which we can force you to think, not about the product itself, but about something bigger, more exciting, certainly more powerful than a bottle of fancy ammonia. The word "like" is used here as a transfer word, which gets you away from the obvious—the odious job of getting down on your hands and knees and scrubbing your kitchen floor—and into the world of fantasy, where we can imply that this little bottle of miracles will supply all the elbow grease you need. Isn't that the name of the game? The whirlwind activity of the tornado replacing the whirlwind motion of your arm? Think about the swirling of the tornado, and all the work it will save you. Think about the power of that devastating windstorm; able to lift houses, overturn cars, and now, pick the dirt up off your floor. And we get the license to do it simply by using the word "like."

It's a copywriter's dream, because we don't have to substantiate 13 anything. When we compare our product to "another leading brand," we'd better be able to prove what we say. But how can you compare ammonia to a windstorm? It's ludicrous. It can't be done. The whole statement is so ridiculous it couldn't be challenged by the government or the networks. So it went on the air, and it worked. Because the little word "like" let us take you out of the world of reality, and into your own fantasies.

Speaking of fantasies, how about the trip to Portugal? Mateus Rosé   14
is actually trying to tell you that you will be transported clear across the Atlantic Ocean merely by sipping their wine. "Oh, come on," you say. "You don't expect me to believe that." Actually, we don't expect you to believe it. But we do expect you to get our meaning. This is called "romancing the product," and it is made possible by the dear little "like." In this case, we deliberately bring attention to the word, and we ask you to join us in setting reality aside for a moment. We take your hand and gently lead you down the path of moonlit nights, graceful dancers, and mysterious women. Are we saying that these things are all contained inside our wine? Of course not. But what we mean is, our wine is part of all this, and with a little help from "like," we'll get you to feel that way, too. So don't think of us as a bunch of peasants squashing a bunch of grapes. As a matter of fact, don't think of us at all. Feel with us.

"Like" is a virus that kills. You'd better get immune to it.   15

OTHER WEASELS

"Help" and "like" are the two weasels so powerful that they can   16
stand on their own. There are countless other words, not quite so potent, but equally effective when used in conjunction with our two basic weasels, or with each other. Let me show you a few.

VIRTUAL *or* VIRTUALLY. How many times have you responded to   17
an ad that said:

Virtually trouble-free . . .
Virtually foolproof . . .
Virtually never needs service . . .

Ever remember what "virtual" means? It means "in essence or effect, but not in fact." Important—"but not in fact." Yet today the word "virtually" is interpreted by you as meaning "almost or just about the same as. . . ." Well, gang, it just isn't true. "Not," in fact, means not, in fact. I was scanning, rather longingly I must confess, through the brochure Chevrolet publishes for its Corvette, and I came to this phrase: "The seats in the 1972 Corvette are virtually handmade." They had me, for a minute. I almost took the bait of that lovely little weasel. I almost decided that those seats were just about completely handmade. And then I remembered. Those seats were not, *in fact,* handmade. Remember, "virtually" means "not, in fact," or you will, in fact, get sold down the river.

ACTS *or* WORKS. These two action words are rarely used alone, and   18
are generally accompanied by "like." They need help to work, mostly
because they are verbs, but their implied meaning is deadly, nonetheless.
Here are the key phrases:

Acts like . . .
Acts against . . .
Works like . . .
Works against . . .
Works to prevent (or help prevent) . . .

You see what happens? "Acts" or "works" brings an action to the product
that might not otherwise be there. When we say that a certain cough
syrup "acts on the cough control center," the implication is that the
syrup goes to this mysterious organ and immediately makes it better. But
the implication here far exceeds what the truthful promise should be.
An act is simply a deed. So the claim "acts on" simply means it performs
a deed on. What that deed is, we may never know.

The rule of thumb is this: if we can't say "cures" or "fixes" or use   19
any other positive word, we'll nail you with "acts like" or "works against,"
and get you thinking about something else. Don't.

CAN BE. This is for comparison, and what we do is to find an   20
announcer who can really make it sound positive. But keep your ears
open. "Crest can be of significant value when used in. . . ," etc., is
indicative of an ideal situation, and most of us don't live in ideal situations.

UP TO. Here's another way of expressing an ideal situation. Re-   21
member the cigarette that said it was aged, or "cured for up to eight
long, lazy weeks"? Well, that could, and should, be interpreted as meaning that the tobaccos used were cured anywhere from one hour to eight
weeks. We like to glamorize the ideal situation; it's up to you to bring it
back to reality.

AS MUCH AS. More of the same. "As much as 20 percent greater   22
mileage" with our gasoline again promises the ideal, but qualifies it.

REFRESHES, COMFORTS, TACKLES, FIGHTS, COMES ON. Just a hand-   23
ful of the same action weasels, in the same category as "acts" and "works,"
though not as frequently used. The way to complete the thought here is
to ask the simple question, "How?" Usually, you won't get an answer.
That's because, usually, the weasel will run and hide.

FEEL *or* THE FEEL OF. This is the first of our subjective weasels.   24
When we deal with a subjective word, it is simply a matter of opinion.
In our opinion, Naugahyde has the feel of real leather. So we can say it.
And, indeed, if you were to touch leather, and then touch Naugahyde,

you may very well agree with us. But that doesn't mean it is real leather, only that it feels the same. The best way to handle subjective weasels is to complete the thought yourself, by simply saying, "But it isn't." At least that way you can remain grounded in reality.

THE LOOK OF *or* LOOKS LIKE. "Look" is the same as "feel," our 25 subjective opinion. Did you ever walk into a Woolworth's and see those $29.95 masterpieces hanging in their "Art Gallery"? "The look of a real oil painting," it will say. "But it isn't," you will now reply. And probably be $29.95 richer for it.

Words That Have No Specific Meaning

If you have kids, then you have all kinds of breakfast cereals in the 26 house. When I was a kid, it was Rice Krispies, the breakfast cereal that went snap, crackle, and pop. (One hell of a claim for a product that is supposed to offer nutritional benefits.) Or Wheaties, the breakfast of champions, whatever that means. Nowadays, we're forced to a confrontation with Quisp, Quake, Lucky-Stars, Cocoa-Puffs, Clunkers, Blooies, Snarkles and Razzmatazz. And they all have one thing in common: they're all "fortified." Some are simply "fortified with vitamins," while others are specifically "fortified with vitamin D," or some other letter. But what does it all mean?

"Fortified" means "added on to." But "fortified," like so many other 27 weasel words of indefinite meaning, simply doesn't tell us enough. If, for instance, a cereal were to contain one unit of vitamin D, and the manufacturers added some chemical which would produce two units of vitamin D, they could then claim that the cereal was "fortified with twice as much vitamin D." So what? It would still be about as nutritional as sawdust.

The point is, weasel words with no specific meaning don't tell us 28 enough, but we have come to accept them as factual statements closely associated with something good that has been done to the product. Here's another example.

ENRICHED

We use this one when we have a product that starts out with 29 nothing. You mostly find it in bread, where the bleaching process combined with the chemicals used as preservatives renders the loaves totally void of anything but filler. So the manufacturer puts a couple of drops of vitamins into the batter, and presto! It's enriched. Sounds great when you say it. Looks great when you read it. But what you have to determine is, is it really great? Figure out what information is missing, and then try to supply that information. The odds are, you won't. Even the breakfast cereals that are playing it straight, like Kellogg's Special K, leave something to be desired. They tell you what vitamins you get, and how much of each in one serving. The catch is, what constitutes a serving? They say, one ounce. So now you have to whip out your baby scale and weigh one serving. Do you have an idea how much that is? Maybe you do. Maybe you don't care. Okay, so you polish off this mound of dried stuff, and now what? You have ostensibly received the minimum, repeat, minimum dosage of certain vitamins for the day. One day. And you still have to go find the vitamins you didn't get. Try looking it up on a box of frozen peas. Bet you won't find it. But do be alert to "fortified" and "enriched." Asking the right questions will prove beneficial.

Did you buy that last sentence? Too bad, because I weaseled you, 30 with the word "beneficial." Think about it.

FLAVOR *and* TASTE

These are two totally subjective words that allow us to claim mar- 31 velous things about products that are edible. Every cigarette in the world has claimed the best taste. Every supermarket has advertised the most flavorful meat. And let's not forget "aroma," a subdivision of this category. Wouldn't you like to have a nickel for every time a room freshener (a weasel in itself) told you it would make your home "smell fresh as all outdoors"? Well, they can say it, because smell, like taste and flavor, is a subjective thing. And, incidentally, there are no less than three weasels in that phrase. "Smell" is the first. Then, there's "as" (a substitute for the ever-popular "like"), and, finally, "fresh," which, in context, is a subjective comparison, rather than the primary definition of "new."

Now we can use an unlimited number of combinations of these 32 weasels for added impact. "Fresher-smelling clothes." "Fresher-tasting tobacco." "Tastes like grandma used to make." Unfortunately, there's no sure way of bringing these weasels down to size, simply because you can't define them accurately. Trying to ascertain the meaning of "taste" in any context is like trying to push a rope up a hill. All you can do is be aware that these words are subjective, and represent only one opinion—usually that of the manufacturer.

STYLE *and* GOOD LOOKS

Anyone for buying a new car? Okay, which is the one with the 33 good looks? The smart new styling? What's that you say? All of them?

Well, you're right. Because this is another group of subjective opinions. And it is the subjective and collective opinion of both Detroit and Madison Avenue that the following cars have "bold new styling": Buick Riviera, Plymouth Satellite, Dodge Monaco, Mercury Brougham, and you can fill in the spaces for the rest. Subjectively, you have to decide on which bold new styling is, indeed, bold new styling. Then, you might spend a minute or two trying to determine what's going on under that styling. The rest I leave to Ralph Nader.

DIFFERENT, SPECIAL, *and* EXCLUSIVE

To be different, you have to be not the same as. Here, you must rely on your own good judgment and common sense. Exclusive formulas and special combinations of ingredients are coming at you every day, in every way. You must constantly assure yourself that, basically, all products in any given category are the same. So when you hear "special," "exclusive," or "different," you have to establish two things: on what basis are they different, and is that difference an important one? Let me give you a hypothetical example. 34

All so-called "permanent" antifreeze is basically the same. It is made from a liquid known as ethylene glycol, which has two amazing properties. It has a lower freezing point than water, and a higher boiling point than water. It does not break down (lose its properties), nor will it boil away. And every permanent antifreeze starts with it as a base. Also, just about every antifreeze has now got antileak ingredients, as well as antirust and anticorrosion ingredients. Now, let's suppose that, in formulating the product, one of the companies comes up with a solution that is pink in color, as opposed to all the others, which are blue. Presto— an exclusivity claim. "Nothing else looks like it, nothing else performs like it." Or how about, "Look at ours, and look at anyone else's. You can see the difference our exclusive formula makes." Granted, I'm exaggerating. But did I prove a point? 35

A FEW MORE GOODIES

At Phillips 66, it's performance that counts
Wisk puts its strength where the dirt is
At Bird's Eye, we've got quality in our corner
Delicious and long-lasting, too

Very quickly now, let's deflate those four lines. First, what the hell does "performance" mean? It means that this product will do what any 36 other product in its category will do. Kind of a backhanded reassurance that this gasoline will function properly in your car. That's it, and nothing more. To perform means to function at a standard consistent with the rest of the industry. All products in a category are basically the same.

Second line: What does "strength" or "strong" mean? Does it mean "not weak"? Or "superior in power"? No, it means consistent with the norms of the business. You can bet your first-born that if Wisk were superior in power to other detergents, they'd be saying it, loud and clear. So strength is merely a description of a property inherent in all similar products in its class. If you really want to poke a pin in a bubble, substitute the word "ingredients" for the word "strength." That'll do it every time. 37

Third line: The old "quality" claim, and you fell for it. "Quality" is not a comparison. In order to do that, we'd have to say, "We've got better quality in our corner than any other frozen food." Quality relates only to the subjective opinion that Bird's Eye has of its own products, and to which it is entitled. The word "quality" is what we call a "parity" statement; that is, it tells you that it is as good as any other. Want a substitute? Try "equals," meaning "the same as." 38

Fourth line: How delicious is delicious? About the same as good-tasting is good-tasting, or fresher-smelling is fresher-smelling. A subjective opinion regarding taste, which you can either accept or reject. More fun, though, is "long-lasting." You might want to consider writing a note to Mr. Wrigley, inquiring as to the standard length of time which a piece of gum is supposed to last. Surely there must be a guideline covering it. The longest lasting piece of gum I ever encountered lasted just over four hours, which is the amount of time it took me to get it off the sole of my shoe. Try expressing the line this way: "It has a definite taste, and you may chew it as long as you wish." Does that place it in perspective? 39

There are two other aspects of weasel words that I should mention here. The first one represents the pinnacle of the copywriter's craft, and I call it the "Weasel of Omission." Let me demonstrate: 40

Of America's best-tasting gums, Trident is sugar-free.

Disregard, for a moment, the obvious subjective weasel "best-tasting." Look again at the line. Something has been left out. Omitted very deliberately. Do you know what that word is? The word that's missing is the word "only," which should come right before the name of the product. But it doesn't. It's gone. Left out. And the question is, why? The answer is, the government wouldn't let them. You see, they start out by making a subjective judgment, that their gum is among the best-tasting. 41

That's fine, as far as it goes. That's their opinion, but it is also the opinion of every other maker of sugar-free gum that his product is also among the best-tasting. And, since both of their opinions must be regarded as having equal value, neither one is allowed the superiority claim, which is what the word "only" would do. So Trident left it out. But the sentence is so brilliantly constructed, the word "only" is so heavily implied, that most people hear it, even though it hasn't been said. That's the Weasel of Omission. Constructing a set of words that forces you to a conclusion that otherwise could not have been drawn. Be on the lookout for what isn't said, and try to fill the gaps realistically.

The other aspect of weasels is the use of all those great, groovy, 42 swinging, wonderful, fantastic, exciting and fun-filled words known as adjectives. Your eyes, ears, mind, and soul have been bombarded by adjectives for so long that you are probably numb to most of them by now. If I were to give you a list of adjectives to look out for, it would require the next five hundred pages, and it wouldn't do any good, anyway. More important is to bear in mind what adjectives do, and then to be able to sweep them aside and distinguish only the facts.

An adjective modifies a noun, and is generally used to denote the 43 quality or a quality of the thing named. And that's our grammar lesson for today. Realistically, an adjective enhances or makes more of the product being discussed. It's the difference between "Come visit Copenhagen," and "Come visit beautiful Copenhagen." Adjectives are used so freely these days that we feel almost naked, robbed, if we don't get at least a couple. Try speaking without adjectives. Try describing something; you can't do it. The words are too stark, too bare-boned, too factual. And that's the key to judging advertising. There is a direct, inverse proportion between the number of adjectives and the number of facts. To put it succinctly, the more adjectives we use, the less we have to say.

You can almost make a scale, based on that simple mathematical 44 premise. At one end you have cosmetics, soft drinks, cigarettes, products that have little or nothing of any value to say. So we get them all dressed up with lavish word and thought images, and present you with thirty or sixty seconds of adjectival puffery. The other end of the scale is much harder to find. Usually, it will be occupied by a new product that is truly new or different. . . . Our craving for adjectives has become so overriding that we simply cannot listen to what is known as "nuts and bolts" advertising. The rest falls somewhere in the middle; a combination of adjectives, weasels, and semitruths. All I can tell you is, try to brush the description aside, and see what's really at the bottom.

Summary

A weasel word is a word that's used to imply a meaning that cannot   45
be truthfully stated. Some weasels imply meanings that are not the same
as their actual definition, such as "help," "like," or "fortified." They can
act as qualifiers and/or comparatives. Other weasels, such as "taste" and
"flavor," have no definite meanings, and are simply subjective opinions
offered by the manufacturer. A weasel of omission is one that implies a
claim so strongly that it forces you to supply the bogus fact. Adjectives
are weasels used to convey feelings and emotions to a greater extent than
the product itself can.

In dealing with weasels, you must strip away the innuendos and try   46
to ascertain the facts, if any. To do this, you need to ask questions such
as: How? Why? How many? How much? Stick to basic definitions of
words. Look them up if you have to. Then, apply the strict definition to
the text of the advertisement or commercial. "Like" means similar to, but
not the same as. "Virtually" means the same in essence, but not in fact.

Above all, never underestimate the devious qualities of a weasel.   47
Weasels twist and turn and hide in dark shadows. You must come to grips
with them, or advertising will rule you forever.

My advice to you is: Beware of weasels. They are nasty and untrain-   48
able, and they attack pocketbooks.

Questions for Study and Discussion

1. What are "weasel words"? Why do advertisers find them useful? Why is it
important for the average American to know about weasel words?

2. Why has Stevens chosen the weasel to describe certain types of advertising language; that is, what characteristics does a weasel have that makes this
association appropriate? Explain.

3. Stevens uses the ad for Mateus Rosé as an example of what he calls "romancing the product." What other examples can you think of? Explain how
each one works.

4. Weasel words help make advertising the fine art of deception. In weasels
like "fortified" and "enriched," the advertisers try to convince us they give
us something "extra." Is this true? What happens in the process of bleaching
flour for "white" bread?

5. How does Stevens organize his classification of weasel words? What is the
purpose of the classification? Does his classification help you understand weasel words and how they are used?

6. Advertisers often create similes, direct comparisons using *like* or *as*: "Ajax
cleans *like* a white tornado." What, according to Stevens, is the advertisers'

intent in using the simile? Outside of the advertising world, similes are not normally used to deceive. What value do similes have for you as a student of composition?

7. Stevens has consciously adopted an informal style in this essay; he wishes to create the impression that he is talking to you, his reader. What devices does Stevens use to establish this informal style? How does his choice of words contribute to this informality?

8. The last four paragraphs serve as the conclusion to Stevens's essay. How effective did you find it? Did he seem to repeat too much from the essay itself, or do you think there was a reason for his doing this?

9. What does Stevens say we should do to protect ourselves from the dangers of deceptive language in ads?

Writing Topics

1. Using the phrase "adjectival puffery," Stevens claims that "our craving for adjectives has become so overriding that we simply cannot listen to what is known as 'nuts and bolts' advertising". Examine several written advertisements with a substantial amount of text for examples of adjectival puffery, weasel words, and semitruths. Is Stevens's claim valid? In an essay describe your findings.

2. As Stevens suggests, "tonight when you plop down in front of the boob tube for your customary three and a half hours of violence and/or situation comedies, take a pad and pencil, and keep score". List the weasels that come up during the commercials. Compare your list with those made by others in your class. Write an essay in which you analyze your reactions to the TV commercials now that you are aware of weasel words.

3. Imagine that you are responsible for preparing the first ad for a new product. Let the product be whatever you wish—a car, a soft drink, disposable paper socks, anything—and let it have whatever features you like. How would you advertise it? Write an ad that will *sell* your product. The ad could be for a newspaper or magazine, or it could be the script for a 60-second spot on TV. The important thing is to write *persuasive* copy.

LEWIS CARROLL

Charles Lutwidge Dodgson was born in 1832 at Daresbury, England, in the country between the great northern cities of Manchester and Liverpool. He attended Oxford University, where he earned honors in classics and mathematics and remained as a teacher of mathematics. Like his father before him, he was ordained a minister in the Church of England, but he rarely preached. He is best known as the author of the two fantastic books he wrote under the pseudonym Lewis Carroll: *Alice's Adventures in Wonderland* (1865) and *Through the Looking-Glass* (1871). Originally written for a little girl Dodgson knew, these books stand among the most popular children's stories ever published. Although "Jabberwocky" is included in *Through the Looking-Glass*, it was written in 1855. Dodgson enjoyed creating puzzles and word games, and "Jabberwocky" has something in it of each. Recently, "Jabber-Whacky," a parody of Carroll's famous poem, was brought to our attention. We include it here for both your study and entertainment. As you read both poems try to determine in what ways one is a parody of the other.

Jabberwocky

'Twas brillig, and the slithy toves
Did gyre and gimble in the wabe;
All mimsy were the borogoves,
And the mome raths outgrabe.

"Beware the Jabberwock, my son!   5
The jaws that bite, the claws that catch!
Beware the Jubjub bird, and shun
The frumious Bandersnatch!"

He took his vorpal sword in hand:
Long time the manxome foe he sought—   10
So rested he by the Tumtum tree,
And stood awhile in thought.

And, as in uffish thought he stood,
The Jabberwock, with eyes of flame,
Came whiffling through the tulgey wood,   15
And burbled as it came!

One, two! One, two! And through and through
The vorpal blade went snicker-snack!
He left it dead, and with its head
He went galumphing back.   20

"And hast thou slain the Jabberwock?
Come to my arms, my beamish boy!
O frabjous day! Callooh! Callay!"
He chortled in his joy.

'Twas brillig, and the slithy toves   25
Did gyre and gimble in the wabe;
All mimsy were the borogoves,
And the mome raths outgrabe.

Jabber-Whacky: Or, On Dreaming, After Falling Asleep Watching TV

'Twas Brillo, and the G.E. Stoves,
Did Procter-Gamble in the Glade;
All Pillsbury were the Taystee loaves,
And in a Minute Maid.

"Beware the Station-Break, my son!   5
The voice that lulls, the ads that vex!
Beware the Doctors Claim, and shun
That horror called Brand-X!"

He took his Q'Tip'd swab in hand;
Long time the Tension Headache fought—   10
So Dristan he by a Mercury,
And Bayer-break'd in thought.

And as in Bufferin Gulf he stood,
The Station-Break, with Rise of Tame,
Came Wisking through the Pride-hazed wood,   15
And Creme-Rinsed as it came!

Buy one! Buy two! We're almost through!
The Q-Tip'd Dash went Spic and Span!
He Tide Air-Wick, and with Bisquick
Went Aero-Waxing Ban.   20

"And has thou Dreft the Station-Break?
Ajax the Breck, Excedrin boy!
Oh, Fab wash day, Cashmere Bouquet!"
He Handi-Wrapped with Joy.

'Twas Brillo, and the G.E. Stoves,   25
Did Procter-Gamble in the Glade;
All Pillsbury were the Taystee loaves,
And in a Minute Maid.

                                                      Anonymous

Questions for Study and Discussion

1. According to *Through the Looking-Glass*, toves are "something like badgers—they're something like lizards—and they're something like corkscrews. . . . also they make their nests under sundials—also they live on cheese." But other unusual words are variations on the familiar: *slithy*, for example, means "lithe and slimy." Find two or three such words and explain their derivations and meaning.

2. Find five words in "Jabberwocky" which you think are pure nonsense, and give your own definitions for them, explaining your definitions as best you can.

3. Since it contains nonsense words, is "Jabberwocky" a nonsense poem? Why, or why not? What is it about?

4. What is a parody? In what ways is "Jabber-Whacky" a parody of Lewis Carroll's poem?

5. What point does "Jabber-Whacky" make?

Writing Topics

1. How are readers at all able to understand a nonsense poem like "Jabberwocky"? What would make the poem completely incomprehensible? What does this suggest about other problems of understanding—for example, reading on an unfamiliar subject or trying to follow a conversation in a foreign

language? Write an essay in which you discuss the language principles that make "Jabberwocky" work.

2. Write a short narrative using words you have invented for the purpose, some of them pure nonsense and others combining the sounds and meanings of familiar words. Or write a parody of "Jabberwocky" on an experience or subject of your choice—a meal in a fast food restaurant, perhaps, or a last-minute drive to score in a football game.

7 The Politics of Technology and Science

Plans to protect air and water, wilderness and wildlife are in fact plans to protect man.
STEWART UDALL

Mankind must put an end to war or war will put an end to mankind.
JOHN F. KENNEDY

The Environment

RACHEL CARSON

Rachel Carson (1907–1964) was born in Springdale, Pennsylvania. A zoologist and accomplished writer, she wrote much about the marine world and taught at Johns Hopkins and the University of Maryland. Her delightfully warm and sensitive interpretations of scientific data in *Under the Sea* (1941), *The Sea Around Us* (1951), and *The Edge of the Sea* (1955) made these books very popular. *The Sea Around Us* won Carson the National Book Award. But it was *Silent Spring* (1962), her study of herbicides and insecticides, that made Carson a controversial figure. Carson's allegations prompted President John F. Kennedy to appoint a commission to study the problem of indiscriminate use of pesticides. Once denounced as an alarmist, she is now recognized as having been a powerful force in the ecology movement.

In "The Obligation to Endure," the second chapter of *Silent Spring*, Carson argues for a more responsible use of pesticides.

The Obligation to Endure

The history of life on earth has been a history of interaction be- 1 tween living things and their surroundings. To a large extent, the physical form and the habits of the earth's vegetation and its animal life have been molded by the environment. Considering the whole span of earthly time, the opposite effect, in which life actually modifies its surroundings, has been relatively slight. Only within the moment of time represented by the present century has one species—man—acquired significant power to alter the nature of his world.

During the past quarter century this power has not only increased 2 to one of disturbing magnitude but it has changed in character. The most alarming of all man's assaults upon the environment is the contamination of air, earth, rivers, and sea with dangerous and even lethal materials. This pollution is for the most part irrecoverable; the chain of evil it initiates not only in the world that must support life but in living tissues

543

is for the most part irreversible. In this now universal contamination of the environment, chemicals are the sinister and little recognized partners of radiation in changing the very nature of the world—the very nature of its life. Strontium 90, released through nuclear explosions into the air, comes to earth in rain or drifts down as fallout, lodges in soil, enters the grass or corn or wheat grown there, and in time takes up its abode in the bones of a human being, there to remain until his death. Similarly, chemicals sprayed on croplands or forests or garden lie long in soil, entering into living organisms, passing from one to another in a chain of poisoning and death. Or they pass mysteriously by underground streams until they emerge and through the alchemy of air and sunlight, combine into new forms that kill vegetation, sicken cattle, and work unknown harm on those who drink from once pure wells. As Albert Schweitzer has said, "Man can hardly even recognize the devils of his own creation."

It took hundreds of millions of years to produce the life that now   3
inhabits the earth—eons of time in which that developing and evolving and diversifying life reached a state of adjustment and balance with its surroundings. The environment, rigorously shaping and directing the life it supported, contained elements that were hostile as well as supporting. Certain rocks gave out dangerous radiation; even within the light of the sun, from which all life draws its energy, there were short-wave radiations with power to injure. Given time—time not in years but in millennia—life adjusts, and a balance has been reached. For time is the essential ingredient; but in the modern world there is no time.

The rapidity of change and the speed with which new situations   4
are created follow the impetuous and heedless pace of man rather than the deliberate pace of nature. Radiation is no longer merely the background radiation of rocks, the bombardment of cosmic rays, the ultraviolet of the sun that have existed before there was any life on earth; radiation is now the unnatural creation of man's tampering with the atom. The chemicals to which life is asked to make its adjustment are no longer merely the calcium and silica and copper and all the rest of the minerals washed out of the rocks and carried in rivers to the sea; they are the synthetic creations of man's inventive mind, brewed in his laboratories, and having no counterparts in nature.

To adjust to these chemicals would require time on the scale that   5
is nature's; it would require not merely the years of a man's life but the life of generations. And even this, were it by some miracle possible, would be futile, for the new chemicals come from our laboratories in an endless stream; almost five hundred annually find their way into actual use in the United States alone. The figure is staggering and its implications are not easily grasped—500 new chemicals to which the bodies of

men and animals are required somehow to adapt each year, chemicals totally outside the limits of biologic experience.

Among them are many that are used in man's war against nature. Since the mid-1940's over 200 basic chemicals have been created for use in killing insects, weeds, rodents, and other organisms described in the modern vernacular as "pests"; and they are sold under several thousand different brand names.

6

These sprays, dusts, and aerosols are now applied almost universally to farms, gardens, forests, and homes—nonselective chemicals that have the power to kill every insect, the "good" and the "bad," to still the song of birds and the leaping of fish in the streams, to coat the leaves with a deadly film, and to linger on in soil—all this though the intended target may be only a few weeds or insects. Can anyone believe it is possible to lay down such a barrage of poisons on the surface of the earth without making it unfit for all life? They should not be called "insecticides," but "biocides."

7

The whole process of spraying seems caught up in an endless spiral. Since DDT was released for civilian use, a process of escalation has been going on in which ever more toxic materials must be found. This has happened because insects, in a triumphant vindication of Darwin's principle of the survival of the fittest, have evolved super races immune to the particular insecticide used, hence a deadlier one has always to be developed—and then a deadlier one than that. It has happened also because destructive insects often undergo a "flareback," or resurgence, after spraying, in numbers greater than before. Thus the chemical war is never won, and all life is caught in its violent crossfire.

8

Along with the possibility of the extinction of mankind by nuclear war, the central problem of our age has therefore become the contamination of man's total environment with such substances of incredible potential for harm—substances that accumulate in the tissues of plants and animals and even penetrate the germ cells to shatter or alter the very material of heredity upon which the shape of the future depends.

9

Some would-be architects of our future look toward a time when it will be possible to alter the human germ plasm by design. But we may easily be doing so now by inadvertence for many chemicals, like radiation, bring about gene mutations. It is ironic to think that man might determine his own future by something so seemingly trivial as the choice of an insect spray.

10

All this has been risked—for what? Future historians may well be amazed by our distorted sense of proportion. How could intelligent beings seek to control a few unwanted species by a method that contaminated the entire environment and brought the threat of disease and death even

11

to their own kind? Yet this is precisely what we have done. We have done it, moreover, for reasons that collapse the moment we examine them. We are told that the enormous and expanding use of pesticides is necessary to maintain farm production. Yet is our real problem not one of *overproduction*? Our farms, despite measures to remove acreages from production and to pay farmers *not* to produce, have yielded such a staggering excess of crops that the American taxpayer in 1962 is paying out more than one billion dollars a year as the total carrying cost of the surplus-food storage program. And is the situation helped when one branch of the Agriculture Department tries to reduce production while another states, as it did in 1958, "It is believed generally that reduction of crop acreages under provisions of the Soil Bank will stimulate interest in use of chemicals to obtain maximum production on the land retained in crops"?

All this is not to say there is no insect problem and no need of control. I am saying, rather, that control must be geared to realities, not to mythical situations, and that the methods employed must be such that they do not destroy us along with the insects.

The problem whose attempted solution has brought such a train of disaster in its wake is an accompaniment of our modern way of life. Long before the age of man, insects inhabited the earth—a group of extraordinarily varied and adaptable beings. Over the course of time since man's advent, a small percentage of the more than half a million species of insects have come into conflict with human welfare in two principal ways: as competitors for the food supply and as carriers of human disease.

Disease-carrying insects become important where human beings are crowded together, especially under conditions where sanitation is poor, as in time of natural disaster or war or in situations of extreme poverty and deprivation. Then control of some sort becomes necessary. It is a sobering fact, however, that the method of massive chemical control has had only limited success, and also threatens to worsen the very conditions it is intended to curb.

Under primitive agricultural conditions the farmer had few insect problems. These arose with the intensification of agriculture—the devotion of immense acreages to a single crop. Such a system set the stage for explosive increases in specific insect populations. Single-crop farming does not take advantage of the principles by which nature works; it is agriculture as an engineer might conceive it to be. Nature has introduced great variety into the landscape, but man has displayed a passion for simplifying it. Thus he undoes the built-in checks and balances by which nature holds the species within bounds. One important natural check is a limit on the amount of suitable habitat for each species. Obviously then, an insect that lives on wheat can build up its population to much higher levels on a farm devoted to wheat than on one in which wheat is intermingled with other crops to which the insect is not adapted.

The same thing happens in other situations. A generation or more 16 ago, the towns of large areas of the United States lined their streets with the noble elm tree. Now the beauty they hopefully created is threatened with complete destruction as disease sweeps through the elms, carried by a beetle that would have only limited chance to build up large populations and to spread from tree to tree if the elms were only occasional trees in a richly diversified planting.

Another factor in the modern insect problem is one that must be 17 viewed against a background of geologic and human history: the spreading of thousands of different kinds of organisms from their native homes to invade new territories. This worldwide migration has been studied and graphically described by the British ecologist Charles Elton in his recent book *The Ecology of Invasions*. During the Cretaceous Period, some hundred million years ago, flooding seas cut many land bridges between continents and living things found themselves confined in what Elton calls "colossal separate nature reserves." There, isolated from others of their kind, they developed many new species. When some of the land masses were joined again, about 15 million years ago, these species began to move out into new territories—a movement that is not only still in progress but is now receiving considerable assistance from man.

The importation of plants is the primary agent in the modern spread 18 of species, for animals have almost invariably gone along with the plants, quarantine being a comparatively recent and not completely effective innovation. The United States Office of Plant Introduction alone has introduced almost 200,000 species and varieties of plants from all over the world. Nearly half of the 180 or so major insect enemies of plants in the United States are accidental imports from abroad, and most of them have come as hitchhikers on plants.

In new territory, out of reach of the restraining hand of the natural 19 enemies that kept down its numbers in its native land, an invading plant or animal is able to become enormously abundant. Thus it is no accident that our most troublesome insects are introduced species.

These invasions, both the naturally occurring and those dependent 20 on human assistance, are likely to continue indefinitely. Quarantine and massive chemical campaigns are only extremely expensive ways of buying time. We are faced, according to Dr. Elton, "with a life-and-death need not just to find new technological means of suppressing this plant or that animal"; instead we need the basic knowledge of animal populations and their relations to their surroundings that will "promote an even balance and damp down the explosive power of outbreaks and new invasions."

Much of the necessary knowledge is now available but we do not use it. We train ecologists in our universities and even employ them in our governmental agencies but we seldom take their advice. We allow the chemical death rain to fall as though there were no alternative, whereas in fact there are many, and our ingenuity could soon discover many more if given opportunity.

Have we fallen into a mesmerized state that makes us accept as inevitable that which is inferior or detrimental, as though having lost the will or the vision to demand that which is good? Such thinking, in the words of the ecologist Paul Shepard, "idealizes life with only its head out of water, inches above the limits of toleration of the corruption of its own environment. . . . Why should we tolerate a diet of weak poisons, a home in insipid surroundings, a circle of acquaintances who are not quite our enemies, the noise of motors with just enough relief to prevent insanity? Who would want to live in a world which is just not quite fatal?"

Yet such a world is pressed upon us. The crusade to create a chemically sterile, insect-free world seems to have engendered a fanatic zeal on the part of many specialists and most of the so-called control agencies. On every hand there is evidence that those engaged in spraying operations exercise a ruthless power. "The regulatory entomologists . . . function as prosecutor, judge and jury, tax assessor and collector and sheriff to enforce their own orders," said Connecticut entomologist Neely Turner. The most flagrant abuses go unchecked in both state and federal agencies.

It is not my contention that chemical insecticides must never be used. I do contend that we have put poisonous and biologically potent chemicals indiscriminately into the hands of persons largely or wholly ignorant of their potentials for harm. We have subjected enormous numbers of people to contact with these poisons, without their consent and often without their knowledge. If the Bill of Rights contains no guarantee that a citizen shall be secure against lethal poisons distributed either by private individuals or by public officials, it is surely only because our forefathers, despite their considerable wisdom and foresight, could conceive of no such problem.

I contend, furthermore, that we have allowed these chemicals to be used with little or no advance investigation of their effect on soil, water, wildlife, and man himself. Future generations are unlikely to condone our lack of prudent concern for the integrity of the natural world that supports all life.

There is still very limited awareness of the nature of the threat. This is an era of specialists, each of whom sees his own problem and is unaware of or intolerant of the larger frame into which it fits. It is also an era dominated by industry, in which the right to make a dollar at whatever cost is seldom challenged. When the public protests, confronted with some obvious evidence of damaging results of pesticide applications, it is fed little tranquilizing pills of half truth. We urgently need an end to these false assurances, to the sugar coating of unpalatable facts. It is the public that is being asked to assume the risks that the insect controllers calculate. The public must decide whether it wishes to continue on the present road, and it can do so only when in full possession of the facts. In the words of Jean Rostand, "The obligation to endure gives us the right to know."

Questions for Study and Discussion

1. Humans in the twentieth century have acquired the power to modify their environment. Why does Rachel Carson find this power so disturbing?

2. What is the "chain of evil" (2) that pollution initiates?

3. Why are the "pace of nature" (4) and the "pace of man" (4) in conflict? What problems are caused by this conflict?

4. Carson devotes much of her essay to a critical examination of the use of insecticides to control the insect population. What are her attitudes toward chemical insecticides and insect control?

5. What is the significance of the title that Carson has given this essay?

6. What types of evidence does Carson use to support her argument? Are you convinced by her evidence? Why or why not?

7. An effective strategy in argumentation is to anticipate and refute an opponent's arguments. Where in this essay does Carson employ this strategy? How effective is her use of the strategy?

8. Carson's essay in large part examines "man's war against nature" (6). Identify those words and phrases that Carson uses to develop and sustain the image of warfare. How appropriate, in your opinion, is this dominant image?

9. What is the connotative value of the italicized words or phrases in each of the following excerpts from the essay?

   a. considering the whole span of *earthly time* (1)
   b. the *chain of evil* it initiates (2)
   c. chemicals are the *sinister* and little recognized *partners* of radiation (2)
   d. through the *alchemy* of air and sunlight (2)
   e. man has displayed a *passion* for simplifying it (15)
   f. most of them have come as *hitchhikers* on plants (18)

g. we allow the *chemical death rain* to fall (21)
h. it is surely only because our *forefathers* (24)
i. it is fed little *tranquilizing pills of half truth* (26)
j. *sugar coating* of unpalatable facts (26)

Writing Topics

1. In 1962, Rachel Carson charged that "we have put poisonous and biologically potent chemicals indiscriminately into the hands of persons largely or wholly ignorant of their potentials for harm." The validity of her charge is everywhere evident today. Write an essay about chemical abuse using specific examples that have been brought to our attention in recent years.

2. Choose from your local newspaper an editorial or article dealing with a controversial environmental issue. Outline the issues involved. Now assume that you have been offered equal space in the newspaper in which to present the opposing viewpoint. Consider the types of evidence you would need to do this, and write a rebuttal.

3. Argue for or against the following proposition: We should ban the use of most herbicides and insecticides.

KELLY DAVIS

Kelly Davis was born in Mt. Kisco, New York, and received two degrees from Syracuse University, one in fine arts and another in journalism. Currently she is director of the Council of Parks Friends, an environmental group concerned with parks and public land. She is responsible for developing nature centers and educational programs at parks in central New York. Davis writes a regular column for *Central New York Environment*, a bimonthly newspaper.

"Health and High Voltage," first published in the July-August 1978 issue of the *Sierra Club Bulletin*, alerts us to the dangers of extra-high-voltage transmission lines and offers some suggestions as to what might be done to minimize their potentially dangerous side effects.

Health and High Voltage

Extra-high-voltage (EHV) transmission lines are on the march across North America; 1400 miles of lines are already in operation in the Midwest and 2500 miles in Quebec. There is an extra-high-voltage DC line running from Oregon to Los Angeles. More EHV lines are planned; five lines will crisscross New York, connecting with others in the Northeast. Electricity from coal-burning plants in Wyoming, Montana and North and South Dakota will be carried by massive lines and steel towers to the cities of the Northwest.   1

A transmission line is simply a pipeline for electricity. In the case of a water pipeline, more water will flow through the pipe as water pressure increases. The same is true of electricity. It is transmitted more economically at high voltages; the more power carried, the less current lost along the lines.   2

We've come a long way from the early low-voltage lines strung on telephone poles. The newest transmission lines carry 765,000 volts (765 kilovolts, or kV) of electricity from power plant to transformer, and they represent only a modest advance in transmission technology. Plans are under way to build lines that will carry 1.2 million and 1.5 million volts. But as voltages have increased, the utility companies' understanding of the effects of these new transmission lines hasn't advanced much from the days when they still used wooden poles. The lines are designed under the assumption that they will not affect the people who work or live near them. Evidence is accumulating, however, that extra-high-voltage lines increase biological stress capable of causing hypertension, ulcers, and abnormal growths. The electric fields are a danger to wild animals, mi-   3

551

gratory birds and livestock pastured near the right-of-way. The lines are noisy, especially when damp from rain, snow or fog. Crops growing near them have shown abnormal growth patterns. Uninsulated wires, carrying thousands of volts of electricity as low as 48 feet overhead, can cause potentially harmful shocks.

Robert Becker, a physician and director of the Orthopedic-Bio-   4
physics Laboratory at the Syracuse, New York, Veterans Administration Hospital–Upstate Medical Center, has been researching the effects of low-frequency electric fields (60 Hz) for fifteen years. Testifying at health and safety hearings for proposed lines in New York, he said that exposure to the fields can produce physiological and functional changes in humans—anything from increased irritability and fatigue to raised cholesterol levels, hypertension and ulcers. Studies of rats exposed to low-level electric fields showed tumor growths and abnormalities in development. Dr. Becker believes we are performing unauthorized medical experiments by exposing people to the electromagnetic fields surrounding the transmission lines.

American utility companies do not take the health hazards of extra-   5
high-voltage lines seriously, but the Russians do. Soviet investigators studied the health of 45 people who had worked in 400kV and 500kV switchyards for about four years. Of the 45 subjects, all but four had some type of disorder. The workers complained of headaches, unusual fatigue, sluggishness and reduced sexual potency. These symptoms occurred during and shortly after field exposure and subsided after the workers stayed away from the lines for a while.

The Russians have instituted strict rules for workers on their lines.   6
Workers must be protected by shields or other devices while working. Workers may spend only limited periods of time near the lines. Conditions the Russians consider dangerous extend beyond the limits to the right-of-way, and use of this area is forbidden. In contrast, American utility companies promote use of the right-of-way for farming and recreation.

An American power company representative has claimed that there   7
have been no "outstanding complaints" against lines currently in operation in this country—although many citizens have, in fact, complained. But even the absence of such complaints, according to Dr. Andrew Marino, a biophysicist working with Dr. Becker, would not prove that electric fields are not dangerous. If very dramatic things happened, says Dr. Marino, such as people falling down from shocks, then the effects of the lines would be more obvious and complaints more frequent. But the public might not yet know about subtle effects of extra-high-voltage lines—effects that they might not even associate with the power lines.

In view of the Russian findings and his own studies, Dr. Marino   8
called for a public research program comparable to the Russians' to investigate the specific effects of transmission lines. In view of the vast
environmental impact of proposed new lines, Marino thinks it is difficult
to justify doing anything less.

The power companies have put only a minuscule amount of money   9
into research. The Electric Power Research Institute is conducting a study
of the effect of electrical fields on workers, but it has not produced any
finished reports on transmission lines and the people living near them.
One EPRI report relied solely upon the unsubstantiated opinion of an
examining physician that individuals examined were normal. No data
were cited, nor were any controls employed. Yet this study is used by
American power companies as evidence of the absence of harmful effects
of transmission lines.

The power companies concede that it is possible for the lines to   10
cause electric shocks by inducing currents in metal objects such as wire
fences, but they insist that such shocks are little more than nuisances,
like the static charges one experiences after walking across certain car-
pets. Farmers who live and work near the lines in Ohio think differently.
"It's like being zapped by 110-volt household current," said one. He
stated that even 400 to 500 feet from the line, the shocks can be quite
severe. "I wouldn't send my boys [sixteen and eighteen years old] to work
under the lines alone," he added.

The power companies can ground all stationary objects such as   11
metal buildings, roofs and fences that they think may be a shock hazard;
the companies also suggest the use of grounding chains for vehicles that
regularly use the right-of-way. But farmers have found that the grounding
methods do not always succeed in warding off strong shocks. Farmers
must take care in getting off farm machinery near the lines. School buses
have to be warned not to pick up or discharge children near them. People
using pacemakers must be warned that the lines can interfere with their
operation.

The most hazardous shocks, those that can do physical harm, are   12
the ones that rise above the "let-go" threshold, the point at which a
person loses voluntary muscle control. The threshold is about 9 milliam-
peres (mA, a standard measure of volts against resistance) for men, 6mA
for women and 4.5mA for children. With lines operating at 800kV (lines
operate within 5% of stated capacity) and a 48-foot clearance, a tractor-
trailer would be subjected to 6.5mA and a school bus to 4.2mA under
the lines. The Russians have recommended a maximum exposure of 4.0.
To meet this requirement, clearances of about 70 feet would be needed.

To minimize the environmental impact of all transmission lines,   13
siting guidelines have been set by the Department of the Interior, the
Department of Agriculture, the Federal Power Commission and others.
Transmission routes, they say, should avoid scenic, historic and recreational areas, prime farm and timber lands, population centers and areas
of valuable natural resources. Where, then, to put the towers? The power
companies naturally want the cheapest route, and farmlands are flat,
relatively bare and offer easy access for construction vehicles. Since it is
cheaper to keep the lines as straight as possible, the power companies
will buy an easement through a farm rather than move the towers to the
edge of a property.

It is estimated that 30 miles of lines with a right-of-way 250 feet   14
wide require 1000 acres—and the 765kV lines need a right-of-way at
least 500 feet wide to operate safely.

The towers supporting the 765kV lines are 135 to 200 feet tall, four   15
or more to a mile, with a "wingspread" of 100 feet. Each tower leg is
four feet in diameter, set in five-foot-wide concrete bases.

The construction vehicles and access roads of the utility companies   16
compact the earth. It can take from four to six years to restore the
damaged land to its original productivity. Drainage patterns may change
because of construction and maintenance crew activity.

Farmers have noted changes in corn planted under the lines; the   17
height of the stalks is not affected, but the ears do not mature. Cattle
pastured under the lines lose as many as half their calves. The egg-laying
capacity of hens also has been significantly altered. As one farmer put
it, "What are they going to do when our farms die, eat electricity?"

Power lines produce a continuous humming and crackling sound   18
that turns into a loud roar when they get wet. The noise 400 feet away
from the line sounds like a small waterfall. Power companies have said
that one of the key factors in assessing public acceptability of the lines
will be the noise. Company figures show 53dB(A) (decibels as perceived
by human hearing) at the edge of a 250-foot right-of-way, but others say
it is nearer 70dB(A). At 60dB(A), one must shout in order to be heard.

A nationally known expert on noise from Stanford University, Dr.   19
Karl Kryter, says that sleep disturbances will occur in some people when
the level reaches only 34dB(A). Long-term effect of exposure to the noise
from extra-high-voltage transmission lines is not known. Americans are
exposed to twice as much noise today as twenty years ago. Clinical evidence shows that excessive exposure to noise constricts the arteries, increases the heartbeat and dilates the pupils of the eye.

Building heavier lines with more cables per bundle would reduce   20
noise as well as radio and TV interference but would be more costly.

Cables for 765kV transmission are made of aluminum reinforced with steel. They consist of a bundle of four conductors, each about 1.3 inches in diameter, approximately 18 inches apart; each circuit is composed of three parallel conductor bundles.

The utilities will build the lightest lines acceptable. In some cases, 21 power companies have come to the agencies for permits only after spending large sums of money on equipment. Faced with a *fait accompli*, power commissions rarely demand costly changes in design.

What are the alternatives to a nationwide grid of potentially dan- 22 gerous, environmentally unsound, land-gulping power lines? Should we delay certification of all proposed extra-high-voltage lines until an adequate research program has resolved questions of their safety?

Transmission lines are used to carry electricity from generating source 23 to consumer. Locating the two closer together, as energy experts such as Amory Lovins have suggested, would eliminate the need for many of the lines. Advocates of decentralized energy call for more smaller local plants and less reliance on energy generated in one region and consumed in another. One problem is that it is cheaper to burn coal at a mine and transport electricity on expensive lines than to ship the coal to plants nearer cities, where compliance with clean-air laws may be more difficult. But should cities be allowed to escape the consequences of their energy consumption in this way?

Extra-high-voltage lines are also well suited to transmitting the high 24 outputs of electricity from nuclear power plants and, in fact, may be designed with that use in mind.

Utilities will argue that increasing the "interties" among their power 25 systems reduces the need for extra capacity within individual systems, thus requiring fewer power plants; the interties permit moving energy from places with excess capacity to areas where power is short because of heavy peak demands or equipment failure.

Where transmission of electricity cannot be avoided, better plan- 26 ning would create a safer and more efficient system. More research and investment is necessary to develop national safety standards. Superconductors (metals that carry power without heat or energy loss) could make present 345kV lines more effective, and eliminate the need for higher-voltage lines; towers can be designed to be more attractive; noise and shock hazards can be reduced.

But the ultimate answer to more and potentially dangerous lines is 27 the conservation of energy. Power companies have a vested interest in expanding their business. The more power they sell, the more profit they make, since state regulations fix profit margins for utility companies at a percentage of total investment.

Forecasts of electricity demand should be made by independent   28
agencies. We should insist that incentives for conservation of energy be
built into rate systems. We should support the decentralization of power
systems, the development of alternative—and safer—sources of energy
closer to the people who will eventually use the energy. In these ways
we can resist the degradation of the land by higher-voltage power lines.

Questions for Study and Discussion

1. Why have utility companies begun to use extra-high-voltage transmission
lines to carry electricity?

2. Identify the potential health and environmental hazards associated with
extra-high-voltage transmission lines.

3. Why does Davis find fault with the American utility companies?

4. What solutions to the prospect of "a nationwide grid of potentially dangerous . . . power lines" (22) does Davis suggest? What, in Davis's view, is
"the ultimate answer" (27)?

5. Davis claims that the harmful effects of extra-high-voltage transmission
lines are (1) biological stress, (2) electric fields, (3) noise, (4) abnormal
growth patterns in crops, and (5) harmful shocks. What types of evidence
does she use to substantiate her claims?

6. Davis anticipates and answers possible counterarguments to her own views.
Identify several passages in which she does this, and explain how this strategy
helps her argument.

7. What evidence do you find in Davis's diction to suggest that her attitude
toward utilities is less than objective?

8. Identify the analogy that Davis uses early in the essay, and explain how it
works.

Writing Topics

1. In "Health and High Voltage" Davis writes that safety, health, and environmental concerns should take precedence over economic factors. Even
though most Americans would seem to agree with Davis's position, in practice economic factors seem always to be of primary importance. Write an
essay in which you analyze what you think the reasons are for this alarming
situation.

2. With the increasing awareness of the detrimental effects of pollution in
general, the controversy over smoking and health has become more complex.
No longer can smokers be concerned only with their health, because non-
smokers now argue that their right to clean air is infringed upon when they
are forced to be in the company of smokers. Write an essay in which you
argue for the individual's right to clean air not polluted by tobacco smoke,
and that smoking should be limited to specific areas on your campus.

A. B. C. WHIPPLE

As our world becomes increasingly industrialized we gradually become more and more accustomed to the by-products of such industrialization—acid rain, choking smog, ground-water contamination, and the barges that take our tons of daily garbage out to sea for dumping. It is when we travel to the unspoiled areas of the world, however, that we become conscious of just how polluted our home environment has become. Such was the case with A. B. C. Whipple in 1970 when an oil spill reached the beaches near his home in the Bahamas. His essay, which appeared in *Life* magazine, describes the coming of pollution to this Caribbean paradise and attempts to analyze the economic and technological forces at the root of the problem.

An Ugly New Footprint in the Sand

There were strangers on our beach yesterday, for the first time in a month. A new footprint on our sand is nearly as rare as in *Robinson Crusoe*. We are at the very edge of the Atlantic; half a mile out in front of us is a coral reef, and then nothing but 3,000 miles of ocean to West Africa. It is a wild and lonely beach, with the same surf beating on it as when Columbus came by. And yet the beach is polluted. 1

Oil tankers over the horizon have fouled it more than legions of picnickers could. The oil comes ashore in floating patches that stain the coral black and gray. It has blighted the rock crabs and the crayfish and has coated the delicate whorls of the conch shells with black goo. And it has congealed upon itself, littering the beach with globes of tar that resemble the cannonballs of a deserted battlefield. The islanders, as they go beachcombing for the treasures the sea has washed up for centuries, now wear old shoes to protect their feet from the oil that washes up too. 2

You have to try to get away from pollution to realize how bad it really is. We have known for the last few years how bad our cities are. Now there is no longer an escape. If there is oil on this island far out in the Atlantic, there is oil on nearly every other island. 3

It is still early here. The air is still clear over the island, but it won't be when they build the airstrip they are talking about. The water out over the reef is still blue and green, but it is dirtier than it was a few years ago. And if the land is not despoiled, it is only because there are not yet enough people here to despoil it. There will be. And so for the moment on this island we are witnesses to the beginning, as it were, of the pollution of our environment. 4

When you watch a bird over the beach or a fish along the reef you   5
realize how ill-adapted man is to this environment anyway. Physically
there is nothing he can do that some other creature cannot do better.
Only his neocortex, the "thinking cap" on top of his brain, has enabled
him to invent and construct artificial aids to accomplish what he could
not do by himself. He cannot fly, so he developed airplanes that can go
faster than birds. He is slower than the horse, so he invented the wheel
and the internal combustion engine. Even in his ancestral element, the
sea, he is clumsy and short of breath. Without his brain, his artificial
aids, his technology, he would have been unable to cope with, even
survive in, his environment. But only after so many centuries is his brain
dimly realizing that while he has managed to control his environment,
he has so far been unable to protect it.

Perhaps he simply is not far enough up the evolutionary ladder to   6
survive on this planet for very much longer. To take only two of his
inefficient physical functions, he is so far unable to control either his
body wastes or his population. Man is a natural polluter, and his invention of the bathroom and the incinerator has, it now becomes evident,
only postponed the problem. On this island we burn our papers, bury
our tin cans and dump our garbage in the bay. It is not very efficient and
perhaps not even very civilized. Yet so long as there are only a few people
here, it has no ill effects. But when the inevitable wave of population
sweeps out from the mainland, the islanders will face the problem of their
own pollution just as the New Yorker does today.

Man's sexual construction is perhaps the biggest accident of his   7
physical makeup: it is only now becoming obvious—when it may well be
too late—that it would have been better if he required artificial aid to
have children, rather than to *avoid* having them.

Until the pollution of our deserted beach, it seemed simple to blame   8
everything on the "population explosion." If the population of this island, for example, could be stabilized at a couple of hundred, there would
be very little problem with the environment in this secluded area. There
would be no pollution of the environment if there were not too many
people using it. And so if we concentrate on winning the war against
overpopulation, we can save the earth for mankind.

But the oil on the beach belies this too-easy assumption. Those   9
tankers are not out there because too many Chinese and Indians are
being born every minute. They are not even out there because there are
too many Americans and Europeans. They are delivering their oil, and
cleaning their tanks at sea and sending the residue up onto the beaches
of the Atlantic and Pacific, in order to fuel the technology of mankind—
and the factories and the power plants, the vehicles and the engines that

have enabled mankind to survive on his planet are now spoiling the planet for life.

The fishermen on this island are perfectly right in preferring the   10
outboard motor to the sail. Their livelihood is involved, and the motor for all its fouling smell, has helped increase the fisherman's catch so that he can now afford to dispense with the far more obnoxious outdoor privy. But the danger of technology is in its escalation, and there has already been a small amount of escalation here. You can see the motor oil slicks around the town dock. Electric generators can be heard over the sound of the surf. And while there are only about two dozen automobiles for the ten miles of road, already there is a wrecked jeep rusting in the harbor waters where it was dumped and abandoned. The escalation of techno-logical pollution is coming here just as surely as it came to the mainland cities that are now shrouded by fly ash.

If the oil is killing the life along the coral heads, what must it not   11
be doing to the phytoplankton at sea which provide 70% of the oxygen we breathe? The lesson of our fouled beach is that we may not even have realized how late it is already. Mankind, because of his technology, may require far more space per person on this globe than we had ever thought, but it is more than a matter of a certain number of square yards per person. There is instead a delicate balance of nature in which many square miles of ocean and vegetation and clean air are needed to sustain only a relatively few human beings. We may find, as soon as the end of this century, that the final despoliation of our environment has been signaled not by starvation but by people choking to death. The tech-nology—the machine—will then indeed have had its ultimate, mindless, all-unintended triumph over man, by destroying the atmosphere he lives in just as surely as you can pinch off a diver's breathing tube.

Sitting on a lonely but spoiled beach, it is hard to imagine but   12
possible to believe.

Questions for Study and Discussion

1. What is Whipple's thesis in this essay? Where does he state it?

2. What is Whipple's attitude toward population? Toward technology? What, specifically, in the text led you to your conclusions? What does Whipple see as the relationship among population, technology, and pollution?

3. Explain the allusions in Whipple's opening paragraph. Why do you sup-pose he chose these particular allusions to introduce his essay?

4. The ocean tankers are the primary cause of the oil pollution on the beach. What, according to Whipple, is the primary cause? Do you agree with his assessment? Explain.

5. If we are unable to protect our environment, to bring pollution under control, what might be the chain of environmental events that we could expect in the future, according to Whipple?

6. "Now there is no longer an escape," Whipple writes in paragraph 3. What does he mean?

Writing Topics

1. Whipple calls humans natural polluters. Using examples from your own experience, observation, and reading, develop this idea in an essay.

2. As a library project, do some reading in one of the following subject areas:
   a. the importation of oil
   b. relaxation of federal pollution standards
   c. offshore oil drilling
   d. strip mining
   e. soil conservation
   f. wilderness areas

   Develop a position statement based on your research and write an argumentative essay in which you support your statement.

MICHAEL BROWN

Born in 1952, Michael Brown is a free-lance writer whose articles have appeared in such popular magazines as *Atlantic Monthly, Saturday Review, New York,* and *Penthouse.* In his most recent book, *Marked to Die,* he tells of one government informant's experiences with the witness protection program. It is for his investigations of environmental issues, however, that he has established a reputation. His investigative reporting on the dumping of toxic wastes has won him three Pulitzer Prize nominations and an award from the Environmental Protection Agency.

Like Rachel Carson before him, Brown is very seriously concerned with the indiscriminate use and careless disposal of toxic chemicals in our environment. In his book *Laying Waste: The Poisoning of America by Toxic Chemicals* (1980), Brown gives an account of the irresponsible waste-disposal practices of industry across America and the awesome difficulty of controlling pollutants in our environment. The following article gives an account of what happened when the Hooker Chemical Company dumped huge quantities of hazardous chemicals into the Love Canal in Niagara Falls, New York.

Love Canal and the Poisoning of America

Niagara Falls is a city of unmatched natural beauty; it is also a tired industrial workhorse, beaten often and with a hard hand. A magnificent river—a strait, really—connecting Lake Erie to Lake Ontario flows hurriedly north, at a pace of a half-million tons a minute, widening into a smooth expanse near the city before breaking into whitecaps and taking its famous 186-foot plunge. Then it cascades through a gorge of overhung shale and limestone to rapids higher and swifter than anywhere else on the continent.   1

The falls attract long lines of newlyweds and other tourists. At the same time, the river provides cheap electricity for industry; a good stretch of its shore is now filled with the spiraled pipes of distilleries, and the odors of chlorine and sulfides hang in the air.   2

Many who live in the city of Niagara Falls work in chemical plants, the largest of which is owned by the Hooker Chemical Company, a subsidiary of Occidental Petroleum since the 1960s. Timothy Schroeder did not. He was a cement technician by trade, dealing with the factories only if they needed a pathway poured, or a small foundation set. Tim and his wife, Karen, lived in a ranch-style home with a brick and wood exterior at 460 99th Street. One of the Schroeders' most cherished pur-   3

561

chases was a Fiberglas pool, built into the ground and enclosed by a redwood fence.

Karen looked from a back window one morning in October 1974,   4
noting with distress that the pool had suddenly risen two feet above the
ground. She called Tim to tell him about it. Karen then had no way of
knowing that this was the first sign of what would prove to be a punishing
family and economic tragedy.

Mrs. Schroeder believed that the cause of the uplift was the unusual   5
groundwater flow of the area. Twenty-one years before, an abandoned
hydroelectric canal directly behind their house had been backfilled with
industrial rubble. The underground breaches created by this disturbance,
aided by the marshland nature of the region's surficial layer, collected
large volumes of rainfall and undermined the back yard. The Schroeders
allowed the pool to remain in its precarious position until the following
summer and then pulled it from the ground, intending to pour a new
pool, cast in cement. This they were unable to do, for the gaping ex-
cavation immediately filled with what Karen called "chemical water,"
rancid liquids of yellow and orchid and blue. These same chemicals had
mixed with the groundwater and flooded the entire yard, attacking the
redwood posts with such a caustic bite that one day the fence simply
collapsed. When the chemicals receded in the dry weather, they left the
gardens and shrubs withered and scorched, as if by a brush fire.

How the chemicals got there was no mystery. In the late 1930s, or   6
perhaps early 1940s, the Hooker Company, whose many processes included the manufacture of pesticides, plasticizers, and caustic soda, began
using the abandoned canal as a dump for at least 20,000 tons of waste
residues—"still-bottoms," in the language of the trade.

Karen Schroeder's parents had been the first to experience problems   7
with the canal's seepage. In 1959, her mother, Aileen Voorhees, encountered a strange black sludge bleeding through the basement walls.
For the next twenty years, she and her husband, Edwin, tried various
methods of halting the irritating intrusion, pasting the cinder-block wall
with sealants and even constructing a gutter along the walls to intercept
the inflow. Nothing could stop the chemical smell from permeating the
entire household, and neighborhood calls to the city for help were fruitless. One day, when Edwin punched a hole in the wall to see what was
happening, quantities of black liquid poured from the block. The cinder
blocks were full of the stuff.

More ominous than the Voorhees basement was an event that oc-   8
curred at 11:12 P.M. on November 21, 1968, when Karen Schroeder gave
birth to her third child, a seven-pound girl named Sheri. No sense of
elation filled the delivery room. The child was born with a heart that

beat irregularly and had a hole in it, bone blockages of the nose, partial deafness, deformed ear exteriors, and a cleft palate. Within two years, the Schroeders realized Sheri was also mentally retarded. When her teeth came in, a double row of them appeared on her lower jaw. And she developed an enlarged liver.

The Schroeders considered these health problems, as well as ill-   9 nesses among their other children, as acts of capricious genes—a vicious quirk of nature. Like Mrs. Schroeder's parents, they were concerned that the chemicals were devaluing their property. The crab apple tree and evergreens in the back were dead, and even the oak in front of the home was sick; one year, the leaves had fallen off on Father's Day.

The canal had been dug with much fanfare in the late nineteenth   10 century by a flamboyant entrepreneur named William T. Love, who wanted to construct an industrial city with ready access to water power and major markets. The setting for Love's dream was to be a navigable power channel that would extend seven miles from the Upper Niagara before falling two hundred feet, circumventing the treacherous falls and at the same time providing cheap power. A city would be constructed near the point where the canal fed back into the river, and he promised it would accommodate half a million people.

So taken with his imagination were the state's leaders that they   11 gave Love a free hand to condemn as much property as he liked, and to divert whatever amounts of water. Love's dream, however, proved grander than his resources, and he was eventually forced to abandon the project after a mile-long trench, ten to forty feet deep and generally twenty yards wide, had been scoured perpendicular to the Niagara River. Eventually, the trench was purchased by Hooker.

Few of those who, in 1977, lived in the numerous houses that had   12 sprung up by the site were aware that the large and barren field behind them was a burial ground for toxic waste. Both the Niagara County Health Department and the city said it was a nuisance condition, but no serious danger to the people. Officials of the Hooker Company refused comment, claiming only that they had no records of the chemical burials and that the problem was not their responsibility. Indeed, Hooker had deeded the land to the Niagara Falls Board of Education in 1953, for a token $1. With it the company issued no detailed warnings of the chemicals, only a brief paragraph in the quitclaim document that disclaimed company liability for any injuries or deaths which might occur at the site.

Though Hooker was undoubtedly relieved to rid itself of the con-   13 taminated land, the company was so vague about the hazards involved that one might have thought the wastes would cause harm only if touched, because they irritated the skin; otherwise, they were not of great concern. In reality, as the company must have known, the dangers of these wastes far exceeded those of acids or alkalines or inert salts. We now know that the drums Hooker had dumped in the canal contained a veritable witch's brew—compounds of truly remarkable toxicity. There were solvents that attacked the heart and liver, and residues from pesticides so dangerous that their commercial sale was shortly thereafter restricted outright by the government; some of them were already suspected of causing cancer.

Yet Hooker gave no hint of that. When the board of education, which wanted the parcel for a new school, approached Hooker, B. Klaussen, at the time Hooker's executive vice president, said in a letter to the board. "Our officers have carefully considered your request. We are very conscious of the need for new elementary schools and realize that the sites must be carefully selected. We will be willing to donate the entire strip of property which we own between Colvin Boulevard and Frontier Avenue to be used for the erection of a school at a location to be determined. . . ."   14

The board built the school and playground at the canal's midsection. Construction progressed despite the contractor's hitting a drainage trench that gave off a strong chemical odor and the discovery of a waste pit nearby. Instead of halting the work, the authorities simply moved the school eighty feet away. Young families began to settle in increasing numbers alongside the dump, many of them having been told that the field was to be a park and recreation area for their children.   15

Children found the "playground" interesting, but at times painful. They sneezed, and their eyes teared. In the days when the dumping was still in progress, they swam at the opposite end of the canal, occasionally arriving home with hard pimples all over their bodies. Hooker knew children were playing on its spoils. In 1958, three children were burned by exposed residues on the canal's surface, much of which, according to residents, had been covered with nothing more than fly ash and loose dirt. Because it wished to avoid legal repercussions, the company chose not to issue a public warning of the dangers it knew were there, nor to have its chemists explain to the people that their homes would have been better placed elsewhere.   16

The Love Canal was simply unfit as a container for hazardous substances, poor even by the standards of the day, and now, in 1977, local authorities were belatedly finding that out. Several years of heavy snowfall and rain had filled the sparingly covered channel like a bathtub. The contents were overflowing at a frightening rate.   17

The city of Niagara Falls, I was assured, was planning a remedial drainage program to halt in some measure the chemical migration off the   18 site. But no sense of urgency had been attached to the plan, and it was stalled in red tape. No one could agree on who should pay the bill—the city, Hooker, or the board of education—and engineers seemed confused over what exactly needed to be done.

Niagara Falls City Manager Donald O'Hara persisted in his view   19
that, however displeasing to the eyes and nose, the Love Canal was not a crisis matter, mainly a question of aesthetics. O'Hara reminded me that Dr. Francis Clifford, county health commissioner, supported that opinion.

With the city, the board, and Hooker unwilling to commit them-   20
selves to a remedy, conditions degenerated in the area between 97th and 99th streets, until, by early 1978, the land was a quagmire of sludge that oozed from the canal's every pore. Melting snow drained the surface soot onto the private yards, while on the dump itself the ground had softened to the point of collapse, exposing the crushed tops of barrels. Beneath the surface, masses of sludge were finding their way out at a quickening rate, constantly forming springs of contaminated liquid. The Schroeder back yard, once featured in a local newspaper for its beauty, had reached the point where it was unfit even to walk upon. Of course, the Schroeders could not leave. No one would think of buying the property. They still owed on their mortgage and, with Tim's salary, could not afford to maintain the house while they moved into a safer setting. They and their four children were stuck.

Apprehension about large costs was not the only reason the city   21
was reluctant to help the Schroeders and the one hundred or so other families whose properties abutted the covered trench. The city may also have feared distressing Hooker. To an economically depressed area, the company provided desperately needed employment—as many as 3000 blue-collar jobs and a substantial number of tax dollars. Hooker was speaking of building a $17 million headquarters in downtown Niagara Falls. So anxious were city officials to receive the new building that they and the state granted the company highly lucrative tax and loan incentives, and made available to the firm a prime parcel of property near the most popular tourist park on the American side.

City Manager O'Hara and other authorities were aware of the na-   22
ture of Hooker's chemicals. In fact, in the privacy of his office, O'Hara, after receiving a report on the chemical tests at the canal, had informed the people at Hooker that it was an extremely serious problem. Even earlier, in 1976, the New York State Department of Environmental Conservation had been made aware that dangerous compounds were present in the basement sump pump of at least one 97th Street home, and soon after, its own testing had revealed that highly injurious halogenated hy-

drocarbons were flowing from the canal into adjoining sewers. Among them were the notorious PCBs; quantities as low as one part PCBs to a million parts normal water were enough to create serious environmental concerns; in the sewers of Niagara Falls, the quantities of halogenated compounds were thousands of times higher. The other materials tracked, in sump pumps or sewers, were just as toxic as PCBs, or more so. Prime among the more hazardous ones was residue from hexachlorocyclopentadiene, or C-56, which was deployed as an intermediate in the manufacture of several pesticides. In certain dosages, the chemical could damage every organ in the body.

While the mere presence of C-56 should have been cause for alarm, 23
government remained inactive. Not until early 1978—a full eighteen months after C-56 was first detected—was testing conducted in basements along 97th and 99th streets to see if the chemicals had vaporized off the sump pumps and walls and were present in the household air.

While the basement tests were in progress, the rains of spring ar- 24
rived at the canal, further worsening the situation. Heavier fumes rose above the barrels. More than before, the residents were suffering from headaches, respiratory discomforts, and skin ailments. Many of them felt constantly fatigued and irritable, and the children had reddened eyes. In the Schroeder home, Tim developed a rash along the backs of his legs. Karen could not rid herself of throbbing pains in her head. Their daughter, Laurie, seemed to be losing some of her hair.

The EPA test revealed that benzene, a known cause of cancer in 25
humans, had been readily detected in the household air up and down the streets. A widely used solvent, benzene was known in chronic-exposure cases to cause headaches, fatigue, loss of weight, and dizziness followed by pallor, nose-bleeds, and damage to the bone marrow.

No public announcement was made of the benzene hazard. Instead, 26
officials appeared to shield the finding until they could agree among themselves on how to present it.

Dr. Clifford, the county health commissioner, seemed unconcerned 27
by the detection of benzene in the air. His health department refused to conduct a formal study of the people's health, despite the air-monitoring results. For this reason, and because of the resistance growing among the local authorities, I went to the southern end of 99th Street to take an informal health survey of my own. I arranged a meeting with six neighbors, all of them instructed beforehand to list the illnesses they were aware of on their block, with names and ages specified for presentation at the session.

The residents' list was startling. Though unafflicted before they 28
moved there, many people were now plagued with ear infections, nervous

disorders, rashes, and headaches. One young man, James Gizzarelli, said he had missed four months of work owing to breathing troubles. His wife was suffering epileptic-like seizures which her doctor was unable to explain. Meanwhile, freshly applied paint was inexplicably peeling from the exterior of their house. Pets too were suffering, most seriously if they had been penned in the back yards nearest to the canal, constantly breathing air that smelled like mothballs and weedkiller. They lost their fur, exhibited skin lesions, and, while still quite young, developed internal tumors. A great many cases of cancer were reported among the women, along with much deafness. On both 97th and 99th streets, traffic signs warned passing motorists to watch for deaf children playing near the road.

Evidence continued to mount that a large group of people, perhaps all of the one hundred families immediately by the canal, perhaps many more, were in imminent danger. While watching television, while gardening or doing a wash, in their sleeping hours, they were inhaling a mixture of damaging chemicals. Their hours of exposure were far longer than those of a chemical factory worker, and they wore no respirators or goggles. Nor could they simply open a door and escape. Helplessness and despair were the main responses to the blackened craters and scattered cinders behind their back yards.   29

But public officials often characterized the residents as hypochondriacs. Every agent of government had been called on the phone or sent pleas for help, but none offered aid.   30

Commissioner Clifford expressed irritation at my printed reports of illness, and disagreement began to surface in the newsroom on how the stories should be printed. "There's a high rate of cancer among my friends," Dr. Clifford argued. "It doesn't mean anything."   31

Yet as interest in the small community increased, further revelations shook the neighborhood. In addition to the benzene, eighty or more other compounds were found in the makeshift dump, ten of them potential carcinogens. The physiological effects they could cause were profound and diverse. At least fourteen of them could impact on the brain and central nervous system. Two of them, carbon tetrachloride and chlorobenzene, could readily cause narcotic or anesthetic consequences. Many others were known to cause headaches, seizures, loss of hair, anemia, or skin rashes. Together, the compounds were capable of inflicting innumerable illnesses, and no one knew what new concoctions were being formulated by their mixture underground.   32

Edwin and Aileen Voorhees had the most to be concerned about. When a state biophysicist analyzed the air content of their basement, he determined that the safe exposure time there was less than 2.4 minutes—   33 the toxicity in the basement was thousands of times the acceptable limit for twenty-four-hour breathing. This did not mean they would necessarily become permanently ill, but their chances of contracting cancer, for example, had been measurably increased. In July, I visited Mrs. Voorhees for further discussion of her problems, and as we sat in the kitchen, drinking coffee, the industrial odors were apparent. Aileen, usually chipper and feisty, was visibly anxious. She stared down at the table, talking only in a lowered voice. Everything now looked different to her. The home she and Edwin had built had become their jail cell. Their yard was but a pathway through which toxicants entered the cellar walls. The field out back, that proposed "park," seemed destined to be the ruin of their lives.

On July 14 I received a call from the state health department with   34
some shocking news. A preliminary review showed that women living at the southern end had suffered a high rate of miscarriages and had given birth to an abnormally high number of children with birth defects. In one age group, 35.3 percent had records of spontaneous abortions. That was far in excess of the norm. The odds against it happening by chance were 250 to one. These tallies, it was stressed, were "conservative" figures. Four children in one small section of the neighborhood had documentable birth defects, club feet, retardation, and deafness. Those who lived there the longest suffered the highest rates.

The data on miscarriages and birth defects, coupled with the other   35
accounts of illness, finally pushed the state's bureaucracy into motion. A meeting was scheduled for August 2, at which time the state health commissioner, Dr. Robert Whalen, would formally address the issue. The day before the meeting, Dr. Nicholas Vianna, a state epidemiologist, told me that residents were also incurring some degree of liver damage. Blood analyses had shown hepatitis-like symptoms in enzyme levels. Dozens if not hundreds of people, apparently, had been adversely affected.

In Albany, on August 2, Dr. Whalen read a lengthy statement in   36
which he urged that pregnant women and children under two years of age leave the southern end of the dump site immediately. He declared the Love Canal an official emergency, citing it as a "great and imminent peril to the health of the general public."

When Commissioner Whalen's words hit 97th and 99th streets, by   37
way of one of the largest banner headlines in the Niagara *Gazette*'s 125-year history, dozens of people massed on the streets, shouting into bullhorns and microphones to voice frustrations that had been accumulating for months. Many of them vowed a tax strike because their homes were rendered unmarketable and unsafe. They attacked their government for ignoring their welfare. A man of high authority, a physician with a title,

had confirmed that their lives were in danger. Most wanted to leave the neighborhood immediately.

Terror and anger roiled together, exacerbated by Dr. Whalen's failure to provide a government-funded evacuation plan. His words were only a recommendation: individual families had to choose whether to risk their health and remain, or abandon their houses and, in so doing, write off a lifetime of work and savings.

On August 3, Dr. Whalen decided he should speak to the people. He arrived with Dr. David Axelrod, a deputy who had directed the state's investigation, and Thomas Frey, a key aide to Governor Hugh Carey.

At a public meeting, held in the 99th Street School auditorium, Frey was given the grueling task of controlling the crowd of 500 angry and frightened people. In an attempt to calm them, he announced that a meeting between the state and the White House had been scheduled for the following week. The state would propose that the Love Canal be classified a national disaster, thereby freeing federal funds. For now, however, he could promise no more. Neither could Dr. Whalen and his staff of experts. All they could say was what was already known: twenty-five organic compounds, some of them capable of causing cancer, were in their homes, and because young children were especially prone to toxic effects, they should be moved to another area.

Dr. Whalen's order had applied only to those living at the canal's southern end, on its immediate periphery. But families living across the street from the dump site, or at the northern portion, where the chemicals were not so visible at the surface, reported afflictions remarkably similar to those suffered by families whose yards abutted the southern end. Serious respiratory problems, nervous disorders, and rectal bleeding were reported by many who were not covered by the order.

Throughout the following day, residents posted signs of protest on their front fences or porch posts. "Love Canal Kills," they said, or "Give Me Liberty, I've Got Death." Emotionally exhausted and uncertain about their future, men stayed home from work, congregating on the streets or comforting their wives. By this time the board of education had announced it was closing the 99th Street School for the following year, because of its proximity to the exposed toxicants. Still, no public relief was provided for the residents.

Another meeting was held that evening, at a firehall on 102nd Street. It was unruly, but the people, who had called the session in an effort to organize themselves, managed to form an alliance, the Love Canal Homeowners Association, and to elect as president Lois Gibbs, a pretty, twenty-seven-year-old woman with jet-black hair who proved remarkably adept at dealing with experienced politicians and at keeping the matter in the news. After Mrs. Gibbs's election, Congressman John LaFalce entered the hall and announced, to wild applause, that the Federal Disaster Assistance Administration would be represented the next morning, and that the state's two senators, Daniel Patrick Moynihan and Jacob Javits, were working with him in an attempt to get funds from Congress.

With the Love Canal story now attracting attention from the national media, the Governor's office announced that Hugh Carey would be at the 99th Street School on August 7 to address the people. Decisions were being made in Albany and Washington. Hours before the Governor's arrival, a sudden burst of "urgent" reports from Washington came across the newswires. President Jimmy Carter had officially declared the Hooker dump site a national emergency. 44

Hugh Carey was applauded on his arrival. The Governor announced that the state, through its Urban Development Corporation, planned to purchase, at fair market value, those homes rendered uninhabitable by the marauding chemicals. He spared no promises. "You will not have to make mortgage payments on homes you don't want or cannot occupy. Don't worry about the banks. The state will take care of them." By the standards of Niagara Falls, where the real estate market was depressed, the houses were in the middle-class range, worth from $20,000 to $40,000 apiece. The state would assess each house and purchase it, and also pay the costs of moving, temporary housing during the transition period, and special items not covered by the usual real estate assessment, such as installation of telephones. 45

First in a trickle and then, by September, in droves, the families gathered their belongings and carted them away. Moving vans crowded 97th and 99th streets. Linesmen went from house to house disconnecting the telephones and electrical wires, while carpenters pounded plywood over the windows to keep vandals away. By the following spring, 237 families were gone; 170 of them had moved into new houses. In time the state erected around a six-block residential area a green chain-link fence, eight feet in height, clearly demarcating the contamination zone. 46

In October 1978, the long-awaited remedial drainage program began at the south end. Trees were uprooted, fences and garages torn down, and swimming pools removed from the area. So great were residents' apprehensions that dangerous fumes would be released over the surrounding area that the state, at a cost of $500,000, placed seventy-five buses at emergency evacuation pickup spots during the months of work, in the event that outlying homes had to be vacated quickly because of an explosion. The plan was to construct drain tiles around the channel's periphery, where the back yards had been located, in order to divert leakage 47 to seventeen-foot-deep wet wells from which contaminated groundwater could be drawn and treated by filtration through activated carbon. (Removing the chemicals themselves would have been financially prohibitive, perhaps costing as much as $100 million—and even then the materials would have to be buried elsewhere.) After the trenching was complete, and the sewers installed, the canal was to be covered by a sloping mound of clay and planted with grass. One day, city officials hoped, the wasteland would become a park.

In spite of the corrective measures and the enormous effort by the state health department, which took thousands of blood samples from past and current residents and made uncounted analyses of soil, water, and air, the full range of the effects remained unknown. In neighborhoods immediately outside the official "zone of contamination," more than 500 families were left near the desolate setting, their health still in jeopardy. The state announced it would buy no more homes.

The first public indication that chemical contamination had probably reached streets to the east and west of 97th and 99th streets, and to the north and south as well, came on August 11, 1978, when sump-pump samples I had taken from 100th and 101st streets, analyzed in a laboratory, showed the trace presence of a number of chemicals found in the canal itself, including lindane, a restricted pesticide that had been suspected of causing cancer in laboratory animals. While probing 100th Street, I had knocked on the door of Patricia Pino, thirty-four, a blond divorcee with a young son and daughter. I had noticed that some of the leaves on a large tree in front of her house exhibited a black oiliness much like that on the trees and shrubs of 99th Street; she was located near what had been a drainage swale.

After I had extracted a jar of sediment from her sump pump for the analysis, we conversed about her family situation and what the trauma now unfolding meant to them. Ms. Pino was extremely depressed and embittered. Both of her children had what appeared to be slight liver abnormalities, and her son had been plagued with "non-specific" allergies, teary eyes, sinus trouble, which improved markedly when he was sent away from home. Patricia told of times, during the heat of summer, when fumes were readily noticeable in her basement and sometimes even upstairs. She herself had been treated for a possibly cancerous condition on her cervix. But, like others, her family was now trapped.

On September 24, 1978, I obtained a state memorandum that said chemical infiltration of the outer regions was significant indeed. The letter, sent from the state laboratories to the U.S. Environmental Protection Agency, said, "Preliminary analysis of soil samples demonstrates extensive migration of potentially toxic materials outside the immediate canal area." There it was, in the state's own words. Not long afterward, the state medical investigator, Dr. Nicholas Vianna, reported indications that residents from 93rd to 103rd streets might also have incurred liver damage.

On October 4, a young boy, John Allen Kenny, who lived quite a   52
distance north of the evacuation zone, died. The fatality was due to the failure of another organ that can be readily affected by toxicants, the kidney. Naturally, suspicions were raised that his death was in some way related to a creek that still flowed behind his house and carried, near an outfall, the odor of chlorinated compounds. Because the creek served as a catch basin for a portion of the Love Canal, the state studied an autopsy of the boy. No conclusions were reached. John Allen's parents, Norman, a chemist, and Luella, a medical research assistant, were unsatisfied with the state's investigation, which they felt was "superficial." Luella said, "He played in the creek all the time. There had been restrictions on the older boys, but he was the youngest and played with them when they were old enough to go to the creek. We let him do what the other boys did. He died of nephrosis. Proteins were passing through his urine. Well, in reading the literature, we discovered that chemicals can trigger this. There was no evidence of infection, which there should have been, and there was damage to his thymus and brain. He also had nosebleeds and headaches, and dry heaves. So our feeling is that chemicals probably triggered it."

The likelihood that water-carried chemicals had escaped from the   53
canal's deteriorating bounds and were causing problems quite a distance from the site was not lost upon the Love Canal Homeowners Association and its president, Lois Gibbs, who was attempting to have additional families relocated. Because she lived on 101st Street, she was one of those left behind, with no means of moving despite persistent medical difficulties in her six-year-old son, Michael, who had been operated on twice for urethral strictures. [Mrs. Gibbs' husband, a worker at a chemical plant, brought home only $150 a week, she told me, and when they subtracted from that the $90 a week for food and other necessities, clothing costs for their two children, $125 a month for mortgage payments and taxes, utility and phone expenses, and medical bills, they had hardly enough cash to buy gas and cigarettes, let alone vacate their house.]

Assisted by two other stranded residents, Marie Pozniak and Grace   54
McCoulf, and with the professional analysis of a Buffalo scientist named Beverly Paigen, Lois Gibbs mapped out the swale and creekbed areas, many of them long ago filled, and set about interviewing the numerous people who lived on or near formerly wet ground. The survey indicated that these people were suffering from an abnormal number of kidney and

bladder aggravations and problems of the reproductive system. In a report to the state, Dr. Paigen claimed to have found, in 245 homes outside the evacuation zone, thirty-four miscarriages, eighteen birth defects, nineteen nervous breakdowns, ten cases of epilepsy, and high rates of hyperactivity and suicide.

In their roundabout way, the state health experts, after an elaborate investigation, confirmed some of the homeowners' worst fears. On February 8, 1979, Dr. David Axelrod, who by then had been appointed health commissioner, and whose excellence as a scientist was widely acknowledged, issued a new order that officially extended the health emergency of the previous August, citing high incidences of birth deformities and miscarriages in the areas where creeks and swales had once flowed, or where swamps had been. With that, the state offered to evacuate temporarily those families with pregnant women or children under the age of two from the outer areas of contamination, up to 103rd Street. But no additional homes would be purchased; nor was another large-scale evacuation, temporary or otherwise, under consideration. Those who left under the new plan would have to return when their children passed the age limit. 55

Twenty-three families accepted the state's offer. Another seven families, ineligible under the plan but of adequate financial means to do so, simply left their homes and took the huge loss of investment. Soon boarded windows speckled the outlying neighborhoods. 56

The previous November and December, not long after the evacuation of 97th and 99th streets, I became interested in the possibility that Hooker might have buried in the Love Canal waste residues from the manufacture of what is known as 2,4,5-trichlorophenol. My curiosity was keen because I knew that this substance, which Hooker produced for the manufacture of the antibacterial agent hexachlorophene, and which was also used to make defoliants such as Agent Orange, the herbicide employed in Vietnam, carries with it an unwanted by-product technically called 2,3,7,8-tetrachlorodibenzo-para-dioxin, or tetra dioxin. The potency of dioxin of this isomer is nearly beyond imagination. Although its toxicological effects are not fully known, the few experts on the subject estimate that if three ounces were evenly distributed and subsequently ingested among a million people, or perhaps more than that, all of them would die. It compares in toxicity to the botulinum toxin. On skin contact, dioxin causes a disfiguration called "chloracne," which begins as pimples, lesions, and cysts, but can lead to calamitous internal damage. Some scientists suspect that dioxin causes cancer, perhaps even malignancies that occur, in galloping fashion, within a short time of contact. At least two (some estimates went as high as eleven) pounds of dioxin 57 were dispersed over Seveso, Italy, in 1976, after an explosion at a tri-chlorophenol plant: dead animals littered the streets, and more than 300 acres of land were immediately evacuated. In Vietnam, the spraying of Agent Orange, because of the dioxin contaminant, was banned in 1970, when the first effects on human beings began to surface, including diox-in's powerful teratogenic, or fetus-deforming, effects.

I posed two questions concerning trichlorophenol: Were wastes from the process buried in the canal? If so, what were the quantities?   58

On November 8, before Hooker answered my queries, I learned   59
that, indeed, trichlorophenol had been found in liquids pumped from the remedial drain ditches. No dioxin had been found yet, and some officials, ever wary of more emotionalism among the people, argued that, because the compound was not soluble in water, there was little chance it had migrated off-site. Officials at Newco Chemical Waste Systems, a local waste disposal firm, at the same time claimed that if dioxin had been there, it had probably been photolytically destroyed. Its half-life, they contended, was just a few short years.

I knew from Whiteside, however, that in every known case, waste   60
from 2,4,5-trichlorophenol carried dioxin with it. I also knew that dioxin *could* become soluble in groundwater and migrate into the neighborhood upon mixing with solvents such as benzene. Moreover, because it had been buried, sunlight would not break it down.

On Friday, November 10, I called Hooker again to urge that they   61
answer my questions. Their spokesman, Bruce Davis, came to the phone and, in a controlled tone, gave me the answer: His firm had indeed buried trichlorophenol in the canal—200 tons of it.

Immediately I called Whiteside. His voice took on an urgent tone.   62
According to his calculation, if 200 tons of trichlorophenol were there, in all likelihood they were accompanied by 130 pounds of tetra dioxin, an amount equaling the estimated total content of dioxin in the thou-sands of tons of Agent Orange rained upon Vietnamese jungles. The seriousness of the crisis had deepened, for now the Love Canal was not only a dump for highly dangerous solvents and pesticides; it was also the broken container for one of the most toxic substances ever synthesized by man.

I reckoned that the main danger was to those working on the re-   63
medial project, digging in the trenches. The literature on dioxin indi-cated that, even in quantities at times too small to detect, the substance possessed vicious characteristics. In one case, workers in a trichloro-phenol plant had developed chloracne, although the substance could not be traced on the equipment with which they worked. The mere tracking of minuscule amounts of dioxin on a pedestrian's shoes in Seveso led to

major concerns, and, according to Whiteside, a plant in Amsterdam, upon being found contaminated with dioxin, had been "dismantled, brick by brick, and the material embedded in concrete, loaded at a specially constructed dock, on ships, and dumped at sea, in deep water near the Azores." Workers in trichlorophenol plants had died of cancer or severe liver damage, or had suffered emotional and sexual disturbances.

Less than a month after the first suspicions arose, on the evening of December 9, I received a call from Dr. Axelrod. "We found it. The dioxin. In a drainage trench behind 97th Street. It was in the part-per-trillion range."   64

The state remained firm in its plans to continue the construction, and, despite the ominous new findings, no further evacuations were announced. During the next several weeks, small incidents of vandalism occurred along 97th and 99th streets. Tacks were spread on the road, causing numerous flat tires on the trucks. Signs of protest were hung in the school. Meetings of the Love Canal Homeowners Association became more vociferous. Christmas was near, and in the association's office at the 99th Street School, a holiday tree was decorated with bulbs arranged to spell "DIOXIN."   65

The Love Canal people chanted and cursed at meetings with the state officials, cried on the telephone, burned an effigy of the health commissioner, traveled to Albany with a makeshift child's coffin, threatened to hold officials hostage, sent letters and telegrams to the White House, held days of mourning and nights of prayer. On Mother's Day this year, they marched down the industrial corridor and waved signs denouncing Hooker, which had issued not so much as a statement of remorse. But no happy ending was in store for them. The federal government was clearly not planning to come to their rescue, and the state felt it had already done more than its share. City Hall was silent and remains silent today. Some residents still hoped that, miraculously, an agency of government would move them. All of them watched with anxiety as each newborn came to the neighborhood, and they looked at their bodies for signs of cancer.   66

One hundred and thirty families from the Love Canal area began leaving their homes last August and September, seeking temporary refuge in local hotel rooms under a relocation plan funded by the state which had been implemented after fumes became so strong, during remedial trenching operations, that the United Way abandoned a care center it had opened in the neighborhood.   67

As soon as remedial construction is complete, the people will probably be forced to return home, as the state will no longer pay for their lodging. Some have threatened to barricade themselves in the hotels.   68

Some have mentioned violence. Anne Hillis of 102nd Street, who told reporters her first child had been born so badly decomposed that doctors could not determine its sex, was so bitter that she threw table knives and a soda can at the state's on-site coordinator.

In October, Governor Carey announced that the state probably would buy an additional 200 to 240 homes, at an expense of some $5 million. In the meantime, lawyers have prepared lawsuits totaling about $2.65 billion and have sought court action for permanent relocation. Even if the latter action is successful, and they are allowed to move, the residents' plight will not necessarily have ended. The psychological scars are bound to remain among them and their children, along with the knowledge that, because they have already been exposed, they may never fully escape the Love Canal's insidious grasp. 69

Questions for Study and Discussion

1. What was the original purpose of the Love Canal? Why was the project abandoned?

2. Why did the Hooker Chemical Company purchase the Love Canal? What were their reasons for disposing of the property?

3. In paragraphs 2–9 Brown gives us the example of the Schroeder family by way of introducing his subject. In what ways is this example both an interesting and appropriate introduction?

4. Why do you think that the town fathers were slow to act against the Hooker Chemical Company when evidence of toxic contamination started to surface? Do you think they were justified?

5. What information finally caused the state's bureaucracy to move on the disaster at Love Canal?

6. Anyone would agree that the tragic story of Love Canal is of great national importance. What is there in Brown's account of the unfolding events at Love Canal that is especially effective and memorable? How does Brown manage to capture the frustrations, the agony, and sense of helplessness that the residents experienced during their ordeal?

7. How did Brown come to suspect that dioxin was present among the toxins? What was the response of the Hooker Chemical Company to his inquiries? Why did the presence of dioxin escalate the urgency of the situation?

Writing Topics

1. Write an essay in which you examine the Love Canal disaster not as an environmental problem but in terms of economics, politics, and negligence.

2. Imagine yourself a homeowner in a neighborhood in which toxic contam-

ination is discovered. Based on your reading of Brown's article, write an essay in which you propose a plan of action for you and your neighbors.

3. For a longer essay or report, you may wish to update events concerning Love Canal. Brown's report was published in 1979. What has happened in the intervening years? What reports have been issued with regard to further health problems? What action has been taken by the EPA? What events have taken place in the courts? What has the Hooker Chemical Company said or done about the tragedy?

JOHN J. McKETTA

John J. McKetta was born in Wyano, Pennsylvania in 1915. A professor of chemical engineering at the University of Texas at Austin, McKetta holds degrees from Tri-State College in Angola, Indiana and the University of Michigan. In addition to having served as the dean of the School of Engineering and executive vice chancellor for academic affairs at the University of Texas at Austin, McKetta has served on numerous advisory boards and commissions, among them the Texas Atomic Energy Commission, the National Air Quality Control Management Committee, and the National Energy Policy Commission.

In "Will Our World Survive?" McKetta shares with us some facts he has learned regarding current beliefs about our environment. Clearly an advocate for business and science, he argues that we are not on the brink of ecological disaster.

Will Our World Survive?

There is an entire spectrum from zero to infinity, of views and actions on almost any problem.

Let's take the pollution problem, for example. We all know there are still some companies and cities who put toxic gases and liquids into our air and streams. It's almost unbelievable that many of our large cities still discharge raw sewage, or only partially treated sewage into our streams. Both industry and the cities should be stopped immediately from these flagrant violations.

On the other extreme, we have those people who wish to have distilled water in the streams and zero particulates in the atmosphere. These are impossible concentrations and could not be attained even if we had no people on this earth. The answer, obviously, is somewhere between these two extremes.

We're all deeply concerned about reports of the destruction of our environment as a result of technological recklessness, overpopulation, and the lack of consideration to the preservation of nature. As chairman of the National Air Quality Management Committee, I have to read great amounts of technical literature in this area. I've turned up a lot of information that I'd like to share with you.

578

Is Our Oxygen Really Disappearing?

My first surprise concerns the air we breathe. You have been reading   5
that we are seriously depleting the oxygen in the atmosphere and replacing it with toxic substances such as carbon monoxide.

We've always been taught that oxygen in our atmosphere is supplied   6
by green plants using the process of photosynthesis. We know that plants
take in carbon dioxide and through activation by sunlight, combine CO_2
with water to make starches and cellulose, and give off oxygen. In this
way the whole chain of plant and animal life is sustained by energy from
the sun. When the vegetable or animal materials thus produced are eaten,
burned, or allowed to decay they combine with oxygen and return to the
carbon dioxide and water from whence they came. We all know this.
Then, what is the surprise?

Surprise number one is that most of the oxygen in the atmosphere   7
doesn't come from photosynthesis. The evidence is now overwhelming
that photosynthesis is just inadequate to have produced the amount of
oxygen that is present in our atmosphere. The amount of oxygen produced by photosynthesis is just exactly enough to convert the plant tissue
back to the carbon dioxide and water from which it came. The net gain
in oxygen due to photosynthesis is extremely small. The oxygen in the
atmosphere had to come from another source. The most likely possibility
involves the photodissociation of water vapor in the upper atmosphere by
high energy rays from the sun and by cosmic rays.

This means that the supply of oxygen in the atmosphere is virtually   8
unlimited. It is not threatened by man's activities in any significant way.
If all the organic material on earth were oxidized, it would reduce the
atmospheric concentration of oxygen by less than 1 per cent. We can
forget the depletion of oxygen in the atmosphere and get on with the
solution of more serious problems.

Will Carbon Monoxide Kill Us All?

As you know, the most toxic component of automobile exhaust is   9
carbon monoxide. Each year man adds 270 million tons of carbon monoxide to the atmosphere. Most of this comes from automobiles.

People are concerned about the accumulation of this toxic material   10
because they know that it has a life in dry air of about three years. Mon-
itoring stations on land and sea have been measuring the carbon monoxide content of the atmosphere.

Since there are nine times more automobiles in the northern hemi- 11
sphere than in the southern hemisphere it is expected that the northern
hemisphere will have a much higher concentration of atmospheric carbon
monoxide. The true measurements show, however, that there is no difference in CO amounts between the hemispheres and that the overall
concentration in the air is not increasing at all. In fact they've found
higher concentrations of CO over the Atlantic and Pacific oceans than
over land.

Early in 1971 scientists at the Stanford Research Institute in Palo 12
Alto disclosed that they had done some experiments in smog cham-
bers containing soil. They reported that carbon monoxide rapidly disappeared from the chamber. After sterilizing the soil they found that the
carbon monoxide did not disappear. They quickly identified that organisms were responsible for CO disappearance. These organisms, on a world
wide basis, are using all of the 270 million tons of the CO made by man
for their own metabolism, thus enriching the soils of the forest and the
fields.

This does not say carbon monoxide is any less toxic. It does say 13
that, in spite of man's activities, carbon monoxide will never build up in
the atmosphere to a dangerous level except on a localized basis. To put
things in perspective, let me point out that the average concentration of
CO in Austin, Texas, is about 1.5 parts per million. In downtown Houston, in heavy traffic, it sometimes builds up to 15 or 20 p.p.m. In Los
Angeles it gets to be as high as 35 p.p.m. In parking garages and tunnels
it is sometimes 50 p.p.m.

Here lies surprise number two for you—do you know that the CO 14
content of cigarette smoke is as high as 42,000 p.p.m.? The CO concentration in practically any smoke-filled room grossly exceeds the safety
standards we allow in our laboratories. Of course 35 to 50 p.p.m. CO
should not be ignored but there are so many of us who subject ourselves
to CO concentrations voluntarily (and involuntarily) that are greater than
those of our worse polluted cities, including those in the Holland Tunnel
in New York, without any catastrophic effects. It it not at all unusual for
CO concentrations to reach 100–200 p.p.m. range in poorly ventilated,
smoke-filled rooms. Incidentally, if a heavy smoker spends several hours
without smoking in highly polluted city air containing 35 p.p.m. of CO
concentration, the concentration of CO in his blood will actually decrease. In the broad expanses of our natural air, CO levels are totally safe
for human beings. We all know that we should not start our automobiles
in closed unventilated garages.

Will Oxides of Nitrogen Choke Us to Death?

One cannot help but be extremely impressed by the various research 15
efforts on the part of petroleum, automotive, and chemical companies to
remove oxides of nitrogen from the products of combustion in the tail
pipe gas of our automobiles. You've read about the brilliant work of Dr.
Haagen-Smit that showed that the oxides of nitrogen play a critical role
in the chain reaction of photochemical smog formation in Los Angeles.
Oxides of nitrogen are definitely problems in places where temperature
inversions trap the air.

But we've all known for many years that nature also produces oxides 16
of nitrogen.

The number three surprise (and shock) is that most of the oxides of 17
nitrogen come from nature. If we consider only nitric oxide and nitrogen
dioxide the best estimates are 97 per cent is natural and only 3 per cent
is man made. If we also consider nitrous oxide and amines, then it turns
out that 99 plus per cent is natural and less than 1 per cent is man made.

The significance of this is that even if we are 100 per cent successful 18
in our removal of the oxides of nitrogen from combustion bases, we will
still have more than 99 per cent left in the atmosphere which is produced
by nature.

Did Lake Erie Really Succumb?

We've all read for some time that Lake Erie is dead. It's true that 19
the beaches are no longer safe in the Cleveland area and the oxygen
content at the bottom of the lake is decreasing. This is called eutrophication. The blame has been placed on phosphates as the cause of this
situation. Housewives were urged to curb the use of phosphate detergents.
In fact, for several years phosphate detergents were taken off the market.
There's been a change in law since scientific evidence proved that the
phosphate detergents were not the only culprits and never should have
been removed from the market in the first place.

Some studies show clearly that the cause of the eutrophication of 20
Lake Erie has not been properly defined. This evidence suggests that if
we totally stopped using phosphate detergents it would have no effect
whatever on the eutrophication of Lake Erie. Many experiments have
now been carried out that bring surprise number four—that it is the organic carbon content from sewage that is using up the oxygen in the lake
and not the phosphates in the detergents. One must be extremely careful

in these studies since the most recent report by Dr. D. W. Shindler states that phosphorus is the culprit rather than the organic carbon. But the reason that the Cleveland area beaches are not swimmable is that the coliform bacterial count is too high, not that there is too much detergent in the water.

Enlarged and improved sewage treatment facilities by Detroit, Toledo, Sandusky, and Cleveland will be required to correct this situation. Our garbage disposal units do far more to pollute Lake Erie than do the phosphate detergents. If we put in the proper sewage treatment facilities, the lake will sparkle blue again in a very few years. [21]

Incidentally, we've all heard that Lake Superior is so much larger, cleaner, and nicer than Lake Erie. It's kind of strange then to learn that in 1972 and 1973 more tons of commercial fish were taken from Lake Erie than were taken from Lake Superior. [22]

Is DDT Really Our Deadly Foe?

DDT and other chlorinated compounds are supposedly endangering the lives of mankind and eliminating some bird species by the thinning of the egg shells of birds. There is a big question mark as to whether or not this is true. Even if it is true, it's quite possible that the desirable properties of DDT so greatly outnumber the undesirable ones that it might prove to be a serious mistake to ban entirely this remarkable chemical. [23]

Many of you heard of Dr. Norman E. Borlaug, the Nobel Peace Prize winner. He is opposed to the banning of DDT. Obviously he is a competent scientist. He won the Nobel prize because he was able to develop a new strain of wheat that can double the food production per acre anywhere in the world that it is grown. [24]

Dr. Borlaug said "If DDT is banned in the United States, I have wasted my life's work. I have dedicated myself to finding better methods of feeding the world's starving population. Without DDT and other important agricultural chemicals, our goals are simply unattainable." [25]

DDT has had a miraculous impact on arresting insect borne diseases and increasing grain production from fields once ravaged by insects. According to the World Health Organization, malaria fatalities alone dropped from 4 million a year in the 1930s to less than 1 million per year in 1968. Other insect borne diseases, such as encephalitis, yellow fever, and typhus fever showed similar declines. [26]

Surprise number five is that it has been estimated that 100 million human beings who would have died of these afflictions are alive today [27] because of DDT. Incidentally, recent tests indicate that the thinning of bird egg shells may have been caused by mercury compounds rather than DDT. . . .

Many people feel that mankind is the one responsible for the disappearance of animal species. The abundance of evidence indicates that he has very little to do with it. About 50 species are expected to disappear during this century. It is also true that 50 species became extinct last century and 50 species the century before that and so on.

Dr. T. H. Jukes of the University of California points out that about 100 million species of plant and animal life have become extinct since life began on this planet, about 3 billion years ago. Animals come and animals disappear. This is the essence of evolution as Mr. Darwin pointed out many years ago. Mankind is a relatively recent visitor here.

Surprise number six is that one of man's failures is that he has not been successful in eliminating a single insect species—in spite of his all-out war on certain undesirable ones in recent years.

Is Mankind the Real Polluter?

Here's the seventh surprise! The late Dr. William Pecora reported that all of man's air pollution during his thousands of years of life on earth does not equal the amount of particulate and noxious gases from just three volcanoes (Krakatoa, near Java—1883; Mt. Katmai, Alaska—1912; Hekla, Iceland—1947).

Dr. Pecora pointed out that nature's pure water is not so pure after all. Here are a few examples:

1. The natural springs feeding the Arkansas and Red Rivers carry approximately 17 tons of salt per minute.

2. The Lemonade Springs in New Mexico carry approximately 900 pounds H_2SO_4 per million pounds of water. (This is more than ten times the acid concentration in coal mine discharges.)

3. The Mississippi River carries over 2 million tons of natural sediment into the Gulf of Mexico each day.

4. The Paria River of Arizona and Utah carries as much as 500 times more natural sediment per unit volume than the Mississippi River. The Mississippi sediment concentration ranges from 100 to 1,000 mg. per liter. The Paria River concentration has been measured as high as 780,000 mg. per liter during 1973.

Should We Go Back to the Good Old Days?

Dr. Isaac Asimov admonishes us not to believe the trash about the   33
happy lives that people once had before all this nasty industrialization
came along. There was no such thing. One of his neighbors once asked
him "What has all these 2,000 years of development of industry and civilization done for us? Wouldn't we have been happier in 100 B.C.?" Dr.
Asimov said "No, chances are 97 out of 100 that, if you were not a poor
slave, you'd be a poor farmer, living at bare subsistence level."

When people think of ancient times, they think of themselves as   34
members of aristocracy. They are never slaves, never peasants, but that's
what most of them would be.

My wife once said to me "If we lived a hundred years ago we'd have   35
no trouble getting servants." I said, "If we'd lived 150 years ago, we'd be
the servants."

Let's consider what life was really like in America just 150 years   36
ago. For one thing we didn't have to worry about pollution very long—
because life was very brief. Life expectancy of males was about 38 years.
The work week was 72 hours. The women's lot was even worse. They
worked 98 hours a week scrubbing floors, making clothes by hand, bringing in fire wood, cooking in heavy iron pots, fighting off insects without
pesticides. Most of the clothes were rags by present day standards. There
were no fresh vegetables in winter. Vitamin deficiency diseases were prevalent. Homes were cold in winter and sweltering in the summer.

Epidemics were expected yearly and chances were high that they   37
would carry off some members of the immediate family. If you think the
water pollution is bad now, it was deadly then. In 1793 one person in
every five in the city of Philadelphia died in a single epidemic of typhoid
as a result of polluted water. Many people of that time never heard a
symphony orchestra or traveled more than 20 miles from their birthplace
during their entire lifetime. Many informed people do not want to return
to the "paradise" of 150 years ago. Perhaps the simple life was not so
simple.

Are Nuclear Plants Latter Day Witches?

Dr. A. Letcher Jones points out that in every age we have people   38
practicing witchcraft in one form or another. We all think the people of
New England were irrational in accusing certain women of being witches
without evidence to prove it.

Suppose someone accused you of being a witch? How could you 39
prove you were not? It is impossible to prove unless you can give evidence. It is precisely this same witchcraft practice that is being used to deter the construction of nuclear power plants. The opponents are saying these plants are witches and it is up to the builders and owners to prove they are not. The scientific evidence is that nuclear power plants constructed to date are the cleanest and least polluting devices for generating electricity so far developed by man. We need electricity to maintain the standard of living we have reached, but to the extreme environmentalists we are witches. We should be burned at the stake.

We hear the same accusations about lead compounds from the gas- 40
oline engine. Our Environmental Protection Agency has no evidence that there has ever been a single case of death, or even illness, from lead in the air coming from burning of gasoline, but they still insist we remove the lead from gasoline.

To the EPA we are witches. They have no evidence—no proof— 41
we are pronounced guilty! And yet you know gasoline needs some additives to prevent engine knocks. If we don't use tetraethyl-lead we'll have to use aromatic compounds. Some aromatics are carcinogenic. We know that! The use of unleaded gasoline also can use up to 12 per cent more crude oil. (Incidentally, the real reason for removing lead from gasoline was because it was suspected that lead poisoned the catalyst in the emission control unit. Now we have some evidence that it isn't the lead but ethylene bromide which is the poisoner.)

Is There Real Hope for Our Survival?

From what we read and hear it would seem we are on the edge of 42
impending doom. A scientific evaluation of the evidence does not support this conclusion. Of course we have many undesirable problems attributed to technological activities. The solution of these problems will require a technical understanding of their nature, not through emotion. They cannot be solved unless properly identified, which will require more technically trained people—not less.

Thomas Jefferson said if the public is properly informed, the people 43
will make wise decisions. The public has not been getting all of the facts on matters relating to ecology. This is the reason some of us are speaking out on this subject today—as technical people and as citizens.

In summary, let me state we are not on the brink of ecological dis- 44
aster. Our O_2 is not disappearing. There will be no build up of poisonous CO. The waters can be made pure again by adequate sewage treatment

plants. The disappearance of species is natural. A large percentage of pollution is natural pollution and would be here whether or not man was on this earth. We cannot solve our real problems unless we attack them on the basis of what we know rather than what we don't know. Let us use our knowledge and not our fears to solve the real problems of our environment.

Questions for Study and Discussion

1. What are the seven surprises McKetta offers in his essay? Why does he call them "surprises"? Did any of these seven pieces of information actually surprise you? Explain.

2. On what grounds does McKetta reject the notion that the "good old days" were, in fact, good?

3. What happens to the 270 million tons of carbon monoxide that man produces each year?

4. Explain how the witchcraft analogy in paragraphs 38–41 works. Do you think the analogy is an effective one? Explain.

5. McKetta identifies himself as the chairman of the National Air Quality Management Committee, but does not identify himself as the chairman of the Texas Atomic Energy Commission. Does this new information alter your sense of his fairness in dealing with these issues, especially the nuclear power issue?

6. McKetta is obviously a proponent of technology. What is his tone in this essay? Is his tone appropriate for his audience and subject matter? Explain.

7. Most readers would agree that McKetta has made a technical subject accessible to a general audience. How has he managed to accomplish this? Consider his diction, tone, organization, and his introduction and conclusion. Has he been equally successful throughout his essay?

Writing Topics

1. Today many people, especially environmentalists, do not have a favorable opinion of industry and technology. In fact, some have gone so far as to suggest that industrial development be limited. Write an essay in which you discuss the various arguments that can be made in favor of technology.

2. In *Future Shock*, Alvin Toffler writes "We cannot and must not turn off the switch of technological progress. Only romantic fools babble about returning to a 'state of nature.' " Is technology really the answer to all our problems? Would it be beneficial to go back in time? In an essay of your own,

argue for or against the idea that technology is the solution to our environmental problems.

3. Carson, Davis, Whipple, and Brown do not share McKetta's optimism about our environment. Write an essay in which you, as a protechnology advocate, respond to the problem addressed by any of these students of the environment.

The Nuclear Predicament

ROBERT J. LIFTON

In 1969 Robert J. Lifton won the National Book Award for *Death in Life: Survivors of Hiroshima*, a book that established Lifton as a preeminent thinker and student of human behavior. Lifton was born in Brooklyn, New York, in 1926 and studied at Cornell University and at New York Medical College, where he received his M.D. in 1948. Since 1967 he has been professor of psychiatry at Yale University. His published works reflect his continued interest in the survivor theme, the psychological paradigm of death and continuity, and the relationship between death imagery and violence, especially in American society. His other books include *Revolutionary Immortality: Mao Tse-Tung and the Chinese Cultural Revolution* (1968), and *Home from the War: Vietnam Veterans—Neither Victims Nor Executioners* (1973).

The following article was published in 1980 in the *Dial*, the subscriber magazine of the Public Broadcasting System. In it Lifton warns us not to fall victim to "psychic numbness," a pervasive lack of concern with respect to the nuclear threat.

Why Aren't We More Afraid of the Bomb?

The atom bomb that struck Hiroshima shortly after 8:00 A.M. on August 6, 1945, was a trifle. Strategic warheads today can create a nuclear explosion over a thousand times more powerful. These devices are infinitely more lethal in the amount of radiation they can spread. We know, nevertheless, what that trifling bomb did to Hiroshima. We know that people by the thousands were incinerated in the streets, many of them as they hurried to work. A white flash, and they were gone. Ninety percent of the people who were outdoors and within six tenths of a mile from where the bomb hit died instantly. All the buildings within two miles crumbled. The blast melted stone.

Surviving the explosion was no guarantee of remaining alive. Within   2

589

days, radiation began its work. People became weak, ran high fevers, developed diarrhea, bled from all their orifices, lost their hair, and died. Death by radiation is in many ways worse than the explosion itself. Radiation is invisible. It was the survivors' second encounter with death after the bomb dropped.

Years later, they had their third encounter. Because of radiation, 3 cases of leukemia, most of them fatal, increased. This was only one kind of cancer that the bomb produced: the incidence of cancer of the thyroid, the lungs, the ovaries, and the cervix also rose. But psychologically, leukemia, particularly in children, was the ultimate horror, the eventual outcome of the first moments after the bomb struck. The fears have not ended. The rate of cancer among survivors continues to increase. They wonder what genetic scars will appear in their children or their children's children.

We can be reminded of the Hiroshima bomb, and we know that 4 many more powerful bombs are aimed right now at cities around the world. So why aren't we frightened by the knowledge that if a one-megaton bomb (the bomb dropped on Hiroshima was only thirteen kilotons) struck a city as densely populated as New York, over two million people would probably die instantly? Cockroaches would survive well. They would be blinded by the flash but still able to resist radiation far better than humans.

I think we are afraid, but we hide our fear. We have done precious 5 little talking about the consequences of Hiroshima and Nagasaki. Yet, my study of Hiroshima survivors and my observations in this country today lead me to believe that those events *have* had an important psychological impact on us. The Hiroshima explosion cannot really represent what would occur today if nuclear weapons were used. Still, Hiroshima has things to tell us, particularly if we look at it not as an obscure event in the past but as a truth dominating our existence today. Ironically, we ourselves experience in muted form much of what happened psychologically to the survivors even though we have never experienced such a holocaust.

Right after the bomb exploded, the survivors ceased to feel, though 6 they were surrounded by destruction and mutilation—people whose flesh fell from their bodies, charred corpses in fantastic positions, screams and moans. "Somehow, I became a pitiless person," one survivor told me, "because if I had had pity, I would not have been able to walk through the city, to walk over those dead bodies, badly injured bodies that had turned black, their eyes looking for someone to come and help them."

The survivors were psychically numb. It was a defense mechanism 7 to close themselves off from death. Their unconscious message: If I feel nothing, then death is not taking place. But such cessation of feeling is itself a symbolic form of death.

There was also another emotion: The survivors felt the need to justify their own survival when so many others had died. An impossible task. The alternative was to feel guilty for being alive, and this turned to shame. Survivors spoke of "the shame of living." They could never simply conclude that by happy chance they had survived. Now, thirty-five years later, some have remained so identified with those who died that they themselves feel as if dead. In daily life, they have been distrustful and suspicious yet have craved human relationships. These have been difficult to find: just as the survivors felt ashamed for themselves, others in Hiroshima have felt them to be tainted by death. Survival became a stigma, and some of that attitude still lingers.

Hiroshima initiated us into the possibility of global destruction. In the United States, that awareness has a special impact on children, according to unpublished studies conducted several years ago by Michael Carey, a historian trained in psychoanalytic methods. He interviewed people who had been schoolchildren in the early 1950s. It was the time when schools across the country held bomb drills, in which pupils were told to crouch under their desks. The Hiroshima and Nagasaki bombs and the fear of a menacing Russia inspired those quaint exercises. Nightmares and fantasies of death and destruction resulted.

The repercussions went far beyond bad dreams. A child must struggle to understand death and come to terms with its inevitability and finality. We all have difficulty doing this, but under ordinary circumstances, we come to accept death as part of life's rhythm. Bomb drills, bomb scares, and images of grotesque, massive death interfere with the capacity of children to think of death as natural. They equate it with annihilation.

The world is insane. This attitude also emerged from Carey's interviews—the bomb is irrational, governments are irrational, and those in authority have no real authority. In such a world, nothing can endure. Awareness of the bomb's potential has thus created an ephemerality; we remain alive at the whim of a craziness that can make us disappear in an instant.

We deal with this by leading double lives. All those whom Carey interviewed spoke of both the possibility of destruction as well as the need to go about their lives as if nothing would happen. Most of us probably lead the same double lives and, in fact, share the themes that appear in Carey's work. We cannot afford to incorporate our knowledge of the destructiveness of nuclear weapons into our emotions. If we allow

8

9

10

11

12

ourselves to feel what we know, we probably could not go on; hence the extraordinary gap we experience between knowledge and feeling.

Becoming numb to the threat of nuclear destruction is perhaps one　13 way to get through daily life, but it is not a solution. Indeed, it may lead us right into extinction. The existence of nuclear weapons and the threat of their use interfere with the human desire for continuity. We need to feel connected, I believe, to those who have existed before and will exist beyond our brief individual life spans. We normally experience this sense of immortality in the idea of living on in our children, our creations, our influences on others, and in something all cultures describe as an individual's relationship to the natural world. We also feel this larger continuity in spiritual, or religious, terms and, finally, in psychic states that we view as transcendent, states so intense that time and death disappear—religious ecstasy, song and dance, sex, or merely the contemplation of beauty.

But in the face of extermination by a nuclear holocaust, who can　14 believe in living on in one's children and their children or by means of spiritual or creative achievement or even in nature, which we now know to be vulnerable to our destructive weapons? Though we may be numb to the danger of destruction, we are aware of the bomb's presence, its weight on us. This, I believe, is why we are hungrier than ever for states of transcendence. We seek highs from drugs, meditation, jogging, and skydiving, and we join extremist religious cults that offer a kind of cosmology that sometimes includes or even welcomes a nuclear event.

Much worse, a religion based solely upon the nuclear threat exists　15 today. It is industrial society's ultimate disease, a condition I call nuclearism. Worshipers passionately embrace nuclear weapons both as a solution to anxiety over possible nuclear holocaust and as a way of restoring a lost sense of immortality. They seek grace and even salvation—the mastery of death and evil—through the power of the new technological deity.

Adherents see the deity as capable not only of apocalyptic destruc-　16 tion but also of unlimited creation. The bomb, they think, can solve diplomatic impasses, force a way to peace, and atomic energy's potential can create a world of milk and honey. Believers come to depend on weapons to keep the world going. Edward Teller, a leader in the development of the hydrogen bomb, has associated unlimited bomb making with the adventurous intellectual experience of Western civilization, derided what he calls "the fallout scare," assured us that we can survive a nuclear attack, and insists above all that we cannot and must not try to limit the use of nuclear weapons.

A dangerous expression of nuclearism in our present weapons policy　17 is the advocacy of "limited nuclear war." Proponents continue to seek from weapons magical solutions to political and military dilemmas while closing their eyes to the unlimited destruction that would result.

We must be able to imagine the consequences of nuclear weapons   18
if we are to stop their use. Coming to terms with massive death, collective death, is asking a great deal of the human imagination. Yet, I do not see how we can ask for less.

That is why we need to remember Hiroshima. Its images give sub-   19
stance to our own intellectual sense of horror. However inadequately that city represents what would happen now if thermonuclear weapons were dropped on a population center, it helps us imagine. Keeping alive Hiroshima's death may help us keep alive.

The proximity of a nuclear holocaust is beginning to break through   20
out numbness, at least for many of us. The accident at Three Mile Island, the near explosion of a Titan II warhead in Damascus, Arkansas, bring the ease of massive death in the nuclear age to the surface of our consciousness. The Iraq–Iran conflict deepens the shadow of possible global destruction. We are beginning to see through the sterility of the nuclear language—"exchanges," "scenarios," "stockpiles"—used by our political and military planners. As we sense the danger increasing, our defenses weaken and our fears increase. This is the beginning of awareness. We now need to go further and place nuclear dangers in the contexts of our lives, our values, and our personal and political advocacies. Unless each one of us knows where he or she stands ethically and politically—what one feels about the future of nations and mankind—a stand on nuclear holocaust may be impossible.

But to gain that perception, one must open oneself to discomfort   21
and anxiety. That poses a formidable historical, even evolutionary, problem. Ordinarily, we are selective in what we experience, feeling just enough and closing ourselves off just enough to function and survive. Technology has upset that equation. What is now required is an unprecedented level of tension and psychic balancing, one that permits us to imagine a nuclear holocaust but does not paralyze us with fear.

Can we speak of a shift in consciousness taking place? We may do   22
better to speak of a struggle against numbing. As reluctant as a turn toward awareness may be, it is an important step along a path to a human future.

Questions for Study and Discussion

1. Why does Lifton recount what happened at Hiroshima in his first three paragraphs? Why does he believe that "we need to remember Hiroshima"?
2. What is Lifton's thesis in this essay? What is his purpose? What is he asking us to do?

3. According to Lifton, what happened to the survivors immediately after the bomb exploded? What does he mean when he says, "Ironically, we ourselves experience in muted form much of what happened psychologically to the survivors even though we have never experienced such a holocaust"?

4. What does Lifton mean by "nuclearism"? Who practices nuclearism? In what sense can it be considered a religion?

5. What recent events have served to awaken us to the possibility of a nuclear holocaust?

6. How persuasive do you find Lifton's argument? What are its strengths? Are there parts of his argument that could have been made more persuasively? If so, explain what you think is needed.

Writing Topics

1. Lifton believes that the threat of nuclear holocaust has caused us to "seek highs from drugs, meditation, jogging, and skydiving, and we join extremist religious cults that offer a kind of cosmology that sometimes includes or even welcomes a nuclear event." Using examples from your own experience or reading, write an essay in which you either agree or disagree with Lifton's position.

2. Write an essay explaining the objectives of one or more of the antinuclear groups active in the world today. You may wish to consider how the group got started, what strategies it employs to keep the nuclear issue before the public, and its proposals for solving the current nuclear impasse.

HELEN CALDICOTT

Pediatrician, educator, and author Helen Caldicott was born in Melbourne, Australia, in 1938. During the early 1970s she became an activist against the use of nuclear technology. Her protests were directed at the French, who were then testing nuclear weapons in the atmosphere over the South Pacific. In time she expanded her activities to include protests against the nonmilitary use of nuclear energy. In 1975 she moved to the United States and two years later became a member of the faculty of the Medical School of Harvard University. After the Three Mile Island nuclear accident Caldicott almost singlehandedly revitalized the Physicians for Social Responsibility and sought to educate the public about the dangers of nuclear energy. She helped to establish antinuclear groups in England and Europe and in 1980 created the Women's Action for Nuclear Disarmament group. Caldicott's two antinuclear books are *Nuclear Madness: What You Can Do!* (1979) and *Missile Envy: The Arms Race and Nuclear War* (1984). Caldicott was also the subject of the Academy Award–winning film *If You Love this Planet.*

In "What You Must Know about Radiation," first published in *Redbook,* Caldicott discusses the various types of radiation to which humans are exposed today and warns us about the dangers of radiation at all levels.

What You Must Know about Radiation

All radiation is dangerous. No radiation is safe, and we live with a   1
certain amount of background radiation all the time. It comes from the sun, and from cosmic rays that originate in outer space. Now, eons of time ago, when we were just amoebae and paramecia and other small organisms and when the ozone layer in the atmosphere was very thin, a lot of radiation came through, and the radiation changed our genes—and genes, I remind you, are the very essence of life; they control everything about us. So as radiation poured in from the sun eons of time ago, the structure and functions of the genes in the amoebae and the paramecia and other small organisms were changed and a process of evolution began, eventually producing fish, birds, plants and living animals, including human beings.

Now, a change in a gene is called a "mutation." And there were   2
some mutations that were good. They allowed fish to develop lungs and birds to develop wings—that sort of thing. But there also were mutations that created disease and deformities, that made many organisms unfit to survive in their environment. Those organisms died off. The others lived.

595

Many people call this process of separation of the fit creatures from the unfit ones an illustration of the Darwinian theory of the "survival of the fittest." In any case, that's how we think human beings evolved. But radiation continues to produce mutations in cells. Some of these mutations cause changes—"cancer."

Today the background radiation from the sun is much less than it   3
was in the beginning, millions of years ago. That's because the ozone layer is thicker—it tends to strain out a lot of the radiation—and we live more or less in equilibrium with background radiation, though we do get a certain amount of cancer from it.

Although we get radiation from natural sources—from air, rocks   4
and our own body cells—we also, in modern times, get it from man-made sources. X-rays, administered in doctors' offices and hospitals, are the commonest source today.

It has been estimated that 40 to 50 percent of all medical x-rays   5
are unnecessary, and since the effect of all radiation is cumulative—that is, each exposure increases the risk of getting cancer—you must never have an x-ray without knowing absolutely why and without being assured that it is truly necessary. If you are a heavy smoker, obviously you will need more chest x-rays than a nonsmoker. Or if you cough up blood or have pneumonia or break your arm, you really need an x-ray. The risk from one x-ray is minimal, and the benefit can be great if it is truly necessary. But keep in mind that doctors often order x-rays without thinking much about it. X-rays have become routine. Instead of putting his hand on a patient's belly, palpating it and working out a clinical diagnosis, a doctor may order an x-ray. And some doctors may simply want to have an x-ray for their files as part of your record.

Then there are dental x-rays. You don't need a dental x-ray every   6
six months; you don't even need one every year. When I was a child my dentist didn't have an x-ray machine, and I've got well-filled teeth. Very occasionally, if you have severe pain or you have a root abscess or something like that, you need a tooth x-rayed. But you see, like doctors, some dentists do not think of the dangers. And some buy x-ray machines and pay for them by taking a lot of x-rays and charging the patients for them.

When a doctor or dentist suggests an x-ray, ask, "Why? What are   7
you going to find out from this x-ray?" Get the doctor to draw a picture and explain the pathology so that you understand; *you* make the decision. But don't ever have an unnecessary x-ray.

The reason for care is that human beings are more sensitive to the   8
effects of radiation than any other animal. We get cancer more readily. We don't know why. And children and fetuses are about 10 to 20 times more sensitive than adults because their cells are rapidly dividing and

growing. It is during the time when a child is growing and the cells are multiplying that radiation damage to the genes can have its most devastating effect.

The British epidemiologist Dr. Alice Stewart has shown that one   9
x-ray of a pregnant abdomen increases the risk of eventual leukemia in the baby by 40 percent above the normal incidence. Fortunately, we don't often x-ray pregnant abdomens nowadays. We use ultrasound to determine where the fetal head is. But if you *have* had an x-ray while pregnant, let me reassure you: The increased incidence of 40 percent isn't much, because normally only about 1 in 40,000 children will develop leukemia.

I have been talking about natural radiation and x-ray radiation.   10
Now let us talk about nuclear radiation. This is the kind that comes from atomic bombs and is developed in nuclear energy plants.

In order to run the atomic reactors that produce energy and make   11
nuclear bombs, we need uranium. Uranium is a natural ore that is found in the ground, and it's safe enough if it's left in the ground. But when it is mined, it emits radioactive byproducts—radium and a radioactive gas called "radon." Unfortunately, uranium is worth a lot of money; both the Government and private utilities pay a very good price for it.

Large-scale uranium mining in the United States started in the '40s,   12
during World War II, in connection with the Manhattan Project, which was created to produce the first atomic bombs. Many of the miners who were doing this work inhaled the radon gas, which attaches itself to tiny dust particles and lodges in the terminal air passages in the lungs. Nothing happened to these men at the time, but 15, 25, 30 years later some of these men found themselves coughing up blood or having other symptoms of chest disease. This time x-rays were definitely in order. So they got x-rays, and on each x-ray plate there was a big mass—a big white mass. It was cancer.

Now, what happened? Well, here are the cells in the lung and here   13
is the radon, which has been continuously emitting its radioactive alpha particles. Inside each cell is a nucleus, which is the "brain" of the cell. In the nucleus are chromosomes, and on the chromosomes are the genes. Now, in every cell in the body there's a gene that controls the rate of cell division, and that is called the "regulatory gene." And what happened to the men who got cancer from the radon gas was that one of the alpha particles in the gas by chance hit the regulatory gene in one of the cells and damaged it. And the cell sat very quietly for all those years until one day, instead of dividing to produce just two daughter cells as it should, it went berserk and produced millions and trillions of daughter cells—a clone of abnormal cells—and that is cancer. In other words,

it may actually take only one alpha particle emitted from one atom, to hit one cell and one gene, to initiate the cancer cycle. And this is very serious, because in this country right now, a lot of the men who mined uranium in the past are dying of lung cancer.

It is a terrible thing that when uranium mining first began in this   14
country none of the big companies paid any attention to the need for safety precautions, in spite of the fact that it was known that men in Europe who had mined other ores that contained some uranium died of cancer. So now there is an epidemic of lung cancer among former American uranium miners. The same kind of indifference to human welfare exists in industries that produce dangerous nonradioactive chemicals.

Regulations of the Environmental Protection Agency are being   15
watered down because of the tremendous pressure that is exerted on government by industry. Industry makes hundreds of new chemicals every year. Very few are tested for their potential as causes of cancer. They are just dumped into the environment, as they were in Love Canal, Niagara Falls, New York, and in many other places around the country, where they become concentrated in the food chains, in our air, in our water, in our soil. Our whole world is rapidly becoming polluted with substances we haven't even looked at from the medical point of view. All to make money, to produce useless objects like plastic bottles that we throw away.

After uranium is mined it is taken to a milling plant. There it is   16
crushed and chemically treated. The uranium is then removed and the stuff produced as a byproduct, called "uranium tailings," is discarded. These tailings, a sandy material, contain the radioactive products of radium and thorium, which continue to emit radon gas for hundreds of thousands of years. If you live next to a uranium tailings dump, you have double the risk of getting cancer, compared to a nonexposed population.

There are millions of tons of tailings lying around in this country.   17
There's a huge pile of uranium tailings right next to Grants, New Mexico. Just last spring the Navaho Indians, many of whom were uranium miners in the early 1950s and are dying of lung cancer, staged an antinuclear demonstration a few miles from Grants. At the same time the people of Grants, which bills itself as "the Uranium Capital of the United States," staged a different demonstration. It was a huge pronuclear parade and rally, which included more than 15 floats, many of them provided by milling and mining companies in the area. One of the floats bore the following statement: "This community lives from uranium—it's our bread and butter." And all the time, tailings were being blown over Grants from that lethal pile, and the people in that area have a double risk of getting lung cancer. But they don't know; they really don't understand the dangers.

They didn't understand the dangers in other places either. In some   18
places tailings were used as landfill, and homes, stores and other structures
were built on top of them. In other places tailings were simply dumped.
Salt Lake City has a uranium tailings dump of 1.7 million tons. It is
called the "Vitro Dump," after the city's Vitro Chemical Company mill.
In New Jersey there are two churches that stand on or next to areas
where tailings were dumped. In addition, because tailings are like sand
and were free for the taking, contractors and builders used them in concrete mix, and in Grand Junction, Colorado, there are thousands of
structures in which tailings were used—among them two schools, three
shopping malls, an airport and many, many houses.

Obviously the people were never told that the tailings might be   19
dangerous, and all the time they were emanating radiation. Then, about
1971, a pediatrician, Dr. Robert M. Ross, Jr., sounded an alarm: He was
finding too many birth defects and too much cancer among his young
patients. A committee composed of doctors and researchers was appointed to investigate, and some months later they compared statistics
from Mesa County, where Grand Junction is located, with those of the
whole state. They found that the death rate from birth defects in Mesa
County was more than 50 percent higher than in all of Colorado from
1965 to 1968. Cleft lip and cleft palate were nearly twice as common in
Mesa County as in all of Colorado, and death from cancer was significantly higher in the Grand Junction area than in the rest of the state.
Though there was controversy about those figures, and there still is,
another statistic was recently added by Dr. Stanley W. Ferguson, of the
Colorado State Health Department: Between 1970 and 1976, the incidence of leukemia in Grand Junction more than doubled. Efforts to remedy this situation began in 1972 and are still going on, but it's a patchwork affair predicated on "permissible levels of radiation." Of course, I'm
convinced that no level of radiation is safe, and since its effects are
cumulative, we'll probably be hearing of case after case of cancer in that
area in the years to come.

It was only about a year ago that the United States Congress passed   20
a bill making it mandatory that all the millions of tons of tailings in this
country be disposed of properly—a practically hopeless task because so
much of the stuff has accumulated. In the meantime a great deal of harm
has been done.

The next step in the nuclear cycle is enrichment. It takes a full   21
ton of uranium ore to make four pounds of pure uranium, and about 99
percent of this pure uranium is unfissionable—not usable for making
energy. This is called Isotope Uranium-238. About a half ounce out of
the four pounds is fissionable; this is called Uranium-235. Uranium-235

is what is used for nuclear power, but the 0.7 percent that is got from the natural ore must be enriched to 3.0 percent to be used in a reactor. If it is enriched to 20 percent or more, it is suitable for making atomic bombs. The bomb used on Hiroshima was a uranium bomb and it was called "Little Boy." They have nice names for their bombs.

After enrichment comes fabrication. If you've seen the film *The China Syndrome*, you know that the enriched uranium is made into little pellets like aspirin tablets and packed into hollow rods that are about three quarters of an inch thick and about 12 feet long. When this has been done the rods are taken to the nuclear plant, where they are packed into the core of the nuclear reactor. When they have finished there are 100 tons of uranium in the reactor core, at which point they submerge it all in water. Now, when you pack uranium so densely and in such a way, it reaches "critical mass." That means that the atoms spontaneously start breaking apart, and this action produces about 200 new radioactive elements called "fission products," which are the broken-down products of the original uranium atoms. These fission products are the same materials that are formed when an atom bomb explodes. 22

An atom bomb explodes as the uranium fissions because it is an uncontrolled reaction. But in a nuclear power plant this process is controlled and the fissioning uranium doesn't explode. Instead, the heat produced by the fission process boils the water in which the uranium-bearing rods have been submerged, and the steam that is formed turns a turbine that makes electricity. 23

So in fact, all a nuclear reactor does is boil water. It's a very sophisticated way to boil water. Because inside of each 1,000-megawatt reactor is as much radioactive material as would be released by the explosion of 1,000 bombs of the size of the one that was dropped on Hiroshima. 24

The reason we are discussing all this is that something happened at Three Mile Island, near Harrisburg, Pennsylvania, last spring. What happened? Well, accident, certainly human error and possibly mechanical failure caused large quantities of water to escape from the container holding the immensely hot uranium rods. Apparently the operators of the plant were unaware of the escaping water. Because the water wasn't immediately replaced, the rods became uncovered and remained uncovered for at least 50 minutes. Looking back at it now, most nuclear engineers can't understand what kept the uranium fuel in the uncovered rods from melting down. 25

What would have happened if there had been a meltdown? The low water level and subsequent inefficient cooling of the rods would have allowed the intrinsic heat of the fission products in the uranium to melt 26 the 100 tons of uranium into a globular mass. It then would have continued to melt right through the bottom of the container and—nuclear experts say—hundreds of feet into the earth "toward China"! That's what is called the "China syndrome" by the nuclear industry.

If a meltdown had occurred at Three Mile Island, a massive steam   27
explosion would have ruptured the reactor container and released all the radiation—as much as in 1,000 Hiroshima-sized bombs—into the air. It would not have been an atomic explosion, but it would have contaminated an area the size of Pennsylvania for thousands of years. Nobody could have lived there any more for thousands of years! And depending on the direction of the wind, other huge areas could have been contaminated.

Such an accident would cost about $17 billion in property damage.   28
And what about human damage? Let's say that as many as 10 million people would have been exposed—that would be entirely possible. Well, some statisticians report that almost immediately about 3,300 people would die of lethal radiation exposure. Two or three weeks later about 10,000 to 100,000 more could die of what is called acute radiation illness. First they'd go bald. Their hair would drop out; we saw this for the first time after the bomb was dropped on Hiroshima. Then they would begin to hemorrhage under the skin. They would develop skin ulcers, awful ulcers in their mouths, vomiting and diarrhea, and they'd die of bleeding or infection.

That would happen in a relatively short time, but there are long-   29
term effects too. Hundreds of thousands of men would be rendered sterile from the radiation damage to their testicles. Hundreds of thousands of women would stop menstruating, many permanently. Thousands of people would develop hypothyroidism. With their thyroid glands damaged, their metabolic rate would slow down, they would become constipated, they would be unable to think properly, they'd lose their appetites and at the same time become fat.

Thousands more would have acute respiratory impairment, the ra-   30
diation having damaged their lungs. Thousands of babies affected by radiation while still in their mothers' wombs would be born with microcephaly, or with very small heads—"pinheads," they called them in Hiroshima, where this happened after the bomb fell. Thousands more would be born cretins, with ablated thyroids and neurological damage.

And five, ten, 20, 30 years later, hundreds of thousands of cases of   31
cancer would occur, to say nothing of the varieties of genetic defects—dwarfism, mental retardation, hemophilia, and others—that would develop and be passed on and on through future generations.

My list of sick, dying and dead comes to just less than half a million   32
people. Possibly the estimate could be for a few less, since Three Mile
Island had been in operation for only three months before the accident
and had only 80 percent of the inventory of radioactive products that a
normal, long-term operating, 1,000-megawatt reactor would contain. But
it would have been a catastrophe such as the world has never seen,
because only 200,000 people died in Hiroshima and Nagasaki, though
the incidence of cancer is still increasing among the bomb survivors
there.

Now, what I want to know is, why doesn't our Government tell us   33
of the dangers to which we are being exposed? Why hasn't it told us
what a meltdown would mean? What can we expect as a result of the
careless dumping of nuclear wastes, which, if not as swiftly devastating
as a meltdown or a bomb, can be just as deadly over a period of time?
Where does the allegiance of our elected representatives belong—to the
utility companies or to us? Did Dwight Eisenhower, when he was President and they were testing hydrogen bombs in Nevada in 1953, set a
permanent policy when he told the Atomic Energy Commission to "keep
the public confused" about radioactive fallout? (The AEC certainly was
receptive to Eisenhower's advice. Recently declassified commission records
show that it repeatedly brushed aside questions about health hazards; and
in February, 1955, Willard F. Libby, a member of the commission, said:
"People have got to learn to live with facts of life, and part of the facts
of life is fallout.")

The accident at Three Mile Island in Pennsylvania revealed still   34
other alarming things. People operating the nuclear plant for Metropolitan Edison didn't know what they were doing. In the first 48 hours after
the accident, primary coolant (water that surrounds the rods) was vented
into the atmosphere as steam. Rule number one in the nuclear energy
business is, Never vent primary coolant! It's like, if you are a surgeon,
you never cut off a head—you just don't do that! But the primary coolant
was vented after the cladding of many of the rods had melted and released
highly radioactive fission products into the water. They weren't measuring anything in the first 48 hours, either, so they don't know exactly
what they let out—plutonium? strontium? cesium? radioactive iodine?
That's the first thing. The second thing is that a whole lot of radioactive
water from the primary coolant spilled onto the reactor floor. An attempt
was made to transfer some of this to a tank in an auxiliary building that
stands beside the reactor, but the tank already contained radioactive
water—perhaps not so radioactive as the primary coolant, but radioactive
just the same. To make room for the primary coolant, 4,000 gallons of
radioactive water from the tank was emptied into the Susquehanna River.

Now, water from that tank is routinely emptied into the Susque-   35
hanna, but first, as Government spokesmen would say, it has to be tested
and diluted to a "permissible level of radioactivity." As I see it, no level
of radioactivity is permissible, so that's bad enough. But during those
first critical 48 hours, the 4,000 gallons of radioactive water they emptied
into the river weren't even tested. They also released a lot of radioactive
gases into the air, many of which are precursors of products such as
Strontium-90, Cesium-137 and Radioactive Iodine-131.

More proof that the people operating that plant didn't know what   36
they were doing: Not only did they make "a series of errors"—I quote
the *New York Times*—"in the operation of the plant," but when the
accident occurred they continued to make errors. A very serious problem.
And because Metropolitan Edison doesn't know how much radioactive
stuff was emptied into the environment, there is no hard data on which
to make predictions about what will happen to people in the Harrisburg
area in the future. And yet Joseph A. Califano, Jr., then Secretary of
the Department of Health, Education and Welfare, said that only one
person—at worst, ten people—would die of cancer as a result of the
accident. He had no primary data on which to base the announcement.
It's very worrying.

Let me tell you about Strontium-90. Strontium-90 stays poisonous   37
for 600 years. Released into the atmosphere, it settles on the grass from
the air, the rain and the dew, and its potency gets compounded many
times over the concentration that is in the air. When this happens in
dairying areas, cattle eat the grass and the Strontium-90 is concentrated
in cow's milk, which both calves and babies drink. It concentrates most
highly in human breast milk, and it gets there when pregnant women
and nursing mothers eat dairy products that are contaminated by Stron-
tium-90. Now, anybody who ingests a radioactive substance can be affected, but it's very important to know that babies are inordinately sensitive to the effects of radiation. You can't taste the radiation. It's odorless,
invisible and tasteless, and when a baby drinks milk containing Stron-
tium-90 the body treats it as if it were calcium; it's deposited in the
growing bones. It causes bone cancer. It also causes leukemia—many of
those children die.

Between January, 1951, and October, 1958, when a large number   38
of atomic and hydrogen bombs were tested in the Nevada desert, the
winds carried the fallout to agricultural as well as populated areas in Utah
and Strontium-90 was found in milk. At that time the Nobel Prize-
winning scientist Linus Pauling said if babies drank milk containing
Strontium-90, they might get leukemia later. And the Government said
Pauling was wrong. Then early this year the New England Journal of

Medicine published a paper saying that the incidence of leukemia in Utah children in the "high fallout" counties who were under 14 at the time of the testing had increased nearly two and a half times above normal level.

Radioactive Iodine-131 also concentrates in milk, and if there are bodies of water nearby, it concentrates in fish. Although it is active for only a few weeks, once it gets into milk or fish its potency is compounded thousands of times. And its effect, when ingested by humans, is vicious and lasting. Taken up by the thyroid, it can cause thyroid cancer. Keep in mind that I have named only three or four dangerous elements. Actually almost 200 of those dangerous elements that are made in nuclear reactors are contained in nuclear waste.   39

Nuclear waste. Garbage. Nobody needs it. Nobody wants it. And nobody knows what to do with it. And it has to be disposed of, isolated from the environment, because many of those elements remain potent for one million years. If those materials leak, they get into our air, they get into our water, they get into our food chain and get recycled through human bodies for hundreds and thousands of years, causing cancers after cancers after cancers, to say nothing of birth deformities and genetic disease.   40

Now, by present methods of technology, nuclear waste, which is active for up to one million years, can be safely stored for only ten to 20 years. But even before that the containers begin to corrode; there are leaks; it gets into all parts of our environment. Even if the most brilliant scientist we have should think he's found the answer for storing nuclear wastes, he'll be dead long before his hypothesis can be verified. This is the heritage we are leaving to our descendents.   41

You can imagine our descendents, like the people at Love Canal, Niagara Falls, New York, where nonnuclear but dangerous chemicals were dumped, waking up one morning with their food already contaminated, their kids already being born deformed and dying of leukemia and cancer, and with adults too dying of cancer. It will be too late. But we're risking millions of lives so we can turn our lights on. And to keep the economy running. And because government and big business have invested a lot of money.   42

In the nuclear industries they say, "Don't worry, we're scientists; we'll find the answer." That's like my saying to a patient, "You have cancer; you have about six months to live; but don't worry, I'm a good doctor and by 1995 I might find a cure."   43

Now let's talk about plutonium, out of which both atomic and hydrogen bombs are made. That's one of the most dangerous elements known. It is manmade in a nuclear reactor; it didn't exist until we fis-   44 sioned uranium. And it's named, appropriately, after Pluto, the god of the underworld. It is so incredibly toxic that a millionth of a gram—and a gram is about the size of a grape—can cause cancer. When plutonium is exposed to the air it produces particles as fine as talcum powder that are totally invisible. And if you inhale any of those particles, they will almost certainly give you lung cancer.

If you took just ten pounds of plutonium and put a speck of it in every human lung, that would be enough to kill every single person on earth. Ten pounds! And each nuclear reactor makes 500 pounds of it every year. Five hundred pounds! What's worse, plutonium remains toxic for half a million years. It is not biodegradable, that is, it doesn't decompose; so the plutonium-contaminated waste remains toxic all that time.

There are areas around Denver, Colorado, that are contaminated by plutonium radiation, and the testicular cancer rate in a suburb next to Rock Flats, about 13 miles from the center of Denver, is 140 percent higher than the normal incidence. You see, plutonium lodges in the testicles and it's in the testicles that the sperm are, where the genes for the future generations are! Plutonium also crosses the placental barrier, where it can damage the developing fetus. It can kill a cell that's going to form the left side of a baby's brain, or, say, the left arm, or whatever. Do you remember what thalidomide did? Plutonium is thalidomide forever! It will damage fetus after fetus after fetus, down the generations, virtually for the rest of time. And, of course, its effects are not limited to the unborn. It causes lung cancer. It causes bone cancer. It causes liver cancer, and more.

The nuclear reactor was first designed as part of the Manhattan Project to make plutonium, the plutonium to be used in making nuclear weapons. And in making bombs and other atomic weapons they have produced 74 million gallons of high-level radioactive waste, and scientists and engineers and environmental specialists all have studied the problem—and nobody seems to know what to do with it.

Nobody has devised a foolproof, leakproof, fail-safe place to sequester those wastes over the thousands and thousands of years they remain dangerous. At the present time, wastes, contained in large carbon-steel tanks, are being stored on the site of the Government's Hanford Reservation, a nuclear complex near Richland, Washington. They are also being stored on the site of the Savannah River Plant, another Government facility that produces nuclear weapons materials, near Aiken, South Carolina. At Hanford the tanks have already leaked 450,000 gallons of poisonous radioactive waste into the soil near the Columbia River. Eventually these radioactive elements will probably enter the Columbia River, where they will become concentrated in the fish we eat, in the water we drink and, if the water is used for irrigation, in plants and animals.

The dangers of nuclear power are not only accidental meltdowns, escaping radiation and all the radioactive wastes we don't know how to dispose of. The dangers are even greater because it is a small step from nuclear power to nuclear weaponry.

When Robert Strange McNamara was U.S. Secretary of Defense he figured out that if the United States had 400 nuclear weapons, we could wipe out one third of the Soviet population and destroy two thirds of her industry—and that would be a deterrent. The United States now has at least 30,000 nuclear warheads and can kill every human being on earth 12 times over. *Overkill*—that's the Pentagon term. The Russians can overkill Americans 20 times.

Do you know that probably every town and city in this country with a population of 25,000 or more is targeted at this instant with a nuclear weapon? The same is true for towns and cities in the U.S.S.R., China, Europe and England. From the moment that a button is pressed in one country and buttons in other countries are pressed in retaliation, it would take about one-half hour to two hours to complete the war. And that would be the end of civilization as we know it. Shelters would be useless. People in shelters would be asphyxiated. That's because a 20-megaton bomb produces a fire storm of 3,000 square miles that uses up all the oxygen, including that in the shelter.

It is known that the man who had his finger on the button in this country five and a half years ago was not what any psychiatrist would term psychiatrically stable at the end of his term in office. Leonid Brezhnev had been a sick man and, people say, has been treated with cortisone. A good drug. But occasionally it can induce acute psychosis. Not long ago, while still in power, the dictator Idi Amin, of Uganda, who is not exactly given to good judgment, let alone respect for human life, bragged that he would have an atomic bomb in a few years. Granted that some leaders seem more stable than others, but ask yourself: Who is there that any of us would entrust with the safety of the world?

There are now 35 countries that have nuclear weapons capability because they have been sold nuclear reactors—some small, some large— by this country and by others. And since each 1,000-megawatt reactor produces about 500 pounds of plutonium every year, so, theoretically, many of those 35 countries could make 50 atomic bombs every year from each 1,000-megawatt reactor.

Albert Einstein said, "The splitting of the atom has changed everything save man's mode of thinking; thus we drift toward unparalleled catastrophe."

What would happen if all the weapons were used? One, the syn- 55
ergistic effects could be so great, with the ozone destroyed, icecaps melting, radiation everywhere, and so on, that probably not an organism
would survive. Maybe the cockroaches would survive because they're
400,000 times more radiation-resistant than humans. Or if you did survive—if there had been no fire storm to eat up all the oxygen in your
shelter—and you stayed in your shelter for at least two weeks (otherwise
you would die from the intense radiation) what would you find when you
came out? There would be countless dead and dying—Guyana, where
the earth was covered with the dead, would have nothing on us. There
would be no doctors, drugs or hospital beds in big cities, because those
are targeted. You might find some doctors in small communities, but
what could they do? Disease would be rampant. And you can imagine
the earth inhabited by bands of roving mutant humanoids generations
hence. This would be like no science fiction story ever invented.

Look at the changing seasons—the spring and the flowers and the 56
trees coming into leaf. Look at the fall of the year and the leaves turning
gold. Look at our growing children. One child. One baby. We're a fantastic species. We're capable of such creativity, love and friendship.

I've got three children. And I am a doctor who treats children, a 57
great many of them having the commonest genetic disease of childhood—
cystic fibrosis. I live with dying children. I live with grieving parents. I
understand the value of every single human life.

The ultimate in preventive medicine is to eliminate nuclear power 58
and nuclear weapons. I look on this as a religious issue too. Because what
is our responsibility to God but to continue creation?

Someone said, "Evil flourishes only when good men and women do 59
nothing." And there are many of us—good men and women—and we
can do a lot.

We have only a short time to turn the destructive powers around. 60
A short time. I appeal especially to women to do this work because we
understand the genesis of life. Our bodies are built to nurture life. We
have wombs; we have breasts; we have periods to remind us that we can
produce life! We also have won a voice in the affairs of the world and
are becoming more influential every day. I beg you—do what you can
today.

Questions for Study and Discussion

1. Caldicott is calling for the elimination of nuclear power and nuclear weapons
because of the catastrophic radiation problems associated with each. Why,
then, does she begin her essay by discussing natural radiation and radiation
from x-rays?

2. Briefly explain the causal link between radiation and cancer. Why is it that children and fetuses are more sensitive than adults to the effects of radiation?

3. Briefly explain the step-by-step process of taking uranium ore from the ground to producing nuclear energy.

4. How does paragraph 10 function in the context of Caldicott's essay?

5. What evidence does Caldicott offer that the people operating the plant at Three Mile Island didn't know what they were doing?

6. Why is the question of nuclear waste such an important one for Caldicott?

7. This essay originally appeared in *Redbook*, a popular women's magazine. In what ways is this article appropriate for her audience?

8. In you own words define the following terms: tailings, meltdown, China Syndrome, and overkill.

Writing Topics

1. Caldicott believes that one of the real culprits in the radiation and nuclear question is "money." What does she mean by this? To what extent do you agree with her? What are the chances of changing the situation? Is the situation different in noncapitalistic countries?

2. In 1986 a nuclear disaster occurred in the Soviet Union at the Chernobyl nuclear power plant. Find out as much as you can about this event and its aftermath. How closely do Caldicott's predictions for human and property damage that would result from a nuclear power plant meltdown coincide with what you have been able to learn about the Chernobyl accident?

3. What has been your own experience with x-rays? Do you think the x-rays you have had in your lifetime have all been necessary? What is normal practice with respect to the taking of x-rays when you go to your doctor or dentist? Are x-rays routinely given, or are you consulted each time?

4. Write an essay in which you argue that all nuclear power plants should be shut down until a satisfactory method of disposing of nuclear wastes is developed.

ROGER FISHER

Roger Fisher was born in Winnetka, Illinois, in 1922 and earned his A.B. and LL. B. from Harvard University. Currently a practicing attorney and professor of law at Harvard Law School, he has been a consultant to the Department of Defense, a member of the Board of Trustees of the Hudson Institute, and a member of the International Peace Academy. He was the originator and the executive editor of *The Advocates* and *Arabs and Israelis*, two national public television series. Fisher is also the author of several books including *International Conflict for Beginners* (1969) and *International Crises and the Role of Law: Points of Choice* (1978).

In the following essay, first published in *The Bulletin of the Atomic Scientists*, Fisher looks at what we can do to prevent, or at least reduce, the chances of a nuclear war.

Preventing Nuclear War

"Preventing Nuclear War"? "Boy, have *you* got a problem." That reaction a few minutes ago to the title of these remarks reminded me of an incident when during World War II, I was a B-17 weather reconnaissance officer. One fine day we were in Newfoundland test-flying a new engine that replaced one we had lost. Our pilot's rank was only that of flight officer because he had been court martialed so frequently for his wild activities; but he was highly skillful.

He took us up to about 14,000 feet and then, to give the new engine a rigorous test, he stopped the other three and feathered their propellers into the wind. It is rather impressive to see what a B-17 can do on one engine. But then, just for a lark, the pilot feathered the fourth propeller and turned off that fourth engine. With all four propellers stationary, we glided, somewhat like a stone, toward the rocks and forests of Newfoundland.

After a minute or so the pilot pushed the button to unfeather. Only then did he remember: In order to unfeather the propeller you had to have electric power, and in order to have electric power you had to have at least one engine going. As we were buckling on our parachutes, the copilot burst out laughing. Turning to the pilot he said, "Boy, have *you* got a problem!"

As with the crew of that B-17, we're all in this together. Professionals, whether lawyers like myself or doctors like you, tend to put the problem of preventing nuclear war on somebody else's agenda. But whoever

609

is responsible for creating the danger, we're all on board one fragile spacecraft. The risk is high. What can we do to reduce it?

There are two kinds of reasons for the high risk: hardware reasons   5
and people reasons. We—and the military—tend to focus on the hardware: nuclear explosives and the means for their delivery. We think about the terrible numbers of terrible weapons. We count them by the hundreds, by the thousands and by the tens of thousands. There are clearly too many. There are too many fingers on the trigger. There are too many hands through which weapons pass in Europe, in the United States and in the Soviet Union.

Yes, changes should be made in the hardware. I believe we should   6
stop all nuclear weapons production; we should cut back on our stockpiles. But even if we should succeed in stopping production, and even if we should succeed in bringing about significant reductions, there will still be thousands of nuclear weapons. We keep our attention on the hardware. The military think it is the answer; we think it is the problem. In my judgment it is not the most serious problem.

The U.S. Air Force and the U.S. Navy both have enough weapons   7
to blow each other up; and they have disagreements. There are serious disputes between the Air Force and the Navy: disputes that mean jobs, careers; disputes that are sometimes more serious in practical consequences than those between the United States and the Soviet Union. But the two services have learned to fight out their differences before the Senate Appropriations Committee, before the Secretary of Defense, in the White House and on the football field.

The case of the Navy and the Air Force demonstrates, in a crude   8
way, that the problem is not just in the hardware; it is in our heads. It lies in the way we think about nuclear weapons. And if the problem lies in the way we think, then that's where the answer lies. In Pogo's immortal phrase, "We have met the enemy and they are us."

The danger of nuclear war is so great primarily because of the men-   9
tal box we put ourselves in. We all have working assumptions that remain unexamined. It is these assumptions that make the world so dangerous. Let me suggest three sets of mistaken assumptions about: (1) our goals, that is, the ends we are trying to pursue; (2) the means for pursuing those ends; and (3) whose job it is to do what.

First, what are our goals? Internationally, we think we want to   10
"win." We go back to primitive notions of victory. We look at a situation and we ask, "Who's winning?" But that is an area in which we must change our thinking. Internationally and domestically, we do not really want a system in which any one side—even our own—wins all the time.

Yet this concept of "winning"—that there is such a thing and that it is our dominant objective—is one of our fundamental beliefs.

In fact, like a poker player, we have three kinds of objectives. One   11
is to win the hand. Whatever it is we think we want, we want it now. We want victory. The second is to be in a good position for future hands. We want a reputation and chips on the table so that we can influence future events. In other words, we want power. Our third objective is not to have the table kicked over, the house burned down, or our opponent pull a gun. We want peace.

We want victory; we want power; we want peace. Exploding nu-   12
clear weapons will not help us achieve any one of them. We have to re-examine rigorously our working assumption that in a future war we would want to "win." What do we mean by "win"? What would our purpose be?

Last spring I gave the officers at the NATO Defense College in Rome   13
a hypothetical war in Europe, and asked them to work out NATO's war aims. The "war" was presumed to have grown out of a general strike in East Germany, with Soviet and West German tanks fighting on both sides of the border. Deterrence had failed. I told the officers: "You are in charge of the hotline message to Moscow. What is the purpose of this war? What are you trying to do?" At first they thought they knew—win! Very simple. But what did that mean? What was the purpose of the war? They began to realize that NATO did not plan to conquer the Soviet Union acre by acre as the Allies had conquered Germany in World War II. They did not plan physically to impose their will on the Soviet Union. They were seeking a Soviet decision. That was the only way they could have a successful outcome.

With further thought they reached a second conclusion; they were   14
not going to ask for unconditional surrender. That gave them a specific task: Just define the Soviet decision that would constitute success for NATO and that NATO could reasonably expect the Soviet Union to make. The officers worked through the day considering how the Russians probably saw their choice, how we wanted them to see it, and what kind of "victory" for us we could realistically expect the Soviet Union to agree to.

It turned out that the only plausible objective was to stop the war.   15
"Winning" meant ending the war on acceptable terms. The goal was some kind of cease-fire, the sooner the better. It was with difficulty and even pain that some officers discovered that winning meant stopping, even if some Soviet troops remained in West Germany; even with only a promise to restore the *status quo ante*.

They found it hard to draft a fair cease-fire that didn't sound like   16
a unilateral Western ultimatum. It might say, "Stop firing at 0100 hours
tomorrow, promise to withdraw, promise to restore the status quo within
48 hours, and we will meet in Vienna to talk about serious problems as
soon as the status quo is 'more or less' restored." But the NATO draftsmen
did not know whether the Soviets would prefer Geneva to Vienna or
whether they wanted 0200 hours instead of 0100 hours, etc.

Someone creatively suggested, "Wouldn't it be a good idea if right   17
now we worked out with the Russians some standby cease-fire terms?
Then in a crisis we wouldn't have to be demanding that they accept our
terms or they demanding that we accept theirs. Let's produce some cease-
fire drafts that we can both accept." One of the other officers was incredulous: "What did you say? You are going to negotiate the armistice
before the war begins? In that case, why have the war?"

The need to re-examine assumptions about our foreign policy ob-   18
jectives is also demonstrated by our self-centered definition of national
security. Typically, political leaders and journalists alike suggest that the
primary goal of foreign policy is national security, and only after that has
been assured should we worry about our relations with the Soviet Union.

Such thinking assumes that we can be secure while the Soviet   19
Union is insecure—that somehow we can be safe while the Soviet Union
faces a high risk of nuclear war. But in any nuclear war between the
United States and the Soviet Union missiles will go both ways. There is
no way we can make the world more dangerous for them without also
making it more dangerous for ourselves. The less secure the Soviets feel,
the more they will be doing about it, and the less secure we will become.
Security is a joint problem.

We must make the Soviet Union share responsibility for our security   20
problem. We should say, "Look, you Russians have to understand why
we built these missiles and how it looks to us when you behave as you
do. You must take some responsibility for helping us deal with our security
problem." Similarly, we must take on responsibility for dealing with their
security problem. We cannot make our end of the boat safer by making
the Soviet end more likely to capsize. We cannot improve our security
by making nuclear war more likely for them. We can't "win" security
from nuclear war unless they win it too. Any contrary assumption is
dangerous.

Here I may point out that we in the peace movement do not always   21
practice what we preach. I am always ready to tell friends at the Pentagon
that it does no good to call Soviet officials idiots, but am likely to add,
"Don't you see that, you idiot?" We who are concerned with reducing
the risks of war often think that our job is to "win" the war against

hawks. In advancing our interests we assume that our adversaries have none worth considering. But our task is not to win a battle. Instead, we have to find out what the other side's legitimate concerns are, and we have to help solve their legitimate problems in order to solve our own. At every level, domestically and internationally, we need to re-examine our working assumptions. We are not seeking to win a war, but to gain a peace.

A second set of dangerous assumptions are those we make about how to pursue our objectives. The basic mistaken assumption is that for every problem there is a military solution. We will first try diplomacy. We will talk about it; we will negotiate. But if that doesn't solve the problem we assume that we can always resort to force. We tend to assume that if we have the will and the courage, and are prepared to pay the price, then we can always solve the problem by military means. Wrong. For the world's big problems there is no military solution. Nuclear war is not a solution. It is worse than any problem it might "solve." 22

We have mislearned from the past. During World War II the Allies could physically impose a result on Hitler and his country. Acre by acre it was done. But the world has changed. We can no longer impose such a result on any nuclear power. We cannot physically make things happen. The only means we have available is to try to change someone's mind. 23

There is no way in which nuclear hardware can bring about a physical solution to any problem we face except the population problem. Just as you cannot make a marriage work by dynamite or make a town work by blowing it up, there is no way we can make the world work by using nuclear bombs. When people hear that they say, "Yes, that's true." Yet they go right ahead, operating on the assumption that there are military solutions. 24

Like Linus in the Charlie Brown comic strip, we cling to our security blanket, military hardware. Both U.S. and Soviet officials clutch their plutonium security blankets as though somehow they offer real security. Somehow, we think, this bomb, this hardware, will give us strength, will protect us. We will be able to avoid the necessity of dealing with the real world. Our assumption is that the problem is simple—it's us against them. We want to believe in a quick fix. It is like cowboys and Indians. Whatever the problem, John Wayne will arrive with his six-guns blazing, and the problem will be solved. 25

Those are our common assumptions about how to deal with international problems. We operate on them although most of us know they are not true. The fact that conventional weapons remain useful and that conventional wars, such as that between Iraq and Iran, continue, reinforces our mistaken assumptions about the use of nuclear weapons. 26

We have far better ways to deal with international problems. Break   27
up big problems into manageable pieces. Look at each item on its merits.
Sit down side-by-side and discuss it. Don't concentrate on what our
adversaries say their positions are, but try to understand and deal with
their interests. Communicate and listen. What's in their minds? What's
bothering them? How would we feel?

If you were sitting in Moscow and looking off to the left saw Japan   28
thinking of rearming; if you saw your long-time strongest ally, China,
with a 2,000-mile common frontier, now your worst enemy; if you saw
Pakistan apparently getting a nuclear bomb; if you heard Western voices
saying, "We must help the rebels in Afghanistan"; if you saw American
military equipment now in the Gulf, in Saudi Arabia, in Egypt and in
Israel; if you saw Greece rejoining NATO and Turkey in the hands of a
military government; and if cruise missiles were about to be located in
West Germany—how must that all look from Moscow? We should put
ourselves in their shoes and understand their problems. The only way we
can succeed is to affect their future thinking. The starting point is to
understand their present thinking.

Second, we have to invent wise solutions. We have to figure out   29
not just good arguments, but good ways to reconcile our differing interests. And they must participate in that process. There is no way, in any
conflict, in which one side can produce the right answer. The understanding that comes from both sides working on a problem, and the
acceptability that comes from joint participation in a solution, make any
good answer better. We need to engage in joint problem-solving.

That same process of working together is equally applicable to our   30
domestic difference. The peace movement is not the only source of wisdom; we are part of the conflict. There are a lot of people in this country
who have legitimate concerns about the Soviet Union. We must try to
understand these concerns and meet them, not carry on a war. We need
to put ourselves in their shoes—in Pentagon shoes. We have to listen as
well as talk. With their participation, we will invent better solutions.

By this process we will promote joint learning, not just at the   31
intellectual level but at the level of feeling, of emotion, of caring, the
level of concern. International conflict is too often dealt with cerebrally,
too often dealt with as a hypothetical problem out there. We need not
only to apply what we know, but to keep on learning about human
behavior, how to affect our own behavior and that of others, not just
manipulate it.

The danger of nuclear war lies largely within us. It lies in how we   32
think about winning, in how we define success, and in our illusions of
being able to impose results.

The danger also comes from my third set of assumptions—about whose job it is to reduce the risk of war. If there were a military solution, there would be a case for leaving it to the military—to policy-science experts, and to professional strategists. Physicians, for example, have said: "We are just concerned with the medical aspects of nuclear war and will limit ourselves to that area. We will tell you how bad a nuclear war would be. It is somebody else's job to prevent it."

Such statements rest on the assumption that the solution is in the hardware department. But we are not facing a technical military problem "out there." The solution lies right here: in changing our own assumptions and those of other people; in growing up; in abandoning our plutonium security blanket.

The Soviet Union and the United States cling to nuclear weapons as symbols of security; other national leaders want them. If someone is clinging to a plutonium blanket which is bad for his health, you do not call in an engineer and say, "Design a better plutonium blanket." The problem is in the heads of those who are clinging to it.

There is no one I know who has a professional license in the skills of reducing the risk of nuclear war. Fortunately, however, no professional license is required. But who are those with skills in dealing with psychological problems like denial, like distancing, like turning flesh and blood issues into abstract problems through the use of jargon? Who is likely to notice that people are denying responsibility because a problem seems too overwhelming? Nuclear engineers? I think not.

A few minutes ago I left you in a B-17 over the hills of Newfoundland. The co-pilot was saying to the pilot: "Boy, do *you* have a problem." Well, we didn't crash; we weren't all killed. On that plane we had a buck sergeant who remembered that back behind the bomb bay we had a putt-putt generator for use in case we had to land at some emergency air field that did not have any electric power to start the engines. The sergeant found it. He fiddled with the carburetor; wrapped a rope around the flywheel a few times; pulled it and pulled it; got the generator going and before we were down to 3,000 feet we had electricity. The pilot restarted the engines, and we were all safe. Now saving that plane was not the sergeant's job in the sense that he created the risk. The danger we were in was not his fault or his responsibility. But it was his job in the sense that he had an opportunity to do something about it.

We professionals tend to define our roles narrowly. I sometimes ask my law students: "What would have been the responsibility of a professional musician judging Nero's performance on the fiddle while Rome burned? Should he limit himself to discussing the music?" A member of the lay public would probably get a bucket and put out the fire. By becoming professionals do we become less responsible? Can we say, "No, I'm a professional. I'm not a firefighter. That's someone else's job."?

Such special knowledge and training as we have may not make it obligatory for us to try to prevent nuclear war. Rather, it gives us an opportunity. My notion of whose job something is is best defined by who has an opportunity. We have an opportunity. I encourage you, as I encourage myself, to use it. The world is at risk. The very danger of nuclear war means that there is more opportunity to make a difference than ever before.

If everyone with any significant power made the right decision every time, that's as near utopia as we can get. There are only three reasons they don't. One is that they are poor decision-makers. Our job is to change them; that is what politics is about. Second, they are operating on bad assumptions, thinking poorly. Our job is to correct their assumptions. And the third possibility is that they are subject to harmful constraints. Our job is to free them from those constraints.

In a simple chart I have put all problems on the left-hand side, divided into those three parts. Across the top are the activities in which we can engage: research on facts and theory; communication in terms of learning ourselves and teaching others; devising things to do (that is, turning a problem into a possible answer, inventing possible proposals or action ideas), getting a proposal onto somebody's agenda; advocating ideas; or doing something ourselves.

Chart of Useful Activities

Avoiding nuclear war will require wise decision-makers, who make wise assumptions on ends and means, and who are free from harmful constraints. Which part of that problem do you want to work on? Which activity will best harness your interests and abilities? To get wise results someone must devote attention to each box in the matrix. To get a wise decision answers are needed in every box.

PROBLEMS	ACTIVITIES					
	Research: facts, theory	Commu- nicate: learn, teach	Devise things to do	Build an agenda	Advocate	Do it yourself
Poor deciders						
Poor thinking on ends on means						
Harmful constraints						

To get a wise decision we need good answers *in every box.* No   42
amount of useful research will overcome poor deciders; no number of
good deciders will overcome bad assumptions or harmful constraints.
Somebody has to invent what's to be done. Somebody has to put it on
the agenda. Somebody has to persuade others that it is a good idea and
somebody has to do it. All those activities are needed for each category
of problem. There is enough to keep all of us busy.

All of us can do any of those things. No single activity will be   43
sufficient. We need theory on how to reduce instability. We need to
develop knowledge about nuclear war, about the consequences and about
ways to reduce the risks. We need to communicate that knowledge both
to the public, who constrain our decision-makers, and to the people who
are making the decisions. We need to communicate both the bad news
and the opportunities for reducing it.

If all we do is deliver bad news and say that there's nothing we can   44
do about it, the bad news does not become operational. We have to turn
that news into something we can do.

My favorite activity is inventing. An early arms control proposal   45
dealt with the problem of distancing that the President would have in
the circumstances of facing a decision about nuclear war. There is a young
man, probably a Navy officer, who accompanies the President. This young
man has a black attaché case which contains the codes that are needed
to fire nuclear weapons. I could see the President at a staff meeting
considering nuclear war as an abstract question. He might conclude: "On
SIOP Plan One, the decision is affirmative. Communicate the Alpha line
XYZ." Such jargon holds what is involved at a distance.

My suggestion was quite simple: Put that needed code number in a   46
little capsule, and then implant that capsule right next to the heart of a
volunteer. The volunteer would carry with him a big, heavy butcher
knife as he accompanied the President. If ever the President wanted to
fire nuclear weapons, the only way he could do so would be for him first,
with his own hands, to kill one human being. The President says, "George,
I'm sorry but tens of millions must die." He has to look at someone and
realize what death is—what an innocent death is. Blood on the White
House carpet. It's reality brought home.

When I suggested this to friends in the Pentagon they said, "My   47
God, that's terrible. Having to kill someone would distort the President's
judgment. He might never push the button."

Whether or not that particular idea has any merit, there is lots to   48
do. Action is required to convince the public that it is in our interest to
have the Soviets feel secure rather than insecure. Much of the press
apparently thinks that the more terrified the Soviets are the more we

benefit. The Committee on the Present Danger (perhaps better called the Committee on Increasing the Present Danger) ignores the fact that if we raise the risk of nuclear war for the Soviet Union we also raise it for ourselves.

If you don't know what to do, that's great. That gives you some-   49
thing to do right there. Get some friends together on Saturday morning and generate some ideas. Separate this inventing process from the later process of deciding among them. Identify three or four other people who might make a decision of some significance. What can you do to increase the chance they'll make some desired decision next week? Whoever it is—journalists, congressmen, governors, legislators, newspaper editors, businessmen, a civic organization, a medical association, a friend of President Reagan's, a school teacher, a publisher—what are some things they might do that would illuminate our faulty working assumptions to help establish better ones? Figuring out what to do is itself an excellent activity. In intellectual efforts, as in gunnery, aiming is crucial.

Don't wait to be instructed. Take charge. This is not an organized   50
campaign that someone else is going to run. If you share these concerns, get involved. There is a lot to do to reduce the risk of nuclear war. Reading, writing, talking, perhaps a radio program, or perhaps a letter-writing campaign to your congressman. Tell him, "Grow up. Give up your plutonium security blanket."

But perhaps you are still holding on to your own security blanket,   51
that neat definition of your job. The security blanket most of us cling to is, "Don't blame me. It's not my job to plan nuclear strategy. I'm not responsible for the risk of nuclear war." You can give up that security blanket any time.

The way to enlist support is not to burden others with guilt but to   52
provide them with an opportunity to volunteer. I find it an exciting venture. It is a glorious world outside. There are people to be loved and pleasures to share. We should not let details of past wars and the threat of the future take away the fun and the joy we can have working together on a challenging task. I see no reason to be gloomy about trying to save the world. There is more exhilaration, more challenge, more zest in tilting at windmills than in any routine job. Be involved, not just intellectually but emotionally. Here is a chance to work together with affection, with caring, with feeling. Feel some of your emotions. Don't be uptight. You don't have to be simply a doctor, a lawyer, or a merchant. We are human beings. Be human.

People have struggled all of their lives to clear ten acres of ground   53
or simply to maintain themselves and their family. Look at the opportunity we have. Few people in history have been given such a chance—

a chance to apply our convictions, our values, our highest moral goals with such competence as our professional skills may give us. A chance to work with others—to have the satisfaction that comes from playing a role, however small, in a constructive enterprise. It's not compulsory. So much the better. But what challenge could be greater? We have an opportunity to improve the chance of human survival.

In medicine there is a traditional call that strikes a nice balance   54
between duty and opportunity, that invites us to lend a hand with all the skill and compassion we can muster: "Is there a doctor in the house?"

Questions for Study and Discussion

1. Fisher says that there is a high risk of war because of hardware reasons and because of people reasons. What does he mean by each? Which does he consider the more serious?

2. What three sets of basic assumptions does Fisher believe make our world so dangerous?

3. What is the purpose of the B-17 bomber story that Fisher uses to introduce his essay? Why does he wait until paragraph 37 before completing the story?

4. What did the officers learn from the exercise that Fisher gave them at the NATO Defense College? What did you learn?

5. According to Fisher, what are the three reasons that leaders do not make a wise decision every time? Explain the purpose of his "Chart of Useful Activities" and how it works. Did you find his chart useful? Why, or why not?

6. This essay was originally given as a speech. What stylistic features in it reveal that it was written to be delivered as a speech?

7. Identify at least two figures of speech that Fisher uses in this essay.

Writing Topics

1. In the concluding paragraphs of his essay Fisher suggests some ways that each of us can begin to contribute to the peace movement. Reflect on Fisher's suggestions and write a more detailed proposal for those who wish to become more involved in efforts to eliminate the potential for nuclear war.

2. What is your reaction to the current peace movement? What contact, if any, have you had with people in the peace movement? What do you know of their philosophy? Their activities? Are they misguided optimists or thoughtful realists? Have you ever participated in a peace demonstration?

3. The beginnings of responsible citizenship are in knowing where your elected officials stand on important issues. Select one person from your state's congressional delegation. What are that person's views on nuclear disarmament? Do you agree with that position? Write a letter in which you either show support for that representative's position or try to persuade him or her to your way of thinking.

COLIN S. GRAY AND KEITH PAYNE

Colin S. Gray currently works as an analyst at the National Institute for Policy in McLean, Virginia. At the time that he coauthored the following essay with Keith Payne, both were strategic analysts with the Hudson Institute, a conservative think tank. Gray has been a consultant for the Department of Defense on the MX missile project and has served on the General Advisory Committee, which regularly advises the Pentagon. Gray has written extensively on the subject of nuclear war, and his books include *The Soviet-American Arms Race* (1976), *MX, ICBM, and National Security* (1981), and *Strategic Studies and Public Policy: The American Experience* (1982). Gray is a proponent of President Reagan's Strategic Defense Initiative.

In "Victory Is Possible," written in 1980 for the journal *Foreign Policy*, Gray and Payne ask us to give up the idea that nuclear war is likely to be a "meaningless, terminal event" and to start developing a strategy whereby we can successfully wage a nuclear war.

Victory Is Possible

Nuclear war is possible. But unlike Armageddon, the apocalyptic war prophesied to end history, nuclear war can have a wide range of possible outcomes. Many commentators and senior U.S. government officials consider it a nonsurvivable event. The popularity of this view in Washington has such a pervasive and malign effect upon American defense planning that it is rapidly becoming a self-fulfilling prophecy for the United States.

Recognition that war at any level can be won or lost, and that the distinction between winning and losing would not be trivial, is essential for intelligent defense planning. Moreover, nuclear war can occur regardless of the quality of U.S. military posture and the content of American strategic theory. If it does, deterrence, crisis management, and escalation control might play a negligible role. Through an inability to communicate or through Soviet disinterest in receiving and acting upon American messages, the United States might not even have the option to surrender and thus might have to fight the war as best it can. Furthermore, the West needs to devise ways in which it can employ strategic nuclear forces coercively, while minimizing the potentially paralyzing impact of self-deterrence.

If American nuclear power is to support U.S. foreign policy objectives, the United States must possess the ability to wage nuclear war rationally. This requirement is inherent in the geography of East-West

621

relations, in the persisting deficiencies in Western conventional and theater nuclear forces, and in the distinction between the objectives of a revolutionary and status quo power.

U.S. strategic planning should exploit Soviet fears insofar as is feasible from the Soviet perspective; take full account of likely Soviet responses and the willingness of Americans to accept those responses; and provide for the protection of American territory. Such planning would enhance the prospect for effective deterrence and survival during a war. Only recently has U.S. nuclear targeting policy been based on careful study of the Soviet Union as a distinct political culture, but the U.S. defense community continues to resist many of the policy implications of Soviet responses to U.S. weapons programs. In addition, the U.S. government simply does not recognize the validity of attempting to relate its freedom of offensive nuclear action and the credibility of its offensive nuclear threat to the protection of American territory.   4

Critics of such strategic planning are vulnerable in two crucial respects: They do not, and cannot, offer policy prescriptions that will insure that the United States is never confronted with the stark choice between fighting a nuclear war or surrendering, and they do not offer a concept of deterrence that meets the extended responsibilities of U.S. strategic nuclear forces. No matter how elegant the deterrence theory, a question that cannot be avoided is what happens if deterrence mechanisms fail? Theorists whose concept of deterrence is limited to massive retaliation after Soviet attack would have nothing of interest to say to a president facing conventional defeat in the Persian Gulf or in Western Europe. Their strategic environment exists only in peacetime. They can recommend very limited, symbolic options but have no theory of how a large-scale Soviet response is to be deterred.   5

Because many believe that homeland defense will lead to a steeper arms race and destabilize the strategic balance, the U.S. defense community has endorsed a posture that maximizes the prospect for self-deterrence. Yet the credibility of the extended U.S. deterrent depends on the Soviet belief that a U.S. president would risk nuclear escalation on behalf of foreign commitments.   6

In the late 1960s the United States endorsed the concept of strategic parity without thinking through what that would mean for the credibility of America's nuclear umbrella. A condition of parity or essential equivalence is incompatible with extended deterrent duties because of the self-deterrence inherent in such a strategic context. However, the practical implications of parity may be less dire in some areas of U.S. vital interest. Western Europe, for example, is so important an American   7 interest that Soviet leaders could be more impressed by the character and duration of the U.S. commitment than by the details of the strategic balance.

A Threat to Commit Suicide

Ironically, it is commonplace to assert that war-survival theories affront the crucial test of political and moral acceptability. Surely no one can be comfortable with the claim that a strategy that would kill millions of Soviet citizens and would invite a strategic response that could kill tens of millions of U.S. citizens would be politically and morally acceptable. However, it is worth recalling the six guidelines for the use of force provided by the "just war" doctrine of the Catholic Church: Force can be used in a just cause; with a right intent; with a reasonable chance of success; in order that, if successful, its use offers a better future than would have been the case had it not been employed; to a degree proportional to the goals sought, or to the evil combated; and with the determination to spare noncombatants, when there is a reasonable chance of doing so.

These guidelines carry a message for U.S. policy. Specifically, as long as nuclear threat is a part of the U.S. diplomatic arsenal and provided that threat reflects real operational intentions—it is not a total bluff—U.S. defense planners are obliged to think through the probable course of a nuclear war. They must also have at least some idea of the intended relationship between force applied and the likelihood that political goals will be achieved—that is, a strategy.

Current American strategic policy is not compatible with at least three of the six just-war guidelines. The policy contains no definition of success aside from denying victory to the enemy, no promise that the successful use of nuclear power would insure a better future than surrender, and no sense of proportion because central war strategy in operational terms is not guided by political goals. In short, U.S. nuclear strategy is immoral.

Those who believe that a central nuclear war cannot be waged for political purposes because the destruction inflicted and suffered would dwarf the importance of any political goals can construct a coherent and logical policy position. They argue that nuclear war will be the end of history for the states involved, and that a threat to initiate nuclear war is a threat to commit suicide and thus lacks credibility. However, they acknowledge that nuclear weapons cannot be abolished. They maintain that even incredible threats may deter, provided the affront in question is sufficiently serious, because miscalculation by an adversary could have

8

9

10

11

terminal consequences; because genuinely irrational behavior is always possible; and because the conflict could become uncontrollable.

In the 1970s the U.S. defense community rejected this theory of deterrence. Successive strategic targeting reviews appeared to move U.S. policy further and further from the declaratory doctrine of mutual assured destruction adopted by former Secretary of Defense Robert S. McNamara. Yet U.S. defense planners have not thoroughly studied the problems of nuclear war nor thought through the meaning of strategy in relation to nuclear war. The U.S. defense community has always tended to regard strategic nuclear war not as war but as a holocaust. Former Secretary of Defense James R. Schlesinger apparently adopted limited nuclear options (LNOs)—strikes employing anywhere from a handful of several dozen warheads—as a compromise between the optimists of the minimum deterrence school and the pessimists of the so-called war-fighting persuasion. By definition, LNOs apply only to the initial stages of a war. But what happens once LNOs have been exhausted? If the Soviets retaliated after U.S. LNOs, the United States would face the dilemma of escalating further or conciliating.

Deterrence may fail to be restored during war for several reasons: The enemy may not grant, in operational practice, the concept of intra-war deterrence and simply wage the war as it is able; and command, control, and communications may be degraded so rapidly that strategic decisions are precluded and both sides execute their war plans. Somewhat belatedly, the U.S. defense community has come to understand that flexibility in targeting and LNOs do not constitute a strategy and cannot compensate for inadequate strategic nuclear forces.

LNOs are the tactics of the strong, not of a country entering a period of strategic inferiority, as the United States is now. LNOs would be operationally viable only if the United States had a plausible theory of how it could control and dominate later escalation.

The fundamental inadequacy of flexible targeting, as presented in the 1970s, is that it neglected to take proper account of the fact that the United States would be initiating a process of competitive escalation that it had no basis for assuming could be concluded on satisfactory terms. Flexible targeting was an adjunct to plans that had no persuasive vision of how the application of force would promote the attainment of political objectives.

War Aims

U.S. strategic targeting doctrine must have a unity of political purpose from the first to the last strikes. Strategic flexibility, unless wedded to a plausible theory of how to win a war or at least insure an acceptable end to a war, does not offer the United States an adequate bargaining position before or during a conflict and is an invitation to defeat. Small, preplanned strikes can only be of use if the United States enjoys strategic superiority—the ability to wage a nuclear war at any level of violence with a reasonable prospect of defeating the Soviet Union and of recovering sufficiently to insure a satisfactory postwar world order.

However, the U.S. government does not yet appear ready to plan   17
seriously for the actual conduct of nuclear war should deterrence fail, in spite of the fact that such a policy should strengthen deterrence. Assured-destruction reasoning is proclaimed officially to be insufficient in itself as a strategic doctrine. However, a Soviet assured-destruction capability continues to exist as a result of the enduring official U.S. disinterest in strategic defense, with potentially paralyzing implications for the United States. No matter how well designed and articulated, targeting plans that allow an enemy to inflict in retaliation whatever damage it wishes on American society are likely to prove unusable.

Four interdependent areas of strategic policy—strategy, weapons de-   18
velopment and procurement, arms control, and defense doctrine—are currently treated separately. Theoretically, strategy should determine the evolution of the other three areas. In practice, it never has. Most of what has been portrayed as war-fighting strategy is nothing of the kind. Instead, it is an extension of the American theory of deterrence into war itself. To advocate LNOs and targeting flexibility and selectivity is not the same as to advocate a war-fighting, war-survival strategy.

Strategists do not find the idea of nuclear war fighting attractive.   19
Instead, they believe that an ability to wage and survive war is vital for the effectiveness of deterrence; there can be no such thing as an adequate deterrent posture unrelated to probable wartime effectiveness; victory or defeat in nuclear war is possible, and such a war may have to be waged to that point; and, the clearer the vision of successful war termination, the more likely war can be waged intelligently at earlier stages.

There should be no misunderstanding the fact that the primary in-   20
terest of U.S. strategy is deterrence. However, American strategic forces do not exist solely for the purpose of deterring a Soviet nuclear threat or attack against the United States itself. Instead, they are intended to support U.S. foreign policy, as reflected, for example, in the commitment to preserve Western Europe against aggression. Such a function requires American strategic forces that would enable a president to initiate strategic nuclear use for coercive, though politically defensive, purposes.

U.S. strategy, typically, has proceeded from the bottom up. Such   21
targeting does not involve any conception of the war as a whole, nor of how the war might be concluded on favorable terms. The U.S. defense

community cannot plan intelligently for lower levels of combat, unless it has an acceptable idea of where they might lead.

Most analyses of flexible targeting options assume virtually perfect   22 stability at the highest levels of conflict. Advocates of flexible targeting assert that a U.S. LNO would signal the beginning of an escalation process that the Soviets would wish to avoid in light of the American threat to Soviet urban-industrial areas. Yet it seems inconsistent to argue that the U.S. threat of assured destruction would deter the Soviets from engaging in escalation following an LNO but that U.S. leaders could initiate the process despite the Soviet threat. What could be the basis of such relative U.S. resolve and Soviet vacillation in the face of strategic parity or Soviet superiority?

Moreover, the desired deterrent effect would probably depend upon   23 the Soviet analysis of the entire nuclear campaign. In other words, Soviet leaders would be less impressed by American willingness to launch an LNO than they would be by a plausible American victory strategy. Such a theory would have to envisage the demise of the Soviet state. The United States should plan to defeat the Soviet Union and to do so at a cost that would not prohibit U.S. recovery. Washington should identify war aims that in the last resort would contemplate the destruction of Soviet political authority and the emergence of a postwar world order compatible with Western values.

The most frightening threat to the Soviet Union would be the de-   24 struction or serious impairment of its political system. Thus, the United States should be able to destroy key leadership cadres, their means of communication, and some of the instruments of domestic control. The USSR, with its gross overcentralization of authority, epitomized by its vast bureaucracy in Moscow, should be highly vulnerable to such an attack. The Soviet Union might cease to function if its security agency, the KGB, were severely crippled. If the Moscow bureaucracy could be eliminated, damaged, or isolated, the USSR might disintegrate into anarchy, hence the extensive civil defense preparations intended to insure the survival of the Soviet leadership. Judicious U.S. targeting and weapon procurement policies might be able to deny the USSR the assurance of political survival.

Once the defeat of the Soviet state is established as a war aim,   25 defense professionals should attempt to identify an optimum targeting plan for the accomplishment of that goal. For example, Soviet political control of its territory in Central Asia and in the Far East could be weakened by discriminate nuclear targeting. The same applies to Transcaucasia and Eastern Europe.

The Ultimate Penalty

Despite a succession of U.S. targeting reviews, Soviet leaders, look- 26
ing to the mid-1980s, may well anticipate the ability to wage World War
III successfully. The continuing trend in the East-West military balance
allows Soviet military planners to design a theory of military victory that
is not implausible and that may stir hopes among Soviet political leaders
that they might reap many of the rewards of military success even without
having to fight. The Soviets may anticipate that U.S. self-deterrence
could discourage Washington from punishing Soviet society. Even if the
United States were to launch a large-scale second strike against Soviet
military and economic targets, the resulting damage should be bearable
to the Soviet Union given the stakes of the conflict and the fact that the
Soviets would control regions abroad that could contribute to its recovery.

In the late 1960s the United States identified the destruction of 27
20–25 percent of the population and 50–75 percent of industrial capacity
as the ultimate penalty it had to be able to inflict on the USSR. In the
1970s the United States shifted its attention to the Soviet recovery economy. The Soviet theory of victory depends on the requirement that the
Soviet Union survive and recover rapidly from a nuclear conflict. However, the U.S. government does not completely understand the details of
the Soviet recovery economy, and the concept has lost popularity as a
result. Highly complex modeling of the Soviet economy cannot disguise
the fact that the available evidence is too rudimentary to permit any
confidence in the analysis. With an inadequate data base it should require
little imagination to foresee how difficult it is to determine targeting
priorities in relation to the importance of different economic targets for
recovery.

Schlesinger's advocacy of essential equivalence called for a U.S. 28
ability to match military damage for military damage. But American strategic development since the early 1970s has not been sufficient to maintain the American end of that balance. Because the U.S. defense community has refused to recognize the importance of the possibility that a
nuclear war could be won or lost, it has neglected to think beyond a
punitive sequence of targeting options.

American nuclear strategy is not intended to defeat the Soviet Union 29
or insure the survival of the United States in any carefully calculated
manner. Instead, it is intended to insure that the Soviet Union is punished increasingly severely. American targeting philosophy today is only
a superficial improvement over that prevalent in the late 1960s, primarily

because U.S. defense planners do not consider anticipated damage to the United States to be relevant to the integrity of their offensive war plans. The strategic case for ballistic missile defense and civil defense has not been considered on its merits for a decade.

In the late 1970s the United States targeted a range of Soviet eco-   30
nomic entities that were important either to war-supporting industry or to economic recovery. The rationale for this targeting scheme was, and remains, fragile. War-supporting industry is important only for a war of considerable duration or for a period of post-war defense mobilization. Moreover, although recovery from war is an integral part of a Soviet the-ory of victory, it is less important than the achievement of military suc-cess. If the USSR is able to win the war, it should have sufficient military force in reserve to compel the surviving world economy to contribute to Soviet recovery. Thus, the current trend is to move away from targeting the recovery economy.

To date, the U.S. government has declined to transcend what   31
amounts to a deterrence-through-punishment approach to strategic war planning. Moreover, the strategic targeting reviews of the 1970s did not address the question of self-deterrence adequately. The United States has no ballistic missile defense and effectively no civil defense, while U.S. air defense is capable of guarding American air space only in peacetime. The Pentagon has sought to compensate for a lack of relative military muscle through more imaginative strategic targeting. Review after review has attempted to identify more effective ways in which the USSR could be hurt. Schlesinger above all sought essential equivalence through a more flexible set of targeting options without calling for extensive new U.S. strategic capabilities. Indeed, he went to some pains to separate the ques-tion of targeting design from procurement issues.

The United States should identify nuclear targeting options that   32
could help restore deterrence, yet would destroy the Soviet state and en-hance the likelihood of U.S. survival if fully implemented. The first priority of such a targeting scheme would be Soviet military power of all kinds, and the second would be the political, military, and economic control structure of the USSR. Successful strikes against military and political control targets would reduce the Soviet ability to project military power abroad and to sustain political authority at home. However, it would not be in the interest of the United States actually to implement an offensive nuclear strategy no matter how frightening in Soviet perspective, if the U.S. homeland were totally naked to Soviet retaliation.

Striking the USSR should entail targeting the relocation bunkers of   33
the top political and bureaucratic leadership, including those of the KGB; key communication centers of the Communist party, the military, and

the government; and many of the economic, political, and military records. Even limited destruction of some of these targets and substantial isolation of many of the key personnel who survive could have revolutionary consequences for the country.

The Armageddon Syndrome

The strategic questions that remain incompletely answered are in some ways more difficult than the practical problems of targeting the political control structure. Is it sensible to destroy the government of the enemy, thus eliminating the option of negotiating an end to the war? In the unlikely event that the United States identifies all of the key relocation bunkers for the central political leadership, who would then conduct the Soviet war effort and to what ends? Since after a large-scale counter-control strike the surviving Soviet leadership would have little else to fear, could this targeting option be anything other than a threat? 34

The U.S. defense community today believes that the political control structure of the USSR is among the most important targets for U.S. strategic forces. However, just how important such targeting might be for deterrence or damage limitation has not been determined. Current American understanding of exactly how the control structure functions is less than perfect. But that is a technical matter that can in principle be solved through more research. The issue of whether the Soviet control structure should actually be struck is more problematic. 35

Strategists cannot offer painless conflicts or guarantee that their preferred posture and doctrine promise a greatly superior deterrence posture to current American schemes. But, they can claim that an intelligent U.S. offensive strategy, wedded to homeland defenses, should reduce U.S. casualties to approximately 20 million, which should render U.S. strategic threats more credible. If the United States developed the targeting plans and procured the weapons necessary to hold the Soviet political, bureaucratic, and military leadership at risk, that should serve as the functional equivalent in Soviet perspective of the assured-destruction effect of the late 1960s. However, the U.S. targeting community has not determined how it would organize this targeting option. 36

A combination of counterforce offensive targeting, civil defense, and ballistic missile and air defense should hold U.S. casualties down to a level compatible with national survival and recovery. The actual number would depend on several factors, some of which the United States could control (the level of U.S. homeland defenses); some of which it could influence (the weight and character of the Soviet attack); and some 37 of which might evade anybody's ability to control or influence (for example, the weather). What can be assured is a choice between a defense program that insures the survival of the vast majority of Americans with relative confidence and one that deliberately permits the Soviet Union to wreak whatever level of damage it chooses.

No matter how grave the Soviet offense, a U.S. president cannot credibly threaten and should not launch a strategic nuclear strike if expected U.S. casualties are likely to involve 100 million or more American citizens. There is a difference between a doctrine that can offer little rational guidance should deterrence fail and a doctrine that a president might employ responsibly for identified political purposes. Existing evidence on the probable consequences of nuclear exchanges suggests that there should be a role for strategy in nuclear war. To ignore the possibility that strategy can be applied to nuclear war is to insure by choice a nuclear apocalypse if deterrence fails. The current U.S. deterrence posture is fundamentally flawed because it does not provide for the protection of American territory.

Nuclear war is unlikely to be an essentially meaningless, terminal event. Instead it is likely to be waged to coerce the Soviet Union to give up some recent gain. Thus, a president must have the ability, not merely to end a war, but to end it favorably. The United States would need to be able to persuade desperate and determined Soviet leaders that it has the capability, and the determination, to wage nuclear war at ever higher levels of violence until an acceptable outcome is achieved. For deterrence to function during a war each side would have to calculate whether an improved outcome is possible through further escalation.

An adequate U.S. deterrent posture is one that denies the Soviet Union any plausible hope of success at any level of strategic conflict; offers a likely prospect of Soviet defeat; and offers a reasonable chance of limiting damage to the United States. Such a deterrence posture is often criticized as contributing to the arms race and causing strategic instability, because it would stimulate new Soviet deployments. However, during the 1970s the Soviet Union showed that its weapon development and deployment decisions are not dictated by American actions. Western understanding of what determines Soviet defense procurement is less than perfect, but it is now obvious that Soviet weapon decisions cannot be explained with reference to any simple action-reaction model of arms-race dynamics. In addition, highly survivable U.S. strategic forces should insure strategic stability by denying the Soviets an attractive first-strike target set.

An Armageddon syndrome lurks behind most concepts of nuclear strategy. It amounts either to the belief that because the United States could lose as many as 20 million people, it should not save the 80 million or more who otherwise would be at risk, or to a disbelief in the serious possibility that 200 million Americans could survive a nuclear war.

There is little satisfaction in advocating an operational nuclear doctrine that could result in the deaths of 20 million or more people in an unconstrained nuclear war. However, as long as the United States relies on nuclear threats to deter an increasingly powerful Soviet Union, it is inconceivable that the U.S. defense community can continue to divorce its thinking on deterrence from its planning for the efficient conduct of war and defense of the country. Prudence in the latter should enhance the former.

42

Questions for Study and Discussion

1. What is the authors' thesis and where is it stated?

2. Upon what assumptions do the authors base their argument? Do you agree with these assumptions? Why or why not?

3. How do the authors answer the critics of strategic planning? Are these counterarguments persuasive?

4. What are the six guidelines of the Catholic Church's "just war" doctrine? In what ways does American strategic policy fail to meet these guidelines?

5. What, according to the authors, would happen if our current policy of deterrence should fail? What do they mean when they say that a plan "for the actual conduct of nuclear war . . . should strengthen deterrence"?

6. What course of action do the authors want our defense community to take? What specific suggestions do the authors make for a possible war with the Soviet Union?

7. What is the Armageddon Syndrome? What do the authors see as the problem with this way of thinking?

Writing Topics

1. Write an essay using the following statement as your thesis: "Nuclear war is unlikely to be an essentially meaningless, terminal event."

2. The area of concern for Gray and Payne in their essay is U.S. strategic planning in the event of a nuclear war, especially if our policy of deterrence should fail. What are the alternatives to nuclear warfare? How can they be achieved?

3. The United States policy is currently one of deterrence. What exactly is a policy of deterrence? What are its strengths? What are its weaknesses?

4. On March 23, 1983, President Reagan gave a speech to the nation on

national security in which he first announced his Strategic Defense Initiative (SDI), a plan further detailed in a White House Paper entitled "The President's Strategic Defense Initiative." A good number of critics have since announced their opposition to the President's plan, but perhaps their position has its best philosophic base in a statement made by Omar Bradley, the last of America's World War II Five-Star Generals: "The central problem of our time . . . is how to employ human intelligence for the salvation of mankind. It is a problem we have put upon ourselves. . . . Missiles will bring antimissiles and antimissiles will bring anti-antimissiles. We are now speeding inexorably toward a day when even the ingenuity of our scientists may be unable to save us." The question is, Do we try to change our thinking about nuclear weapons or do we try to build better gadgets than our adversaries? After doing some library research, write a report on SDI and the opposition to it.

CARL SAGAN

Carl Sagan has established a considerable reputation in astronomy, biology, and physics, as well as in the emerging science of exobiology, the study of extraterrestrial life. Born in 1934 in New York City, Sagan was educated at the University of Chicago. After receiving his doctorate in 1960, he taught and did research at Harvard University and at the University of California, Berkeley, before settling at Cornell, where he is professor of astronomy and space sciences. He was awarded a 1978 Pulitzer Prize for *The Dragons of Eden: Speculations on the Evolution of Human Intelligence* (1977), the first book for a popular audience to delve into the human brain. He followed this with *Murmurs of Earth: The Voyager Interstellar Record* (1978), *Broca's Brain: Reflections on the Romance of Science* (1979), *Cosmos* (1980), an adaptation of public television's most highly rated series, and *Contact* (1985), a novel. These books have helped to make Sagan one of modern science's most popular spokesmen.

A member of the Union of Concerned Scientists, Sagan coauthored a petition calling for an international treaty to ban all nuclear weapons from space. The petition was signed by forty of the world's leading scientists. In the following essay, first published in the widely circulated Sunday newspaper supplement *Parade*, Sagan continues his antinuclear campaign. He warns us of the frightening effects that nuclear war would have on our planet Earth.

The Nuclear Winter

"Into the eternal darkness, into fire, into ice."
—DANTE, *The Inferno*

Except for fools and madmen, everyone knows that nuclear war 1 would be an unprecedented human catastrophe. A more or less typical strategic warhead has a yield of 2 megatons, the explosive equivalent of 2 million tons of TNT. But 2 million tons of TNT is about the same as all the bombs exploded in World War II—a single bomb with the explosive power of the entire Second World War but compressed into a few seconds of time and an area 30 or 40 miles across . . .

In a 2-megaton explosion over a fairly large city, buildings would 2 be vaporized, people reduced to atoms and shadows, outlying structures blown down like matchsticks and raging fires ignited. And if the bomb were exploded on the ground, an enormous crater, like those that can be seen through a telescope on the surface of the Moon, would be all that remained where midtown once had been. There are now more than

633

50,000 nuclear weapons, more than 13,000 megatons of yield, deployed in the arsenals of the United States and the Soviet Union—enough to obliterate a million Hiroshimas.

But there are fewer than 3000 cities on the Earth with populations of 100,000 or more. You cannot find anything like a million Hiroshimas to obliterate. Prime military and industrial targets that are far from cities are comparatively rare. Thus, there are vastly more nuclear weapons than are needed for any plausible deterrence of a potential adversary.

Nobody knows, of course, how many megatons would be exploded in a real nuclear war. There are some who think that a nuclear war can be "contained," bottled up before it runs away to involve much of the world's arsenals. But a number of detailed analyses, war games run by the U.S. Department of Defense, and official Soviet pronouncements all indicate that this containment may be too much to hope for: Once the bombs begin exploding, communications failures, disorganization, fear, the necessity of making in minutes decisions affecting the fates of millions, and the immense psychological burden of knowing that your own loved ones may already have been destroyed are likely to result in a nuclear paroxysm. Many investigations, including a number of studies for the U.S. government, envision the explosion of 5000 to 10,000 megatons—the detonation of tens of thousands of nuclear weapons that now sit quietly, inconspicuously, in missile silos, submarines and long-range bombers, faithful servants awaiting orders.

The World Health Organization, in a recent detailed study chaired by Sune K. Bergstrom (the 1982 Nobel laureate in physiology and medicine), concludes that 1.1 billion people would be killed outright in such a nuclear war, mainly in the United States, the Soviet Union, Europe, China and Japan. An additional 1.1 billion people would suffer serious injuries and radiation sickness, for which medical help would be unavailable. It thus seems possible that more than 2 billion people—almost half of all the humans on Earth—would be destroyed in the immediate aftermath of a global thermonuclear war. This would represent by far the greatest disaster in the history of the human species and, with no other adverse effects, would probably be enough to reduce at least the Northern Hemisphere to a state of prolonged agony and barbarism. Unfortunately, the real situation would be much worse.

In technical studies of the consequences of nuclear weapons explosions, there has been a dangerous tendency to underestimate the results. This is partly due to a tradition of conservatism which generally works well in science but which is of more dubious applicability when the lives of billions of people are at stake. In the Bravo test of March 1, 1954, a 15-megaton thermonuclear bomb was exploded on Bikini Atoll. It had about double the yield expected, and there was an unanticipated last-minute shift in the wind direction. As a result, deadly radioactive fallout came down on Rongelap in the Marshall Islands, more than 200 kilometers away. Almost all the children on Rongelap subsequently developed thyroid nodules and lesions, and other long-term medical problems, due to the radioactive fallout.

Likewise, in 1973, it was discovered that high-yield airbursts will 7
chemically burn the nitrogen in the upper air, converting it into oxides of nitrogen; these, in turn, combine with and destroy the protective ozone in the Earth's stratosphere. The surface of the Earth is shielded from deadly solar ultraviolet radiation by a layer of ozone so tenuous that, were it brought down to sea level, it would be only 3 millimeters thick. Partial destruction of this ozone layer can have serious consequences for the biology of the entire planet.

These discoveries, and others like them, were made by chance. 8
They were largely unexpected. And now another consequence— by far the most dire—has been uncovered, again more or less by accident.

The U.S. Mariner 9 spacecraft, the first vehicle to orbit another 9
planet, arrived at Mars in late 1971. The planet was enveloped in a global dust storm. As the fine particles slowly fell out, we were able to measure temperature changes in the atmosphere and on the surface. Soon it became clear what had happened:

The dust, lofted by high winds off the desert into the upper Martian 10
atmosphere, had absorbed the incoming sunlight and prevented much of it from reaching the ground. Heated by the sunlight, the dust warmed the adjacent air. But the surface, enveloped in partial darkness, became much chillier than usual. Months later, after the dust fell out of the atmosphere, the upper air cooled and the surface warmed, both returning to their normal conditions. We were able to calculate accurately, from how much dust there was in the atmosphere, how cool the Martian surface ought to have been.

Afterwards, I and my colleagues, James B. Pollack and Brian Toon 11
of NASA's Ames Research Center, were eager to apply these insights to the Earth. In a volcanic explosion, dust aerosols are lofted into the high atmosphere. We calculated by how much the Earth's global temperature should decline after a major volcanic explosion and found that our results (generally a fraction of a degree) were in good accord with actual measurements. Joining forces with Richard Turco, who has studied the effects of nuclear weapons for many years, we then began to turn our attention to the climatic effects of nuclear war. [The scientific paper, "Global Atmospheric Consequences of Nuclear War," is written by R. P. Turco, O. B. Toon, T. P. Ackerman, J. B. Pollack and Carl Sagan.

From the last names of the authors, this work is generally referred to as "TTAPS."]

We knew that nuclear explosions, particularly groundbursts, would lift an enormous quantity of fine soil particles into the atmosphere (more than 100,000 tons of fine dust for every megaton exploded in a surface burst). Our work was further spurred by Paul Crutzen of the Max Planck Institute for Chemistry in Mainz, West Germany, and by John Birks of the University of Colorado, who pointed out that huge quantities of smoke would be generated in the burning of cities and forests following a nuclear war.

Groundbursts—at hardened missile silos, for example—generate fine dust. Airbursts—over cities and unhardened military installations—make fires and therefore smoke. The amount of dust and soot generated depends on the conduct of the war, the yields of the weapons employed and the ratio of groundbursts to airbursts. So we ran computer models for several dozen different nuclear war scenarios. Our baseline case, as in many other studies, was a 5000-megaton war with only a modest fraction of the yield (20 percent) expended on urban or industrial targets. Our job, for each case, was to follow the dust and smoke generated, see how much sunlight was absorbed and by how much the temperatures changed, figure out how the particles spread in longitude and latitude, and calculate how long before it all fell out of the air back onto the surface. Since the radio-activity would be attached to these same fine particles, our calculations also revealed the extent and timing of the subsequent radioactive fallout.

Some of what I am about to describe is horrifying. I know, because it horrifies me. There is a tendency—psychiatrists call it "denial"—to put it out of our minds, not to think about it. But if we are to deal intelligently, wisely, with the nuclear arms race, then we must steel ourselves to contemplate the horrors of nuclear war.

The results of our calculations astonished us. In the baseline case, the amount of sunlight at the ground was reduced to a few percent of normal—much darker, in daylight, than in a heavy overcast and too dark for plants to make a living from photosynthesis. At least in the Northern Hemisphere, where the great preponderance of strategic targets lies, an unbroken and deadly gloom would persist for weeks.

Even more unexpected were the temperatures calculated. In the baseline case, land temperatures, except for narrow strips of coastline, dropped to minus 25° Celsius (minus 13° Fahrenheit) and stayed below freezing for months—even for a summer war. (Because the atmospheric structure becomes much more stable as the upper atmosphere is heated and the lower air is cooled, we may have severely *under*estimated how long the cold and the dark would last.) The oceans, a significant heat reservoir, would not freeze, however, and a major ice age would probably not be triggered. But because the temperatures would drop so catastrophically, virtually all crops and farm animals, at least in the Northern Hemisphere, would be destroyed, as would most varieties of uncultivated or domesticated food supplies. Most of the human survivors would starve.

In addition, the amount of radioactive fallout is much more than expected. Many previous calculations simply ignored the intermediate time-scale fallout. That is, calculations were made for the prompt fallout—the plumes of radioactive debris blown downwind from each target—and for the long-term fallout, the fine radioactive particles lofted into the stratosphere that would descend about a year later, after most of the radioactivity had decayed. However, the radioactivity carried into the upper atmosphere (but not as high as the stratosphere) seems to have been largely forgotten. We found for the baseline case that roughly 30 percent of the land at northern midlatitudes could receive a radioactive dose greater than 250 rads, and that about 50 percent of northern midlatitudes could receive a dose greater than 100 rads. A 100-rad dose is the equivalent of about 1000 medical X-rays. A 400-rad dose will, more likely than not, kill you.

The cold, the dark and the intense radioactivity, together lasting for months, represent a severe assault on our civilization and our species. Civil and sanitary services would be wiped out. Medical facilities, drugs, the most rudimentary means for relieving the vast human suffering, would be unavailable. Any but the most elaborate shelters would be useless, quite apart from the question of what good it might be to emerge a few months later. Synthetics burned in the destruction of the cities would produce a wide variety of toxic gases, including carbon monoxide, cyanides, dioxins and furans. After the dust and soot settled out, the solar ultraviolet flux would be much larger than its present value. Immunity to disease would decline. Epidemics and pandemics would be rampant, especially after the billion or so unburied bodies began to thaw. Moreover, the combined influence of these severe and simultaneous stresses on life are likely to produce even more adverse consequences—biologists call them synergisms—that we are not yet wise enough to foresee.

So far, we have talked only of the Northern Hemisphere. But it now seems—unlike the case of a single nuclear weapons test—that in a real nuclear war, the heating of the vast quantities of atmospheric dust and soot in northern midlatitudes will transport these fine particles toward and across the Equator. We see just this happening in Martian dust storms. The Southern Hemisphere would experience effects that, while less severe than in the Northern Hemisphere, are nevertheless extremely ominous. The illusion with which some people in the Northern Hemisphere reassure themselves—catching an Air New Zealand flight in a time of serious international crisis, or the like—is now much less tenable, even on the narrow issue of personal survival for those with the price of a ticket.

But what if nuclear wars *can* be contained, and much less than 5000 megatons is detonated? Perhaps the greatest surprise in our work was that even small nuclear wars can have devastating climatic effects. We considered a war in which a mere 100 megatons were exploded, less than one percent of the world arsenals, and only in low-yield airbursts over cities. This scenario, we found, would ignite thousands of fires, and the smoke from these fires alone would be enough to generate an epoch of cold and dark almost as severe as in the 5000-megaton case. The threshold for what Richard Turco has called The Nuclear Winter is very low.

Could we have overlooked some important effect? The carrying of dust and soot from the Northern to the Southern Hemisphere (as well as more local atmospheric circulation) will certainly thin the clouds out over the Northern Hemisphere. But, in many cases, this thinning would be insufficient to render the climatic consequences tolerable—and every time it got better in the Northern Hemisphere, it would get worse in the Southern.

Our results have been carefully scrutinized by more than 100 scientists in the United States, Europe and the Soviet Union. There are still arguments on points of detail. But the overall conclusion seems to be agreed upon: There are severe and previously unanticipated global consequences of nuclear war—subfreezing temperatures in a twilit radioactive gloom lasting for months or longer.

Scientists initially underestimated the effects of fallout, were amazed that nuclear explosions in space disabled distant satellites, had no idea that the fireballs from high-yield thermonuclear explosions could deplete the ozone layer and missed altogether the possible climatic effects of nuclear dust and smoke. What else have we overlooked?

Nuclear war is a problem that can be treated only theoretically. It is not amenable to experimentation. Conceivably, we have left something important out of our analysis, and the effects are more modest than we calculate. On the other hand, it is also possible—and, from previous experience, even likely—that there are further adverse effects that no one has yet been wise enough to recognize. With billions of lives at stake, where does conservatism lie—in assuming that the results will be better than we calculate, or worse?

Many biologists, considering the nuclear winter that these calculations describe, believe they carry somber implications for life on Earth. Many species of plants and animals would become extinct. Vast numbers of surviving humans would starve to death. The delicate ecological relations that bind together organisms on Earth in a fabric of mutual dependency would be torn, perhaps irreparably. There is little question that our global civilization would be destroyed. The human population would be reduced to prehistoric levels, or less. Life for any survivors would be extremely hard. And there seems to be a real possibility of the extinction of the human species.

It is now almost 40 years since the invention of nuclear weapons. 26 We have not yet experienced a global thermonuclear war—although on more than one occasion we have come tremulously close. I do not think our luck can hold forever. Men and machines are fallible, as recent events remind us. Fools and madmen do exist, and sometimes rise to power. Concentrating always on the near future, we have ignored the long-term consequences of our actions. We have placed our civilization and our species in jeopardy.

Fortunately, it is not yet too late. We can safeguard the planetary 27 civilization and the human family if we so choose. There is no more important or more urgent issue.

Questions for Study and Discussion

1. How does Sagan answer those who feel that a limited nuclear war is possible?

2. How does Sagan make us aware of the tremendous explosive power of a typical nuclear weapon?

3. In paragraph 6 Sagan presents the example of the Bravo test on Bikini Atoll. What point is he trying to illustrate with this example?

4. Sagan describes the mission of the U.S. Mariner 9 spacecraft to Mars. How are the findings of this space probe related to Sagan's discussion of nuclear warfare? Why does he stress the chance nature of these discoveries?

5. How does Sagan assure us that his group's findings are not flawed?

6. Identify several metaphors and similes that Sagan uses in his essay and explain how each works.

Writing Topics

1. Imagine yourself the survivor of a nuclear holocaust. Describe what it might be like to endure the ensuing nuclear winter.

2. Both Lifton (pp. 589–594) and Sagan acknowledge that people find comfort in denying reality with respect to nuclear warfare. Why do people put the nuclear issue out of their minds? Why is it so necessary for us all to first recognize and then deal with this denial? How can we get people to engage in the debate over nuclear disarmament and to change national policies?

8 The Individual and Society

True democracy is based on the fact that in essence we are all equal and perfect.
OSCAR ICHAZO

Nations will rise and fall, but equality remains the ideal. The universal aim is to achieve respect for the entire race, not for the dominant few.
CARLOS P. ROMULO

Isn't the real question of abortion one of mandated pregnancy—the right of self-determination and control over the use of one's body versus the rights of an unborn potential human being?
SHIRLEY K. BELL

The quality, not the longevity, of one's life is what is important.
MARTIN LUTHER KING, JR.

Some Classic Statements

THOMAS JEFFERSON

In June 1776 the Continental Congress chose a committee of five to draft a justification for revolution, with Benjamin Franklin, John Adams, and Thomas Jefferson among its members. The committee in turn asked Jefferson to write a first draft. Born in 1743 in Albemarle County, Virginia, Jefferson was the youngest delegate to the Congress. He was, in time, to become a governor, secretary of state, and president before he died on July 4, 1826, but in 1776 he was known only as a talented lawyer out of William and Mary College with a gift for words. His draft was lightly revised by Adams and Franklin and amended during the Congress's debate, but it remains essentially the work not of a committee but of one man with the political insight, the vision, and the rhetorical skill to speak for his people.

The Declaration of Independence

When in the course of human events, it becomes necessary for one people to dissolve the political bands which have connected them with another, and to assume among the Powers of the earth, the separate and equal station to which the Laws of Nature and of Nature's God entitle them, a decent respect to the opinions of mankind requires that they should declare the causes which impel them to the separation. 1

We hold these truths to be self-evident, that all men are created equal, that they are endowed by their Creator with certain unalienable Rights, that among these are Life, Liberty and the pursuit of Happiness. That to secure these rights, Governments are instituted among Men deriving their just powers from the consent of the governed. That whenever any Form of Government becomes destructive of these ends, it is the Right of the People to alter or to abolish it, and to institute new Government, laying its foundation on such principles and organizing its powers in such form, as to them shall seem most likely to effect their Safety and Happiness. Prudence, indeed, will dictate that Governments 2

643

long established should not be changed for light and transient causes; and accordingly all experience hath shown, that mankind are more disposed to suffer, while evils are sufferable, than to right themselves by abolishing the forms to which they are accustomed. But when a long train of abuses and usurpations pursuing invariably the same Object evinces a design to reduce them under absolute Despotism, it is their right, it is their duty, to throw off such government, and to provide new Guards for their future security. Such has been the patient sufferance of these Colonies; and such is now the necessity which constrains them to alter their former Systems of Government. The history of the present King of Great Britain is a history of repeated injuries and usurpations, all having in direct object the establishment of an absolute Tyranny over these States. To prove this, let Facts be submitted to a candid world.

He has refused his Assent to laws, the most wholesome and necessary for the public good. 3

He has forbidden his Governors to pass Laws of immediate and pressing importance, unless suspended in their operation till his Assent should be obtained; and when so suspended, he has utterly neglected to attend to them. 4

He has refused to pass other Laws for the accommodation of large districts of people, unless those people would relinquish the right of Representation in the Legislature, a right inestimable to them and formidable to tyrants only. 5

He has called together legislative bodies at places unusual, uncomfortable, and distant from the depository of their Public Records, for the sole purpose of fatiguing them into compliance with his measures. 6

He has dissolved Representative Houses repeatedly, for opposing with manly firmness his invasions on the rights of the people. 7

He has refused for a long time, after such dissolutions, to cause others to be elected; whereby the Legislative Powers, incapable of Annihilation, have returned to the People at large for their exercise; the State remaining in the mean time exposed to all the dangers of invasion from without, and convulsions within. 8

He has endeavoured to prevent the population of these States; for that purpose obstructing the Laws of Naturalization of Foreigners; refusing to pass others to encourage their migration hither, and raising the conditions of new Appropriations of Lands. 9

He has obstructed the Administration of Justice, by refusing his Assent to Laws for establishing Judiciary Powers. 10

He has made Judges dependent on his Will alone, for the tenure of their offices, and the amount and payment of their salaries. 11

He has erected a multitude of New Offices, and sent hither swarms   12
of Officers to harass our People, and eat out their substance.

He has kept among us, in time of peace, Standing Armies without   13
the Consent of our Legislature.

He has affected to render the Military independent of and superior   14
to the Civil Power.

He has combined with others to subject us to jurisdictions foreign   15
to our constitution, and unacknowledged by our laws; giving his Assent
to their acts of pretended Legislation:

For quartering large bodies of armed troops among us: 16

For protecting them, by a mock Trial, from Punishment for any   17
Murders which they should commit on the Inhabitants of these States:

For cutting off our Trade with all parts of the world: 18

For imposing Taxes on us without our Consent: 19

For depriving us in many cases, of the benefits of Trial by Jury: 20

For transporting us beyond Seas to be tried for pretended offenses: 21

For abolishing the free System of English Laws in a Neighbouring   22
Province, establishing therein an Arbitrary government, and enlarging
its boundaries so as to render it at once an example and fit instrument
for introducing the same absolute rule into these Colonies:

For taking away our Charters, abolishing our most valuable Laws,   23
and altering fundamentally the Forms of our Governments:

For suspending our own Legislatures, and declaring themselves in-   24
vested with Power to legislate for us in all cases whatsoever.

He has abdicated Government here, by declaring us out of his   25
Protection and waging War against us.

He has plundered our seas, ravaged our Coasts, burnt our towns   26
and destroyed the Lives of our people.

He is at this time transporting large Armies of foreign Mercenaries   27
to compleat works of death, desolation and tyranny, already begun with
circumstances of Cruelty & perfidy scarcely paralleled in the most barbarous ages, and totally unworthy the Head of a civilized nation.

He has constrained our fellow Citizens taken Captive on the high   28
Seas to bear Arms against their Country, to become the executioners of
their friends and Brethren, or to fall themselves by their Hands.

He has excited domestic insurrections amongst us, and has endeav-   29
oured to bring on the inhabitants of our frontiers, the merciless Indian
Savages, whose known rule of warfare, is an undistinguished destruction
of all ages, sexes and conditions.

In every stage of these Oppressions We Have Petitioned for Redress   30
in the most humble terms: Our repeated petitions have been answered
only by repeated injury. A Prince, whose character is thus marked by

every act which may define a Tyrant, is unfit to be the ruler of a free People.

Nor have We been wanting in attention to our British brethren. We have warned them from time to time of attempts by their legislature to extend an unwarrantable jurisdiction over us. We have reminded them of the circumstances of our emigration and settlement here. We have appealed to their native justice and magnanimity and we have conjured them by the ties of our common kindred to disavow these usurpations, which would inevitably interrupt our connections and correspondence. They too have been deaf to the voice of justice and of consanguinity. We must, therefore, acquiesce in the necessity, which denounces our Separation, and hold them, as we hold the rest of mankind, Enemies in War, in Peace Friends.   31

We, therefore, the Representatives of the United States of America, in General Congress, Assembled, appealing to the Supreme Judge of the world for the rectitude of our intentions, do, in the Name, and by Authority of the good People of these Colonies, solemnly publish and declare, That these United Colonies are, and of Right ought to be Free and Independent States; that they are Absolved from all Allegiance to the British Crown, and that all political connection between them and the State of Great Britain, is and ought to be totally dissolved; and that as Free and Independent States, they have full power to levy War, conclude Peace, contract Alliances, establish Commerce, and to do all other Acts and Things which Independent States may of right do. And for the support of this Declaration, with a firm reliance on the protection of Divine Providence, we mutually pledge to each other our lives, our Fortunes and our sacred Honor.   32

Questions for Study and Discussion

1. What, according to the Declaration of Independence, is the purpose of government? Are there other legitimate purposes that governments serve? If so, what are they?

2. What is the chief argument offered by the Declaration for "abolishing" English rule over the American colonies? How is that argument supported?

3. What argument does the Declaration make for overthrowing any unacceptable government? What assumptions underlie this argument? Where does sovereignty lie, according to the Declaration?

4. According to the Declaration, how did the colonists try to persuade the English king to rule more justly?

5. Is the language of the Declaration of Independence coolly reasonable or emotional, or does it change from one to the other? Give examples to support your answer.

Writing Topics

1. The adoption of the Declaration of Independence was, among other things, a matter of practical politics. Using library sources, research the deliberations of the Continental Congress and explain how and why the final version of the Declaration differs from Jefferson's first draft.

2. To some people the Declaration of Independence still accurately reflects America's political philosophy and way of life; to others it does not. What is your own position? Discuss your analysis of the Declaration's contemporary relevance.

In 1845, at the age of twenty-eight, Henry David Thoreau built a cabin in the woods near Walden Pond and moved in. He wanted to live alone with nature and hoped to simplify his life to be free of materialistic concerns. He stayed there for more than two years, an experience he later described in his greatest literary work, *Walden, or Life in the Woods* (1854).

Thoreau was born in 1817 in Concord, Massachusetts. After graduating from Harvard College, he worked as a schoolteacher, a house-painter, and a handyman—the latter for his mentor and friend, Ralph Waldo Emerson. Thoreau was always an activist, once going to jail rather than pay a poll tax to a government that made war with Mexico and supported slavery. This act of civil disobedience in protest of actions that he considered unjust is the subject of his essay "Civil Disobedience" (1849), which later inspired both Gandhi and Martin Luther King, Jr., in their nonviolent protests. Thoreau died in 1862.

Civil Disobedience

I heartily accept the motto, "That government is best which governs least;" and I should like to see it acted up to more rapidly and systematically. Carried out, it finally amounts to this, which also I believe—"That government is best which governs not at all;" and when men are prepared for it, that will be the kind of government which they will have. Government is at best but an expedient; but most governments are usually, and all governments are sometimes, inexpedient. The objections which have been brought against a standing army, and they are many and weighty, and deserve to prevail, may also at last be brought against a standing government. The standing army is only an arm of the standing government. The government itself, which is only the mode which the people have chosen to execute their will, is equally liable to be abused and perverted before the people can act through it. Witness the present Mexican war, the work of comparatively a few individuals using the standing government as their tool; for, in the outset, the people would not have consented to this measure. 1

This American government—what is it but a tradition, though a recent one, endeavoring to transmit itself unimpaired to posterity, but each instant losing some of its integrity? It has not the vitality and force of a single living man; for a single man can bend it to his will. It is a sort of wooden gun to the people themselves. But it is not the less necessary for this; for the people must have some complicated machinery 2 or other, and hear its din, to satisfy that idea of government which they have. Governments show thus how successfully men can be imposed on, even impose on themselves, for their own advantage. It is excellent, we must all allow. Yet this government never of itself furthered any enterprise, but by the alacrity with which it got out of its way. *It* does not keep the country free. *It* does not settle the West. *It* does not educate. The character inherent in the American people has done all that has been accomplished; and it would have done somewhat more, if the government had not sometimes got in its way. For government is an expedient by which men would fain succeed in letting one another alone; and, as has been said, when it is most expedient, the governed are most let alone by it. Trade and commerce, if they were not made of india-rubber, would never manage to bounce over the obstacles which legislators are continually putting in their way; and, if one were to judge these men wholly by the effects of their actions and not partly by their intentions, they would deserve to be classed and punished with those mischievous persons who put obstructions on the railroads.

But, to speak practically and as a citizen, unlike those who call   3
themselves no-government men, I ask for, not at once no government, but *at once* a better government. Let every man make known what kind of government would command his respect, and that will be one step toward obtaining it.

After all, the practical reason why, when the power is once in the   4
hands of the people, a majority are permitted, and for a long period continue, to rule is not because they are most likely to be in the right, nor because this seems fairest to the minority, but because they are physically the strongest. But a government in which the majority rule in all cases cannot be based on justice, even as far as men understand it. Can there not be a government in which majorities do not virtually decide right and wrong, but conscience?—in which majorities decide only those questions to which the rule of expediency is applicable? Must the citizen ever for a moment, or in the least degree, resign his conscience to the legislator? Why has every man a conscience, then? I think that we should be men first, and subjects afterwards. It is not desirable to cultivate a respect for the law, so much as for the right. The only obligation which I have a right to assume is to do at any time what I think right. It is truly enough said that a corporation has no conscience; but a corporation of conscientious men is a corporation *with* a conscience. Law never made men a whit more just; and, by means of their respect for it, even the well-disposed are daily made the agents of injustice. A common and natural result of an undue respect for law is, that you may see a file of soldiers, colonel, captain, corporal, privates, powder-monkeys, and all,

marching in admirable order over hill and dale to the wars, against their wills, ay, against their common sense and consciences, which makes it very steep marching indeed, and produces a palpitation of the heart. They have no doubt that it is a damnable business in which they are concerned; they are all peaceably inclined. Now, what are they? Men at all? or small movable forts and magazines, at the service of some unscrupulous man in power? Visit the Navy-Yard, and behold a marine, such a man as an American government can make, or such as it can make a man with its black arts—a mere shadow and reminiscence of humanity, a man laid out alive and standing, and already, as one may say, buried under arms with funeral accompaniments, though it may be,—

Not a drum was heard, not a funeral note,
    As his corse to the rampart we hurried;
Not a soldier discharged his farewell shot
    O'er the grave where our hero was buried.[1]

The mass of men serve the state thus, not as men mainly, but as   5
machines, with their bodies. They are the standing army, and the militia, jailers, constables, *posse comitatus*, etc. In most cases there is no free exercise whatever of the judgment or of the moral sense; but they put themselves on a level with wood and earth and stones; and wooden men can perhaps be manufactured that will serve the purpose as well. Such command no more respect than men of straw or a lump of dirt. They have the same sort of worth only as horses and dogs. Yet such as these even are commonly esteemed good citizens. Others—as most legislators, politicians, lawyers, ministers, and office-holders—serve the state chiefly with their heads; and, as they rarely make any moral distinctions, they are as likely to serve the devil, without *intending* it, as God. A very few— as heroes, patriots, martyrs, reformers in the great sense, and *men*—serve the state with their consciences also, and so necessarily resist it for the most part; and they are commonly treated as enemies by it. A wise man will only be useful as a man, and will not submit to be "clay," and "stop a hole to keep the wind away,"[2] but leave that office to his dust at least:—

I am too high-born to be propertied,
To be a secondary at control,
Or useful serving-man and instrument
To any sovereign state throughout the world.[3]

---

[1]Charles Wolfe, "Burial of Sir John Moore at Corunna" (1817).
[2]*Hamlet*, V, i, ll. 236–237.
[3]*King John*, V, ii, ll. 79–82.

He who gives himself entirely to his fellow-men appears to them   6
useless and selfish; but he who gives himself partially to them is pronounced a benefactor and philanthropist.

How does it become a man to behave toward this American gov-   7
ernment today? I answer, that he cannot without disgrace be associated
with it. I cannot for an instant recognize that political organization as
my government which is the *slave's* government also.

All men recognize the right of revolution; that is, the right to refuse   8
allegiance to, and to resist, the government, when its tyranny or its
inefficiency are great and unendurable. But almost all say that such is
not the case now. But such was the case, they think, in the Revolution
of '75. If one were to tell me that this was a bad government because it
taxed certain foreign commodities brought to its ports, it is most probable
that I should not make an ado about it, for I can do without them. All
machines have their friction; and possibly this does enough good to counter-
balance the evil. At any rate, it is a great evil to make a stir about it.
But when the friction comes to have its machine, and oppression and
robbery are organized, I say, let us not have such a machine any longer.
In other words, when a sixth of the population of a nation which has
undertaken to be the refuge of liberty are slaves, and a whole country is
unjustly overrun and conquered by a foreign army, and subjected to
military law, I think that it is not too soon for honest men to rebel and
revolutionize. What makes this duty the more urgent is the fact that the
country so overrun is not our own, but ours is the invading army.

Paley,[4] a common authority with many on moral questions, in his   9
chapter on the "Duty of Submission to Civil Government," resolves all
civil obligation into expediency; and he proceeds to say that "so long as
the interest of the whole society requires it, that is, so long as the established government cannot be resisted or changed without public incon-
veniency, it is the will of God . . . that the established government be
obeyed—and no longer. This principle being admitted, the justice of
every particular case of resistance is reduced to a computation of the
quantity of the danger and grievance on the one side, and of the probability and expense of redressing it on the other." Of this, he says, every
man shall judge for himself. But Paley appears never to have contemplated those cases to which the rule of expediency does not apply, in
which a people, as well as an individual, must do justice, cost what it
may. If I have unjustly wrested a plank from a drowning man, I must

---

[4]Rev. William Paley, *Principles of Moral and Political Philosophy* (1785), a text Thoreau
is known to have studied at Harvard College.

restore it to him though I drown myself.[5] This, according to Paley, would be inconvenient. But he that would save his life, in such a case, shall lose it.[6] This people must cease to hold slaves, and to make war on Mexico, though it cost them their existence as a people.

In their practice, nations agree with Paley; but does any one think   10
that Massachusetts does exactly what is right at the present crisis?

A drab of state, a cloth-o'-silver slut,
To have her train borne up, and her soul trail in the dirt.

Practically speaking, the opponents to a reform in Massachusetts are not a hundred thousand politicians at the South, but a hundred thousand merchants and farmers here, who are more interested in commerce and agriculture than they are in humanity, and are not prepared to do justice to the slave and to Mexico, *cost what it may.* I quarrel not with far-off foes, but with those who, near at home, coöperate with, and do the bidding of, those far away, and without whom the latter would be harmless. We are accustomed to say, that the mass of men are unprepared; but improvement is slow, because the few are not materially wiser or better than the many. It is not so important that many should be as good as you, as that there be some absolute goodness somewhere; for that will leaven the whole lump.[7] There are thousands who are *in opinion* opposed to slavery and to the war, who yet in effect do nothing to put an end to them; who, esteeming themselves children of Washington and Franklin, sit down with their hands in their pockets, and say that they know not what to do, and do nothing; who even postpone the question of freedom to the question of free trade, and quietly read the prices-current along with the latest advices from Mexico, after dinner, and, it may be, fall asleep over them both. What is the price-current of an honest man and patriot today? They hesitate, and they regret, and sometimes they petition; but they do nothing in earnest and with effect. They will wait, well disposed, for others to remedy the evil, that they may no longer have it to regret. At most, they give only a cheap vote, and a feeble countenance and God-speed, to the right, as it goes by them. There are nine hundred and ninety-nine patrons of virtue to one virtuous man. But it is easier to deal with the real possessor of a thing than with the temporary guardian of it.

All voting is a sort of gaming, like checkers or backgammon, with   11
a slight moral tinge to it, a playing with right and wrong, with moral

---

[5]Cited by Cicero, *De Officiis*, III, a text Thoreau knew at college.
[6]Luke IX: 24; Matthew X: 39.
[7]I Corinthians V: 6.

questions; and betting naturally accompanies it. The character of the voters is not staked. I cast my vote, perchance, as I think right; but I am not vitally concerned that that right should prevail. I am willing to leave it to the majority. Its obligation, therefore, never exceeds that of expediency. Even voting *for the right* is *doing* nothing for it. It is only expressing to men feebly your desire that it should prevail. A wise man will not leave the right to the mercy of chance, nor wish it to prevail through the power of the majority. There is but little virtue in the action of masses of men. When the majority shall at length vote for the abolition of slavery, it will be because they are indifferent to slavery, or because there is but little slavery left to be abolished by their vote. *They* will then be the only slaves. Only *his* vote can hasten the abolition of slavery who asserts his own freedom by his vote.

I hear of a convention to be held at Baltimore, or elsewhere, for   12
the selection of a candidate for the Presidency, made up chiefly of editors, and men who are politicians by profession; but I think, what is it to any independent, intelligent, and respectable man what decision they may come to? Shall we not have the advantage of his wisdom and honesty, nevertheless? Can we not count upon some independent votes? Are there not many individuals in the country who do not attend conventions? But no: I find that the respectable man, so called, has immediately drifted from his position, and despairs of his country, when his country has more reason to despair of him. He forthwith adopts one of the candidates thus selected as the only *available* one, thus proving that he is himself *available* for any purposes of the demagogue. His vote is of no more worth than that of any unprincipled foreigner or hireling native, who may have been bought. O for a man who is a *man*, and, as my neighbor says, has a bone in his back which you cannot pass your hand through! Our statistics are at fault: the population has been returned too large. How many *men* are there to a square thousand miles in this country? Hardly one. Does not America offer any inducement for men to settle here? The American has dwindled into an Odd Fellow—one who may be known by the development of his organ of gregariousness, and a manifest lack of intellect and cheerful self-reliance; whose first and chief concern, on coming into the world, is to see that the almshouses are in good repair; and, before yet he has lawfully donned the virile garb, to collect a fund for the support of the widows and orphans that may be; who, in short, ventures to live only by the aid of the Mutual Insurance company, which has promised to bury him decently.

It is not a man's duty, as a matter of course, to devote himself to   13
the eradication of any, even the most enormous, wrong; he may still properly have other concerns to engage him; but it is his duty, at least,

to wash his hands of it, and, if he gives it no thought longer, not to give it practically his support. If I devote myself to other pursuits and contemplations, I must first see, at least, that I do not pursue them sitting upon another man's shoulders. I must get off him first, that he may pursue his contemplations too. See what gross inconsistency is tolerated. I have heard some of my townsmen say, "I should like to have them order me out to help put down an insurrection of the slaves, or to march to Mexico;— see if I would go"; and yet these very men have each, directly by their allegiance, and so indirectly, at least, by their money, furnished a substitute. The soldier is applauded who refuses to serve in an unjust war by those who do not refuse to sustain the unjust government which makes the war; is applauded by those whose own act and authority he disregards and sets at naught; as if the state were penitent to that degree that it hired one to scourge it while it sinned, but not to that degree that it left off sinning for a moment. Thus, under the name of Order and Civil Government, we are all made at last to pay homage to and support our own meanness. After the first blush of sin comes its indifference; and from immoral it becomes, as it were, *unmoral*, and not quite unnecessary to that life which we have made.

The broadest and most prevalent error requires the most disinterested virtue to sustain it. The slight reproach to which the virtue of patriotism is commonly liable, the noble are most likely to incur. Those who, while they disapprove of the character and measures of a government, yield to it their allegiance and support are undoubtedly its most conscientious supporters, and so frequently the most serious obstacles to reform. Some are petitioning the State to dissolve the Union, to disregard the requisitions of the President. Why do they not dissolve it themselves—the union between themselves and the State—and refuse to pay their quota into its treasury? Do not they stand in the same relation to the State that the State does to the Union? And have not the same reasons prevented the State from resisting the Union which have prevented them from resisting the State?   14

How can a man be satisfied to entertain an opinion merely, and enjoy *it*? Is there any enjoyment in it, if his opinion is that he is aggrieved? If you are cheated out of a single dollar by your neighbor, you do not rest satisfied with knowing that you are cheated, or with saying that you are cheated, or even with petitioning him to pay you your due; but you take effectual steps at once to obtain the full amount, and see that you are never cheated again. Action from principle, the perception and the performance of right, changes things and relations; it is essentially revolutionary, and does not consist wholly with anything which   15 was. It not only divides States and churches, it divides families; ay, it divides the *individual*, separating the diabolical in him from the divine.

Unjust laws exist: shall we be content to obey them, or shall we endeavor to amend them, and obey them until we have succeeded, or shall we transgress them at once? Men generally, under such a government as this, think that they ought to wait until they have persuaded the majority to alter them. They think that, if they should resist, the remedy would be worse than the evil. But it is the fault of the government itself that the remedy *is* worse than the evil. *It* makes it worse. Why is it not more apt to anticipate and provide for reform? Why does it not cherish its wise minority? Why does it cry and resist before it is hurt? Why does it not encourage its citizens to be on the alert to point out its faults, and *do* better than it would have them? Why does it always crucify Christ, and excommunicate Copernicus and Luther, and pronounce Washington and Franklin rebels?   16

One would think, that a deliberate and practical denial of its authority was the only offence never contemplated by government; else, why has it not assigned its definite, its suitable and proportionate, penalty? If a man who has no property refuses but once to earn nine shillings for the State, he is put in prison for a period unlimited by any law that I know, and determined only by the discretion of those who placed him there; but if he should steal ninety times nine shillings from the State, he is soon permitted to go at large again.   17

If the injustice is part of the necessary friction of the machine of government, let it go, let it go: perchance it will wear smooth—certainly the machine will wear out. If the injustice has a spring, or a pulley, or a rope, or a crank, exclusively for itself, then perhaps you may consider whether the remedy will not be worse than the evil; but if it is of such a nature that it requires you to be the agent of injustice to another, then, I say, break the law. Let your life be a counter friction to stop the machine. What I have to do is to see, at any rate, that I do not lend myself to the wrong which I condemn.   18

As for adopting the ways which the State has provided for remedying the evil, I know not of such ways. They take too much time, and a man's life will be gone. I have other affairs to attend to. I came into this world, not chiefly to make this a good place to live in, but to live in it, be it good or bad. A man has not everything to do, but something; and because he cannot do *everything*, it is not necessary that he should do *something* wrong. It is not my business to be petitioning the Governor or the Legislature any more than it is theirs to petition me; and if they should not hear my petition, what should I do then? But in this case the State has provided no way: its very Constitution is the evil. This may   19 seem to be harsh and stubborn and unconciliatory; but it is to treat with the utmost kindness and consideration the only spirit that can appreciate or deserves it. So is all change for the better, like birth and death, which convulse the body.

I do not hesitate to say, that those who call themselves Abolitionists   20 should at once effectually withdraw their support, both in person and property, from the government of Massachusetts, and not wait till they constitute a majority of one, before they suffer the right to prevail through them. I think that it is enough if they have God on their side, without waiting for that other one. Moreover, any man more right than his neighbors constitutes a majority of one already.

I meet the American government, or its representative, the State   21 government, directly, and face to face, once a year—no more—in the person of its tax-gatherer; this is the only mode in which a man situated as I am necessarily meets it; and it then says distinctly, Recognize me; and the simplest, the most effectual, and, in the present posture of affairs, the indispensablest mode of treating with it on this head, of expressing your little satisfaction with and love for it, is to deny it then. My civil neighbor, the tax-gatherer, is the very man I have to deal with—for it is, after all, with men and not with parchment that I quarrel—and he has voluntarily chosen to be an agent of the government. How shall he ever know well what he is and does as an officer of the government, or as a man, until he is obliged to consider whether he shall treat me, his neighbor, for whom he has respect, as a neighbor and well-disposed man, or as a maniac and disturber of the peace, and see if he can get over this obstruction to his neighborliness without a ruder and more impetuous thought or speech corresponding with his action. I know this well, that if one thousand, if one hundred, if ten men whom I could name—if ten *honest* men only—ay, if *one* HONEST man, in this State of Massachusetts, *ceasing to hold slaves*, were actually to withdraw from this copartnership, and be locked up in the county jail therefor, it would be the abolition of slavery in America. For it matters not how small the beginning may seem to be: what is once well done is done forever. But we love better to talk about it: that we say is our mission. Reform keeps many scores of newspapers in its service, but not one man. If my esteemed neighbor, the State's ambassador,[8] who will devote his days to the settlement of the question of human rights in the Council Chamber, instead of being threatened with the prisons of Carolina, were to sit down the prisoner

---

[8]In 1844, Samuel Hoar, the statesman of Concord, was sent to Charleston, South Carolina, on behalf of Negro seamen from Massachusetts threatened with arrest and slavery on entering the port, and was rudely expelled from Charleston.

of Massachusetts, that State which is so anxious to foist the sin of slavery upon her sister—though at present she can discover only an act of inhospitality to be the ground of a quarrel with her—the Legislature would not wholly waive the subject the following winter.

Under a government which imprisons any unjustly, the true place   22
for a just man is also a prison. The proper place to-day, the only place which Massachusetts has provided for her freer and less desponding spirits, is in her prisons, to be put out and locked out of the State by her own act, as they have already put themselves out by their principles. It is there that the fugitive slave, and the Mexican prisoner on parole, and the Indian come to plead the wrongs of his race should find them; on that separate, but more free and honorable, ground, where the State places those who are not *with* her, but *against* her—the only house in a slave State in which a free man can abide with honor. If any think that their influence would be lost there, and their voices no longer afflict the ear of the State, that they would not be as an enemy within its walls, they do not know by how much truth is stronger than error, nor how much more eloquently and effectively he can combat injustice who has experienced a little in his own person. Cast your whole vote, not a strip of paper merely, but your whole influence. A minority is powerless while it conforms to the majority; it is not even a minority then; but it is irresistible when it clogs by its whole weight. If the alternative is to keep all just men in prison, or give up war and slavery, the State will not hesitate which to choose. If a thousand men were not to pay their tax-bills this year, that would not be a violent and bloody measure, as it would be to pay them, and enable the State to commit violence and shed innocent blood. This is, in fact, the definition of a peaceable revolution, if any such is possible. If the tax-gatherer, or any public officer, asks me, as one has done, "But what shall I do?" my answer is, "If you really wish to do anything, resign your office." When the subject has refused allegiance, and the officer has resigned his office, then the revolution is accomplished. But even suppose blood should flow. Is there not a sort of blood shed when the conscience is wounded? Through this wound a man's real manhood and immortality flow out, and he bleeds to an everlasting death. I see this blood flowing now.

I have contemplated the imprisonment of the offender, rather than   23
the seizure of his goods—though both will serve the same purpose—because they who assert the purest right, and consequently are most dangerous to a corrupt State, commonly have not spent much time in accumulating property. To such the State renders comparatively small service, and a slight tax is wont to appear exorbitant, particularly if they are obliged to earn it by special labor with their hands. If there were one

who lived wholly without the use of money, the State itself would hesitate to demand it of him. But the rich man—not to make any invidious comparison—is always sold to the institution which makes him rich. Absolutely speaking, the more money, the less virtue; for money comes between a man and his objects, and obtains them for him; and it was certainly no great virtue to obtain it. It puts to rest many questions which he would otherwise be taxed to answer; while the only new question which it puts is the hard but superfluous one, how to spend it. Thus his moral ground is taken from under his feet. The opportunities of living are diminished in proportion as what are called the "means" are increased. The best thing a man can do for his culture when he is rich is to endeavor to carry out those schemes which he entertained when he was poor. Christ answered the Herodians according to their condition. "Show me the tribute-money," said he;—and one took a penny out of his pocket;—if you use money which has the image of Caesar on it, and which he has made current and valuable, that is, *if you are men of the State*, and gladly enjoy the advantages of Caesar's government, then pay him back some of his own when he demands it. "Render therefore to Caesar that which is Caesar's, and to God those things which are God's"— leaving them no wiser than before as to which was which; for they did not wish to know.

When I converse with the freest of my neighbors, I perceive that,   24
whatever they may say about the magnitude and seriousness of the question, and their regard for the public tranquillity, the long and the short of the matter is, that they cannot spare the protection of the existing government, and they dread the consequences to their property and families of disobedience to it. For my own part, I should not like to think that I ever rely on the protection of the State. But, if I deny the authority of the State when it presents its tax-bill, it will soon take and waste all my property, and so harass me and my children without end. This is hard. This makes it impossible for a man to live honestly, and at the same time comfortably, in outward respects. It will not be worth the while to accumulate property; that would be sure to go again. You must hire or squat somewhere, and raise but a small crop, and eat that soon. You must live within yourself, and depend upon yourself always tucked up and ready for a start, and not have many affairs. A man may grow rich in Turkey even, if he will be in all respects a good subject of the Turkish government. Confucius said: "If a state is governed by the principles of reason, poverty and misery are subjects of shame; if a state is not governed by the principles of reason, riches and honors are the subjects of shame." No: until I want the protection of Massachusetts to be extended to me in some distant Southern port, where my liberty is

endangered, or until I am bent solely on building up an estate at home by peaceful enterprise, I can afford to refuse allegiance to Massachusetts, and her right to my property and life. It costs me less in every sense to incur the penalty of disobedience to the State than it would to obey. I should feel as if I were worth less in that case.

Some years ago, the State met me in behalf of the Church, and commanded me to pay a certain sum toward the support of a clergyman whose preaching my father attended, but never I myself. "Pay," it said, "or be locked up in the jail." I declined to pay.[9] But, unfortunately, another man saw fit to pay it. I did not see why the schoolmaster should be taxed to support the priest, and not the priest the schoolmaster; for I was not the State's schoolmaster, but I supported myself by voluntary subscription. I did not see why the lyceum should not present its tax-bill, and have the State to back its demand, as well as the Church. However, at the request of the selectmen, I condescended to make some such statement as this in writing:—"Know all men by these presents, that I, Henry Thoreau, do not wish to be regarded as a member of any incorporated society which I have not joined." This I gave to the town clerk; and he has it. The State, having thus learned that I did not wish to be regarded as a member of that church, has never made a like demand on me since; though it said that it must adhere to its original presumption that time. If I had known how to name them, I should then have signed off in detail from all the societies which I never signed on to; but I did not know where to find a complete list.

I have paid no poll-tax for six years. I was put into a jail once on this account, for one night; and, as I stood considering the walls of solid stone, two or three feet thick, the door of wood and iron, a foot thick, and the iron grating which strained the light, I could not help being struck with the foolishness of that institution which treated me as if I were mere flesh and blood and bones to be locked up. I wondered that it should have concluded at length that this was the best use it could put me to, and had never thought to avail itself of my services in some way. I saw that, if there was a wall of stone between me and my townsmen, there was a still more difficult one to climb or break through before they could get to be as free as I was. I did not for a moment feel confined, and the walls seemed a great waste of stone and mortar. I felt as if I alone of all my townsmen had paid my tax. They plainly did not know how to treat me, but behaved like persons who are underbred. In every threat and in every compliment there was a blunder; for they thought that my

25

26

---

[9]Thoreau's first act on returning to Concord after leaving college was to "sign off" from the Church.

chief desire was to stand the other side of that stone wall. I could not but smile to see how industriously they locked the door on my meditations, which followed them out again without let or hindrance, and *they* were really all that was dangerous. As they could not reach me, they had resolved to punish my body; just as boys, if they cannot come at some person against whom they have a spite, will abuse his dog. I saw that the State was half-witted, that it was timid as a lone woman with her silver spoons, and that it did not know its friends from its foes, and I lost all my remaining respect for it, and pitied it.

Thus the State never intentionally confronts a man's sense, intel-   27
lectual or moral, but only his body, his senses. It is not armed with superior wit or honesty, but with superior physical strength. I was not born to be forced. I will breathe after my own fashion. Let us see who is the strongest. What force has a multitude? They only can force me who obey a higher law than I. They force me to become like themselves. I do not hear of *men* being *forced* to live this way or that by masses of men. What sort of life were that to live? When I meet a government which says to me, "Your money or your life," why should I be in haste to give it my money? It may be in a great strait, and not know what to do: I cannot help that. It must help itself; do as I do. It is not worth the while to snivel about it. I am not responsible for the successful working of the machinery of society. I am not the son of the engineer. I perceive that, when an acorn and a chestnut fall side by side, the one does not remain inert to make way for the other, but both obey their own laws, and spring and grow and flourish as best they can, till one, perchance, overshadows and destroys the other. If a plant cannot live according to its nature, it dies; and so a man.

The night in prison was novel and interesting enough. The pris-   28
oners in their shirt-sleeves were enjoying a chat and the evening air in the doorway, when I entered. But the jailer said, "Come, boys, it is time to lock up"; and so they dispersed, and I heard the sound of their steps returning into the hollow apartments. My room-mate was introduced to me by the jailer as "a first-rate fellow and a clever man." When the door was locked, he showed me where to hang my hat, and how he managed matters there. The rooms were whitewashed once a month; and this one, at least, was the whitest, most simply furnished, and probably the neatest apartment in the town. He naturally wanted to know where I came from, and what brought me there; and, when I had told him, I asked him in my turn how he came there, presuming him to be an honest man, of course; and, as the world goes, I believe he was. "Why," said he, "they accuse me of burning a barn; but I never did it." As near as I could discover, he had probably gone to bed in a barn when drunk, and smoked

his pipe there; and so a barn was burnt. He had the reputation of being a clever man, had been there some three months waiting for his trial to come on, and would have to wait as much longer; but he was quite domesticated and contented, since he got his board for nothing, and thought that he was well treated.

He occupied one window, and I the other; and I saw that if one stayed there long, his principal business would be to look out the window. I had soon read all the tracts that were left there, and examined where former prisoners had broken out, and where a grate had been sawed off, and heard the history of the various occupants of that room; for I found that even here there was a history and a gossip which never circulated beyond the walls of the jail. Probably this is the only house in the town where verses are composed, which are afterward printed in a circular form, but not published. I was shown quite a long list of verses which were composed by some young men who had been detected in an attempt to escape, who avenged themselves by singing them. 29

I pumped my fellow-prisoner as dry as I could, for fear I should never see him again; but at length he showed me which was my bed, and left me to blow out the lamp. 30

It was like travelling into a far country, such as I had never expected to behold, to lie there for one night. It seemed to me that I never had heard the town clock strike before, nor the evening sounds of the village; for we slept with the windows open, which were inside the grating. It was to see my native village in the light of the Middle Ages, and our Concord was turned into a Rhine stream, and visions of knights and castles passed before me. They were the voices of old burghers that I heard in the streets. I was an involuntary spectator and auditor of whatever was done and said in the kitchen of the adjacent village inn—a wholly new and rare experience to me. It was a closer view of my native town. I was fairly inside of it. I never had seen its institutions before. This is one of its peculiar institutions; for it is a shire town. I began to comprehend what its inhabitants were about. 31

In the morning, our breakfasts were put through the hole in the door, in small oblong-square tin pans, made to fit, and holding a pint of chocolate, with brown bread, and an iron spoon. When they called for the vessels again, I was green enough to return what bread I had left; but my comrade seized it, and said that I should lay that up for lunch or dinner. Soon after he was let out to work at haying in a neighboring field, whither he went every day, and would not be back till noon; so he bade me good-day, saying that he doubted if he should see me again. 32

When I came out of prison—for some one interfered, and paid that tax—I did not perceive that great changes had taken place on the com- 33 mon, such as he observed who went in a youth and emerged a tottering and gray-headed man; and yet a change had to my eyes come over the scene—the town, and State, and country—greater than any that mere time could effect. I saw yet more distinctly the State in which I lived. I saw to what extent the people among whom I lived could be trusted as good neighbors and friends; that their friendship was for summer weather only; that they did not greatly propose to do right; that they were a distinct race from me by their prejudices and superstitions, as the China-men and Malays are; that in their sacrifices to humanity they ran no risks, not even to their property; that after all they were not so noble but they treated the thief as he had treated them, and hoped, by a certain outward observance and a few prayers, and by walking in a particular straight though useless path from time to time, to save their souls. This may be to judge my neighbors harshly; for I believe that many of them are not aware that they have such an institution as the jail in their village.

It was formerly the custom in our village, when a poor debtor came out of jail, for his acquaintances to salute him, looking through their fingers, which were crossed to represent the grating of a jail window, "How do ye do?" My neighbors did not thus salute me, but first looked at me, and then at one another, as if I had returned from a long journey. I was put into jail as I was going to the shoemaker's to get a shoe which was mended. When I was let out the next morning, I preceeded to finish my errand, and, having put on my mended shoe, joined a huckleberry party, who were impatient to put themselves under my conduct; and in half an hour—for the horse was soon tackled—was in the midst of a huckleberry field, on one of our highest hills, two miles off, and then the State was nowhere to be seen. 34

This is the whole history of "My Prisons." 35

I have never declined paying the highway tax, because I am as desirous of being a good neighbor as I am of being a bad subject; and as for supporting schools, I am doing my part to educate my fellow-coun-trymen now. It is for no particular item in the tax-bill that I refuse to pay it. I simply wish to refuse allegiance to the State, to withdraw and stand aloof from it effectually. I do not care to trace the course of my dollar, if I could, till it buys a man or a musket to shoot one with—the dollar is innocent—but I am concerned to trace the effects of my alle-giance. In fact, I quietly declare war with the State, after my fashion, though I will still make what use and get what advantage of her I can, as is usual in such cases. 36

If others pay the tax which is demanded of me, from a sympathy with the State, they do but what they have already done in their own case, or rather they abet injustice to a greater extent than the State 37 requires. If they pay the tax from a mistaken interest in the individual taxed, to save his property, or prevent his going to jail, it is because they have not considered wisely how far they let their private feelings interfere with the public good.

This, then, is my position at present. But one cannot be too much 38
on his guard in such a case, lest his action be biased by obstinacy or an undue regard for the opinions of men. Let him see that he does only what belongs to himself and to the hour.

I think sometimes, Why, this people mean well, they are only 39
ignorant; they would do better if they knew how: why give your neighbors this pain to treat you as they are not inclined to? But I think again, This is no reason why I should do as they do, or permit others to suffer much greater pain of a different kind. Again, I sometimes say to myself, When many millions of men, without heat, without ill will, without personal feeling of any kind, demand of you a few shillings only, without the possibility, such is their constitution, of retracting or altering their present demand, and without the possibility, on your side, of appeal to any other millions, why expose yourself to this overwhelming brute force? You do not resist cold and hunger, the winds and the waves, thus obstinately; you quietly submit to a thousand similar necessities. You do not put your head into the fire. But just in proportion as I regard this as not wholly a brute force, but partly a human force, and consider that I have relations to those millions as to so many millions of men, and not of mere brute or inanimate things, I see that appeal is possible, first and instantaneously, from them to the Maker of them, and, secondly, from them to themselves. But if I put my head deliberately into the fire, there is no appeal to fire or to the Maker of fire, and I have only myself to blame. If I could convince myself that I have any right to be satisfied with men as they are, and to treat them accordingly, and not according, in some respects, to my requisitions and expectations of what they and I ought to be, then, like a good Mussulman and fatalist, I should endeavor to be satisfied with things as they are, and say it is the will of God. And, above all, there is this difference between resisting this and a purely brute or natural force, that I can resist this with some effect; but I cannot expect, like Orpheus, to change the nature of the rocks and trees and beasts.

I do not wish to quarrel with any man or nation. I do not wish to 40
split hairs, to make fine distinctions, or set myself up as better than my neighbors. I seek rather, I may say, even an excuse for conforming the laws of the land. I am but too ready to conform to them. Indeed, I have reason to suspect myself on this head; and each year, as the tax-gatherer comes round, I find myself disposed to review the acts and positions of

the general and State governments, and the spirit of the people, to discover a pretext for conformity.

> We must affect our country as our parents,
> And if at any time we alienate
> Our love or industry from doing it honor,
> We must respect effects and teach the soul
> Matter of conscience and religion,
> And not desire of rule or benefit.

I believe that the State will soon be able to take all my work of this sort out of my hands, and then I shall be no better a patriot than my fellow-countrymen. Seen from a lower point of view, the Constitution, with all its faults, is very good; the law and the courts are very respectable; even this State and this American government are, in many respects, very admirable, and rare things, to be thankful for, such as a great many have described them; but seen from a point of view a little higher, they are what I have described them; seen from a higher still, and the highest, who shall say what they are, or that they are worth looking at or thinking of at all?

However, the government does not concern me much, and I shall   41
bestow the fewest possible thoughts on it. It is not many moments that I live under a government, even in this world. If a man is thought-free, fancy-free, imagination-free, that which *is not* never for a long time appearing *to be* to him, unwise rulers or reformers cannot fatally interrupt him.

I know that most men think differently from myself; but those   42
whose lives are by profession devoted to the study of these or kindred subjects content me as little as any. Statesmen and legislators, standing so completely within the institution, never distinctly and nakedly behold it. They speak of moving society, but have no resting-place without it. They may be men of a certain experience and discrimination, and have no doubt invented ingenious and even useful systems, for which we sincerely thank them; but all their wit and usefulness lie within certain not very wide limits. They are wont to forget that the world is not governed by policy and expediency. Webster never goes behind government, and so cannot speak with authority about it. His words are wisdom to those legislators who contemplate no essential reform in the existing government; but for thinkers, and those who legislate for all time, he never once glances at the subject. I know of those whose serene and wise speculations on this theme would soon reveal the limits of his mind's range and hospitality. Yet, compared with the cheap professions of most reformers, and the still cheaper wisdom and eloquence of politicians in

general, his are almost the only sensible and valuable words, and we thank Heaven for him. Comparatively, he is always strong, original, and, above all, practical. Still, his quality is not wisdom, but prudence. The lawyer's truth is not Truth, but consistency or a consistent expediency. Truth is always in harmony with herself, and is not concerned chiefly to reveal the justice that may consist with wrong-doing. He well deserves to be called, as he has been called, the Defender of the Constitution. There are really no blows to be given by him but defensive ones. He is not a leader, but a follower. His leaders are the men of '87. "I have never made an effort," he says, "and never propose to make an effort; I have never countenanced an effort, and never mean to countenance an effort, to disturb the arrangement as originally made, by which the various States came into the Union." Still thinking of the sanction which the Constitution gives to slavery, he says, "Because it was a part of the original compact—let it stand." Notwithstanding his special acuteness and ability, he is unable to take a fact out of its merely political relations, and behold it as it lies absolutely to be disposed of by the intellect—what, for instance, it behooves a man to do here in America today with regard to slavery—but ventures, or is driven, to make some such desperate answer as the following, while professing to speak absolutely, and as a private man—from which what new and similar code of social duties might be inferred? "The manner," says he, "in which the governments of those States where slavery exists are to regulate it is for their own consideration, under their responsibility to their constituents, to the general laws of propriety, humanity, and justice, and to God. Associations formed elsewhere, springing from a feeling of humanity, or any other cause, have nothing whatever to do with it. They have never received any encouragement from me, and they never will."[10]

They who know of no purer sources of truth, who have traced up   43
its stream no higher, stand, and wisely stand, by the Bible and the Constitution, and drink at it there with reverence and humility; but they who behold where it comes trickling into this lake or that pool, gird up their loins once more, and continue their pilgrimage toward its fountain-head.

No man with a genius for legislation has appeared in America. They   44
are rare in the history of the world. There are orators, politicians, and eloquent men, by the thousand; but the speaker has not yet opened his mouth to speak who is capable of settling the much-vexed questions of the day. We love eloquence for its own sake, and not for any truth which it may utter, or any heroism it may inspire. Our legislators have not yet

---

[10]These extracts have been inserted since the lecture was read. [Author's note.]

learned the comparative value of free trade and of freedom, of union, and of rectitude, to a nation. They have no genius or talent for comparatively humble questions of taxation and finance, commerce and manufactures and agriculture. If we were left solely to the wordy wit of legislators in Congress for our guidance, uncorrected by the seasonable experience and the effectual complaints of the people, America would not long retain her rank among the nations. For eighteen hundred years, though perchance I have no right to say it, the New Testament has been written; yet where is the legislator who has wisdom and practical talent enough to avail himself of the light which it sheds on the science of legislation?

The authority of government, even such as I am willing to submit   45
to—for I will cheerfully obey those who know and can do better than I, and in many things even those who neither know nor can do so well—is still an impure one: to be strictly just, it must have the sanction and consent of the governed. It can have no pure right over my person and property but what I concede to it. The progress from an absolute to a limited monarchy, from a limited monarchy to a democracy, is a progress toward a true respect for the individual. Even the Chinese philosopher was wise enough to regard the individual as the basis of the empire. Is a democracy, such as we know it, the last improvement possible in government? Is it not possible to take a step further towards recognizing and organizing the rights of man? There will never be a really free and enlightened State until the State comes to recognize the individual as a higher and independent power, from which all its own power and authority are derived, and treats him accordingly. I please myself with imagining a State at least which can afford to be just to all men, and to treat the individual with respect as a neighbor; which even would not think it inconsistent with its own repose if a few were to live aloof from it, not meddling with it, nor embraced by it, who fulfilled all the duties of neighbors and fellow-men. A State which bore this kind of fruit, and suffered it to drop off as fast as it ripened, would prepare the way for a still more perfect and glorious State, which also I have imagined, but not yet anywhere seen.

Questions for Study and Discussion

1. What, according to Thoreau, is the purpose of government? What does he believe government should do? What does he think government can do? What does he believe government can't do?

2. Why was Thoreau jailed? Even though jailed, why did he consider himself free?

3. What, according to Thoreau, should people do about laws they consider unjust? What other alternatives are available? Do governments have a conscience? Should they have a conscience?

4. What is Thoreau's tone in this essay? Who is his audience? What is his attitude toward his audience?

5. What is Thoreau's purpose in this essay? Is he merely trying to rationalize his own behavior or does he have a deeper purpose?

6. On what grounds does Thoreau find fault with Daniel Webster? Do you agree with his assessment?

7. What types of evidence does Thoreau use both to support and to document his claims?

Writing Topics

1. Thoreau wrote, "Under a government which imprisons any unjustly, the true place for a just man is also a prison." Using examples from recent history, argue for or against the validity of Thoreau's statement.

2. Write an essay in which you attempt to reconcile individual conscience with majority rule.

3. Read "Letter from Birmingham Jail" by Martin Luther King, Jr. (pp. 694–709), and write an essay in which you discuss the influences of Thoreau's "Civil Disobedience."

ELIZABETH CADY STANTON

Elizabeth Cady Stanton (1815–1902), American reformer and leader of the women's rights movement, was born in Johnstown, New York. She was admitted to the Johnstown Academy, an all-male institution, by special arrangement. Stanton excelled in Greek and went on to study at the Emma Willard Academy in Troy, New York, graduating in 1832. Emma Willard was the best school Stanton could attend; all other degree-granting institutions at the time excluded women. After college Stanton studied law with her father, but again, because of her sex, was not able to gain admission to the bar.

Influenced by the legal restrictions placed upon women and the discriminations shown against them, Stanton also showed early interest in the temperance and antislavery movements. In 1840 she married Henry Brewster Stanton, an abolitionist and journalist, but in a not uncharacteristic fashion refused to "obey" him or be referred to as Mrs. Stanton. After a brief period in which the couple lived in Boston, they moved to Seneca Falls, New York, where in July of 1848 the Seneca Falls Convention, which she helped to organize, was held. At the convention, generally regarded as the beginning of the women's rights movement, Elizabeth Cady Stanton read her "Declaration of Sentiments," a list of grievances against existing laws and customs that restricted the rights of all women. Because of her pioneering work and tireless efforts on behalf of women, Stanton was elected president of the National American Woman Suffrage Association in 1890.

Declaration of Sentiments and Resolutions

Adopted by the Seneca Falls Convention,
July 19–20, 1848

When, in the course of human events, it becomes necessary for one portion of the family of man to assume among the people of the earth a position different from that which they have hitherto occupied, but one to which the laws of nature and of nature's God entitle them, a decent respect to the opinions of mankind requires that they should declare the causes that impel them to such a course.

We hold these truths to be self-evident: that all men and women are created equal; that they are endowed by their Creator with certain inalienable rights; that among these are life, liberty, and the pursuit of happiness; that to secure these rights governments are instituted, deriving their just powers from the consent of the governed. Whenever any form of government becomes destructive of these ends, it is the right of those who suffer from it to refuse allegiance to it, and to insist upon the institution of a new government, laying its foundation on such principles, and organizing its powers in such form, as to them shall seem most likely to effect their safety and happiness. Prudence, indeed, will dictate that governments long established should not be changed for light and transient causes; and accordingly all experience hath shown that mankind are more disposed to suffer, while evils are sufferable, than to right themselves by abolishing the forms to which they were accustomed. But when a long train of abuses and usurpations, pursuing invariably the same object, evinces a design to reduce them under absolute despotism, it is their duty to throw off such government, and to provide new guards for their future security. Such has been the patient sufferance of the women under this government, and such is now the necessity which constrains them to demand the equal station to which they are entitled.

The history of mankind is a history of repeated injuries and usurpations on the part of man toward woman, having in direct object the establishment of an absolute tyranny over her. To prove this, let facts be submitted to a candid world. 3

He has never permitted her to exercise her inalienable right to the elective franchise. 4

He has compelled her to submit to laws, in the formation of which she had no voice. 5

He has withheld from her rights which are given to the most ignorant and degraded men—both natives and foreigners. 6

Having deprived her of this first right of a citizen, the elective franchise, thereby leaving her without representation in the halls of legislation, he has oppressed her on all sides. 7

He has made her, if married, in the eye of the law, civilly dead. 8

He has taken from her all right in property, even to the wages she earns. 9

He has made her, morally, an irresponsible being, as she can commit many crimes with impunity, provided they be done in the presence of her husband. In the covenant of marriage, she is compelled to promise obedience to her husband, he becoming to all intents and purposes, her master—the law giving him power to deprive her of her liberty, and to administer chastisement. 10

He has so framed the laws of divorce, as to what shall be the proper causes, and in case of separation, to whom the guardianship of the children shall be given, as to be wholly regardless of the happiness of women—the law, in all cases, going upon a false supposition of the supremacy of man, and giving all power into his hands. 11

After depriving her of all rights as a married woman, if single, and the owner of property, he has taxed her to support a government which recognizes her only when her property can be made profitable to it.

He has monopolized nearly all the profitable employments, and from those she is permitted to follow, she receives but a scanty remuneration. He closes against her all the avenues to wealth and distinction which he considers most honorable to himself. As a teacher of theology, medicine, or law, she is not known.

He has denied her the facilities for obtaining a thorough education, all colleges being closed against her.

He allows her in Church, as well as State, but a subordinate position, claiming Apostolic authority for her exclusion from the ministry, and, with some exceptions, from any public participation in the affairs of the Church.

He has created a false public sentiment by giving to the world a different code of morals for men and women, by which moral delinquencies which exclude women from society, are not only tolerated, but deemed of little account in man.

He has usurped the prerogative of Jehovah himself, claiming it as his right to assign for her a sphere of action, when that belongs to her conscience and to her God.

He has endeavored, in every way that he could, to destroy her confidence in her own powers, to lessen her self-respect, and to make her willing to lead a dependent and abject life.

Now, in view of this entire disfranchisement of one-half the people of this country, their social and religious degradation—in view of the unjust laws above mentioned, and because women do feel themselves aggrieved, oppressed, and fraudulently deprived of their most sacred rights, we insist that they have immediate admission to all the rights and privileges which belong to them as citizens of the United States.

In entering upon the great work before us, we anticipate no small amount of misconception, misrepresentation, and ridicule; but we shall use every instrumentality within our power to effect our object. We shall employ agents, circulate tracts, petition the State and National legislatures, and endeavor to enlist the pulpit and the press in our behalf. We hope this Convention will be followed by a series of Conventions embracing every part of the country.

[The following resolutions were discussd by Lucretia Mott, Thomas and Mary Ann McClintock, Amy Post, Catharine A. F. Stebbins, and others, and were adopted:]

WHEREAS, The great precept of nature is conceded to be, that "man 22
shall pursue his own true and substantial happiness." Blackstone[1] in his
Commentaries remarks, that this law of Nature being coeval[2] with mankind, and dictated by God himself, is of course superior in obligation to
any other. It is binding over all the globe, in all countries and at all
times; no human laws are of any validity if contrary to this, and such of
them as are valid, derive all their force, and all their validity, and all
their authority, mediately and immediately, from this original; therefore,

Resolved, That such laws as conflict, in any way, with the true and 23
substantial happiness of woman, are contrary to the great precept of
nature and of no validity, for this is "superior in obligation to any other."

Resolved, That all laws which prevent woman from occupying such 24
a station in society as her conscience shall dictate, or which place her
in a position inferior to that of man, are contrary to the great precept of
nature, and therefore of no force or authority.

Resolved, That woman is man's equal—was intended to be so by 25
the Creator, and the highest good of the race demands that she should
be recognized as such.

Resolved, That the women of this country ought to be enlightened 26
in regard to the laws under which they live, that they may no longer
publish their degradation by declaring themselves satisfied with their present
position, nor their ignorance, by asserting that they have all the rights
they want.

Resolved, That inasmuch as man, while claiming for himself intel- 27
lectual superiority, does accord to woman moral superiority, it is pre-
eminently his duty to encourage her to speak and teach, as she has an
opportunity, in all religious assemblies.

Resolved, That the same amount of virtue, delicacy, and refinement 28
of behavior that is required of woman in the social state, should also be
required of man, and the same transgressions should be visited with equal
severity on both man and woman.

Resolved, That the objection of indelicacy and impropriety, which 29
is so often brought against woman when she addresses a public audience,
comes with a very ill-grace from those who encourage, by their attendance, her appearance on the stage, in the concert, or in feats of the
circus.

Resolved, That woman has too long rested satisfied in the circum- 30

---

[1]Sir William Blackstone (1723–1780): The most influential of English scholars of the
law. His *Commentaries of the Laws of England* (4 vols., 1765–1769) form the basis of
the study of law in England.

[2]coeval: Existing simultaneously.

scribed limits which corrupt customs and a perverted application of the Scriptures have marked out for her, and that it is time she should move in the enlarged sphere which her great Creator has assigned her.

Resolved, That it is the duty of the women of this country to secure to themselves their sacred right to the elective franchise.

Resolved, That the equality of human rights results necessarily from the fact of the identity of the race in capabilities and responsibilities.

Resolved, therefore, That, being invested by the Creator with the same capabilities, and the same consciousness of responsibility for their exercise, it is demonstrably the right and duty of woman, equally with man, to promote every righteous cause by every righteous means; and especially in regard to the great subjects of morals and religion, it is self-evidently her right to participate with her brother in teaching them, both in private and in public, by writing and by speaking, by any instrumentalities proper to be used, and in any assemblies proper to be held; and this being a self-evident truth growing out of the divinely implanted principles of human nature, any custom or authority adverse to it, whether modern or wearing the hoary sanction of antiquity, is to be regarded as a self-evident falsehood, and at war with mankind.

[At the last session Lucretia Mott[3] offered and spoke to the following resolution:]

Resolved, That the speedy success of our cause depends upon the zealous and untiring efforts of both men and women, for the overthrow of the monopoly of the pulpit, and for the securing to woman an equal participation with men in the various trades, professions, and commerce.

Questions for Study and Discussion

1. The opening paragraphs of the Seneca Falls declaration closely parallel those of the Declaration of Independence. Why do you suppose Stanton chose to start in this manner?

2. What is a parody? Is Stanton's essay a parody of the Declaration of Independence? Why, or why not?

3. What is it that Elizabeth Cady Stanton and the other women at the Seneca Falls convention want?

---

[3]Lucretia Mott (1793–1880): One of the founders of the 1848 convention at which these resolutions were presented. She is one of the earliest and most important of the feminists who struggled to proclaim their rights. She was also a prominent abolitionist.

4. What is the "elective franchise"? Why is it so fundamental to Stanton's argument?

5. What does Stanton mean when she says, "He has made her, if married, in the eye of the law, civilly dead"?

6. In paragraphs 4–18 Stanton catalogs the abuses women suffer. Who is the "He" referred to in each of the statements? What is the rhetorical effect of listing these abuses and starting each one with similar phrasing?

7. At what audience is Stanton's declaration aimed? What in the declaration itself led you to this conclusion?

8. What is the function of the resolutions that conclude the declaration? What would have been gained or lost if Stanton had concluded the declaration with paragraph 20?

9. Is there anything in the style, tone, or voice of this document that would lead you to call it "feminine" or "female"? Explain.

Writing Topics

1. Write a report updating Stanton's declaration. What complaints have been resolved? Which still need to be redressed? What new complaints have been voiced by women in the last twenty years?

2. Write an essay in which you compare and contrast the Declaration of Independence with Stanton's declaration. You should consider such things as purpose, audience, and style in your essay.

Born around 1786, Seattle was chief of the Suquamish Indians and leader of other tribes in the area around Puget Sound. He was a loyal friend of the white settlers who in the early nineteenth century were coming to the region in increasing numbers. In 1853, during the administration of President Franklin Pierce, the region was organized as the Washington Territory, with Isaac Stevens as governor. The next year Stevens, on behalf of the federal government, offered to buy two million acres of land from Seattle's people, and the Indians agreed. In later years, the settlers named their growing city after him, though Seattle consented to this reluctantly, believing that after death his spirit would be disturbed every time his name was mentioned. He died in 1866.

The following is Seattle's reply to Governor Stevens's offer. Though the great Indian relocations and massacres that were to begin in the 1860s were still in the future, and Indians were still the chief inhabitants of nearly half of the continent, Seattle clearly understood what was to come. His words are a prophecy—and a warning.

My People

Yonder sky that has wept tears upon my people for centuries untold, and which to us appears changeless and eternal, may change. Today is fair. Tomorrow may be overcast with clouds. My words are like the stars that never change. Whatever Seattle says the great chief at Washington can rely upon with as much certainty as he can upon the return of the sun or the seasons. The White Chief says that Big Chief at Washington sends us greetings of friendship and goodwill. That is kind of him for we know he has little need of our friendship in return. His people are many. They are like the grass that covers vast prairies. My people are few. They resemble the scattering trees of a storm-swept plain. The great, and—I presume—good, White Chief sends us word that he wishes to buy our lands but is willing to allow us enough to live comfortably. This indeed appears just, even generous, for the Red Man no longer has rights that he need respect, and the offer may be wise also, as we are no longer in need of an extensive country. . . . I will not dwell on, nor mourn over, our untimely decay, nor reproach our paleface brothers with hastening it, as we too may have been somewhat to blame.

Youth is impulsive. When our young men grow angry at some real or imaginary wrong, and disfigure their faces with black paint, it denotes that their hearts are black, and then they are often cruel and relentless,

674

and our old men and old women are unable to restrain them. Thus it has ever been. Thus it was when the white men first began to push our forefathers further westward. But let us hope that the hostilities between us may never return. We would have everything to lose and nothing to gain. Revenge by young men is considered gain, even at the cost of their own lives, but old men who stay at home in times of war, and mothers who have sons to lose, know better.

Our good father at Washington—for I presume he is now our father as well as yours, since King George has moved his boundaries further north—our great good father, I say, sends us word that if we do as he desires he will protect us. His brave warriors will be to us a bristling wall of strength, and his wonderful ships of war will fill our harbors so that our ancient enemies far to the northward—the Hydas and Tsimpsians—will cease to frighten our women, children, and old men. Then in reality will he be our father and we his children. But can that ever be? Your God is not our God! Your God loves your people and hates mine. He folds his strong and protecting arms lovingly about the paleface and leads him by the hand as a father leads his infant son—but He has forsaken His red children—if they really are his. Our God, the Great Spirit, seems also to have forsaken us. Your God makes your people wax strong every day. Soon they will fill the land. Our people are ebbing away like a rapidly receding tide that will never return. The white man's God cannot love our people or He would protect them. They seem to be orphans who can look nowhere for help. How then can we be brothers? How can your God become our God and renew our prosperity and awaken in us dreams of returning greatness? If we have a common heavenly father He must be partial—for He came to his paleface children. We never saw Him. He gave you laws but He had no word for His red children whose teeming multitudes once filled this vast continent as stars fill the firmament. No; we are two distinct races with separate origins and separate destinies. There is little in common between us.

To us the ashes of our ancestors are sacred and their resting place is hallowed ground. You wander far from the graves of your ancestors and seemingly without regret. Your religion was written upon tables of stone by the iron finger of your God so that you could not forget. The Red Man could never comprehend nor remember it. Our religion is the traditions of our ancestors—the dreams of our old men, given them in solemn hours of night by the Great Spirit; and the visions of our sachems;[1] and it is written in the hearts of our people.

---

[1]Indian chiefs.

Your dead cease to love you and the land of their nativity as soon   5
as they pass the portals of the tomb and wander way beyond the stars.
They are soon forgotten and never return. Our dead never forget the
beautiful world that gave them being.

Day and night cannot dwell together. The Red man has ever fled   6
the approach of the White Man, as the morning mist flees before the
morning sun. However, your proposition seems fair and I think that my
people will accept it and will retire to the reservation you offer them.
Then we will dwell apart in peace, for the words of the Great White
Chief seem to be the words of nature speaking to my people out of dense
darkness.

It matters little where we pass the remnant of our days. They will   7
not be many. A few more moons; a few more winters—and not one of
the descendants of the mighty hosts that once moved over this broad
land or lived in happy homes, protected by the Great Spirit, will remain
to mourn over the graves of a people once more powerful and hopeful
than yours. But why should I mourn at the untimely fate of my people?
Tribe follows tribe, and nation follows nation, like the waves of the sea.
It is the order of nature, and regret is useless. Your time of decay may
be distant, but it will surely come, for even the White Man whose God
walked and talked with him as friend with friend, cannot be exempt from
the common destiny. We may be brothers after all. We will see.

We will ponder your proposition, and when we decide we will let   8
you know. But should we accept it, I here and now make this condition
that we will not be denied the privilege without molestation of visiting
at any time the tombs of our ancestors, friends and children. Every part
of this soil is sacred in the estimation of my people. Every hillside, every
valley, every plain and grove, has been hallowed by some sad or happy
event in days long vanished. . . . The very dust upon which you now
stand responds more lovingly to their footsteps than to yours, because it
is rich with the blood of our ancestors and our bare feet are conscious of
the sympathetic touch. . . . Even the little children who lived here and
rejoiced here for a brief season will love these somber solitudes and at
eventide they greet shadowy returning spirits. And when the last Red
Man shall have perished, and the memory of my tribe shall have become
a myth among the White Men, these shores will swarm with the invisible
dead of my tribe, and when your children's children think themselves
alone in the field, the store, the shop, upon the highway, or in the
silence of the pathless woods, they will not be alone. . . . At night when
the streets of your cities and villages are silent and you think them
deserted, they will throng with the returning hosts that once filled and
still love this beautiful land. The White Man will never be alone.

Let him be just and deal kindly with my people, for the dead are   9
not powerless. Dead, did I say? There is not death, only a change of
worlds.

Questions for Study and Discussion

1. What are Chief Seattle's purposes in his speech? Whom is it addressed to?

2. What condition does Seattle demand before yielding the land to the U.S. government? How does he prepare for this condition in his speech?

3. What is Seattle's attitude toward the white men, their president, and their god? How do you know? Seattle refers to the president as the Indians' "father." What does this signify? Why might Seattle presume that the White Chief is good as well as great?

4. What, for you, is the most powerful part of the speech? What gives it its power? Did anything in his speech surprise you? If so, why?

5. What differences between red men and white men does Seattle describe? Why do you think he chooses to mention those particular differences? What other differences might he have included, and why do you think he didn't?

6. Chief Seattle's address is rich in figures of speech, beginning with "My words are like the stars that never change." What areas of knowledge and experience does he continually draw on for his analogies and metaphors? Give examples.

Writing Topics

1. Throughout his speech, Chief Seattle quietly registers a complaint that was to become a battle cry in later years. This sentiment can be summed up by his pessimistic view, "not one of the descendants of the mighty hosts that once moved over this broad land or lived in happy homes, protected by the Great Spirit, will remain to mourn over the graves of a people once more powerful and hopeful than yours." Write an essay in which you explain what in the history of the American Indians may have led Chief Seattle to make this prediction, and what later events seemed almost to fulfill it. Use library resources to support your answer.

2. Despite his obvious regret, Chief Seattle worked out an accommodation with the more powerful forces of the United States. If you were in his position, would you have done the same or would you have led your people to fight for its land and independence? Write an essay in which you explain your choice.

Little is known about Saint Matthew, the tax collector called by Jesus to be one of his disciples. The Gospel attributed to him was probably written by one or more anonymous Christians toward the end of the first century A.D., but legend says that it contains many sayings of Jesus that were collected and preserved by Matthew, sayings that are missing from the other Gospels.

Modern scholarship is divided on whether the Sermon is a single utterance or an anthology of sayings from different times and occasions, for it is episodic rather than tightly organized, with sudden shifts in subject. The late classicist Gilbert Highet suggests that it reflects Jesus's epigrammatic style, that instead of making a speech he would have delivered such sayings one at a time, with pauses in between so that his listeners could absorb and reflect on them.

The Sermon on the Mount

Blessed are the poor in spirit: for theirs is the kingdom of heaven. 1

Blessed are they that mourn: for they shall be comforted. 2

Blessed are the meek: for they shall inherit the earth. 3

Blessed are they which do hunger and thirst after righteousness: for 4 they shall be filled.

Blessed are the merciful: for they shall obtain mercy. 5

Blessed are the pure in heart: for they shall see God. 6

Blessed are the peacemakers: for they shall be called the children 7 of God.

Blessed are they which are persecuted for righteousness' sake: for 8 theirs is the kingdom of heaven.

Blessed are ye, when men shall revile you, and persecute you, and 9 shall say all manner of evil against you falsely, for my sake. Rejoice, and be exceeding glad: for great is your reward in heaven: for so persecuted they the prophets which were before you.

Ye are the salt of the earth: but if the salt have lost his savour, 10 wherewith shall it be salted? it is thenceforth good for nothing, but to be cast out, and to be trodden under foot of men.

Ye are the light of the world. A city that is set on a hill cannot be 11 hid. Neither do men light a candle, and put it under a bushel, but on a candlestick; and it giveth light unto all that are in the house. Let your light so shine before men, that they may see your good works, and glorify your Father which is in heaven.

Think not that I am come to destroy the law, or the prophets; I   12
am not come to destroy, but to fulfil. For verily I say unto you, Till
heaven and earth pass, one jot or one tittle shall in no wise pass from
the law, till all be fulfilled. Whosoever therefore shall break one of these
least commandments, and shall teach men so, he shall be called the least
in the kingdom of heaven: but whosoever shall do and teach them, the
same shall be called great in the kingdom of heaven. For I say unto you,
That except your righteousness shall exceed the righteousness of the
scribes and Pharisees,[1] ye shall in no case enter into the kingdom of
heaven.

Ye have heard that it was said by them of old time, Thou shalt not   13
kill; and whosoever shall kill shall be in danger of the judgment: but I
say unto you, That whosoever is angry with his brother without a cause
shall be in danger of the judgment: and whosoever shall say to his brother,
Raca,[2] shall be in danger of the council: but whosoever shall say, Thou
fool, shall be in danger of hell fire. Therefore if thou bring thy gift to
the altar, and there rememberest that thy brother hath ought against
thee; leave there thy gift before the altar, and go thy way; first be reconciled to thy brother, and then come and offer thy gift. Agree with
thine adversary quickly, while thou art in the way with him; lest at any
time the adversary deliver thee to the judge, and the judge deliver thee
to the officer, and thou be cast into prison. Verily I say unto thee, Thou
shalt by no means come out thence, till thou hast paid the uttermost
farthing.

Ye have heard that it was said by them of old time, Thou shalt not   14
commit adultery; but I say unto you, That whosoever looketh on a woman
to lust after her hath committed adultery with her already in his heart.
And if thy right eye offend thee, pluck it out, and cast it from thee: for
it is profitable for thee that one of thy members should perish, and not
that thy whole body should be cast into hell. And if thy right hand
offend thee, cut it off, and cast it from thee: for it is profitable for thee
that one of thy members should perish, and not that thy whole body
should be cast into hell.

It hath been said, Whosoever shall put away his wife, let him give   15
her a writing of divorcement: but I say unto you, That whosoever shall
put away his wife, saving for the cause of fornication, causeth her to
commit adultery: and whosoever shall marry her that is divorced com-
mitteth adultery.

---

[1]The scribes among the ancient Jews were dedicated to copying their holy scriptures;
the Pharisees were an extremely devout Jewish sect.

[2]Emptyhead; a term of hatred and contempt.

Again, ye have heard that it hath been said by them of old time,   16
Thou shalt not forswear thyself, but shalt perform to the Lord thine oaths:
but I say unto you, Swear not at all; neither by heaven; for it is God's
throne: nor by the earth; for it is his footstool: neither by Jerusalem; for
it is the city of the great King. Neither shalt thou swear by thy head,
because thou canst not make one hair white or black. But let your communication be, Yea, yea; Nay, nay: for whatsoever is more than these
cometh of evil.

Ye have heard that it hath been said, An eye for an eye, and a   17
tooth for a tooth: but I say unto you, That ye resist not evil: but whosoever shall smite thee on thy right cheek, turn to him the other also.
And if any man will sue thee at the law, and take away thy coat, let
him have thy cloak also. And whosoever shall compel thee to go a mile,
go with him twain. Give to him that asketh thee, and from him that
would borrow of thee turn not thou away.

Ye have heard that it hath been said, Thou shalt love thy neighbor,   18
and hate thine enemy. But I say unto you, Love your enemies, bless them
that curse you, do good to them that hate you, and pray for them which
despitefully use you, and persecute you; that ye may be the children of
your Father which is in heaven; for he maketh his sun to rise on the evil
and on the good, and sendeth rain on the just and on the unjust. For if
ye love them which love you, what reward have ye? do not even the
publicans the same? And if ye salute your brethren only, what do ye
more than others? do not even the publicans so? Be ye therefore perfect,
even as your Father which is in heaven is perfect.

Take heed that ye do not your alms before men, to be seen of them: 19
otherwise ye have no reward of your Father which is in heaven.

Therefore when thou doest thine alms, do not sound a trumpet   20
before thee, as the hypocrites do in the synagogues and in the streets,
that they may have glory of men. Verily I say unto you, They have their
reward. But when thou doest alms, let not thy left hand know what thy
right hand doeth: that thine alms may be in secret: and thy Father which
seeth in secret himself shall reward thee openly.

And when thou prayest, thou shalt not be as the hypocrites are: 21
for they love to pray standing in the synagogues and in the corners of
the streets, that they may be seen of men. Verily I say until you, They
have their reward. But thou, when thou prayest, enter into thy closet,
and when thou hast shut thy door, pray to thy Father, which is in secret;
and thy Father which seeth in secret shall reward thee openly.

But when ye pray, use not vain repetitions, as the heathen do: for   22
they think that they shall be heard for their much speaking. Be not ye

therefore like unto them: for your Father knoweth what things ye have need of, before ye ask him. After this manner therefore pray ye:

Our Father which art in heaven, Hallowed be thy name. Thy king- 23
dom come. Thy will be done in earth, as it is in heaven. Give us this day our daily bread. And forgive us our debts, as we forgive our debtors. And lead us not into temptation, but deliver us from evil: for thine is the kingdom, and the power, and the glory, for ever. Amen.

For if ye forgive men their trespasses, your heavenly Father will also 24
forgive you: but if ye forgive not men their trespasses, neither will your Father forgive your trespasses.

Moreover when ye fast, be not, as the hypocrites, of a sad coun- 25
tenance: for they disfigure their faces, that they may appear unto men to fast. Verily I say unto you, They have their reward. But thou, when thou fastest, anoint thine head, and wash thy face; that thou appear not unto men to fast, but unto thy Father which is in secret; and thy Father, which seeth in secret, shall reward thee openly.

Lay up not for yourselves treasures upon earth, where moth and 26
rust doth corrupt, and where thieves break through and steal: but lay up for yourselves treasures in heaven, where neither moth nor rust doth corrupt, and where thieves do not break through nor steal: for where your treasure is, there will your heart be also.

The light of the body is the eye: if therefore thine eye be single, 27
thy whole body shall be full of light. But if thine eye be evil, thy whole body shall be full of darkness. If therefore the light that is in thee be darkness, how great is that darkness!

No man can serve two masters: for either he will hate the one, and 28
love the other; or else he will hold to the one, and despise the other. Ye cannot serve God and mammon.

Therefore I say unto you, Take no thought for your life, what ye 29
shall eat, or what ye shall drink; nor yet for your body, what ye shall put on. Is not the life more than meat, and the body than raiment? Behold the fowls of the air: for they sow not, neither do they reap, nor gather into barns; yet your heavenly Father feedeth them. Are ye not much better than they? Which of you by taking thought can add one cubit unto his stature? And why take ye thought for raiment? Consider the lilies of the field, how they grow; they toil not, neither do they spin: and yet I say unto you, That even Solomon in all his glory was not arrayed like one of these. Wherefore, if God so clothe the grass of the field, which to day is, and to morrow is cast into the oven, shall he not much more clothe you, O ye of little faith? Therefore taken no thought, saying, What shall we eat? or, What shall we drink? or, Wherewithal shall we be clothed? (For after all these things do the Gentiles seek:) for your

heavenly Father knoweth that ye have need of all these things. But seek
ye first the kingdom of God, and his righteousness; and all these things
shall be added unto you.

Take therefore no thought for the morrow: for the morrow shall   30
take thought for the things of itself. Sufficient unto the day is the evil
thereof.

Judge not, that ye be not judged. For with what judgment ye judge,   31
ye shall be judged: and with what measure ye mete, it shall be measured
to you again. And why beholdest thou the mote that is in thy brother's
eye, but considerest not the beam that is in thine own eye? Or how wilt
thou say to thy brother, Let me pull out the mote out of thine eye; and
behold, a beam is in thine own eye? Thou hypocrite, first cast out the
beam out of thine own eye; and then shalt thou see clearly to cast out
the mote of thy brother's eye.

Give not that which is holy unto the dogs, neither cast ye your   32
pearls before swine, lest they trample them under their feet, and turn
again and rend you.

Ask, and it shall be given you; seek and ye shall find; knock, and   33
it shall be opened unto you: for every one that asketh receiveth; and he
that seeketh findeth; and to him that knocketh it shall be opened. Or
what man is there of you, whom if his son ask bread, will he give him a
stone? Or if he ask a fish, will he give him a serpent? If ye then, being
evil, know how to give good gifts unto your children, how much more
shall your Father which is in heaven give good things to them that ask
him? Therefore all things whatsoever ye would that men should do to
you, do ye even so to them: for this is the law and the prophets.

Enter ye in at the strait gate: for wide is the gate, and broad is the 34
way, that leadeth to destruction, and many there be which go in thereat:
because strait is the gate, and narrow is the way, which leadeth unto
life, and few there be that find it.

Beware of false prophets, which come to you in sheep's clothing,   35
but inwardly they are ravening wolves. Ye shall know them by their
fruits. Do men gather grapes of thorns, or figs of thistles? Even so every
good tree bringeth forth good fruit; but a corrupt tree bringeth forth evil
fruit. A good tree cannot bring forth evil fruit, neither can a corrupt tree
bring forth good fruit. Every tree that bringeth not forth good fruit is
hewn down, and cast into the fire. Wherefore by their fruits ye shall
know them.

Not every one that saith unto me, Lord, Lord, shall enter into the   36
kingdom of heaven; but he that doeth the will of my Father which is in
heaven. Many will say to me in that day, Lord, Lord, have we not
prophesied in thy name? And in thy name have cast out devils? and in

thy name done many wonderful works? And then will I profess unto them, I never knew you: depart from me, ye that work iniquity.

Therefore whosoever heareth these sayings of mine, and doeth them,   37
I will liken him unto a wise man, which built his house upon a rock: and the rain descended, and the floods came, and the winds blew, and beat upon that house; and it fell not: for it was founded upon a rock. And every one that heareth these sayings of mine, and doeth them not, shall be likened unto a foolish man, which built his house upon the sand: and the rain descended, and the floods came, and the winds blew, and beat upon that house; and it fell: and great was the fall of it.

Questions for Study and Discussion

1. What is the purpose of the Sermon on the Mount? To whom is it addressed? How do you know? Cite passages from the text to support your answer.

2. What is the essential message of the Sermon on the Mount?

3. Are there attitudes and practices mentioned in the Sermon that you think irrelevant to contemporary life? If so, what are they? How do such references affect your response to the Sermon?

4. The Sermon is much concerned with social ethics. According to Jesus, how should people behave toward one another? Given human nature, do you think the ethical prescriptions of the Sermon realistic or idealistic? What kind of society would result if everyone followed them?

5. What, according to the Sermon, is the relationship between individuals and God? How should this be reflected in religious observance? In our attitudes toward life?

6. In the Sermon on the Mount, Jesus often teaches through analogies and metaphors. Identify some of each, and explain what they mean and why they are appropriate.

Writing Topics

1. Whether or not one is a Christian, the Sermon on the Mount offers a challenge to lead a just and moral life. Write an essay in which you discuss those injunctions you find relevant to your own life and explain why you find them important.

2. How, if at all, do you think Christianity or any religion should influence American politics and government? Given the constitutional separation of church and state, are there any ways in which government properly may influence the practice of religion? Write an essay in which you present your position on this important issue.

Contemporary Issues
Equality

WILLIAM RYAN

What is equality? For whom is it an issue? Should everyone be absolutely equal? Is equality even possible? These are puzzling questions that challenge a person's deepest and most basic beliefs. It should come as no surprise, then, that the subject of equality can move writers to passion and eloquence and reasoning of the highest order. There are, of course, no simple answers; but, because the quest for equality has come to touch all aspects of American life and to involve all segments of American society, the subject is one that every individual must approach thoughtfully and without prejudice. William Ryan has long been interested in the subject of equality. Born in 1923, Ryan received his Ph.D. from Boston University in 1958. He is a professor of psychology at Boston College and works actively for the extension of civil rights and reformation of the penal system. Among his books are *Distress in the City*, *Blaming the Victim*, and *Equality*.

In this essay from *Equality*, published in 1981, Ryan sets out the central terms of the equality question and describes the ambiguity inherent in Thomas Jefferson's ideal.

The Equality Dilemma: Fair Play or Fair Shares

Thinking about equality makes people fidgety. Insert the topic into   1
a conversation and listen: voices rise, friends interrupt each other, utter conviction mingles with absolute confusion. The word slips out of our grasp as we try to define it. How can one say who is equal to whom and in what way? Are not some persons clearly superior to others, at least in some respects? Can superiority coexist with equality, or must the one demolish the other? Most important, are the existing inequalities such

that they should be redressed? If they are, what precisely should be equalized? And by whom?

We feel constrained by the very word—to deny equality is almost   2
to blaspheme. Yet, at the same time, something about the idea of equality
is dimly sinful, subject to some obscure judgment looming above us. It
is not really adequate to be "as good as." We should be "better than."
And the striving for superiority fills much of the space in our lives, even
filtering into radio commercials. Listen to a chorus of little boys singing,
"My dog's better than your dog; my dog's better than yours." They are
selling dog food, it turns out, and apparently successfully, which must
mean that a lot of people want very much to have their dogs be better
than your dogs. Their *dogs!*

This passing example suggests how far it is possible to carry the   3
competition about who and whose is better. The young voices sing fear-
lessly. There is little danger that some fanatic will leap up and denounce
the idea of one dog's being superior to another or quote some sacred text
that asserts the equality of all dogs. In regard to people, however, we do
hesitate to claim superiority or to imply inferiority. No commercials announce, "My son's better than your son" or "My wife's better than yours"
or, most directly, "I'm better than you." That we remain reticent about
flaunting such sentiments and yet devote ourselves to striving for superiority signals the clash of intensely contradictory beliefs about equality
and inequality.

We all know, uneasily but without doubt, that our nation rests on   4
a foundation of documents that contain mysterious assertions like "all
men are created equal," and we comprehend that such phrases have
become inseparable components of our license to nationhood. Our le-
gitimacy as a particular society is rooted in them, and [they] bound and
limit our behavior. We are thus obliged to agree that all men are created
equal—whatever that might mean to us today.

But our lives are saturated with reminders about whose dog is better.   5
In almost all our daily deeds, we silently pledge allegiance to inequality,
insisting on the continual labeling of winners and losers, of Phi Beta
Kappas and flunkouts, and on an order in which a few get much and the
rest get little.

We re-create the ambiguity in the minds of our children as we   6
teach them both sides of the contradiction. "No one is better than anyone else," we warn. "Don't act snotty and superior." At the same time
we teach them that all are obliged to get ahead, to compete, to achieve.
Everyone is equal? Yes. Everyone must try to be superior? Again, yes.
The question reverberates.

As a nation we grow more troubled about many issues that in large   7
part touch on questions of equality, although they are not defined in
such terms.

Consider several examples: 8

Regarding racial equality there is swelling bitterness as one side
calls for affirmative action and the other side curses reverse discrimination—and both are attending to the same phenomenon.

Then there is the astonishing failure to achieve rapid passage of
the equal rights for women amendment. The simple sentence that was
supposed to become the twenty-sixth amendment is so innocuous as to
be almost banal, almost like the casual correction of an oversight. At
first there was no dispute, no controversy; rapid ratification seemed certain. The process started just that way. Then, suddenly, the equal-rights
amendment was becalmed. The obvious had somehow become obscure,
the undisputed controversial; the simple sentence was scribbled over with
complicated interpretation and exegesis. "Are you *against* equal rights for
women?" one asks, aghast. "Of course not! But it's not as simple as it
seems. You don't understand . . ."

Even events that have been lumped together under the cliché "middle-class tax revolt" have the flavor of perceived violations of principles
of equality. Although such events as the passage of Proposition 13 in
California, which drastically cut back property taxes, were facilely interpreted as protests against "big government," what the voters themselves
said to interviewers does not support this interpretation. It seems clear
that voters were enraged because they felt they were being treated un-
fairly. Why, they asked, should they have to pay such enormous fractions
of their incomes in taxes on the homes that many of them had struggled
so hard to buy? What were they paying so much money *for?* And whom
was it going *to?* They were convinced that they were paying *more* and
getting back *less* than their fair share. If that is a correct interpretation,
it certainly places the issue squarely in the domain of equality.

It is true that many home owners on a strained budget have been   9
persuaded that the poor are the cause of all their troubles. "Why," they
ask, "should I pay my hard-earned money to support people who won't
even work?" "Why," they inquire indignantly, "should I pay someone
else's hospital bills? I still owe my own doctor." The feeling that emerges
reflects a belief that rules about equality and fairness are being violated.

Then listen to the answers to their questions: "Why should anybody   10
be able to *buy* necessary medical care? Why should health—even life—
be put up for auction?" and "If a person can't work and has no money,
what should happen? Should we let him *starve?*" That's another way of
appealing to principles of equality.

Looking into the near future, we see national issues beginning to   11
be analyzed in terms of conflicting definitions of equality. What should
we do if there is a long-term gasoline shortage? One answer is to impose
the rule of the free market: let everyone be free to buy as much gasoline
as he can afford, allowing rising prices to balance supply and demand.
The other answer, drawing on a different conception of equality, is formal
rationing: gasoline is provided to each driver in accordance with his need.

The latent conflicts and ambiguities in our views about equality   12
have struck many observers of American life from Tocqueville[1] to the
compiler of a joke book published in 1896. Appropriately, the observation on equality that I found was an ethnic joke. As there are Italian
and Polish jokes today, with a fixed form, there was an equivalent form
then, called the Irish Bull, which was a joke illustrating the inferior
capacity for logic of the slow-witted Irishman, the "thick Mick" of that
generation's ethnic mythology. A rally is being addressed by an eloquent
and passionate egalitarian, whose peroration begins with the cry "One
man is as good as another!" To which the Irishman in the audience,
leaping to his feet and applauding wildly, shouts back, "Sure, and a great
deal better!"

That may be as good a summation as any of the great American   13
equality dilemma.

The source of the dilemma, the mystery of equality, can be traced   14
back more than two centuries to the time of our nation's birth and the
startling words of Jefferson's "self-evident" truth: all men are created
equal. The words are in many ways like a promissory note on which the
date and the amount of payment are omitted. What the devil did Jefferson mean by that? And did Hancock and the other cosigners of the
note—did they all agree on what it meant? Was it clear to them then?
It certainly is puzzling and ambiguous to us today and many minds have,
over the centuries, struggled to construe the mysterious words of the
powerful talismanic phrase and have come to vastly different conclusions.
If we are to understand our dilemma today, we must begin with those
three words: men, created, equal. What are we to make of them?

Men, but not women? In 1776, probably not. We have, however,   15
progressed somewhat, and, formally at least, we here use the term "men"
to denote species rather than gender. Winking for the moment at eight-
eenth-century sexism, we can agree that "men" equals "persons," but
where does that get us? Men, but not animals? Although wise dolphins
and chimps that can chat with us have struck glancing blows at our self-

---

[1]Alexis de Tocqueville (1805–1859), a French politician, published his observations
of American life *Democracy in America* in 1835.

esteem, we remain fairly certain that we are superior to other animals. Men as opposed to what then? Are there *nonmen?* Our history gives clues, such as the Dred Scott[2] decision, which ruled that slaves are a form of living property, and this must remind us that the author of the phrase himself owned slaves. So it would seem that, at least at times, and in the view of some, there exist men who are not men. Another of our foundation documents seems to confirm such an assumption. The arithmetic of Article I, Section 2, of the Constitution is unequivocal: the equation of political power is that three "free men" are equal to five of "all other persons"—that is, black slaves. And many, probably most, read this to mean that blacks are, at best, 60 percent human and thus not really men. The question whether some persons are less *human* than others, or whether they can be declared to be so, was presumably decided in the negative a century ago. We now agree that a person's humanity cannot be forfeited, but the barbarous idea that it can remains unspoken in the minds of many.

We come next to "created." Why created? Why not just men *are*   16 equal? The next phrase—"that they are endowed by their Creator with certain unalienable rights"—suggests the answer. Persons are seen as existing within a larger framework—encompassing other creatures, other forms of life, and the vast realm of what we think of as nonliving—that has a Creator. As His creatures we are equal in the *form* of our creation, as members of the human species. Whatever is universally entailed in being human—in this instance the reference is to certain rights—holds equally true for all humans. All human beings share those rights equally. This theme of the universal and natural rights of man formed a dominant strain in the political philosophy of the eighteenth century, and we can, I believe, safely construe that the Founding Fathers were referring to equal *rights*, not dependent on law but deriving from one's status as a human being, which were then spelled out as including "life, liberty and the pursuit of happiness." It is not, then, the idea that all men are created equal that is mysterious or ambiguous, nor, in a general sense, is it unclear that the words were intended to mean that all human beings share equally in the specified rights. The equality dilemma arises when we move from the abstract to the concrete, when we begin to define the meaning of these rights. This is where the disputes and disagreements begin.

What is disputed? The right to life seems fairly simple and straight-   17 forward: no one should kill me or you; we are equally entitled to live. But if it were indeed that simple, why even bother to make the point?

---

[2]In 1857 the U.S. Supreme Court ruled that Dred Scott, a slave petitioning for his freedom, was not entitled to the rights of a Federal citizen.

If we think about it for a while, the idea that all human beings have the right to life is a profound and weighty claim. For example, if you and I have really and truly been endowed by our Creator with an unalienable *right* to life, does it not follow necessarily and logically that we have a *right* to the means of sustaining life? If this assertion does not include the associated right of all to food, shelter, clothing, and other necessities, then it carries very little meaning at all. If the idea of a right is to have concrete significance, it must be possible to exercise that right. Therefore, the right to means of exercising it is linked with it and is itself a right. No one will quarrel with you if you keep it general and say, "Everyone has the right to life." Who could argue with that? But try saying, "Everyone has the right to all that is necessary to sustain life," and someone will start disagreeing with you. That is the basis of dispute number one.

Dispute number two arises when we start digging into the right to 18 liberty. There is broad agreement on the equation of liberty with maximum freedom to think and do what one wishes—up to the point of harming others. But calling liberty freedom is just interchanging synonyms. Freedom—or liberty—certainly implies more than some detached and floating right to *do* something. If we all share equally in the right to liberty, we must be free from arbitrary and unreasonable compulsion and coercion. No one may dictate my religious or political opinions, no one may enslave me (just as important, I may not enslave myself). It would seem, furthermore, that this right suggests that everyone has the right to participate in the political process, since a rule cannot be applied to persons who were completely excluded from the process of making the rule.

The right to freedom also necessarily includes the means to execute 19 that right. If I have no income and no resources whatever and am then offered a job at two dollars an hour, am I really free not to take it? Or does such a situation imply some compulsion to work? Am I free to be a Jew or a "radical" only if I am willing to forgo privileges that are granted to Christians and "moderates"? The right to liberty, then, is also not as simple as it might at first seem. Its meaning must encompass the fact that one person's existence is inextricably bound up with that of many others who could—but may not—coerce him or her and whom he or she could—but may not—coerce; moreover, in order to be guaranteed protection against coercion, one must possess certain means of resistance that are also guaranteed. Thus we see there is a necessary conjoining of the right to life and the right to liberty, since a person is not free if he is subject to coercion because he is deprived of the means of sustaining life.

We come, finally, to the "pursuit of happiness," the interpretation 20
of which is the most obvious source of disagreement. According to the
modern consensus, this phrase clearly means that every individual has
the right to pursue his or her own particular desires and visions, which
tend, of course, to be quite different for each person. In other words, in
the current dialogue about equality, this particular issue tends to be defined as the individual's own pursuit of *private* happiness. (There are other
plausible interpretations that stress *public* happiness, but this line of analysis has received little attention in modern times.) The source of conflict
here is manifest: it might very well happen that one individual can successfully pursue his own dream of happiness only if he may critically
diminish the means available to others to sustain life or if he may in
some measure coerce others. If pursuing happiness is taken to mean primarily achieving command over resources—and it is frequently given that
primary meaning—then it involves an immediate clash of interests between the individual pursuers and those who must have a certain stock
of resources if they are to preserve their own rights to life and liberty.
The latter's right of access to resources limits somewhat the former's
efforts to obtain resources in order to insure his own happiness.

It should not surprise us, then, that the clause "all men are created 21
equal" can be interpreted in quite different ways. Today, I would like to
suggest, there are two major lines of interpretation: one, which I will
call the "Fair Play" perspective, stresses the individual's right to pursue
happiness and obtain resources; the other, which I will call the "Fair
Shares" viewpoint, emphasizes the right of access to resources as a necessary condition for equal rights to life, liberty, and happiness.

Almost from the beginning, and most apparently during the past 22
century or so, the Fair Play viewpoint has been dominant in America.
This way of looking at the problem of equality stresses that each person
should be equally free from all but the most minimal necessary interference with his right to "pursue happiness." It is frequently stressed that
all are equally free to *pursue*, but have no guarantee of *attaining*, happiness. The right to obtain and keep property is often subsumed under this
larger right. . . . The main outward sign of this condition of equality is
the absence of encumbrances on the individual—encumbrances deriving
from status at birth, from family position, from skin color, sex, age, and
the like. Given significant differences of interests, of talents, and of
personalities, it is assumed that individuals will be variably successful in
their pursuits and that society will consequently propel to its surface what
Jefferson called a "natural aristocracy of talent," men who because of
their skills, intellect, judgment, character, will assume the leading positions in society that had formerly been occupied by the hereditary ar-

istocracy—that is, by men who had simply been born into positions of wealth and power. In contemporary discussions, the emphasis on the individual's unencumbered pursuit of his own goals is summed up in the phrase "equality of opportunity." Given at least an approximation of this particular version of equality, Jefferson's principle of a natural aristocracy—spoken of most commonly today as the idea of "meritocracy"—will insure that the ablest, most meritorious, ambitious, hardworking, and talented individuals will acquire the most, achieve the most, and become the leaders of society. The relative inequality that this implies is seen not only as tolerable, but as fair and just. Any effort to achieve what proponents of Fair Play refer to as "equality of results" is seen as unjust, artificial, and incompatible with the more basic principle of equal opportunity.

The Fair Shares perspective, as compared with the Fair Play idea, concerns itself much more with equality of rights and of access, particularly the implicit rights to a reasonable share of society's resources, sufficient to sustain life at a decent standard of humanity and to preserve liberty and freedom from compulsion. Rather than focusing on the individual's pursuit of his own happiness, the advocate of Fair Shares is more committed to the principle that all members of the society obtain a reasonable portion of the goods that society produces. From this vantage point, the overzealous pursuit of private goals on the part of some individuals might even have to be bridled. From this it follows, too, that the proponent of Fair Shares has a different view of what constitutes fairness and justice, namely, an appropriate distribution throughout society of sufficient means for sustaining life and preserving liberty. 23

So the equality dilemma is built into everyday life and thought in America; it comes with the territory. Rights, equality of rights—or at least interpretations of them—clash. The conflict between Fair Play and Fair Shares is real, deep, and serious, and it cannot be easily resolved. Some calculus of priorities must be established. Rules must be agreed upon. It is possible to imagine an almost endless number of such rules: 24

Fair Shares until everyone has enough; Fair Play for the surplus

Fair Shares in winter; Fair Play in summer

Fair Play until the end of a specified "round," then "divvy up" Fair Shares, and start Fair Play all over again (like a series of Monopoly games)

Fair Shares for white men; Fair Play for blacks and women

Fair Play all the way, except that no one may actually be allowed to starve to death.

The last rule is, I would argue, a perhaps bitter parody of the prevailing one in the United States. Equality of opportunity and the principle of meritocracy are the clearly dominant interpretation of "all men 25 are created equal," mitigated by the principle (usually defined as charity rather than equality) that the weak, the helpless, the deficient will be more or less guaranteed a sufficient share to meet their minimal requirements for sustaining life.

Questions for Study and Discussion

1. State in your own words the "equality dilemma" that Ryan discusses in this article. He claims that the "equality dilemma arises when one moves from the abstract to the concrete", when people try to define the meaning of the rights set forth by the founding fathers. What does he mean specifically?

2. Ryan says that "the clause 'all men are created equal' can be interpreted in quite different ways". He uses the terms "Fair Play" and "Fair Shares" to label the two major lines of interpretation. What does he mean by his use of each term?

3. Ryan ends his article with a short list of "rules." What are these rules? Explain in greater detail what Ryan means by them.

4. In paragraph 7, Ryan asserts that a number of issues in fact touch upon questions of equality even though they do not appear on the surface to do so. What are some of the issues Ryan discusses? Can you add any of your own?

5. "The Equality Dilemma" is an essay of definition. What specific techniques does Ryan use to help him define the concept of equality?

Writing Topics

1. Write an essay in which you give a definition of equality and how equality might be achieved in a democratic society. You may wish to consider any or all of the following questions: What is equality? For whom is equality an issue? Should everyone be absolutely equal? Is equality possible?

2. Many companies advertise themselves as "Equal Opportunity Employers." Interview someone in the personnel office of one such company to determine exactly what is meant by the phrase "Equal Opportunity Employer." What practical consequences does the phrase have in terms of hiring/firing practices and general working conditions? Write a report based on your findings.

3. Closely related to the equality question is the problem of poverty. What is the federal government's current official definition of poverty? What government programs are now in place to help the poor? In your opinion, is the government doing enough? Too much? What should be added to its programs, or dropped from them? In relation to other government expenses, what priority should be given to helping the poor?

Martin Luther King, Jr., was born in 1929 in Atlanta, Georgia. The son of a Baptist minister, he was himself ordained at the age of eighteen and went on to study at Morehouse College, Crozer Theological Seminary, Boston University, and Chicago Theological Seminary. He first came to prominence in 1955, in Montgomery, Alabama, when he led a successful boycott against the city's segregated bus system. As the first president of the Southern Christian Leadership Conference, King promoted a policy of massive but non-violent resistance to racial injustice, and in 1964 he was awarded the Nobel Peace Prize. He was assassinated in Memphis, Tennessee, in 1968.

Dr. King dated his landmark letter from Birmingham jail April 16, 1963. He appended the following note to the published version:

> This response to a published statement by eight fellow clergymen from Alabama (Bishop C. C. J. Carpenter, Bishop Joseph A. Durick, Rabbi Hilton L. Grafman, Bishop Paul Hardin, Bishop Holan B. Harmon, the Reverend George M. Murray, the Reverend Edward V. Ramage and the Reverend Earl Stallings) was composed under somewhat constricting circumstances. Begun on the margins of the newspaper in which the statement appeared while I was in jail, the letter was continued on scraps of writing paper supplied by a friendly Negro trusty, and concluded on a pad my attorneys were eventually permitted to leave me. Although the text remains in substance unaltered, I have indulged in the author's prerogative of polishing it for publication.

Letter from Birmingham Jail

My Dear Fellow Clergymen:

While confined here in the Birmingham city jail, I came across   1
your recent statement calling my present activities "unwise and untimely." Seldom do I pause to answer criticism of my work and ideas. If I sought to answer all the criticisms that cross my desk, my secretaries would have little time for anything other than such correspondence in the course of the day, and I would have no time for constructive work. But since I feel that you are men of genuine good will and that your criticisms are sincerely set forth, I want to try to answer your statement in what I hope will be patient and reasonable terms.

I think I should indicate why I am here in Birmingham, since you have been influenced by the view which argues against "outsiders coming in." I have the honor of serving as president of the Southern Christian Leadership Conference, an organization operating in every southern state, with headquarters in Atlanta, Georgia. We have some eighty-five affiliated organizations across the South, and one of them is the Alabama Christian Movement for Human Rights. Frequently we share staff, educational, and financial resources with our affiliates. Several months ago the affiliate here in Birmingham asked us to be on call to engage in a nonviolent direct-action program if such were deemed necessary. We readily consented, and when the hour came we lived up to our promise. So I, along with several members of my staff, am here because I was invited here. I am here because I have organizational ties here.

But more basically, I am in Birmingham because injustice is here. Just as the prophets of the eighth century B.C. left their villages and carried their "thus saith the Lord" far beyond the boundaries of their home towns, and just as the Apostle Paul left his village of Tarsus and carried the gospel of Jesus Christ to the far corners of the Greco-Roman world, so am I compelled to carry the gospel of freedom beyond my own home town. Like Paul, I must constantly respond to the Macedonian call for aid.

Moreover, I am cognizant of the interrelatedness of all communities and states. I cannot sit idly by in Atlanta and not be concerned about what happens in Birmingham. Injustice anywhere is a threat to justice everywhere. We are caught in an inescapable network of mutuality, tied in a single garment of destiny. Whatever affects one directly, affects all indirectly. Never again can we afford to live with the narrow, provincial, "outside agitator" idea. Anyone who lives inside the United States can never be considered an outsider anywhere within its bounds.

You deplore the demonstrations taking place in Birmingham. But your statement, I am sorry to say, fails to express a similar concern for the conditions that brought about the demonstrations. I am sure that none of you would want to rest content with the superficial kind of social analysis that deals merely with effects and does not grapple with underlying causes. It is unfortunate that demonstrations are taking place in Birmingham, but it is even more unfortunate that the city's white power structure left the Negro community with no alternative.

In any nonviolent campaign there are four basic steps: collection of the facts to determine whether injustices exist; negotiation; self-purification; and direct action. We have gone through all these steps in Birmingham. There can be no gainsaying the fact that racial injustice engulfs this community. Birmingham is probably the most thoroughly segregated city in the United States. Its ugly record of brutality is widely known. Negroes have experienced grossly unjust treatment in courts. There have been more unsolved bombings of Negro homes and churches in Birmingham than in any other city in the nation. These are the hard, brutal facts of the case. On the basis of these conditions, Negro leaders sought to negotiate with the city fathers. But the latter consistently refused to engage in good-faith negotiation.

Then, last September, came the opportunity to talk with leaders 7 of Birmingham's economic community. In the course of the negotiations, certain promises were made by the merchants—for example, to remove the stores' humiliating racial signs. On the basis of these promises, the Reverend Fred Shuttlesworth and the leaders of the Alabama Christian Movement for Human Rights agreed to a moratorium on all demonstrations. As the weeks and months went by, we realized that we were the victims of a broken promise. A few signs, briefly removed, returned; the others remained.

As in so many past experiences, our hopes had been blasted, and 8 the shadow of deep disappointment settled upon us. We had no alternative except to prepare for direct action, whereby we would present our very bodies as means of laying our case before the conscience of the local and the national community. Mindful of the difficulties involved, we decided to undertake a process of self-purification. We began a series of workshops on nonviolence, and we repeatedly asked ourselves: "Are you able to accept blows without retaliating?" "Are you able to endure the ordeal of jail?" We decided to schedule our direct-action program for the Easter season, realizing that except for Christmas, this is the main shopping period of the year. Knowing that a strong economic-withdrawal program would be the by-product of direct action, we felt that this would be the best time to bring pressure to bear on the merchants for the needed change.

Then it occurred to us that Birmingham's mayoral election was 9 coming up in March, and we speedily decided to postpone action until after election day. When we discovered that the Commissioner of Public Safety, Eugene "Bull" Connor, had piled up enough votes to be in the run-off, we decided again to postpone action until the day after the run-off so that the demonstrations could not be used to cloud the issues. Like many others, we waited to see Mr. Connor defeated, and to this end we endured postponement after postponement. Having aided in this community need, we felt that our direct-action program could be delayed no longer.

You may well ask, "Why direct action? Why sit-ins, marches, and   10
so forth? Isn't negotiation a better path?" You are quite right in calling
for negotiation. Indeed, this is the very purpose of direct action. Nonviolent direct action seeks to create such a crisis and foster such a tension
that a community which has constantly refused to negotiate is forced to
confront the issue. It seeks so to dramatize the issue that it can no longer
be ignored. My citing the creation of tension as part of the work of the
nonviolent-resister may sound rather shocking. But I must confess that
I am not afraid of the word "tension." I have earnestly opposed violent
tension, but there is a type of constructive, nonviolent tension which is
necessary for growth. Just as Socrates[1] felt that it was necessary to create
a tension in the mind so that individuals could rise from the bondage of
myths and half-truths to the unfettered realm of creative analysis and
objective appraisal, so must we see the need for nonviolent gadflies to
create the kind of tension in society that will help men rise from the
dark depths of prejudice and racism to the majestic heights of understanding and brotherhood.

The purpose of our direct-action program is to create a situation so   11
crisis-packed that it will inevitably open the door to negotiation. I therefore concur with you in your call for negotiation. Too long has our
beloved Southland been bogged down in a tragic effort to live in mon-
ologue rather than dialogue.

One of the basic points in your statement is that the action that I   12
and my associates have taken in Birmingham is untimely. Some have
asked: "Why didn't you give the new city administration time to act?"
The only answer that I can give to this query is that the new Birmingham
administration must be prodded about as much as the outgoing one,
before it will act. We are sadly mistaken if we feel that the election of
Albert Boutwell as mayor will bring the millennium to Birmingham.
While Mr. Boutwell is a much more gentle person than Mr. Connor,
they are both segregationists, dedicated to maintenance of the status quo.
I have hoped that Mr. Boutwell will be reasonable enough to see the
futility of massive resistance to desegregation. But he will not see this
without pressure from devotees of civil rights. My friends, I must say to
you that we have not made a single gain in civil rights without determined legal and nonviolent pressure. Lamentably, it is an historical fact
that privileged groups seldom give up their privileges voluntarily. Individuals may see the moral light and voluntarily give up their unjust

---

[1]The greatest of the ancient Greek philosophers, Socrates was sentenced to death
because he persisted in raising difficult questions of authority.

posture; but, as Reinhold Niebuhr[2] has reminded us, groups tend to be more immoral than individuals.

We know through painful experience that freedom is never vol- 13 untarily given by the oppressor; it must be demanded by the oppressed. Frankly, I have yet to engage in a direct-action campaign that was "well timed" in the view of those who have not suffered unduly from the disease of segregation. For years now I have heard the word "Wait!" It rings in the ear of every Negro with piercing familiarity. This "Wait" has almost always meant "Never." We must come to see, with one of our distinguished jurists, that "justice too long delayed is justice denied."

We have waited for more than 340 years for our constitutional and 14 God-given rights. The nations of Asia and Africa are moving with jetlike speed toward gaining political independence, but we still creep at horse-and-buggy pace toward gaining a cup of coffee at a lunch counter. Perhaps it is easy for those who have never felt the stinging darts of segregation to say, "Wait." But when you have seen vicious mobs lynch your mothers and fathers at will and drown your sisters and brothers at whim; when you have seen hate-filled policemen curse, kick, and even kill your black brothers and sisters; when you see the vast majority of your twenty million Negro brothers smothering in an airtight cage of poverty in the midst of an affluent society; when you suddenly find your tongue twisted and your speech stammering as you seek to explain to your six-year-old daughter why she can't go to the public amusement park that has just been advertised on television, and see tears welling up in her eyes when she is told that Funtown is closed to colored children, and see ominous clouds of inferiority beginning to form in her little mental sky, and see her beginning to distort her personality by developing an unconscious bitterness toward white people; when you have to concoct an answer for a five-year-old son who is asking, "Daddy, why do white people treat colored people so mean?"; when you take a cross-country drive and find it necessary to sleep night after night in the uncomfortable corners of your automobile because no motel will accept you; when you are humiliated day in and day out by nagging signs reading "white" and "colored"; when your first name becomes "nigger," your middle name becomes "boy" (however old you are) and your last name becomes "John," and your wife and mother are never given the respected title "Mrs."; when you are harried by day and haunted by night by the fact that you are a Negro, living constantly at tiptoe stance, never quite knowing what to expect next, and are plagued with inner fears and outer resentments; when you

---

[2]Niebuhr (1892–1971), an American theologian, attempted to establish a practical code of social ethics, based in religious conviction.

are forever fighting a degenerating sense of "nobodiness"—then you will understand why we find it difficult to wait. There comes a time when the cup of endurance runs over, and men are no longer willing to be plunged into the abyss of despair. I hope, sirs, you can understand our legitimate and unavoidable impatience.

You express a great deal of anxiety over our willingness to break laws. This is certainly a legitimate concern. Since we so diligently urge people to obey the Supreme Court's decision of 1954 outlawing segregation in the public schools, at first glance it may seem rather paradoxical for us consciously to break laws. One may well ask: "How can you advocate breaking some laws and obeying others?" The answer lies in the fact that there are two types of laws: just and unjust. I would be the first to advocate obeying just laws. One has not only a legal but a moral responsibility to obey just laws. Conversely, one has a moral responsibility to disobey unjust laws. I would agree with St. Augustine[3] that "an unjust law is no law at all."

Now, what is the difference between the two? How does one determine whether a law is just or unjust? A just law is a manmade code that squares with the moral law or the law of God. An unjust law is a code that is out of harmony with the moral law. To put it in the terms of St. Thomas Aquinas[4]: An unjust law is a human law that is not rooted in eternal law and natural law. Any law that uplifts human personality is just. Any law that degrades human personality is unjust. All segregation statutes are unjust because segregation distorts the soul and damages the personality. It gives the segregator a false sense of superiority and the segregated a false sense of inferiority. Segregation, to use the terminology of the Jewish philosopher Martin Buber, substitutes an "I-it" relationship for an "I-thou" relationship and ends up relegating persons to the status of things. Hence segregation is not only politically, economically, and sociologically unsound, it is morally wrong and sinful. Paul Tillich[5] has said that sin is separation. Is not segregation an existential expression of man's tragic separation, his awful estrangement, his terrible sinfulness? Thus it is that I can urge men to obey the 1954 decision of the Supreme Court, for it is morally right; and I can urge them to disobey segregation ordinances, for they are morally wrong.

---

[3]An early bishop of the Christian church, St. Augustine (354–430) is considered the founder of theology.

[4]The wide-embracing Christian teachings of medieval philosopher St. Thomas Aquinas (1225–1274) have been applied to every realm of human activity.

[5]Tillich (1886–1965) and Buber (1878–1965) are both important figures in twentieth-century religious thought.

Let us consider a more concrete example of just and unjust laws.   17
An unjust law is a code that a numerical or power majority group compels
a minority group to obey but does not make binding on itself. This is
difference made legal. By the same token, a just law is a code that a
majority compels a minority to follow and that it is willing to follow
itself. This is *sameness* made legal.

Let me give another explanation. A law is unjust if it is inflicted   18
on a minority that, as a result of being denied the right to vote, had no
part in enacting or devising the law. Who can say that the legislature of
Alabama which set up that state's segregation laws was democratically
elected? Throughout Alabama all sorts of devious methods are used to
prevent Negroes from becoming registered voters, and there are some
counties in which, even though Negroes constitute a majority of the
population, not a single Negro is registered. Can any law enacted under
such circumstances be considered democratically structured?

Sometimes a law is just on its face and unjust in its application.   19
For instance, I have been arrested on a charge of parading without a
permit. Now, there is nothing wrong in having an ordinance which
requires a permit for a parade. But such an ordinance becomes unjust
when it is used to maintain segregation and to deny citizens the First
Amendment privilege of peaceful assembly and protest.

I hope you are able to see the distinction I am trying to point out.   20
In no sense do I advocate evading or defying the law, as would the rabid
segregationist. That would lead to anarchy. One who breaks an unjust
law must do so openly, lovingly, and with a willingness to accept the
penalty. I submit that an individual who breaks a law that conscience
tells him is unjust, and who willingly accepts the penalty of imprisonment
in order to arouse the conscience of the community over its injustice, is
in reality expressing the highest respect for law.

Of course, there is nothing new about this kind of civil disobedi-   21
ence. It was evidenced sublimely in the refusal of Shadrach, Meshach,
and Abednego to obey the laws of Nebuchadnezzar,[6] on the ground that
a higher moral law was at stake. It was practiced superbly by the early
Christians, who were willing to face hungry lions and the excruciating
pain of chopping blocks rather than submit to certain unjust laws of the
Roman Empire. To a degree, academic freedom is a reality today because
Socrates practiced civil disobedience. In our own nation, the Boston Tea
Party represented a massive act of civil disobedience.

---

6. When Shadrach, Meshach, and Abednego refused to worship an idol, King Nebuchadnezzar had them cast into a roaring furnace; they were saved by God. [See
Daniel 1:7–3:30]

We should never forget that everything Adolf Hitler did in Germany was "legal" and everything the Hungarian freedom fighters[7] did in Hungary was "illegal." It was "illegal" to aid and comfort a Jew in Hitler's Germany. Even so, I am sure that, had I lived in Germany at the time, I would have aided and comforted my Jewish brothers. If today I lived in a Communist country where certain principles dear to the Christian faith are suppressed, I would openly advocate disobeying that country's antireligious laws.   22

I must make two honest confessions to you, my Christian and Jewish brothers. First, I must confess that over the past few years I have been gravely disappointed with the white moderate. I have almost reached the regrettable conclusion that the Negro's great stumbling block in his stride toward freedom is not the White Citizen's Counciler[8] or the Ku Klux Klanner, but the white moderate, who is more devoted to "order" than to justice; who prefers a negative peace which is the absence of tension to a positive peace which is the presence of justice; who constantly says, "I agree with you in the goal you seek, but I cannot agree with your methods of direct action"; who paternalistically believes he can set the timetable for another man's freedom; who lives by a mythical concept of time and who constantly advises the Negro to wait for a "more convenient season." Shallow understanding from people of good will is more frustrating than absolute misunderstanding from people of ill will. Lukewarm acceptance is much more bewildering than outright rejection.   23

I had hoped that the white moderate would understand that law and order exist for the purpose of establishing justice and that when they fail in this purpose they become the dangerously structured dams that block the flow of social progress. I had hoped that the white moderate would understand that the present tension in the South is a necessary phase of the transition from an obnoxious negative peace, in which the Negro passively accepted his unjust plight, to a substantive and positive peace, in which all men will respect the dignity and worth of human personality. Actually, we who engage in nonviolent direct action are not the creators of tension. We merely bring to the surface the hidden tension that is already alive. We bring it out in the open, where it can be seen and dealt with. Like a boil that can never be cured so long as it is covered up but must be opened with all its ugliness to the natural medicines of air and light, injustice must be exposed, with all the tension its exposure   24

7. In 1956 Hungarian nationalists revolted against Communist rule, but were quickly put down with a violent show of Soviet force.

8. Such councils were organized in 1954 to oppose school desegregation.

creates, to the light of human conscience and the air of national opinion, before it can be cured.

In your statement you assert that our actions, even though peaceful, must be condemned because they precipitate violence. But is this a logical assertion? Isn't this like condemning a robbed man because his possession of money precipitated the evil act of robbery? Isn't this like condemning Socrates because his unswerving commitment to truth and his philosophical inquiries precipitated the act by the misguided populace in which they made him drink hemlock? Isn't this like condemning Jesus because his unique God-consciousness and never-ceasing devotion to God's will precipitated the evil act of crucifixion? We must come to see that, as the federal courts have consistently affirmed, it is wrong to urge an individual to cease his efforts to gain his basic constitutional rights because the quest may precipitate violence. Society must protect the robbed and punish the robber.

I had also hoped that the white moderate would reject the myth concerning time in relation to the struggle for freedom. I have just received a letter from a white brother in Texas. He writes: "All Christians know that the colored people will receive equal rights eventually, but it is possible that you are in too great a religious hurry. It has taken Christianity almost two thousand years to accomplish what it has. The teachings of Christ take time to come to earth." Such an attitude stems from a tragic misconception of time, from the strangely irrational notion that there is something in the very flow of time that will inevitably cure all ills. Actually, time itself is neutral; it can be used either destructively or constructively. More and more I feel that the people of ill will have used time much more effectively than have the people of good will. We will have to repent in this generation not merely for the hateful words and actions of the bad people, but for the appalling silence of the good people. Human progress never rolls in on wheels of inevitability; it comes through the tireless efforts of men willing to be co-workers with God, and without this hard work, time itself becomes an ally of the forces of social stagnation. We must use time creatively, in the knowledge that the time is always ripe to do right. Now is the time to make real the promise of democracy and transform our pending national elegy into a creative psalm of brotherhood. Now is the time to lift our national policy from the quicksand of racial injustice to the solid rock of human dignity.

You speak of our activity in Birmingham as extreme. At first I was rather disappointed that fellow clergymen would see my nonviolent efforts as those of an extremist. I began thinking about the fact that I stand in the middle of two opposing forces in the Negro community. One is a force of complacency, made up in part of Negroes who, as a result of long years of oppression, are so drained of self-respect and a sense of "somebodiness" that they have adjusted to segregation; and in part of a few middle-class Negroes who, because of a degree of academic and economic security and because in some ways they profit by segregation, have become insensitive to the problems of the masses. The other force is one of bitterness and hatred, and it comes perilously close to advocating violence. It is expressed in the various black nationalist groups that are springing up across the nation, the largest and best-known being Elijah Muhammad's Muslim movement. Nourished by the Negro's frustration over the continued existence of racial discrimination, this movement is made up of people who have lost faith in America, who have absolutely repudiated Christianity, and who have concluded that the white man is an incorrigible "devil."

I have tried to stand between these two forces, saying that we need emulate neither the "do-nothingism" of the complacent nor the hatred and despair of the black nationalist. For there is the more excellent way of love and nonviolent protest. I am grateful to God that, through the influence of the Negro church, the way of nonviolence became an integral part of our struggle. [28]

If this philosophy had not emerged, by now many streets of the South would, I am convinced, be flowing with blood. And I am further convinced that if our white brothers dismiss as "rabble-rousers" and "outside agitators" those of us who employ nonviolent direct action, and if they refuse to support our nonviolent efforts, millions of Negroes will, out of frustration and despair, seek solace and security in black-nationalist ideologies—a development that would inevitably lead to a frightening racial nightmare. [29]

Oppressed people cannot remain oppressed forever. The yearning for freedom eventually manifests itself, and that is what has happened to the American Negro. Something within has reminded him of his birthright of freedom, and something without has reminded him that it can be gained. Consciously or unconsciously, he has been caught up by the *Zeitgeist*,[9] and with his black brothers of Africa and his brown and yellow brothers of Asia, South America, and the Caribbean, the United States Negro is moving with a sense of great urgency toward the promised land of racial justice. If one recognizes this vital urge that has engulfed the Negro community, one should readily understand why public demonstrations are taking place. The Negro has many pent-up resentments and latent frustrations, and he must release them. So let him march; let him make prayer pilgrimages to the city hall; let him go on freedom rides— [30]

---

9. *Zeitgeist*: German word for "the spirit of the times."

and try to understand why he must do so. If his repressed emotions are not released in nonviolent ways, they will seek expression through violence; this is not a threat but a fact of history. So I have not said to my people, "Get rid of your discontent." Rather, I have tried to say that this normal and healthy discontent can be channeled into the creative outlet of nonviolent direct action. And now this approach is being termed extremist.

But though I was initially disappointed at being categorized as an extremist, as I continued to think about the matter I gradually gained a measure of satisfaction from the label. Was not Jesus an extremist for love: "Love your enemies, bless them that curse you, do good to them that hate you, and pray for them which despitefully use you, and persecute you." Was not Amos an extremist for justice: "Let justice roll down like waters and righteousness like an ever-flowing stream." Was not Paul an extremist for the Christian gospel: "I bear in my body the marks of the Lord Jesus." Was not Martin Luther an extremist: "Here I stand; I cannot do otherwise, so help me God." And John Bunyan: "I will stay in jail to the end of my days before I make a butchery of my conscience." And Abraham Lincoln: "This nation cannot survive half slave and half free." And Thomas Jefferson: "We hold these truths to be self-evident, that all men are created equal. . . ." So the question is not whether we will be extremists, but what kind of extremists we will be. Will we be extremists for hate or for love? Will we be extremists for the preservation of injustice or for the extension of justice? In that dramatic scene on Calvary's hill three men were crucified. We must never forget that all three were crucified for the same crime—the crime of extremism. Two were extremists for immorality, and thus fell below their environment. The other, Jesus Christ, was an extremist for love, truth, and goodness, and thereby rose above his environment. Perhaps the South, the nation, and the world are in dire need of creative extremists.

I had hoped that the white moderate would see this need. Perhaps I was too optimistic; perhaps I expected too much. I suppose I should have realized that few members of the oppressor race can understand the deep groans and passionate yearnings of the oppressed race, and still fewer have the vision to see that injustice must be rooted out by strong, persistent, and determined action. I am thankful, however, that some of our white brothers in the South have grasped the meaning of this social revolution and committed themselves to it. They are still all too few in quantity, but they are big in quality. Some—such as Ralph McGill, Lillian Smith, Harry Golden, James McBride Dabbs, Ann Braden, and Sarah Patton Boyle—have written about our struggle in eloquent and prophetic terms. Others have marched with us down nameless streets of the South. They have languished in filthy, roach-infested jails, suffering the abuse and brutality of policemen who view them as "dirty nigger-lovers." Unlike so many of their moderate brothers and sisters, they have recognized the urgency of the moment and sensed the need for powerful "action" antidotes to combat the disease of segregation.

Let me take note of my other major disappointment. I have been so greatly disappointed with the white church and its leadership. Of course, there are some notable exceptions. I am not unmindful of the fact that each of you has taken some significant stands on this issue. I commend you, Reverend Stallings, for your Christian stand on this past Sunday, in welcoming Negroes to your worship service on a nonsegregated basis. I commend the Catholic leaders of this state for integrating Spring Hill College several years ago. 33

But despite these notable exceptions, I must honestly reiterate that I have been disappointed with the church. I do not say this as one of those negative critics who can always find something wrong with the church. I say this as a minister of the gospel, who loves the church; who was nurtured in its bosom; who has been sustained by its spiritual blessings and who will remain true to it as long as the cord of life shall lengthen. 34

When I was suddenly catapulted into the leadership of the bus protest in Montgomery, Alabama, a few years ago, I felt we would be supported by the white church. I felt that the white ministers, priests, and rabbis of the South would be among our strongest allies. Instead, some have been outright opponents, refusing to understand the freedom movement and misrepresenting its leaders; all too many others have been more cautious than courageous and have remained silent behind the anesthetizing security of stained-glass windows. 35

In spite of my shattered dreams, I came to Birmingham with the hope that the white religious leadership of this community would see the justice of our cause and, with deep moral concern, would serve as the channel through which our just grievances could reach the power structure. I had hoped that each of you would understand. But again I have been disappointed. . . . 36

There was a time when the church was very powerful—in the time when the early Christians rejoiced at being deemed worthy to suffer for what they believed. In those days the church was not merely a thermometer that recorded the ideas and principles of popular opinion; it was a thermostat that transformed the mores of society. Whenever the early Christians entered a town, the people in power became disturbed and 37 immediately sought to convict the Christians for being "disturbers of the peace" and "outside agitators." But the Christians pressed on, in the conviction that they were "a colony of heaven," called to obey God rather than man. Small in number, they were big in commitment. They were too God-intoxicated to be "astronomically intimidated." By their effort and example they brought an end to such ancient evils as infanticide and gladiatorial contests.

Things are different now. So often the contemporary church is a weak, ineffectual voice with an uncertain sound. So often it is an arch-defender of the status quo. Far from being disturbed by the presence of the church, the power structure of the average community is consoled by the church's silent—and often even vocal—sanction of things as they are. 38

But the judgment of God is upon the church as never before. If today's church does not recapture the sacrificial spirit of the early church, it will lose its authenticity, forfeit the loyalty of millions, and be dismissed as an irrelevant social club with no meaning for the twentieth century. Every day I meet young people whose disappointment with the church has turned into outright disgust. 39

Perhaps I have once again been too optimistic. Is organized religion too inextricably bound to the status quo to save our nation and the world? Perhaps I must turn my faith to the inner spiritual church, the church within the church, as the true *ekklesia*[10] and the hope of the world. But again I am thankful to God that some noble souls from the ranks of organized religion have broken loose from the paralyzing chains of conformity and joined us as active partners in the struggle for freedom. They have left their secure congregations and walked the streets of Albany, Georgia, with us. They have gone down the highways of the South on torturous rides for freedom. Yes, they have gone to jail with us. Some have been dismissed from their churches, have lost the support of their bishops and fellow ministers. But they have acted in the faith that right defeated is stronger than evil triumphant. Their witness has been the spiritual salt that has preserved the true meaning of the gospel in these troubled times. They have carved a tunnel of hope through the dark mountain of disappointment. 40

I hope the church as a whole will meet the challenge of this decisive hour. But even if the church does not come to the aid of justice, I have no despair about the future. I have no fear about the outcome of our 41

---

10. *ekklesia*: word referring to the early Church and its spirit; from the Greek New Testament.

struggle in Birmingham, even if our motives are at present misunderstood. We will reach the goal of freedom in Birmingham and all over the nation, because the goal of America is freedom. Abused and scorned though we may be, our destiny is tied up with America's destiny. Before the pilgrims landed at Plymouth, we were here. Before the pen of Jefferson etched the majestic words of the Declaration of Independence across the pages of history, we were here. For more than two centuries our forebears labored in this country without wages; they made cotton king; they built the homes of their masters while suffering gross injustice and shameful humiliation— and yet out of a bottomless vitality they continued to thrive and develop. If the inexpressible cruelties of slavery could not stop us, the opposition we now face will surely fail. We will win our freedom because the sacred heritage of our nation and the eternal will of God are embodied in our echoing demands.

Before closing I feel impelled to mention one other point in your 42 statement that has troubled me profoundly. You warmly commended the Birmingham police force for keeping "order" and "preventing violence." I doubt that you would have so warmly commended the police force if you had seen its dogs sinking their teeth into unarmed, nonviolent Negroes. I doubt that you would so quickly commend the policemen if you were to observe their ugly and inhumane treatment of Negroes here in the city jail; if you were to watch them push and curse old Negro women and young Negro girls; if you were to see them slap and kick old Negro men and young boys; if you were to observe them, as they did on two occasions, refuse to give us food because we wanted to sing our grace together. I cannot join you in your praise of the Birmingham police department.

It is true that the police have exercised a degree of discipline in 43 handling the demonstrators. In this sense they have conducted themselves rather "nonviolently" in public. But for what purpose? To preserve the evil system of segregation. Over the past few years I have consistently preached that nonviolence demands that the means we use must be as pure as the ends we seek. I have tried to make clear that it is wrong to use immoral means to attain moral ends. But now I must affirm that it is just as wrong, or perhaps even more so, to use moral means to preserve immoral ends. Perhaps Mr. Connor and his policemen have been rather nonviolent in public, as was Chief Pritchett in Albany, Georgia, but they have used the moral means of nonviolence to maintain the immoral end of racial injustice. As T. S. Eliot has said, "The last temptation is the greatest treason: To do the right deed for the wrong reason."

I wish you had commended the Negro sit-inners and demonstrators   4
of Birmingham for their sublime courage, their willingness to suffer, and
their amazing discipline in the midst of great provocation. One day the
South will recognize its real heroes. They will be the James Merediths,[11]
with the noble sense of purpose that enables them to face jeering and
hostile mobs, and with the agonizing loneliness that characterizes the life
of the pioneer. They will be old, oppressed, battered Negro women,
symbolized in a seventy-two-year-old woman in Montgomery, Alabama,
who rose up with a sense of dignity and with her people decided not to
ride segregated buses, and who responded with ungrammatical profundity
to one who inquired about her weariness: "My feets is tired, but my soul
is at rest." They will be the young high school and college students, the
young ministers of the gospel and a host of their elders, courageously and
nonviolently sitting in at lunch counters and willingly going to jail for
conscience' sake. One day the South will know that when these disin-
herited children of God sat down at lunch counters, they were in reality
standing up for what is best in the American dream and for the most
sacred values in our Judaeo-Christian heritage, thereby bringing our nation back to those great wells of democracy which were dug deep by the
founding fathers in their formulation of the Constitution and the Declaration of Independence.

Never before have I written so long a letter. I'm afraid it is much   45
too long to take your precious time. I can assure you that it would have
been much shorter if I had been writing from a comfortable desk, but
what else can one do when he is alone in a narrow jail cell, other than
write long letters, think long thoughts, and pray long prayers?

If I have said anything in this letter that overstates the truth and   46
indicates an unreasonable impatience, I beg you to forgive me. If I have
said anything that understates the truth and indicates my having a patience that allows me to settle for anything less than brotherhood, I beg
God to forgive me.

I hope this letter finds you strong in the faith. I also hope that   47
circumstances will soon make it possible for me to meet each of you, not
as an integrationist or a civil-rights leader but as a fellow clergyman and
a Christian brother. Let us all hope that the dark clouds of racial prejudice
will soon pass away and the deep fog of misunderstanding will be lifted
from our fear-drenched communities, and in some not too distant to-

---

11. In 1961 James Meredith became the first black student to enroll at the University
of Mississippi, sparking considerable controversy and confrontation.

morrow the radiant stars of love and brotherhood will shine over our great nation with all their scintillating beauty.

Yours for the cause of Peace and Brotherhood,

MARTIN LUTHER KING, JR.

Questions for Study and Discussion

1. Why did King write this letter? What was he doing in Birmingham? What kinds of "direct action" did he take there and why? What did he do that caused him to be jailed?

2. King says that he "stands in the middle of two opposing forces in the Negro community". What are those forces and why does he see himself between them?

3. What does King find wrong with the contemporary church as opposed to the early Christian church?

4. What specific objections to his activities have been presented in the statement that King is responding to? How does he answer each objection?

5. What does King call upon the clergy to do? What actions does he wish them to take, and what beliefs to hold?

6. King says that he advocates nonviolent resistance. What does he mean? In his letter he notes that the Birmingham Police Department has been praised for its nonviolent response to demonstrations. What is King's response to this claim?

7. King's letter was written in response to a statement sent him by eight fellow clergymen. While these men are his primary audience, he would appear to have a secondary audience, as well. What is that audience? How does King show himself to be a man of reason and thoughtfulness in his letter of response?

Writing Topics

1. Write an essay in which you discuss how Martin Luther King's actions as well as his "Letter from Birmingham Jail" exemplify Thoreau's principle of civil disobedience (pp. 648–666).

2. King advocates nonviolent resistance as a way of confronting oppression. What other means of confronting oppression were available to him? What are the strengths and weaknesses of those alternatives? Write an essay in which you assess the effectiveness of nonviolent resistance in the light of its alternatives.

In 1985 Steven Spielberg brought out the highly acclaimed movie *The Color Purple*. Based on Alice Walker's novel of the same name which won both the Pulitzer Prize and American Book Award for fiction in 1983, the movie put her name boldly in front of the American public. But this was not always the case. Alice Walker was born in 1944 in Eatonton, Georgia, the eighth child of black sharecroppers. She grew up in the pre-Civil Rights South and was greatly influenced by the early work of Dr. Martin Luther King, Jr. Walker attended Spelman College in Atlanta on scholarship and later graduated from Sarah Lawrence College, where during her senior year she wrote her first book of poems, *Once* (1965). After graduation her essays and stories started to appear with some regularity in magazines and newspapers like *American Scholar*, *The New York Times*, *Mother Jones*, and *Ms.* During the late 1960s and early 1970s while in Jackson, Mississippi, with her husband, a prosecutor of school-desegregation cases, Walker taught at Jackson State College and continued to write industriously. It was during this period that she produced *The Third Life of Grange Copeland* (1970), her first novel; *Revolutionary Petunias and Other Poems* (1973); *In Love and Trouble: Stories of Black Women* (1973); and a biography of Langston Hughes for young readers. Since that time she has written two more books of poetry, a collection of essays, another book of short stories, and two more novels, one of them *The Color Purple* (1982).

"The Civil Rights Movement: What Good Was It?" was Walker's first published essay. Written in 1967, it won the *American Scholar* essay contest. Later Walker included this essay in her collection *In Search of Our Mothers' Gardens* (1983). Here she takes a thoughtful look at what the Civil Rights Movement has meant for black Americans.

The Civil Rights Movement: What Good Was It?

Someone said recently to an old black lady from Mississippi, whose legs had been badly mangled by local police who arrested her for "disturbing the peace," that the Civil Rights Movement was dead, and asked, since it was dead, what she thought about it. The old lady replied, hobbling out of his presence on her cane, that the Civil Rights Movement was like herself, "if it's dead, it shore ain't ready to lay down!"

This old lady is a legendary freedom fighter in her small town in the Delta. She has been severely mistreated for insisting on her rights as an American citizen. She has been beaten for singing Movement songs, placed in solitary confinement in prisons for talking about freedom, and placed on bread and water for praying aloud to God for her jailers' deliverance. For such a woman the Civil Rights Movement will never be over as long as her skin is black. It also will never be over for twenty million others with the same "affliction," for whom the Movement can never "lay down," no matter how it is killed by the press and made dead and buried by the white American public. As long as one black American survives, the struggle for equality with other Americans must also survive. This is a debt we owe to those blameless hostages we leave to the future, our children.

Still, white liberals and deserting Civil Rights sponsors are quick 3 to justify their disaffection from the Movement by claiming that it is all over. "And since it is over," they will ask, "would someone kindly tell me what has been gained by it?" They then list statistics supposedly showing how much more advanced segregation is now than ten years ago—in schools, housing, jobs. They point to a gain in conservative politicians during the last few years. They speak of ghetto riots and of the survey that shows that most policemen are admittedly too anti-Negro to do their jobs in ghetto areas fairly and effectively. They speak of every area that has been touched by the Civil Rights Movement as somehow or other going to pieces.

They rarely talk, however, about human attitudes among Negros 4 that have undergone terrific changes just during the past seven to ten years (not to mention all those years when there was a Movement and only the Negroes knew about it). They seldom speak of changes in personal lives because of the influence of people in the Movement. They see general failure and few, if any, individual gains.

They do not understand what it is that keeps the Movement from 5 "laying down" and Negroes from reverting to their former *silent* second-class status. They have apparently never stopped to wonder why it is always the white man—on his radio and in his newspaper and on his television—who says that the Movement is dead. If a Negro were audacious enough to make such a claim, his fellows might hanker to see him shot. The Movement is dead to the white man because it no longer interests him. And it no longer interests him because he can afford to be uninterested: he does not have to live by it, with it, or for it, as Negroes must. He can take a rest from the news of beatings, killings, and arrests that reach him from North and South—if his skin is white. Negroes cannot now and will never be able to take a rest from the injustices that plague them, for they—not the white man—are the target.

Perhaps it is naïve to be thankful that the Movement "saved" a 6 large number of individuals and gave them something to live for, even if it did not provide them with everything they wanted. (Materially, it provided them with precious little that they wanted.) When a movement awakens people to the possibilities of life, it seems unfair to frustrate them by then denying what they had thought was offered. But what was offered? What was promised? What was it all about? What good did it do? Would it have been better, as some have suggested, to leave the Negro people as they were, unawakened, unallied with one another, unhopeful about what to expect for their children in some future world?

I do not think so. If knowledge of my condition is all the freedom I get from a "freedom movement," it is better than unawareness, forgottenness, and hopelessness, the existence that is like the existence of a beast. Man only truly lives by knowing; otherwise he simply performs, copying the daily habits of others, but conceiving nothing of his creative possibilities as a man, and accepting someone else's superiority and his own misery.

When we are children, growing up in our parents' care, we await the spark from the outside world. Sometimes our parents provide it—if we are lucky—sometimes it comes from another source far from home. We sit, paralyzed, surrounded by our anxiety and dread, hoping we will not have to grow up into the narrow world and ways we see about us. We are hungry for a life that turns us on; we yearn for knowledge of living that will save us from our innocuous lives that resemble death. We look for signs in every strange event; we search for heroes in every unknown face.

It was just six years ago that I began to be alive. I had, of course, been living before—for I am now twenty-three—but I did not really know it. And I did not know it because nobody told me that I—a pensive, yearning, typical high-school senior, but Negro—existed in the minds of others as I existed in my own. Until that time my mind was locked apart form the outer contours and complexion of my body as if it and the body were strangers. The mind possessed both thought and spirit—I wanted to be an author or a scientist—which the color of the body denied. I had never seen myself and existed as a statistic exists, or as a phantom. In the white world I walked, less real to them than a shadow; and being young and well hidden among the slums, among people who also did not exist—either in books or in films or in the government of their own lives—I waited to be called to life. And, by a miracle, I was called.

There was a commotion in our house that night in 1960. We had managed to buy our first television set. It was battered and overpriced, but my mother had gotten used to watching the afternoon soap operas at the house where she worked as maid, and nothing could satisfy her

7

8

9

10

on days when she did not work but a continuation of her "stories." So she pinched pennies and bought a set.

I remained listless throughout her "stories," tales of pregnancy, abortion, hypocrisy, infidelity, and alcoholism. All these men and women were white and lived in houses with servants, long staircases that they floated down, patios where liquor was served four times a day to "relax" them. But my mother, with her swollen feet eased out of her shoes, her heavy body relaxed in our only comfortable chair, watched each movement of the smartly coiffed women, heard each word, pounced upon each innuendo and inflection, and for the duration of these "stories" she saw herself as one of them. She placed herself in every scene she saw, with her braided hair turned blond, her two hundred pounds compressed into a sleek size-seven dress, her rough dark skin smooth and *white*. Her husband became "dark and handsome," talented, witty, urbane, charming. And when she turned to look at my father sitting near her in his sweat shirt with his smelly feet raised on the bed to "air," there was always a tragic look of surprise on her face. Then she would sigh and go out to the kitchen looking lost and unsure of herself. My mother, a truly great woman who raised eight children of her own and half a dozen of the neighbors' without a single complaint, was convinced that she did not exist compared to "them." She subordinated her soul to theirs and became a faithful and timid supporter of the "Beautiful White People." Once she asked me, in a moment of vicarious pride and despair, if I didn't think that "they" were "jest naturally smarter, prettier, better." My mother asked this· a woman who never got rid of any of her children, never cheated on my father, was never a hypocrite if she could help it, and never even tasted liquor. She could not even bring herself to blame "them" for making her believe what they wanted her to believe: that if she did not look like them, think like them, be sophisticated and corrupt-for-comfort's-sake like them, she was a nobody. Black was not a color on my mother; it was a shield that made her invisible.

Of course, the people who write the soap-opera scripts always made the Negro maids in them steadfast, trusty, and wise in a home-remedial sort of way; but my mother, a maid for nearly forty years, never once identified herself with the scarcely glimpsed black servant's face beneath the ruffled cap. Like everyone else, in her daydreams at least, she thought she was free.

Six years ago, after half-heartedly watching my mother's soap operas and wondering whether there wasn't something more to be asked of life, the Civil Rights Movement came into my life. Like a good omen for the future, the face of Dr. Martin Luther King, Jr., was the first black face I saw on our new television screen. And, as in a fairy tale, my soul was

11

12

13

stirred by the meaning for me of his mission—at the time he was being rather ignominiously dumped into a police van for having led a protest march in Alabama—and I fell in love with the sober and determined face of the Movement. The singing of "We Shall Overcome"—that song betrayed by nonbelievers in it—rang for the first time in my ears. The influence that my mother's soap operas might have had on me became impossible. The life of Dr. King, seeming bigger and more miraculous than the man himself, because of all he had done and suffered, offered a pattern of strength and sincerity I felt I could trust. He had suffered much because of his simple belief in nonviolence, love, and brotherhood. Perhaps the majority of men could not be reached through these beliefs, but because Dr. King kept trying to reach them in spite of danger to himself and his family, I saw in him the hero for whom I had waited so long.

What Dr. King promised was not a ranch-style house and an acre of manicured lawn for every black man, but jail and finally freedom. He did not promise two cars for every family, but the courage one day for all families everywhere to walk without shame and unafraid on their own feet. He did not say that one day it will be us chasing prospective buyers out of our prosperous well-kept neighborhoods, or in other ways exhibiting our snobbery and ignorance as all other ethnic groups before us have done; what he said was that we had a right to live anywhere in this country we chose, and a right to a meaningful well-paying job to provide us with the upkeep of our homes. He did not say we had to become carbon copies of the white American middle class; but he did say we had the right to become whatever we wanted to become. 14

Because of the Movement, because of an awakened faith in the newness and imagination of the human spirit, because of "black and white together"—for the first time in our history in some human relationship on and off TV—because of the beatings, the arrests, the hell of battle during the past years, I have fought harder for my life and for a chance to be myself, to be something more than a shadow or a number, than I had ever done before in my life. Before, there had seemed to be no real reason for struggling beyond the effort for daily bread. Now there was a chance at that other that Jesus meant when He said we could not live by bread alone. 15

I have fought and kicked and fasted and prayed and cursed and cried myself to the point of existing. It has been like being born again, literally. Just "knowing" has meant everything to me. Knowing has pushed me out into the world, into college, into places, into people. 16

Part of what existence means to me is knowing the difference between what I am now and what I was then. It is being capable of looking 17 after myself intellectually as well as financially. It is being able to tell when I am being wronged and by whom. It means being awake to protect myself and the ones I love. It means being a part of the world community, and being *alert* to which part it is that I have joined, and knowing how to change to another part if that part does not suit me. To know is to exist: to exist is to be involved, to move about, to see the world with my own eyes. This, at least, the Movement has given me.

The hippies and other nihilists would have me believe that it is all the same whether the people in Mississippi have a movement behind them or not. Once they have their rights, they say, they will run all over themselves trying to be just like everybody else. They will be well fed, complacent about things of the spirit, emotionless, and without that marvelous humanity and "soul" that the Movement has seen them practice time and time again. "What has the Movement done," they ask, "with the few people it has supposedly helped?" "Got them white-collar jobs, moved them into standardized ranch houses in white neighborhoods, given them nondescript gray flannel suits?" "What are these people now?" they ask. And then they answer themselves, "Nothings!"

I would find this reasoning—which I have heard many, many times from hippies and nonhippies alike—amusing if I did not also consider it serious. For I think it is a delusion, a cop-out, an excuse to dissociate themselves from a world in which they feel too little has been changed or gained. The real question, however, it appears to me, is not whether poor people will adopt the middle-class mentality once they are well fed; rather, it is whether they will ever be well fed enough to be able to choose whatever mentality they think will suit them. The lack of a movement did not keep my mother from *wishing* herself bourgeois in her daydreams.

There is widespread starvation in Mississippi. In my own state of Georgia there are more hungry families than Lester Maddox would like to admit—or even see fed. I went to school with children who ate red dirt. The Movement has prodded and pushed some liberal senators into pressuring the government for food so that the hungry may eat. Food stamps that were two dollars and out of the reach of many families not long ago have been reduced to fifty cents. The price is still out of the reach of some families, and the government, it seems to a lot of people, could spare enough free food to feed its own people. It angers people in the Movement that it does not; they point to the billions in wheat we send free each year to countries abroad. Their government's slowness while people are hungry, its unwillingness to believe that there are Americans starving, its stingy cutting of the price of food stamps, make many Civil Rights workers throw up their hands in disgust. But they do not

18

19

20

give up. They do not withdraw into the world of psychedelia. They apply what pressure they can to make the government give away food to hungry people. They do not plan so far ahead in their disillusionment with society that they can see these starving families buying identical ranch-style houses and sending their snobbish children to Bryn Mawr and Yale. They take first things first and try to get them fed.

They do not consider it their business, in any case, to say what kind of life the people they help must lead. How one lives is, after all, one of the rights left to the individual—when and if he has opportunity to choose. It is not the prerogative of the middle class to determine what is worthy of aspiration. There is also every possibility that the middle-class people of tomorrow will turn out ever so much better than those of today. I even know some middle-class people of today who are not *all* bad.   21

I think there are so few Negro hippies because middle-class Negroes, although well fed, are not careless. They are required by the treacherous world they live in to be clearly aware of whoever or whatever might be trying to do them in. They are middle class in money and position, but they cannot afford to be middle class in complacency. They distrust the hippie movement because they know that it can do nothing for Negroes as a group but "love" them, which is what all paternalists claim to do. And since the only way Negroes can survive (which they cannot do, unfortunately, on love alone) is with the support of the group, they are wisely wary and stay away.   22

A white writer tried recently to explain that the reason for the relatively few Negro hippies is that Negroes have built up a "supercool" that cracks under LSD and makes them have a "bad trip." What this writer doesn't guess at is that Negroes are needing drugs less than ever these days for any kind of trip. While the hippies are "tripping," Negroes are going after power, which is so much more important to their survival and their children's survival than LSD and pot.   23

Everyone would be surprised if the Israelis ignored the Arabs and took up "tripping" and pot smoking. In this country we are the Israelis. Everybody who can do so would like to forget this, of course. But for us to forget it for a minute would be fatal. "We Shall Overcome" is just a song to most Americans, *but we must do it.* Or die.   24

What good was the Civil Rights Movement? If it had just given this country Dr. King, a leader of conscience, for once in our lifetime, it would have been enough. If it had just taken black eyes off white television stories, it would have been enough. If it had fed one starving child, it would have been enough.   25

If the Civil Rights Movement is "dead," and if it gave us nothing 26
else, it gave us each other forever. It gave some of us bread, some of us
shelter, some of us knowledge and pride, all of us comfort. It gave us our
children, our husbands, our brothers, our fathers, as men reborn and
with a purpose for living. It broke the pattern of black servitude in this
country. It shattered the phony "promise" of white soap operas that
sucked away so many pitiful lives. It gave us history and men far greater
than Presidents. It gave us heroes, selfless men of courage and strength,
for our little boys and girls to follow. It gave us hope for tomorrow. It
called us to life.

Because we live, it can never die. 27

Questions for Study and Discussion

1. What is Walker's thesis in this essay? Where is it most clearly and succinctly expressed?

2. How, according to Walker, do white liberals justify their disaffection with the Civil Rights Movement? Why does Walker believe that the Movement is dead for whites?

3. On a personal level, what has the Movement provided Walker? What has the Movement provided black people in general?

4. In paragraph 6, Walker asks a series of questions. What is the purpose of these questions? How do they function in the context of the essay?

5. Walker begins her essay with the example of the old black lady from Mississippi. What, if anything, does she gain by starting with this story? What is the connection between Walker's opening and her conclusion?

6. In paragraphs 10–12, Walker discusses her mother and her fascination with the soap operas. What point does Walker make with this extended example?

7. How did Walker first become aware of Dr. Martin Luther King, Jr.? In what ways was he a hero for her? What lasting influence did he have on Walker?

Writing Topics

1. Write an essay in which you give your own views on the impact that the Civil Rights Movement has had on you and/or other Americans.

2. Write an essay in which you argue that much still needs to be done to achieve racial equality in the United States.

3. The Women's Movement, like the Civil Rights Movement, seeks to heighten awareness of the inequalities that exist between the sexes in this country and to work toward their elimination. The Women's Movement has also had its share of supporters who eventually fell by the wayside. Using Walker's essay as a model, write an essay in which you answer the question: What good is the Women's Movement?

W. H. AUDEN

Wystan Hugh Auden was born in York, England, in 1907, and was educated at Oxford University. While a student at Christ Church College there, he began to write the poems that brought him attention as an original, modern voice in English letters. During the 1930s Auden developed his special kind of direct, often political poetry and also wrote plays, a movie script, and books that grew out of journeys to Iceland and China with such friends and fellow writers as Louis MacNeice and Christopher Isherwood. At the end of the thirties, he left England for the United States, later to become an American citizen. As he grew older, his poetry became more introspective, less "public" and political. He died in 1973. Many countries have monuments dedicated to their "unknown soldier," a soldier killed on the battlefield who symbolizes the ideals of national service and sacrifice. "The Unknown Citizen" suggests what might be written on a monument for a symbolic civilian, who represents his society's peacetime values.

The Unknown Citizen

(To JS/07/M/378
This Marble Monument
Is Erected by the State)

He was found by the Bureau of Statistics to be
One against whom there was no official complaint,
And all the reports on his conduct agree
That, in the modern sense of an old-fashioned word, he was a saint,
For in everything he did he served the Greater Community.   5
Except for the War till the day he retired
He worked in a factory and never got fired,
But satisfied his employers, Fudge Motors Inc.
Yet he wasn't a scab or odd in his views,
For his Union reports that he paid his dues,   10
(Our report on his Union shows it was sound)
And our Social Psychology workers found
That he was popular with his mates and liked a drink.
The Press are convinced that he bought a paper every day
And that his reactions to advertisements were normal in every way.   15
Policies taken out in his name prove that he was fully insured,
And his Health-card shows he was once in hospital but left it cured.
Both Producers Research and High-Grade Living declare
He was fully sensible to the advantages of the Instalment Plan

And had everything necessary to the Modern Man,   2(
A phonograph, a radio, a car and a frigidaire.
Our researchers into Public Opinion are content
That he held the proper opinions for the time of year;
When there was peace, he was for peace; when there was war, he
    went.
He was married and added five children to the population,   25
Which our Eugenist says was the right number for a parent of his
    generation,
And our teachers report that he never interfered with their education.
Was he free? Was he happy? The question is absurd:
Had anything been wrong, we should certainly have heard.

Questions for Study and Discussion

1. Do the words in this poem literally express Auden's own views? What makes you think so? If not, whose views are they meant to express?

2. Why do you think Auden presents this poem as an inscription on a public monument? What is the advantage of this choice? Why would a society erect a monument to its "unknown citizen"?

3. What does the poem tell us about the unknown citizen? What doesn't it tell us? What do its inclusions and omissions reveal about the state's official attitudes and values? How do these attitudes and values compare with Auden's? How do you know?

4. Look at the inscription following the title. What can you say about its content and style? How does it affect your understanding of the poem?

5. Comment on Auden's use of capitalization, citing examples from the poem. How does it affect the poem's meaning?

6. How do you think Auden meant readers to respond to this poem? Cite evidence from the poem to support your answer. How do you respond to it? Why do you respond that way?

Writing Topics

1. Auden wrote his poem in 1939. Using whatever information you think relevant, write an essay in which you describe the "unknown citizen" of the 1980s.

2. Suppose that in the year 2000 the state were to erect a monument to you, and that you could write the inscription yourself, within a limit of 500 words. What would you want your monument to say? Write your own inscription.

3. The United States government relies heavily on statistical information about its citizens, information that depersonalizes them in various ways. What sort of information does the government collect? What are the advantages and uses of having such information? What are the disadvantages and abuses? Write an essay in which you discuss the pros and/or the cons of extensive information gathering by the government.

KURT VONNEGUT, JR.

Our Declaration of Independence states as a "self-evident truth" that all men are created equal. But what does it mean to be "equal"? In the following story, Kurt Vonnegut, Jr., shows what it does *not* mean. Vonnegut was born in 1922 in Indianapolis, Indiana. While he was a student at Cornell University, he joined the Army to serve in World War II and was sent to Europe. Taken prisoner by the German Army, he witnessed the Allied firebombing of Dresden in 1945, a bloody and pointless incident that inspired his novel *Slaughterhouse-Five* (1969). After the war he completed his education at the University of Chicago, then from 1947 to 1950 worked in the public relations department of General Electric; since then, he has worked full-time as a writer. Probably his best known novels, besides *Slaughterhouse-Five*, are *Player Piano* (1952) and *Cat's Cradle* (1963), and some of his short stories have been collected in *Welcome to the Monkey House* (1968). "Harrison Bergeron," from this collection, is set in 2081, but like much science fiction it offers a critique of the present as much as a prediction of the future.

Harrison Bergeron

The year was 2081, and everybody was finally equal. They weren't only equal before God and the law. They were equal every which way. Nobody was smarter than anybody else. Nobody was better looking than anybody else. Nobody was stronger or quicker than anybody else. All this equality was due to the 211th, 212th, and 213th Amendments to the Constitution, and to the unceasing vigilance of agents of the United States Handicapper General.

Some things about living still weren't quite right, though. April, for instance, still drove people crazy by not being springtime. And it was in that clammy month that the H-G men took George and Hazel Bergeron's fourteen-year-old son, Harrison, away.

It was tragic, all right, but George and Hazel couldn't think about it very hard. Hazel had a perfectly average intelligence, which meant she couldn't think about anything except in short bursts. And George, while his intelligence was way above normal, had a little mental handicap radio in his ear. He was required by law to wear it at all times. It was tuned to a government transmitter. Every twenty seconds or so, the transmitter would send out some sharp noise to keep people like George from taking unfair advantage of their brains.

George and Hazel were watching television. There were tears on Hazel's cheeks, but she'd forgotten for the moment what they were about.

On the television screen were ballerinas.   5

A buzzer sounded in George's head. His thoughts fled in panic, like   6
bandits from a burglar alarm.

"That was a real pretty dance, that dance they just did," said   7
Hazel.

"Huh?" said George.   8

"That dance—it was nice," said Hazel.   9

"Yup," said George. He tried to think a little about the ballerinas.   10
They weren't really very good—no better than anybody else would have
been, anyway. They were burdened with sashweights and bags of birdshot,
and their faces were masked, so that no one, seeing a free and graceful
gesture or a pretty face, would feel like something the cat drug in. George
was toying with the vague notion that maybe dancers shouldn't be handicapped. But he didn't get very far with it before another noise in his ear
radio scattered his thoughts.

George winced. So did two out of the eight ballerinas.   11

Hazel saw him wince. Having no mental handicap herself, she had   12
to ask George what the latest sound had been.

"Sounded like somebody hitting a milk bottle with a ball peen   13
hammer," said George.

"I'd think it would be real interesting, hearing all the different   14
sounds," said Hazel, a little envious. "All the things they think up."

"Um," said George.   15

"Only, if I was Handicapper General, you know what I would do?"   16
said Hazel. Hazel, as a matter of fact, bore a strong resemblance to the
Handicapper General, a woman named Diana Moon Glampers. "If I was
Diana Moon Glampers," said Hazel, "I'd have chimes on Sunday—just
chimes. Kind of in honor of religion."

"I could think, if it was just chimes," said George.   17

"Well—maybe make 'em real loud," said Hazel. "I think I'd make   18
a good Handicapper General."

"Good as anybody else," said George.   19

"Who knows better'n I do what normal is?" said Hazel.   20

"Right," said George. He began to think glimmeringly about his   21
abnormal son who was now in jail, about Harrison, but a twenty-one
gun salute in his head stopped that.

"Boy!" said Hazel, "that was a doozy, wasn't it?"   22

It was such a doozy that George was white and trembling, and tears   23
stood on the rims of his red eyes. Two of the eight ballerinas had collapsed
to the studio floor, were holding their temples.

"All of a sudden you look so tired," said Hazel. "Why don't you   24
stretch out on the sofa, so's you can rest your handicap bag on the pillows,

honeybunch." She was referring to the forty-seven pounds of birdshot in a canvas bag, which was padlocked around George's neck. "Go on and rest the bag for a little while," she said. "I don't care if you're not equal to me for a while."

George weighed the bag with his hands. "I don't mind it," he said. "I don't notice it any more. It's just a part of me."   25

"You been so tired lately—kind of wore out," said Hazel. "If there was just some way we could make a little hole in the bottom of the bag, and just take out a few of them lead balls. Just a few."   26

"Two years in prison and two thousand dollars fine for every ball I took out," said George. "I don't call that a bargain."   27

"If you could just take a few out when you came home from work," said Hazel. "I mean—you don't compete with anybody around here. You just set around."   28

"If I tried to get away with it," said George, "then other people'd get away with it—and pretty soon we'd be right back to the dark ages again, with everybody competing against everybody else. You wouldn't like that, would you?"   29

"I'd hate it," said Hazel.   30

"There you are," said George. "The minute people start cheating on laws, what do you think happens to society?"   31

If Hazel hadn't been able to come up with an answer to this question, George couldn't have supplied one. A siren was going off in his head.   32

"Reckon it'd fall all apart," said Hazel.   33
"What would?" said George blankly.   34
"Society," said Hazel uncertainly. "Wasn't that what you just said?"   35
"Who knows?" said George.   36

The television program was suddenly interrupted for a news bulletin. It wasn't clear at first as to what the bulletin was about, since the announcer, like all announcers, had a serious speech impediment. For about half a minute, and in a state of high excitement, the announcer tried to say, "Ladies and gentlemen—"   37

He finally gave up, handed the bulletin to a ballerina to read.   38

"That's all right—" Hazel said of the announcer, "he tried. That's the big thing. He tried to do the best he could with what God gave him. He should get a nice raise for trying so hard."   39

"Ladies and gentlemen—" said the ballerina, reading the bulletin. She must have been extraordinarily beautiful, because the mask she wore was hideous. And it was easy to see that she was the strongest and most graceful of all the dancers, for her handicap bags were as big as those worn by two-hundred-pound men.   40

And she had to apologize at once for her voice, which was a very 41
unfair voice for a woman to use. Her voice was a warm, luminous, timeless
melody. "Excuse me—" she said, and she began again, making her voice
absolutely uncompetitive.

"Harrison Bergeron, age fourteen," she said in a grackle squawk, 42
"has just escaped from jail, where he was held on suspicion of plotting
to overthrow the government. He is a genius and an athlete, is under-
handicapped, and should be regarded as extremely dangerous."

A police photograph of Harrison Bergeron was flashed on the screen— 43
upside down, then sideways, upside down again, then right side up. The
picture showed the full length of Harrison against a background calibrated
in feet and inches. He was exactly seven feet tall.

The rest of Harrison's appearance was Halloween and hardware. 44
Nobody had ever born heavier handicaps. He had outgrown hindrances
faster than the H-G men could think them up. Instead of a little ear radio
for a mental handicap, he wore a tremendous pair of earphones, and
spectacles with thick wavy lenses. The spectacles were intended to make
him not only half blind, but to give him whanging headaches besides.

Scrap metal was hung all over him. Ordinarily, there was a certain 45
symmetry, a military neatness to the handicaps issued to strong people,
but Harrison looked like a walking junkyard. In the race of life, Harrison
carried three hundred pounds.

And to offset his good looks, the H-G men required that he wear 46
at all times a red rubber ball for a nose, keep his eyebrows shaved off,
and cover his even white teeth with black caps at snaggle-tooth random.

"If you see this boy," said the ballerina, "do not—I repeat, do not— 47
try to reason with him."

There was the shriek of a door being torn from its hinges. 48

Screams and barking cries of consternation came from the television 49
set. The photograph of Harrison Bergeron on the screen jumped again
and again, as though dancing to the tune of an earthquake.

George Bergeron correctly identified the earthquake, and well he 50
might have—for many was the time his own home had danced to the
same crashing tune. "My God—" said George, "that must be Harrison!"

The realization was blasted from his mind instantly by the sound 51
of an automobile collision in his head.

When George could open his eyes again, the photograph of Har- 52
rison was gone. A living, breathing Harrison filled the screen.

Clanking, clownish, and huge, Harrison stood in the center of the 53
studio. The knob of the uprooted studio door was still in his hand.
Ballerinas, technicians, musicians, and announcers cowered on their knees
before him, expecting to die.

"I am the Emperor!" cried Harrison. Do you hear? I am the Em-   54
peror! Everybody must do what I say at once!" He stamped his foot and
the studio shook.

"Even as I stand here—" he bellowed, "crippled, hobbled, sick-   55
ened—I am a greater ruler than any man who ever lived! Now watch
me become what I *can* become!"

Harrison tore the straps of his handicap harness like wet tissue   56
paper, tore straps guaranteed to support five thousand pounds.

Harrison's scrap-iron handicaps crashed to the floor.   57

Harrison thrust his thumbs under the bar of the padlock that secured   58
his head harness. The bar snapped like celery. Harrison smashed his
headphones and spectacles against the wall.

He flung away his rubber-ball nose, revealed a man that would have   59
awed Thor, the god of thunder.

"I shall now select my Empress!" he said, looking down on the   60
cowering people. "Let the first woman who dares rise to her feet claim
her mate and her throne!"

A moment passed, and then a ballerina arose, swaying like a willow.   61

Harrison plucked the mental handicap from her ear, snapped off   62
her physical handicaps with marvelous delicacy. Last of all, he removed
her mask.

She was blindingly beautiful.   63

"Now—" said Harrison, taking her hand, "shall we show the people   64
the meaning of the word dance? Music!" he commanded.

The musicians scrambled back into their chairs, and Harrison stripped   65
them of their handicaps, too. "Play your best," he told them, "and I'll
make you barons and dukes and earls."

The music began. It was normal at first—cheap, silly, false. But   66
Harrison snatched two musicians from their chairs, waved them like
batons as he sang the music as he wanted it played. He slammed them
back into their chairs.

The music began again and was much improved.   67

Harrison and his Empress merely listened to the music for a while—   68
listened gravely, as though synchronizing their heartbeats with it.

They shifted their weights to their toes.   69

Harrison placed his big hands on the girl's tiny waist, letting her   70
sense the weightlessness that would soon be hers.

And then, in an explosion of joy and grace, into the air they sprang!   71

Not only were the laws of the land abandoned, but the law of   72
gravity and the laws of motion as well.

They reeled, whirled, swiveled, flounced, capered, gamboled, and   73
spun.

They leaped like deer on the moon.   74

The studio ceiling was thirty feet high, but each leap brought the   75
dancers nearer to it.

It became their obvious intention to kiss the ceiling.   76

They kissed it.   77

And then, neutralizing gravity with love and pure will, they re-   78
mained suspended in air inches below the ceiling, and they kissed each
other for a long, long time.

It was then that Diana Moon Glampers, the Handicapper General,   79
came into the studio with a double-barreled ten-gauge shotgun. She fired
twice, and the Emperor and the Empress were dead before they hit the
floor.

Diana Moon Glampers loaded the gun again. She aimed it at the   80
musicians and told them they had ten seconds to get their handicaps
back on.

It was then that the Bergerons' television tube burned out.   81

Hazel turned to comment about the blackout to George. But George   82
had gone out into the kitchen for a can of beer.

George came back in with the beer, paused while a handicap signal   83
shook him up. And then he sat down again. "You been crying?" he said
to Hazel.

"Yup," she said.   84

"What about?" he said.   85

"I forget," she said. "Something real sad on television."   86

"What was it?" he said.   87

"It's all kind of mixed up in my mind," said Hazel.   88

"Forget sad things," said George.   89

"I always do," said Hazel.   90

"That's my girl," said George. He winced. There was the sound of   91
a rivetting gun in his head.

"Gee—I could tell that one was a doozy," said Hazel.   92

"You can say that again," said George.   93

"Gee—" said Hazel, "I could tell that one was a doozy."   94

Questions for Study and Discussion

1. In what ways is Vonnegut's world of 2081 little changed from the present?
What is different? What can you infer from this about Vonnegut's intention?

2. Why does George refer to the competitive past as the "dark ages"? What
solution does "handicapping" offer? In what ways does being under-handi-
capped make Harrison dangerous?

3. Consider the specific handicaps that above-average people have to wear

in the story. How do you respond to Vonnegut's descriptions? What do those handicaps suggest about the collective mentality of 2081 society?

4. Why does Vonnegut make Harrison a fourteen-year-old child? What childish qualities does Harrison display?

5. Vonnegut's story is plausible up to the point where Harrison and the ballerina "defy the law of gravity and the laws of motion. . . ." Why do you think Vonnegut shifts to fantasy at this point? Would the story have been better or worse if he had kept to the physically possible? Why do you think so?

6. What can you say about the Handicapper General, Diana Moon Glampers? What does the story tell you, or allow you to infer, about her position in 2081 society and her way of doing her job?

7. The words *equality* and *average* refer to similar but essentially different concepts. In what significant way do they differ? How does this difference relate to the theme of Vonnegut's story?

Writing Topics

1. Is there a typical American attitude toward people of exceptional talent or achievement? What is your attitude? Are there dangers in too much respect for such people—or too little? Write an essay in which you present your views on this important social issue. Use examples from your own experiences whenever appropriate.

2. Choose an area of contemporary society in which handicaps are imposed to achieve social ends, such as affirmative action in employment, open admissions in schools and colleges, or the progressive income tax. What social ends does the handicap serve? What are its benefits? What harm does it do? Write an essay in which you discuss the pros and/or cons of imposing handicaps to achieve equality in the area of contemporary society you have selected.

3. In an essay, compare and contrast "Harrison Bergeron" with W. H. Auden's "The Unknown Citizen" (page 719) as depictions of society.

Abortion

SHIRLEY CHISHOLM

Shirley Chisholm, the first black woman ever elected to Congress, was for fourteen years a member of the United States House of Representatives, serving Brooklyn, New York. Born in 1924, Chisholm graduated from Brooklyn College and Columbia University. From 1964 to 1968 she was a member of the New York State Assembly. She is an outspoken advocate of the rights of all minorities, an authority on child welfare, and an educational consultant. Her books *Unbought and Unbossed* (1970) and *The Good Fight* (1973) are records of her experiences as a black female politician. Currently, she is on the advisory council of the National Organization for Women and serves as a director of Americans for Democratic Action.

The following essay, the introduction to the feminist anthology *Abortion Rap* (1971), was written two years before the *Roe v. Wade* decision made abortion on demand legal. Chisholm's essay highlights some of the arguments and captures the strong emotions of the proabortion movement in the years before the issue was ruled on by the Supreme Court.

Outlawing Compulsory Pregnancy Laws

There are many political, legal, social, moral and economic issues involved in government-sponsored birth control programs and policies. I will address myself to some of those issues that surround the most widely used method of birth control in the world today—abortion.

Alice S. Rossi, in an excellent article in the July–August 1969 issue of *Dissent*, made this most cogent comment about the word *abortion*:

"Free association to the word *abortion* would probably yield a fantastic array of emotional responses: pain, relief, murder, crime, fear, freedom, genocide, guilt, sin. Which of these associations people have no doubt reflects their age, marital status, religion or nationality. To a forty-four-year-old Japanese or Hungarian woman, the primary response might be 'freedom' and 'relief'; to an unmarried American college girl,

729

'fear' and 'pain'; to a Catholic priest, 'murder' and 'sin'; to some black militants, 'genocide.' "

There are many ways to avoid the negative associations and con-   4
notations that surround the word. We could, for example, borrow the term advanced by the British when they recently rewrote their laws— "pregnancy termination."

I believe that that would get us closer to the heart of the issue but   5
it would still not be close enough.

Not close enough because the basic issue—and the only real choice   6
of alternatives for the pregnant woman who does not want the child— is abortion or compulsory pregnancy. If we view the issue in this per- spective we are at what one might call "ground zero."

Does our government or any other government have the right by   7
which to force a woman to have a child that she does not want? In Hungary, Gyorgy Peters, the chief government statistician, has answered (presumably with backing from high officials) with an emphatic "No!" He reportedly has said, "The introduction of regulations with which the state would interfere with the freedom of the parents contradicts our political and moral concepts." What then must we, as representatives of a democracy, answer to the question?

The majority of family-planning advocates would be aghast if our   8
government were to suggest laws *requiring* the use of any contraceptive, or, as in a recent case in California, legal sterilization.

Yet it has been government policy in this country that compels   9
pregnant women to carry a full-term pregnancy, often against the wishes of both parents.

Dr. Garrett Hardin has, perhaps rightly, equated this situation with   10
compulsory servitude and has said, "When we recognize that these (abor- tion or compulsory pregnancy) are the real operational alternatives (for the pregnant woman), the false problems created by the pseudo-alter- natives disappear."

What has been the situation in Washington, that showplace of the   11
nation, under the compulsory pregnancy law?

Dr. Milan Vuitch, who was the central figure in Judge Gessel's   12
recent ruling on the District's compulsory pregnancy law, estimates that more than 20,000 abortions a year are performed in the greater Wash- ington area. He further estimates that only 25 percent of them are per- formed in hospitals. That means that there are more than 15,000 illegal abortions performed in or near Washington.

The municipal hospitals in the District have the same anti-black,   13
anti-poor policies in effect that I find in the New York City hospitals. D.C. General, for instance, reports 80 therapeutic abortions for 1968.

That is roughly .016 percent for the legal abortions in the greater Washington area. That figure has even more impact, I believe, when one realizes that it is only .004 percent of the total abortions performed, both legally and illegally, in this area.

The impact multiplies dramatically when we consider that D.C. 14
General also reports between 800 and 1,000 incomplete abortions. Incomplete means that the abortion was induced, either by drugs, instrument or naturally, but that it did not complete naturally . . . therefore it must be completed by a physician.

In short, they expended 10 to 12 times more effort on repairing 15
botched, non-professional surgery than they did on performing medically safe, professional surgery. That is nothing short of complete absurdity. Botched abortions are the single largest cause of maternal deaths in the United States, and it is evidently going to be government policy to keep it that way.

There are no clear statistics on exactly how many illegal abortions 16
there are each year in this country. Estimates range from as low as 200,000 to 1.5 million. One thing that is clear, however, is that if we repealed our compulsory pregnancy laws the incidents would be reduced.

There are many statistics from other countries that support my 17
contention. But let me quote from an article about the new British law that appeared in the *Washington Post* in June of 1969.

"Some doctors contend the only value of the bill is to prevent the 18
harm done by secret abortionists. They say Hungary allows abortions for anyone who wants one, and illegal operations have reportedly faded away. Czechoslovakia has a 'social clause' similar to Britain's, and clandestine abortions have dropped to 4,000 a year instead of 100,000."

If there are now 1,500,000 illegal abortions in this country, a drop 19
of the same percentage would reduce the number of illegal operations performed to about 30,000; that is only about twice as many as are now performed in the District of Columbia alone.

Let us look briefly at some of the countries where the compulsory 20
pregnancy laws have been weakened or, if you prefer, where abortion laws have been liberalized:

Experience in Sweden and Denmark has shown that as legal abor- 21
tions increased the death rate associated with it decreased.

In 1967 in Hungary there were 187,000 legal abortions as against 22
148,000 live births. Similarly Czechoslovakia's birth rate has been reduced but not as drastically as Hungary's.

Rumania, after substituting a more restrictive law in 1966, discov- 23
ered that its birth rate almost tripled in one year, the previous rate being 13.7 per 1,000.

It would seem that the absence of compulsory pregnancy laws alone   24
can contribute a great deal to the control of the population growth,
especially when one considers that at least the Eastern bloc countries
mentioned do not widely practice the more modern methods of contraception.

Of course no discussion of abortion would be complete without   25
discussing the politically volatile issue of religious and moral concepts.

Since we are already outside of the country, let's stay there mo-   26
mentarily to inspect the abortion rates of a few countries with large
Catholic populations:

The illegal abortion rate in Uruguay is almost two and one half   27
times the number of annual live births.

In Roman Catholic Chile, 27 percent of the women reported that   28
they had had abortions at one time or another.

In Roman Catholic France, the annual number of abortions equals   29
the annual number of live births.

Coming back to this country, we find that in a poll conducted in   30
1967, no less than 72 percent of the Catholics polled favored abortion
reform, as did 83 percent of the Protestants and 98 percent of the Jewish.

No lesser a Catholic luminary than Cardinal Cushing of Boston   31
was quoted as having said, "It does not seem reasonable to me to forbid
in civil law a practice that can be considered a matter of private morality."

Outlawing compulsory pregnancy laws, which some might still pre-   32
fer to call legalizing abortion, would not be forcing doctors or hospitals
to perform abortions against their beliefs. By outlawing these laws we
would instead be honoring the basic and individual right of a woman to
terminate an unwanted pregnancy.

The basic underlying question in any discussion of compulsory preg-   33
nancy laws (which I choose to use rather than the term *abortion laws*) is
what should a woman who is pregnant against *her* will do, and what
should the professional and public response toward her be if she chooses
to terminate the pregnancy?

If the underlying thesis of family planning is to reduce even the   34
number of wanted pregnancies, is it not illogical then to continue to
force women with unwanted pregnancies to have the child? I think that
it is!

Questions for Study and Discussion

1. What is Chisholm's thesis in this essay? Where is the thesis stated?
2. Why do you think Alice Rossi might associate "genocide" with the word *abortion*?

3. What problem does Chisholm hope to solve by using the term "pregnancy termination" instead of the word *abortion*? Do you think this change will really eliminate the problem? In terms of her argument what does Chisholm gain or lose by referring to abortion laws as "compulsory pregnancy laws"?

4. Chisholm's article was published in 1971, two years before *Roe v. Wade*, the Supreme Court's decision to legalize abortion. Even with this Supreme Court decision the debate over abortion continues. What elements of Chisholm's argument are persuasive today? Are there any parts of her argument that fail to persuade you? If so, why?

5. In paragraphs 11–15 Chisholm discusses the situation in Washington, D. C. under the "compulsory pregnancy" law. In your own words, what point is she trying to make with this extended example?

6. Knowing that some people would object to legalized abortion on moral and religious grounds, how does Chisholm anticipate these objections? What weight does Chisholm's quotation of Cardinal Cushing lend to her argument?

Writing Topics

1. Write an essay in which you discuss the abortion question as a conflict between public and private morality.

2. In 1971 Chisholm wrote that abortion is "the most widely used method of birth control in the world today." Write an argument against abortion as a form of birth control.

After working as an advertising copywriter, Linda Bird Francke became an editor at *New York* magazine and *Newsweek*. She was born in New York City in 1939 and attended Bradford Junior College. In 1980 she began a career as a free-lance writer and has since published *Fathers and Daughters* (1980) and *Growing Up Divorced* (1983).

In 1973 Francke had an abortion; as a result of the confusion and guilt she felt afterwards, she wrote "There Just Wasn't Room in Our Lives for Another Baby" and published it anonymously in the *New York Times*. In response to the essay, hundreds of women wrote to the newspaper describing their experiences with abortion. This prompted Francke to interview yet other women and to write *The Ambivalence of Abortion* (1978). The following selection has been excerpted from Francke's book and includes the original *New York Times* essay together with her response to the letters the newspaper received.

The Right to Choose

"Jane Doe," thirty-eight, had an abortion in New York City in 1973. The mother of three children, then three, five, and eleven, Jane had just started a full-time job in publishing. She and her husband, an investment banker, decided together that another baby would add an almost unbearable strain to their lives, which were already overfull. What Jane had not anticipated was the guilt and sadness that followed the abortion. She wrote about the experience shortly thereafter and filed the story away. Three years later she reread it and decided it might be helpful to other women who experience the ambivalence of abortion. The *New York Times* ran it on their Op-Ed page in May 1976. This is what she wrote:

> We were sitting in a bar on Lexington Avenue when I told my husband I was pregnant. It is not a memory I like to dwell on. Instead of the champagne and hope which had heralded the impending births of the first, second and third child, the news of this one was greeted with shocked silence and Scotch. "Jesus," my husband kept saying to himself, stirring the ice cubes around and around. "Oh, Jesus."
>
> Oh, how we tried to rationalize it that night as the starting time for the movie came and went. My husband talked about his plans for a career change in the next year, to stem the staleness that fourteen years with the same investment-banking firm had brought him. A new baby would preclude that option.

The timing wasn't right for me either. Having juggled pregnancies and child care with what freelance jobs I could fit in between feedings, I had just taken on a full-time job. A new baby would put me right back in the nursery just when our youngest child was finally school age. It was time for *us*, we tried to rationalize. There just wasn't room in our lives now for another baby. We both agreed. And agreed. And agreed.

How very considerate they are at the Women's Services, known formally as the Center for Reproductive and Sexual Health. Yes, indeed, I could have an abortion that very Saturday morning and be out in time to drive to the country that afternoon. Bring a first morning urine specimen, a sanitary belt and napkins, a money order or $125 cash—and a friend.

My friend turned out to be my husband, standing awkwardly and ill at ease as men always do in places that are exclusively for women, as I checked in at nine A.M. Other men hovered around just as anxiously, knowing they had to be there, wishing they weren't. No one spoke to each other. When I would be cycled out of there four hours later, the same men would be slumped in their same seats, locked downcast in their cells of embarrassment.

The Saturday morning women's group was more dispirited than the men in the waiting room. There were around fifteen of us, a mixture of races, ages and backgrounds. Three didn't speak English at all and a fourth, a pregnant Puerto Rican girl around eighteen, translated for them.

There were six black women and a hodge-podge of whites, among them a T-shirted teenager who kept leaving the room to throw up and a puzzled middle-aged woman from Queens with three grown children.

"What form of birth control were you using?" the volunteer asked each one of us. The answer was inevitably "none." She then went on to describe the various forms of birth control available at the clinic, and offered them to each of us.

The youngest Puerto Rican girl was asked through the interpreter which she'd like to use: the loop, diaphragm, or pill. She shook her head "no" three times. "You don't want to come back here again, do you?" the volunteer pressed. The girl's head was so low her chin rested on her breastbone. "Si," she whispered.

We had been there two hours by that time, filling out endless forms, giving blood and urine, receiving lectures. But unlike any other group of women I've been in, we didn't talk. Our common denominator, the one which usually floods across language and economic barriers into familiarity, today was one of shame. We were losing life that day, not giving it.

The group kept getting cut back to smaller, more workable units, and finally I was put in a small waiting room with just two other women. We changed into paper bathrobes and paper slippers, and we rustled whenever we moved. One of the women in my room was shivering and an aide brought her a blanket.

4

5

6

7

8

9

10

11

12

"What's the matter?" the aide asked her. "I'm scared," the woman   13
said. "How much will it hurt?" The aide smiled. "Oh, nothing worse than
a couple of bad cramps," she said. "This afternoon you'll be dancing a
jig."

I began to panic. Suddenly the rhetoric, the abortion marches I'd   14
walked in, the telegrams sent to Albany to counteract the Friends of the
Fetus, the Zero Population Growth buttons I'd worn, peeled away, and I
was all alone with my microscopic baby. There were just the two of us
there, and soon, because it was more convenient for me and my husband,
there would be one again.

How could it be that I, who am so neurotic about life that I step   15
over bugs rather than on them, who spend hours planting flowers and
vegetables in the spring even though we rent out the house and never see
them, who make sure the children are vaccinated and inoculated and filled
with vitamin C, could so arbitrarily decide that this life shouldn't be?

"It's not a life," my husband had argued, more to convince himself   16
than me. "It's a bunch of cells smaller than my fingernail."

But any woman who has had children knows that certain feeling in   17
her taut, swollen breasts, and the slight but constant ache in her uterus
that signals the arrival of a life. Though I would march myself into blisters
for a woman's right to exercise the option of motherhood, I discovered
there in the waiting room that I was not the modern woman I thought I
was.

When my name was called, my body felt so heavy the nurse had to   18
help me into the examining room. I waited for my husband to burst through
the door and yell "stop," but of course he didn't. I concentrated on three
black spots in the acoustic ceiling until they grew in size to the shape of
saucers, while the doctor swabbed my insides with antiseptic.

"You're going to feel a burning sensation now," he said, injecting   19
Novocaine into the neck of the womb. The pain was swift and severe,
and I twisted to get away from him. He was hurting my baby, I reasoned,
and the black saucers quivered in the air. "Stop," I cried. "Please stop."
He shook his head, busy with his equipment. "It's too late to stop now,"
he said. "It'll just take a few more seconds."

What good sports we women are. And how obedient. Physically the   20
pain passed even before the hum of the machine signaled that the vac-
uuming of my uterus was completed, my baby sucked up like ashes after a
cocktail party. Ten minutes start to finish. And I was back on the arm of
the nurse.

There were twelve beds in the recovery room. Each one had a gaily   21
flowered draw sheet and a soft green or blue thermal blanket. It was all
very feminine. Lying on these beds for an hour or more were the shocked
victims of their sex, their full wombs now stripped clean, their futures less
encumbered.

It was very quiet in that room. The only voice was that of the nurse,   22 locating the new women who had just come in so she could monitor their blood pressure, and checking out the recovered women who were free to leave.

Juice was being passed about, and I found myself sipping a Dixie cup   23
of Hawaiian Punch. An older woman with tightly curled bleached hair was just getting up from the next bed. "That was no goddamn snap," she said, resting before putting on her miniskirt and high white boots. Other women came and went, some walking out as dazed as they had entered, others with a bounce that signaled they were going right back to Bloomingdale's.

Finally then, it was time for me to leave. I checked out, making an   24
appointment to return in two weeks for a IUD insertion. My husband was slumped in the waiting room, clutching a single yellow rose wrapped in a wet paper towel and stuffed into a baggie.

We didn't talk the whole way home, but just held hands very tightly.   25
At home there were more yellow roses and a tray in bed for me and the children's curiosity to divert.

It had certainly been a successful operation. I didn't bleed at all for   26
two days just as they had predicted, and then I bled only moderately for another four days. Within a week my breasts had subsided and the tenderness vanished, and my body felt mine again instead of the eggshell it becomes when it's protecting someone else.

My husband and I are back to planning our summer vacation and   27
his career switch.

And it certainly does make more sense not to be having a baby right   28
now—we say that to each other all the time. But I have this ghost now. A very little ghost that only appears when I'm seeing something beautiful, like the full moon on the ocean last weekend. And the baby waves at me. And I wave at the baby. "Of course, we have room," I cry to the ghost. "Of course, we do."

I am "Jane Doe." Using a pseudonym was not the act of cowardice   29
some have said it was, but rather an act of sympathy for the feelings of my family. My daughters were too young then to understand what an abortion was, and my twelve-year-old son (my husband's stepson) reacted angrily when I even broached the subject of abortion to him. Andrew was deeply moralistic, as many children are at that age, and still young enough to feel threatened by the actions of adults; his replies to my "suppose I had an abortion" queries were devastating. "I think abortion is okay if the boy and girl aren't married, and they just made a mistake," he said. "But if you had an abortion, that would be different. You're married, and there is no reason for you not to have another baby. How could you just kill something—no matter how little it is—that's going to grow and have legs and wiggle its fingers?

"I would be furious with you if you had an abortion. I'd lose all   3
respect for you for being so selfish. I'd make you suffer and remind you
of it all the time. I would think of ways to be mean. Maybe I'd give you
the silent treatment or something.

"If God had meant women to have abortions, He would have put   3:
buttons on their stomachs."

I decided to wait until he was older before we discussed it again.   3:

There were other considerations as well. My husband and I had   3:
chosen not to tell our parents about the abortion. My mother was very
ill at the time and not up to a barrage of phone calls from her friends
about "what Linda had written in the newspaper." And there were my
parents-in-law, who had always hoped for a male grandchild to carry on
the family name. So I avoided the confessional and simply wrote what I
thought would be a helpful piece for other women who might have shared
my experience.

The result was almost great enough to be recorded on a seismo-   34
graph. Interpreting the piece as anti-abortion grist, the Right-to-Lifers
reproduced it by the thousands and sent it to everyone on their mailing
lists. In one Catholic mailing, two sentences were deleted from the article: one that said I was planning to return to the clinic for an IUD
insertion, and the other the quote from a middle-aged woman, "That
was no goddamn snap." Papers around the country and in Canada ran
it, culminating in its appearance in the Canadian edition of the *Reader's
Digest*, whose staff took it upon their editorial selves to delete the last
paragraph about the "little ghost" because they considered it "mawkish."
They also changed the title from "There Just Wasn't Room in Our Lives
for Another Baby" to "A Successful Operation" in hopes that it would
change their magazine's pro-abortion image.

Hundreds of letters poured into the *New York Times*, some from   35
Right-to-Lifers, who predictably called me a "murderer," and others from
pro-choice zealots who had decided the article was a "plant" and might
even have been written by a man. Women wrote about their own abortions, some of which had been positive experiences and some disastrous.
One woman even wrote that she wished her own mother had had an
abortion instead of subjecting her to a childhood that was "brutal and
crushing." Many of the respondents criticized me, quite rightly, for not
using birth control in the first place. I was stunned, and so was the *New
York Times*. A few weeks later they ran a sampling of the letters and my
reply, which follows:

> The varied reactions to my abortion article do not surprise me at   36
> all. They are all right. And they are all wrong. There is no issue so

fundamental as the giving of life, or the cessation of it. These decisions are the most personal one can ever make and each person facing them reacts in her own way. It is not black-and-white as the laws governing abortion are forced to be. Rather it is the gray area whose core touches our definition of ourselves that produces "little ghosts" in some, and a sense of relief in others.

I admire the woman who chose not to bear her fourth child because she and her husband could not afford to give that child the future they felt necessary. I admire the women who were outraged that I had failed to use any form of contraception. And I ache for the woman whose mother had given birth to her even though she was not wanted, and thus spent an empty, lonely childhood. It takes courage to take the life of someone else in your own hands, and even more courage to assume responsibility for your own.   37

I had my abortion over two years ago. And I wrote about it shortly thereafter. It was only recently, however, that I decided to publish it. I felt it was important to share how one person's abortion had affected her, rather than just sit by while the pro and con groups haggled over legislation.   38

The effect has indeed been profound. Though my husband was very supportive of me, and I, I think, of him, our relationship slowly faltered. As our children are girls, my husband anguished at the possibility that I had been carrying a son. Just a case of mule macho, many would argue. But still, that's the way he feels, and it is important. I hope we can get back on a loving track again.   39

Needless to say, I have an IUD now, instead of the diaphragm that is too easily forgotten. I do not begrudge my husband his lack of contraception. Condoms are awkward. Neither do I feel he should have a vasectomy. It is profoundly difficult for him to face the possibility that he might never have that son. Nor do I regret having the abortion. I am just as much an avid supporter of children by choice as I ever was.   40

My only regret is the sheer irresponsibility on my part to become pregnant in the first place. I pray to God that it will never happen again. But if it does, I will be equally thankful that the law provides women the dignity to choose whether to bring a new life into the world or not.   41

Questions for Study and Discussion

1. How does the husband react at the news that his wife is pregnant? Why doesn't he want another child? What are Francke's reasons?

2. If you were to read her original article for the *New York Times* (paragraphs 2–28), would you think that Francke was proabortion or antiabortion? Why?

3. What is Francke's attitude toward the other women at the center that morning? What common denominator did these women share?

4. What does Francke mean when she says, "I discovered there in the waiting room that I was not the modern woman I thought I was"?

5. The story of Francke's abortion was written for the *New York Times*. What features of the style clearly identify it as a newspaper piece? How does the style of the newspaper account differ from the surrounding text?

6. Francke's story for the *New York Times* is replete with carefully chosen details. For example, she tells us that her husband held "a single yellow rose wrapped in a wet paper towel and stuffed into a Baggie." Cite other examples of Francke's use of details and explain the effect that they have on you as a reader.

7. Identify any metaphors and similes that Francke uses in her essay and explain how each one works.

Writing Topics

1. One issue that Francke is not ambivalent about is birth control. Write an essay in which you argue for or against birth control.

2. Francke discovers that having an abortion is different from having certain political views on the subject. Write an essay describing how your views on a subject were altered by a firsthand experience with it. For example, you may hold views regarding the extent of hunger that exists in America that were sharply altered by work as volunteer in a soup kitchen. Or, you may be basically trusting of people but have had some very bad experiences that caused you to become much more cautious in dealing with other people.

RONALD REAGAN

Ronald Reagan, the fortieth president of the United States, was born February 6, 1911 in Tampico, Illinois. After earning his B.A. from Eureka College in 1932, Reagan went on to a career as a sports announcer and editor before signing a contract with Warner Brothers in 1937. Reagan has appeared in some fifty feature-length films. Originally a Democrat, he became a Republican in 1962 and was elected governor of California for two terms starting in 1966. After two unsuccessful attempts to gain the Republican party presidential nomination, Reagan became his party's standard bearer and was elected president in 1980. In 1984 he was reelected, beating his Democratic opponent Walter Mondale in a landslide election.

The following essay was published in 1983 on the tenth anniversary of *Roe v. Wade*, the Supreme Court decision granting women the limited right to abortion.

Abortion and the Conscience of the Nation

The 10th Anniversary of the Supreme Court decision in *Roe v. Wade* is a good time for us to pause and reflect. Our nationwide policy of abortion-on-demand through all nine months of pregnancy was neither voted for by our people nor enacted by our legislators—not a single State had such unrestricted abortion before the Supreme Court decreed it to be national policy in 1973. But the consequences of this judicial decision are now obvious: since 1973, more than 15 million unborn children have had their lives snuffed out by legalized abortions. That is over ten times the number of Americans lost in all our nation's wars. 1

Make no mistake, abortion-on-demand is not a right granted by the Constitution. No serious scholar, including one disposed to agree with the Court's result, has argued that the framers of the Constitution intended to create such a right. Shortly after the *Roe v. Wade* decision, Professor John Hart Ely, now Dean of Stanford Law School, wrote that the opinion "is not constitutional law and gives almost no sense of an obligation to try to be." Nowhere do the plain words of the Constitution even hint at a "right" so sweeping as to permit abortion up to the time the child is ready to be born. Yet that is what the Court ruled. 2

As an act of "raw judicial power" (to use Justice White's biting phrase), the decision by the seven-man majority in *Roe v. Wade* has so far been made to stick. But the Court's decision by no means settled the debate. Instead, *Roe v. Wade* has become a continuing prod to the conscience of the nation. 3

741

Abortion concerns not just the unborn child, it concerns every one   4
of us. The English poet, John Donne, wrote: ". . . any man's death
diminishes me, because I am involved in mankind; and therefore never
send to know for whom the bell tolls; it tolls for thee."

We cannot diminish the value of one category of human life—the   5
unborn—without diminishing the value of all human life. We saw tragic
proof of this truism last year when the Indiana courts allowed the starvation death of "Baby Doe" in Bloomington because the child had Down's
Syndrome.

Many of our fellow citizens grieve over the loss of life that has   6
followed *Roe v. Wade.* Margaret Heckler, soon after being nominated to
head the largest department of our government, Health and Human
Services, told an audience that she believed abortion to be the greatest
moral crisis facing our country today. And the revered Mother Teresa,
who works in the streets of Calcutta ministering to dying people in her
world-famous mission of mercy, has said that "the greatest misery of our
time is the generalized abortion of children."

Over the first two years of my Administration I have closely fol-   7
lowed and assisted efforts in Congress to reverse the tide of abortion—
efforts of Congressmen, Senators and citizens responding to an urgent
moral crisis. Regrettably, I have also seen the massive efforts of those
who, under the banner of "freedom of choice," have so far blocked every
effort to reverse nationwide abortion-on-demand.

Despite the formidable obstacles before us, we must not lose heart.   8
This is not the first time our country has been divided by a Supreme
Court decision that denied the value of certain human lives. The *Dred
Scott* decision of 1857 was not overturned in a day, or a year, or even a
decade. At first, only a minority of Americans recognized and deplored
the moral crisis brought about by denying the full humanity of our black
brothers and sisters; but that minority persisted in their vision and finally
prevailed. They did it by appealing to the hearts and minds of their
countrymen, to the truth of human dignity under God. From their example, we know that respect for the sacred value of human life is too
deeply engrained in the hearts of our people to remain forever suppressed.
But the great majority of the American people have not yet made their
voices heard, and we cannot expect them to—any more than the public
voice arose against slavery—*until* the issue is clearly framed and presented.

What, then, is the real issue? I have often said that when we talk   9
about abortion, we are talking about two lives—the life of the mother
and the life of the unborn child. Why else do we call a pregnant woman
a mother? I have also said that anyone who doesn't feel sure whether we

are talking about a second human life should clearly give life the benefit of the doubt. If you don't know whether a baby is alive or dead, you would never bury it. I think this consideration itself should be enough for all of us to insist on protecting the unborn.

The case against abortion does not rest here, however, for medical   10
practice confirms at every step the correctness of these moral sensibilities. Modern medicine treats the unborn child as a patient. Medical pioneers have made great breakthroughs in treating the unborn—for genetic problems, vitamin deficiencies, irregular heart rhythms, and other medical conditions. Who can forget George Will's moving account of the little boy who underwent brain surgery six times during the nine weeks before he was born? Who is the *patient* if not that tiny unborn human being who can feel pain when he or she is approached by doctors who come to kill rather than to cure?

The real question today is not when human life begins, but, *What*   11
is the value of human life? The abortionist who reassembles the arms and legs of a tiny baby to make sure all its parts have been torn from its mother's body can hardly doubt whether it is a human being. The real question for him and for all of us is whether that tiny human life has a God-given right to be protected by the law—the same right we have.

What more dramatic confirmation could we have of the real issue   12
than the Baby Doe case in Bloomington, Indiana? The death of that tiny infant tore at the hearts of all Americans because the child was undeniably a live human being—one lying helpless before the eyes of the doctors and the eyes of the nation. The real issue for the courts was *not* whether Baby Doe was a human being. The real issue was whether to protect the life of a human being who had Down's Syndrome, who would probably be mentally handicapped, but who needed a routine surgical procedure to unblock his esophagus and allow him to eat. A doctor testified to the presiding judge that, even with his physical problem corrected, Baby Doe would have a "non-existent" possibility for "a minimally adequate quality of life"—in other words, that retardation was the equivalent of a crime deserving the death penalty. The judge let Baby Doe starve and die, and the Indiana Supreme Court sanctioned his decision.

Federal law does not allow Federally-assisted hospitals to decide that   13
Down's Syndrome infants are not worth treating, much less to decide to starve them to death. Accordingly, I have directed the Departments of Justice and HHS to apply civil rights regulations to protect handicapped newborns. All hospitals receiving Federal funds must post notices which will clearly state that failure to feed handicapped babies is prohibited by Federal law. The basic issue is whether to value and protect the lives of

the handicapped, whether to recognize the sanctity of human life. This is the same basic issue that underlies the question of abortion.

The 1981 Senate hearings on the beginning of human life brought out the basic issue more clearly than ever before. The many medical and scientific witnesses who testified disagreed on many things, but not on the *scientific* evidence that the unborn child is alive, is a distinct individual, or is a member of the human species. They did disagree over the *value* question, whether to give value to a human life at its early and most vulnerable stages of existence. 14

Regrettably, we live at a time when some persons do *not* value all human life. They want to pick and choose which individuals have value. Some have said that only those individuals with "consciousness of self" are human beings. One such writer has followed this deadly logic and concluded that "shocking as it may seem, a newly born infant is not a human being." 15

A Nobel Prize winning scientist has suggested that if a handicapped child "were not declared fully human until three days after birth, then all parents could be allowed the choice." In other words, "quality control" to see if newly born human beings are up to snuff. 16

Obviously, some influential people want to deny that every human life has intrinsic, sacred worth. They insist that a member of the human race must have certain qualities before they accord him or her status as a "human being." 17

Events have borne out the editorial in a California medical journal which explained three years before *Roe v. Wade* that the social acceptance of abortion is a "defiance of the long-held Western ethic of intrinsic and equal value for every human life regardless of its stage, condition, or status." 18

Every legislator, every doctor, and every citizen needs to recognize that the real issue is whether to affirm and protect the sanctity of all human life, or to embrace a social ethic where some human lives are valued and others are not. As a nation, we must choose between the sanctity of life ethic and the quality of life ethic. 19

I have no trouble identifying the answer our nation has always given to this basic question, and the answer that I hope and pray it will give in the future. America was founded by men and women who shared a vision of the value of each and every individual. They stated this vision clearly from the very start in the Declaration of Independence, using words that every schoolboy and schoolgirl can recite: 20

We hold these truths to be self-evident, that all men are created equal, that they are endowed by their Creator with certain unalienable rights, that among these are life, liberty, and the pursuit of happiness.

We fought a terrible war to guarantee that one category of man-   21
kind—black people in America—could not be denied the inalienable rights with which their Creator endowed them. The great champion of the sanctity of all human life in that day, Abraham Lincoln, gave us his assessment of the Declaration's purpose. Speaking of the framers of that noble document, he said:

> This was their majestic interpretation of the economy of the Universe. This was their lofty, and wise, and noble understanding of the justice of the Creator to His creatures. Yes, gentlemen, to all His creatures, to the whole great family of man. In their enlightened belief, nothing stamped with the divine image and likeness was sent into the world to be trodden on. . . . They grasped not only the whole race of man then living, but they reached forward and seized upon the farthest posterity. They erected a beacon to guide their children and their children's children, and the countless myriads who should inhabit the earth in other ages.

He warned also of the danger we would face if we closed our eyes   22
to the value of life in any category of human beings:

> I should like to know if taking this old Declaration of Independence, which declares that all men are equal upon principle and making exceptions to it where will it stop. If one man says it does not mean a Negro, why not another say it does not mean some other man?

When Congressman John A. Bingham of Ohio drafted the Four-   23
teenth Amendment to guarantee the rights of life, liberty, and property to all human beings, he explained that *all* are "entitled to the protection of American law, because its divine spirit of equality declares that all men are created equal." He said the rights guaranteed by the amendment would therefore apply to "any human being." Justice William Brennan, writing in another case decided only the year before *Roe v. Wade*, referred to our society as one that "strongly affirms the sanctity of life."

Another William Brennan—not the Justice—has reminded us of   24
the terrible consequences that can follow when a nation rejects the sanctity of life ethic:

> The cultural environment for a human holocaust is present whenever any society can be misled into defining individuals as less than human and therefore devoid of value and respect.

As a nation today, we have *not* rejected the sanctity of human life.   25
The American people have not had an opportunity to express their view on the sanctity of human life in the unborn. I am convinced that Amer-

icans do not want to play God with the value of human life. It is not for us to decide who is worthy to live and who is not. Even the Supreme Court's opinion in *Roe v. Wade* did not explicitly reject the traditional American idea of intrinsic worth and value in all human life; it simply dodged this issue.

The Congress has before it several measures that would enable our   26
people to reaffirm the sanctity of human life, even the smallest and the youngest and the most defenseless. The Human Liberty Bill expressly recognizes the unborn as human beings and accordingly protects them as persons under our Constitution. This bill, first introduced by Senator Jesse Helms, provided the vehicle for the Senate hearings in 1981 which contributed so much to our understanding of the real issue of abortion.

The Respect Human Life Act, just introduced in the 98th Con-   27
gress, states in its first section that the policy of the United States is "to protect innocent life, both before and after birth." This bill, sponsored by Congressman Henry Hyde and Senator Roger Jepsen, prohibits the Federal government from performing abortions or assisting those who do so, except to save the life of the mother. It also addresses the pressing issue of infanticide which, as we have seen, flows inevitably from permissive abortion as another step in the denial of the inviolability of innocent human life.

I have endorsed each of these measures, as well as the more difficult   28
route of constitutional amendment, and I will give these initiatives my full support. Each of them, in different ways, attempts to reverse the tragic policy of abortion-on-demand imposed by the Supreme Court ten years ago. Each of them is a decisive way to affirm the sanctity of human life.

We must all educate ourselves to the reality of the horrors taking   29
place. Doctors today know that unborn children can feel a touch within the womb and that they respond to pain. But how many Americans are aware that abortion techniques are allowed today, in all 50 states, that burn the skin of a baby with a salt solution, in an agonizing death that can last for hours?

Another example: two years ago, the *Philadelphia Inquirer* ran a   30
Sunday special supplement on "The Dreaded Complication." The "dreaded complication" referred to in the article—the complication feared by doctors who perform abortions—is the *survival* of the child despite all the painful attacks during the abortion procedure. Some unborn children *do survive the late-term abortions* the Supreme Court has made legal. Is there any question that these victims of abortion deserve our attention and protection? Is there any question that those who *don't* survive were living human beings before they were killed?

Late-term abortions, especially when the baby survives, but is then   31
killed by starvation, neglect, or suffocation, show once again the link
between abortion and infanticide. The time to stop both is now. As my
Administration acts to stop infanticide, we will be fully aware of the real
issue that underlies the death of babies before and soon after birth.

Our society has, fortunately, become sensitive to the rights and   32
special needs of the handicapped, but I am shocked that physical or
mental handicaps of newborns are still used to justify their extinction.
This Administration has a Surgeon General, Dr. C. Everett Koop, who
has done perhaps more than any other American for handicapped children, by pioneering surgical techniques to help them, by speaking out
on the value of their lives, and by working with them in the context of
loving families. You will not find his former patients advocating the so-
called quality of life ethic.

I know that when the true issue of infanticide is placed before the   33
American people, with all the facts openly aired, we will have no trouble
deciding that a mentally or physically handicapped baby has the same
intrinsic worth and right to life as the rest of us. As the New Jersey
Supreme Court said two decades ago, in a decision upholding the sanctity
of human life, "a child need not be perfect to have a worthwhile life."

Whether we are talking about pain suffered by unborn children, or   34
about late-term abortions, or about infanticide, we inevitably focus on
the humanity of the unborn child. Each of these issues is a potential
rallying point for the sanctity of life ethic. Once we as a nation rally
around any one of these issues to affirm the sanctity of life, we will see
the importance of affirming this principle across the board.

Malcolm Muggeridge, the English writer, goes right to the heart of   35
the matter: "Either life is always and in all circumstances sacred, or
intrinsically of no account; it is inconceivable that it should be in some
cases the one, and in some the other." The sanctity of innocent human
life is a principle that Congress should proclaim at every opportunity.

It is possible that the Supreme Court itself may overturn its abortion   36
rulings. We need only recall that in *Brown v. Board of Education* the
Court reversed its own earlier "separate-but-equal" decision. I believe if
the Supreme Court took another look at *Roe v. Wade*, and considered
the real issue between the sanctity of life ethic and the quality of life
ethic, it would change its mind once again.

As we continue to work to overturn *Roe v. Wade*, we must also   37
continue to lay the groundwork for a society in which abortion is not
the accepted answer to unwanted pregnancy. Pro-life people have already
taken heroic steps, often at great personal sacrifice, to provide for unwed
mothers. I recently spoke about a young pregnant woman named Vic-

toria, who said, "In this society we save whales, we save timber wolves and bald eagles and Coke bottles. Yet, everyone wanted me to throw away my baby." She has been helped by Sav-a-Life, a group in Dallas, which provides a way for unwed mothers to preserve the human life within them when they might otherwise be tempted to resort to abortion. I think also of House of His Creation in Coatesville, Pennsylvania, where a loving couple has taken in almost 200 young women in the past ten years. They have seen, as a fact of life, that the girls are *not* better off having abortions than saving their babies. I am also reminded of the remarkable Rossow family of Ellington, Connecticut, who have opened their hearts and their home to nine handicapped adopted and foster children.

The Adolescent Family Life Program, adopted by Congress at the request of Senator Jeremiah Denton, has opened new opportunities for unwed mothers to give their children life. We should not rest until our entire society echoes the tone of John Powell in the dedication of his book, *Abortion: The Silent Holocaust,* a dedication to every woman carrying an unwanted child: "Please believe that you are not alone. There are many of us that truly love you, who want to stand at your side, and help in any way we can." And we can echo the always-practical woman of faith, Mother Teresa, when she says, "If you don't want the little child, that unborn child, give him to me." We have so many families in America seeking to adopt children that the slogan "every child a wanted child" is now the emptiest of all reasons to tolerate abortion.   38

I have often said we need to join in prayer to bring protection to the unborn. Prayer and action are needed to uphold the sanctity of human life. I believe it will not be possible to accomplish our work, the work of saving lives, "without being a soul of prayer." The famous British Member of Parliament, William Wilberforce, prayed with his small group of influential friends, the "Clapham Sect," for *decades* to see an end to slavery in the British empire. Wilberforce led that struggle in Parliament, unflaggingly, because he believed in the sanctity of human life. He saw the fulfillment of his impossible dream when Parliament outlawed slavery just before his death.   39

Let his faith and perseverance be our guide. We will never recognize the true value of our own lives until we affirm the value in the life of others, a value of which Malcolm Muggeridge says: ". . . however low it flickers or fiercely burns, it is still a Divine flame which no man dare presume to put out, be his motives ever so humane and enlightened."   40

Abraham Lincoln recognized that we could not survive as a free land when some men could decide that others were not fit to be free and should therefore be slaves. Likewise, we cannot survive as a free nation   41 when some men decide that others are not fit to live and should be abandoned to abortion or infanticide. My Administration is dedicated to the preservation of America as a free land, and there is no cause more important for preserving that freedom than affirming the transcendent right to life of all human beings, the right without which no other rights have any meaning.

Questions for Study and Discussion

1. Who was Dred Scott? What was the Supreme Court decision in 1857 that bears his name? What parallels does Reagan see between the Dred Scott decision and *Roe v. Wade*?

2. Reagan uses the phrase "raw judicial power" (borrowed from Justice White) to characterize *Roe v. Wade*. Why do Reagan and White see the decision in this light?

3. Reagan believes that the American people cannot voice their opinions until the abortion issue is "clearly framed and presented." What, for Reagan, is the real issue of abortion?

4. Reagan believes that the abortion question comes down to a choice between the "sanctity of life ethic" and the "quality of life ethic." Briefly describe each philosophy. Which one does Reagan support? Why?

5. What does Reagan see as the link between abortion and infanticide? What use does he make of the link in his overall argument? How convincing is the link for you?

6. In paragraph 37, Reagan makes reference to Victoria, the House of His Creation, and the Rossow family. What does his use of these specific examples add to his argument?

7. How optimistic is Reagan that *Row v. Wade* can be overturned? What specific suggestions does he make for achieving this goal?

Writing Topics

1. Reagan seems to believe that there is a need for the American people to be heard on the question of abortion-on-demand. Write an argument for or against a national referendum on legalized abortion in the United States.

2. Reagan, in echoing John Donne's remarks, writes that the loss of any human life diminishes the value of all human life. Write an essay in which you discuss the truth of this statement with respect to any of the following: the physically or mentally handicapped, the terminally ill, the unborn, or the elderly.

3. What is the place of men in the abortion question? Should fathers be accorded any rights or should the issue be left solely to women?

The Right to Die?

EVAN R. COLLINS, JR.

"Death is not the greatest loss in life," writes Norman Cousins. "The greatest loss is what dies inside us while we live. The unbearable tragedy is to live without dignity or sensitivity." In short, this is the central argument of the Right to Die movement. Many believe that Americans have an unrealistic fear of death and, as a result, are willing to try any means to prolong life. In the process, they have managed to dehumanize death, often making it a rather mechanical, sterile hospital experience. Members of the Society for the Right to Die believe that the individual should have control over his or her death and advocate the use of a "living will." In the following essay from *USA Today* (November 1984), Evan R. Collins, Jr., vice president and resident officer of Kidder, Peabody & Company and president of the Society for the Right to Die, establishes the basic position of his organization and sets forth its goals and programs. He echoes the words of Dr. Joseph Fletcher, a noted bioethicist and former president of the society, who once wrote, "Good dying must at last find its place in our scheme of things, along with good birthing, good living and good loving. After all, it makes perfectly sound sense to strive for quality straight across the board, as much in our dying as in our living."

The Right to Choose Life or Death

The public indignation that followed Gov. Richard D. Lamm's speech in March, 1984, to the Colorado Health Lawyers Association was, the Governor has said, largely caused by reporters misinterpreting his statements and quoting them out of context. Certainly, many people, especially the elderly, reacted with outrage when they read in their newspapers, "We've got a duty to die, to get out of the way with our machines and our artificial hearts and everything else like that, and let the other society, our kids, build a reasonable life." His paraphrase of a statement later attributed to Leon Kass, writing in *American Scholar* magazine—"It's like if leaves fall off a tree forming the humus for the other plants

751

to grow"—did not help. Unthinkable historical analogies were conjured up, including genocide under the Nazi regime (an angry responding article by Nat Hentoff in New York's *Village Voice* was illustrated by a photograph of Hitler), or, on another scale, the "final solution" once practiced by hard-pressed Eskimo families scrabbling for survival in the farthest reaches of the Arctic: when grandmother lost her usefulness, she was left on the ice floe, possibly to become food for the polar bear that might later be hunted to feed her own family. Grandmother, it was said, stoically accepted her fate. We are not about to do the same. The idea of any of us having a "duty to die" is abhorrent.

Whatever legitimate outrage Gov. Lamm's reckless remarks caused, 2
he struck a responsive chord when warned that "we should be very careful in terms of our technological miracles that we don't impose life on people who, in fact, are suffering beyond our ability to help." He might also have included people who are beyond suffering, in irreversible coma, their brain function permanently destroyed. Patients of both kinds are a common occurrence in hospitals everywhere. Typical is the inert body of an 82-year-old woman, victim of a massive coronary, lying day after day hooked up to tubes and wires with no prospect of returning to consciousness, much less to last week's exceptional vitality which her daughter remembers as she says, "That's not my mother lying there." Less typical only because it was taken to court is the case of Abe Perlmutter, presenting the distressing picture of man mortally ill with ALS ("Lou Gehrig's disease"); fully aware and desperate, wrenching out with his own hands the mechanical respirator attached to his trachea in a failed attempt to die (the hospital alarm sounded). What are we to think of Karen Ann Quinlan, who, more than eight years after the court permitted termination of life-support apparatus, still occupies a bed in a New Jersey nursing home—weighing 60-odd pounds, usually in fetal position, and kept "alive" by the artificially given food and water that her parents can't bring themselves to stop?

It has been estimated that the medical advances of the last 10 years 3
exceed all the medical progress achieved in the preceding 100 years. The miracles continue to multiply, most of them beneficial in preserving life and the ability to enjoy it. However, new technology has also confronted us with dilemmas we've never had to consider before. As the distinguished bioethicist, Joseph Fletcher, expressed it, "Ethical questions jump out at us from every laboratory and clinic." The answers to those questions are not easy to find—not for ethicists, clergymen, doctors, nurses, hospital caseworkers, lawyers, judges, government agency officials, legislators, or you and me.

How do we determine the line between prolonging life and pro-   4
longing dying? How far should we go to sustain a life whose quality is at
best only marginal? Can anyone define unacceptable "quality of life" for
anyone else? If a hospital's life-sustaining equipment is limited, who is
to decide its allocation, and how? Is the life of a 65-year-old upright
citizen less "worth saving" than the life of a 25-year-old confirmed criminal? Should the wishes of an intermittently "confused" 90-year-old woman
be heeded if she refuses recommended surgery? The list of questions could
go on and on, repeatedly echoing "Who's to decide?" No wonder the
elderly were alarmed by the implications of Gov. Lamm's quoted statements, envisioning a lifetime of control over their own lives eroded at
the end by a battery of medical decision-makers.

Dr. Fletcher, professor emeritus of Christian ethics and Pastoral   5
Theology at the Episcopal Divinity School in Cambridge, Mass., is also
president emeritus of the Society for the Right to Die, an organization
that was founded nearly a half-century ago. His philosophy emphasizes
the human need to be in control. The Society stresses the fundamental
right of self-determination—the right to determine what shall and shall
not be done to one's own body. This right, established by common law
and the constitutional right of privacy, includes the right to refuse treatment—the corollary of informed consent. A surprising number of patients
are unaware that they can say no in a hospital, just as they are unsure
of their right to leave a hospital at will.

Knowing these rights can be important to patients who have the   6
capacity to listen, understand, make decisions, and communicate or act
on them. However, critically ill or injured patients are often helpless—
debilitated by disease, incapacitated by pain or other medication, mentally impaired or unconscious. Many of them have no prospect of recovery
and would, if they could, choose not to prolong a hopeless situation.

It is to protect the rights of these patients that the Society for the   7
Right to Die offers "living will" forms—documents which, with or without personalized modifications and specific additions, may be executed
in advance by competent adults to serve as written evidence of their
preferences regarding terminal treatment. It can be a help to their doctors
when communication is impossible, and a relief to their families who
may otherwise have to bear the entire burden of making painful decisions
for them. A living will can be revoked at any time. The wishes expressed
by the terminally ill patient, which may contradict the preferences stated
in the document, always supersede it.

In addition to supplying living will forms, the Society supports   8
enactment of state laws that give legal recognition to these advance
directives, make them binding on doctors and other health care profes-

sionals, and provide immunity from liability for complying with them. So far, 21 states (Alabama, Arkansas, California, Delaware, Florida, Georgia, Idaho, Illinois, Kansas, Mississippi, Nevada, New Mexico, North Carolina, Oregon, Texas, Vermont, Virginia, Washington, West Virginia, Wisconsin, and Wyoming) and the District of Columbia have enacted such laws. While many other legislatures have failed year after year to pass them, living will bills proliferate and support for them grows. Twenty-five states considered them during the 1984 legislative session, and six were enacted in the spring.

Although only two living will laws are exactly alike, most of them 9 contain specific wording of the living will "declaration"—to be followed precisely or "substantially"—that expresses the desire not to have one's dying artificially prolonged by life-sustaining procedures if one's condition has been medically certified as terminal. The Society distributes on request the forms contained specifically in the statutes, as well as its own "Living Will Declaration," made available to people who live in states that have not yet passed living will laws. It is impossible to estimate just how many people have signed living wills in states both that have and have not passed laws recognizing them, but millions of forms have been distributed.

An added protection is the naming of another person to make 10 treatment decisions on behalf of the patient, in keeping with the patient's known wishes. This is provided in some of the more recent living will laws, and is contained in the Society's Living Will Declaration form. The proxy is an optional election; not everyone has someone to appoint—especially the childless elderly, who may have no surviving family or close friends. If there is an appropriate person available, however, the proxy appointment may be helpful, providing someone on the spot to press for decisions that honor the patient's wishes with specific reference to the patient's condition and treatment options, which can never be fully foreseen.

Another way of extending the rights and protecting the interests 11 of patients who have lost the ability to make or communicate decisions is through a durable power of attorney appointment. All 50 states have durable power of attorney statutes which would theoretically permit decisions about medical treatment, as well as about property matters. Two states—California and Pennsylvania—have amended those laws expressly to cover health care decisions. California, characteristically avant garde, was the first state to pass a living will law of any kind—but its 1976 Natural Death Act is relatively restrictive and the 1983 amended durable power statute can compensate for its limitations. Pennsylvania has yet to enact a living will law.

The application to medical treatment decisions of durable powers   12
of attorney in states that don't specify this use is uncertain. As a presidential commission pointed out in its March, 1983, report, *Deciding to Forego Life-Sustaining Treatment*, these laws need to be studied further with a view to safeguarding them from possible abuse in connection with health care matters. Their use, even coupled with living will directives, has not been tested to any extent.

Nor have living wills been widely tested in the courts. They have   13
figured in only two known cases—peripherally in one, significantly in the other. In Texas, the issue was muddied by the fact that the patient had executed a living will quite different from the document form prescribed by the Texas Natural Death Act. The case was ultimately resolved by declaring the patient brain-dead—an anomaly, since, if he was found to meet the generally accepted medical criteria for brain death, what was his case doing in court?

In Florida, a living will case was carried to the state's highest court   14
following an appellate court decision. The lower court had ruled that, although a comatose patient's living will could be admitted as evidence, it was not sufficient in itself to guarantee immunity to physicians acting in accordance with it, and that life support could be withdrawn only if a court-appointed guardian had obtained court approval to do so. Although the patient had already died, the hospital appealed the case to the Florida Supreme Court, hoping for guidance in the treatment of some 40 other comatose patients. During the last week of May, 1984—the same week that saw enactment, finally, of a Florida living will law—the high court overturned the appellate court's ruling. It affirmed the validity of the living will, gave the right of decision to a comatose patient's family, and removed the necessity for court intervention before life support could be terminated.

Patients' deaths have preceded judicial resolutions in the majority   15
of right-to-die cases that have made their way up to state supreme courts. While living wills have not played a part in them—none of the other dying patients had executed these—one notable case has been decided on the basis of "clear and convincing evidence" of the patient's prior wishes, which a living will can without doubt provide. The case concerned Brother Fox, a member of the Catholic Marianist order in a religious community in New York. At the time when the newspapers were full of the Karen Ann Quinlan case, he had expressed his own feelings about being kept alive "as a vegetable." Ironically, three and a half years later, he lapsed into a permanent coma following surgery. His superior, Father Eichner, petitioned the court for permission to withdraw Brother Fox's respirator. Though permission was granted two months

later, it was not acted on. Because of the importance of the issue, the case was appealed to the Appellate Division (at which point, Brother Fox, despite continuing respiratory support, had died), and finally to the Court of Appeals, New York's highest court. The court's opinion was handed down a full year and a half after Father Eichner had initiated legal action and 14 months after Brother Fox's death. In addition to the "clear and convincing evidence" of his earlier statements, the court based its findings on Brother Fox's common law right to refuse treatment.

In one way or another—which is to say, on one ground or an-   16
other—the highest state courts have upheld the terminal patient's right to be allowed to die in all but one major decision (*In re Storar,* New York Court of Appeals, 1981, which involved a retarded adult who had never been competent. He had terminal cancer of the liver, but the treatment in question was blood transfusion, and the court considered bleeding treatable and in a different category from untreatable cancer. The court also relied on the role of the state as surrogate parent with an interest in protecting the health of a child, which, for legal purposes, Storar was considered to be). All but one of the rulings have concerned patients whose decision-making capacity was lost; only Abe Perlmutter, mentioned above, was judged competent.

Aside from the support it implies of living will declarations, Brother   17
Fox's case is significant because the petitioner on his behalf was a Catholic priest and Brother Fox a member of the same order. A lot of the opposition to living will legislation has come from sectors of the Catholic community, despite the 1980 Vatican Declaration reiterating the church's position that, when death is inevitable and imminent, treatment which would secure only a "precarious and burdensome prolongation of life" may be, in conscience, refused.

Devout Catholic Peter Cinque might be viewed as an indirect vic-   18
tim of that opposition in New York State, which has yet to enact a living will statute. Diabetic, blind, and a multiple amputee, having endured enough, Cinque consulted with his priest and his family before asking his hospital to take him off the dialysis machine that was keeping him alive. Hospital agreement was slow in coming, and Cinque spent many days in an anguish of uncertainty. He suffered severe pain as well, since hospital authorities took him off all medication in order to assure themselves of his complete competency to make a rational decision to die. Then, abruptly, despite statements he had signed relieving them of all responsibility for the outcome (hospital personnel had supplied him with the forms refusing treatment), the hospital sent its lawyers to obtain a court order to continue the dialysis. Cinque's shock and despair may have accelerated his deterioration. At any rate, the next day, he lapsed

into coma. There was a hearing in his hospital room a few days later in which, as the judge discovered, Cinque was unable to participate. A lawyer was appointed his guardian and, after more testimony, his request was finally granted. He died an hour after dialysis was discontinued.

Needed: Guidelines

The yes-no shift in this hospital's position is perhaps an extreme example of the uncertainties and fears that not only propel right-to-die cases into the courts, but also cause foot-dragging, half measures, fruitless treatment, and general stonewalling when it comes to deciding whether or not what doctors call "aggressive treatment" can be stopped. Not that there aren't plenty of instances where a determination to stop it is reached between doctors and dying patients' families and quietly carried out. However, as technology advances and malpractice actions proliferate, some clarifying guidelines are sorely needed in the medical community. What is appropriate care for the dying patient? [19]

One response has been the issuance of suggested "Do Not Resuscitate" policies and procedures by a handful of medical societies and many hospitals. These, in effect, are intended to eliminate the absurdity of rushing to restore respiration and heartbeat to patients for whom the failure of these functions is associated with their terminal condition; to revive them is only to prolong their dying, and serves no purpose. Sensible systems for regulating DNR orders and their implementation include appropriate communication and documentation. This point was driven home in early 1984, when a special grand jury investigating a death in a Queens, New York, hospital reported its findings. The hospital had been using an informal "purple dot" system to denote which of the patients were not to be resuscitated if they went into cardiac or pulmonary arrest. Their nursing cards, purple decal and all, were destroyed after the patients died. The system meant secrecy (there was no assurance that patients or their families were aware of the DNR decision), possible error (one nursing card was found to have *two* purple decals fixed to it—if this could happen, what else could?), and unaccountability. [20]

Another response to the need came out of a conference of distinguished doctors, sponsored by the Society for the Right to Die, who met to develop guidelines on "The Physician's Responsibility Toward Hopelessly Ill Patients"—the title of the resulting article that was published in *The New England Journal of Medicine* in April, 1984. The 10 physician co-authors represent various medical disciplines and institutions in a number of states. The conclusions they reached were based on two premises: the [21] patient has a primary role in making treatment decisions, and there should be a decrease in aggressive treatment when it would only prolong the dying process. The article spells out in detail the care its authors consider ethically correct and desirable at various stages of illness, for both competent and incompetent patients. These range from emergency resuscitation and intensive care, if wanted, to giving comfort care only. They suggest procedures that may be withdrawn or withheld under certain conditions and if patient or family have agreed. In including artificially given food and water among these procedures, the authors confront an emotionally charged subject, one that was at issue in court cases still unresolved at the time of the article's publication. Depriving patients of nourishment is a step more freighted with feeling—and controversy—than disconnecting mechanisms such as respirators. In considering it, as in all matters affecting terminal patients, the authors urge clear communication, including telling the patient the truth about his or her condition. "The anxiety of dealing with the unknown can be far more upsetting than the grief of dealing with a known, albeit tragic, truth."

The article also confronts squarely the influences on doctors that may keep them from accepting the idea that "less" often can be "more" in treating terminal patients: training and tradition that emphasizes keeping the patient alive no matter what; the great temptation to use all the sophisticated medical technology that is there for the using; personal values and unconscious motivations; equating a patient's death with professional failure; and insistence on impossibly absolute prognostic certainty. In addition, of course, there is fear of liability, often more exaggerated than it need be, and often a deterrent to sensible, humane treatment.   22

The authors touch briefly on the astronomical cost of high-tech medicine, which strains public funds, escalates health insurance premiums, and can wipe out family finances. They note the increasing pressure on doctors for cost constraint. Gov. Lamm's statements highlighted this admittedly difficult and delicate point. No one would measure the value of a human life against the dollars it costs to sustain it—the thought is repugnant. Still, when it comes to perpetuating meaningless existences of thousands of comatose dying patients, it seems anything but heartless to talk about costs in money as well as in family anguish.   23

Pointing out that terminally ill patients are often cared by specialists or members of hospital staffs who can not possibly know what the patient's wishes would be (unless the patient is competent to tell them), the authors recommend advance statements of those wishes—a living will—or, alternatively, the advance designation of a proxy. These devices, even though they do not necessarily solve every dilemma faced   24 by a physician, can be of real help in deciding the best treatment course to recommend.

Hospitals' Viewpoints

It is reassuring that these 10 prestigious physicians have so strongly supported the patient's right to exercise control over terminal treatment and have recognized the usefulness of the living will. While you and I can hardly anticipate with pleasure a future time and circumstance when our own living will may be a significant piece of paper, can we at least anticipate with confidence that its instructions will be respected whenever we need them to be? Will hospitals honor them?

During the past year, at the suggestion of the Society for the Right to Die, hundreds of people have written to their local hospitals asking how their living will documents would be regarded if they became critically ill patients with no hope of recovery. Would the hospital honor the instructions? Did the hospital have a policy and a procedure on this?

Hospitals' responses were for the most part attentive and thoughtful, often formulated with legal counsel. Some of them said that the questions had spurred the creation of committees to develop living will policies. Others mentioned the risk of liability in the absence of a state law setting guidelines and offering protection. A few hospitals in states where living will laws do exist seemed not to know of them, but most in that category knew and referred to the statute. It is difficult to analyze the results of this "survey" in terms of categorical yes or no responses to the question of complying with the living will; some hospitals were clear, some waffled in their answers. However, one response appeared over and over again: hospitals do not initiate services or procedures, but produce them on doctors' orders. The obvious conclusion we *can* make is that we had better be sure to talk to our doctors about how we feel about terminal treatment.

If tubes and machines are abhorrent to us, what do we want as our lives are ending? What are we entitled to? Ease of pain, certainly, and, insofar as possible, relief from emotional discomfort; but beyond these considerations, it is the assurance that we will be permitted to die with, to quote Dr. Fletcher again, "that quality of humanness, the preservation of which is what the concepts of loving concern and social justice are built upon."

As he wrote, "Good dying must at last find its place in our scheme

25

26

27

28

29

of things, along with good birthing, good living and good loving. After all, it makes perfectly sound sense to strive for quality straight across the board, as much in our dying as in our living."

LIVING WILL DECLARATION
To My Family, Physician and Medical Facility

I, _____ , being of sound mind voluntarily make known my desire that my dying shall not be artificially prolonged under the following circumstances:

If I should have an injury, disease or illness regarded by my physician as incurable and terminal, and if my physician determines that the application of life-sustaining procedures would serve only to prolong artificially the dying process, I direct that such procedures be withheld or withdrawn and that I be permitted to die. I want treatment limited to those measures that will provide me with maximum comfort and freedom from pain. Should I become unable to participate in decisions with respect to my medical treatment, it is my intention that these directions be honored by my family and physician(s) as a final expression of my legal right to refuse treatment, and I accept the consequences of this refusal.

Signed _____ Date _____

Witness _____ Witness _____

DESIGNATION CLAUSE (optional*)

Should I become comatose, incompetent or otherwise mentally or physically incapable of communication, I authorize _____

presently residing at _____
to make treatment decisions on my behalf in accordance with my Living Will Declaration. I have discussed my wishes concerning terminal care with this person, and I trust his/her judgment on my behalf.

Signed _____ Date _____

Witness _____ Witness _____

*If I have not designated a proxy as provided above, I understand that my Living Will Declaration shall nevertheless be given effect should the appropriate circumstances arise.

Questions for Study and Discussion

1. What is Collins's main point in this essay? What is his purpose in making that point? Is he primarily interested in informing us about the issue or in persuading us to some action?

2. Comment on the effectiveness of Collins's introduction. What is he trying to achieve in his first two paragraphs?

3. What is a "living will"? Why has the Society for the Right to Die developed the "living will" form? What is your reaction to the sample living will at the end of the essay? What would be lost if Collins did not include this sample?

4. What point does Collins make in citing the cases of Brother Fox and Peter Cinque? How do these cases further his purpose in the essay?

5. What kind of guidelines does Collins feel are needed with respect to the treatment of the terminally ill and living wills?

6. What has been the response of hospitals to living wills?

7. What is the tone of Collins's essay? Is it appropriate for both his subject and his audience?

Writing Topics

1. Write an essay in which you discuss the status of living wills in your state. How do hospitals in your area regard living wills? Does your state have any laws that control living wills?

2. Collins quotes Dr. Fletcher as saying, "Good dying must at last find its place in our scheme of things, along with good birthing, good living and good loving. After all, it makes perfectly sound sense to strive for quality straight across the board, as much in our dying as in our living." Write an essay in which you discuss the issue of "good dying" and the various attempts—like hospice programs—that have been made to achieve it.

MORTIMER OSTOW

Mortimer Ostow was born in New York City in 1918 and graduated from Columbia University in 1937. A psychiatrist and neurologist in private practice since 1954, Ostow has been affiliated with many hospitals in New York City, including Mt. Sinai Hospital. Ostow has also been a visiting professor of pastoral psychiatry at the Jewish Theological Seminary and since 1965 the director of the Bernstein Center for Pastoral Counseling. Ostow is the author of numerous technical articles and books in his field of study, including many on the relationship of drugs and psychology.

In the following Letter to the Editor which first appeared in *The New York Times* on May 25, 1977, Ostow takes issue with an editorial titled "Who Shall Make the Ultimate Decision?" He believes that decisions about matters of life and death belong to the state, and not to the individual.

That Right Belongs Only to the State

To the Editor:

Nine members of the Kennedy Institute for the Study of Human   1
Reproduction and Bioethics commented on May 18 on your May 2 editorial "Who Shall Make the Ultimate Decision?" Their assertion that it is important to establish precise criteria to guide the judgment of reasonable people cannot be faulted.

I believe comment is called for, however, on your argument that   2
vital decisions respecting life and death belong to the patient or, when he is incompetent to make them, to those who are presumed to have his best interests at heart. The members of the Kennedy Institute concur.

It is a basic assumption of our society that individual members   3
possess no right to determine matters of life and death respecting other individuals, or even themselves. That right belongs only to the state. The prohibition of murder, suicide, and, until recently, abortion, has rested on this assumption. The right to determine whether life-preserving efforts are to be continued or discontinued therefore belongs neither to the physician nor to the patient or his guardian, but to the state.

In practical terms, when such a decision is called for, the decision   4
is to be made only by some agency or agent of the state, and it is to be made only by due process. To cede the right to the individuals involved is to license murder.

Aside from the philosophic argument, which not everyone will find   5

762

cogent, there are two practical reasons for requiring due process in such instances. In discussion of matters of continuing or withholding life-support systems and euthanasia, the arguments usually offered relate to the best interests of the patient or to the economic cost to society. Abortion, too, is discussed in these terms. A far more important consideration, it seems to me, is what making life-and-death decisions does to the individuals who decide.

While most of us will doubt that having made a decision to terminate life support to a suffering relative will then incline one to commit murder, still, making such a decision does condition the unconditional respect for life, and does weaken the concept of the distinction between what is permitted and what is forbidden.   6

One can see a tendency to pass from withdrawing life support from the moribund to facilitating the death of the suffering, and from there to the neglect or even abandonment of the profoundly defective, and from there to the degradation or liquidation of any whom society might consider undesirable. The undisciplined making of life-and-death decisions tends to corrupt the individual who makes them, and corrupted individuals tend to corrupt society.   7

Second, it is not necessarily true that the individual himself has his own interests at heart. Afflicted with a painful and long-drawn-out illness, many individuals will wish for death, even when objectively there is a reasonable possibility of recovery. Permitting the patient to make the decision to die may amount to encouraging his suicide. Anyone familiar with the ambivalence which prevails in family relationships will not take it for granted that family members will necessarily represent the patient's best interests.   8

It is important for the morale and morality of our society that "the ultimate decision" be made only by a disinterested agent or agency of our society, and only by due process.   9

Mortimer Ostow, M.D.
Bronx, May 25, 1977

Questions for Study and Discussion

1. What assumption about life and death in American society does Ostow invoke in his argument? Does legalized abortion undermine this assumption? Explain.

2. Ostow believes that when individuals are given the right to determine whether life-preserving efforts are made or not, they are given license to murder. Do you agree, or is this an exaggeration of reality?

3. What, according to Ostow, will be the impact of life-and-death decisions on individuals making them? What evidence does Ostow give to substantiate his opinion?

4. Does the fact that Ostow is himself a doctor influence your opinion of his argument? Explain.

Writing Topics

1. Write an essay in which you compare and contrast the articles by Mortimer Ostow and Evan Collins (pp. 751–761) on the advisability of leaving life-and-death decisions to individuals. What are the strongest arguments for each position? The weakest? Where do you stand on the right-to-die issue?

2. Ostow believes that making a decision to terminate life support "does condition the unconditional respect for life, and does weaken the concept of the distinction between what is permitted and what is forbidden." Write an essay in which you agree or disagree with Ostow's view.

JAMES RACHELS

Suppose that someone is dying and is experiencing great pain which no medicine can relieve. Is it better to keep that person alive as long as possible, despite the suffering, or to end the suffering quickly through euthanasia? Active euthanasia, or "mercy killing," is legally considered murder, but passive euthanasia—withholding treatment that would keep the patient alive—is not; indeed, it is even endorsed by the American Medical Association. James Rachels, a professor of philosophy who is particularly concerned with ethical issues, disputes this position. Born in 1941 in Columbus, Georgia, Rachels earned degrees at Mercer University and the University of California, and has taught at the University of Miami, Coral Gables, since 1972. He is the editor of *Moral Problems*, a reader in the ethical dimensions of contemporary social issues.

"Active and Passive Euthanasia" was first published in *The New England Journal of Medicine* in 1975, and has since been often reprinted and widely discussed. Arguing that mercy killing is morally no worse than allowing people to die, Rachels challenges doctors—and indeed all of us—to reconsider some basic assumptions.

Active and Passive Euthanasia

The distinction between active and passive euthanasia is thought to be crucial for medical ethics. The idea is that it is permissible, at least in some cases, to withhold treatment and allow a patient to die, but it is never permissible to take any direct action designed to kill the patient. This doctrine seems to be accepted by most doctors, and it is endorsed in a statement adopted by the House of Delegates of the American Medical Association on December 4, 1973:

> The intentional termination of the life of one human being by another—mercy killing—is contrary to that for which the medical profession stands and is contrary to the policy of the American Medical Association.
>
> The cessation of the employment of extraordinary means to prolong the life of the body when there is irrefutable evidence that biological death is imminent is the decision of the patient and/or his immediate family. The advice and judgment of the physician should be freely available to the patient and/or his immediate family.

However, a strong case can be made against this doctrine. In what follows I will set out some of the relevant arguments, and urge doctors to reconsider their views on this matter.

765

To begin with a familiar type of situation, a patient who is dying   2
of incurable cancer of the throat is in terrible pain, which can no longer
be satisfactorily alleviated. He is certain to die within a few days, even
if present treatment is continued, but he does not want to go on living
for those days since the pain is unbearable. So he asks the doctor for an
end to it, and his family joins in the request.

Suppose the doctor agrees to withhold treatment, as the conven-   3
tional doctrine says he may. The justification for his doing so is that the
patient is in terrible agony, and since he is going to die anyway, it would
be wrong to prolong his suffering needlessly. But now notice this. If one
simply withholds treatment, it may take the patient longer to die, and
so he may suffer more than he would if more direct action were taken
and a lethal injection given. This fact provides strong reason for thinking
that, once the initial decision not to prolong his agony has been made,
active euthanasia is actually preferable to passive euthanasia, rather than
the reverse. To say otherwise is to endorse the option that leads to more
suffering rather than less, and is contrary to the humanitarian impulse
that prompts the decision not to prolong his life in the first place.

Part of my point is that the process of being "allowed to die" can   4
be relatively slow and painful, whereas being given a lethal injection is
relatively quick and painless. Let me give a different sort of example. In
the United States about one in 600 babies is born with Down's syndrome.
Most of these babies are otherwise healthy—that is, with only the usual
pediatric care, they will proceed to an otherwise normal infancy. Some,
however, are born with congenital defects such as intestinal obstructions
that require operations if they are to live. Sometimes, the parents and
the doctor will decide not to operate, and let the infant die. Anthony
Shaw describes what happens then:

> . . . When surgery is denied [the doctor] must try to keep the infant
> from suffering while natural forces sap the baby's life away. As a surgeon
> whose natural inclination is to use the scalpel to fight off death, standing
> by and watching a salvageable baby die is the most emotionally exhausting
> experience I know. It is easy at a conference, in a theoretical discussion,
> to decide that such infants should be allowed to die. It is altogether dif-
> ferent to stand by in the nursery and watch as dehydration and infection
> wither a tiny being over hours and days. This is a terrible ordeal for me
> and the hospital staff—much more so than for the parents who never set
> foot in the nursery.[1]

I can understand why some people are opposed to all euthanasia, and

---

[1]A. Shaw, "Doctor, Do We Have a Choice?" *The New York Times Magazine*, January
30, 1972, p. 54. (Author's note.)

insist that such infants must be allowed to live. I think I can also understand why other people favor destroying these babies quickly and painlessly. But why should anyone favor letting "dehydration and infection wither a tiny being over hours and days?" The doctrine that says that a baby may be allowed to dehydrate and wither, but may not be given an injection that would end its life without suffering, seems so patently cruel as to require no further refutation. The strong language is not intended to offend, but only to put the point in the clearest possible way.

My second argument is that the conventional doctrine leads to   5
decisions concerning life and death made on irrelevant grounds.

Consider again the case of the infants with Down's syndrome who   6
need operations for congenital defects unrelated to the syndrome to live.
Sometimes, there is no operation, and the baby dies, but when there is
no such defect, the baby lives on. Now, an operation such as that to
remove an intestinal obstruction is not prohibitively difficult. The reason
why such operations are not performed in these cases is, clearly, that the
child has Down's syndrome and the parents and doctor judge that because
of that fact it is better for the child to die.

But notice that this situation is absurd, no matter what view one   7
takes of the lives and potentials of such babies. If the life of such an
infant is worth preserving, what does it matter if it needs a simple operation? Or, if one thinks it better that such a baby should not live on,
what difference does it make that it happens to have an unobstructed
intestinal tract? In either case, the matter of life and death is being
decided on irrelevant grounds. It is the Down's syndrome, and not the
intestines, that is the issue. The matter should be decided, if at all, on
that basis, and not be allowed to depend on the essentially irrelevant
question of whether the intestinal tract is blocked.

What makes this situation possible, of course, is the idea that when   8
there is an intestinal blockage, one can "let the baby die," but when
there is no such defect there is nothing that can be done, for one must
not "kill" it. The fact that this idea leads to such results as deciding life
or death on irrelevant grounds is another good reason why the doctrine
should be rejected.

One reason why so many people think that there is an important   9
moral difference between active and passive euthanasia is that they think
killing someone is morally worse than letting someone die. But is it? Is
killing, in itself, worse than letting die? To investigate this issue, two
cases may be considered that are exactly alike except that one involves
killing whereas the other involves letting someone die. Then, it can be
asked whether this difference makes any difference to the moral assessments. It is important that the cases be exactly alike, except for this one

difference, since otherwise one cannot be confident that it is this difference and not some other that accounts for any variation in the assessments of the two cases. So, let us consider this pair of cases:

In the first, Smith stands to gain a large inheritance if anything   10
should happen to his six-year-old cousin. One evening while the child
is taking his bath, Smith sneaks into the bathroom and drowns the child,
and then arranges things so that it will look like an accident.

In the second, Jones also stands to gain if anything should happen   11
to his six-year-old cousin. Like Smith, Jones sneaks in planning to drown
the child in his bath. However, just as he enters the bathroom Jones
sees the child slip and hit his head, and fall face down in the water.
Jones is delighted; he stands by, ready to push the child's head back
under if it is necessary, but it is not necessary. With only a little thrashing
about, the child drowns all by himself, "accidentally," as Jones watches
and does nothing.

Now Smith killed the child, whereas Jones "merely" let the child   12
die. That is the only difference between them. Did either man behave
better, from a moral point of view? If the difference between killing and
letting die were in itself a morally important matter, one should say that
Jones's behavior was less reprehensible than Smith's. But does one really
want to say that? I think not. In the first place, both men acted from
the same motive, personal gain, and both had exactly the same end in
view when they acted. It may be inferred from Smith's conduct that he
is a bad man, although that judgment may be withdrawn or modified if
certain further facts are learned about him—for example, that he is mentally deranged. But would not the very same thing be inferred about
Jones from his conduct? And would not the same further considerations
also be relevant to any modification of this judgment? Moreover, suppose
Jones pleaded, in his own defense, "After all, I didn't do anything except
just stand there and watch the child drown. I didn't kill him; I only let
him die." Again, if letting die were in itself less bad than killing, this
defense should have at least some weight. But it does not. Such a "defense" can only be regarded as a grotesque perversion of moral reasoning.
Morally speaking, it is no defense at all.

Now, it may be pointed out, quite properly, that the cases of eu-   13
thanasia with which doctors are concerned are not like this at all. They
do not involve personal gain or the destruction of normal healthy children. Doctors are concerned only with cases in which the patient's life
is of no further use to him, or in which the patient's life has become or
will soon become a terrible burden. However, the point is the same in
these cases: the bare difference between killing and letting die does not,
in itself, make a moral difference. If a doctor lets a patient die, for

humane reasons, he is in the same moral position as if he had given the patient a lethal injection for humane reasons. If his decision was wrong— if, for example, the patient's illness was in fact curable—the decision would be equally regrettable no matter which method was used to carry it out. And if the doctor's decision was the right one, the method used is not in itself important.

The AMA policy statement isolates the crucial issue very well; the crucial issue is "the intentional termination of the life of one human being by another." But after identifying this issue, and forbidding "mercy killing," the statement goes on to deny that the cessation of treatment is the intentional termination of a life. This is where the mistake comes in, for what is the cessation of treatment, in these circumstances, if it is not "the intentional termination of the life of one human being by another"? Of course it is exactly that, and if it were not, there would be no point to it.

Many people will find this judgment hard to accept. One reason, I think, is that it is very easy to conflate the question of whether killing is, in itself, worse than letting die, with the very different question of whether most actual cases of killing are more reprehensible than most actual cases of letting die. Most actual cases of killing are clearly terrible (think, for example, of all the murders reported in the newspapers), and one hears of such cases every day. On the other hand, one hardly ever hears of a case of letting die, except for the actions of doctors who are motivated by humanitarian reasons. So one learns to think of killing in a much worse light than of letting die. But this does not mean that there is something about killing that makes it in itself worse than letting die, for it is not the bare difference between killing and letting die that makes the difference in these cases. Rather, the other factors—the murderer's motive of personal gain, for example, contrasted with the doctor's humanitarian motivation—account for different reactions to the different cases.

I have argued that killing is not in itself any worse than letting die; if my contention is right, it follows that active euthanasia is not any worse than passive euthanasia. What arguments can be given on the other side? The most common, I believe, is the following:

"The important difference between active and passive euthanasia is that, in passive euthanasia, the doctor does not do anything to bring about the patient's death. The doctor does nothing, and the patient dies of whatever ills already afflict him. In active euthanasia, however, the doctor does something to bring about the patient's death: he kills him. The doctor who gives the patient with cancer a lethal injection has himself caused his patient's death; whereas if he merely ceases treatment, the cancer is the cause of the death."

A number of points need to be made here. The first is that it is not exactly correct to say that in passive euthanasia the doctor does nothing, for he does do one thing that is very important: he lets the patient die. "Letting someone die" is certainly different, in some respects, from other types of action—mainly in that it is a kind of action that one may perform by way of not performing certain other actions. For example, one may let a patient die by way of not giving medication, just as one may insult someone by way of not shaking his hand. But for any purpose of moral assessment, it is a type of action nonetheless. The decision to let a patient die is subject to moral appraisal in the same way that a decision to kill him would be subject to moral appraisal: it may be assessed as wise or unwise, compassionate or sadistic, right or wrong. If a doctor deliberately let a patient die who was suffering from a routinely curable illness, the doctor would certainly be to blame for what he had done, just as he would be to blame if he had needlessly killed the patient. Charges against him would then be appropriate. If so, it would be no defense at all for him to insist that he didn't "do anything." He would have done something very serious indeed, for he let his patient die.

Fixing the cause of death may be very important from a legal point of view, for it may determine whether criminal charges are brought against the doctor. But I do not think that this notion can be used to show a moral difference between active and passive euthanasia. The reason why it is considered bad to be the cause of someone's death is that death is regarded as a great evil—and so it is. However, if it has been decided that euthanasia—even passive euthanasia—is desirable in a given case, it has also been decided that in this instance death is no greater an evil than the patient's continued existence. And if this is true, the usual reason for not wanting to be the cause of someone's death simply does not apply.

Finally, doctors may think that all of this is only of academic interest—the sort of thing that philosophers may worry about but that has no practical bearing on their own work. After all, doctors must be concerned about the legal consequences of what they do, and active euthanasia is clearly forbidden by the law. But even so, doctors should also be concerned with the fact that the law is forcing upon them a moral doctrine that may well be indefensible, and has a considerable effect on their practices. Of course, most doctors are not now in the position of being coerced in this matter, for they do not regard themselves as merely going along with what the law requires. Rather, in statements such as the AMA policy statement that I have quoted, they are endorsing this doctrine as a central point of medical ethics. In that statement, active euthanasia is condemned not merely as illegal but as "contrary to that for which the medical profession stands," whereas passive euthanasia is approved. However, the preceding considerations suggest that there is really no moral difference between the two, considered in themselves (there may be important moral differences in some cases in their *consequences*, but, as I pointed out, these differences may make active euthanasia, and not passive euthanasia, the morally preferable option). So, whereas doctors may have to discriminate between active and passive euthanasia to satisfy the law, they should not do any more than that. In particular, they should not give the distinction any added authority and weight by writing it into official statements of medical ethics.

Questions for Study and Discussion

1. What is Rachels's thesis? Is he in favor of euthanasia? Support your answer.

2. According to Rachels, what is the difference between active and passive euthanasia? Which is generally considered more ethical? Which is more humane in Rachels's view? What do you think?

3. Is the example in paragraph 4 and the following discussion relevant to Rachels's thesis? Why does he include it?

4. What is the purpose of the hypothetical case involving Smith and Jones? Why do you think Rachels invented an example instead of drawing it from real life? What are the example's advantages and its limitations?

5. What was Rachels's purpose in writing this article? Who are his expected readers? How can you tell? Why is the article relevant to other readers?

Writing Topics

1. Are there any circumstances in which you might wish for euthanasia? If so, what are the circumstances and what would be your reasons? If not, what are your objections to euthanasia? Write an essay in which you explain your position.

2. As doctors have discovered means of prolonging the lives of terminally ill people, the debate over euthanasia has intensified. Some terminally ill people have taken their lives and their deaths into their own hands. This of course amounts to suicide and is prohibited by law. It is defended, however, under the banner of "death with dignity." Research the issues involved and discuss

the pros and cons of euthanasia, taking medical, legal, and moral considerations into account.

3. As Rachels's article shows, the law often intervenes in moral questions. Do you think this is a proper function of the law? When, if ever, should we seek to legislate morality? How effective is such legislation? How should we respond when the law compels us to act against our moral sense? Write an essay in which you address one or more of these questions.

JOHN DONNE

John Donne's writings encompass both worldly and religious concerns, as did his life. He was born in London in 1572 and, after attending Oxford, Cambridge, and the law school at Lincoln's Inn, he began his public career as an officer on a warship headed for action against Spain. After two years of service he returned to England and in 1598 became secretary to a leading statesman of the day, with excellent prospects for a career at court. Those prospects were ruined in 1601, however, when Donne eloped with a member of the statesman's family, for which he not only lost his position but was briefly imprisoned. For the next fifteen years he sought a position at court, but in vain; King James saw in him the makings of an excellent preacher and would offer him no other appointment. Finally Donne agreed to take holy orders and in 1615 was appointed Reader in Divinity at Lincoln's Inn. He distinguished himself as the most eloquent preacher of the day and became Dean of Saint Paul's Cathedral in 1621. "Death, Be Not Proud," the tenth of a series of nineteen *Holy Sonnets*, was evidently written around 1609 though not published until 1633. In it Donne uses a lawyer's reasoning and a Christian's faith to refute Death's claim to power.

Death, Be Not Proud

Death, be not proud, though some have callèd thee
Mighty and dreadful, for thou are not so;
For those whom thou think'st thou dost overthrow
Die not, poor Death, nor yet canst thou kill me.
From rest and sleep, which but thy pictures be,   5
Much pleasure; then from thee much more must flow,
And soonest our best men with thee do go,
Rest of their bones, and soul's delivery.
Thou'art slave to fate, chance, kings, and desperate men,
And dost with poison, war, and sickness dwell,   10
And poppy'or charms can make us sleep as well
And better than thy stroke; why swell'st thou then?
One short sleep past, we wake eternally
And death shall be no more; Death, thou shalt die.

Questions for Study and Discussion

1. How does Donne characterize death? How does he contrive to turn death into an almost human figure?

2. Why does Donne say that death should not be proud? What is the underlying assumption of the poem?

3. What does Donne mean by these two paradoxes:

 a. For those whom thou think'st thou dost overthrow
 Die not, poor Death, nor yet canst thou kill me.

 b. One short sleep past, we wake eternally
 And death shall be no more; Death, thou shalt die.

4. Paraphrase lines 5 and 6 to make their meaning clear.

5. What is Donne's tone in this poem? How does it suit his theme and his point of view?

6. The poem is divisible into several sections. Where do the divisions come, and how are they marked? What does each part of the poem contribute?

Writing Topics

1. The immortality of the soul is one of the great promises of several religions. Do you believe the soul will exist in an afterlife? How does your belief, or lack of it, affect your outlook on life and your attitude toward death?

2. Though death lies ahead for all of us, it has long been an "unthinkable" topic. Americans generally avoid discussing the topic, and consequently have had much difficulty in dealing with friends and relatives they know to be dying. Recent books and articles on death and dying may be changing this, however. Do some research into the subject, and report on those analyses and proposals that interest you.

Glossary

Abstract: See *Concrete/Abstract.*

Action is the series of events in a narrative. It is also called the story line. See also *Plot.*

Alliteration: See *Sound.*

Allusion is a passing reference to a person, place, or thing. Often drawn from history, the Bible, mythology, or literature, allusions are an economical way for a writer to convey the essence of an idea, atmosphere, emotion, or historical era. Some examples of allusion are "The scandal was his Watergate," "He saw himself as a modern Job," and "The campaign ended not with a bang but a whimper." An allusion should be familiar to the reader; if it is not, it will neither add to the meaning of a text nor enrich an emotion.

Analogy is a special form of comparison in which the writer explains something unfamiliar by comparing it to something familiar: "A transmission line is simply a pipeline for electricity. In the case of a water pipeline, more water will flow through the pipe as water pressure increases. The same is true of electricity in a transmission line."

Analysis is a type of exposition in which the writer considers a subject in terms of its parts or elements. For example, one may analyze a movie by considering its subject, its plot, its dialogue, its acting, its camera work, and its set. See also *Cause and Effect, Classification, Process Analysis.*

Anecdote. An anecdote is a brief story told to illustrate a concept or support a point. Anecdotes are often used to open essays because of the inherent interest of a story.

Antagonist. An antagonist is a character who struggles against the central character, or protagonist, in a conflict. Chillingworth in *The Scarlet Letter* is a villainous antagonist; Jim in *The Adventures of Huckleberry Finn*, a virtuous antagonist. See also *Protagonist.*

Aphorism. An aphorism is a short, concise statement embodying a general truth.

Appropriateness: See *Diction.*

Argument is one of the four basic forms of discourse. (Narration, description, and exposition are the other three.) To argue is to attempt to persuade a reader to agree with a point of view or to pursue a particular course of action by appealing to the reader's rational or intellectual faculties. See also *Deduction, Induction, Logical Fallacies,* and *Persuasion.*

Assonance: See *Sound.*

Assumptions are things one believes to be true, whether or not their truth can be proven. All writing includes many unstated assumptions as well as some that are stated, and an active reader seeks to discover what those assumptions are and to decide whether they are acceptable.

Attitude is the view or opinion of a person; in writing, the author's attitude is reflected in its tone. See also *Tone.*

Audience is the expected readership for a piece of writing. For example, the readers of a national weekly newsmagazine come from all walks of life and have diverse interests, opinions, and educational backgrounds. In contrast, the readership for an organic chemistry journal is made up of people whose interests and education are quite specialized.

Cause and Effect is a form of analysis that answers the question *why.* It explains the reasons for an occurrence or the consequences of an action. Determining causes and effects is usually thought-provoking and quite complex. One reason for this is that there are two types of causes: (1) *immediate causes,* which are readily apparent because they are closest to the effect, and (2) *ultimate causes,* which are somewhat removed, not so apparent, or perhaps even obscure. Furthermore, ultimate causes may bring about effects which themselves become causes, thus creating what is called a *causal chain.* For example, the immediate cause of a flood may be the collapse of a dam, and the ultimate cause might be an engineering error. An intermediate cause, however, might be faulty construction of the dam owing to corruption in the building trades.

Character. A character is a person in a story. Characters are generally regarded as being one of two types: flat or round. A flat character is one who exhibits a single trait, such as the devoted husband, the kind grandmother, or the shrewd businessman; such a character is stereotypic, unwavering, and thoroughly predictable. A round character, on the other hand, displays various traits and is complex and at times unpredictable—in short, very much like most of us. The chief character in a story is often called the *protagonist,* whereas the character or characters who oppose the protagonist are the *antagonists.*

Classification, sometimes called classification and division, is a form of exposition. When classifying, the writer sorts and arranges people, places, or things into categories according to their differing characteristics. When dividing, the writer creates new, smaller categories within a large category, usually for purposes of classification. For example, a writer might divide the large category *books* into several smaller ones: textbooks, novels, biographies, reference books, and so on. Then specific books could be classified by assigning them to these categories.

Cliché. A cliché is a trite or hackneyed expression, common in everyday speech but avoided in most serious writing.

Climax. In a work of fiction or drama, the climax is the point of highest tension, sometimes identical with the turning point of the narrative.

Coherence is a quality of good writing that results when all sentences, paragraphs, and longer divisions of an essay are naturally connected. Coherent writing is achieved through (1) a logically organized sequence of ideas, (2) the repetition of key words and ideas, (3) a pace suitable for the topic and the reader, and (4) the use of transitional words and expressions. See also *Organization, Transitions.*

Colloquial Expressions: See *Diction.*

Comparison and Contrast is a form of exposition in which the writer points out the similarities and differences between two or more subjects in the same class or category. The function of any comparison and contrast is to clarify— to reach some conclusion about the items being compared and contrasted. The writer's purpose may be simply to inform, or to make readers aware of similarities or differences that are interesting and significant in themselves. Or, the writer may explain something unfamiliar by comparing it to something very familiar, perhaps explaining squash by comparing it to tennis. Finally, the writer can point out the superiority of one thing by contrasting it with another—for example, showing that one product is the best by contrasting it with all its competitors.

Conclusion. The conclusion of an essay is the sentences or paragraphs that sum up the main points and suggest their significance or in some other way bring the essay to a satisfying end. See also *Introduction.*

Concrete/Abstract. A concrete word names a specific object, person, place, or action: *bicycle, milkshake, building, book, John F. Kennedy, Chicago,* or *hiking.* An abstract word, in contrast, refers to general qualities, conditions, ideas, actions, or relationships which cannot be directly perceived by the senses: *bravery, dedication, excellence, anxiety, stress, thinking,* or *hatred.* Although writers must use both concrete and abstract language, good writers avoid too many abstract words. Instead, they rely on concrete words to define and illustrate abstractions.

Conflict in a story is the clash of opposing characters, events, and ideas. A resolution of the conflict is necessary in order for the story to conclude.

Connotation/Denotation refer to the meanings of words. Denotation is the literal meaning of a word. Connotation, on the other hand, is the implied or suggested meaning of a word, including its emotional associations. For example, the denotation of *lamb* is "a young sheep." The connotations of lamb are numerous: *gentle, docile, weak, peaceful, blessed, sacrificial, blood, spring, frisky, pure, innocent,* and so on. Good writers are sensitive to both the denotations and connotations of words.

Consonance: See *Sound.*

Contrast: See *Comparison and Contrast.*

Deduction is a method of reasoning from the general to the particular. The most common form of deductive reasoning is the *syllogism*, a three-part argument that moves from a general statement (major premise) and a specific statement (minor premise) to a logical conclusion, as in the following example:

a. All women are mortal. (major premise)
b. Judy is a woman. (minor premise)
c. Therefore, Judy is mortal. (conclusion)

The conclusion to a deductive argument is persuasive only when both premises are true and the form of the syllogism is correct. Then it is said that the argument is sound.

Definition is a statement of the meaning of a word, or of an idea or even an experience. A definition may be brief or extended, the latter requiring a paragraph of an essay or even an entire essay. There are two basic types of brief definitions, each useful in its own way. The first method is to give a *synonym*, a word that has nearly the same meaning as the word you wish to define: *dictionary* for *lexicon*, *nervousness* for *anxiety*. No two words ever have exactly the same meaning, but you can, nevertheless, pair a familiar word with an unfamiliar one and thereby clarify your meaning. The other way to define quickly, often with a single sentence, is to give a *formal definition;* that is, to place the term to be defined in a general class and then to distinguish it from other members of that class by describing its particular characteristics. For example:

WORD	CLASS	CHARACTERISTICS
A *canoe*	is a *small boat*	that has *curved sides* and *pointed ends* and is *narrow, made of lightweight materials,* and *propelled by paddles.*
A *rowboat*	is a *small boat*	that has a *shallow draft* and usually a *flat* or *rounded bottom,* a *squared-off* or *V-shaped stern,* and *oarlocks* for the *oars with which it is propelled.*

Denotation: See *Connotation/Denotation.*

Denouement is the resolution or conclusion of a narrative.

Description is one of the four basic forms of discourse. (Narration, exposition, and argument are the other three.) To describe is to give a verbal picture of a person, a place, or a thing. Even an idea or a state of mind can be made vividly concrete, as in, "The old woman was as silent as a ghost." Although descriptive writing can stand alone, description is often used with other rhetorical strategies; for instance, description can make examples more interesting, explain the complexities of a process, or clarify a definition or comparison. A good writer selects and arranges descriptive details to create a *dominant impression* that reinforces the point or the atmosphere of a piece of writing.

Objective description emphasizes the *object* itself and is factual without resorting to such scientific extremes that the reader cannot understand the facts. *Subjective* or *impressionistic description,* on the other hand, emphasizes the *observer* and gives a personal interpretation of the subject matter through language rich in modifiers and figures of speech.

Dialogue is the conversation that is recorded in a piece of writing. Through dialogue writers reveal important aspects of characters' personalities as well as events in the plot.

Diction refers to a writer's choice and use of words. Good diction is precise and appropriate—the words mean exactly what the writer intends and are well suited to the writer's subject, intended audience, and purpose in writing. There are three main levels of diction, each with its own uses: formal, for grand occasions; colloquial, or conversational, especially for dialogue; and informal, for most essay writing. See also *Connotation/Denotation, Concrete/Abstract, Specific/General.*

Discourse, Forms of. The four traditional forms of discourse are narration, description, exposition, and argument. Depending on the purpose, a writer may use one or more than one of these forms in a piece of writing. For more information see *Argument, Description, Exposition,* and *Narration.*

Division: See *Classification.*

Dominant Impression: See *Description.*

Draft. A draft is a version of a piece of writing at a particular stage in the writing process. The first version produced is usually called the rough draft or first draft and is a writer's beginning attempt to give overall shape to his or her ideas. Subsequent versions are called revised drafts. The copy presented for publication is the final draft.

Editing. During the editing stage of the writing process, the writer makes his or her prose conform to the conventions of the language. This includes making final improvements in sentence structure and diction and proofreading for wordiness and errors in grammar, usage, spelling, and punctuation. After editing, the writer is ready to type a final copy.

Effect: See *Cause and Effect.*

Emphasis is the placement of important ideas and words within sentences and longer units of writing so that they have the greatest impact. In general, the end has the most impact, and the beginning nearly as much; the middle has the least. See also *Organization*.

Essay. An essay, traditionally, is a piece of nonfiction prose, usually fairly brief, in which the writer explores his or her ideas on a subject. Essays come in many forms including personal narratives and scientific and theoretical inquiries, as well as critical, humorous, and argumentative pieces. The word *essay* presently is used fairly loosely to include not only personal writing but most short nonfiction prose pieces.

Evaluation of a piece of writing is the assessment of its effectiveness or merit. In evaluating a piece of writing, one should ask the following questions: What does the writer have to say? Are the writer's ideas challenging or thought-provoking? What is the writer's purpose? Is it a worthwhile purpose? Does the writer achieve the purpose? Is the writer's information sufficient and accurate? What are the strengths of the essay? What are its weaknesses? Depending on the type of writing and the purpose, more specific questions can also be asked. For example, with an argument one could ask: Does the writer follow the principles of logical thinking? Is the writer's evidence convincing?

Evidence is the data on which a judgment or argument is based or by which proof or probability is established. Evidence usually takes the form of statistics, facts, names, examples, illustrations, and opinions of authorities, and always involves a clear indication of its relevance to the point at issue.

Example. An example is a person, place, or thing used to represent a group or explain a general statement. Many entries in this glossary contain examples used in both ways. Examples enable writers to show and not simply to tell readers what they mean. The terms *example* and *illustration* are sometimes used interchangeably. See also *Specific/General*.

Exposition is one of the four basic forms of discourse. (Narration, description, and argument are the other three.) The purpose of exposition is to clarify, explain, and inform. The methods of exposition are analysis, definition, classification, comparison and contrast, cause and effect, and process analysis. For a discussion of each of these methods of exposition, see *Analysis, Cause and Effect, Classification, Comparison and Contrast, Definition,* and *Process Analysis*.

Fallacy: See *Logical Fallacies*.

Figures of Speech are words and phrases that are used in an imaginative rather than literal way. Figurative language makes writing vivid and interesting and therefore more memorable. The most common figures of speech are:

Simile. An explicit comparison introduced by *like* or *as:* "The fighter's hands were like stone."

Metaphor. An implied comparison which uses one thing as the equivalent of another: "All the world's a stage."

Personification. The attributing of human traits to an inanimate object: "The engine coughed and then stopped."

Hyperbole. A deliberate exaggeration or overstatement: "I am so hungry I could eat a horse."

Metonymy. A type of comparison in which the name of one thing is used to represent another, as in the words *White House* used to represent the President of the United States.

Synecdoche. Another comparison in which a part stands for the whole, as in the word *crown* used to represent a king or the word *sail* to represent a ship.

See also *Symbol.*

Focus. Focus is the limitation that a writer gives his or her subject. The writer's task is to select a manageable topic given the constraints of time, space, and purpose. For example, within the general subject of sports, a writer could focus on government support of amateur athletes or narrow the focus further to government support of Olympic athletes.

General: See *Specific/General.*

Genre. A genre is a type or form of literary writing, such as poetry, fiction, or the essay; the term is also used to refer to more specific literary forms, as to an epic poem, novel, or detective story.

Hyperbole: See *Figures of Speech.*

Illustration: See *Example.*

Imagery is the verbal representation of a sensory experience: sight, hearing, touch, smell, taste, even the sensations one feels inside one's own body. Writers use imagery to create details in their descriptions. Effective images can make writing come alive and enable the reader to experience vicariously what is being described.

Induction is a method of reasoning that moves from particular examples to a general statement. In doing so, the writer makes what is known as an *inductive leap* from the evidence to the generalization, which can never offer the absolute certainty of deductive reasoning. For example, after examining enrollment statistics, we can conclude that students do not like to take courses offered early in the morning or late in the afternoon. See also *Argument*.

Introduction. The introduction of an essay consists of the sentences or paragraphs in which the author captures the reader's interest and prepares for what is to come. An introduction normally identifies the topic, indicates what purpose the essay is to serve, and often states or implies the thesis. See also *Conclusion*.

Irony is the use of language to suggest other than its literal meaning. *Verbal irony* uses words to suggest something different from their literal meaning. For example, when Jonathan Swift writes in *A Modest Proposal* that Ireland's population problem should be solved through cannibalism, he means that almost any other solution would be preferable. *Dramatic irony*, in literature, presents words or actions that are appropriate in an unexpected way. For example, Oedipus promises to find and punish the wrongdoer who has brought disaster on Thebes, then discovers that the criminal is himself. *Irony of situation* involves a state of affairs the opposite of what one would expect: a pious man is revealed as a hypocrite, or an athlete dies young.

Jargon refers to specialized terms associated with a particular field of knowledge. Also, it sometimes means pseudotechnical language used to impress readers.

Logic, in writing, is the orderly, coherent presentation of a subject. As a subdivision of philosophy, logic is both the study and the method of correct reasoning, using the techniques of deduction or induction to arrive at conclusions.

Logical Fallacies are errors in reasoning that render an argument invalid. Some of the more common logical fallacies are:

Oversimplification. The tendency to provide simple solutions to complex problems: "The reason we have inflation today is that OPEC has unreasonably raised the price of oil."

Non sequitur ("It does not follow"). An inference or conclusion that does not follow from the premises or evidence: "He was a brilliant basketball player; therefore, he will be an outstanding Supreme Court justice."

Post hoc, ergo propter hoc ("After this, therefore because of this"). Confusing chance or coincidence with causation. Because one event comes after another one, it does not necessarily mean that the first event caused the second: "I know I caught my cold at the hockey game, because I didn't have it before I went there."

Begging the question. Assuming in a premise that which needs to be proved: "Government management of a rail system is an economic evil because it is socialistic."

Either/or thinking. The tendency to see an issue as having only two sides: "America—love it or leave it."

Metaphor: See *Figures of Speech.*

Meter: See *Sound.*

Metonymy: See *Figures of Speech.*

Modes, Rhetorical: See *Discourse, Forms of.*

Mood is the emotional effect or feeling that a literary work evokes in the reader.

Narration is one of the four basic forms of discourse. (Description, exposition, and argument are the other three.) To narrate is to tell a story, to tell what happened. Whenever you relate an incident or use an anecdote to make a point, you use narration. In its broadest sense, narration includes all writing that provides an account of an event or a series of events.

Objective/Subjective. Objective writing is impersonal in tone and relies chiefly on facts and logical argument. Subjective writing refers to the author's personal feelings and may appeal not to reasons but to the reader's emotions. A writer may modulate between the two within the same essay, according to his or her purpose, but one or the other is usually made to dominate.

Opinion. An opinion is a belief or conclusion not substantiated by positive knowledge or proof. An opinion reveals personal feelings or attitudes or states a position. Opinion should not be confused with argument.

Organization is the plan or scheme by which the contents of a piece of writing are arranged. Some often-used plans of organization are *chronological order,* which relates people and events to each other in terms of time, for example, as one event coming before another, or two conditions existing simultaneously; *spatial order,* which relates objects and events in space, for example, from far to near or from top to bottom; *climactic order,* which presents ideas and evidence in order of increasing importance, power, or magnitude to heighten emphasis; and its opposite, *anticlimactic order.*

Paradox. A paradox is a self-contradictory statement that yet has truth in it, for example: "Less is more."

Paragraph. The paragraph, the single most important unit of thought in an essay, is a series of closely related sentences. These sentences adequately develop the central or controlling idea of the paragraph. This central or controlling idea, usually stated in a topic sentence, is necessarily related to the purpose of the whole composition. A well-written paragraph has several distinguishing characteristics: a clearly stated or implied topic sentence, adequate development, unity, coherence, and an appropriate organizational strategy.

Parallelism. Parallel structure is the repetition of word order or form either within a single sentence or in several sentences that develop the same central idea. As a rhetorical device, parallelism can aid coherence and add emphasis. Roosevelt's statement, "I see one third of the nation ill-housed, ill-clad, and ill-nourished," illustrates effective parallelism.

Persona, or speaker, is the "voice" you can imagine uttering the words of a piece of writing. Sometimes the speaker is recognizably the same as the author, especially in nonfiction prose. Often, however, the speaker is a partly or wholly fictional creation, as in short stories, novels, poems, and some essays.

Personification: See *Figures of Speech.*

Persuasion is the effort to make one's audience agree with one's thesis or point of view and thus accept a belief or take a particular action. There are two main kinds of persuasion: the appeal to reason (see *Argument*) and the appeal to an audience's emotions; both kinds are often blended in the same piece of writing.

Plot is the sequence or pattern of events in a short story, novel, film, or play. The chief elements of plot are its *action,* the actual event or events; *conflict,* the struggle between opposing characters or forces; the *climax,* the turning point of the story; and the *denouement,* the final resolution or outcome of the story.

Poetry is a rhythmical, imaginative, and intense form of expression. Poetry achieves its intensity by not only saying things in the fewest possible words but also in relying more heavily than other forms of literature on such language devices as metaphor, symbol, connotation, allusion, sound repetition, and imagery.

Point of View, as a technical term in writing, refers to the grammatical person of the speaker in a piece of writing. For example, a first-person point of view uses the pronoun *I* and is commonly found in autobiography and the personal essay; a third-person point of view uses the pronouns *he, she,* or *it* and is commonly found in objective writing. Both are used in the short story to characterize the narrator, the one who tells the story. The narrator may be *omniscient*—that is, telling the actions of all the characters whenever and wherever they take place, and reporting the characters' thoughts and atti- tudes as well. A less knowing narrator, such as a character in the story, is said to have a *limited,* or restricted, point of view.

Prewriting. Prewriting is a name applied to all the activities that take place before a writer actually starts a rough draft. During the prewriting stage of the writing process, the writer will select a subject area, focus on a particular topic, collect information and make notes, brainstorm for ideas, discover connections between pieces of information, determine a thesis and purpose, rehearse portions of the writing in the mind and/or on paper, and make a scratch outline.

Process Analysis answers the question *how* and explains how something works or gives step-by-step directions for doing something. There are two types of process analysis: directional and informational. The *directional* type provides instructions on how to do something. These instructions can be as brief as the directions for making instant coffee printed on a label or as complex as the directions in a manual for building your own home computer. The purpose of directional process analysis is simple: the reader can follow the directions and achieve the desired results. The *informational* type of process analysis, on the other hand, tells how something works, how some- thing is made, or how something occurred. You would use informational process analysis if you wanted to explain to a reader how the human heart functions, how hailstones are formed, how an atomic bomb works, how iron ore is made into steel, how you selected the college you are attending, or how the Salk polio vaccine was developed. Rather than giving specific di- rections, the informational type of process analysis has the purpose of ex- plaining and informing.

Protagonist. The protagonist is the central character in the conflict of a story. He or she may be either a sympathetic character (Hester Prynne in *The Scarlet Letter*) or an unsympathetic one (Captain Ahab in *Moby-Dick*).

Publication. The publication stage of the writing process is when the writer shares his or her writing with the intended audience. Publication can take the form of a typed or oral presentation, a dittoed or xeroxed copy, or a commercially printed rendition. What's important is that the writer's words are read in what amounts to their final form.

Purpose. The writer's purpose is what he or she wants to accomplish in a particular piece of writing. Sometimes the writer may state the purpose openly, but sometimes the purpose must be inferred from the written work itself.

Revision. During the revision stage of the writing process, the writer determines what in the draft needs to be developed or clarified so that the essay says what the writer intends it to say. Often the writer needs to revise several times before the essay is "right." Comments from peer evaluators can be invaluable in helping writers determine what sorts of changes need to be made. Such changes can include adding material, deleting material, changing the order of presentation, and substituting new material for old.

Rhetoric is the effective use of language, traditionally the art of persuasion, though the term is now generally applied to all purposes and kinds of writing.

Rhyme: See *Sound*.

Rhythm: See *Sound*.

Satire is a literary composition, in prose or poetry, in which human follies, vices, or institutions are held up to scorn.

Setting is the time and place in which the action of a narrative occurs. Many critics also include in their notion of setting such elements as the occupations and lifestyles of characters as well as the religious, moral, and social environment in which they live.

Short Story. The short story, as the name implies, is a brief fictional narrative in prose. Short stories range in length from about 500 words (a short short story) to about 15,000–20,000 words (a long short story or novella).

Simile: See *Figures of Speech*.

Sound. Writers of prose and especially of poetry pay careful attention to the sounds as well as the meanings of words. Whether we read a piece aloud or simply "hear" what we read in our mind's ear, we are most likely to notice the following sound features of the language:
 Rhythm. In language, the *rhythm* is mainly a pattern of stressed and unstressed syllables. The rhythm of prose is irregular, but prose writers sometimes cluster stressed syllables for emphasis: "Théy sháll nót páss." Much

poetry is written in highly regular rhythms called *meters*, in which a pattern of stressed and unstressed syllables is set and held to: "Th' ĕxpénse | ŏf spír | ĭt iń | ă wáste | ŏf sháme." Even nonmetrical poetry may sometimes use regular rhythms, as in this line by Walt Whitman: "Ĭ célĕbráte mўsélf aňd síng mўsélf."

Assonance, Consonance, and Rhyme. The repetition of a consonant is called *consonance,* and the repetition of a vowel is called *assonance.* The following line of poetry uses consonance of *l* and *d,* and assonance of *o:* "Roll on, thou deep and dark blue ocean—roll!" When two nearby words begin with the same sound, like *deep* and *dark* above, that sound pattern is called *alliteration.* And when two words end with whole syllables that sound the same, and one of those syllables is stressed, the result is called *rhyme,* as in strong/along and station/gravitation.

Specific/General. General words name groups or classes of objects, qualities, or actions. Specific words, on the other hand, name individual objects, qualities, or actions within a class or group. To some extent the terms *general* and *specific* are relative. For example, *dessert* is a class of things. *Pie,* however, is more specific than *dessert* but more general than *pecan pie* or *chocolate cream pie.* Good writing judiciously balances the general with the specific. Writing with too many general words is likely to be dull and lifeless. General words do not create vivid responses in the reader's mind as concrete specific words can. On the other hand, writing that relies exclusively on specific words may lack focus and direction, the control that more general statements provide. See also *Example.*

Style is the individual manner in which a writer expresses his or her ideas. Style is created by the author's particular selection of words, construction of sentences, and arrangement of ideas. A skillful writer adapts his or her style to the purpose and audience at hand. Some useful adjectives for describing styles include literary or journalistic, ornamental or economical, personal or impersonal, formal or chatty, among others. But these labels are very general, and an accurate stylistic description or analysis of a particular author or piece of writing requires consideration of sentence length and structure, diction, figures of speech, and the like.

Subjective: See *Objective/Subjective.*

Symbol. A symbol is a person, place, or thing that represents something beyond itself. For example, the eagle is a symbol of the United States, and the cross, a symbol of Christianity.

Synecdoche: See *Figures of Speech.*

Theme is the central idea in a piece of writing. In fiction, poetry, and drama, the theme may not be stated directly, but it is then presented through the characters, actions, and images of the work. In nonfiction prose the theme is often stated explicitly in a thesis statement. See also *Thesis*.

Thesis. The thesis of an essay is its main idea, the point it is trying to make. The thesis is often expressed in a one- or two-sentence statement, although sometimes it is implied or suggested rather than stated directly. The thesis statement controls and directs the content of the essay: Everything that the writer says must be logically related to the thesis. Some therefore prefer to call the thesis the *controlling idea.*

Tone. Comparable to "tone of voice" in conversation, the tone of a written work reflects the author's attitude toward the subject and audience. For example, the tone of a work might be described by such terms as friendly, serious, distant, angry, cheerful, bitter, cynical, enthusiastic, morbid, resentful, warm, playful, and so forth.

Transitions are words or phrases that link sentences, paragraphs, and larger units of a composition in order to achieve coherence. These devices include connecting words and phrases like *moreover, therefore,* and *on the other hand,* and the repetition of key words and ideas.

Unity. A well-written essay should be unified; that is, everything in it should be related to its thesis, or main idea. The first requirement for unity is that the thesis itself be clear, either through a direct statement, called the thesis statement, or by implication. The second requirement is that there be no digressions, no discussion or information that is not shown to be logically related to the thesis. A unified essay stays within the limits of its thesis.

Writing Process. The writing process consists of five major stages: prewriting, writing drafts, revision, editing, and publication. The process is not inflexible, but there is no mistaking the fact that most writers follow some version of it most of the time. Although orderly in its basic components and sequence of activities, the writing process is nonetheless continuous, creative, and unique to each individual writer. See also *Prewriting, Draft, Revision, Editing,* and *Publication.*

Acknowledgments (continued from p. iv)

Caroline Bird, "College is a Waste of Time and Money," from THE CASE AGAINST COLLEGE, 1975. Reprinted by permission of the author.

Anthony Brandt, "Rite of Passage," from *The Atlantic Monthly*, February 1981. Reprinted by permission of the author.

Brigid Brophy, "Women: Invisible Cages," from DON'T NEVER FORGET: COLLECTED VIEWS AND REVIEWS (Holt, Rinehart and Winston, 1966). Reprinted by permission of the author.

Michael Brown, "Love Canal and the Poisoning of America," Copyright © 1979 by Michael Brown. Reprinted from LAYING WASTE: LOVE CANAL AND THE POISONING OF AMERICA, by Michael Brown, by permission of Pantheon Books, a division of Random House, Inc.

Alexander Calandra, "Angels on a Pin," from *The Saturday Review*, December 12, 1968. Reprinted by permission of the author.

Helen Caldecott, "What You Must Know About Radiation," from *Redbook*, November 1979. Reprinted by permission of the author.

Rachel Carson, "The Obligation to Endure," from SILENT SPRING. Copyright © 1962 by Rachel L. Carson. Reprinted by permission of Houghton-Mifflin Company.

Shirley Chisolm, "Outlawing Compulsory Pregnancy Laws," from ABORTION RAP, edited by Diane Schulder and Florynce Kennedy (McGraw-Hill, 1971). Reprinted by permission of McGraw-Hill Book Company.

John Ciardi, "Is Everyone Happy?," from *The Saturday Review*, March 14, 1964. Copyright © 1964 by Saturday Review Magazine. Reprinted by permission.

Evan R. Collins, Jr., "The Right to Choose Life or Death," Reprinted from USA Today, November 1984. Copyright © 1984 by The Society for the Advancement of Education.

Norman Cousins, "How to Make People Smaller than They Are," from *The Saturday Review*. Copyright © 1978 by Saturday Review Magazine. Reprinted by permission.

Donna Woolfolk Cross, "Propaganda: How Not to Be Bamboozled," from SPEAKING OF WORDS: A LANGUAGE READER. Reprinted by permission of the author.

Harvey A. Daniels, "Is There Really a Language Crisis?," from FAMOUS LAST WORDS: THE AMERICAN LANGUAGE CRISIS RECONSIDERED, by Harvey A. Daniels. Copyright © 1983 by Southern Illinois University Board of Trustees. Reprinted by permission of Southern Illinois University Press, publishers.

Kelley Davis, "Health and High Voltage," reprinted from *Sierra*, the Sierra Club Bulletin, July/ August, 1978, by permission.

Joan Didion, "On Going Home," from SLOUCHING TOWARD BETHLEHEM by Joan Didion. Copyright © 1967, 1968 by Joan Didion. Reprinted by permission of Farrar, Straus, and Giroux, Inc.

Annie Dillard, "Sight into Insight," published in *Harper's*, 1974. Reprinted by permission of the author and her agent Blanche C. Gregory, Inc. Copyright © 1974 by Annie Dillard.

Index of Authors and Titles